EXTERNAL POSSESSION

TYPOLOGICAL STUDIES IN LANGUAGE (TSL)

A companion series to the journal "STUDIES IN LANGUAGE"

Volumes in this series will be functionally and typologically oriented, covering specific topics in language by collecting together data from a wide variety of languages and language typologies. The orientation of the volumes will be substantive rather than formal, with the aim of investigating universals of human language via as broadly defined a data base as possible, leaning toward cross-linguistic, diachronic, developmental and live-discourse data. The series is, in spirit as well as in fact, a continuation of the tradition initiated by C. Li (*Word Order and Word Order Change, Subject and Topic, Mechanisms for Syntactic Change*) and continued by T. Givón (*Discourse and Syntax*) and P. Hopper (*Tense-Aspect: Between Semantics and Pragmatics*).

Volume 39

Doris L. Payne and Immanuel Barshi (eds)

External Possession

EXTERNAL POSSESSION

Edited by

DORIS L. PAYNE
IMMANUEL BARSHI
University of Oregon

JOHN BENJAMINS PUBLISHING COMPANY
AMSTERDAM/PHILADELPHIA

The paper used in this publication meets the minimum requirements of American National Standard for Information Sciences — Permanence of Paper for Printed Library Materials, ANSI Z39.48-1984.

Library of Congress Cataloging-in-Publication Data

External possession / edited by Doris L. Payne, Immanuel Barshi.
p. cm. -- (Typological studies in language, ISSN 0167-7373; v. 39)
Includes bibliographical references and index.
1. Grammar, Comparative and general--Possessives. I. Payne. Doris I., 1952- . II. Barshi, Immanuel. III. Series.
P299.P67E94 1999
415--dc21 99-22381
ISBN 90 272 2938 4 (Eur.) / 1 55619 652 0 (US) (Hb; alk. paper) CIP
ISBN 90 272 2941 4 (Eur.) / 1 55619 655 5 (US) (Pb; alk. paper)

John Benjamins Publishing Co. • P.O.Box 75577 • 1070 AN Amsterdam • The Netherlands
John Benjamins North America • P.O.Box 27519 • Philadelphia PA 19118-0519 • USA

Table of Contents

Acknowledgments

We are grateful to numerous people who supported, challenged, and enriched this project intellectually and practically by participating in the Conference on External Possession and Related Noun Incorporation, held at the University of Oregon, September 1997. These include but are not limited to the authors represented in the current volume, Melissa Bowerman, Ursula Brinkmann, Robert Carlson, Bill Croft, Robert Davis, Scott DeLancey, Zygmunt Frajzyngier, Aya Katz, Suzanne Kemmer, Aleksandr Kibrik, Michael Kliffer, Silvia Luraghi, Marianne Mithun, Wataru Nakamura, Mickey Noonan, Tom Payne, Carol Rosen, Veerle van Geenhoven, and Cynthia Vakareliyska. Doris Payne's focus on the typology of EP constructions was honed by participants in the Spring 1997 course on external possession associated with the III Jornadas de Lingüística Aborigen, organized by Ana Gerzenstein, Ana Fernández Garay, Lucía Goluscio, Cristina Messineo, Pedro Viegas Barros, and Alejandra Vidal. We are also grateful to a number of anonymous reviewers and to students at the University of Oregon who assisted with the conference. This project could not have been completed without the extensive contributions of Gwen Frishkoff, Wendy Ames, Mitzi Barker, and Mickey Noonan, to whom we are not only indebted, but grateful.

The EP conference and this research project were partially supported by NSF Grant SBR-9616482, which we gratefully recognize. Research of the quality, extent, and focus represented here would be much less likely to emerge without such support.

Part I

Introduction

External Possession

What, Where, How, and Why

Doris L. Payne
University of Oregon

Immanuel Barshi
University of Colorado

We take core instances of *external possession* (EP) to be constructions in which a semantic possessor-possessum relation is expressed by coding the possessor (PR) as a core grammatical relation of the verb and in a constituent separate from that which contains the possessum (PM). The PR may be expressed as subject, direct object, indirect object or dative, or as ergative or absolutive depending on the language type — but not, for example, as an oblique. That is, the PR is expressed like a direct, governed, argument of one of the three universally attested basic predicate types (intransitive, transitive, or ditransitive). In addition to being expressed as a core grammatical relation, in some languages the PR can simultaneously be expressed by a pronoun or pronominal affix internal to the NP containing the PM; but this Genitive-NP-internal coding cannot be the only expression of the PR. Furthermore, the possessor-possessum relationship cannot reside in a possessive lexical predicate such as *have, own* or *be located at* and the lexical verb root does not in any other way have a PR within its core argument frame. Thus, despite being coded as a core argument, the PR is not licensed by the argument frame of the verb root itself — and herein resides the intrinsic fascination of EP constructions.

To illustrate the problem, consider the following examples from the IlKeekonyokie dialect of Maasai (Payne 1997a). *E-yshu* '3SG-be.alive' is one of the most highly intransitive Maasai verbs. It cannot take transitive inverse prefixes, and it cannot be transitivized via a morphological causative (which is otherwise productive for almost every verb in the language). Normally, *ishu*'s single allowable argument would be understood as a Patient-of-State (or Theme). (In the gloss, "3>1" indicates a third person subject and 1st person singular object inverse form; cf., Tucker & Mpaayei 1955; Payne, Hamaya & Jacobs 1994.)

(1) a. *é-yshú*
3–be.alive
'He/she/they are alive.'
Subject = Patient

b. **áa-yshú*
3>1–be.alive
'He/she/they cause me to be alive; He/she/they enliven me.'

However, with no additional morphology, the verb can occur in what appears to be a normal transitive clause, with inverse prefixes, if and only if the lexically-expressed subject participant can be interpreted as possessed by the object of the (otherwise intransitive) clause:

c. *áa-yshú en-tító*
3>1–be.alive FEM.SG-girl.NOM
'My girl is alive (with presumably positive effect on me).'
Subject = Possessed Patient & source of impact on possessor;
Object = Affected Possessor.

In IlKeekonyokie Maasai, other intransitives including unergatives, morphological antipassives, and morphological middle forms can similarly occur in formally transitive structures if and only if the object is interpretable as the PR of a lexically-expressed subject.[1]

Similarly, otherwise divalent verbs can act trivalently, without addition of causative, applicative, or any other morphology, if and only if the object can be interpreted as the semantic PR of some lexical expression in what is otherwise a clause with one-too-many core participants:

(2) a. *k-é-ból ɔl-páyyàn ɛn-káŋ*
DSCN-3–open MASC.SG-man.NOM FEM.SG-kraal.ACC
'The man will open the kraal.'

b. **k-áa-ból ɔl-páyyàn*
DSCN-3>1–open MASC.SG-man.NOM
'The man will open me.' (pragmatically nonsensical)

c. *k-áa-ból ɔl-páyyàn ɛn-kishómì*
DSCN-3>1–open MASC.SG-man.NOM FEM.SG-gate.ACC
'My husband/man will open the gate.'
(Literally: 'The man will open me the gate.')

d. *k-áa-ból ɔl-páyyàn ɛn-kʊ́tʊ́k*
DSCN-3>1–open MASC.SG-man.NOM FEM.SG-mouth.ACC
'The man will open my mouth.'
(Literally: 'The man will open me the mouth.')

One way to describe what goes on in these examples is to say that EP constructions have an extra participant; the possessor is treated as an additional argument of the clause. The papers in this volume document numerous additional "mismatches" between the argument structures of basic verb roots and clause structures. Some papers probe how they are handled by language processors, and many explore their implications for an adequate theory of syntax.

1. The ubiquity of external possession

Some EP constructions (EPCs) have been described in the past as instances of possessor raising.[2] Until fairly recently possessor raising may have been viewed as something belonging to the margins of relatively exotic languages — akin to the exotica of hundreds of classifiers in Southeast Asian languages, South American ideophones, Amerindian noun incorporation, or rhinoglottophilia (the last made exotic at least by virtue of its name). In the 1980's and continuing into the 1990's a number of studies argued for PR raising in languages of North and Meso-America (e.g., Aissen 1987; Allen, Gardiner & Frantz 1984, 1990; Carden, Gordon & Munro 1982; Davies 1984; Marlett 1986; Martin 1993; Munro 1984; Munro & Gordon 1982; O'Connor 1996; Rude 1985). Many of the earlier papers were largely from within or inspired by Relational Grammar. They documented some range of typological variation and discussed the extent to which the phenomenon did, or did not obey proposed universals such as the Relational Succession Law (Perlmutter and Postal 1983) and the Projection Principle of Government and Binding theory (Chomsky 1982; cf. Carden, Gordon & Munro 1982; Munro 1984). A few early papers dealt with languages outside the Americas, focusing on the involvement of direct object versus indirect object relations in raising processes (cf. Blake 1984 on some Australian languages; Bickford 1986, Hyman, Alford and Akpati 1970, Kimenyi 1980 on various African languages), and "topic" involvement in Cebuano (Bell 1983). And in the 1990's, additional studies attested to some variety of raising or external possession in additional languages of Africa (Ameka 1995; Barshi and Payne 1996; Hyman 1995; Payne 1997a; Schaefer 1995), some families of Asia and Southeast Asia (Chappell 1995; Clark 1995; multiple studies on Korean and Japanese), additional languages of Australia (multiple papers in Chappell and McGregor 1995b), and the Pacific (Foley 1991). If we were to include the dative EP type (see below), then Semitic (Berman 1982), Caucasian (Harris 1976, 1981), and Indo-European would be added to the geographic spread. Numerous papers have illustrated some interaction with noun incorporation, particularly throughout the

Americas (for a small sampling, see Mithun 1984, 1986; T. Payne 1995; Velázquez-Castillo 1995a, 1995b, 1996; Weir 1990; Wilhelm 1992).

When added to the preceding studies, the papers in this volume[3] lead to the solid conclusion that *external possession* is found in all parts of the globe: Asia (multiple Sinitic languages: Chappell), the Pacific region (Austronesian: Donohue), Australia (Nyulnyulan: McGregor), all across the Americas from North America (Muskogean: Martin, Munro; Sahaptian: Rude; Iroquoian: Baker), through Meso-America (Totonacan: Levy; Mixe-Zoquean: Zavala; Mayan: Aissen), and in South America (Tupi-Guaraní: Velázquez-Castillo), Europe (various areas and subfamilies within Europe: Haspelmath, Fried, Podlesskaya & Rakhilina), and Africa (Benue-Congo: Schaefer; Nilotic: Payne & Barshi). It seems safe to say that there is no geographical area of the world where the phenomenon does not occur, and it is hardly exotic. Its sheer ubiquity suggests it must be a linguistically natural phenomenon, serving some central human communicative need — as equally central as that served by active-passive-antipassive choices, causativization, and a host of other well-documented alternations.

2. The family of EP constructions and possessor raising

The definition of EP advanced above actually delimits a family of constructions. The term *external possessor* has previously been used for French and other European dative constructions which code the PR as dative and the PM as direct object (Vergnaud & Zubizarreta 1992; König & Haspelmath 1997). König and Haspelmath also use the term for constructions in which the PR may be coded in some type of locative, as in Swedish, Norwegian, and Icelandic. Whether Indo-European locative PRs fall within the core definition advanced above depends, we suggest, on whether there are basic verbal predicates which require locative-marked core arguments, and on whether the EPC has been diachronically and metaphorically modeled on such basic predicates in a schema-like or construction-like fashion (cf. O'Connor 1996; Heine 1997; Fried; Schaefer).

EPCs can also result from the type of noun incorporation (NI) that leaves the PR of an incorporated noun external to the verb as an object or intransitive subject (Mithun's 1984 Type II NI; Mohawk: Baker; Totonac: Levy; Guaraní: Velázquez-Castillo; Oluta Popoluca: Zavala). A common EPC type involves an applicative, such that the PR is expressed as object (Martin, Rude, Zavala). For some languages the applicative is argued to create a "double object" construction without the consequence that the PM is accorded chômeur status (Martin, Zavala). In yet other languages, "double object" EPCs may occur with no involvement of an applicative, as in Korean. In the Maasai EPC, the PR is simply coded as an object (possibly a Primary Object in the sense of Dryer 1986), with no applicative, noun incorporation, or dative encoding. In Tukang Besi, EPCs formed from transitive roots are highly similar (Donohue). There are also "double subject" (generally unaccusative) EPCs, as in Korean (e.g., Gerdts 1992; Youn 1989), Japanese (e.g., Shibatani 1994; Uehara) and Sinitic (Chappell 1995, this volume). Nyulnyulan displays other types of double case marking EPCs (McGregor).

The extent to which core external possession coincides with *possessor raising/ascension* entirely depends on definitions of the latter.[4] Briefly, PR raising falls within the set of EPCs as defined above; but not all EPCs are uniformly viewed as raising. Typically, definitions of raising assume that a PR viewed as having a semantic or argument-structure dependency on an element within a "lower" constituent is structurally realized in a "higher" syntactic unit. Fox (1981) nevertheless includes English sentences like *The dog bit him in the leg* as instances of PR raising; this codes a supposed PR as object and a supposed PM as locative. However, this English construction is not universally regarded as PR raising, although it may show certain semantic and functional affinities with EPCs. The primary reason not to consider it raising is that *The dog bit him* is a complete predication with *him* as the affected undergoer of the action, licensed and governed by the argument frame of *bite*. The presence of *him* does not have a semantic dependency relation to *leg*. The locative oblique *in the leg* just further refines the exact location at which the undergoer was affected. Thus, there is no "raising" of anything.[5]

Croft (1985), Fox (1981) and others include dative PRs as instances of raising, as in Spanish *Le secó las lágrimas* 'To:her$_i$ he:dried the (=her$_i$) tears.' In contrast, Tuggy (1980) argues that the Spanish possessive dative does not involve raising. Tuggy notes that meaning equivalence between supposed raising and non-raising possessive constructions does not exist, which a transformational analysis would presumably imply (cf. Chappell and McGregor 1995a). In Tuggy's view, Spanish merely adds an extra "ethical dative" which refers to affected participants. Under the right circumstances it can also refer to affected PRs (cf. Shibatani 1994), but this does not make it a specifically PR raising construction. Langacker (1993) also rejects a raising analysis for French. With regard to EP, in this volume we neither assume nor expect meaning or functional equivalence for external versus internal possession (IP) construction pairs,[6] because the motivation for the development of two separate constructions in a language resides precisely in the fact that there are distinct meanings or functions.

In some contrast to Tuggy's conclusion for Spanish, Fried gives a carefully argued treatise on the Czech dative EPC, showing that not all "extra" possessive datives in Czech merely occur because the PR is especially affected — but rather that an EP dative is sometimes *required* for the meaning of possession, and an IP counterpart simply cannot occur. Thus in Czech, as apparently in certain other Slavic languages (cf. Podlesskaya & Rakhilina), some sentences may be best described as *EP constructions*[7] and not just the result of adding extra "ethical datives" which sometimes have a possessive nuance.

Similar debates surround other EPC types. For example, a raising analysis has been argued for a number of applicative-EPCs (Aissen 1979, 1987; Constable 1989; Marlett 1986). But Zavala argues against a raising analysis for applicative-EPCs in Oluta Popoluca. The same debate surrounds the analysis of Japanese "double subject" EPCs (Uehara).

If the definition of EPCs is broadened to include all constructions that express a PR in a distinct constituent from the PM (Velázquez-Castillo), it then brings into our purview external possessors expressed in non-core argument positions, e.g., as structural topics which have delimiting (Dooley 1982) frame of reference, or reference point (Langacker 1993) functions. This broader definition opens the door to understanding how some EPCs develop. Langacker (1993) notes that both topics and possessives function to name one entity as a reference point for establishing mental contact with another entity. Thus, there is an understandable functional motivation for expressing a PR as a structural topic. Once established, these extended-EPCs have sometimes almost certainly undergone grammaticization from possessor-as-topic into possessor-as-subject constructions (cf. Tz'utujil: Aissen; Creek versus Chickasaw: Martin; Sinitic: Chappell; see also Langacker 1993 on Luiseño). Munro carefully discusses the extent to which EPRs are accorded some (but not all) subject (and object) properties in Chickasaw, which we might interpret as suggesting gradual grammaticalization from one construction to the other.

3. Typological variability in EP constructions

Within the family of what we have defined as core EPCs, some structures combine EP with NI, and some combine it with applicatives; yet others do not carry in the verb (phrase) any derivational marking that correlates with EP. Typological variability in EP constructions concerns (1) the grammatical relation of the EPR, (2) the grammatical relation of the PM both in the EPC and in the analogous IPC counterpart, (3) the range of participating predicate types, (4) the semantic range of nouns which can be construed as possessed, and (5) the semantics of the PR.

3.1 *Grammatical relation of the external possessor (EPR)*

The grammatical relation that the EPR assumes in the clause does not seem to be governed by any particular implicational hierarchy, either language-internal or cross-linguistic. As papers in this volume show, EPRs may be expressed as dative, primary object, direct object, intransitive subject, or (structural) topic, depending on the language and the particular EPC.

During the 1980's, work in Relational Grammar showed that EP phenomena sometimes obey the Relational Succession Law (Perlmutter and Postal 1983) in that the raised PR takes on the grammatical relation that the possessed NP would have had (cf. Tukang Besi; Donohue). But in other languages, the Relational Succession Law does not hold. Some scholars concluded that whenever it did not hold, the PR would then always assume an indirect object (or dative) role (Blake 1984; see also Croft 1985). Indeed, there is a widespread attestation of dative EPRs (Fried, Gerdts, Haspelmath, Martin, Munro, Podlesskaya & Rakhilina). Diachronically, the dative type of EPC likely develops by extension of a locative/goal or dative schema (Heine 1997; Schaefer) to the possession domain, based on conceptualizing the PR as the relevant affected "endpoint" of an action or situation (Croft 1994; Fried).

But yet further data show that even put together, these two proposals (the Relational Succession Law and the dative possibility) are still far too restrictive. Maasai intransitive verbs allow EP and express the PR simply as an object (perhaps Primary Object in the sense of Dryer 1986). The Relational Succession Law is not observed.[8] The only reason for positing an indirect object "stage" for a Maasai clause like (1c) would be to satisfy some requirements of a theory — not because there is any clear evidence for it in Maasai itself. There is, in fact, quite widespread attestation of an object EPR form (Gerdts), in some cases with the involvement of an applicative (Martin, Rude, Zavala). Important insight into the diachronic rise of applicatives and how some come to participate in EPCs is provided by Levy's discussion of Totonac.

An absolutive EPR typically surfaces in combination with Mithun's Type II NI (cf. Weir 1990; Baker, Levy, Velázquez-Castillo, Zavala). Type II NI/EP typically adheres to the Relational Succession Law, though as Baker shows for Mohawk, this is not universal. EPRs not resulting from NI may also assume an absolutive relation — though the surface case marking in intransitive subject and transitive object EPCs may actually differ (e.g., Korean).

An EPR may take the intransitive subject relation (Chappell, Donohue, Martin, Munro). For the EPR to assume a transitive subject relation is extremely rare cross-linguistically, and even where it does occur (Payne 1997a; McGregor), it may mostly surface with rather stative transitive predicates (cf. Uehara). This suggests that the grammatical relation of the EPR is not completely independent from other parameters. It is particularly not independent of the predicate type in the sentence, and this in turn also constrains issues of semantic role. (These intersecting parameters are considered below.)

Aissen argues for an additional EPC in which the EPR occurs in a clausal Topic position, and does not assume a core grammatical relation. Diachronically this construction may develop from structural Topic (perhaps a functional "delimiting phrase," Dooley 1982; Payne 1995: 454–455) into a (double) subject construction (Aissen, Chappell, Martin, Uehara). If such development does occur, the resultant EPC would then fit within the core definition advanced earlier.

Chickasaw subject EPCs (Munro) present a particularly interesting synthesis of both the topic>subject type, and the dative EPR types. The lexical EPR takes on a number of subject properties, but is simultaneously registered in the Dative applicative-pronominal prefix on the verb.[9] Munro speculates that for some particular verbs, there has been a full reanalysis of subjects as accusative objects, along with loss of possessive interpretation.

3.2 *Grammatical relation and semantic role of the PM*

Two questions concerning the grammatical relation and thematic role of the PM are: What relation does the PM have in the EPC? And, what range of possessa is accessible to being externally possessed relative to otherwise analogous IP constructions?

In NI EPCs, the PM is incorporated into the verb and does not have argument status. In other cases, the PM is shunted off as a non-incorporated oblique (roughly akin to English *She cut me on the leg*); or the PM has chômeur status even if retaining subject or object case marking (e.g., Korean: Gerdts 1992; Chickasaw and Choctaw subject possessor raising: Munro & Gordon 1982; Munro). In a third pattern, there is no particular evidence that the PM has chômeur status in the EPC (e.g., Zavala).

The second question concerns the range of accessible possessa. Cross-linguistically, EP is preferentially associated with direct objects and/or subjects of unaccusative verbs, i.e., the O/S_o grouping. The involvement of unergative subjects is attested but less common; transitive subject possessa appear to be extremely rare (Youn 1989; but see Payne 1997a; McGregor). From this distribution, it is clear that the patient or theme semantic role is also privileged in EPCs. The primacy of the patient/theme role is, of course, not idiosyncratic to EPCs, as it also correlates with morphosyntactic asymmetries in stative/active languages, universal NI patterns, and 'object' classifiers in various Native American languages. Why the patient/theme role is privileged in such constructions surely derives from the particularly tight-knit co-dependent "interpretive bond" between this role and its predicate (Keenan 1984). In fact, we might say that the theme/patient and verbal predicate together tend to *comprise* complex semantic predicates — and some constructions in some languages simply give overt expression of this complexity.

Altogether, different EPCs follow *different* hierarchies relative to what grammatical relation/semantic role is most accessible. Moreover, Donohue argues that in some languages accessibility to EP is constrained by the semantic role of the PM, while in others it is constrained by its grammatical relation. The particular hierarchy for a given construction most certainly depends on the diachronic origin of the EPC in question.

One proposed hierarchy governing accessibility of possessa to EP is: *PP < direct object < unaccusative subject < unergative subject < transitive subject* (Haspelmath). By this hierarchy Haspelmath means that "if an EP construction is possible for a position at any point of the hierarchy, then that EP construction is also possible with all the positions that are to the left on the hierarchy." This hierarchy was worked out largely on the basis of European languages. Fried, Podlesskaya and Rakhilina, and Velázquez-Castillo corroborate the accessibility of oblique locatives in Czech, Russian, and Spanish respectively. Possessed locatives as well as direct objects are also highly accessible in Totonac (Levy) and Oluta Popoluca (Zavala) (both of these latter cases also involving NI).

However, other studies show that this hierarchy is not universal. Haspelmath hesitates over the universal position of PPs on this hierarchy, and the studies in this volume and elsewhere (cf. Youn 1989; Payne 1997a) suggest that oblique possessa or possessa expressed in PPs which are not within the argument structure of the basic verb, are not universally favored in EPCs. Simply, numerous languages allow EPCs for possessed objects and unaccusative subjects, but not for possessed obliques. For a range of Maasai dialects, for example, there is reasonable synchronic evidence, even in the absence of historical documents, to hypothesize that the expansion of the EP construction across dialects proceeded from *direct object → unaccusative subject → unergative subject → transitive subject*, excluding *oblique* and *dative/indirect object* (thus supporting part of Haspelmath's hierarchy; Payne 1997a). Emai (Schaefer) allows EPCs only for direct objects and (presumably governed) locative complements of verbs like 'put.'

Some languages privilege intransitive unaccusative arguments over transitive objects. There appear to be both semantic and discourse-pragmatic motivations for this pattern. Polinsky and Comrie show that possessors can be relativized on in Tsez (Northeast Caucasian) only if the relative clause has an unaccusative predicate which expresses an obvious change-of-state and if the PR-PM relationship is essentially inalienable. These factors are primarily semantic or pragmatic. Some Sinitic languages (Chappell) have EPCs just for unaccusative subjects (an NP-V_i-NP construction for process unaccusatives, and an NP-NP-V_i construction for stative unaccusatives). To understand the discrepancy between Maasai and Chinese, we are obliged to see that the EPCs in the two languages have markedly different diachronic sources. Chappell (1995) notes that the two Sinitic EPCs conform to the Chinese Topic-Comment structure, that is, a conjunction of NP_{TOP} + Sentence; though in the EPCs the Sentence is semantically related to the initial NP. The two NPs are furthermore semantically related as Part-to-Whole. Similarly, Rude claims that also EPRs in Sahaptian intransitive clauses are topics.[10] Chappell (1995) cites Chao (1968) in observing that most commonly, the Chinese construction "describes the state or characteristic, less commonly an event, about the main subject." This is akin to Hopper's (1987) observation that NP-initial sentences in NV/VN languages like Austronesian and Old English "describe" rather than "narrate." That is, the function of Topic-Comment and NV sentences in these languages is to describe a state or characteristic of something. Describing a state or a characteristic is typically the discourse-pragmatic job of an *unaccusative intransitive* clause (which has only a subject), and not of a transitive clause (which allows an object).

To our knowledge, indirect object possessa of underived divalent predicates have almost never been mentioned in the literature as being accessible to EP, and some studies report its impossibility (Payne 1997a; Schaefer) In fact, for those languages which express the EPR as a dative/indirect object or as a primary object, we should generally expect the universal restriction on multiple instances of a given grammatical relation in a clause to disfavor accessibility of possessa in dative/indirect object or primary object roles — since that is the grammatical relation which the EPR assumes.[11] Having said that, we note that McGregor argues that Nyulnyulan languages are particularly liberal in what roles are accessible to external possession, including arguments of unergative reflexive intransitives and the ergative of transitive predicates.

3.3 *Predicate types*

EPCs may also be constrained by predicate type, which is not unrelated to the grammatical relation of the PM (Section 3.2). There are two dominant patterns. A particular EPC may privilege change of state predicates, or stative unaccusative predicates.[12]

There is considerable evidence that for some constructions, predicates that express change of state most easily allow EPCs. For European languages, Haspelmath suggests a hierarchy of predicate types: *patient-affecting* < *dynamic non-affecting* < *stative*. In support of this, Podlesskaya and Rakhilina describe what they call "PR raising" versus "PR splitting" constructions in Russian. The former has the familiar Indo-European dative PR, while the PR splitting construction usually expresses the PR as a core accusative-case object; the PM occurs in a directional oblique phrase as object of a preposition. Predicates that express greater affectedness of the PR allow "raising"; predicates which do not convey such affectedness motivate splitting. The privileged status of change-of-state verbs is also found outside of Indo-European languages. In Tsez, only unaccusative predicates which express an obvious change-of-state allow possessor relatives (Polinsky & Comrie). In Emai, verbs that code a change of state are allowed in EPCs, while those encoding perceptions, statives, and activities with no inherent change tend not to admit EP (Schaefer).

But Haspelmath's hierarchy does not hold universally. The starting point for Sinitic EPCs appears to be stative intransitive predicates (Chappell). Baker also notes the primacy of intransitive stative verbs for NI and certain subtypes of EPCs in Mohawk. Totonac locative EPCs are allowed from just one of four Locative Existentials (these verbs subcategorize for a locative complement; Levy).[13]

Regardless of transitivity and the unaccusative/unergative distinction, quite a number of languages require that EPCs be used only when there is the possibility of effect on the PR. In some languages, EFFECT must be a lexical feature of the verb, while in others it can be conceptually construed. Chappell claims that Sinitic unaccusative verbs must convey a sufficiently adversative effect on the PR in order to allow the EPC. For Totonac, Levy argues that in one type of EPC, the verb must express high effect on, and physical contact with, the undergoer such that a change of state is usually expressed. In Czech (Fried), predicates that do not have any affected argument are less likely to welcome EPCs (e.g., verbs of perception, sensation, or unergative predicates); Russian also disallows the dative EPC for such verbs (Podlesskaya & Rakhilina). For Tukang Besi, Donohue claims that the lexical verb must express adverse effect on theme/patient (i.e., a subclass of the absolutive role); the adverse effect cannot just be construable from context, but must be part of the lexical meaning of the predicate. In Russian, by contrast, lexical predicates which allow "raising" must have a lexical feature of "affectedness". A given Russian lexeme like 'touch' or 'kiss' can be construed on one occasion as having such a feature; but on other occasions as not having such a feature.

It may well be that some languages are not sensitive to the stative/effect feature but simply prefer unaccusative predicates. Aissen notes that Tz'utujil EPCs occur preferably with unaccusatives, while questionable judgments surface for unergatives or subjects of transitives. Unaccusative predicates are preferred over (object of) transitive predicates.

For Chickasaw, Munro notes that possessor raising applies primarily with intransitive verbs, though it can occur with verbs of all sorts: agentive or non-agentive, volitional or not, controlled or not. Munro importantly notes that verbs are *lexically marked* for whether they undergo possessor raising, as one member of a semantically similar pair may participate (e.g., 'be hungry'), while the other does not (e.g., 'be thirsty').

Finally, some languages are very liberal in what predicates allow EPCs (Japanese: Uehara; Nyulnyulan languages: McGregor).

3.4 *Semantics of the PM and of the PR*

Velázquez-Castillo (1996), drawing particularly on Seiler (1983) and Langacker (1993, 1995a), gives an excellent discussion of the semantic and cognitive bases for hierarchies governing accessibility of both PM and PR. Relative accessibility is grounded in the degree of *conceptual closeness* between PR and PM.

First, it appears non-controversial that there is a universal semantic hierarchy constraining accessible possessa in EPCs. Most broadly, this is *inalienable < alienable*; more finely we suggest *body part < part-whole < other inalienable < alienable + proximate < alienable + distal < non-possessable*. What counts as "other inalienable", "alienable", and as "non-possessable" varies from language to language and from culture to culture (e.g., Chappell notes the privileged accessibility of kin terms in Sinitic; McGregor elaborates on what falls within the "personal domain" in Nyulnyulan languages). The exact specification of accessible PM-nouns may be more grammaticized in one language, and more pragmatic/statistical in another. Some languages (e.g., Japanese: Uehara) are extremely liberal in what possessa are accessible to EPCs.

There also is a cross-linguistic hierarchy governing the PR in EP constructions. External possessors are most typically animate, human, and ego. Schaefer argues that the relevant hierarchy for Emai is *1st pronoun < 2nd pronoun < 3rd pronoun < proper name < human < other animate < inanimate*. Haspelmath suggests a slightly more general hierarchy as universally relevant. Donohue claims that only pronominal PRs are accessible in Tukang Besi. Thus, languages grammaticize a certain cut-off point for accessibility, but still support the universal nature of the proposed hierarchy.

4. Processing challenges presented by EPCs

The cognitive demands associated with the processing of "extra" participants have not received much psycholinguistic study (we note that English does not have "extra participant" EPCs and most psycholinguistic research continues to be English-based). Most current models of psycholinguistics have been largely built around theories that assume clause structure depends on verbal argument structure. Given that core EPCs contain an extra participant in terms of the expected argument structure of the verb, their acquisition and processing, both at the sentence level (Mitchell 1994) and at the text level (Gernsbacher 1990; Kintsch 1988), seem to be outside most models. In particular, models of sentence processing often assume a verb-driven syntactic parser. In such a model, the expected argument structure of the verb guides the parsing (cf. Boland 1993; Clifton, Speer & Abney 1991). If that is the case, EPCs would be expected to constitute a "garden path" experience (Singer). Given the wide distribution of EPCs in the world's languages, and the fact that language users seem to have no difficulty in producing and comprehending them, we might predict that processing models which predict EPCs to be garden paths are clearly inadequate. Singer reviews studies which suggest that argument-structure based garden paths are not as taxing as are other types of garden path phenomena. Nevertheless, Uehara argues on the basis of off-line experimental evidence that Japanese EPCs are more difficult to process than are center-embedding sentences. Altogether, the constructions may be more challenging for comprehension than for production, but to our knowledge there are no studies comparing the production of EPCs with the comprehension of EPCs.

5. The theoretical significance of EPCs

EPCs bring together central questions in language processing and in syntax, including the intersection of verbal valence, and — as we argue below — event construal and voice. Their particular interest is that they are a limiting case in terms of argument structure, and thus hold some fundamental keys for understanding the connection between verbal argument structure and syntactic clause structure. As noted, certain EPC types appear to "break the rules" about how many arguments a verb of a given valence can have, and challenge the notion that clause-level syntax depends directly on the argument structure and subcategorization frames of individual verbs or verb stems.

Because the clausal syntax of some EPCs does not seem to match the (expected) argument structure of the lexical verb, such constructions present challenges to several rules and constraints that were proposed in the 1980's and 1990's.[14] Pertinent proposals include the Government and Binding Projection Principle (informally, syntax is determined by lexical properties of predicates) and Theta Criterion (informally, any sentence is ungrammatical if an NP does not have one and only one theta-role; and roles are assigned only under subcategorization); the Lexical Functional Grammar Coherence Principle (informally, every argument must be governed by a local predicate or ungrammaticality results); and the Relational Grammar Relational Succession Law (a raised argument must assume the grammatical relation that its host held to the matrix verb, which as we have noted was quickly found not to be universally true). As we have noted, assumptions in these proposals are at the foundation of most psycholinguistic models of language processing, as well as theories of language acquisition and second language learning (Barshi & Payne 1998). By challenging fundamental premises that nearly all these proposals make, EPCs raise important questions not only for syntactic theory but also for developing adequate models of language processing and language acquisition.

If we set aside three EPC types — those that result from Type II NI, those for which the PM can be argued to be a chômeur (Munro), and those involving valence-increasing applicatives — then we find that EPCs appear to have one more argument than even the derived verb stem in the clause would normally appear to allow; that is, otherwise intransitive predicates appear to take two arguments, and otherwise transitive predicates appear to take three arguments. (We questioned earlier the ease with which ditransitive predicates allow EPCs.) The semantic role of what behaves grammatically as one of the core arguments of the verb is also arguably anomalous, necessarily being a semantic (affected) possessor — rather than, say, the agent or patient/theme or whatever roles are provided by the predicate frame. That is, some participant *other* than the possessor is understood as having the agent or patient/theme role normal to the argument structure of the verb in question.

If it is the case that "syntax is projected from the lexicon," or that argument structure of verbs determines the syntactic structure of the clause, then the Maasai EP data presented earlier would seem impossible. This is because the verb stem in (1) is a basic intransitive with a theme/patient as its single argument, and the stem in (2) is a basic transitive with an agent-patient argument frame; so neither one should take a Genitive or PR core argument.

In terms of cognitive processing, especially when one considers the time course of processing in a verb initial language like Maasai, we might expect that every encounter with an EP sentence would constitute a "garden path" experience for the listener (Singer). This is because the first argument frame to build upon encountering a verb like that in (2c) would be an agent-patient frame (as is necessary for 2a), not an agent-possessor frame. Then, when one more non-oblique phrase is encountered than the argument structure a particular verb would allow, the hearer has to reject the analysis so far developed, and re-posit something like an agent-possessor-patient frame for (2c–d), or a patient-possessor frame (for 1c) in order for the sentence to be processable (Payne & Barshi 1995a). Yet this frame is arguably required in order to interpret the entire sentence in (2c).

Thus, both in terms of speaker's production and hearer's comprehension, EP phenomena have important implications for descriptively and explanatorily adequate theories of language (Payne & Barshi 1995b). Any theory which assumes that clausal syntax is entirely dependent on lexical predicates (whether simple or derived) would be challenged to account for the Maasai EP sentences, because the basic argument structure of the verb (stem) in question presumably demands both fewer arguments, and arguments with different semantic roles, than what actually occurs. The unusualness of data such as these has led to several proposed theoretical modifications. It also raises the question of what is stored in the lexicon: a verb with its argument structure(s), or such predicates as well as more complex *constructions* (as in Construction Grammar, Goldberg 1995; Fried).

One possible approach to solving the general problem might be along the lines of Baker's (1988, 1992, 1996, this volume) proposals, wherein the argument structure of the verb is adjusted by a *lexical operation* (e.g., NI, or addition of an applicative) such that the "extra" argument is in fact no longer ungoverned or extra. And we have seen that it is extremely common for EPCs to correlate with the addition of an applicative to the verb stem (Aissen 1987; Kimenyi 1980; Marlett 1986; Martin; Zavala; see also Croft 1994); or with Type II NI (Baker, Levy, Velázquez-Castillo, Zavala).

In some EPC cases, a causative analysis might be initially suggested by the fact that something about what is happening to the PM is necessarily understood as the cause of some emotional or psychological effect on the PR. For example, a literal Maasai EP sentence like 'The goat (subject) fats me (object)' is necessarily understood to mean 'My goat is fat with some positive/negative affect on me' (see also (1c) above). The difficulty of a causative analysis, however, is that clear causative morphology is not known to surface in EPCs (and to our knowledge, a causative solution for EP has never been proposed in the literature for any language).[15] In the case of Maasai and Tukang Besi specifically, there do exist overt dative and instrumental applicative morphemes, and overt causative morphemes — but none of these surfaces in the EPCs.

Vergnaud and Zubizarreta's (1992) solution for the one-too-many arguments problem in French is a *small clause* analysis. Like a number of other Indo-European languages, French allows external dative possessors of direct object body parts. Vergnaud and Zubizarreta propose that the dative indirect object and the direct object form a small clause constituent, and it is this *constituent* which satisfies the normal patient/object argument requirements of the transitive verb involved. This proposal accommodates the assumption that clause structure is projected from, or dependent on, the nature of particular lexical entries.

A difficulty with the small clause analysis is that, beyond stating that the PR and PM have some relationship to each other (which is also true for IPCs), it is not clear what explanation the proposal is really providing. If the crucial claim is that the direct and dative objects somehow form a syntactic constituent, then this proposal arguably would not extend to cover the more classic core cases of PR raising because the very basis of the raising analysis is that the possessor and possessed items no *longer* form a constituent but behave as syntactically independent NPs — one now holding a core grammatical relation to the verb (and the other possibly having chômeur status). Nor would the constituency implications of the small clause analysis cover core EPCs as defined here. If the claim concerns a semantic relationship, it is not clear why a language should have both Genitive-NPs and EPCs, because in both there is an obvious semantic relationship between the PM and PR.

Shibatani (1994) suggests that the one-too-many arguments problem is not so much a problem of syntax or of changing grammatical relations, as it is a problem of semantic *relevance* of a PR or other participant to the scene depicted by the verb. Shibatani (see also O'Connor 1992) defines *relevance* in terms of two parameters: (a) physical proximity, and (b) affecting or affectedness. The more relevant a participant is to a given scene, the more easily it can be *integrated* into the scene, even if it is not otherwise included in the scene by virtue of having the agent or patient role dictated by the verb and despite any extra-thematicity.

Shibatani's relevance framework is intended to cover variations in acceptability of the EPC depending on semantic transitivity of the verb, inalienability of the PM, person of the PR, and physical proximity. Different languages can grammaticize different cut-off relevance points. For example, with intransitive verbs, Spanish, German, and French form a cline with respect to whether non-body parts in close physical proximity to an affected participant can code the affected participant in an extra-thematic dative phrase. A promising aspect of Shibatani's analysis is that it aims to provide a comprehensive semantic framework not only for possessor raising constructions and for the Indo-European type of "ethical datives," but also for (Japanese) adversative passives which similarly have one-too-many arguments. One limitation is that it does not address the typical syntactic properties of some EPCs, such as why stative unaccusative subjects may be the most likely items with which PRs can be construed (a transitivity-based argument is suggested for direct object possessa).

Within a Cognitive Grammar framework, Langacker (1993, 1995a, 1995b) develops a Reference-Point model for understanding possessive constructions generally. Langacker argues that, conceptually, there isn't really an "extra" argument. The reference point model is based on "our basic cognitive ability to invoke one entity [=the PR] as a reference point for establishing mental contact with another [=the PM]" (1995b: 27). The relationship between the reference point and the "target" (=PM) is just a special case of metonymy, and thus one might further argue that there is no real "extra" argument. This is, of course, most persuasive in the case of part-whole relationship and inalienable possession.

Insofar as Polinsky and Comrie are concerned with possessive relative clauses in Tsez, they are not actually faced with the one-too-many argument problem of (some) EPCs. Nevertheless, their work does suggest a solution to this very problem for languages which restrict EPCs to highly inalienable possessa. They suggest that relational nouns, part nouns, and other inalienable possessa have a type of argument structure of their own, in that such items do not have "independent existence." The very mention of such nouns evokes a *frame* (Fillmore 1982, 1985) which includes a possessor (or a whole), and it is this frame which licenses the PR.

Finally, a Construction Grammar (Goldberg 1995) approach to the one-too-many argument problem is proposed by Fried for Czech, who also invokes the notion of a frame. Construction Grammar does not attribute exclusive responsibility for clause structure to the argument structure of the verb, but claims that particular *constructions* may have their own unique argument structure arrangements, which language learners acquire along with individual lexemes. The construction itself constrains the range of verbs that may occur in that particular construction. The diachronic rise of a construction is not too dissimilar in notion from Heine's (1997) notion of how a schema may be extended to cover new situations (Martin, Schaefer), and perhaps eventually be grammaticized in a new way.

Some of these proposals are more semantic and others are more structural, but all attempt to deal with the argument structure problem. Without further debating these proposals and the insights they offer here, we propose that the primary explanation of EPCs lies in the domain of voice and differing construals of an event or situation.

6. External possession and the domain of voice and event structure

EPCs manipulate which participants or semantic roles receive prominent syntactic coding as core grammatical relations of the clause. EPCs are likely widespread for the same sorts of reasons that voice alternations are widespread. Classic voice and diathesis phenomena involve manipulations of how agents and patients/themes are morphosyntactically expressed, giving one or the other more or less syntactic prominence. Though there is some division in the field as to exactly what counts as "voice," versus "diathesis," versus "event structure," these domains are typically considered to motivate the existence of, and alternation between active, passive, antipassive, middle, and more recently some types of inverse versus direct constructions (whether defined structurally or functionally, depending on the scholar; cf., Fox & Hopper 1994; Givón 1994; Kemmer 1993, 1994; Thompson 1989).

Croft (1994) and others have extended the discussion of event structure and voice to include applicatives and causatives because these are similarly employed when speakers construe alternative mental models as to what is the initiating agent and what is the end point — as is also true for classic voice phenomena. Almost in passing, Croft mentions possessor ascension as being akin to applicative situations, which he brings into the functional domain of voice. Most typically, the EPC represents a different construal of what is the primary affected end point of an event (Croft 1994; Payne 1997b), and this may motivate coding the PR as an object (whether a primary object, applicative object, an object left outside the verb with NI, etc.) When a speaker construes the PR to be most affected, the PR is the *salient* endpoint of the action or situation. Its affectedness accords it with cognitive saliency. These are precisely the kinds of beginning/end-point construals that can motivate more classic voice alternations.[16]

Such construals are not independent of varying discourse statuses that different participants have. Topical participants (or those in the cognitive focus of attention; Tomlin 1995) are more likely construed as the *relevant* starting points and end points of given actions or situations, and this also plays into voice alternations (cf. Givón 1983, 1994; Thompson 1989). As a case in point, Schaefer claims that Emai EPCs are triggered when the PR has the discourse status of being a predication-affected (secondary) topic. Velázquez-Castillo argues that for Spanish and Guaraní, it is not *affectedness* of the PR that motivates the EPC so much as the speaker's *empathy with* or *adopting the point of view of* the PR. Even so, the PR is likely to be cast as the relevant starting or ending point of the situation. Aissen and Polinsky and Comrie similarly appeal to topicality of the possessor (or an "aboutness" condition) as relevant to EPCs in Tz'utujil and to possessor relatives, respectively.[17]

Less frequently, scholars have described the choice between EPCs and IPCs as based on co-reference clarification (e.g., Aissen 1987; Marlett 1986; Martin, Rude, Schaefer; see also Podlesskaya & Rakhilina for evidence of this motivation in Russian). To our knowledge, this reference clarification always involves EPCs with transitive stems. In particular, EP is motivated when the PR of an object is *not* co-referential with the subject. Although not widely reported, we suspect that this functional correlation with EPCs is in fact quite common, at least statistically. The effect of this may perhaps be appreciated by examining the following set of simple Hebrew clauses:

(3) a. *Hu roxets yadaim.*
he wash hands
'He$_i$ is washing his$_i$ hands.'

b. *Hu roxets et hayadaim shelo.*
he wash DEF:DIRECT:OBJ DEF.hands POSS:3:SG:MASC
'He$_i$ is washing his$_i$ hands.'

c. *Hu roxets lo (et ha)yadaim.*
he wash to:him (DEF:DIRECT:OBJ DEF)hands
'He$_i$ is washing his$_j$ hands.' (strongest reading)
('He$_i$ is washing his$_i$ hands' is also a possible interpretation, but is less strong.)

In (3a), there is no overt internal possessor, but the subject is interpreted as the possessor of hands (similarly to Spanish, Velázquez-Castillo). In (3b) there is an internally possessed object, and the subject is likewise interpreted as coreferential with the possessor. In (3c), however, the possessor is expressed in the external dative, and the strongest interpretation is that subject and possessor are *not* co-referential (though other contextual factors, such as if there is something unusual about the washing, may override this interpretation).

One motivation for this specific pattern of co-reference interpretation may be grounded in iconicity (Haiman 1980), in that an EPC presents an iconic relation between referential distinctness and syntactic distinctness. As Podlesskaya and Rakhilina allude, if the subject and the possessor of a body part (i.e., the most accessible PM) object are co-referential, then the action is essentially a reflexive one, and the subject and PR are referentially or semantically non-distinct (see also, Wierzbicka 1988). In the Hebrew examples above, this correlates with either internal possession (3b), or a straightforward interpretation that the subject must be the possessor of the object (3a). When a PR is well-individuated from (i.e., non-coreferential with) other participants in the scene, iconically coding the PR as a core (often dative or direct object) argument syntactically individuates the PR, as in (3c). In sum, an EPC externalizes the possessor-as-reference-point (Langacker 1993), making it syntactically more distinct from other participants or referents in the clause.

At first glance, there may seem to be no obvious connection between co-referential distinctness and affectedness, or between co-reference and topic, as motivations for structurally similar constructions. However, if external possession is seen as ultimately grounded in issues of *reference point* or *point-of-view*, then a connection begins to suggest itself: if something is construed as a reference point distinct from the subject, it may for that very fact serve as a conceptually prominent (affected) endpoint.

Croft (1994) proposes that the *idealized cognitive model* of an event is "self-contained" as to its causal starting point (expressed as subject) and necessarily includes an endpoint or a "final result" (expressed as object or stative subject).[18] Croft particularly notes that a state is a "final result" of an event, and thus he includes statives as being endpoint oriented. He suggests that this model accounts for the existence of derived causative and applicative verbal forms, as "these forms describe events that are causally more complex than the event type represented by the 'basic' verb form;" however, they subsume that more complex event to the idealized cognitive model by re-arranging what is conceived of as the cognitive starting point or endpoint. Croft goes on to say that derived causative and applicative forms "appear to be related to voice functions" (94). Similarly, EPCs take more complex participant situations (involving a possessor), and due to the speaker's construal of the possessor as the primary affected endpoint, express the possessor as object (whether primary object, direct object, or indirect object) or as stative subject. Thus, EPCs belong to the domain of voice in the same extended sense as do causatives and applicatives.

Notes

1 Other dialects of Maasai are more conservative in terms of the types of verbs they will allow in EPCs (Payne 1997a).

2 We will shortly discuss the distinction between *possessor raising* and *external possession*.

3 Author's names which are not followed by a year of publication refer to chapters in this volume.

4 On accounts of *raising* per se, see Postal 1974, Chomsky 1982, and Langacker 1995b, *inter alia*.

5 Whether this should even count as an instance of external possession is debatable because *him* is clearly governed by the core argument frame of the basic predicate *bit*. Any sense of a

possessor is collapsed into the same participant as the patient. The construction would, however, probably fit within the extended sense in which Velázquez-Castillo uses the term *external possession* for Spanish examples like *Ella lavó las manos* 'She washed the hands' (i.e., She_i washed her_i hands). In this Spanish example, the agent and understood possessor are collapsed into the same argument.

6 Internal Possession (IP) is a construction in which the PR is internal to the constituent containing the PM, as in Genitive-NP constructions like *my hat.*

7 Note, however, that this is not necessarily the same thing as a raising analysis.

8 Some Maasai dialects allow EPCs for unergative arguments and some even for transitive agents; in these types the EPR is still expressed as primary object and so the Relational Succession Law is even more clearly violated.

9 Munro does not particulary discuss topic issues for Chickasaw, though she does mention "discourse importance." Martin speculates on the role of topic in the diachronic development of EPCs in Western Muskogean generally.

10 Sahaptian also has transitive object EPRs which involve an applicative. Rude claims these EPRs have "secondary topic" status. Schaefer appeals to "secondary topic" or "predication-affected topic" status as a motivation for EPCs in Emai. For Emai and for the Sahaptian transitives, we offer the hypothesis that the "secondary topic" or "predication-affected topic" likely pertains to the domain of what is construed as the primary affected endpoint of an event, which we will discuss shortly.

11 Multiple instances of "identical" GRs may possibly be allowed where there is a part-whole or co-referential relationship between referents. And we note (at least surface) "double case" constructions.

12 The ease with which underived ditransitive predicates allow EPCs requires more research. Maasai (Payne 1997a) and Tukang Besi (Donohue) disfavor them.

13 The relative status of *patient-affecting* versus *dynamic non-affecting* in Haspelmath's hierarchy also merits further investigation. If the English *She cut me on the leg* is included as an EPC, *cut* is certainly not as patient-affecting as is *break*; yet *break* disallows the construction (cf. **She broke me on the leg*.) This English construction is apparently limited to verbs which Fillmore (1977) describes as AGENT–GOAL verbs (cf. *She gave me*=goal/dative *a cut*=patient *on the leg*), and not as AGENT–PATIENT verbs (compare **She broke me*=patient *on the arm*/**She gave me a break on the arm*).

14 We particularly have in mind dative, double-case marking, and the Maasai and Tukang Besi-type of EPCs which do not involve applicatives or noun incorporation. Baker (1988) argues that applicatives and NI do yield lexical entries that govern the "extra" argument (so that there is, in fact, no extra argument). Though analyses certainly can, and have, been developed within the mentioned theories (cf. Vergnaud and Zubizaretta 1992; Donohue), the point is that how to do so is not always straightforward.

15 Gerdts notes that Relational Grammar "possessor union analyses" of EPCs structurally parallel causative clause union analyses, in that the PR and PM are seen as occupying an embedded "clause" (though there is no overt predicate morpheme in the "embedded clause"). This is not entirely dissimilar from Vergnaud and Zubizarreta's (1992) "small clause" proposal, discussed shortly.

16 We recognize that some languages require an EPC under certain inalienability conditions. Since there is then no choice in the coding, one might object that in such cases it cannot be a voice(-like) phenomenon, under the presupposition that *voice* is always a discourse-pragmatic option.

However, we see this just as a matter of grammaticalization. Because a structure is required under certain semantic conditions does not entail that the phenomenon is thereby disconnected from the domain of what motivates voice options. To the contrary, it is presumably because the indicated inalienability conditions so often coincide with pragmatic affectedness and reference-point salience of the PR, that the construction eventually becomes required under the indicated semantic conditions. The required-EPC situations seem to us completely analogous to requiring an inverse construction if the object is a speech-act participant; or requiring object coding of a human recipient (e.g., "obligatory indirect object advancement" as in Tzotzil; Aissen 1987).

17 In contrast to voice and topic motivations, Uehara notes Kuno's (1973) and Takahashi's (1996) claims that Japanese EPCs are motivated by (contrastive) focus on the PR. This reported function merits careful study, as it is reported almost nowhere else in the literature. Uehara does note that no corpus studies examining the distribution of EPCs exist for Japanese.

18 Croft's elaboration of semantic event structure is presaged by DeLancey (1982), who describes an event as having an Onset/Agent/Source and a Termination/Patient/Goal.

References

Aissen, Judith. 1979. "Possessor Ascension in Tzotzil." In Laura Martin (ed.), *Papers in Mayan Linguistics*. Colombia, Missouri: Lucas Brothers, 89–108.

Aissen, Judith. 1987. *Tzotzil Clause Structure*. Dordrecht: Reidel.

Allen, Barbara, Donald Gardiner and Donald Frantz. 1984. "Noun Incorporation in Southern Tiwa." *International Journal of American Linguistics* 52: 388–403.

Allen, Barbara, Donald Gardiner and Donald Frantz. 1990. "Verb Agreement, Possessor Ascension, and Multistratal Representation in Southern Tiwa." In Paul Postal and Brian Joseph (eds.), *Studies in Relational Grammar 3*. Chicago: University of Chicago Press, 321–382.

Ameka, Felix. 1995. "Body parts in Ewe grammar." In Hilary Chappell and William McGregor (eds.), *The Grammar of Inalienability*. Berlin: Mouton de Gruyter, 783–840.

Baker, Mark. 1988. *Incorporation: A Theory of Grammatical Function Changing*. Chicago: University of Chicago Press.

Baker, Mark. 1992. "Structure Preservation and Mohawk Inchoative Verbs." *Berkeley Linguistics Society* 11: 261–275.

Baker, Mark. 1996. *The Polysynthesis Parameter*. New York: Oxford University Press.

Barshi, Immanuel and Doris Payne. 1996. "The Interpretation of 'Possessor Raising' in a Maasai Dialect." In Lionel Bender and Thomas Hinnebusch (eds.) *Afrikanistische Arbeitspapiere 45*. Köln: Universität zu Köln, 207–226.

Barshi, Immanuel and Doris Payne. 1998. "Argument Structure and Maasai Possessive Interpretation: Implications for Language Learning." In Alice Healy and Lyle Bourne, Jr. (eds.), *Foreign Language Learning: Psycholinguistic Experiments on Training and Retention*. Mahwah, NJ: Erlbaum, 213–229.

Bell, Sarah. 1983. "Advancements and Ascensions in Cebuano." In David M. Perlmutter (ed.), *Studies in Relational Grammar I*. Chicago: University of Chicago Press, 143–218.

Berman, Ruth. 1982. "Dative Marking of the Affectee Role: Data from Modern Hebrew." *Hebrew Annual Review* 6: 35–59.

Bickford, J. Albert. 1986. "Possessor Ascension in Kinyarwanda." *Chicago Linguistic Society* 22: 129–143.

Blake, Barry. 1984. "Problems for Possessor Ascension: Some Australian Examples." *Linguistics* 22: 437–453.

Boland, Julie E. 1993. "The Role of Verb Argument Structure in Sentence Processing: Distinguishing Between Syntactic and Semantic Effects." *Journal of Psycholinguistic Research* 22: 133–152.

Carden, Guy, Lynn Gordon, and Pamela Munro. 1982. "Raising Rules and the Projection Principle." Paper presented at the 1982 Annual Meeting of the Linguistics Society of America.

Chao, Yuen Ren. 1968. *A Grammar of Spoken Chinese*. Berkeley: UC Press.

Chappell, Hilary. 1995. "Inalienability and the Personal Domain in Mandarin Chinese Discourse." In Hilary Chappell and William McGregor (eds.), *The Grammar of Inalienability: A Typological Perspective on Body Part Terms and the Part-Whole Relation.* Berlin: Mouton de Gruyter, 465–527.

Chappell, Hilary, and William McGregor. 1995a. "Prolegomena to a Theory of Inalienability." In Hilary Chappell and William McGregor (eds.), *The Grammar of Inalienability: A Typological Perspective on Body Part Terms and the Part-Whole Relation.* Berlin: Mouton de Gruyter, 3–30.

Chappell, Hilary, and William McGregor (eds.). 1995b. *The Grammar of Inalienability: A Typological Perspective on Body Part Terms and the Part-Whole Relation.* Berlin: Mouton de Gruyter.

Chomsky, Noam. 1982. *Lectures on Government and Binding*. Dordrecht: Foris.

Clark, Marybeth. 1995. "Where Do You Feel? — Stative Verbs and Body-part Terms in Mainland Southeast Asia." In Hilary Chappell and William McGregor (eds.), *The Grammar of Inalienability*. Berlin: Mouton de Gruyter, 529–564.

Clifton, Charles, Shari Speer, and Steven Abney. 1991. "Parsing Arguments: Phrase Structure and Argument Structure as Determinants of Initial Parsing Decisions." *Journal of Memory and Language* 30: 251–271.

Constable, Peter. 1989. *Basic Clause Structure in Veracruz Huastec.* M.A. Thesis, University of North Dakota.

Croft, William. 1985. "Indirect Object 'Lowering'" *Berkeley Linguistics Society* 11: 39–51.

Croft, William. 1994. "Voice: Beyond Control and Affectedness." In Barbara Fox and Paul Hopper (eds.), *Voice: Form and Function.* Amsterdam: John Benjamins, 89–117.

Davies, William. 1984. "Inalienable Possession and Choctaw Referential Coding." *International Journal of American Linguistics* 50: 384–402.

DeLancey, Scott. 1982. "Aspect, Transitivity, and Viewpoint." In Paul Hopper (ed.), *Tense-Aspect: Between Semantics and Pragmatics*. Amsterdam: John Benjamins, 167–183.

Dooley, Robert. 1982. "Options in the Pragmatic Structuring of Guaraní Sentences." *Language* 58: 307–331.

Dryer, Matthew. 1986. "Primary Objects, Secondary Objects, and Antidative." *Language* 62: 808–845.

Fillmore, Charles. 1977. "The Case for Case Reopened." In Peter Cole and Jerrold M. Sadock (eds.), *Grammatical Relations.* (Syntax and Semantics, 8.). New York: Academic Press, 59–81.

Fillmore, Charles. 1982. "Frame Semantics." *Linguistics in the Morning Calm.* Seoul: Hanshin, 111–138.

Fillmore, Charles. 1985. "Frames and the Semantics of Understanding." *Quaderni di Semantica* 6/2: 222–254.

Foley, William. 1991. *The Yimas Language of New Guinea.* Stanford: Stanford University Press.

Fox, Barbara. 1981. "Body Part Syntax: Towards a Universal Characterization." *Studies in Language* 5: 323–342.

Fox, Barbara and Paul Hopper (eds). 1994. *Voice: Form and Function.* Amsterdam: John Benjamins.

Gerdts, Donna. 1992. "The Syntax of Case-Marked Possessors in Korean." In C. Lee (ed.), *Proceedings of the Korean Syntax and Semantics Workshop (Linguistic Society of America Summer Institute, University of California, Santa Cruz, July 1991),* 11–26.

Gernsbacher, Morton Ann. 1990. *Language Comprehension as Structure Building.* Hillsdale, NJ: Erlbaum.

Givón, T. (ed.) 1983. *Topic Continuity in Discourse: Quantified Cross-Language Studies.* Amsterdam: John Benjamins.

Givón, T. (ed.) 1994. *Voice and Inversion.* Amsterdam: John Benjamins.

Goldberg, Adele. 1995. *A Construction Grammar Approach to Argument Structure.* Chicago: University of Chicago Press.

Haiman, John. 1980. "The Iconicity of Grammar: Isomorphism and Motivation." *Language* 56: 515–540.

Harris, Alice. 1976. *Grammatical Relations in Modern Georgian.* Ph.D. dissertation, Harvard University.

Harris, Alice. 1981. *Georgian Syntax.* Cambridge: Cambridge University Press.

Heine, Bernd. 1997. *Possession: Cognitive Sources, Forces, and Grammaticalization.* New York: Cambridge University Press.

Hopper, Paul. 1987. "Stability and Change in VN/NV Alternating Languages: A Study in Pragmatics and Linguistic Typology." In Jef Verschueren and Marcella Bertuccelli-Papi (eds.), *The Pragmatic Perspective.* Amsterdam: John Benjamins, 455–476.

Hyman, Larry. 1995. "The Syntax of Body Parts in Haya." In Hilary Chappell and William McGregor (eds.), *The Grammar of Inalienability.* Berlin: Mouton de Gruyter, 865–890.

Hyman, Larry, Danny Alford, and Elizabeth Akpati. 1970. "Inalienable Possession in Igbo." *Journal of West African Languages* 7: 85–101.

Keenan, Edward. 1984. "Semantic Correlates of the Ergative/Absolutive Distinction." *Linguistics* 22: 197–223.

Kemmer, Suzanne. 1993. *The Middle Voice*. Amsterdam: John Benjamins.

Kemmer, Suzanne. 1994. "Middle Voice, Transitivity, and the Elaboration of Events." In Barbara Fox and Paul Hopper (eds.), *Voice: Form and Function*. Amsterdam: John Benjamins, 179–228.

Kimenyi, Alexandre. 1980. *A Relational Grammar of Kinyarwanda*. Berkeley: University of California Press.

Kintsch, Walter. 1988. "The Use of Knowledge in Discourse Processing: A Construction Integration Model." *Psychological Review* 95: 163–182.

König, Ekkehard and Martin Haspelmath. 1997. "Les constructions à possesseur externe dans les langues de l'Europe." In Jack Feuillet (ed.), *Actance et Valence dans les Langues d'Europe*. Berlin: Mouton de Gruyter, 525–606.

Kuno, Susumu. 1973. *The Structure of the Japanese Language*. Cambridge, MA: MIT Press.

Langacker, Ronald. 1993. "Reference-Point Constructions." *Cognitive Linguistics* 4: 1–38.

Langacker, Ronald. 1995a. "Possession and Possessive Constructions." In John Taylor and Robert MacLaury (eds.), *Language and the Cognitive Construal of the World*. Berlin: Mouton de Gruyter, 51–79.

Langacker, Ronald. 1995b. "Raising and Transparency." *Language* 71: 1–62.

Marlett, Stephen. 1986. "Syntactic Levels and Multiattachment in Sierra Popoluca." *International Journal of American Linguistics* 52: 359–387.

Martin, Jack. 1993. "'Inalienable Possession' in Creek (and its Possible Origin)." *International Journal of American Linguistics* 59: 442–452.

Mitchell, Don. 1994. "Sentence Parsing." In Morton Ann Gernsbacher (ed.), *Handbook of Psycholinguistics*. New York: Academic Press, 375–409.

Mithun, Marianne. 1984. "The Evolution of Noun Incorporation." *Language* 60: 847–894.

Mithun, Marianne. 1986. "On the Nature of Noun Incorporation." *Language* 62: 32–37.

Munro, Pamela. 1984. "The Syntactic Status of Object Possessor Raising in Western Muskogean." *Berkeley Linguistics Society* 10: 634–649.

Munro, Pamela and Lynn Gordon. 1982. "Syntactic Relations in Western Muskogean: a Typological Perspective." *Language* 58: 81–115.

O'Connor, Mary Catherine. 1992. *Topics in Northern Pomo Grammar*. New York: Garland.

O'Connor, Mary Catherine. 1996. "The Situated Interpretation of Possessor Raising." In Masayoshi Shibatani and Sandra Thompson (eds.). *Grammtical Constructions: Their Form and Meaning*. Oxford: Oxford University Press, 125–156.

Payne, Doris L. 1995. "Verb Initial Languages and Information Order." In Pamela Downing and Michael Noonan (eds.), *Word Order in Discourse*. Amsterdam: John Benjamins, 449–485.

Payne, Doris L. 1997a. "The Maasai External Possessor Construction." In Joan Bybee, John Haiman, and Sandra Thompson (eds.), *Essays on Language Function and Language Type*. Amsterdam: John Benjamins, 395–422.

Payne, Doris L. 1997b. "Argument Structure and Locus of Affect in the Maasai External Possession Construction." *Berkeley Linguistics Society 23. Special Session on African Languages*, 98–115.

Payne, Doris, and Immanuel Barshi. 1995a. "A Sentence-Processing Account of Possessor Raising in Maasai." Paper presented at the Eighth CUNY Conference on Sentence Processing, Tucson, Arizona.

Payne, Doris, and Immanuel Barshi. 1995b. "A Holistic Account of Possessor Raising in Maasai." Paper presented at the Conference on Functional Approaches to Grammar, Albuquerque, New Mexico. Linguistics Society of America Summer Institute conference.

Payne, Doris, Mitsuyo Hamaya, and Peter Jacobs. 1994. "Active, Inverse and Passive in Maasai." In T. Givón (ed.), *Voice and Inversion*. Amsterdam: John Benjamins, 283–315.

Payne, Thomas. 1995. "Object Incorporation in Panare." *International Journal of American Linguistics* 61: 295–311.

Perlmutter, David and Paul Postal. 1983. "The Relational Succession Law." In David Perlmutter (ed.), *Studies in Relational Grammar 1*. Chicago: University of Chicago Press, 30–80.

Postal, Paul. 1974. *On Raising*. Cambridge, MA: MIT Press.

Rude, Noel. 1985. *Studies in Nez Perce Grammar and Discourse*. Ph.D. dissertation, University of Oregon.

Schaefer, Ronald. 1995. "On the Discourse Function of Possessor Movement in Emai Prose Narratives." In Pamela Downing and Michael Noonan (eds.), *Word Order in Discourse*. Amsterdam: John Benjamins, 487–515.

Seiler, Hansjakob 1983. *Possession as an Operational Dimension of Language*. Tübingen: Gunter Narr Verlag.

Shibatani, Masayoshi. 1994. "An Integrational Approach to Possessor Raising, Ethical Datives, and Adversative Passives." *Berkeley Linguistic Society* 20: 461–486.

Takahashi, Chioko. 1996. *Multiplicity, Optimality, and Constraints on the Distribution of Nominative Case in Japanese*. Ph.D. dissertation, Cornell University.

Thompson, Chad. 1989. *Voice and Obviation in Athabaskan and Other Languages*. Ph.D. dissertation, University of Oregon.

Tomlin, Russell. 1995. "Focal Attention, Voice, and Word Order." In Pamela Downing and Michael Noonan (eds.), *Word Order in Discourse*. Amsterdam: John Benjamins, 517–554.

Tucker, A. N. and J. Tompo Ole Mpaayei. 1955. *A Maasai Grammar with Vocabulary*. London: Longmans, Green and Co.

Tuggy, David. 1980. "Ethical Dative and Possessor Omission *si*, Possessor Ascension *no*!" *Working Papers of the Summer Institute of Linguistics* 24: 97–141.

Velázquez-Castillo, Maura. 1995a. "Noun Incorporation and Object Placement in Discourse: The Case of Guaraní." In Pamela Downing and Michael Noonan (eds.), *Word Order in Discourse*. Amsterdam: John Benjamins, 555–579.

Velázquez-Castillo, Maura. 1995b. "Noun Incorporation in Guaraní: A Functional Analysis." *Linguistics* 33: 673–709

Velázquez-Castillo, Maura. 1996. *The Grammar of Possession: Inalienability, Incorporation and Possessor Ascension in Guaraní.* (Studies in Language Companion Series 33.) Amsterdam: John Benjamins.

Vergnaud, Jean-Roger and Maria Luisa Zubizarreta. 1992. The Definite Determiner and the Inalienable Constructions in French and English." *Linguistic Inquiry* 23: 595–652.

Weir, E. M. Helen. 1990. "Incorporation in Nadëb." In Doris L. Payne (ed.), *Amazonian Linguistics: Studies in Lowland South American Languages.* Austin: University of Texas Press, 321–363.

Wierzbicka, Anna. 1988. *The Semantics of Grammar.* Amsterdam: John Benjamins.

Wilhelm, Andrea. 1992. *Noun Incorporation in Northern Athapaskan.* M.A. thesis, University of Calgary.

Youn, Cheong. 1989. *A Relational Analysis of Korean Multiple Nominative Constructions.* Ph.D. dissertation, SUNY at Buffalo.

Part II

Psycholinguistic Perspectives on External Possession

External Possession and Language Processes

Murray Singer
University of Manitoba

External possession (EP) refers to the expression of semantic possessor (PR) and possessed (PM) in separate constituents, with at least the PR as a core grammatical relation of the verb. The particular grammatical case (e.g., accusative, dative) of the possessor varies from language to language (Barshi & Payne 1996; Payne & Barshi, this volume). One type is exemplified by the Spanish for 'The mother cut her hair', namely *La mamá le cortó el pelo*. This sentence is literally translated as 'The mother to.her cut the hair.' A striking feature of many EP constructions (EPCS) is that they are marked by an "extra" argument, relative to the usual argument structure of the verb in question. The appearance of the extra case, such as 'to.her' in the present example, appears to signal the interpretation of possession.

This chapter was designed to address the study of EP from the framework of experimental psychology, with particular reference to the work of Barshi and Payne (1996, 1997) and Uehara (this volume). In turn, I will address (a) the experimental methodology of these studies, (b) the inferential elements of the comprehension of EP, and (c) the relevance of individual differences in language processes for the study of EP.

1. Experimental methods of inspecting external possession

1.1 *Sentence completions*

Sentence completion and other production techniques have long been used to derive respondents' grammatical insights (Fletcher 1984; Reder 1983). This technique is exemplified by Uehara's exploration of EP in Japanese (this volume). Her participants were asked to form complete sentences from 2–*ga* and 3–*ga* strings. Consider example (1):

(1)	a.	*Sobo-ga*	*kaseihu-ga*	*Takahashi-san-ni*
	b.	My grandmother	housekeeper	PN-Ms./Mr.
		-NOM	-NOM	-DAT

One reading of the 2–*ga* string in (1) is the EP, 'the grandmother's housekeeper.' Uehara reported an appreciable number of such interpretations by her respondents, especially for 3–*ga* strings.

Sentence completions provide access to people's conscious reflections about sentences and text. The benefits of this measure are balanced by certain disadvantages. First, the generation of sentence completions may intrude on ordinary language processes (Christensen 1988). As such, it reflects what people can do, but not necessarily what they ordinarily do. Second, sentence completion occurs after, rather than during, the reading of a text segment. "Off-line" measures of this sort are considered to reflect language processes somewhat less faithfully than behaviors that are measured concurrently with comprehension.

The shortcomings of sentence completion may be mitigated by pairing it with an on-line measure of processing. This approach is exemplified in a study of the implicit causality of verbs (Vonk 1985). In that investigation, participants were asked to complete sentence fragments such as 'Harry won the money from Albert because …' Insofar as this sequence tends to designate 'Harry' as the causal agent of winning, people typically generated completions such as 'he played skillfully'. This sentence-completion experiment was complemented by another one, in which the participants' eye movements were tracked when they read stimuli which began with phrases such as (2a) and (2b).

(2) a. Harry won the money from Mary because he …
b. Harry won the money from Mary because she …

All of the stimuli were complete sentences, such as 'Harry won the money from Mary because she played carelessly'. Each sentence ended with a congruent clause, in the sense that Mary playing carelessly is consistent with Harry winning. However, the readers fixated the pronoun for 50 milliseconds longer when the pronoun was inconsistent with the implicit causality of the verb (i.e., 2b) than when it was consistent (i.e., 2a). Thus, the sentence completion data were corroborated by the eyetracking data. In general, sentence completions can suggest valuable hypotheses that may be further explored using on-line measures.

1.2 *Syntactic judgements*

Syntactic judgements reveal people's linguistic intuitions. For example, respondents can be asked to assess the grammaticality of an entire string of words

(McElree 1993), or to signal the point at which a string ceases to be grammatical (Mauner, Tanenhaus, & Carlson 1995). In this regard, Barshi and Payne (1996; Payne & Barshi, this volume) asked Maasai respondents to identify the possessed entity in sequences bearing possible EP interpretations. Barshi and Payne (1996) varied the degree to which the discourse context supported one noun phrase or the other as identifying the possessed item, as well as the order of appearance of noun phrases competing for the "possessed" assignment. Barshi and Payne reported that context predominates in influencing the respondent's interpretation.

Like sentence completion, syntactic judgment is an off-line measure. Therefore, it too may be fruitfully complemented with on-line measures. Pertinent to this suggestion is Payne and Barshi's observation (this volume) that EPCS may "garden-path" the understander. Garden-pathing occurs when the beginning of a sentence favors a grammatical analysis that must ultimately be rejected. For example, when one reads 'The florist sent the flowers was very pleased', one may initially misinterpret the florist to be the agent of the action (Rayner, Carlson, & Frazier 1983). Garden-pathing may be experimentally studied by scrutinizing the reading times of, and eye fixations upon, critical regions of the sentence (Ferreira & Clifton 1986; Rayner et al. 1983).

Garden-pathing in the comprehension of EP sentences may result when a transitive verb creates the expectation that the sentence object will function as a patient. The object may consequently have to be reinterpreted as a possessor. As a result, the measurement of reading times in the comprehension of EP sentences would likely yield data that converges with syntactic judgements.

In summary, investigators have already applied several familiar off-line measures to the study of EP. These measures could be beneficially complemented with others that are made concurrently with reading and comprehension.

2. External possession and inference processes

Inference is so pervasive in language understanding that it has been characterized as the core of the comprehension process (Schank 1976; Singer 1994). It is worthwhile to examine the inferential features of the comprehension of EPCS. One may gain insight in this endeavor by first considering the role of inference in argument constructions more typical than EP.

2.1 *Non-EP constructions*

Understanding even simple clauses requires a deceptively complex array of mechanisms to determine (a) which cases are entailed by the intended sense of the verb, (b) which of those cases are explicitly mentioned in the clause, and (c) which nouns or other parts of speech correspond to each case. Each of these issues will be considered in turn.

2.1.1 *Inferring which cases are relevant*
The problem of identifying the entailed cases is illustrated by (3).

(3) a. Frank was walking.
b. Frank was walking the dog.

Although 'walk' is typically intransitive, the reader cannot determine definitively, upon encountering 'walking' in (3a) and (3b), which sense of 'walk' is under consideration (Charniak 1981). Rather, the entire clause must be examined before the intended interpretation of 'walking' is inferred, and the corresponding constellation of cases consequently invoked. The related problem of whether verbs such as 'walk' have one or more lexical entries remains controversial in the study of language processes (Carlson & Tanenhaus 1988; Charniak 1981; Cottrell & Small 1985).

2.1.2 *Inferring case assignments*
Once the verb sense has been selected, there remains the nontrivial problem of determining the case assignment for each noun. In certain examples, such as 'The teacher read the principal's announcement to the class', this may be relatively straightforward. However, theorists have identified a variety of subproblems in case assignment. First, it is necessary to determine which of the relevant cases have corresponding nouns at all. Consider set (4).

(4) a. Sally read to the child.
b. Sally read the child the story.

Both (4a) and (4b) are grammatical. However, for (4a), the reader must determine that no patient has been specified. For (4b), case assignment is complicated by the appearance of 'the child' immediately after the verb, and without the preposition 'to.' A satisfactory case assignment for (4b) must be inferred with reference to the meaning of the sentence nouns.

I am not suggesting that verb sense selection strictly *precedes* the assignment of nouns to their cases. For example, in comprehending 'Frank was walking', the reader might tentatively adopt the preferred, intransitive, interpretation of 'walking', and assign 'Frank' as the agent. Only upon encountering 'the dog' could a revision of sense selection be made. In general, the strictly serial execution of syntactic and semantic decisions is considered untenable (Waltz & Pollack 1985).

2.1.3 *Are empty cases included in sentence representation?*
A second subproblem of case assignment is whether null, or empty, cases, such as the patient for (4a), appear in the mental representation of a sentence. In an investigation of this problem, Mauner et al. (1995) proposed that the representation of "short passive" sentences such as 'The game show's wheel was spun' includes an agent case, albeit an empty one. To test this hypothesis, they examined the processing of sentences such as those in set (5).

(5) a. The game show's wheel was spun to win a prize and lots of cash. (short passive)
b. The game show's wheel spun to win a prize and lots of cash. (intransitive)

Both (5a) and (5b) included a clause specifying the rationale of the action. On the assumption that a rationale requires a agent, Mauner et al. (1995) argued that (5a) is felicitous whereas (5b) is not. In the experiment, for each word in the stimulus sentence, the participants pressed a "yes" button to signal that the sentence was still sensible, and to view the next word. They pressed "no" as soon as the sentence no longer made sense. Consistent with Mauner et al.'s hypothesis, the readers registered "no" responses for 41% of the intransitive sentences but only 12% of the short passives. In addition, reading time was higher in the rationale clause for the intransitive sentences than the short passives. The researchers concluded that understanding short passives results in the representation of empty cases.

2.1.4 *Is garden-pathing in case assignment demanding of cognitive resources?*
As discussed earlier, a reader is garden-pathed when a preliminary syntactic or semantic decision is refuted by a later portion of the sentence. Carlson and Tanenhaus (1988) advanced the hypothesis that, in contrast with most instances of garden-pathing, case reassignment would not consume extra processes and time. Their rationale for this proposal was that verbs have only a single lexical entry. Although this entry may be associated with different constellations of cases, all of the cases are activated when any token of the verb is encountered. Reinterpreting a verb as transitive rather than intransitive, for example, would not result in greatly increased demands on cognitive resources.

To evaluate this hypothesis, Carlson and Tanenhaus (1988) contrasted garden-pathing in semantic decisions as opposed to case assignment decisions. On each trial of the experiment, the participants read a sentence and pressed a key to indicate whether it was sensible. The semantic materials are illustrated by set (6):

(6) a. Bill set the alarm clock onto the shelf.
b. Bill put the alarm clock onto the shelf.

Because 'set' in (6a) is ambiguous, the reader has the opportunity to select the wrong sense. Consistent with this observation, sensibility judgements took longer for (6a) than (6b).

Set (7) shows a parallel set of sentences in which the ambiguity of (7a) results from the case-assignment alternatives.

(7) a. Sue loaded the truck with bricks.
b. Sue filled the truck with bricks.

Whereas (7b) is unambiguous, (7a) may be initially interpreted to mean either that the truck was loaded with something or on something. In spite of this ambiguity, there was no statistical difference between the sensibility judgment times for (7a) and (7b). The joint pattern of results for sets such as (6) and (7) caused Carlson and Tanenhaus (1988) to conclude that case assignment garden-pathing is not taxing of cognitive resources. Other studies of this sort would be useful to assess the robustness of this outcome.

2.1.5 *Conclusion*

Successful case assignment in sentence processing routinely requires a wide variety of inferences. The role of these inferences in comprehending EP will be considered next. The next section will also address the factors that guide case assignment in EP.

2.2 *The external possession construction*

Comprehending EP clauses involves two of the fundamental features of case inference that were considered earlier. First, the identification of which cases are relevant to the ongoing clause results in the determination that the current construction is indeed EP. Second, the case assignments must be performed. For EP, the latter problem may be subdivided into the identification of the possessor and the assignment of the other cases. Each of these processing problems will be considered in turn.

2.2.1 *Which cases are relevant? Inferring EP*

To determine that the current construction is one of EP, the understander must infer which cases are relevant to the current construction. Consider again set (1):

(1)	a.	*Sobo-ga*	*kaseihu-ga*	*Takahashi-san-ni*
	b.	My grandmother	housekeeper	PN-Ms./Mr.
		-NOM	-NOM	-DAT

String (1a) is exceptional in its presentation of consecutive nominative phrases, marked by *-ga* strings. The Japanese reader must consider at least three alternatives in the interpretation of (1a) (Uehara, this volume): First, (1a) might initiate an EPC. Second, it might initiate a competing construction, such as center-embedding or a parallel subject construction. Third, it might simply be ungrammatical. Indeed, the ostensive appearance of two or more nouns in the same grammatical case is typical of EP (e.g., Barshi & Payne 1996).

Few psychological investigations of EP have been conducted to date. As a result, existing studies tend more to suggest appealing solutions to the problem of how the understander identifies an EPC than to definitively select among those solutions. Uehara's investigation (this volume) of sequences such as (1a) highlighted the role of noun-phrase order and semantics in EP identification. With regard to order, she reported that respondents who generated sentence completions to 3–*ga* strings generally extracted EP interpretations that grouped noun phrases 2 and 3 rather than 1 and 2. However, the same pattern emerged for sequences that prohibited an EP reading by the inclusion of a *-wa* noun phrase (Uehara's Dataset 2). This discounted noun-phrase order as a factor specific to the organization of noun phrases in EPCS.

Conversely, Uehara's findings tended to implicate clause semantics in the comprehension of EPCS. First, certain *-ga* strings prohibit an EP interpretation by their meaning (e.g., her transcribed translation, 'father-Nom PN-NOM famous-writer-Nom'). Second, she observed that inalienable possession may be more subject to EP interpretation than is alienable possession.

At a level of analysis different from distinguishing the trade-off between phrase order and semantics in guiding EP interpretations, Payne and Barshi review several general solutions to the problem of EP. Meriting special consideration is their reference to Shibatani's (1994) proposal that the appearance of "too many arguments" in EP is a problem of the *relevance* of the arguments to the current clause. The concept of discourse relevance has received extensive consideration in psycholinguistics (Clark 1982; Grice 1975; Sperber & Wilson 1986). Clark (1982) argued that many expressions, such as (8), have a sense specifically relevant to the current context.

(8) Linda managed to porch the newspaper.

Clark observed that (8) should stymie any traditional parser, simply because *porch* is a noun, not a verb. To the contrary, Clark observed that people have little difficulty understanding "contextual expressions" of this sort. He concluded that the pervasiveness of contextual expressions suggests that the mental processes that contribute to their comprehension constitute the typical processes of sentence comprehension, rather than exceptional ones.

The alternative to Clark's (1982) analysis is that, for case assignment, pronoun resolution, and other facets of sentence processing, there exist default procedures that usually yield a satisfactory result. Only when the default procedures occasionally fail does the understander resort to complex reasoning to comprehend the sentence (Murphy 1985).

These alternatives are worthy of consideration with respect to EP. I speculate that if the parsing of EP phrases depends on conscious reasoning, processing time ought to be longer than for non-EP phrases with comparable superficial features such as length. If, on the other hand, EP is a *bona fide*, albeit rare, case construction, then its parsing processes should not be particularly time-consuming. This would be consistent with the finding, discussed earlier, that garden paths that are due to case-assignment ambiguities are not especially taxing of cognitive resources (Carlson & Tanenhaus 1988).

2.2.2 *Case assignment*

Having definitively or tentatively interpreted a construction as EP, the reader is still faced with the problem of case assignment. Barshi and Payne (1996) addressed the factors that influence case assignment in EP comprehension. They focused on a Maasai construction in which there are two possible objects, a first person object marked on the verb plus a noun in another case, such as the nominative or the accusative. Their literal translation of one of their examples is shown in (9):

(9) CN-3>1SG-take MASC.SG-warrior.NOM FEM.SG-goat.ACC

According to Barshi and Payne's (1996) analysis, having two different arguments ('me' (>1SG) and 'goat') competing for the single object slot in the argument structure of the verb results in the EP interpretation that 'me' refers to the possessor. However, the possessed entity could be either 'warrior' ('my warrior took a/the goat') or 'goat' ('a/the warrior took my goat'). Barshi and Payne manipulated the order of appearance of the two non-possessor nouns ('warrior,' 'goat') and whether the discourse favored one or the other as the possessed item. The experimental participants were overwhelmingly influenced by discourse context rather than order of appearance in their designation of the possessed entity.

This outcome carries two suggestions about the study of the assignment of the non-possessor cases in EP. First, factors such as discourse context and surface order may be effectively pitted against other ones, such as grammatical markers, part of speech of the word, and agreement. This might achieve a complete assessment of the variables that influence the identification of the possessed entity in EP. Second, as discussed in the methodology section, on-line measures of this phenomenon might provide evidence that effectively converged with that derived from Barshi and Payne's (1996) respondents' grammatical interpretations.

3. Parsing processes and individual differences

Findings concerning individual differences in sentence processing offer an important caveat for the study of the comprehension of EP. There is emerging evidence that individuals differing in their information processing characteristics and reading skill may process complex linguistic constructions in qualitatively different ways. This can be illustrated with reference to sentence (10):

(10) The soldiers warned about the dangers before the midnight raid.

Sentence (10) is ambiguous at the verb 'warned'. ' Warned' could function as the main verb; or be part of a reduced relative clause, as in 'The soldiers warned about the dangers conducted the midnight raid.' Theorists have asked whether readers maintain a single interpretation or multiple interpretations at the point of such an ambiguity (Just & Carpenter 1992).

Just and Carpenter (1992) evaluated this question with reference to people's reading span (Daneman & Carpenter 1980), a measure that reflects the trade-off between the processing and storage functions of working memory (the antecedent notion of "short-term memory" highlighted only storage characteristics). Just and Carpenter reported that elevated reading time at the disambiguating word 'raid' is measured in sentence (10), but only for individuals of *high* reading span. This outcome is ostensively paradoxical. Typically, it is low span readers who are hampered in language processing (Daneman & Carpenter 1980). Just and Carpenter proposed that the high span readers maintained two interpretations of 'warned' in sentence (10), whereas the low span readers represented only the "main verb" interpretation. As a result, only the high span readers were hampered when the sentence ended at 'raid,' thereby denying the reduced relative interpretation.

This outcome carries important implications for the comprehension of EP and other linguistic constructions. The hypothesis that all individuals process a construction in a uniform fashion is a parsimonious one. However, it may oversimplify the true state of affairs in the realm of parsing processes.

4. Conclusions

The central proposal of this chapter is that achieving a proper grasp of EP might be most readily attained by applying the methods of linguistics and psychology in a converging way. Attaining this goal has the potential to identify important principles of linguistics. It might also significantly clarify the nature of language processing. In the latter regard, EP sequences ostensively demand that the understander engage in reasoning, which is taxing of cognitive resources. However, if, according to psychological measures, people exhibit little difficulty in comprehending EP clauses, it would tend to confirm that the analysis of core grammatical relations does not entail complex problem solving, in the form of reasoning.

Acknowledgments

This research was supported by Grant OGP9800 from the Natural Sciences and Engineering Research Council of Canada. Please address correspondence to Murray Singer, Department of Psychology, University of Manitoba, Winnipeg, Canada R3T 2N2, e-mail m_singer@umanitoba.ca.

References

Barshi, Immanuel, and Doris Payne. 1996. "The Interpretation of "Possessor Raising" in a Maasai Dialect." *Afrikanistische Arbeitspapiere* 45: 207–226.

Barshi, Immanuel, and Doris Payne. 1997, September. "Experimental Design in Processing of Arguments Structures: Maasai External Possession." Paper presented at the *Conference on External Possession and Noun Incorporation*. University of Oregon, Eugene.

Carlson, Greg N. and Michael K. Tanenhaus. 1988. "Thematic Roles and Language Comprehension." In W. Wilkins (ed.), *Syntax and Semantics, Vol. 21: Thematic Relations*. New York: Academic Press.

Charniak, Eugene. 1981. "The Case-Slot Identity Theory." *Cognitive Science* 5: 285–292.

Christensen, Larry B. 1988. *Experimental Methodology*, 4th edition. Boston: Allyn and Bacon.

Clark, Herbert H. 1982. "Making Sense of Nonce Sense." In G. Flores d'Arcais and R. Jarvella (eds.), *The Process of Language Understanding*. New York: John Wiley & Sons, 297–331.

Cottrell, Garrison W. and Steven L. Small. 1983. "A Connectionist Scheme for Modelling Word Sense Disambiguation." *Cognition and Brain Theory* 6: 89–120.

Daneman, Meredyth and Patricia A. Carpenter. 1980. "Individual Differences in Working Memory and Reading." *Journal of Verbal Learning and Verbal Behavior* 19: 450–466.

Grice, H. P. 1975. William James Lectures, Harvard University, 1967. Published in part as "Logic and Conversation." In P. Cole and J. L. Morgan (eds.). *Syntax and Semantics Volume III: Speech Acts.* New York: Seminar Press, 41–58.

Ferreira, Fernanda and Charles C. Clifton Jr. 1986. "The Role of Context in Resolving Syntactic Ambiguity." *Journal of Memory and Language* 25: 348–368.

Fletcher, Charles. 1984. "Markedness and Topic Continuity and Discourse Processing." *Journal of Verbal Learning and Verbal Behavior* 23: 487–493.

Just, Marcel A. and Patricia A. Carpenter. 1992. "A Capacity Theory of Comprehension: Individual Differences in Working Memory." *Psychological Review* 99: 122–149.

Mauner, Gail, Michael K. Tanenhaus, and Greg N. Carlson. 1995. "Implicit Arguments in Sentence Processing." *Journal of Memory and Language* 34: 357–382.

McElree, Brian. 1993. "The Locus of Lexical Preference Effects in Sentence Comprehension: A Time-Course Analysis." *Journal of Memory and Language* 32: 536–571.

Murphy, G. L. 1985. "Processes of Understanding Anaphora." *Journal of Memory and Language* 24: 290–303.

Rayner, Keith, Marcia Carlson and Lyn Frazier. 1983. "The Interaction of Syntax and Semantics During Sentence Processing: Eye Movements in the Analysis of Semantically Biased Sentences." *Journal of Verbal Learning and Verbal Behavior* 22: 358–374.

Reder, Lynne M. 1983. "What Kind of Pitcher Can a Catcher Fill? Effects of Priming in Sentence Comprehension." *Journal of Verbal Learning and Verbal Behavior* 22: 189–202.

Schank, Roger C. 1976. "The Role of Memory in Language Processing." In C. Cofer (ed.), *The Nature of Human Memory*. San Francisco: W. H. Freeman Press, 162–189.

Shibatani, Masayoshi. 1994. "An Integrational Approach to Possessor Raising, Ethical Datives, and Adversative Passives." *Berkeley Linguistic Society* 20: 461–486.

Singer, Murray. 1994. "Discourse Inference Processes". In Morton Ann Gernsbacher (ed.), *Handbook of Psycholinguistics*. San Diego: Academic Press, 479–515.

Sperber, Dan and Deirdre Wilson. 1986. *Relevance: Communication and Cognition.* Cambridge, MA: Harvard University Press.

Vonk, Wietske. 1985. "The Immediacy of Inferences in the Understanding of Pronouns." In G. Rickheit and H. Strohner (eds.), *Advances in Psychology, 29: Inferences in Text Processing*. Amsterdam: North-Holland, 205–218.

Waltz, David N. and Jordan B. Pollack. 1985. "Massively Parallel Parsing: A Strongly Interactive Model of Natural Language Interpretation." *Cognitive Science* 9: 51–74.

External Possession Constructions in Japanese

A Psycholinguistic Perspective

Keiko Uehara
The Graduate Center of The City University of New York

1. Introduction

This paper reports two off-line sentence-completion experiments in Japanese, in which stimulus items permitted (but crucially did not require) interpretation as the External Possession Construction (hereafter, EPC). The study has two functions: it illustrates one way to study EPCs psycholinguistically, and it provides some preliminary indication of the difficulties that EPCs may present in sentence processing. As in many other languages, the EPC in Japanese makes the possessor NP (not marked as genitive) an external argument, above the normal valence of the predicate. In this sense, the EPC exhibits unique characteristics in its syntax and argument structure; Section 2 of the paper offers a sketch of the relevant facts, as these are usually construed for Japanese.

Psycholinguistic research assumes that hypotheses about structure emerge as an early and important step in comprehension. These will be driven in very precise ways by the properties of the input and the syntax of the language, but will also be constrained by the parsing priorities set up by universal principles. It is potentially of great interest to discover how a construction as special as the EPC is handled; this can tell us both more about EPCs, and more about language processing mechanisms.

The experiments reported in this paper utilize the fact that the language processor builds structures incrementally, often in the face of ambiguity: in Japanese, sentences employing the EPC begin in a way that does not distinguish them from sentences employing quite different constructions. Just this ambiguity is exploited to ask how likely the EPC is as a structural hypothesis, relative to its possible competitors, and answers are sought by analyzing the variety of structures imposed on ambiguous sentence beginnings (see Section 3). The data show quite clearly that the EPC is much less likely than are alternative hypotheses (see Section 4). This finding is interpreted as indicating that substantial difficulty arises in processing the EPC. After surveying possible sources of that difficulty, Section 5 of the paper presents a proposal that has implications for the EPC both in Japanese and in other languages. The proposal is that transparency of Case interpretation is an important priority in sentence processing, to the routine detriment of structures that, like the EPC, employ non-standard usages of Case.

2. External possession constructions in Japanese

This section describes characteristics of EPCs in Japanese and briefly reviews their analysis in the generative framework. As shown in (1a), EPCs in Japanese mark both the possessor NP (hereafter, PR) and the possessum NP (hereafter, PM) with the same case-marker *-ga* (NOM).[1] Although the case-marking of the PR in EPCs is nominative, it is naturally interpreted as having genitive force, i.e., as indicating that the entity represented by NP1 possesses the entity represented by NP2. In contrast, in (1b), an Internal Possessor Construction (hereafter IPC) parallel to (1a), the PR is explicitly marked with the genitive case-marker *-no*. (Note that English translations in (1) to (8) below do not attempt to capture the EPC's focus effects; we will take up issues of focus later in this section.)

(1) a. *John-ga oneesan-ga totemo kirei-da* EPC
John-NOM older:sister-NOM very pretty-is
'John's older sister is very pretty.'

b. *John-no oneesan-ga totemo kirei-da* IPC
John-GEN older:sister-NOM very pretty-is
'John's older sister is very pretty.'

Japanese allows EPCs only for nominative NPs. In this way it differs from Korean, which allows EPCs for nominative, accusative, and dative NPs, the PR assuming the Case of the PM (Nakamura 1997). Thus, although Japanese is generally considered to be similar to Korean syntactically, EPCs in Japanese are structurally more limited than those in Korean. As illustrated in (2a) and (3a), EPCs in Japanese are not in general possible (whereas they would be possible in Korean), when the intended PR is case-marked as accusative or dative to match the case-marking of the PM.[2] In contrast, IPC equivalents (2b) and (3b) are both perfectly grammatical.

(2) a. **Mary-ga John-o oneesan-o hometa* *EPC (ACC)
Mary-NOM John-ACC older:sister-ACC praised
'*(intended)* Mary praised John's older sister.'
b. *Mary-ga John-no oneesan-o hometa* IPC (ACC)
Mary-NOM John-GEN older:sister-ACC praised
'Mary praised John's older sister.'

(3) a. **Mary-ga John-ni oneesan-ni atta* *EPC (DAT)
Mary-NOM John-DAT older:sister-DAT met
'*(intended)* Mary met John's older sister.'
b. *Mary-ga John-no oneesan-ni atta* IPC (DAT)
Mary-NOM John-GEN older:sister-DAT met
'Mary met John's older sister.'

The well-studied instances of EPCs in Japanese are those in which it is a subject PM that is nominatively marked (and it is just these instances that are examined in the psycholinguistic studies set out in Section 4). However, a detail of the grammar of Japanese requires that we ask whether it is the PM's *-ga* marking *per se* that makes EPCs possible, or its subjecthood: for a special set of predicates, those with [+stative] features, objects are also marked with *-ga* in the so-called Nominative Object Construction (Dubinsky 1992; Kuno 1973a; Tada 1992; Takahashi 1996). Nominative objects occur with simplex predicates such as *wakaru* (understand), *iru* (need), and *suki-da* (be fond of), and with complex predicates such as *V+eru* (can V) and *V+tai* (want to V). Recent analyses have begun to ask whether EPCs are possible with nominative objects (as well as with subjects), and in fact EPCs in nominatively marked object position do seem to be possible (see Morikawa 1993; Tada 1992). But unlike EPCs in subject position, their occurrence is apparently idiosyncratic; (4a), for example, shows an EPC that is as acceptable as its IPC counterpart (in which *sono hon-no* is used for *sono hon-ga*), but (4b) is awkward although its IPC counterpart is perfectly fine. EPCs of this special kind have not yet been discussed much in the literature, and it is not clear whether there is any systematicity in the pattern of their occurrence.[3] For this reason, all further discussion of EPCs in this paper is restricted to those occurring in subject position.

(4) a. *Mary-ga sono hon-ga naiyoo-ga wakara-nai*
Mary-NOM that book-NOM content-NOM understand-not
'Mary does not understand that book's content.' EPC (object)

b. ?**Mary-ga sono hito-ga kimoti-ga wakara-nai*
Mary-NOM that person-NOM feeling-NOM understand-not
?*EPC (object)
'*(intended)* Mary does not understand that person's feelings.'

Just as the IPC allows PRs to stack up without limit, to give NP1's NP2's NP3's … NP, the EPC in Japanese is said to allow multiple PRs (Kuno 1973a; Takahashi 1996; Tateishi 1991; cf. Kubo 1992).[4] Example (5a) illustrates the possibility of double EPC, i.e., an EPC containing two PRs, and (5b) illustrates the IPC counterpart:

(5) a. *John-ga oneesan-ga kami-ga totemo kirei-da*
John-NOM older:sister-NOM hair-NOM very pretty-is
'John's older sister's hair is very pretty.' double EPC
b. *John-no oneesan-no kami-ga totemo kirei-da*
John-GEN older:sister-GEN hair-NOM very pretty-is
'John's older sister's hair is very pretty.' double IPC

The EPC in Japanese is generally analyzed as involving PR-raising; that is, a PR modifying the PM within a host DP, where *-no* (GEN) case-marking is required, is raised out of that DP and adjoined to a higher position, creating a new nominative argument (Kitagawa 1986; Kuno 1973a; Kuroda 1992; Morikawa 1993; Shibatani 1977; Tada 1992; Takahashi 1996; Tateishi 1991; Ueda 1990; Whitman 1998). Since an EPC is derived from [$_{DP}$ NP-*no* NP]-*ga* by raising, a sentence containing an EPC in Japanese always has an IPC counterpart (Kuno 1973a). The examples given previously in (1) are repeated below as (6), to make explicit the structural difference between an EPC and its corresponding IPC under this raising analysis.

(6) a. *John-ga*$_i$ [$_{DP}$ t$_i$ *oneesan*]-*ga totemo kirei-da* EPC
John-NOM older:sister-NOM very pretty-is
'John's older sister is very pretty.'
b. [$_{DP}$ *John-no oneesan*]-*ga totemo kirei-da* IPC
John-GEN older:sister-NOM very pretty-is
'John's older sister is very pretty.'

Opinions differ as to where the EPC's raised PR is adjoined. For example, Kuno (1973a) assumes adjunction to IP, whereas Tateishi (1991) assumes adjunction inside IP (to Spec of AgrP), and Ueda (1990) assumes adjunction to a special focus phrase outside IP. Such differences of opinion arise in part as a consequence of changes in syntactic theory, and in part as a consequence of differences in the specificity of the analysis. A now-extensive literature has often treated the EPC under the rubric "Multiple Subject Construction", along with other constructions involving special *ga*-marked arguments (e.g., Kuno 1973a; Shibatani 1977).[5] It is only recently that fine-grained analyses have begun to tease out facts about the EPC, in particular, distinguishing it from other types (e.g., Tateishi 1991).[6]

Alternatives to the raising analysis exist in the literature on the EPC in Japanese. Some researchers have proposed that the EPC is base-generated in Japanese (Saito 1982, 1985; Takezawa 1987),[7] or even that it is a hybrid phenomenon, involving raising in some instances and base-generation in others (Ura 1996).[8] But whether the EPC is seen as involving PR-raising or base-generation, all analyses agree that the PR is outside the DP containing the PM. Thus, EPC sentences contain an additional nominative argument, above the usual valence of the predicate, and the different accounts sketched here diverge chiefly in how that additional argument arises and how it is to be accommodated. This paper assumes, following the majority, that in the EPC the PR is raised out of its host DP; but takes no position on the location of the PR's adjunction site.

As we have seen in (6), PR-raising in the EPC creates an additional nominative argument. The externality of the NP-*ga* PR (cf. the internality of an NP-*no* PR) is confirmed in (7), which illustrates a contrast in acceptability between EPC and IPC when a sentential adverb is placed between PR and PM. A comparison of ungrammatical (7b) with grammatical (7a) shows that PR and PM form a single constituent in an IPC but not in an EPC; the EPC's raised PR forms a constituent of its own outside the host DP (Shibatani 1977; Ueda 1990; Ura 1996).

(7) a. *John-ga*$_i$ *totemo* [$_{DP}$ t$_i$ *oneesan*]-*ga* *kirei-da* EPC
John-NOM very older:sister-NOM pretty-is
'John's older sister is very pretty.'

b. *[$_{DP}$ *John-no totemo oneesan*]-*ga* *kirei-da* *IPC
John-GEN very older:sister-NOM pretty-is
'*(intended)* John's older sister is very pretty.'

The externality of the PR in the EPC is also confirmed in tests involving coordinate and cleft constructions: since only a single constituent can be coordinated or clefted, the pattern in (7) is reversed, i.e., these constructions are grammatical with an IPC but ungrammatical with an EPC (Ueda 1990).

We now turn to a consideration of possible content constraints on the freedom with which EPCs can occur in Japanese. It has been observed cross-linguistically that, in EPCs, PRs are most likely to refer to humans, and that PR and PM most typically stand in an inalienable relation;[9] some languages even restrict PMs to, e.g., body-parts (Payne 1997a, b). Japanese does not exhibit any such obvious content restriction on EPCs. We have already seen that *John-ga oneesan-ga* (John's older sister) in (5a) involves human terms for PR and PM in an inalienable kinship relation, and that *oneesan-ga kami-ga* (older sister's hair) involves a body-part PM. In addition to such examples, EPCs like (8a) involving alienable possession are also possible, and (8b) shows that a human PR is not required, either, whether inalienably or alienably related to the PM.

(8) a. *John-ga gakkoo-ga totemo yuumei-da*
John-NOM school-NOM very famous-is
'John's school is very famous.'

b. *sono neko-ga sippo-ga / kubiwa-ga totemo nagai*
that cat-NOM tail-NOM collar-NOM very long
'That cat's tail / collar is very long.'

It has also been observed across languages that there is a strong preference in constructing EPCs for predicates of particular types, unaccusative intransitive verbs or active transitive verbs of physical contact being most likely (Payne 1997b, c). However, EPCs in Japanese exhibit no such restriction as to the type of predicate (Takahashi 1996; cf. Kubo 1992).[10] For example, an EPC like *John-ga oneesan-ga* (John's sister) can equally naturally be the subject of unaccusative intransitive verbs, e.g., *iku* 'go'; transitive verbs taking a direct object, a sentential complement, or an indirect object, e.g., *homeru* 'praise', *iu* 'say', *au* 'meet', respectively; or ditransitive verbs, e.g., *shookaisuru* 'introduce'. Roughly, it can be said that whenever the PR and PM have lexical content to support a plausible IPC relation (and the PM is the subject), the EPC is possible with any predicate in Japanese.

EPCs in Japanese have their motivation in focus requirements. The *ga*-marked thematic subject in an IPC normally receives focus, as shown in (9a); however, focus shifts to the raised PR in (9b) and (9c), in which EPCs are differently sited. Note that, unlike (1) to (8) above, English translations here attempt to give a sense of the focus of the Japanese sentences.

(9) a. *John-no oneesan-no syuzin-ga totemo hansamu-da*
John-GEN older:sister-GEN husband-NOM very handsome-is
'It is John's older sister's husband who is very handsome.'
double IPC

b. *John-ga oneesan-no syuzin-ga totemo hansamu-da*
John-NOM older:sister-GEN husband-NOM very handsome-is
'It is John whose older sister's husband is very handsome.'
EPC, NP1 NP2

c. *John-no oneesan-ga syuzin-ga totemo hansamu-da*
John-GEN older:sister-NOM husband-NOM very handsome-is
'It is John's older sister whose husband is very handsome.'
EPC, NP2 NP3

Kuno (1973a, b) argues that the leftmost NP-*ga* takes precedence for focus. The occurrence of double EPC, however, presents an instance in which multiple focus may be possible. Certainly, some researchers, e.g., Takahashi (1996), have made this claim for examples like that in (10), at the same time noting the inherent difficulty of double focus readings. (English has no natural device for expressing multiple focus, and the translation offered in (10) is necessarily awkward.)

(10) *John-ga oneesan-ga syuzin-ga totemo hansamu-da*
John-NOM older:sister-NOM husband-NOM very handsome-is
'It is the older sister (in particular) of John (in particular) whose husband is very handsome.' double EPC

No corpus studies exist through which we can determine how often EPCs are used in daily conversation in Japanese; however, the author's intuition is that they are not frequent. As we have seen, EPCs place focus on the PR (cf. the PM in IPC), and discourse contexts in which a speaker will be inclined to do that seem likely to have a special character; presumably the speaker wishes to emphasize the PR (and only the PR, drawing a contrast with other contextually relevant candidates), while simultaneously encoding the possession relationship. While we can readily imagine various settings in which an EPC would be used for those purposes, it seems highly relevant that the language offers alternative devices that achieve the same end. Instead of an EPC, we could (in speech) use an IPC and put a strong stress on the PR term, or (in print) an IPC with an added phrase, e.g., 'John's sister and nobody else's'. We could also employ a cleft construction. The EPC is undoubtedly chosen when it encodes the speaker's communicative intent better than these alternatives; but it will require a good deal of discourse-oriented research to tease out the relevant facts.

To round out this brief sketch of the EPC in Japanese, we should note that judgements about the construction can be variable.[11] Some speakers find EPCs to be "awkward" and "hard to understand" to the point of unacceptability, particularly when multiple possession is involved, as in examples (5) and (10), above. Here, it is likely to be important that such sentences contain three consecutive NP-*ga*'s (hereafter, 3*ga*). Uehara (1997a) found evidence for an independent processing cost associated with 3*ga*; the judged processability of 3*ga* sentences was notably lower than that of their minimally different counterparts in which the 3*ga* sequence was avoided by, e.g., thematization of an NP. The acceptability of EPCs may also depend to some extent on the alienability of the PR-PM relation, though (to the author's knowledge) this has yet to be studied systematically for Japanese.

3. External possessor constructions in Japanese: Psycholinguistic considerations

3.1 *Ambiguity in sentence processing*

In a language like Japanese — SOV, head-final, with flexible word order (scrambling) — sentence beginnings consisting of a sequence of case-marked NPs are very typical. For the language processing mechanism, such sequences represent instances of temporary (or even global) syntactic ambiguity; many different structural analyses are possible, and the ambiguity is resolved (if at all) only by later sentence content, e.g., verbs, complementizers, further argument phrases. Despite this, the available evidence suggests that in Japanese, just as in other languages, sentences are processed incrementally, so that analyses are proposed as inputs are being received. The implication is that hypotheses about structure are routinely being made in advance of disambiguating information (Inoue and Fodor 1995). The consensus among researchers is that among the alternative structural analyses compatible with an ambiguous input, some will clearly be preferred — and further, that the pattern of preferences will in some systematic way reflect the character of the processor's normal computational routines (Frazier 1978). For this reason, studies exploiting structural ambiguity have been an important source of evidence in the development of models of sentence processing.

Consider the problem of structural ambiguity as it applies to the EPC in Japanese, taking as an example the phrases *John-ga oneesan-ga* (John-NOM older sister-NOM) used to illustrate many of the characteristics of EPC in Section 2. When a sentence beginning presents two such adjacent NP-*ga*'s with lexical contents appropriate to a PR-PM relation, the fragment offers an EPC opportunity — it *can* be interpreted as an EPC, 'John's older sister'. But other structural analyses are also possible (see Section 3.2, below, for a sketch of those that are most salient), and we can therefore ask: what is the likelihood that the structure imposed on a sentence-initial 2*ga* string is an EPC, rather than one or other of its competitors? Is it high, or is it low? In the end, answers here will speak to the way in which EPCs are handled by the sentence processor.

The sentence completion task can be used to provide preliminary information about the likely ranking among competing analyses of an ambiguous input. The task presents a sentence beginning, and asks for a continuation that results in a natural, well-formed sentence. No constraint is imposed on what can be added, except that changes or insertions internal to the material given are ruled out. Completion responses are examined to determine the structure that was imposed on the stimulus fragment, in effect running in reverse the steps underlying performance in the task. (For the respondent in sentence completion, the way a stimulus fragment is parsed constrains what can be added.) Many responses are collected for a variety of fragment types, so that systematicity in the patterns of response can be identified.

3.2 *EPC's structural competitors*

In Japanese, the nominative case-marker has a variety of syntactic functions. Although *-ga* has its prototypical usage as a marker for thematic subjects, special usages exist in which *-ga* is interpreted with something other than nominative force, as Section 2 has shown with respect to the EPC. The Nominative Object Construction (hereafter, NOC) mentioned earlier represents another such usage; a 2*ga* string can be interpreted as a sequence of subject (NP1-*ga*) and object (NP2-*ga*), requiring a predicate with [+stative] features, as shown in (11). The NOC occurs frequently in daily conversation, and this is not surprising given the variety and frequency of the predicates that trigger this construction.[12]

(11) $[_{IP}$ *John-ga oneesan-ga daisuki-da*] NOC
John-NOM older:sister-NOM much:fond-is
'John likes his older sister very much.'

A second competitor for EPC is one that gives *-ga* its prototypical interpretation as a marker of subjects, but quite exceptionally assigns two independent subjects to just one clause, as shown in (12). This so-called Parallel Subjects Construction (hereafter, PSC) is especially emphatic, and occurs rarely in daily conversation because of its poetic or literary quality.

(12) $[_{IP}$ *John-ga oneesan-ga sorezore tomodati-o annaisata*] PSC
John-NOM older:sister-NOM each friend-ACC showed:around
'John and his older sister each showed the friend around.'

A third competitor for EPC arises when each NP-*ga* of a *2ga* string is given an interpretation that is both prototypical and unexceptional, as the subject of its own clause. As illustrated in (13), the result is a sentence in which one clause is center-embedded in another:

(13) [$_{IP}$ *John-ga* [$_{IP}$ *oneesan-ga* *tomodati-o annaisuru*] *to itta*]
John-NOM older:sister-NOM friend-ACC showed:around that said
'John said that his older sister showed the friend around.'
EMBEDDING

3.3 *EPC's structural preference in sentence completion*

Which of the EPC and the three structural types outlined above might be preferred in the sentence completion task, when a stimulus fragment offers an EPC opportunity? It may be pertinent that NOCs and PSCs, like EPCs, are "same clause" interpretations (both NP-*ga*'s are assigned to a single clause), cf. the less compact "separate clause" interpretation of an embedding. A different grouping of the alternatives makes reference to the frequency with which these structures usually occur, EPCs and PSCs being less common (and notably so, in the case of PSCs). Yet another grouping notices the prototypicality with which case-marker *-ga* is used: PSCs and structures involving embedding interpret *-ga* (NOM) as a marker of thematic subjects, transparently, while EPCs and NOCs do not. To the extent that compactness, structural frequency, and transparency in the interpretation of case-markers have any impact in sentence completion (separately, or in combination), different patterns of response frequencies will emerge for EPC-opportunity fragments.

On this point, the author's previous research with sentence completion (see Uehara 1997b, c; Uehara and Bradley 1998) provides relevant background information. That earlier project (in which the possibility of EPCs was excluded by design) established a database of completion responses for fragments that exhausted the possible orders of NP-*ga*, NP-*ni* (DAT) and/or NP-*o* (ACC), with only NP-*ga* phrases being allowed two appearances.[13] Over this wide variety of word orders, the data exhibited a striking regularity — overwhelmingly, completion responses assigned NP-*ga* phrases to separate clauses, whether or not these were consecutive in the stimulus fragment. Apparently, economy in clause building is not a priority. However, it was noteworthy that the generalization "Assign each NP-*ga* to a separate clause" was very powerful but not absolute. Violations occurred on 11% of possible occasions, and all involved PSCs (never NOCs). The evidence in hand suggests, then, that transparency (but not structural frequency) might be an important determinant of response patterns in sentence completion.

It is necessarily the case that findings in the sentence completion task are to be interpreted cautiously. Given its paper-and-pencil format, the situation confronting an incremental processor is mimicked only crudely (as in any other unspeeded task), and there can be no guarantee that the rankings of response likelihood that emerge in sentence completion will exactly reflect the preferences of the processor in first-pass parsing, so-called. For the latter, a long-standing assumption has been that relative processing cost decides among competing analyses (see, e.g., Frazier 1978); that is, the structures most likely to be initially hypothesized are those that require least effort to compute. But though there can be no legitimate *direct* inference from relative likelihood in sentence completion to claims about relative processing cost, an *indirect* inference can be supported in the right circumstances.

Suppose that the sentence completion data rank the EPC between structures for which the facts about processing cost have been established independently, and that the impact of possibly confounding factors can be ruled out or minimized. Then sentence completion data can provide a preliminary estimate of the EPC's likely processing cost, to generate hypotheses for follow-up studies employing, e.g., on-line paradigms like self-paced reading. This is the approach adopted in the studies reported in Section 4 where, crucially, the EPC's salient competitors will include single center-embedding, on the one hand, and double center-embedding, on the other.

4. EPC in sentence-completion responses

Analyses of sentence completion responses are presented in this section, for two data sets. Data Set I was drawn from a sentence completion questionnaire in which the 8 fragment stimuli of interest (among 32 filler stimuli) had 2*ga* strings with lexical contents compatible with an EPC interpretation.[14] Data were gathered from 23 respondents who were paid for their participation; all were students learning English at the International Center of New York who had lived in Japan at least until they graduated from a Japanese high school; their average age was 32 years. They were told that the aim of the study was to investigate how native speakers understand difficult and easy Japanese sentences, and received standard task instructions, i.e., they could add anything they wanted to the given fragments to make natural, well-formed sentences. The paper-and-pencil questionnaire was written in Japanese characters and the entire procedure was conducted in Japanese.

The responses in Data Set II were gathered in the course of Uehara's (1997b, c) database project, and the 8 fragments of interest were simply additional stimulus types intermingled with Uehara's word order variants. The task procedure was exactly the same as that for Data Set I, and there were 18 respondents who were either faculty or graduate students at Gunma University in Japan; again, average age was 32 years.

4.1 *Data Set I: Single EPC opportunity*

The fragments considered here all included two consecutive NPs setting up an opportunity for an EPC, i.e., NP1-*ga* could be taken as a PR of NP2-*ga*. NP1-*ga* was always a human role term, and two fragment subgroups were defined by the lexical content of NP2. For the fragments listed in (14a–d), a noun specifying a human role filled this position, while for those listed in (15a–d), the noun was inanimate. The latter was intended to rule out the PSC (the most likely structural competitor for the EPC when both NP-*ga*'s are assigned to a single clause); the pairing of NP1's human role term and NP2's inanimate noun is simply not appropriate for a PSC, under any normal interpretation. Within each subgroup, the number of terms in a fragment varied. Fragments (14a) and (15a) presented only the two NP-*ga* phrases, thus allowing an NOC interpretation; but the NOC was blocked in fragments (14b–d) and (15b–d) which added argument phrases marked as NP-*o* or NP-*ni*, or both. In (14) and (15) below, the 2*ga* string providing an EPC opportunity is shown in boldface. (The appendix shows these fragments in Japanese orthography, as they appeared in the questionnaire.)

(14) a. ***shachoo-ga untenshu-ga***
president-NOM driver-NOM

b. ***okumanchooja-ga monban-ga*** *yuubinbutu-o*
billionaire-NOM gatekeeper-NOM mail-ACC

c. ***senmu-ga hisho-ga*** *shain-ni*
managing:director-NOM secretary-NOM company:worker-DAT

d. ***eigahaiyuu-ga koibito-ga*** *direkutaa-ni shutuen-o*
movie:actor-NOM lover-NOM director-DAT appearance (in a show)-ACC

(15) a. *yuukaihannin*-***ga seimeibun-ga***
kidnapper-NOM threatening:letter-NOM

b. ***taipisuto-ga kompuutaa-ga*** *joohoo-o*
typist-NOM Computer-NOM information-ACC

c. ***yuumeisakka-ga genkoo-ga*** *siriai-ni*
famous:writer-NOM draft-NOM acquaintance-DAT

d. ***kaishain-ga kyuuryoo-ga*** *kodomo-ni omocha-o*
office:worker-NOM salary-NOM child-DAT toy-ACC

The sentences produced as completions for these fragments were analyzed to determine the extent to which the "separate clause" pattern (see Section 3.3) observed in the author's earlier studies with non-EPC fragments held, when NP strings presented an EPC opportunity. That is, did the structure imposed on fragments assign each NP-*ga* as the subject of a separate clause (in compliance with Uehara's generalization), or were these assigned instead to the same clause as required for the EPC? And, among "same clause" responses, what was the frequency of EPCs (interpreting NP1-*ga* with genitive force) relative to PSCs (interpreting both NP-*ga*'s as subjects, transparently)? The data presented in Table 1 are summarized in these terms. The table gives response frequencies for "Separate" and "Same Clause" categories, the latter being divided among subcategories "EPC", "PSC", and "Other" (representing instances of remaining special usages of -*ga*); a small proportion of globally ambiguous responses, interpretable as either EPCs or PSCs, are represented in a joint category "EPC/PSC":[15]

Table 1. *Completion Response Frequency, as a Function of Structural Interpretation*

	Separate Clause	Same Clause				Total
		EPC	EPC PSC	PSC	Other	
(14a) ***-ga -ga***	17	0	2	4	0	23
(14b) ***-ga -ga*** *-o*	21	0	1	1	0	23
(14c) ***-ga -ga*** *-ni*	20	0	1	2	0	23
(14d) ***-ga -ga*** *-ni -o*	18	0	2	3	0	23
	76	0	6	10	0	92
(15a) ***-ga -ga***	22	0	0	0	1[a]	23
(15b) ***-ga -ga*** *-o*	20	0	2	0	0	22[b]
(15c) ***-ga -ga*** *-ni*	23	0	0	0	0	23
(15d) ***-ga -ga*** *-ni -o*	20	1	0	0	1	22[b]
	85	1	2	0	2	90

[a] Response ambiguous between EPC and NOC
[b] N=1 response incomprehensible

The data of Table 1 exhibit a very clear pattern. Despite lexical contents providing an opportunity for EPCs, the overwhelming majority of sentence completions handled consecutive NP-*ga*'s in the input string by imposing structures that involve an embedding. For the fragments taken together, this characterization takes in 88% of the analyzable responses. Considering the fragment subgroups separately gives figures of 83% and 94%, for fragment subgroups (14a–d) and (15a–d), respectively, so that the effect of ruling out PSC in the latter has been to increase the likelihood of embedding, rather than anything else.

Among the minority of responses assigning NP-*ga*'s to the same clause, there was only 1 instance of a response unambiguously involving EPC, as compared to 10 clearcut instances of PSC for (14a–d) (recall that inanimate NP2 in (15a–d) was designed to block PSC). Although ambiguity was minimal in this collection of sentence completions (because respondents were sufficiently informative to make their intended meanings clear), 9 sentences were ambiguous; note that 2 ambiguous responses for fragment (15b) involved an unanticipated metaphoric reading of NP2 "computer" as animate. The ambiguity in all instances but one involved EPC versus PSC. Given the highly implausible assumption that all such ambiguities were intended as EPCs, the likelihood that an EPC opportunity in this set of fragments was taken up is estimated as 5.5%, *at maximum*. (Reversing that assumption leads to a minimum estimate of 0.5%.) Clearly, the strong preference in sentence completion for strings beginning NP-*ga* NP-*ga* is one that makes each -*ga* phrase the single subject of its own clause. The EPC has markedly lower preference. When lexical content makes the EPC's "same clause" competitor unlikely — compare the frequencies of responses using the PSC, in Table 1's upper and lower panels — the effect is not to increase the frequency of the EPC, but rather the frequency of embedding. It seems plausible, therefore, that the EPC is less likely to be imposed even than the PSC, despite the very special character of the latter.

4.2 *Data Set II: Double EPC opportunity*

In Data Set I, very few EPCs were observed when the possibility of this structural interpretation was simply offered by an input fragment, and the dominant preference was for a center-embedded structure. Section 4.2.1 reports on an exploratory EPC test in which, by design, more opportunities were offered in 3NP fragments, and at the same time this most likely alternative would result in a structure that is known to be difficult to process, i.e., double center-embedding.[16] Anticipating the (partial) success of this ploy, we also assess the structural configuration in which EPCs were imposed, and provide evidence (in Section 4.2.2) as to why this might have a particular clause boundary pattern.

4.2.1 *EPC versus double center-embedding*

Two EPC-potential fragments were constructed as the starting point for Data Set II. One fragment, given in (16a), consisted of a string in which three consecutive NPs were marked with *-ga*; the other, given in (16b), avoided the processing cost known to be associated with 3*ga* strings (Uehara 1997a; see also Section 2) by thematization of NP1, now marked with topic marker *-wa.* Kuno (1973a) demonstrates that the raised PR of an EPC can be thematized; thus, the two fragments are equivalent in their EPC opportunities, though (16a) with a 3*ga* string is likely to incur higher processing cost than (16b).

(16) a. ***Sonii-ga shain-ga taido-ga***
SONY-NOM employee-NOM attitude-NOM
b. ***Kyojin-wa tooshu-ga wanryoku-ga***
Giants-TOP pitchers-NOM arm:power-NOM

These fragments offer opportunities for EPC with more insistence than those in Data Set I. Since the lexical content of the three NPs in either of the fragments supports a possession relation between NP1 and NP2 and between NP2 and NP3, an EPC opportunity is available at two sites, *simultaneously.* Thus, the fragments can be seen as offering either one opportunity for a double EPC, or two independent opportunities for a single EPC. Moreover, lexical content makes the PSC, one of the EPC's rivals, semantically impossible. The fragments took a human collective term at NP1, a human role term NP2, and a property noun at NP3. Thus, no pair of nouns (let alone the triplet) has the balance in status required for the PSC. Finally — and most importantly — the structural alternative which Data Set I has shown to be strongly preferred to the EPC in more neutral circumstances, embedding, can now be taken up only with substantial processing difficulty. Should each of the three NPs in these fragments be treated as the subject of its own clause, the result is double center-embedding.

The presence of two EPC opportunities per fragment raises an interesting problem. If both of those opportunities were exploited (double EPC), the resulting structure would involve two syntactic operations of the same kind, PR-raising, and it is possible that the processing system itself imposes a limit which is absent in the grammar. A standard account of the special difficulty associated with double self-embedding supposes that there are costs associated with the iterative application of any syntactic operation (Chomsky and Miller 1963; Lewis 1993, 1996; Miller and Chomsky 1963; Stabler 1994). Whether this holds at the DP level, as well as at the clause level, is not known.

It is thus an open question whether the two EPC opportunities are ignored entirely, taken up only in part, or exploited fully. That is, by examining the sentence completion responses for the fragments in (16), we find out about response preferences as these range from double center-embedding on the one hand, to double EPC on the other. Respondents in the sentence completion task can avoid the problem associated with two embeddings by constructing a double EPC. And if constructing a double EPC is not optimal, either, then a middle course is available, in structures involving one embedding and one EPC. The data are shown in Table 2, which for convenience maintains the same format as Table 1 earlier. Note, however, that "Separate Clause" now means that each of the fragment NPs was assigned to its own clause, and "Same Clause" now means that at least two of the three NPs were treated as clausemates.

Table 2. *Completion Response Frequency, as a Function of Structural Interpretation*

	Separate Clause	Same Clause			Total
		2EPC	1EPC	Other	
(16a) ***-ga -ga -ga***	0	1	16	0	17 [a]
(16b) ***-wa -ga -ga***	1	0	16	0	17 [a]

[a] N=1 response ambiguous between categories

The outcomes for fragments (16a) and (16b) are remarkably alike, and very clear. For the two fragments taken together, 94% of responses treated the inputs as beginning sentences with two clauses, resulting in a single embedding plus a single EPC. Respondents avoided both double EPCs and double center-embeddings, and took up the EPC opportunity only partially. Putting the findings for Data Sets I and II together, we can say that likelihood of the EPC falls between that for single and double embedding. EPCs may indeed be unlikely, but they are not extraordinarily unlikely.

The sentences produced by respondents, taking up the EPC opportunity only partially, have an interesting property which is not evident in Table 2. Responses involving a single embedding plus a single EPC could involve an EPC at either of two sites, as shown in (17):

(17) a. NP1's NP2 [NP3
b. NP1 [NP2's NP3

It was surprising that, for responses to fragments (16a) and (16b) taken together, not one employed the pattern shown in (17a), with a complex subject in a higher clause and a simple subject in a lower clause. Rather, all responses took the pattern shown in (17b), in which the complex subject occurs in the embedded clause.

It is possible that this strikingly asymmetric outcome arises because of the kind of possession implied by the lexical contents of the test fragments, schematized in (18). The potential PR-PM relation for NP1 and NP2 is alienable under usual assumptions (but see Note 9), while that for NP2 and NP3 is inalienable. Although the literature holds that the EPC in Japanese is allowed for both kinds of possession (see Section 2), data from other languages have suggested to many researchers that inalienable possession is the unmarked case for the EPC. Thus, the outcome might reflect a previously unobserved impact of alienability on the EPC in Japanese.

(18)	**SONY**	**employee**	**attitude**
	Giants	**pitcher**	**arm-power**
	human collective	human role	property

alienable (human collective – human role)   inalienable (human role – property)

Before any launch into a research program committed to varying the intricacies of potential PR-PM relations in EPC-opportunity fragments,[17] it seems worth considering an alternative source of the asymmetry observed for fragments (16a, b). That is, the outcome might have nothing to do with the EPC in particular, but might simply reflect a preferred pattern in the siting of clause boundaries — in which case the pattern observed in the EPC responses would also emerge in sentence completions for *any* 3NP fragment allowing either that clause boundary pattern or its competitor. It was this alternative possibility which was assessed in the second part of Data Set II.

There is an inevitable problem in constructing stimulus fragments consisting of three case-marked NPs for which both the boundary patterns of interest, NP1 [NP2 NP3 and NP1 NP2 [NP3, are freely available. Uehara's (1997b, c) sentence completion project has shown that the occurrence and order of case-markers powerfully constrains the siting of clause boundaries under normal circumstances. Stimulus items designed to test for preferred patterns must therefore have a special character. The section that follows sets out the logic under which the topic-marker *-wa* can be used to neutralize thematic influences on boundary patterns, at least partially, and presents sentence completion data for non-EPC fragments using only the case-markers *-ga* (NOM) and *-wa* (TOP).

4.2.2 *Clause boundary patterns in 3NP strings*

In Japanese, the topic marker *-wa* can be used to thematize not only NP-*ga*, but also non-subject phrases, i.e., NP-*ni* (DAT) and NP-*o* (ACC) (Kuno 1973a).[18]

What follows from this is that an NP-*wa* encountered in an input is, strictly speaking, ambiguous — it *can* be interpreted in any of three ways, and therefore provides a means by which thematic influences on boundary placement can be minimized. It must be noted, however, that the neutrality of *-wa* is not an entirely balanced one, since the most frequent target for thematization is a subject phrase.

The strategy for discovering how a 3NP string is most characteristically broken into clauses therefore uses NP-*wa* phrases, but not exclusively; phrases were also marked with nominative *-ga*. Here, it is relevant that Uehara's generalization about the influence of *-ga* on the clause-building (see Section 3.3) is one that makes *-ga* a constraint on clause pattern but not a position-specific trigger. Consider, for example, a string of the form NP-*ga* NP-*wa* NP-*ga*, and the injunction to assign NP-*ga*'s to separate clauses; nothing dictates whether NP-*wa* is assigned to the higher or lower clause.

In the end, five fragments were constructed to allow interpretations placing a single clause boundary internal to a 3NP string. These exhaust the relevant orders, and are listed in (19) (see also the appendix):

(19) a. *haha-ga* *shuninishi-wa* *Takashi-ga*
mother-NOM chief:doctor-TOP Takashi-NOM
b. *oba-ga* *tenshu-wa* *gakusei-wa*
my:aunt-NOM store:owner-TOP college:student-TOP
c. *ryoosin-wa* *untenshu-ga* *Susumu-wa*
parents-TOP driver-NOM Susumu-TOP
d. *mago-wa* *Shimizu-san-wa* *seinen-ga*
grandchild-TOP Shimizu-Mr/Ms-TOP young:man-NOM
e. *chuugakusei-wa* *hanayome-wa* *Imai-san-wa*
junior:high:school:student-TOP bride-TOP Imai-Mr/Ms-TOP

None of these fragment stimuli contains sequences of adjacent NP-*ga*'s to trigger a clause boundary at a particular site, and no adjacent NP pair has lexical contents appropriate for a PR-PM relation.

Data for one further fragment stimulus, given in (20), are relevant to the point at hand. This was a non-EPC string with all three terms marked by *-ga*, against which it was possible to assess whether the use of *-wa* in (19a–e) indeed encouraged responses with just one clause boundary internal to the fragment.

(20) *titioya-ga* *Michio-ga* *yuumeisakka-ga*
father-NOM Michio-NOM famous:writer-NOM

A breakdown of the sentence completion data is presented in Table 3, which differs in format from the earlier tables. Here, *x* represents an NP, and *bracket* represents the site of a clause boundary internal to the stimulus fragment. The body of the table shows the frequencies with which sentence completion responses fell into three broadly defined clause-pattern categories, abstracting away from further structural detail. Responses that were ambiguous between analysis categories are excluded from the table, as are those that were uninterpretable or incomplete. Data for EPC fragments (16a) and (16b) are also included in the table, in the upper panel, under the same analysis categories.

Table 3. *Completion Response Frequency, as a Function of Clause Boundary Site*

	x [x [x	x [x x	x x [x	Total
(16a) ***-ga -ga -ga***	0	16	0	16[a,b]
(16b) ***-wa -ga -ga***	1	16	0	17[a]
(19a) *-ga -wa -ga*	16	2	0	18
(19b) *-ga -wa -wa*	13	3	0	16[c]
(19c) *-wa -ga -wa*	14	1	0	15[a,d]
(19d) *-wa -wa -ga*	6	12	0	18
(19e) *-wa -wa -wa*	11	5	0	16[d]
(20) *-ga -ga -ga*	17	1	0	18

[a] N=1 response ambiguous between categories
[b] N=1 response double EPC
[c] N=2 responses ambiguous between categories
[d] N=2 responses uninterpretable/incomplete

For non-EPC fragments (19a–e) together, using NP-*ga* and NP-*wa*, 28% of responses unambiguously imposed just one boundary internal to the fragment. Although double-embedding was the predominant response, we see a fivefold increase (relative to non-EPC fragment (20) with NP-*ga* only) in the kind of response needed to answer our inquiry: what is the routine grouping of an NP1 NP2 NP3 string? The table shows that *all* such non-EP responses with a single internal boundary imposed that boundary after NP1, so that NP2 and NP3 were assigned to the same clause; no responses grouped NP1 and NP2 (cf. for EPC fragments, all NP2's NP3, no NP1's NP2). Thus, the outcome indicates that whatever it is that makes a clause boundary between NP1 and NP2 preferred, it is *not* something special about EPCs — it is a fact about the typical pattern of response in the sentence completion task, more generally.

The intriguing possibility raised by the asymmetric pattern of responses to fragments offering two EPC opportunities simultaneously, in the first part of

Data Set II, is that in Japanese, as in many other languages, EPCs might show real sensitivity to the alienability of the PR-PM relation. The assessment undertaken in the second part of Data Set II suggests, however, that it would be premature to assume that responses of the form NP1's NP2 were blocked (and responses of the form NP2's NP3 were encouraged) by alienability *per se* — the data are entirely compatible with an alternative account, one referring only to the preferred siting of clause boundaries. But the argument here is indirect, necessarily, and leaves open the possibility that alienability has to some extent contributed to the pattern observed. Given the importance of the issue, and the cross-linguistic facts, a direct assessment remains as an important priority for future research.

5. General discussion

The exploratory studies presented in this paper have been built around the fact that occurrences of the EPC in Japanese inevitably involve temporary structural ambiguity. Because EPCs mark both PM and PR with nominative *-ga*, and because *-ga* serves many syntactic functions, an EPC interpretation is only one of several possible analyses for a sentence fragment in which *ga*-marked phrases have appropriate lexical content. The sentence completion data reported in Section 4 indicate that the EPC is not a likely interpretation by any means. As we have seen, responses to the EPC-opportunity fragments of Data Set I rarely imposed an EPC. Instead, each NP-*ga* was more usually made the subject of its own clause, to produce a sentence with embedding; less commonly, the NP-*ga* phrases were taken to be two independent subjects within a single clause, in the PSC. EPC interpretations did finally emerge in Data Set II, when NP-*ga/wa* NP-*ga* NP-*ga* fragments offered two EPC opportunities simultaneously (and lexical content ruled out the possibility of a PSC).

Can this outcome pattern be taken to mean that, in general, the EPC is not a likely structural hypothesis? One immediate problem is that EPCs were perhaps not tested in a fair way in the completion task, so that the outcome pattern might be specific to this experimental setting. For example, frequency considerations might weigh against the EPC since it does not often occur in daily conversation. It seems, however, that frequency cannot account for the data patterns. Recall that in sentence completion responses, the PSC is more than occasionally imposed while the NOC is not (see Section 3.3), entirely reversing what is rare and what is common in normal language production. Uehara and Bradley (1998) have also noted that sentences with scrambling arise in sentence completion even where alternative non-scrambled interpretations are available, though scrambling is claimed to occur infrequently (indeed, in less than 1% of sentences in Yamashita's (1998) corpus study).

A more serious concern would be that the absence of appropriate contexts for the EPC in the completion task might have discouraged its occurrence. That is, if the EPC normally arises in a discourse context that justifies its focus effects, the simple presence in fragment stimuli of NP-*ga*'s with lexical content supporting a possession relation might be insufficient for EPCs to occur. As with frequency, we could try to argue that the occurrence of PSCs (both in the current study, and those of Uehara 1997b, c) constitutes evidence against the importance of a triggering context: if PSCs can occur outside their normal poetic/literacy register, why should EPCs not occur outside their normal discourse contexts? But there is a problem with this approach; arguably, PSCs are in effect self-justifying constructions in the sense that a special register might declare itself phrase- or sentence-internally. Discourse context is another matter altogether. Consider the so-called "exhaustive listing" reading that Kuno (1973a) supposes to be associated with a *ga*-marked possessor; for "president-*ga* driver-*ga*" in (14a), say, this reading has the force "It is the president (and only the president) whose driver …". By this account, the external PR is contrasted with other candidate PRs *in the universe of discourse* (see also Shibatani 1977); certainly, this kind of context cannot be established sentence-internally. If discourse-oriented research confirms Kuno's intuition, and if context is indeed a crucial determinant of the occurrence of EPCs, then the sentence completion task would be doomed as a means of investigating EPCs in Japanese psycholinguistically (and different methods must be sought).[19] That is, providing a supporting context for an EPC-opportunity fragment that has this degree of specificity would in all probability force an EPC reading in any off-line task, and we would no longer be able to exploit the structural ambiguity associated with NP-*ga* NP-*ga*.

However, one serious difficulty arises with any purely contextual account of the distribution of response types in the completion task. It does not explain the fact that EPCs *did* occur even without supporting contexts in Data Set II, in a situation where the usual preference for embedding would (if applied blindly) result in structures with double center-embedding. This observation has two consequences. First, contextual support cannot be the sole determinant of the occurrence of EPCs. Second, issues of processing difficulty are indeed relevant to the kinds of responses produced in the sentence completion task; it was not single embedding but double embedding (associated with a substantial processing cost) that brought out the EPC. This fact leads us to claim that structural factors *are* an important determinant of EPC occurrences, and that they outweigh contextual considerations. It was a striking property of Data Set II that all responses but two involved a single EPC together with a single embedding. Taking this together with the findings for Data Set I (occurrences of the EPC, 0.5% – 5.5%; cf. embedding, 83% – 94%), the EPC is ranked between single and double embedding in structural preference. We therefore propose as a working hypothesis that there is a more-than-moderate processing cost associated with EPC.

If there is real processing cost associated with the EPC, what kind of difficulty might it be that the processor is encountering in parsing these structures? Processing models generally assume that the language processing mechanism is economical, so that the parser prefers "compact structure" (Fodor 1995). This implies a preference for single-clause over embedded-clause structures, all other things being equal. The current data (see also Uehara 1997b, c) suggest a preference for an embedded structure over a single-clause structure involving EPCs and NOCs, and (to a lesser extent) PSCs. There *is* something to be explained, some cost that means things are *not* equal.

Current processing models include a mechanism that might be the basis for an account. They assume not only that the parser is economical about proposing clauses, but also that it is economical about hypothesizing movement chains. That is, if a structure involves a chain, it will be costly to process relative to one that does not (De Vincenzi 1991). Note that the raising analysis generally offered for the EPC (see Section 2) creates a chain, and on these grounds EPCs are predicted to be costly; and if the NOC also involves movement (Dubinsky 1992; Morikawa 1993; Koizumi 1994), the same consideration would apply. If there were an independent reason for supposing the cost of a chain to be substantially greater than that of building a new clause, a uniform account could be given of the similarly low structural preference rankings of the EPC and the NOC. Two problems emerge at this point: no grounds exist for weighing the costs of chains versus clause-building in this way; and the NOC may not involve a movement chain, at all. The NOC may be base-generated, triggered by the predicate's lexical feature specification (Kuno 1973a; Saito 1985).

Alternatively, the EPC and the NOC have in common a non-transparent use of the nominative case-marker *-ga,* and this may be the source of the processing problem. Recall that the prototypical use of NP-*ga* is the thematic subject of a clause; PSCs adhere to this prototypical use (and are exceptional only in having more than one subject), while EPCs require NP-*ga* to be used as a non-subject, just as NOCs do. Uehara (1997b, c), having found that NOCs were essentially never imposed on fragment stimuli in the sentence completion task (even though respondents did occasionally use NOCs in material *added* to that already given), suggested that non-transparent use of Case is problematic in comprehension but not in production; her proposal was that such usages specifically violate a priority for the parser. An account of the current findings for EPCs falls quite naturally under the same analysis. This proposal gains support from a study outside the possibly special circumstances of the sentence completion task. Sekerina (1997), employing an on-line sentence-reading task, found evidence indicating that constructions in Russian involving exceptional dative-marked subjects are misinterpreted in first-pass parsing; apparently, NP (DAT) was interpreted prototypically, i.e., as an indirect object.

The proposal that the parser prefers transparent interpretation of Case is an addition to existing models of the sentence processor, and clearly requires extensive assessment with a variety of constructions, in many languages. But it is an addition that seems very natural for languages like Japanese and Russian in which word order is flexible. It enables the parser to utilize the information provided by overt case-markers straightforwardly, so as to propose structural hypotheses incrementally. When sentence beginnings consist of NP strings (as is typical for Japanese), Case may be all that the parser has in hand. Researchers have only recently begun to examine the processing of scrambled sentences in Japanese, and the evidence is therefore quite slim. It can be said, however, Japanese native speakers have no notable problems in processing scrambled sentences when all case-markers are present (see Yamashita 1997; Uehara & Bradley 1998).

In this paper, we have used the term "transparency" with reference to the interpretation of the nominative case-marker *-ga* to mean simply its use as the natural (thematic) subject. We have noticed that a preference for transparent interpretation of Case does seem to give a uniform account for the low likelihood that EPC and NOC interpretations of fragment stimuli will arise in sentence completion responses (cf. the markedly greater likelihood of embeddings, and even of PSCs). The background assumption is that the explanatory devices currently available in our models of sentence processing (e.g., the chain principle) will not be able to provide a satisfactory account, without some addition.

What remains to be specified, of course, is the precise sense in which the processor requires Case interpretation to be transparent. Is this structural ("Interpret NP-*ga* as a subject")? This being so, we ask whether nominatively marked external PRs in Japanese share any structural properties with natural subjects. Is this thematic ("Interpret NP-*ga* as agent")? This being so, we ask whether non-agent subjects are disadvantaged in the way external PRs seem to be.

6. Concluding remarks

This study aimed to look at the EPC in Japanese from a psycholinguistic viewpoint, using the sentence completion task. The data outcomes revealed that EPC interpretations were rarely imposed on fragment stimuli offering EPC opportunities. A possible explanation for the relative absence of EPC responses, turning on the lack of any context that might justify the EPC's focus effects, was rejected; EPCs in fact did occur even without such contexts, in special circumstances, so that the contextual factors could not be seen as controlling the completion responses. Under an alternative view emphasizing the costs of structure-building, the likelihood ranking provided by completion responses was taken to suggest that there is a more-than-moderate processing cost associated with the EPC; and further, that this cost may arise because transparent interpretation of Case is a priority in sentence processing. Clearly, a suggestion like this has for now only the status of a working hypothesis, and must be confirmed in a variety of settings, and in more sensitive on-line paradigms, in particular. But the hypothesis is an important one since, cross-linguistically, external PRs are rarely marked (morphologically or syntactically) as genitives. If it is correct to claim that a processing cost arises for the EPC because its PR is non-transparently case-marked, this has an immediate consequence for similarly structured EPCs in other languages.

In Japanese, we are able to evaluate the Case transparency hypothesis, as it applies to the EPC, only in terms of exceptional nominative *-ga*, since this construction occurs almost exclusively with subject PMs. A strong test of that hypothesis arises when we ask whether *any* non-genitive case-marking leads to the processing cost we have seen for the EPC. It is conceivable, for example, that phrases (mis)interpretable as subjects have a particular salience for the processor; this being so, processability might differ when EPCs occur in non-subject position (cf. subject position). A test of this kind would be achievable in languages in which EPCs are marked not only with nominative but also with other case-markers, e.g., EPCs with accusative and dative PMs (and thus PRs), as in Korean.

Acknowledgments

I would like to acknowledge the contributions made by Dianne Bradley, in particular, and also those of Janet Dean Fodor and William McClure who provided comments in the course of this project. I would also like to thank Takeo Shimizu who recruited participants for experiments conducted at Gunma University, and James Sangenito and Rebecca Ibanéz who organized the setting for data collection at The International Center of New York. Finally, I would like to acknowledge an anonymous reviewer whose comments proved very useful.

Notes

1 Both PR and PM in the EPC in Japanese are marked with *-ga* except when the PR is optionally thematized and so marked with *-wa* (Kuno 1973a). We will refer to thematization of external PRs in Section 4.2.

2 An anonymous reviewer has suggested that EPCs in which the PR is marked by the accusative case-marker may be possible in the Hachijoojima dialects. Since an accusatively marked PR is otherwise disallowed in Japanese, it is outside the focus of the current study.

3 Morikawa (1993) and Tada (1992) present just a few sentences illustrating the possibility of EPCs with nominative object PMs. As in (4a), all have complex predicates; simplex predicates also seem to allow some nominative object EPCs. Usually, [+stative] predicates are classified into subtypes (see Dubinsky 1992; Takahashi 1996), but it seems that the distribution of EPCs with nominative objects does not reflect that classification. Nor is there predictability in the PR-PM relation for which EPCs in object position are acceptable.

4 Kubo (1992) claims that her dialect allows at most two *ga*-marked phrases in a single clause, and thus judges the sentences in (i-a) and (i-b) as ungrammatical. Her judgments disagree with those of Kuno (1973a) and Tateishi (1991), respectively.

(i) a. *Bunmeikoku-ga dansei-ga heikinzyumyoo-ga mizikai.*
civilized:countries-NOM male-NOM average:life:span-NOM short
'The average life-span of males of civilized countries is short.'
(Kuno 1973a: 34, judged as grammatical)

b. *Taro-ga chichioya-ga otooto-ga nyuin-shi-ta*
Taro-NOM father-NOM brother-NOM hospitalized-do-PAST
'Taro's father's younger brother was hospitalized.'
(Tateishi 1991: 27, judged as grammatical)

5 In the literature, the terms "subjectivization" (Kuno 1973a) or "nominativization" (Shibatani 1977; cf. Morikawa 1993) are frequently used to refer both to the EPC (genitive-driven multiple subject construction, so-called) and to other multiple subject constructions which are not genitive-driven.

6 Tateishi (1991) uses the term "genitive raising construction" to distinguish the EPC from other (non-genitive-driven) multiple subject constructions, e.g., the "major subject construction". He shows that these differ syntactically.

7 Although both Saito (1982, 1985) and Takezawa (1987) propose base-generated EPCs, they disagree about whether nominative Case is assigned to the PR independently of the abstract Case system (Saito), or within that system (Takezawa).

8 In a novel analysis, Ura (1996) proposes that PR-raising is possible only for inalienable possession, universally. Thus the syntax of inalienable possession is seen to differ from that of alienable possession, even in the IPC; Ura treats the former as involving DP-internal PR-raising (from Spec of NP to Spec of DP), while alienable PRs are base-generated at the higher node. In the EPC, the same contrast is drawn, so that only inalienable PRs are sited external to the host DP via a raising operation. For Ura, EPCs in Japanese involving alienable possession are classified with the so-called "major subject" construction (for which no movement is proposed, apparently, but rather base-generation). The analysis depends on the demonstration that, where the intended PR-PM relation is alienable rather than inalienable, EPCs and major subject constructions are constrained in the same way (there can be no more than one major subject or external PR). Here, Ura's examples are less than compelling; other native speakers (including

the author) disagree with his judgments, and counterexamples are readily constructed. Thus, provocative though Ura's proposal might be, it is not considered further in this paper.

9 I assume Croft's (1990: 175) definition; an inalienable relation refers to "a permanent relationship between two entities", such as body-parts and kinship relations, whereas an alienable relation refers to "a relationship that can be temporary". However, the distinction between inalienable and alienable is not clear-cut, and varies among authors: Kitagawa (1986), for example, seems to interpret the notion of inalienable possession more narrowly, to include body-parts such as *me* (eye) but to exclude kinship terms such as *go-choonan* (son). Ura (1996) accepts Croft's now-standard definition, but reads it in a way that suggests that decisions about (in)alienability may turn on quite subtle distinctions. He presents *Handai-ga gakuchoo-ga* (Osaka University-Nom president-Nom) as involving an inalienable relation, presumably favoring the permanence of the *office* over the temporary tenure of any given *office-holder*.

10 For a thorough examination of the freedom with which EPCs can be constructed, with respect to predicate types, see Takahashi (1996). It should be noted that, contrary to Takahashi and other authors, Kubo (1992) reports that her dialect restricts EPCs to stative predicates. (See also Footnote 4.)

11 An anonymous reviewer provided helpful comments on this issue.

12 According to Kuno (1973a), the predicates that allow the NOC include all transitive adjectives, all nominal adjectives, and all transitive stative verbs.

13 In Uehara's database project, consecutive NP-*ga's* never supported the PR-PM relation required for EPCs. Possession interpretations were made impossible or implausible either by the order of NPs, e.g., *classmate*-Nom *Sachiko*-Nom (*classmate's Sachiko), or by lexical content, e.g., *Hiroshi*-Nom *criminal*-Nom (?? Hiroshi's criminal).

14 Data Set I here replaces that presented in the author's paper at the Conference on External Possessors and Related Noun Incorporation held at University of Oregon in September 1997. The earlier data set suffered a good deal of ambiguity arising from special (non-standard) task instructions.

15 Examples (ii-a, b) present typical sentence-completion responses illustrating instances unambiguously involving the EPC and the PSC, respectively. Examples (ii-c) presents a typical instance of a response interpretable either as an EPC or as a PSC. The sentence content constituting the stimulus fragment is shown in boldface:

(ii) a. [$_{IP}$ ***kaishain-ga*** ***kyuuryoo-ga kodomo-ni omocha-o*** *katte-yar-eta*]
office:worker-NOM salary-NOM child-Dat toy-ACC buy-give-could
'The office worker's salary was enough to buy a toy for his child.'

b. [$_{IP}$ ***shachoo-ga*** ***untenshu-ga*** *sosite hisho-made-ga sorotte uso-o*
president-NOM driver-NOM and secretary-even-NOM all lie-ACC
tuite-iru]
telling-be
'The president, the driver, and even the secretary are all telling a lie.'

c. [$_{IP}$ ***shachoo-ga*** ***untenshu-ga*** *genkan-no mae-ni tatte-iru*]
president-NOM driver-NOM entrance-GEN front-at standing-be
'The president's driver is standing in front of the entrance.'
'The president and the driver are (both) standing in front of the entrance.'

16 The psycholinguistics literature has often focused on a particular kind of double center-embedding, i.e., double self-embedding, in which two embedded clauses are of the same type. While self-embedding certainly increases difficulty, it is clear (both in English and in Japanese) that any double center-embedding is burdensome for the processor. See, e.g., Gibson (1991).

17 In an informal check on the possible impact of alienability on the preferred site of single EPC when stimulus fragments offer two EPC opportunities, responses were collected for the following fragment (included among the fillers for Data Set I):

(iii) *Kyojin-ga tooshu-ga kooti-ga*
Giants-NOM pitcher-NOM coach-NOM

Crucially, either EPC site in this example involves alienable possession (*Giants' pitcher, pitcher's coach*). Among a total of 10 responses imposing a single EPC, only 1 took the form NP1's NP2 and 9 took the form NP2's NP3, i.e., the asymmetry observed in Data Set II still held. (It is curious that almost 50% of responses imposed two fragment-internal clause boundaries, alleviating the cost of double embedding by making one clause an adverbial adjunct.)

18 When NP-*ga* and NP-*o* are thematized, -*ga* and -*o* are replaced by -*wa*. When NP-*ni* is thematized, it is either replaced by -*wa*, making the form NP-*wa*, or -*wa* is attached after -*ni*,making the form NP-*ni-wa*. There are no differences in meaning between the latter two forms.

19 More accurately, sentence completion would be doomed as a means of investigating certain kinds of question about the processing of EPCs in Japanese, namely, those concerned with the *parsing* of these constructions. Other questions would remain viable, e.g., those concerned with what aspects, exactly, of discourse context are the most effective in triggering occurrences of the EPC.

References

Chomsky, Noam and George Miller. 1963. "Introduction to the Formal Analysis of Natural Languages." In R. Duncan Luce, Robert R. Bush, and Eugene Galanter (eds.), *Handbook of Mathematical Psychology, II.* New York: John Wiley and Sons, 269–321.

Croft, William. 1990. *Typology and Universals.* Cambridge: Cambridge University.

De Vincenzi, Marica. 1991. *Syntactic Parsing Strategies in Italian.* Dordrecht: Kluwer.

Dubinsky, Stanley. 1992. "Case Assignment to VP-adjoined Positions: Nominative Objects in Japanese." *Linguistics,* 30: 873–910.

Fodor, Janet D. 1995. "Comprehending Sentence Structure." In Lila R. Gleitman and Mark Liberman (eds.), *An Invitation to Cognitive Science, Volume 1: Language* (Second Edition). Cambridge: MIT Press, 209–246.

Frazier, Lyn. 1978. *On Comprehending Sentences: Syntactic Parsing Strategies.* Unpublished doctoral dissertation, University of Massachusetts. Reproduced by Indiana University Linguistics Club, 1979.

Gibson, Edward. 1991. *A Computational Theory of Human Linguistic Processing: Memory Limitations and Processing Breakdown.* Unpublished doctoral dissertation, Carnegie Mellon University.

Inoue, Atsu and Janet D. Fodor. 1995. "Information-paced Parsing of Japanese." In Reiko Mazuka and Noriko Nagai (eds.), *Japanese Sentence Processing.* Hillsdale: Lawrence Erlbaum Associates, 9–55.

Kitagawa, Yoshihisa. 1986. *Subjects in Japanese and English.* Unpublished doctoral dissertation, University of Massachusetts.

Koizumi, Masatoshi. 1994. "Nominative Objects: The Role of TP in Japanese." In Masatoshi Koizumi and Hiroyuki Ura (eds.), *MIT Working Papers in Linguistics 24: Formal Approaches to Japanese Linguistics 1.* Cambridge: MIT, 211–230.

Kubo, Miori. 1992. *Japanese Syntactic Structures and their Constructional Meanings.* Unpublished doctoral dissertation, Massachusetts Institute of Technology.

Kuno, Susumu. 1973a. *The Structure of the Japanese Language.* Cambridge: MIT Press.

Kuno, Susumu. 1973b. *Nihon Bonpoo Kenkyuu.* Tokyo: Taishuukan.

Kuroda, Shige-Yuki. 1992. *Japanese Syntax and Semantics: Collected Papers.* Dordrecht: Kluwer.

Lewis, Richard L. 1993. *An Architecturally-Based Theory of Human Sentence Comprehension.* Unpublished doctoral dissertation, Carnegie Mellon University.

Lewis, Richard L. 1996. "Interference in Short-term Memory: The Magical Number Two (or Three) in Sentence Processing." *Journal of Psycholinguistic Research,* 25: 93–115.

Miller, George and Noam Chomsky. 1963. "Finitary Models of Language Users." In R. Duncan Luce,

Morikawa, Masahiro. 1993. *A Parametric Approach to Case Alternation Phenomena.* Tokyo: Hituzi Syobo.

Nakamura, Wataru. 1997. "On the Argument Structure of Inalienable Possession Constructions." Paper presented at the Conference on External Possession and Noun Incorporation, Eugene.

Payne, Doris. 1997a. "Prolegomenon to a Typology of EP Constructions." *Handbook of the Conference on External Possession and Noun Incorporation*, Eugene: vi-vii.

Payne, Doris. 1997b. "The Maasai External Possessor Construction." In J. Bybee, J. Haiman, and S. A. Thompson (eds.), *Essays on Language Function and Language Type: Dedicated to T. Givón.* Amsterdam: John Benjamins, 395–422.

Payne, Doris. 1997c. "Argument Structure and Locus of Affect in the Maasai External Possession Construction." *Berkeley Linguistic Society 23. Special Session on African Linguages*, 98–115.

Saito, Mamoru. 1982. *Case-Marking in Japanese: A Preliminary Study.* Unpublished manuscript, Massachusetts Institute of Technology.

Saito, Mamoru. 1985. *Some Asymmetries in Japanese and their Theoretical Implications.* Unpublished doctoral dissertation, Massachusetts Institute of Technology.

Sekerina, Irina. 1997. *The Syntax and Processing of Scrambling Constructions in Russian.* Unpublished doctoral dissertation, The City University of New York.

Shibatani, Masayoshi. 1977. "Grammatical Relations and Surface Cases." *Language,* 53: 798–809.

Stabler, Edward P. 1994. "The Finite Connectivity of Linguistic Structure." In C. Clifton, Jr., L. Frazier, and K. Rayner (eds.), *Perspectives on Sentence Processing.* Hillsdale, NJ: Lawrence Erlbaum Associates, 303–336.

Tada, Hiroaki. 1992. "Nominative Objects in Japanese." *Journal of Japanese Linguistics,* 14: 91–108.

Takahashi, Chioko. 1996. *Multiplicity, Optimality, and Constraints on the Distribution of Nominative Case in Japanese.* Unpublished doctoral dissertation, Cornell University.

Takezawa, Koichi. 1987. *A Configurational Approach to Case-Marking in Japanese.* Unpublished doctoral dissertation, University of Washington.

Tateishi, Koichi. 1991. *The Syntax of 'Subjects'.* Unpublished doctoral dissertation, University of Massachusetts.

Ueda, Masanobu. 1990. *Japanese Phrase Structure and Parameter Setting.* Unpublished doctoral dissertation, University of Massachusetts.

Uehara, Keiko. 1997a. "Judgments of Processing Load: The effect of NP-*ga* sequences." *Journal of Psycholinguistics Research,* 26: 255–263.

Uehara, Keiko. 1997b. "Structuring Japanese Argument Sequences: A Sentence-completion Study." Poster presented at the 10th Annual CUNY Conference on Human Sentence Processing, Santa Monica.

Uehara, Keiko. 1997c. "Clause Segmentation Strategies in Japanese." Paper presented at the Annual Student/Faculty Conference, Ph.D. Program in Linguistics, The Graduate Center of The City University of New York.

Uehara, Keiko and Dianne C. Bradley. 1998. "Processing Scrambled Argument Structures in Japanese." Paper presented at the 72nd Annual Meeting of The Linguistic Society of America, New York.

Ura, Hiroyuki. 1996. *Multiple Feature-Checking: A Theory of Grammatical Function Splitting.* Unpublished doctoral dissertation, Massachusetts Institute of Technology.

Yamashita, Hiroko. 1997. "The Effects of Word-order and Case Marking Information on the Processing of Japanese." *Journal of Psycholinguistics Research,* 26: 159–188.

Yamashita, Hiroko. 1998. "Performance and Pragmatic Accounts of the Distribution of Scrambled Sentences in Colloquial Japanese." Paper presented at the Psycholinguistics Supper Club, The Graduate Center of The City University of New York.

Whitman, John B. 1998. "Kayne 1994: p.143, FN.3." Unpublished manuscript, Cornell University.

Appendix: Sentence-Completion Fragments

Example numbers correspond to those in the text.

(14) a. 社長が運転手が ...

b. 億万長者が門番が郵便物を ...

c. 専務が秘書が社員に ...

d. 映画俳優が恋人がディレクターに出演を ...

(15) a. 誘拐犯人が声明文が ...

b. タイピストがコンピューターが情報を ...

c. 有名作家が原稿が知り合いに ...

d. 会社員が給料が子供におもちゃを ...

(16) a. ソニーが社員が態度が ...

b. 巨人は投手が腕力が ...

(19) a. 母が主任医師は孝が ...

b. 叔母が店主は学生は ...

c. 両親は運転手が進は ...

d. 孫は清水さんは青年が ...

e. 中学生は花嫁は今井さんは ...

(20) 父が道夫が有名作家が ...

PART III

Comparative Studies

Body-Part EP Constructions

A Cognitive/Functional Analysis

Maura Velázquez-Castillo
Colorado State University

1. Preliminaries

The aim of this paper is to offer a structural and functional characterization of two different types of external possessor (EP) constructions, as found in Spanish and the South American language Guaraní. These two languages are typologically very different, and exhibit EP constructions with obvious structural differences which nevertheless share identifiable semantic and functional commonalties.

Typical EP constructions in both Spanish and Guaraní involve: i) a body-part term (BPT) directly involved in some activity or state, or characterized by a descriptive attribute; and ii) a human possessor portrayed as the primary experiencer of the activity/state involving its body-parts, or as the main bearer of the descriptive attributes of its body parts. Examples (1–10) contrast Spanish non-thematic "possessive dative" (1–3), "body-move" (4), and "attributive *tener*" (5) constructions with their incorporating EP Guaraní counterparts (6–10):

(1) *Julio le atravesó el corazón con el arma.*
'Julio cut him through the heart with the weapon.'

(2) *Me lavé las manos.*
'I washed me the hands (=my hands).'

(3) *Me da vueltas la cabeza.*
'To me turns the head = I'm dizzy'

(4) *Cerré los ojos.*
'I closed the eyes (=my eyes).'

(5) *Tenía las piernas delgadas.*
'S/he had the legs thin (=thin legs).'

(6) *Julio oi-py'a-kutu chupe kysé-pe*
3ACT-chest-stab to=him knife-with
'Julio cut him through the heart with the weapon.'

(7) *A-je-po-héi.*
1ACT-REFL-hand-wash
'I washed me the hands (=my hands).'

(8) *Che akã-jere.*
1INACT head-turn
'To me turns the head = I'm dizzy'

(9) *A-je-sa-pymi.*
1ACT-REFL-eye-sink
'I closed the eyes (=my eyes).'

(10) *Hetymã-po'i*
3INACT=leg-thin
'S/he had the legs thin (=thin legs).'

Spanish BPTs feature the definite article as their determiner and are coded in independent NPs, while Guaraní BPTs are normally incorporated into the main predicator stem with no modifier. Often, but not always, an alternative non-EP construction exists for each EP construction type. In Spanish, the alternative is marked by the presence of the possessive adjective in lieu of the definite article as the BPT determiner. In Guaraní, the non-EP counterpart involves the use of a person/number prefix on an unincorporated BPT.

To start, I will first define how the term "external possession" is used in this paper. I use EP in a broad sense that includes any construction in which a possessor (PR) NP is coded in a syntactic constituent different from that which contains the possessum (PM). Almost always, this means that the PR is coded as a core verbal argument in the same clause as its PM. For example, in a typical Spanish EP construction involving BPTs, the PR appears syntactically as an indirect object (*Me rompí la pierna* 'I broke to me the leg') or as the clausal subject, often marked on the verb (*Levanté la pierna* 'I raised the leg'). In an EP construction, the PM is sometimes coded as an oblique or as a verbal argument, as in the Spanish examples above; or is incorporated into the verb, as in Guaraní (6–10).

Formal-theoretical accounts of EP generally concentrate on offering a structural account of the puzzling fact that the clausal arguments of some EP constructions seem not to be licensed by the valence of the verb. In striving for an economic grammar, these accounts tend to reduce EP constructions to other types of theoretically sanctioned phenomena, such as "raising" or "movement" in multi-tier grammatical representations (e.g., Bell 1983; Baker 1988), or reanalysis in lexical representation (e.g., Vandeweghe 1987). One important contribution of these studies is the identification of the strong association of EP phenomena with absolutive arguments, typically the object of a transitive clause or an unaccusative intransitive subject. The problem I find with these accounts is that, in their reductionism, they invariably exclude a subset of EP and related constructions for no other reason than theory-internal constraints. For instance, examples like (3) and (8) would not be included in the category of EP constructions simply because the PR cannot be analyzed as "extracted" from an underlying object. In addition, these accounts frequently leave out defining semantic and communicative factors whose consideration could include related constructions and result in a more unified account of the phenomenon.

There have been some studies of EP which suggest that EP is invariably accompanied by semantic constraints. According to Croft (1985: 46–47), the primary fact which licenses EP is that "something can be beneficially/adversely affected by an action by virtue of being the possessor of the entity which is directly affected by an action." He adds, "the more intimate the possession relation, the more likely one will find PA [possessor ascension]." Wierzbicka (1988) has an analysis in which EP is a function of the degree of conceptual differentiation between a body-part and its PR. She finds that EP is the formal device of choice to express a portrayal of body-parts as integrally connected with their PRs. She notes that EP is permissible only with a limited number of nouns among which BPTs figure prominently.

Functional accounts of EP tend to suffer from a different kind of reductionism, one that originates from a premature semantic delimitation of the phenomenon that tends to impose artificially rigid boundaries between core manifestations of EP and other clearly related constructions. This is particularly true of analyses which propose the notion of "affectedness" as a necessary semantic component of EP constructions (e.g., Durie 1987: 389). The primacy of this notion in defining EP tends to be overstated, as evidenced by the existence of EP constructions (broadly understood) that involve non-patient roles. Again, (3) and (8), as well as (5) and (10) would be left out of the family of EP constructions, despite their clear connection to more central members of the EP category.

The analysis proposed here integrates semantic and functional aspects in the explanation of the formal features of EP, and builds on Velázquez-Castillo's (1996) use of cognitive linguistics and functional models for the analysis of inalienable possession constructions. An aspect of cognitive linguistics which will prove useful for a unified explanation of EP phenomena is the fact that formal variations in grammatical constructions are not exclusively linked to verbal semantics and are viewed as codifications of alternate semantic construals.

Cognitive and functional linguistics recognize the existence of canonical patterns, as well as deviations from these patterns in response to the confluence of special semantic configurations. My analysis acknowledges the existence of these "prototype effects" in the multiple manifestations of EP, and at the same time proposes a general characterization that includes and unifies all types of EP phenomena.

My analysis of EP constructions and corresponding construals assumes Langacker's (1991) reference-point model, which was devised to explain possessive, and other types of constructions involving an asymmetric prominence relation between two nominals. Semantically salient entities often serve as reference points for less salient entities (*targets*) which are connected semantically to them. In other words, entities with lesser salience are accessed mentally via their reference points. The set of entities accessible through a reference point is called the *dominion* of that reference point. In a possessive relation, for example, there is always an asymmetric relation between the PR and the PM, where the PR is conceptually more prominent and serves as the reference point for the PM. Thus a part-whole possessive relation is always expressed with the whole as PR and the part as PM and not vice-versa. Humans, being higher in the empathy hierarchy than their body-parts, are natural reference points for their body-parts. Unlike other entities, body-parts are inherently dependent on their semantically obligatory reference points.

The data sample on which this study is based is drawn from written narrative texts: a compilation of folk tales in the case of Guaraní, and fragments of literary narrative in the case of Spanish. The author's native knowledge of both languages has provided a source of grammaticality judgments on constructed variations of examples found in the data, and has facilitated the identification of sometimes subtle semantic and functional differences and commonalties. These constructed variations are marked with a (*) when ungrammatical, and with a (?) when they are pragmatically odd in the context in which they occur.

2. Spanish EP constructions: functional and structural profile

2.1 *Externally possessed BPTs: functional and grammatical roles*

My discussion of Spanish EP constructions begins with an assessment of the discourse topicality of Spanish BPTs and their PRs in EP constructions and non-EP constructions. According to Givón (1984a: 138), "the main behavioral manifestation of important topics in discourse is *continuity*, as expressed by frequency of occurrence." The topicality measures shown in Table 1 were obtained applying Givón's (1983) quantitative method of topicality assessment. RD stands for "referential distance" (number of clauses separating the present occurrence of the referent from its last mention within the 15 preceding clauses). TP stands for "topic persistence" (number of recurrences of the referent in the 15 subsequent clauses).

Table 1: *Discourse topicality measures of BPTs and their PRs in Spanish EP and non-EP constructions*

	Mean RD (1–15 scale)	Mean TP (0–15 scale)	Total (=N)
EP construction BPTs	**15.00**	**0.05**	**60**
PRs	0.20	6.90	60
Non-EP construction BPTs	**13.95**	**0.32**	**56**
PRs	1.43	5.50	56

Not surprisingly, Table 1 shows that BPTs in general have low discourse topicality (high RD and low TP), while their PRs show considerable topicality (low RD and high TP). As the RD and TP figures indicate, most BPTs in EP constructions tend to be first mentions and are not able to sustain referential continuity. Comparing the topicality measures of article-modified BPTs with those of possessive-modified BPTs, a subtle but significant difference can be noted: while article-modified BPTs have the maximum referential distance considered, possessive-modified BPTs have a somewhat reduced number, suggesting that at least in some cases, these BPTs have been mentioned before and therefore have a degree of familiarity attached to them. The measures also suggest a relatively greater ability of possessive-modified BPTs to persist as topics once introduced. Noteworthy as the numeric differences given in Table 1 are, they do not capture the longer-range discourse continuity that the possessive often signals. The reference to *cuerpo* 'body' in *El coronel no supo qué hacer con su cuerpo* 'The colonel did not know what to do with his body'(GM 87) is clearly resumed in a second mention three paragraphs later: *El coronel recuperó su cuerpo* 'The colonel recovered his body'. Even longer-range resumptions of reference are not uncommon with the use of possessive-modified BPTs. The following reference to the intensely green eyes of one character *El coronel eludió los penetrantes ojos verdes de Germán* 'The colonel avoided the penetrating green eyes of Germán' (GM 77) is resumed four pages later, emphasizing the same qualities, using a possessive with the BPT: *Germán lo penetró con sus pupilas* 'Germán penetrated him with his eyes'(GM 81).

Grammatically, discourse topicality is manifested by access to the case roles of subject and object. Of the two "the subject tends to code the most important, recurrent, continuous topic" while "the direct object codes the topic next in importance, recurrence or continuity" (Givón 1984: 138). In general, I am assuming a grammatical role prominence hierarchy in which SUBJ > DO > IO > OBL. Table 2 shows the distribution of BPTs in EP constructions by grammatical function.

Table 2: *Distribution of BPTs in EP Constructions According to Grammatical Function*

Grammatical Function	*Total N*	*Percentage*
Subject	21	6.6
Objects	137	43.2
Object of attributive *tener*	18	6.7
Object in body-move construction.	45	14.2
Other objects	74	23.3
Obliques	120	37.9
Descriptive apposition	14	4.4
Genitive complement	10	3.2
Other	15	4.7
Total	317	100

The incidence of BPTs in subject position is low (6.6%). Contrast this with 23% of possessive-modified BPTs in subject position (Velázquez-Castillo, to appear). Since the subject role correlates strongly with the semantic role of action initiator/agent, it is significant that this is one of the most common roles born by possessive-modified BPTs, while its association with article-modified BPTs is weak. The semantic role of agent/initiator is also manifested grammatically as an agentive complement, which possessive-modified BPTs are capable of bearing and article-modified BPTs are not (Velázquez-Castillo, to appear). The number of article-modified BPTs in the role of object is considerably higher (43.2%); but, as we will see, these "objects" exhibit grammatical and pragmatic features of weak objecthood. Although discourse participants coded in object and subject roles are expected to have considerable topicality, BPTs in these roles exhibit low topicality levels, as shown in Table 3.

The structure types found in the corpus are illustrated in examples (11)–(20). Both the BPT and the PR are underlined in the examples whenever possible:

Table 3: *Topicality Measures of externally possessed BPTs in the role of subjects and objects*

	Mean RD (0–15 scale)	*Mean TP (0–15 scale)*	*Total number*
Externally possessed BTPs as Subjects	14.5	0.19	21
Externally possessed BTPs as Objects	14.8	0.11	137

BPT in a manner complement- PR in subject role

(11) *...el coronel le preguntó en voz baja, con los dientes apretados: — ¿Cuánto le debemos, doctor?* (GM 41)
'the colonel$_1$ asked him, clenching the (his)$_1$ teeth, — How much do we owe you, doctor?'

BPT in descriptive apposition qualifying a subject or object PR

(12) *El cuello y los muslos pelados y cárdenos, la cresta rebanada, el animal había adquirido una figura escueta, un aire indefenso.* (GM 124)
'The (his$_1$)neck and thighs, hairless and red, the (his$_1$)comb drooping, the animal$_1$ appeared thin and defenseless.'

"Object" of attributive *tener*- PR in subject role

(13) *Teng-o las piernas rotas.* (F 177)
'have-1SG (=I have) the (=my) legs broken (My legs are broken.)'

BPT in a locative complement- PR in subject or object role

(14) *Examin-ó la pastilla en la palma de la mano.* (GM 86)
'examine-3SG (=He$_1$ examined) the pill in the palm of the (=his$_1$) hand.'

(15) *...alguien lo agarró por el brazo...* (GM 19)
'Somebody grabbed him$_1$ by the (=his$_1$) arm.'

BPT in an instrument complement- PR in subject role

(16) *...clav-ó [el arma] en la espalda de Zagal y con el brazo derecho rodeó el cuello del coronel.* (F 199)
'...stab-3SG (=he$_1$ stabbed) Zagal in the back and wrapped the (=his$_1$) right arm around the colonel's neck....'

"Object" and PM of subject in body-move constructions

(17) *El prisionero levantó el rostro y dejó que los ojos se le perdieran en el paisaje seco.*
'The prisoner$_1$ raised *the (=his$_1$) head* and let the (=his$_1$) eyes wander over the parched landscape.' (F 182)

"Object" or subject in possessive dative constructions — PR in dative role

(18) *Don Sabas se secó el cuello con un pañuelo impregnado de lavanda.* (GM 89)
'Don Sabas$_1$ dried himself$_1$ the (=his$_1$) neck with a lavender-soaked handkerchief.'

(19) *Me suda mucho la espalda*. (F 192)
'The (=my) back is sweating me a lot. (My back is sweating a lot)'.

Sentential subject

(20) *Junt-ó los puños sobre el estómago y el rostro se torció de dolor.* (F 202)
Press-3SG (he$_1$ pressed) the (=his$_1$) fists into the (=his$_1$) stomach and the (=his$_1$) face contorted in pain.'

A linguistic element which contributes to the advancement of the plot is considered to be part of the narrative mode, while those elements which describe, orient, categorize, establish relations or otherwise serve purely expressive purposes are considered to be part of the descriptive mode (Du Bois 1980: 227). As can be noted, one of the most prevalent patterns for externally possessed BPTs in discourse is in conjunction with descriptive modifiers. This indicates that their discourse role is more descriptive than narrative. Other obvious descriptive uses of externally possessed BPTs is in appositive constructions and descriptive manner complements (11–13). The descriptive elements that accompany BPTs in these examples are oriented towards developing and characterizing the highly topical PRs, which are the real discourse entities as far as the writer is concerned. All these sentences feature the PR in grammatically prominent positions, rendering it a clear sentential topic, capable of absorbing the descriptive qualities attributed to its body-part.

The same primarily descriptive role is also observable in BPTs as "objects" of the verb of possession *tener* 'have' ((13), repeated below as (21)). This verb can hardly be said to predicate possession in (21); its function is clearly not to inform that the subject has a forehead, a head or legs. Thus, a substitution of *tener* with *poseer* 'to possess' is not allowed:

(21) *Tengo/(*poseo) las piernas rotas.* (F 177)
(lit.) 'My legs are broken/*I have the legs broken.'

Significantly, without the descriptive modifier *rotas* 'broken', the use of the definite article with the object of *tener* renders the sentence anomalous, as shown in **Tengo las piernas*. 'I have the legs.' A primarily possessive sense of this verb is not possible with a definite article as the BPT determiner.[1] With an article-modified BPT, then, the possessive sense of *tener* is weakened to become a primarily attributive predicate. The construction is typically used to depict the physical image intended for a discourse participant. Similar semantic effects are discussed extensively in Tellier's (1992) article on the attributive and possessive use of the French verb *avoir* 'have'. Though clauses involving a verb of possession are not usually considered to be part of the family of EP constructions, I am including the Spanish attributive *tener* construction among them because of the parallels it features with other recognized Spanish EP constructions, i.e., the obligatory use of the definite article as the determiner of the BPT, and the strong association of BPTs with the construction.

One of the most frequent grammatical roles of externally possessed BPTs in Spanish (close to 23%) is that of locative oblique (14). Locatives can be considered to fall in the peripheries of the descriptive discourse mode. They do not typically provide a description of a participant's current predisposition or characterizing trait. They fulfill an orienting role, however, by providing a setting for a narrated event or an evaluative activity. Since BPTs in this role have the ability to be part of a narrated event, they can be said to be more relevant to the narrative mode than the other clearly descriptive uses of BPTs. A somewhat more narrative role, but with clear descriptive effects, is exhibited by externally possessed BPTs as instrumental obliques (16). The increased relevance of this construction to the narrative mode lies in the fact that the instrumental role signals the presence of an agentive subject.

The most common grammatical role borne by article-modified BPTs is that of object (over 43%), a role considered to be next to that of subject in topicality, and therefore with potential narrative function. However, the narrative role of these objects is rather limited, as suggested by their low topicality measures (Table 3). Moreover, the vast majority of them are less than prototypical objects. Standard tests of objecthood usually applied to Spanish NPs are their ability to undergo i) passivization, ii) nominalization, and iii) cliticization with a direct object clitic pronoun. BPT objects do not undergo all these processes; consider the performance of the construction types "body-move", and "possessive dative", given in (22) and (23) below, in these tests. Both examples are constructed sentences.

(22) *El soldado cerró los ojos por un minuto.*
'The soldier$_1$ closed the (=his$_1$) eyes for a minute.'

(23) *El coronel se llevó las manos al pecho al sentir el impacto del disparo.*
'The colonel$_1$ drew the (=his$_1$) hands towards the (=his$_1$) chest as he felt the impact of the bullet.'

(22) a. **Los ojos fueron cerrados (por el soldado)....* (Passivization)
b. **Los ojos se cerraron (por el soldado) por un minuto.*

(23) a. **Las manos fueron llevadas al pecho al sentir el impacto del disparo.*
b. **Se llevaron las manos al pecho (por el coronel) ...*

(22) c. **El cierre de los ojos ...* (Nominalization)

(23) c. **La llevada de manos al pecho...*

(22) d. *El soldado los cerró por un minuto.* (Cliticization)

(23) d. *El coronel se las llevó al pecho al sentir el impacto del disparo.*

The a- and b-examples illustrate a complete inability to passivize: neither the periphrastic passive nor the *se*- passive are suitable structures for these BPT objects; and, as shown by the c-examples, most article-modified BPTs perform dismally in the nominalization test. Both tests represent a measure of the effectiveness characteristic of a canonical transitive event; i.e., the degree to which the object is affected by the event. Naturally, the texts examined did not contain a single case of article-modified BPT objects in passive or nominalized structures.

The cliticization of article-modified BPTs in object position often elicits a positive grammaticality judgment in isolated, constructed sentences (d-examples). This judgment is not to be discounted since other clearly intransitive sentences would most likely elicit a negative reaction. It is fair to say then that the test points to some level of individuality attributed to the body-part object and hence to some degree of transitivity. However, in real discourse, pronoun substitution for "object" BPTs is rare. The corpus used for this study contains only two such cases of pronominalization, one of which is given in (24).

(24) '*Se llevó los dedos a las sienes y las acarició.* (F180)
'He$_1$ raised the (=his$_1$) fingers to the (=his$_1$) temples and rubbed them.'

For the most part, subsequent mention of an object BPT with some degree of continuity is realized by overtly restating the whole NP each time, as in (25). A pronominal substitution would be highly unnatural in this context (25a):

(25) *"Cierra la boca un minuto"... Ella se llevó efectivamente las manos a la boca.*
'"Shut the (=your) mouth for a minute". She indeed placed the (=her) hands over the (=her) mouth.' (GM 89)

(25) a. ?*Ella la cerró y no la volvió a abrir en todo el día.*
'She shut it (=the mouth) and did not open it again all day long.'

Furthermore, a subsequent object clitic pronoun tends to refer to the PR rather than to the body-part, as shown in (26).

(26) *...entonces llegó la tropa federal y empezó a cortarles las manos a los hombres y a perseguirlos por el monte.* (F 190)
'...then the federal troops arrived and began cutting off the (the men's) hands to the men and pursuing them (=the men/*the hands) into the mountains.'

"Objects" of the attributive *tener* construction exhibit similar signs of weak objecthood. Note in this regard their inability to passivize: From *El gallo tenía las patas amarillas* 'The rooster had the legs yellow' one cannot obtain either a periphrastic passive, **Las patas amarillas fueron tenidas por el gallo*, or a *se* passive construction **Se tenían las patas amarillas (por el gallo)*.[2]

I will now consider briefly the limited access these BPTs have to the role of subject, a role with a potentially high narrative status. Consider examples (20) above, 'the (=his) face contorted in pain,' and (27) below:

(27) *El brazo y la pierna, magullados por la caída, le colgaban inertes.*
'The (=his$_i$) arm and the (=his$_i$) leg, badly injured by the fall, hung lifelessly to him$_i$.' (F 175)

Cases in which the BPT is a clausal subject are rare and constitute a potential problem for the reference point model, since one would expect BPTs' grammatical roles to be low in the grammatical role hierarchy while that of their PRs to be high. Particularly troubling in this regard are cases exemplified by (27), where the PR is coded as an indirect object, a role lower in the hierarchy than that of subject occupied by the BPT. However, this is a problem only if one limits oneself to the clausal level. It is evident from a look at the immediate discourse context that the PR is, in fact, the dominant topic of the episode. In (20), for example, the subject *el rostro* is preceded by a coordinated sentence featuring the PR as its subject. Example (27) follows a sentence with a pronominal reference to the PR, which in turn follows a full paragraph describing the mental state of the PR and protagonist. The higher contextual prominence of the PR vis-à-vis the BPT is evident and I would argue that its topicality is maintained despite the subject coding of the BPT. Since the body-part is construed as an integral part of the PR's personhood, coding the BPT as a clausal subject does not interrupt the thematic continuity of the PR. Furthermore, these BPT subjects are not agentive, the subject type that is considered to be characteristic of narrative clauses. In (20), *el rostro* is construed as an experiencer and, in (27), *el brazo y la pierna* are construed as the static themes of a spatial disposition. These sentences are clearly intended to depict the lamentable physical state of the protagonic BPT PRs. Despite their access to subjecthood, which suggests some degree of individuation, these BPTs in fact make a metonymic reference to their PRs. In (20), for example, the body-part is presented as an experiencer of pain, when in fact the PR's painful experience is being described. It is telling in this regard that the sporadic access to subjecthood does not result in an overall increase in the topicality level of BPTs (Table 3). Their local topicality is not maintained beyond the sentence, suggesting that these rare instances of subjecthood are indeed figurative and stylistic in nature.

The difference in semantic, grammatical and discourse prominence between the BPT and its PR, with the PR consistently ranking higher in salience, is fully predicted by the reference point model. It is this type of pronounced asymmetrical relation, characteristic of the relation of the reference point with its target, which leads the reader to link the article-modified BPT to the intended reference point. The definite article is not an explicit indicator of a possessive relationship in an EP construction, but in fulfilling its normal function of signaling connectedness, it instructs the reader to search for the intended reference point in current mental representation. The discourse referent to which the article-modified BPT is linked must be maximally *proximal*, not only in the sense that its conceptual prominence makes it readily identifiable, but also in the sense that it must be found within the same minimal domain as that within which the BPT occurs. This minimal domain of occurrence is usually assumed to be the clause. While this is certainly the norm in the corpus examined, the scope of PR availability can also be cross-sentential, as shown in (28):

(28) *Se arrastró, con el brazo y la pierna adoloridos, hacia una roca gigantesca.... Pero la mano derecha, tullida por el dolor, apenas podía sostener la pistola.* (F 174)
'He$_i$ crawled, with his injured arm and legs, towards a gigantic rock... But the (=his$_i$) right arm, racked with pain, could barely support the pistol.'

This example suggests that the cross-sentential referential link for the definite article is licensed by a topical co-designator, present within the boundaries of an equi-topical discourse chain. The definite article is not acceptable if the equi-topical chain is broken. The fact remains that the PR to which the article-modified BPT is linked must be maximally proximal in terms of availability in current mental representation. The cross-sentential nature of the linguistic distance allowed for the externalization of the PR suggests that perhaps EP is not strictly syntactic in nature. A discourse-based account of the phenomenon has therefore the potential to unify sentential and cross-sentential cases of EP.

While definiteness is typically associated with discourse continuity, the definite marking of externally possessed BPTs in Spanish has very little to do with discourse continuity, as shown by low topicality measurements for BPTs. Since a mental file is not activated to keep track of them in the unfolding discourse, the use of the definite article must respond to a type of definiteness other than familiarity by previous mention. Velázquez-Castillo (to appear) follows recent definiteness studies in analyzing the use of the definite article with externally possessed BPTs as belonging to the class of inferable definites. In that article I argue that the definite article in this case refers not to a uniquely identifiable entity, as most instances of the definite article do, but to a familiar *slot* in a human body frame activated by a previous mention of the PR. In this sense, the level of referential specificity of an article-modified BPT is closer to a type rather than to a token. This low level of body-part individuation results from a construal of integral association between body-part and PR.

2.2 *The PR: Grammatical and discourse roles*

The grammatical roles of a BPT's external PR are that of subject, (dative) indirect object, and less commonly, direct object (11–20). Significantly, the roles most commonly assumed by the PR (SUBJ and IO) are not only high in the grammatical role prominence hierarchy adopted here, SUBJ > DO > IO > OBL,[3] but are also prototypically human, which places them high in the empathy hierarchy as well (Kuno 1976: 431–437). As we will see, empathy, i.e., the degree of the speaker's identification with an event or discourse participant, is a crucial licensing factor for EP constructions. Mental awareness is focused on the PR because the narrator/speaker can relate to it and vicariously live its experiences.

I will argue, in particular, that the EP construction embodies a subjective construal where the subject and dative roles of external PRs of BPTs signal that the events or descriptions must be interpreted from the perspective of the PR, rather than from the perspective of an external observer. I use the term subjectivity in the sense of Langacker (1990a), which can be broadly characterized as a relative approximation between elements of the deictic center or *ground* (primarily the speaker, or the narrator in this case) and the scene referred to. A construal is maximally objective when the speaker construes a given element of the scene as maximally distinct from herself; and is maximally subjective when the speaker views herself as an intimate part of her conceptualization. In highly subjective construals, the speaker is often unaware of her mental involvement in the conceptualization because the mental proximity is such that the distinction between conceptualizer and conception is blurred. For this reason, constructions designating maximally subjective construals tend not to include reference to the ground. The EP constructions examined here involve an implicit omniscient narrator who establishes an empathetic link between herself and a protagonic participant. The latter in turn can establish empathetic connections with other discourse participants, thus creating an empathy chain within the discourse. Each point of empathetic connection set up by the narrator can be considered a "surrogate ground" which mediates the involvement of the narrator in the scene. With each empathetic link, the narrator adopts the point of view of the selected discourse participant and reveals the manner in which this participant views or construes a given scene. A possessive relation is subjectively construed when the PR is part of an empathy chain which links to the narrator or initial ground. If this is the case, the PR-PM relation is construed as proximal, with a reduced conceptual distance between PM and PR. The implicit nature of the possessive relation in EP constructions suggests precisely this type of integrative relation.

Let us consider now the role of external PRs and EP constructions in general in terms of the subjectivity-objectivity opposition. I will first examine the PR in subject role. Citing Kuno, Kemmer (1995: 73) states that "there is a natural tendency for subjects to be taken as the point of view in a sentence." This observation is clearly confirmed in the case of subject PRs of external BPTs, as the following brief analyses show. Example (11) appears in an episode which describes the doctor's visit to the Colonel's house and tells how the Colonel asked the doctor, through clenched teeth, how much he owed him. The events are presented as the colonel experiences them: they give account of his actions, feelings and thoughts and those aspects of the actions, feelings and thoughts of others of which he is aware. The reader knows, from previous episodes, that it hurts the Colonel's pride to receive free services because of his scarce economic resources. The clenched teeth, a characteristic gesture of the Colonel in similar situations, reveals an awareness on the part of the narrator of the Colonel's emotional state. A non-EP construction, *?con sus dientes apretados*, would conflict with the intended perspective by suggesting that the narrator (and indirectly the reader) is unaware of the now familiar feeling of shame that the colonel experiences in these situations.

The PR is the subject of a verb of possession in (13), *Tengo las piernas rotas* 'I have the legs broken'. The observable fact reported is that the legs are broken, but the selection of the PR as the subject portrays this fact as concerning the PR. This sentence is uttered by the companion of the protagonist soldier to explain why the soldier should not attempt taking him along in a difficult escape maneuver. Coding this participant as subject sets him as the surrogate ground from which the broken legs are viewed. The construction provides a holistic construal of the PR, sustaining focus on it as a discourse participant and maintaining the intended perspective. The perfectly grammatical non-EP alternative, ?*Mis piernas están rotas,* would be inappropriate in this context, where the PR's physical ability to partake in the escape is the relevant issue. It portrays a situation with no bearing on the PR, suggesting a certain degree of psychological removal of the PR with respect to the broken legs.

Body-move constructions also have the PR as subject. The body-part is involved in a "spontaneous, non-manual activity" (Diffloth 1974: 129), and is coded as an object, as in (17) *El prisionero levantó el rostro,* 'The prisoner raised the (=his) head.' Maldonado (1992: 141) speaks of an "internal energy transfer" as responsible for the body-move. To the extent that access to this energy source requires that the body-part be viewed "from within," the possessive relation can be said to be construed subjectively. The correctness of this analysis seems evident from the context in which (17) appears. The sentence is followed by a description of what the prisoner sees upon lifting his head, a clear indication that the point of view taken is that of the PR and not that of an outside observer. A non-EP version of this construction, **El rostro del prisionero se levantó,* with the BPT as subject, is never used, even though it is the body-part that is moving. This construction would suggest an autonomous movement of the body-part in total disconnection from its PR, a construal that is totally inappropriate to describe the simple and routine gesture of lifting one's gaze. Since the body-part would be construed as disconnected from its PR, in this particular instance it would be in total clash with the view point adopted in this episode. Another possibility, *El prisionero levantó *su rostro.* 'The prisoner raised *his head' would have the PR as subject and a possessive pronoun in the body-part NP. But the possessive is incompatible with body-move constructions. As shown in Velázquez-Castillo (to appear), the possessive pronoun objectivizes the body-part, creating a sense of separateness between body-part and PR. The subjective construal embodied in the body-move construction and the objectivizing effect of the possessive create a semantic incongruence, resulting in grammatical unacceptability.

To summarize, EP constructions featuring the PR as subject occur in discourse contexts where the narrator (or some character in the narrative) takes the perspective of the PR. This construal is a subjective one in that it sets the PR as a surrogate ground, bringing about, through an empathy chain, the implicit presence of the narrator in the narrative world.

The subjective construal signaled by EP constructions is even clearer in cases where the PR is coded as an indirect object (possessive dative) because this grammatical role involves the notion of affectedness, an obvious internal element that must be accessed by the speaker/narrator. In (18), *Don Sabas se secó el cuello…* 'Don Sabas dried himself the (=his) neck', the BPT is an object and PM of a reflexive dative PR *se*. The PR is coded twice, once as subject and a second time as dative. The subjective construal is clear: the PR's subject role signals that the perspective taken is that of the PR, and the dative conveys affectedness, an important element in the construal of the PR. In the episode which contains this example, the Colonel witnesses an exchange between Don Sabas and his wife. Don Sabas, who is already feeling some physical discomfort, gets exasperated at his wife's impertinent questions to the Colonel and asks her to shut up. The woman leaves slamming the door and Don Sabas, relieved, dries his neck with his handkerchief. The context suggests that the Colonel is aware of and identifies with Don Sabas' feelings of discomfort and exasperation. The non-EP variant, **Don Sabas secó su cuello*, is unacceptable in this (and most) situations because it suggests a complete disconnection between the body-part and its PR. This sentence would require a situation in which Don Sabas is unable to feel the impact of, or is unaware of, his own action. Since the PR would still be coded as the subject, the intended perspective would be maintained. However, a construal of complete separation between body-part and PR would render the statement irrelevant in this context and would therefore be incompatible with the adopted perspective. Another variant, **Don Sabas se secó su cuello…*, retains the PR as dative but replaces the definite article with a possessive. This alternative is completely inadmissible regardless of context.[4] Since the unacceptability of the possessive extends to all construction types involving the dative, there must be something in the meaning of the dative that motivates this incompatibility. Following Langacker, Maldonado (1992: 112) defines the indirect object as "an active participant in the target domain that holds some abstract possessive relationship with respect to a theme." Since the dative already subsumes the concept of possession, the possessive adjective is not necessary to establish the possessive relation.

Examples like (19), *Me suda mucho la espalda* 'To me, the back is sweating a lot', where the BPT is the subject, are equally crucial to establishing or maintaining a subjective perspective. Example (19) is part of an exchange between the novel's protagonist and a companion, both awaiting execution in a military jail. The companion notes that it is almost dawn, when they expect to be executed. The protagonist advises the other not to think about it, to which the latter responds with the utterance in (19). With the dative, the utterance is a clear allusion to the character's fear of death. The speaker adopts his own perspective, viewing subjectively the event involving his body-part. Without the dative, ?*Mi espalda suda mucho,* no such effect is obtained. The utterance reveals an objective construal, where the speaker is psychologically removed from the event involving his body-part. This would be an incoherent comment, with no relevance to the clear emotional emphasis of the description.

I have argued that Spanish EP constructions embody a subjective construal in which the narrator establishes a covert presence in the described events through an empathetic link to a body-part PM. This is evidenced in discourse by the adoption of the PR's perspective in the description of characters and narration of events, and in the direct or indirect accessibility of the internal state of participants to the narrator. In addition to an approximation of the *ground* to the described event, this subjective construal entails a proximal (i.e., inalienable) view of the PR/body relation, whereby a body-part is construed as integrated into the PR's animacy and humanness. This construal of organic linkage between body and PR is evident in the fact that the PR is portrayed as a co-initiator or a co-patient of an action that directly involves only its body-part, or as the co-bearer of a quality that characterizes its body-part. I am suggesting then that the notion of "inalienability" is conceptually derived from a subjective construal that requires a holistic view of a PR that is empathically linked to the ground. In Spanish (as in other Indo-European languages), the use of the possessive adjective in lieu of an EP construction signals a more objective construal in which the body-part is viewed as "an entity in and of itself" (Wierzbicka 1988: 171), and therefore not integral to the PR's personhood. This is discussed in detail in Velázquez-Castillo (to appear), so I will limit myself to one discourse example of the possessive adjective used in lieu of an EP construction. The distancing effect is evident when one contrasts (29) with the examples of subjective construal presented thus far:

(29) *El cerró los puños alrededor de los barrotes oxidados y observó el perfil chato de su guardián. Los mechones negros brotaban de la gorra de lona y se agotaban en el pómulo cuadrado y lampiño. El prisionero*$_1$ *buscó* <u>*su*$_1$ *mirada*</u> *y el cabo respondió con un gesto rápido....* (F 188)

'He closed the (=his) fists around the rusted bars and stared at the flattened profile of his guard. Tufts of black hair sprouted from beneath the (the guard's) burlap cap and petered out on the (the guard's) square and hairless cheekbones. The prisoner$_1$ sought <u>his</u> $_1$ <u>gaze</u> (the guard's) and the corporal responded with a brisk gesture....'

The perspective adopted in this episode is the prisoner's, referred to by *El* in the first clause and 0–anaphora in the second. The second clause introduces the guardian, which becomes the implicit topic of the next two coordinated clauses. The description of the guard in these two sentences is presented as it is observed by the prisoner. The prisoner resumes the subject role in the third sentence. An EP alternative to the possessive adjective would include a dative pronominal referring to the guard: *El prisionero le buscó la mirada* (the guard's). The EP construction, as opposed to the possessive, signals a subjective construal whereby the body-part is viewed by the prisoner (the surrogate ground) from the perspective of the PR. The EP construction would portray the prisoner's gesture as reaching into the guardian's thoughts or feelings. On the other hand, the possessive construes the body-part as an entity in and of itself, not necessarily integrally identified with the possessor's personhood. Example (29) depicts the prisoner's attempt at eye contact with the guard and beyond that, his *failed* attempt to get an empathetic response regarding a great concern of his: the place where he is scheduled to be executed in the morning. The reader finds out in the ensuing conversation that the guard offers only minimal, objective information. The choice of the possessive over the EP construction anticipates this lack of empathetic connection between the newly introduced temporary participant and the character whose perspective was adopted.

Before closing the discussion on the grammatical role of external PRs in Spanish, I will briefly address the issue of their impact on the argument frame of the verb. All of the EP constructions involving the PR as subject exhibit the same number of arguments normally required by the verb and therefore do not pose the "one-too-many argument" problem which has attracted the attention of syntacticians interested in "raising" phenomena. The only EP construction that exhibits this "problem" is the possessive dative, where the BPT maintains its syntactic status as a core verbal argument while the noun referring to the PR is "added" to the verb frame. This explains why most studies on the syntax of Spanish inalienable possession typically concentrate on the possessive dative construction to the exclusion of all the others.[5] This is indeed highly problematic for traditional possessor raising or possessor ascension analyses because it violates theoretical laws such as the Relational Succession Law (Relational Grammar) or the Projection Principle (GB), designed to constrain syntactic possibilities based on verbal argument structure.

In this cognitive/functional analysis, the one-too-many-argument problem does not arise because verbal semantics, though highly influential, does not have a deterministic role in defining sentence structure. Construction types reflect verbal semantics but are also sensitive to the convergence of additional semantic elements stemming from the lexical content of the NPs involved and the particular ways in which the situation is construed. To explain the "addition" of the dative to the verb frame in Spanish EP constructions, we need to understand the meaning of the dative role itself, and the special semantic relation that holds between a BPT and its PR in the particular construal embodied by these constructions. I have demonstrated the existence of a pronounced salience asymmetry between a BPT and its PR and I have argued that EP constructions signal a subjective construal whereby the speaker identifies with the PR's perspective. Since the interest of the speaker focuses holistically on the PR rather than on any given part of it, the PR and the body-part are viewed as integrally connected. From a cognitive/functional perspective, the important question is how the linguistic resources available in Spanish are used to signal these important meaning components. When the PR/body-part doublet is construable as the point of departure of an event, action, state or situation, the PR/body-part asymmetry is signaled by coding the PR as subject and the BPT in a variety of lower roles, including object. Since the subject role is one of the default ways of signaling perspective, the speaker's empathetic relation to the PR is easily accommodated. When the PR/body-part doublet is on the receiving end of an action, the choices are more limited since the subject is not normally available in this case. The highest available role in this case is normally an object, the default coding devise for a patient or affectee, which means that the PR and the body-part PM are in competition for access to the object role. The existence of the dative as a distinct grammaticalized role in the language solves this apparent limitation in the pool of available coding devices and obviates the need for any kind of "object demotion" mechanism to accommodate the asymmetric relation between PR and body-part. First, it accommodates the PR/body-part asymmetry by providing a coding choice for the human PR that is higher than the (object) body-part PM in the empathy hierarchy. Second, the general meaning of an indirect object includes two crucial aspects relevant to a subjective construal of the body-PR relation: a sense of affectedness that captures the empathetic link between speaker and PR, and a sense of possession which obviates the need for an explicit coding of the possessive relation, as explained above. Of all the EP constructions examined here so far, possessive datives are the ones that most overtly retain the possessive relation between the PR and its body-part. In other words, the externalization of the PR results in minimal loss of semantic transparency.

According to the reference-point based analysis proposed here, the interpretation of the PR-PM relation in this construction is derived from three linguistic cues: i) the pronounced prominence asymmetry between the PR and its body-part PM, ii) the sense of possession contained in the meaning of the dative, and iii) the sense of relatedness expressed by the definite article.

The different constructions with a subject PR are also analyzed as EP constructions here. In these, an explicit linguistic coding of the possessive relation is lacking. The sense of possession is derived from the asymmetrical relation between PR and PM, plus the sense of relatedness conveyed by the article. Since the conceptualization of a body-part must be anchored to a reference point, any mention of a body-part in a given discourse naturally compels the hearer to do a mental search for an appropriate reference point in the immediate discourse or situational context. The reference point model accounts for the selection of the participant with maximal prominence in the immediate domain.

3. Paraguayan Guaraní EP constructions: Functional and structural profile

In Velázquez-Castillo (1996: 132–148), I show that in Guaraní the grammatical roles of inalienably possessed body-parts are usually characterized by inactivity and a limited role in narrativity. Inalienably possessed entities have low topicality; their function in story-telling is more descriptive, fulfilling evaluative and orienting functions. In what follows, I will summarize the basic facts and relevant findings concerning Guaraní EP constructions presented in other works, and reanalyze representative data in terms of subjectivity to facilitate comparison with the Spanish EP constructions.

It will first be useful to mention a few general facts about the language. Paraguayan Guaraní is part of the larger Tupí-Guaraní family, which is spoken in the area known as Lowland South America. In terms of traditional morphological typology, Guaraní presents polysynthetic, as well as agglutinating characteristics in the sense that words often contain a sequence of identifiable forms (root/s plus affixes) in a relatively loose morphological connection. Guaraní exhibits an active-stative alignment, also called a split-S system. This alignment is most notably manifested in the existence of two sets of cross-referencing personal prefixes for the coding of active and inactive participants. Velázquez-Castillo (1991) characterizes activeness as a combination of inherent changeability of the process designated by the verb, and a subject involvement characterized by control and volitionality.

Examples (30a)–(33a) illustrate incorporating structures involving BPTs, which invariably externalize the PR. Examples (30b)–(33b) are the unincorporated versions:

(30)	a.	*(Che) che-resa-rovy* I 1INACT-eye-blue 'I am blue-eyed.'	b.	*Che-resa hovy* 1INACT-eye 3INACT=blue 'My eyes are blue.'
(31)	a.	*(Che) che-resay-syry* I 1INACT-tear-flow 'I cried profusely.'	b.	*Che-resay o-syry* 1INACT-tear 3ACT-flow 'My tears flowed.'
(32)	a.	*A-j-ova-héi-ta* 1ACT-REFL-face-wash-FUT 'I'll face-wash myself.'	b.	*A-johéi-ta che-rova* 1ACT-wash-FUT 1INACT-face 'I'll wash my face.'
(33)	a.	*A-hova-hei-ta pe-mitã* 1ACT-face-wash-FUT that-child 'I'll face-wash that child.'		
	b.	*A-johei-ta pe-mitã rova* 1ACT-wash-FUT that-child face 'I'll wash that child's face.'		

The incorporating EP sentences (30a-33a) are ordered according to an increasing degree of transitivity and narrativity, starting with clearly non-transitive and descriptive constructions and ending with relatively more transitive and narrative ones. Unlike externally possessed BPTs in Spanish which can have a limited narrative role, incorporated BPTs themselves seem to have no part in narrativity.

Topicality measures of Guaraní incorporated BPTs and their PRs, taken from Velázquez-Castillo (1996: 171), reveal a pattern very similar to that found for analogous participant types in Spanish EP constructions. Table 4 shows that, like Spanish externally possessed BPTs, Guaraní incorporated BPTs, which also externalize the PR, have practically no discourse topicality (high RD and low TP), suggesting limited narrative relevance. PRs of incorporated BPTs also parallel the high topicality levels of Spanish external PRs, revealing a pronounced asymmetry between BPT and PR.

The limited number of unincorporated BPTs in the corpus precluded the availability of similar topicality measures for unincorporated BPTs. However, a careful analysis of the instances that do occur in the corpus shows that they are capable of a limited narrative role, and a degree of topic continuity not found in the case of incorporated BPTs (Velázquez-Castillo 1996: 189–196).

The grammatical roles borne by incorporated BPTs and their PRs confirm the topicality pattern revealed in Table 4 in a clearer way, perhaps, than in Spanish. PRs of incorporated BPTs can occupy the syntactic positions of either subject or object, while the incorporated BPT has only one grammatical possibility, that of a verb-satellite, to be explained later. As is probably already evident,

Table 4: *Measures of thematic importance of incorporated BPTs and their PRs*

Participant type	*Mean RD* (0–10 scale)	*Mean TP* (0–10 scale)	*Total Number*
Incorporated BPTs	9.9	0.05	37
PRs of Incorporated BPTs	1.6	6.1	37

the most important differences between EP constructions in Spanish and those in Guaraní are manifested in the grammatical codings of the relevant participant types. I will first address the codings of the PR, as well as the functional motivations for these codings.

3.1 *PRs of incorporated BPTs: Functional and grammatical roles*

Velázquez-Castillo (1996: 132–143) demonstrates that the PR, not the incorporated BPT, is the subject in a one-participant EP structure, and the object in a two-participant incorporating EP construction. One-participant EP constructions, as exemplified in (30a) and (31a), have only one focused participant and take inactive agreement prefixes. The unincorporated (b)-examples show one-place predicators agreeing in person with the body-part terms, not with the PR. In the incorporated (a)-examples, the PR NP, not the body-part term, controls agreement. In the same work, I argue that, semantically, the PR subject can be viewed in two complementary ways: as setting-subjects or as reference-point subjects. These PR subjects are interpretable as non-canonical locations where the relations or processes designated by the predicates evolve. Their humanness and their empathetic relation to the speaker makes them inherently more prominent and participant-like than canonical settings; hence their subject coding. These participant-like characteristics bring these setting-subjects closer to Langacker's (1991) notion of reference-points. As stated earlier, because of the inherent higher prominence of people in relation to their body-parts, the former are natural reference points for the latter. The inactive marking in these sentences is explained by the static setting/reference point role of the PR subject.

Two-participant incorporating EP constructions (32a and 33a) take active agreement and have a subject and an independent NP following the incorporating verb complex. Both sentences fit the semantic profile of activeness (Velázquez-Castillo 1991), namely inherent changeability of the process denoted by the verb, and a subject involvement characterized by control and volitionality. Velázquez-Castillo (1996: 134–135) cites four pieces of evidence that the PR NP, not the incorporated BPT, functions as the clausal object: i) the PR fills the normal object slot following the verb (33a); ii) with a reflexive morpheme, the PR is the same as the subject (32a); iii) passivization renders the PR, not the BPT, the subject of the passive sentence; and iv) a portmanteau pronominal prefix indexes first-person subject and second-person object when the subject is first person and the PR is second person, as in (38), Section 3.2 below. In addition, the PR meets the semantic characterization of a prototypical object: i) high degree of individuation, ii) complete affectedness by the designated action, and iii) high degree of salience. Coding of the PR as object of a verb designating an action addressed to its body-part sets up a construal in which the PR is portrayed as affected by the action. Without neglecting the direct involvement of the body-part, this construal focuses holistically on the PR as the experiencer of the event.

As for Spanish, an analysis of the discourse use of these constructions demonstrates that they embody a subjective construal whereby an empathetic narrator adopts the point of view of the PR or otherwise enters the narrative world. Subjective construals signaled by subject and object PRs will be illustrated with some of the of incorporating EP constructions found in a folk tale about the monkey and the crocodile (Ñemity 7:23). The monkey is at the edge of a river, gets excited at the sight of trees full of ripe wild fruit on the other side, and tries to find a way to cross the river. The crocodile comes swimming down the river and the monkey tries to flatter him with the purpose of getting the crocodile to help him cross the river. The story tells how the crafty monkey got his way by taking advantage of the naiveté of the crocodile and is clearly told from the perspective of the monkey.

Line (34) contains the first set of incorporated structures in the story:

(34) *Ka'i* <u>*o-ñe-ndy-moko,*</u> <u>*o-ñe-mbe-su'u,*</u>
monkey 3ACT-REFL-saliva-swallow 3ACT-REFL-lip-bite
<u>*o-jete-poka.*</u>
3ACT-body-twist
'The monkey's mouth waters, he bites his lips, twists his body.'

The discourse function of these incorporated structures is to describe *evaluative* actions that reveal not only the emotional effect that the sight of the ripe fruit had on the monkey, but also some characteristic personality traits. Using a pseudo-narrative mode (note the active agreement marking), the monkey's emotional state is portrayed in a physically active way, suggesting that he is a hyper-active individual (Velázquez-Castillo (1996: 172–188). The construal is subjective: the narrator is empathically linked to the monkey and takes a perspective that allows access to the emotional state of the character. An unincorporated structure (34') cannot be interpreted as a bodily manifestation of an emotional state, and would therefore not cohere with the immediately following line, which informs the listener why the monkey was so uneasy.

(34′) *Ka'i o-moko h-endy, oi-su'u h-embe,*
monkey 3ACT-swallow his-saliva 3ACT-bite his-lips
oi-poka h-ete.
3ACT-twist his-body

Another example of evaluative action is given in (35):

(35) *Neipamiro guãrã o-hecha Jakare <u>huguai-vava-vava</u>*
In.no.time 3ACT-see crocodile his.tail-wag-wag
'Hardly any time passes before (the monkey) sees the crocodile with his tail wagging back and forth (as he comes down the river).'

The perspective taken is, again, clearly that of the monkey, which is coded as the main subject. The incorporated structure describes the crocodile as the monkey sees him while assessing his chances of tricking the crocodile: a slow, tail-wagging, naive individual. The tail-wagging image evoked by the incorporating construction suggests a laid-back attitude and slowness of movement, and perhaps, in the monkey's eyes, mental slowness. Again, the unincorporated version of (35), given in (35′), would not carry any evaluative or interpretational comment superimposed on the described event. The bodily actions are not portrayed as characteristic of the crocodile in a context where a characterization of the characters' nature is important. The body-part's action will have to be interpreted as a significant event on its own, drawing attention to the body-part as a relatively individuated entity, differentiated from its PR. Note, in this regard, the active marking on the verb, a sign of the dynamicity (a participant-like quality) attributed to the body-part.

(35′) *... o-hecha jakare ruguai o-vava-vava*
3ACT-see crocodile tail 3ACT-wag-wag
'...he saw the crocodile's tail wag back and forth.'

Line (36) does not involve an evaluative event. It is clearly descriptive, with one-place inactive predicates (*mburukuja* 'passion flower', *syi* 'soft', and *pyta* 'red') featuring an incorporated BPT and the PR as subject. The monkey tries to flatter the crocodile by telling him that the women think he is very handsome:

(36) *Karia'y pora <u>resa-mburukuja,</u> <u>ape-syi-asy,</u>*
young.man handsome eye-passionflower surface-soft-nice
<u>rembe-pyta</u> jakarati'a-aju, he'i nde-rehe.
lip-red fruit-ripe say=they you-about

'He's a handsome young man with eyes like passion flowers, with nice soft skin, with red lips like ripe fruit. — that's what they say about you.'

Since the monkey's intent here is to flatter the crocodile, he must communicate that he attributes the positive qualities to the crocodile as an individual, rather than to his body-parts only. The positive qualities of the different parts are important only insofar as they serve to suggest the attractiveness of the crocodile. The description is construed from the perspective of an observer that identifies (or pretends to identify) with the crocodile as an individual.

As we can see, there are obvious semantic and functional commonalties between the Spanish EP constructions and the Guaraní incorporating structures. Apart from the obvious fact that these constructions involve BPTs and their PRs as central participants, the central semantic aspect that differentiates EP constructions in both languages from their non-EP equivalents is a subjective construal of the possessive relation.

There are also significant differences. In regard to the coding of the external PR, the most notable difference is the central role played by the dative in Spanish and its absence in Guaraní. While Spanish has a distinct indirect object grammatical role, Guaraní does not have a clear grammaticalized indirect object. Recipients and experiencers (the prototypical semantic roles associated with indirect objects) are generally marked with the postposition *-pe*, which is also the basic locative postposition. The only recipients with a special marking are first and second (singular) person pronouns, and here, the postposition added to the pronoun, *-ve*, looks suspiciously like the locative-*pe*. It seems, then, that Guaraní has, at most, a relatively new and restricted grammaticalized indirect object. The grammatical role hierarchy for Guaraní, then looks like: SUBJ > DO > OBL. This reduces the coding possibilities for external PRs to SUBJ and DO. This limited pool of coding devices for the PR has significant grammatical consequences, since it sets up the need for a "demoting" mechanism, such as NI, to code the body-part directly involved in the event or scene. As a result, external PRs in Guaraní *substitute* or "take the place of" BPTs in the core grammatical roles. This substitution at the grammatical level mirrors a metonymic substitution at the semantic level in which the speaker/narrator construes an event originated by, or affecting, a body-part as involving the PR as the initiator or experiencer of such event, or as the bearer of a quality which characterizes a part of its body.

The most common cases of EP in Guaraní involve PRs with an inherited patient role (Velázquez-Castillo 1996: 105), which means that the EP prototype for Guaraní also involves the notion of affectedness. Less central representatives of the EP construction comprise structures with non-patient PRs, as in the case of reference-point subjects (36), which are portrayed as the bearers of their body-parts' physical attributes. This analysis captures the semantic and formal relatedness of all BPT incorporating structures, while at the same time acknowledging the special status of those constructions which involve the affectedness notion. Neither the prototype, nor the more peripheral representatives of EP in Guaraní contain any linguistic expression of the possessive relation. This is derived from the maximal asymmetry between PM and PR, with the latter occupying the upper end of the prominence axis, plus the inherent semantics of the BPTs, which includes an obligatory reference point.

3.2 *Incorporated BPTs: Functional and grammatical roles*

Incorporated BPTs exhibit poor "nouny" behavior in the sense that they lack general grammatical and discourse manipulability (Velázquez-Castillo 1996). This is manifested in their inability to be accompanied with modifying and inflecting forms, and to introduce and deploy a participant in discourse. These signs of low categoriality do not make them easily analyzable as objects or subjects, or, for that matter, as any of the traditionally acknowledged grammatical relations. I have analyzed them as *verb satellites*, a special grammatical role originally proposed in Talmy (1985) to categorize identifiable linguistic elements internal to the verb-complex which form a semantic and formal unit with the verb-stem.We saw that Spanish features a variety of coding alternatives for externally possessed BPTs: object, oblique and occasionally, even subject roles. This flexibility at the clause level is mirrored by a relative flexibility when it comes to the discourse mode in which Spanish BPTs can participate. While their role is predominantly descriptive, they can play a peripheral role in narrative mode. In contrast, incorporated BPTs in Guaraní play no role in narrative mode, their contribution to discourse being strictly descriptive. These BPTs cannot be subject to subsequent reference of any kind, suggesting that they designate untraceable elements and that their mention does not introduce an entity into the discourse (Velázquez-Castillo 1996: 136). In Spanish, on the other hand, externally possessed BPTs can occasionally be subject to pronominal anaphora, though their overall discourse continuity does not amount to significant figures. These facts point to the conclusion that while externally possessed Guaraní BPTs designate entities that are not discourse participants in any sense, their Spanish counterparts refer to body-parts as if they were peripheral discourse participants. The greater morphosyntactic autonomy and flexibility of Spanish externally possessed body-parts vis-à-vis their Guaraní counterparts suggests to me a greater conceptual individuation of externally possessed BPTs, and therefore, a greater conceptual differentiation between PR and PM.

4. Summary and concluding remarks

The foregoing discussion outlines the structural and functional profiles of two different EP constructions as they appear in two typologically different languages. This section summarizes the main facts, draws some generalizations, and explores their implications.

As we have seen, the most apparent differences between Spanish and Guaraní EP constructions are: i) the presence of noun incorporation with a concomitant syntactic demotion of the BPT in Guaraní and its absence in Spanish; and ii) the availability of a grammatical indirect object role in Spanish and its absence in Guaraní. Guaraní, being a polysynthetic/agglutinative language, features a strong "verbal attraction" tendency. The main predicate (verbal or nominal) attracts grammatical and lexical morphemes whose semantic contents are of relevance to the meaning of the predicate. These combinations often form varying degrees of lexicalized units, where the attached elements lose morphological and semantic autonomy to become meaning components of the resulting complex unit. Spanish, being an inflectional language, indexes grammatical relations on its verbs with linguistic elements that are fused or morphologically integrated to the verb stem, and for the most part, does not allow the attachment of otherwise free-standing linguistic elements. The presence of the dative case in Spanish and its absence in Guaraní is a likely result of the accusative case alignment system of Spanish and the active alignment that characterizes Guaraní. Klimov (1984) notes that it is characteristic of accusative systems to make coding distinctions among object types, while active systems tend not to differentiate them.

There is a demonstrably higher level of individuation and potential discourse topicality in article-modified Spanish BPTs, with a corresponding greater grammatical independence, vis-à-vis their Guaraní counterparts. Conversely, the complete lack of syntactic versatility of incorporated BPTs in Guaraní corresponds to a lack of individuation, which in turn facilitates a construal of virtual identification between body-part and PR to an extent not encountered in Spanish.

In Spanish, the PR assumes the grammatical role of indirect object, a role that is *"added"* to the verbal frame. In Guaraní, the PR *substitutes* the BPT, preserving the canonical verb frame. This formal substitutability of BPTs by their PRs as clausal arguments corresponds to a construal of close *identification* between the two at the semantic level. Thus, the PR is construed as the main undergoer of an action or the bearer of a quality that involves its body-part. In Spanish, on the other hand, the fact that the dative PR does not displace the BPT from its verbal argument position favors a construal in which the change of state or condition described by the verb or adjective is registered on the BPT, and at the same time, "*transferred*" or extended to the PR.

Grammatically, what unifies the constructions analyzed in both languages is the fact that the PR is coded outside of the NP that hosts their BPT PMs, and furthermore, that the PRs' syntactic position is a prominent one. I argue that the coding of PRs of BPTs as subjects or objects in Guaraní, and as subjects or indirect objects in Spanish, signals a subjective construal where the speaker/narrator sets up covert presence in the described events through an empathetic chain that indirectly links the PR to the main ground. The empathetic link between the deictic center and the PR, which characterizes the subjective construal, results in the asymmetry of focus assigned to the entities involved in the relation. This concentration of mental awareness on the PR requires a holistic view where constituent parts are construed as integrated aspects of the entity of interest. Though the involvement of body-parts as defocused event participants often results in low-transitivity events, EP was not found to be a syntactic detransitivizer in either language examined. Instead, EP implements an assignment of core grammatical roles that favors semantic prominence over direct involvement in the event. As such, EP perspectivizes the PR in relation to the BPT, asserting its semantic prominence and its pragmatic relevance to the discourse.

It has been noted that, like incorporation, EP is a process primarily associated with absolutive arguments; more precisely, with a patient role, which is typically coded as the object of a transitive clause or an unaccusative intransitive subject. The importance of the patient role in EP phenomena is indisputable. However, its primacy tends to be exaggerated as evidenced by the existence of EP constructions based on non-patient roles. We have seen that relatively active roles, such as that of MOVER (Langacker 1990b: 209–260), can license EP (examples like (3) and (8)). Noteworthy in this regard is the fact that in Guaraní one does not find a neat line-up of EP phenomena with inactive nominals (i.e., those that are marked with the inactive agreement prefixes). Since active languages constitute the most clearly semantically driven case alignment where the active-inactive divide sets agents and non-agents apart, one would expect a clearer association of EP phenomena with inactive arguments.

If the connection with a patient role is not the defining feature of EP constructions, then what is? As stated before, the notion of affectedness, which invariably accompanies the patient role, has been proposed as the main semantic motivator of EP constructions. When applied to EP, this notion must involve a construal that features a *sentient PR* as the locus of affectedness. While affectedness is characteristic of patient roles, not all patients can license EP because the effect of an action is not always construable as affecting a sentient PR. It seems clear from the data analyzed here that EP must have a more general semantic motivation than transferability of affectedness. There are examples, such as (5) and (10), where the PR can hardly be construed as affected, yet the EP construction is required. As I explained, these subject PRs are construed as reference points for the attribution of body-part qualities, and no sense of affectedness can be derived from these constructions. The thesis defended in this paper, namely that the one constant trait of EP phenomena is the perspectivization of a prominent sentient PR which is empathetically linked to the speaker, offers one possible unifying and inclusive framework for the explanation of the commonalties and differences found in the multiple manifestations of this phenomenon.

Acknowledgments

I am thankful to Doris Payne and an anonymous reviewer for numerous insightful comments on earlier versions of this paper and to the participants of the EP conference at the University of Oregon, who kindly offered many comments and suggestions.

Abbreviations

Abbreviations used in this paper: ACT active, BPT body-part term, CAUS causative, DIM diminutive, EP external possession, F Fuentes, FUT future, GM García Márquez, INACT inactive, INCH inchoative, NI noun incorporation, PL plural, PM possessum, PR possessor, RD referential distance, REFL reflexive, TP topic persistence.

Notes

1 Possession of a body-part is possible, however, with *tener* plus an indefinite modifier, as can be seen in: *Tobías tenía un rostro…* (F 187) 'Tobías did have a face.' The modifier *un* confers a more individuated and objective construal to the body-part, allowing for a more object-like quality.

2 Some objects of grooming verbs, however, perform better in some of these objecthood tests: cliticization (*puso las manos bajo la llave y las lavó*), passivization with *se (?Se le lavaron las manos),* in limited contexts. Nominalization, however, is generally ruled out (*el lavado de las manos).* Kliffer (1983: 767) gives an example of a nominalized grooming verb, but this cannot contain an article-modified BPT: *Cambié de peluquera porque los cortes de Inés siempre me resultaban antecuados.* 'I changed hairdressers because Ines's cuts always looked old fashioned

to me.' **No quiero* <u>un corte</u> *del pelo en este lugar, me parece muy anticuado.* 'I don't want a haircut in this place, it seems very old fashioned.

3 Although the direct object is generally considered to be second in syntactic prominence to the subject, a typical dative is higher in discourse prominence due to the human nature of its referent (c.f., Givón 1984b).

4 The possessive in combination with the dative of possession is acceptable in some varieties of Spanish, however. Colloquial Paraguayan Spanish, for example, allows this combination in sentences such as *Se golpeó su dedito* 'S/he hurt her/his finger', and *Me corté mi pelo* 'I cut my hair' (Velázquez-Castillo 1995). Colloquial Mexican Spanish, at least in some parts of Mexico, also allows this combination.

5 Exceptions are Kliffer (1983), and especially Spanoghe (1993), both extensive studies on the syntax of Spanish inalienable possession.

References

Baker, Mark. 1988. *Incorporation: A Theory of Grammatical Relation Changing*. Chicago: The University of Chicago Press.

Bell, Sarah. 1983. "Advances and Ascensions in Cebuano." In David Perlmutter (ed.), *Studies in Relational Grammar 1*. Chicago: The University of Chicago Press, 143–218.

Croft, William. 1985. "Indirect Object Lowering." *Proceedings of the 11th Annual Meeting of the Berkeley Linguistics Society*, 39–51.

Diffloth, Gérard. 1974. "Body Moves in Semai and French." *Proceedings of the 10th Annual Meeting of the Chicago Linguistics Society*, 128–138.

Du Bois, John W. 1980. "Beyond Definiteness: The Trace of Identity in Discourse." In Wallace Chafe, *The Pear Stories: Cognitive, Cultural, and linguistic Aspects of Narrative Production*. Norwood, N.J.: Ablex, 203–274.

Durie, Mark. 1987. "Grammatical Relations in Acehnese." *Studies in Language* 11–2: 365–399.

Fuentes, Carlos. 1962. *La Muerte de Artemio Cruz*. México: Fondo de Cultura Económica.

García-Márquez, Gabriel. 1961 [1984]. *El Coronel No Tiene Quien Le Escriba*. Barcelona: Editorial Bruguera.

Givón, Talmy (ed). 1983. *Topic Continuity in Discourse: Quantitative Cross-Language Studies*. (=Typological Studies in Language, 3). Amsterdam: John Benjamins.

Givón, Talmy. 1984a. *Syntax, Vol. 1*. Amsterdam: John Benjamins

Givón, Talmy. 1984b. "Direct Object and Dative Shifting: Semantic and Pragmatic Case." In Frans Plank (ed.). *Objects: Towards a Theory of Grammatical Relations*. London and New York: Academic Press, 151–182

Kemmer, Suzanne. 1995. "Emphatic and Reflexive-Self: Expectations, Viewpoint, and Subjectivity." In Dieter Stein and Susan Wright (eds.), *Subjectivity and Subjectification*. Cambridge: Cambridge University Press, 55–82

Kliffer, Michael D. 1983. "Beyond Syntax: Spanish Inalienable Possession." *Linguistics* 21: 759–794.

Klimov, G. A. 1984. "Object Relations in the Ergative System." In Frans Plank (ed.), *Objects: Towards a Theory of Grammatical Relations*. London and New York: Academic Press, 211–219.

Kuno, Susumo. 1976. "Subject, Theme and Speaker's Empathy: A Re-examination of Relativization Phenomena." In Charles N. Li, (ed.), *Subject and Topic*, New York: Academic Press, 137–153.

Langacker, Ronald. 1991. *Foundations of Cognitive Grammar, Vol. 2. Descriptive Application*. Stanford: Stanford University Press.

Langacker, Ronald. 1990a. "Subjectification." *Cognitive Linguistics* 1: 5–38

Langacker, Ronald. 1990b. *Concept, Image and Symbol: The Cognitive Basis of Grammar*. Berlin: Mouton de Gruyter.

Maldonado, Ricardo. 1992. *Middle Voice: The Case of the Spanish* se. Ph. D. Dissertation. La Jolla: University of California, San Diego.

Ñemity: Revista Bilingüe de Cultura. 1980. 7:23. Asunción, Paraguay: Emasa.

Talmy, Leonard. 1985. "Lexicalization Patterns: Semantic Structure in Lexical Form." In T. Shopen (ed.), *Language Typology and Syntactic Description*. Cambridge: Cambridge University Press, 57–149.

Tellier, Christine. 1992. "Remarques sur Avoir Attributif et Possessif." *Revue Québécoise de Linguistique* 22, 1: 166–181.

Spanoghe, Anne Marie. 1993. *La Syntaxe de la Possession Inalienable en Francais, en Espagnol et en Portugais*. Ph.D. Dissertation. Rijksuniversiteit Te Gent. Belgium.

Vandeweghe. Willy. 1987. "The Possessive Dative in Dutch: Syntactic Reanalysis and Predicate Formation." In Johan Van der Auwera and Louis Goossens (eds.), *Ins and Outs of Predication*. Dordrecht: Foris, 137–151.

Velázquez-Castillo, Maura. 1991. "The Semantics of Guaraní Agreement Markers." *Proceedings of the 17th Annual Meeting of the Berkeley Linguistics Society*, 324–335.

Velázquez-Castillo. 1995. "Possessive Constructions in Paraguayan Spanish: the Influence of Guaraní." *Romance Language Annual* 4: 607–613.

Velázquez-Castillo, Maura. 1996. *The Grammar of Possession: Inalienability, Incorporation and Possessor Ascension in Guaraní.* Amsterdam: John Benjamins.

Velázquez-Castillo, Maura. To appear. "Posesión Inalienable y Tematicidad en Español." In Ricardo Maldonado (ed.), *Estudios Cognoscitivos del Español,* Mexico City: Universidad Autónoma de México.

Wierzbicka, Anna. 1988. *The Semantics of Grammar*. Amsterdam and Philadelphia: John Benjamins.

External Possession in a European Areal Perspective

Martin Haspelmath
Max-Planck-Institut für Evolutionäre Anthropologie, Leipzig

1. Introduction

In an external-possession construction, a possessive modifier does not occur as a dependent constituent of the modified NP, but NP-externally as a constituent of the clause. Many European languages have an external-possession construction similar to the constructions exemplified in (1)–(3). Here the possessive NPs expressing 'child's', 'his', and 'my' are not constituents of an NP, but contrary to the English translation, they occur NP-externally. (Throughout this paper, external-possessor phrases are printed in boldface for clarity.)

(1) German
Die Mutter wusch ***dem Kind*** *die Haare.*
the mother washed the:DAT child the:ACT hairs
'The mother washed the child's hair.'

(2) French (Hatcher 1944: 157)
Les larmes ***lui*** *vinrent aux yeux.*
the tears him:DAT came to.the eyes
'Tears welled up in his eyes.'

(3) Russian (Rakhilina 1982: 25)
On njančil ***mne*** *detej.*
he babysat me:DAT children:ACT
'He babysat my children.'

In this paper I will argue that this construction, which I will call DATIVE EXTERNAL POSSESSOR, is a characteristic feature of a European linguistic area (or *Sprachbund*). Although many of the European languages showing this construction belong to the Indo-European family, it can be demonstrated that it must be regarded as an areal feature, not a genetic feature. In §2 of this paper I will describe the main features of this European areal prototype, which is characterized by dative case-marking on the external possessor and a fairly strict affectedness condition. In §3 I will present the case for its areal distribution, and in §4 I will place the European EP (= external-possession) construction in a worldwide perspective, arguing that the European prototype occurs only marginally in the rest of the world, while the world's three most common types of EP constructions occur only marginally in Europe.

Following these areal-typological considerations, I will go on to ask the more general question whether there are any other typological features of the European languages from which the occurrence of the dative EP construction could be predicted (§5). It turns out that the answer to this question is not straightforward, because two proposed typological correlations turn out to be illusory. In §6 I will propose to describe the meaning of case-markers by means of a universal semantic map, which helps explain why languages such as English or Turkish do not have dative EP constructions.

2. The European external-possession prototype

In the European EP prototype, the external possessor (EPR) is represented by a clause-level dative-marked NP argument, while the possessum is a direct object, a locative argument marked by a prepositional phrase, or an unaccusative subject. The four most common patterns are shown schematically in (4).

				possessor		possessum
(4)	a.	Subj	V	Dat		Obj
	b.	Subj	V	Dat	Obj	PP
	c.	Subj	V	Dat		PP
	d.		V	Dat		Subj

These four patterns are exemplified in (5a–d) from some of the languages that come close to the European prototype. These are, in particular, German and Dutch, the Romance languages, the Slavic languages, and the members of the Balkan linguistic area.

(5) a. Slovene (Sandi Kodrič, p.c.)
Zdravnik ***jim*** *je pregledal želodec.*
doctor them:DAT AUX examined stomach
'The doctor examined their stomachs.'

b. Dutch (Vandeweghe 1987: 145)
Fred gooit ***Sylvia*** *een krant naar het hoofd.*
Fred throws Sylvia a paper at the head
'Fred throws a newspaper at Sylvia's head.'

c. Modern Greek (Tassos Kristopoulos, p.c.)
Tu *épese mja pétra sto kapó.*
him:DAT fell a stone on.the hood
'A stone fell on his hood.'

d. Spanish (Roldán 1972: 29)
Se ***le*** *dobló el tobillo.*
REFL him:DAT turned the ankle
'His ankle turned (on him).'

The two most important characteristics of the European EP prototype are (i) the marking of the EPR by the dative case, and (ii) the strict affectedness condition, i.e., external possessors are only possible if the possessor is thought of as being mentally affected by the described situation. This latter restriction also explains the syntactic restriction to PPs, direct objects and unaccusative subjects that was noted at the beginning of this section: these syntactic functions normally express affected semantic roles such as patient, theme or goal, whereas unergative and transitive subjects normally express non-affected semantic roles such as initiator or agent.

The dative case-marking is found wherever there is an unambiguous dative case (i.e., a morphological marker of indirect objects and similar participants), i.e., in German, Slavic (with the exception of Bulgarian and Macedonian), Romance, Basque, and Maltese.[1] In most Romance languages, only clitic pronouns have preserved the dative case, and interestingly, the EPR may then be restricted to pronominal NPs, e.g., in French (cf. Barnes 1985: 161; see also §7 below).

(6) a. *Elle* ***lui*** *a tiré dans le ventre.*
she him:DAT has shot in the stomach
'She shot at his stomach.'

b. **Elle a tiré dans le ventre* ***à Jean***.
she has shot in the stomach to Jean
'She shot at Jean's stomach.'

"Dative" external possessors also exist in several languages which do not strictly speaking have a dative case. Thus, in the Balkan languages there is only one case for genitive and dative functions. However, the syntactic position of the genitive-dative NP in EP constructions like (5c) from Modern Greek is analogous to the indirect-object uses of the genitive-dative case, so the Balkan languages can be grouped with the prototype in this respect. In Dutch (cf. 5b, 13), only a nominative-oblique case distinction has been preserved (and only in pronouns), but again the syntactic position of the EPR allows us to identify it as an "indirect-object" external possessor, still close to the European prototype.

Since at least Havers (1911) and Bally (1926), the affectedness condition has been described in almost all contributions dealing with the EP construction in the various European languages (see König & Haspelmath 1997 for a detailed bibliography). For instance, Roldán (1972: 27) observes that the two sentences in (7a–b) are by no means synonymous, and that it is not true that (7a) is ungrammatical, contrary to what has been claimed.

(7) Spanish

a. *Sus ojos se llenaron de lágrimas.*
his eyes REFL filled of tears

b. *Los ojos se* ***le*** *llenaron de lágrimas.*
the eyes REFL him:DAT filled of tears
'His eyes filled with tears.'

The correct way to describe the contrast is by saying that in (7b) the dative participant (i.e., the possessor) is presented as affected by the situation, whereas in (7a) the possessor is not thought of as mentally affected. Normally one assumes that a person whose eyes are filling with tears is affected by this event, so (7b) is pragmatically unmarked, whereas (7a) requires a special context (e.g., eye surgery during which the patient is anesthetized). Incidentally, this example also shows that it is mental affectedness, not affectedness in general, which is relevant for EP constructions: physically, the possessor is affected also in the internal-possession construction (7a), while the possessor is not affected physically, but only mentally in cases such as (3).

The meaning component of affectedness always seems to be either positive ('benefactive') or negative ('malefactive', 'adversative'). When the possessor is positively affected, constructions with external dative possessors may often be paraphrased by means of a benefactive preposition. Thus, Rakhilina (1982: 25) renders the meaning of (8) as 'I hung a rug + over her bed + for her (*dlja nee*)'.

(8) Russian

Ja povesil ***ej*** *nad krovat'ju kovrik.*
I hung her:DAT over bed rug
'I hung a rug over her bed.'

But when the affectedness meaning is negative (as for instance in (5b–d) above), there is rarely a paraphrase that comes even close to the meaning of the dative possessor. In some cases, a sentence is vague with respect to a positive or negative interpretation, but it seems that we cannot easily conceive of "neutral" affectedness that is neither negative nor positive.

The affectedness condition is not equally strong in all languages, and it has been conventionalized in various ways by different languages. In the European languages studied by König & Haspelmath 1997, evidence surfaces (albeit not always fully conclusive) for four implicational hierarchies which reflect the strength of the affectedness condition in one way or another. EP constructions are favored cross-linguistically if they are high on the hierarchies in (9a–d) (section numbers refer to König & Haspelmath 1997):

(9) a. **The Animacy Hierarchy** (§7.1; cf. Havers 1911; Seiler 1983: 76)
(EP constructions are favored if the possessor is a)
1st/2nd p. pronoun ⊂ 3rd p. pronoun ⊂ proper name ⊂ other animate ⊂ inanimate

b. **The Situation Hierarchy** (§6)
(EP constructions are favored if the predicate is)
patient-affecting ⊂ dynamic non-affecting ⊂ stative

c. **The Inalienability Hierarchy** (§7.2)
(EP constructions are favored if the possessum is a)
body part ⊂ garment ⊂ other contextually unique item

d. **The Syntactic Relations Hierarchy** (§2.6)
(EP constructions are favored if the syntactic relation of the possessum is)
PP ⊂ direct object ⊂ unaccusative subject ⊂ unergative subject ⊂ transitive subject

The statement "EP constructions are favored" means that if an EP construction is possible for a position at any point of the hierarchy, then that EP construction is also possible with all the positions that are higher (= further to the left) on the hierarchy. Among European languages, no counterexamples to these implicational claims have been found, and it seems certain that their application is not restricted to Europe. In fact, these hierarchies cannot be illustrated very well by data from Europe, because most European languages conform more or less to the European prototype, and variation within Europe is not particularly great. Before these hierarchies can be regarded as true implicational universals, they need to be tested on a world-wide sample, and that will probably mean that they have to be revised somewhat (e.g., the high position of PPs on the Syntactic Relations Hierarchy does not appear to be universal).

On all these hierarchies, European languages place fairly strict requirements on their EP constructions. On the Animacy Hierarchy (9a), all European languages seem to restrict their EP constructions to animate possessors. The following example from German is typical (Neumann 1996: 749):

(10) *Der Stein fällt* ***dem Mann*** *auf den Kopf/ **___dem Auto___
the stone falls the:DAT man on the head the:DAT car
aufs Dach.
on.the roof
'The stone falls on the man's head/*on the roof of the car.'

On the Situation Hierarchy (9b), usually only verbs denoting an event may occur in this construction in Europe, i.e., states are generally excluded. Thus, (11) and (12) are not acceptable.[2]

(11) Spanish (Roldán 1972: 30)
*__A estos autores les__ *es errada la construcción.*
to these authors them:DAT is wrong the construction
'The construction of these authors is incorrect.'

(12) Polish (Wierzbicka 1986)
Widziałem* ***mu* *zęby.*
I.saw him:DAT teeth
'I saw his teeth.'

On the Inalienability Hierarchy (9c), the dative EP construction is sometimes restricted to situations in which the possessum is a body part term and hence the possessor is maximally affected. This is the case, for instance, in Dutch (as well as in French, not illustrated here):

(13) Dutch (Vandeweghe 1987: 137, 140)
a. *Anita wierp* { *een vaas naar mijn hoofd.*
Anita threw { a vase at my head
{ ***mij*** *een vaas naar het hoofd.*
{ me:OBL a vase at the head
'Anita threw a vase at my head.'
b. *Ik gooide* { *het rapport op zijn bureau.*
I threw { the report on his desk
{ ****hem*** *het rapport op het bureau.*
{ him:OBL the report on the desk
'I threw the report on his desk.'

However, while body parts are certainly the most typical possessa in EP constructions, most Romance, Slavic, and Balkan languages languages as well as German do not restrict EP constructions to body parts (cf. examples 3, 5c, 8).

Finally, with respect to the Syntactic Relations Hierarchy (9d), we already saw in (4) that in European languages the possessum is generally a prepositional phrase (cf. examples 2, 5b–c, 6a, 8, 10, 13, 18), a direct object (cf. 1, 3, 5a, 39e, 40e), or an unaccusative subject (cf. 5d, 7b). Unergative subjects are very rare (cf. Buchholz & Fiedler 1987: 232 on Albanian), and I know of no case of a possible possessum that is a transitive subject. A language which puts the cut-off point after the direct object is Russian, where examples like (3) with a direct object possessum are possible, but (14) with an unaccusative subject possessum is impossible.

(14) **Mne drožat ruki.*
I:DAT tremble hands
'My hands are trembling.'

Dutch is the only language which puts the cut-off point directly after PPs, so that constructions like (5d) and (13a) are possible, but (15) is not.

(15) **Men heeft hem de arm gebroken.*
one has him:OBL the arm broken
'They have broken his arm.' (cf. French: *On lui a cassé le bras.*)

The affectedness condition and its effects are of course also widely attested elsewhere in the world, but its interpretation in European languages seems to be particularly strict. In non-European languages, examples like those in (16) and (17) seem to be much more common than in Europe.

(16) Sierra Popoluca (Elson & Marlett 1983)
šiwan ***a****-ˀiš-aˀy aŋ-kawah*
John 1ABS-see-APPL my-horse
'John saw my horse.'
(Lit. 'John saw me (dir. obj., absolutive-marked) my horse.')

(17) Korean (Chun 1986: 56)
Mary-ka ***ku namwu-lul*** *kaci-lul cal-ass-ta.*
Mary-NOM that tree-ACT branch-ACT cut-PAST-DECL
'Mary cut the branches of the tree.'

In (16), the possessor is not affected by the action of the verb and the possessum is not inalienable; in (17), the possessor is not animate. Such sentences are generally impossible in European languages.

3. The dative external possessor as an areal feature

Now that we have seen what the European EP prototype looks like, let us examine its geographical distribution. This is shown schematically on the map in Figure 1, where language names are placed approximately at the position of the center of the area where they are spoken. The solid line encloses those languages in Europe which have an EP construction that comes close to the European prototype. Only those languages for which we have reasonably detailed data are included in the map.[3]

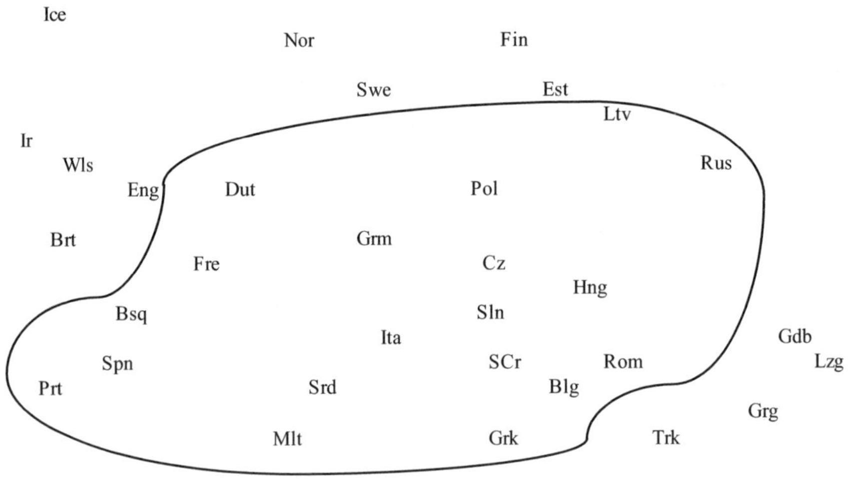

Figure 1: *The geographical distribution of the dative EP construction in Europe*

As can be easily seen, the languages displaying the dative EP construction form a contiguous area in the center and the south of Europe. We have argued elsewhere (König & Haspelmath 1997; Haspelmath 1998) that the existence of dative external possessors is a characteristic feature of the European linguistic area known as STANDARD AVERAGE EUROPEAN (SAE).

One might object to this claim by observing that almost all of the languages sharing this isogloss are Indo-European, and that the dative EP construction was in all likelihood inherited from Proto-Indo-European (PIE). Judging from the rich data on dative external possessors in ancient Indo-European languages that are presented in Havers (1911), it does indeed seem likely that this feature goes back to an early stage of the history of the Indo-European family. However, this does not necessarily mean that it cannot be an areal feature of the European *Sprachbund*. As I show in Haspelmath (1998), the Standard Average European linguistic area is fairly young and came into existence long after the breakup of the unitary proto-language. While this particular feature seems to have been inherited from PIE, most of the other characteristic features of SAE languages are innovations with respect to PIE.

There are three good arguments in favor of the areal interpretation. First, the EPR is also found in some non-Indo-European languages of Europe, specifically Basque, Maltese, and Hungarian. Examples are given in (18)–(20).

(18) Basque (Karmele Rotaetxe, p.c.)
Lagun-a-ri *apurtu d-i-o-gu* *beso-a.*
friend-DEF-DAT break 3SG.ABS-AUX-SG.DAT-1PL.ERG arm-DEF:ABS
'We broke the friend's arm.' (Lit. 'We broke the arm to the friend.')

(19) Maltese (Ray Fabri, p.c.)
It-tabib ***lill-pazjent*** *ittawwal-lu* *f' ħalqu.*
the-doctor DAT:the-patient he:looked-DAT:him in mouth.3SG
'The doctor looked into the mouth of the patient.'

(20) Hungarian (Katalin É. Kiss, p.c.)
A kutya beleharapott a ***szomszéd-nak*** *a lábá-ba.*
the dog into:bit the neighbor-DAT the leg:3SG-LOC
'The dog bit (into) the neighbor's leg.'

The Maltese and Hungarian constructions are different from the European prototype in that the possessor is also marked NP-internally by a pronominal affix, in addition to being expressed as an external dative NP. Nevertheless, the existence of a dative EPR in these languages is very likely to be due to areal convergence with the Indo-European languages of Europe, i.e., to borrowing from them. In the case of Maltese, this is confirmed by the fact that its close non-European cognate Classical Arabic completely lacks external possessors.

The second argument is that not all Indo-European languages of Europe have dative external possessors. As I emphasize in Haspelmath (1998), the nucleus of SAE languages is comprised of the central European languages (Dutch, German, French, northern Italian), corresponding to van der Auwera's (1998) "Charlemagne Sprachbund". The core consists of the other Romance and Germanic languages as well as West and South Slavic and the Balkan languages, and the periphery comprises East Slavic, Baltic, Balto-Finnic and Hungarian, plus Basque, Maltese, Armenian and Georgian. Importantly, there is one group of Indo-European languages that clearly do not belong to the SAE area: the Celtic languages. And interestingly, we do not find external possessors at all in Welsh and Breton. These languages require NP-internal possessors, as shown in (21)–(22). It may not be an accident that English, a language geographically close to Celtic, also lacks EP constructions of the SAE type.

(21) Breton (Pierre-Yves Lambert, p.c.)
Meratae t eneus he diouc'har dezi.
massaged has her legs of.her
'He massaged her legs.' (cf. French *Il lui a massé les jambes.*)

(22) Welsh (Pierre-Yves Lambert, p.c.)
Y mae ef wedi ysgwyd ei law.
is he after shaking his hand
'He shook his hand.' (cf. German *Er schüttelte ihm die Hand.*)

Irish has non-dative external possessors, as have the Nordic languages, the Balto-Finnic languages, and Russian (the latter two belonging to the periphery of SAE also with respect to other features). Thus, all of the nuclear SAE languages have the dative EP construction, and some peripheral SAE or non-SAE Indo-European languages lack it. This is precisely the kind of picture that we usually find in areal typology.

And third, the Indo-European languages spoken outside Europe generally lack the EP construction. Havers (1911) noted that Armenian is the only ancient Indo-European language lacking the dative possessor, and while Old Indic and Old Iranian showed clear traces of this construction in the oldest texts, the modern Iranian and Indic languages seem to have lost this feature entirely. The sentences in (23)–(25) illustrate this.

(23) Persian (Mitra Sharifi, p.c.)
Mâdar sar-e bače râ šost.
mother head-POSS child ACT washed
'The mother washed the child's hair.'

(24) Kurdish (Kurmancî, Geoff Haig, p.c.)
di-ya wî por-ê wî sust
mother-FEM:POSS 3SG:POSS hair-MASC:POSS 3SG:POSS washed
'His mother washed his hair.'

(25) Hindi (Hans Henrich Hock, p.c.)
Vah apne baal dho rah-ii hai.
s/he self's hair wash PROG-FEM:SG is
'She is washing her hair.'

Similarly, the non-Indo-European languages just outside Europe generally have only NP-internal possessors, as far as I am aware (e.g., Biblical Hebrew, Classical Arabic, Amharic; Turkish; Lezgian (northeastern Caucasus); but see (36) below for Georgian.)

Thus, while the dative EPR probably started as a genetic feature of the Indo-European family, it now has a distribution that lends itself primarily to a geographical generalization, although it is still true that most of the SAE languages are genetically Indo-European.

4. Europe vs. the rest of the world

The identification of the dative EPR as a European areal characteristic becomes even more convincing if we now take a world-wide perspective. EP constructions are widely found in the languages of the Americas, Africa, Asia and the Pacific, but I have not come across a single example in the literature of a non-European EP construction showing a possessor marked with a dative case. In the large majority of cases reported in the literature, non-European EP constructions show an EPR that does not occupy an additional clause-level position, but takes the syntactic relation of the possessum (i.e., generally object or subject; in Relational Grammar, this is referred to as "relational succession", cf. Perlmutter & Postal 1983). I will use the established metaphorical term POSSESSOR RAISING for these constructions (without implying a transformational analysis, of course). Possessor raising constructions in non-European languages can be classified into three broad categories:

(A) Possessor raising with possessum demotion
(B) Possessor raising with possessum incorporation
(C) Possessor raising with applicative marking on the verb

An example of type (A), raising with possessum demotion, is shown in (26).

(26) Yoruba (Rowlands 1969: 22)
*ó jí **mi** l' ówó gbé*
he steal me in money take
'He stole my money.' (lit. 'He stole me in money.')

The possessum is "demoted" in these constructions (to "chômeur status"), i.e., it either shows oblique case-marking (cf. 26) or no special case marking and reduced behavioral properties (cf. (32) below).

A more radical form of demotion is incorporation into the verb, i.e. type (B). An example is (27).

(27) Chukchi (Chukotko-Kamchatkan; Nedjalkov 1976: 158)
ətləg-e ***ekək*** *lelu-nimen-nin*
father-ERG son:ABS moustache-shave-3SG:PAST
'The father shaved the son's moustache.' (lit. 'The father moustache-shaved the son.')

In type (C), the possessor also takes the grammatical relation of the possessum (generally the direct object), but here the relation-changing is indicated by an applicative affix on the verb. An example is (28).

(28) Kalkatungu (Australian; Blake 1984: 439)
Kalpin-tu lha-nytyama-mi-kin ***nyini*** *thuku?*
man-ERG hit-APPL-FUT-INTERROG you:ABS dog:ABS
'Will the man hit your dog?'

The examples in (26)–(28) from Africa, Asia and Australia are fairly typical of the kind of patterns that we find in the world's languages. These patterns are not completely unrelated to the European prototype: In all these cases, the possessor is an NP-external, clause-level participant that is not required by the verb's valence. Moreover, in some languages the constructions in (26)–(28) also serve to express recipient or addressee relations, like the dative in Europe. For instance, in Yoruba the recipient of a verb of giving always appears in the direct-object relation, like the possessor in (26):

(29) Yoruba (Rowlands 1969: 21)
a. *ó fún mi l' ówó*
he give me in money
'He gave me money.'

And in Chukchi, the incorporation construction in (27) can serve as a recipient-theme construction as well:

(30) Chukchi (Nedjalkov 1976: 199)
ətləg-e ekək qaa-nm-ənen
father-ERG son:ABS reindeer-slaughter-3SG:PAST
'The father slaughtered a reindeer for the son.'

The same is true of applicative constructions, which in many languages are the normal way of expressing recipient-theme relations (e.g., in Tzotzil, cf. Aissen 1987).

However, I am aware of only a few cases that structurally come close to the European prototype. One of these is Yimas, a non-Austronesian language of New Guinea. In this language, there is an EPR expressed as a pronominal affix on the verb that otherwise marks recipients (there are several pronominal affix classes on verbs: transitive subject ('ACT'), ditransitive theme ('TH'), recipient ('REC'), and others, cf. Foley 1991).

(31) Yimas (New Guinea; Foley 1991: 301)
yampaŋ *k-mpu-**ŋa**-kra-t*
head:SG[GVI] GVI:SG:TH-3PL:act-1SG:REC-cut-PERF
'They cut my hair.'

The EPR is thus treated like a European dative indirect object, except that there is no case-marking in Yimas, a strongly head-marking language.[4] Similarly, in Chickasaw the EPR appears as an indirect object, marked by a pronominal affix of the recipient class on the verb:

(32) Chickasaw (Muskogean; Munro 1984: 637)
Ofi'-at ***ihoo-ã*** *paska* ***im**-apa-tok.*
dog-NOM woman-OBL bread 3SG:REC-eat-PAST
'The dog ate the woman's bread.'

Chickasaw does have some limited case-marking, but the theme-recipient distinction in ditransitive verbs is only shown by head-marking on the verb.

Thus, although the European EP prototype shows some similarities with what we see elsewhere in the world, an EPR marked by a dative case is apparently quite uncommon outside Europe.

However, the dative EP construction does not exhaust the possibilities of EP constructions in European languages. Apart from the locative EP constructions to be discussed in the next section, each of the three majority types (A–C) described earlier can also be found in Europe, though marginally. Relation-inheriting EP with possessum demotion (type A) is of course found widely in cases where a metonymic interpretation is readily available, e.g., with verbs of contact (*He kissed her on the forehead* 'He kissed her forehead'; French *Il la tira par la manche* 'He pulled her by the sleeve = He pulled her sleeve'), and with certain states (e.g. *She was sick at heart/Her heart was sick*). These constructions are unremarkable because in a situation of bodily contact, the contact is established with the whole body and with the body part. Crucially, European languages never allow such patterns when the corresponding expression without the locative-marked possessum would not make sense (e.g. **He is long in the toes* for 'His toes are long', because this does not entail 'He is long').

Thus, in these constructions the demoted possessum is locative-marked, and the locative can normally be interpreted quite directly, as indicating the more specific place of which the predicate is true. There is one isolated construction in Homeric

Greek that deviates from this pattern: With verbs of contact, both the raised possessor and the possessum may be in the same case, generally accusative ("double-case EP", also called "partitive apposition"; cf. Hahn 1954; Jacquinod 1989).

(33) Homeric Greek (Iliad 11, 240)
tòn d' áori plẽks' aukhéna
him:ACT PART sword:DAT hit:3SG:AOR neck:ACT
'He hit him on the neck with a sword.' (lit. 'hit him, the neck')

Type (B), possessor raising with possessum incorporation, at first looks quite exotic to European eyes, but it is not entirely unattested in Europe: Catalan has a moderately productive process of N–V compounding, where the noun is most often a body part, and the direct object of the verb is interpreted as its possessor (cf. Gràcia & Fullana 1996 for a description and analysis of this construction). In (34), the dative EP construction and the incorporating EP construction are shown side by side, and (35) shows an intransitive variant.[5]

Catalan (Gràcia & Fullana 1996: 2)
(34) a. *El caçador va trencar la cama* ***a l' ocell.***
the hunter PAST break the leg to the bird
'The hunter broke the bird's leg.'
b. *El caçador va cama-trencar* ***l' ocell.***
the hunter PAST leg-break the bird
'The hunter broke the bird's leg(s).' (lit. 'leg-broke the bird')

(35) ***L' home*** *cor-batega.*
the man heart-beats
'The man's heart is beating.'

The closest analog to this in English are verbs like *brainwash* (*They brainwashed him* ≈ 'They washed his brain'), but the pattern is unproductive in English and arises only through back-formation (cf. Rice & Prideaux 1991 for some discussion).

Finally, type (C), possessor raising with applicative marking, is attested in the Kartvelian languages Georgian and Laz. When the possessum is a body-part noun, the possessor-raising construction is obligatory, but in (36) it is optional (cf. Harris 1981: 288 for Georgian).

(36) Georgian (Harris 1981: 87)
a. *Mzia c'mends d-is pexsacml-eb-s.*
Mzia cleans sister-GEN shoe-PL-DAT
'Mzia is cleaning her sister's shoes.'

b. *Mzia **u**-c'mends* ***da-s*** *pexsacml-eb-s.*
Mzia 3SG.APPL-cleans sister-DAT shoe-PL-DAT
'Mzia is cleaning her sister's shoes.'

This construction is analogous to the Kalkatungu construction in (28). A slight complication lies in the fact that it is not always possible to neatly separate the applicative prefix from the pronominal affix, and that in Georgian the raised possessor is not a direct object, but a dative-marked indirect object (cf. Harris 1981). Thus, the Georgian construction combines the "non-European" applicative marking with the "European" dative marking.

5. Deviations from the European prototype

Some European languages that belong to the SAE *Sprachbund* deviate from the European prototype characterized in §2 by employing a locative rather than a dative case for their EP construction. Interestingly, these cases also seem to display an areal pattern of their own: locative-marked external possessors occur in the north of Europe, from Irish through Nordic (Icelandic, Norwegian, Swedish, Danish) to Balto-Finnic (Finnish, Estonian) and Russian. In Irish, the locative EP preposition *ag* literally means 'at'. It is a superessive preposition ('on') in Nordic, cf. (37).

(37) Icelandic (Katrín Sverisdottir, p.c.)
Það blæðir úr munninum ***á honom***.
it bleeds from mouth.the on him
'He is bleeding from the mouth.'
(cf. German: *Es blutet ihm aus dem Mund*)

The locative marker is the adessive case in Finnish and Estonian, and the use of Russian *u* 'at' must be due to Finno-Ugrian influence (cf. 38). (In Russian, both the dative EP construction, cf. (3) and (8), and the adessive EP construction exist; see Cienki 1993 for the subtle semantic differences in cases where both are possible.)

(38) Russian (Cienki 1993: 78)
U nego *vyrvali sumku iz ruk.*
at him tore.out bag from hands
'They tore the bag out of his hands.'

Although these northern European languages diverge from the European prototype, they are still reasonably close to it because the locative markers resemble the dative case in that they are dependent-marking elements signaling a non-nuclear grammatical relation. Particularly the use of the adessive is not surprising because this marker is also widely found in predicative possessive constructions (e.g., Finnish ***Hän-ellä*** *on paljon ystäviä*, Russian ***U nee*** *est' mnogo druzej* 'She has many friends'). I am not aware of locative case-markers or adpositions being used as markers of external possessors anywhere else in the world, so this pattern, too, is peculiar to Europe.

6. Typological connections of the European EP prototype

Let us now ask whether in addition to the geographical generalizations, it is possible to make some typological generalizations, i.e., to link the structural properties of the European EP construction to some other properties of Standard Average European languages. Let us begin with some minimal requirements: European languages are largely dependent-marking and have an indirect-object pattern for a recipient-theme configuration (rather than a secondary-object pattern; cf. Dryer 1986). The existence of dative-marked indirect objects seems to be a typological prerequisite for the European EP construction, and to the extent that non-European (and European non-SAE) languages lack these features, we can explain why they lack the European EP construction. However, there are also non-SAE languages that have a dative case and an indirect-object pattern but still lack the dative EP construction, so we must try to be more specific.

Linguists who wonder about the typological conditions of the EP construction in Europe are often struck immediately by the fact that English, the best-studied European language, lacks the SAE EP construction almost entirely. So by comparing English with French and German it might be possible to get a better answer to this question. In practice, however, things are much more complicated, and we are still far from understanding the precise typological conditions of the EP construction.

Vergnaud & Zubizarreta (1992) base their theory of external possession almost entirely on English and French. Their story is much too complicated to be discussed here, but they conclude that the difference between English and French ultimately results from the fact that the French definite article agrees with the noun in gender, whereas the English definite article does not do so. The implicit prediction that languages with genderless definite articles should lack the dative EP construction is falsified by Basque, Maltese and Modern Hebrew, which have a French-type EP construction but an English-type genderless definite article. Conversely, Amharic has a French-type gender-agreeing definite article, but like English it lacks the EP construction.

A more straightforward hypothesis would link the absence of an EP construction in English to the lack of a morphological dative case in this language (cf. Frajzyngier 1997). There are three difficulties with this proposal. First, Dutch, too, lacks a dative-accusative distinction, but it preserves its old EP construction (cf. Burridge 1996 for Middle Dutch) to a much greater extent than English (cf. 5b, 13 above). To this one might reply that English is generally more advanced on its path away from a case-marking language, and the fact that Dutch too is losing its EP construction confirms rather than weakens the hypothesis. But the second difficulty is that by no means all languages with a dative case have a dative external-possession construction (e.g., Turkish and Lezgian have a dative case, but they lack EP), so we still have to explain what allows the dative EP construction in SAE. And thirdly, one wonders why the "new dative" of English, the preposition *to* (or perhaps the benefactive preposition *for*) could not play the same role as the synthetic dative case in the other languages (e.g., **The hands are trembling to/for me.*) Finally, there is no obvious reason why English could not have developed a locative-marked EP construction, like some of the other northern European languages (e.g., **The doctor looked on/at me into the mouth*).

It appears that easy typological generalizations are not possible, and that we have to be content for the moment with the areal generalization, while hoping to find more subtle connections in the future. One concrete suggestion where to look next will be made in in the next section, where I will propose a tentative answer to the question why English *to/for* cannot play the role of a new dative in a dative EP construction.

7. The external possessor's place on a semantic map

So far in this paper I have not said anything about why it should be the dative case that marks the EPR, rather than any other case. Clearly, the external possessor is semantically related to other typical dative uses, such as the marking of a beneficially affected participant (benefactive) or the marking of a possessor in a predicative construction. These relationships have often been noted in the literature, but it is difficult to make them precise.

In this section I would like to propose a new technique for representing these semantic relationships. This technique is methodologically based on the observation of cross-linguistic patterns rather than on a semantic analysis, namely, a SEMANTIC MAP. A semantic map is a spatial representation of various meanings that a linguistic element may have, such that those meanings which are sometimes expressed by the same element are adjacent. The idea is that it is possible to draw a map of some semantic domain that is valid for all languages and thus can be taken as a representation of a universal "semantic space" (see Haspelmath 1997:Ch. 4 for some general discussion of semantic maps). Simultaneously, semantic maps summarize similarities and differences between the semantic properties of related elements in different languages, thus serving as a powerful tool for typological linguistics.

Figure 2 shows a semantic map of some grammatical meanings that are commonly associated with "dative" cases and related prepositions in European languages (in other languages, these meanings may of course be expressed by different means, e.g. by applicative marking on the verb).

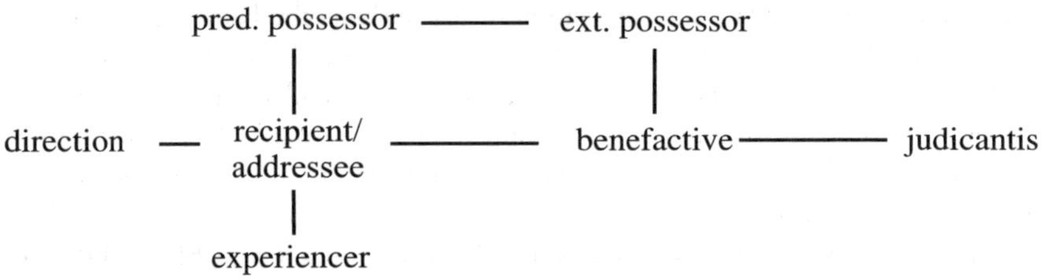

Figure 2: *A semantic map of "dative" functions*

This map was established inductively, i.e., I examined a number of languages and compared their polysemy patterns in this semantic domain. Since I have so far looked only at a few European languages, it is quite tentative at this stage, but my main purpose in this section is to show how such a map would work. The fundamental presupposition of the semantic-map methodology is that polysemy (or more generally polyfunctionality) is not arbitrary, but is based on similarity of conceptual meaning (or function). Since conceptual similarities are by definition universal (if conceptualization is defined as the language-independent level of meaning), it should be possible to arrive at a universal representation of the mutual relations of meaning/conceptualization by comparing polysemy patterns in different languages (thus, an alternative term for these universal semantic maps is "cognitive maps"). To illustrate this, let us look at the polysemy patterns of dative-like case-markers in three languages, Russian, English, and French. In Russian, the dative case can express five of the seven meanings of Fig. 2, all except 'direction' and 'predicative possession', as shown in (39).

(39) Russian

a. direction:
**My poexali Odesse.*
we went Odessa:DAT
'We went to Odessa.'

b. recipient:
Ja emu dam knigu.
I him:DAT I.give book:ACT
'I'll give him (DAT) the book.'

c. predicative possessor:
**Mne est' mnogo knig./ U menja est' mnogo knig.*
me:DAT there's many books at me there's many books
'I (DAT) have many books.'

d. benefactive:
Mama kupila synu velosiped.
mom bought son:DAT bike
'Mom bought a bike for the son (DAT).'

e. external possessor:
Ja tebe vse kosti perelomaju. (cf. also ex. 38)
I you:DAT all bones:ACT I.break
'I'll break all your (DAT) bones.'

f. judicantis:
Èto mne sliškom trudno.
that me:DAT too difficult
'That is too difficult for me (DAT).'

g. experiencer:
Mne stydno.
I:DAT ashamed
'I (DAT) am ashamed.'

The preposition *u* 'at' is used for predicative possession (cf. 39c) and external possession (cf. 38). The distribution of these two grams[6] (dative case and adessive preposition *u*) can be represented as in Figure 3, where each marker occupies a contiguous area on the map. As Figure 3 also shows, various grams can of course show overlaps — (rough) synonymy is not uncommon in grammatical semantics.

If we can draw a semantic map in such a way that the meanings expressed by a polysemous marker in quite a few languages cover a contiguous area on the map (i.e., a set of meanings which are directly linked to each other by lines), then there are good reasons to assume that this map is universal, and that it can

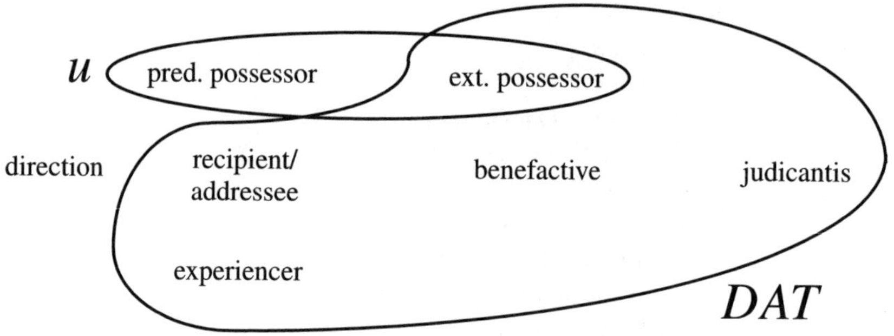

Figure 3: *The distribution of two grams in Russian*

be taken as a reflection of a universal semantic space. Thus, proposing a hypothetical semantic map such as Figure 2 amounts to making a strong universal claim: it is claimed that the meanings expressed by a gram in any language will cover a contiguous area on the map. For instance, if a gram (adposition or case) expresses 'direction' and 'experiencer' (two non-adjacent meanings), it will also express the intermediate meaning 'recipient/addressee'.

Let us now look at English and French. In English, the three meanings 'experiencer', 'possessor', and 'external possessor' are not expressed by prepositions (in fact, the latter meaning or function does not exist in English at all, unless one includes the *on*-construction). The distribution of the two prepositions *to* and *for* is shown in Figure 4 (for English examples, see the translations of the sentences in (39) and (40)).

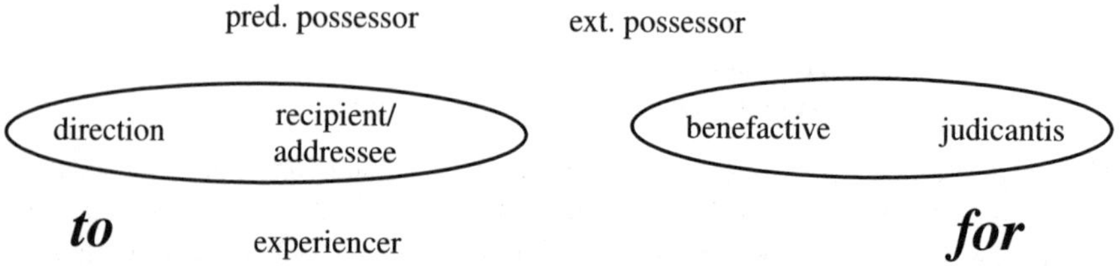

Figure 4: *The distribution of two prepositions in English*

In French, the two grams of interest to us are the dative case of the (clitic) personal pronouns (e.g., *lui* in the 3rd person singular) and the preposition *à*. While these both occur in the central dative use 'recipient/addressee', their distribution is otherwise quite different, as shown in (40).

(40) French
 a. direction:
  *On est allé à Odessa./*On lui est allé.*
  'We went to Odessa./We went there.'
 b. recipient:
  Je donne le livre à Martine./Je lui donne le livre.
  'I'll give Martine the book./I'll give her the book.'
 c. pred. possessor:
  *Ce livre est à Pierre-Yves./*Ce livre lui est.*
  'This book belongs to Pierre-Yves/This book is his.'
 d. benefactive:
  **J'ai trouvé un emploi à Mahmoud./Je lui ai trouvé un emploi.*
  'I found a job for Mahmoud./I found a job for him.'
 e. ext. possessor:
  **On a cassé la jambe à Benoît./On lui a cassé la jambe.*
  'They broke Benoît's leg./They broke his leg.'
 f. judicantis:
  **Cette valise lui est trop lourde./Cette valise est trop lourde pour elle.*
  'This suitcase is too heavy for her.'
 g. experiencer:
  Ce livre plaît à Thierry./Ce livre lui plaît.
  'Thierry likes this book/He likes this book.'

As (40f) shows, neither the dative nor *à* can be used in the judicantis function, where another preposition, *pour*, is required. The distribution of the three grams is shown in Figure 5.

The semantic map in Figure 2 would have to be tested against many more languages before it can be regarded as more than an initial hypothesis, and it will have to be refined by defining the various meanings in a rigorous way and adding quite a few minor distinctions. Moreover, ultimately we need a semantic or cognitive explanation for why the arrangement of meanings is the way it is, i.e., a deductive method for deriving this map that converges with the inductive results on independent grounds. But even in this preliminary form, the map offers some insights into the nature of dative external possessors.[7]

The map is also useful for diachronic considerations: as a marker is

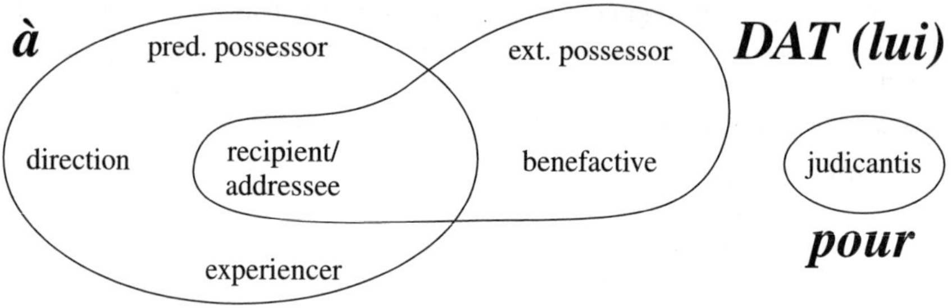

Figure 5: *The distribution of three grams in French*

grammaticalized, it is extended gradually to further functions that are adjacent on the map. We thus also have a spatial representation of the desemanticization or semantic bleaching that is part of the grammaticalization process (cf. Haspelmath 1997:ch. 6 for a defense of this view). Dative-like markers very often seem to be derived from direction markers, i.e., they start out on the left of the map and gradually work their way to the other meanings further to the right. As they acquire new meanings on the right, they necessarily lose meanings on the left, because for obvious reasons a grammatical marker cannot have too many too distantly related meanings.[8] Thus, while the Latin dative could still be used in directional function (e.g., *it clamor caelo* (Virgil) 'the cry goes up to heaven (DAT)'), this is no longer possible in French. The newly grammaticalized dative preposition *à,* whose only function in Latin was to express direction, has come to express a number of further meanings, but it has not reached any of the meanings on the right-hand side yet. This is probably the reason (or at least part of the reason) why *à* cannot be used to mark external possessors — it has not been desemanticized sufficiently. The EPR expresses affectedness in European languages, but not a specific kind of affectedness, i.e., its meaning is more general than the benefactive meaning.

From this perspective, it may also become somewhat clearer why English *to* cannot be used with external possessors (**They broke the leg to him*). Like French *à*, it is still too "fresh" — perhaps markers that span four meanings from 'direction' to external 'possessor' are not easily tolerated. Interestingly, in some of the other languages which have a dative case but lack external possession, e.g., Turkish and Lezgian, the dative case is also used to mark direction (e.g., Turkish *Ankara-ya* 'to Ankara (DAT)'), i.e., it is not as old and desemanticized as the Indo-European dative. It seems that a fair amount of desemanticization is necessary before a gram can mark external possessors. While this cannot be the whole story, it certainly does provide a new perspective that should be explored further in future research.

8. Summary

Let us briefly recapitulate the main results of this paper. I have described a prototype of an EP construction that is found in an areal cluster of central and southern European languages, which I take as further confirmation of the *Sprachbund* status of these European languages (§§2–3). I contrasted this prototype with the three main formal types of EP construction found in the world's languages, concluding that the European dative EP construction is quite peculiar to this part of the world (§4). I briefly mentioned a few northern European languages that have peculiar locative EP constructions, which deviate from the European prototype and display an areal pattern of their own (§5). I then discussed some attempts at connecting the existence of the dative EP construction with other properties of the languages that have it, and I showed that this is not straightforward (§6). As a more subtle instrument of typological analysis, I proposed the semantic-map methodology in §7 and applied it to the dative gram in EP constructions, thus exploring a relatively new way of expressing the relationships between similar constructions and capturing cross-linguistic generalizations.

Acknowledgments

This paper is based to some extent on a comparative study of external-possession constructions in 28 European languages conducted together with Ekkehard König (cf. König & Haspelmath 1997). I am grateful to Ekkehard König for the fruitful cooperation, as well as the other members of the EUROTYP Theme Group 'Actance and Valence', of which this work was part, and all those colleagues who took the trouble to answer our questions on their languages.

Abbreviations

Abbreviations used in this paper: ACT actor, ABS absolutive, ACT accusative, AOR aorist, APPL applicative, ART article, AUX auxiliary, DAT dative, DECL declarative, EP external possession, EPR external possessor, ERG ergative, FEM feminine, FUT future, G gender, GEN genitive, INTERROG interrogative, LOC locative, NOM nominative, OBL oblique, PAST past tense, PERF perfect, PIE Proto-Indo-European, PL plural, POSS possessive marker, PP prepositional phrase, PROG progressive, PART particle, REC recipient, REFL reflexive, SAE Standard Average European, SG singular, TH theme.

Notes

1 An exception to this generalization is Icelandic, which has preserved the dative case, but does not have dative external possessors (cf. (35) in §5 below); Irish, too, technically has a dative case, but this has almost disappeared. The Maltese prefixal dative case (*li-*) is sometimes regarded as a preposition (in accordance with the Semitic grammatical tradition), but it is written bound and there are sufficient reasons for regarding it as an affix.

2 However, Roldán notes that the equivalent of (11) is acceptable in Portuguese (*Lhes é errada a construcção*), and Wierzbicka notes that the equivalent of (12) is grammatical in Italian (*Gli vidi i denti*). Still, even in these languages most stative predicates do not admit dative possessors. The precise limits of the EP construction are still unknown in many languages.

3 Abbreviations of language names should be largely self-explanatory (some less known languages: Gdb Godoberi, Lzg Lezgian, Sln Slovene, Srd Sardinian)

4 The closest parallels to the Yimas situation in Europe are provided by Basque and Maltese, where the verb agrees with the dative-marked participant (cf. 18–19). However, both Basque and Maltese are double-marking languages that have dative case-marking in addition to head-marking on the verb.

5 Catalan also has incorporating adjectives, e.g., *ala-llarg* [wing-long], as in *L'ocell és alallarg* 'the bird is long-winged, the bird's wings are long'. Adjectival compounds with body part nouns are common in Indo-European, but they normally show the reverse pattern, e.g., Old English *hāt-heart* 'hot-hearted', German *bar-fuß* 'bare-footed', Classical Greek *ōkú-pous* 'swift-footed'. However, the Catalan pattern is also attested in ancient Indo-European, e.g., Classical Greek *pod-ōkēs* 'foot-swift' (see Meid 1967: 31–35).

6 *Gram* is short for 'grammatical marker' (cf. Bybee et al. 1994 for this term).

7 For studying cross-linguistic variation, semantic maps are a much more useful tool than formulations of general meanings. For example, consider the following formulations given as characterizations of the dative function in individual languages: 'non-active involvement in an activity' (Burridge 1996, on Middle Dutch); 'the dative clitic always represents an oblique argument of the verb which is a 'theme' of the sentence, i.e., the center of attention' (Barnes 1985: 161, on French); 'the dative serves as the limit of the predicate in the sense that it indicates the ultimate term towards which the action or process referred to tends' (Van Hoecke 1996: 31, on Latin).

8 If the grammatical marker is the sole bearer of this meaning, as in prepositions of European languages, the polysemy pattern will be fairly limited. In languages with one or two all-purpose adpositions/cases, a larger part of the meaning is expressed by other elements (especially the verb). I have not yet explored the problems that are posed for semantic maps by such cases of distributed expression.

References

Aissen, Judith. 1987. *Tzotzil Clause Structure.* Dordrecht: Reidel.

Bally, Charles. 1926. "L'expression des idées de sphère personnelle et de solidarité dans les langues indo-européennes." In F. Fankhauser and J. Jud (eds.), *Festschrift Louis Gauchat.* Aarau: Sauerländer, 68–78. (English translation in Chappell and McGregor 1996: 31–61)

Barnes, Betsy K. 1985. "A Functional Explanation of French Nonlexical Datives." *Studies in Language* 9.2: 159–195. (= *Lingvisticae Investigationes* 4: 245–292)

Blake, Barry J. 1984. "Problems for Possessor Ascension: Some Australian Examples." *Linguistics* 22: 437–453.

Buchholz, Oda and Wilfried Fiedler. 1987. *Albanische Grammatik.* Leipzig: Enzyklopädie.

Burridge, Kate. 1996. "Degenerate Cases of Body Parts in Middle Dutch." In Chappell and McGregor (eds.), 679–710.

Bybee, Joan L. and Revere Perkins and William Pagliuca. 1994. *The Evolution of Grammar.* Chicago: The University of Chicago Press.

Chappell, Hilary and William McGregor (eds). 1996. *The Grammar of Inalienability: A Typological Perspective on Body Part Terms and the Part-Whole Relation.* Berlin: Mouton de Gruyter [*Empirical Approaches to Language Typology* 14].

Chun, Soon Ae. 1986. "Possessor Ascension in Korean", *Buffalo Working Papers in Linguistics* 1: 51–97.

Cienki, Alan. 1993. "Experiencers, Possessors, and Overlap between Russian Dative and *u* + Genitive." *Berkeley Linguistics Society* 19: 76–89.

Dryer, Matthew. 1986. "Primary Objects, Secondary Objects, and Antidative." *Language* 62.4: 808–845.

Elson, Benjamin and Stephen A. Marlett. 1983. "Popoluca Evidence for Syntactic Levels." In Desmond C. Derbyshire (ed.), *Work Papers of the Summer Institute of Linguistics, Univerity of North Dakota Session* 27: 107–134.

Foley, William A. 1991. *The Yimas Language of New Guinea.* Stanford: Stanford University Press.

Frajzyngier, Zygmunt. 1997. "EP and NI as Coding Means: A System Interactional Approach." Abstract, EP/NI Conference, University of Oregon, September 1997.

Gràcia, Lluïsa and Olga Fullana. 1996. *On Catalan Verbal Compounds.* Ms., Universitat de Girona.

Hahn, E. Adelaide. 1954. "Partitive Apposition in Homer and the Greek Accusative." *Transactions and Proceedings of the American Philological Association* 85:82–113.

Harris, Alice C. 1981. *Georgian Syntax.* Cambridge: Cambridge University Press.

Haspelmath, Martin. 1997. *Indefinite Pronouns.* Oxford: Clarendon Press.

Haspelmath, Martin. 1998. "How Young is Standard Average European?" *Language Sciences* 20.3: 271–87.

Hatcher, Anna G. 1944. "Il me prend le bras vs. il prend mon bras." *The Romanic Review* 35.2: 156–164.

Havers, Wilhelm. 1911. *Untersuchungen zur Kasussyntax der indogermanischen Sprachen.* Straßburg: Trübner.

Jacquinod, Bernard. 1989. *Le double accusatif en grec d'Homère à la fin du Ve siècle avant J.-C.* Louvain-la-Neuve: Peeters.

König, Ekkehard and Martin Haspelmath. 1997. "Les constructions à possesseur externe dans les langues d'Europe." In Jack Feuillet (ed.), *Actance et valence dans les langues de l'Europe.* (Empirical Approaches to Language Typology/EUROTYP, 20–2.) Berlin: Mouton de Gruyter, 525–606.

Meid, Wolfgang. 1967. *Germanische Sprachwissenschaft, vol. III: Wortbildungslehre.* Berlin: de Gruyter.

Munro, Pamela. 1984. "The Syntactic Status of Object Possessor Raising in Western Muskogean." *Berkeley Linguistics Society* 10: 634–649.

Nedjalkov, Vladimir P. 1976. "Diathesen und Satzstruktur im Tschuktschischen." In Ronald Lötzsch and Rudolf Růžička (eds.), *Satzstruktur und Genus verbi.* Berlin: Akademie-Verlag, 181–211.

Neumann, Dorothea. 1996. "The Dative and the Grammar of Body Parts in German." In Chappell and McGregor (eds.), 745–779.

Perlmutter, David M. and Paul M. Postal. 1983. "The Relational Succession Law." In: David M. Perlmutter (ed.), *Studies in Relational Grammar 1.* Chicago: The University of Chicago Press, 30–80.

Rakhilina, Elena V. 1982. "Otnošenie prinadležnosti i sposoby ego vyraženija v russkom jazyke (datel'nyj possessivnyj)." *Naučno-texničeskaja informacija, serija 2,* 1982: 24–30.

Rice, Sally and Gary Prideaux. 1991. "Event-Packaging: The Case of Object Incorporation in English." *Berkeley Linguistics Society* 17: 283–298.

Roldán, Mercedes. 1972. "Concerning Spanish Datives and Possessives." *Language Sciences* 21: 27–32.

Rowlands, E.C. 1969. *Yoruba.* Sevenoaks, Kent: Hodder & Stoughton [*Teach Yourself Books*].

Seiler, Hansjakob. 1983. *Possession as an Operational Dimension of Language.* Tübingen: Gunter Narr [*Language Universals Series* 2].

Van der Auwera, Johan. 1998. "Introduction." In Johan van der Auwera (ed.), *Adverbial Constructions in the Languages of Europe.* Berlin: Mouton de Gruyter, 1–23.

Vandeweghe, Willy. 1987. "The Possessive Dative in Dutch: Syntactic Reanalysis and Predicate Formation." In Johan van der Auwera and Louis Goossens (eds.), *Ins and Outs of Predication.* Dordrecht: Foris, 137–151.

Van Hoecke, Willy. 1996. "The Latin Dative." In William Van Belle and Willy Van Langendonck (eds). 1996. *The Dative, vol. 1: Descriptive studies.* Amsterdam and Philadelphia: Benjamins, 3–37.

Vergnaud, Jean-Roger and Maria-Louise Zubizarreta. 1992. "The Definite Determiner and the Inalienable Constructions in French and English." *Linguistic Inquiry* 23: 595–652.

Wierzbicka, Anna. 1986. "The Meaning of a Case: a Study of the Polish Dative." In Richard D. Brecht and James S. Levine (eds.), *Case in Slavic.* Columbus/OH: Slavica.

Mapping Possessors

Parameterizing the External Possession Construction

Donna B. Gerdts
Simon Fraser University

Introduction

Many languages of the world exhibit External Possessor Constructions (EPCs), in which a nominal occupying a core syntactic position (subject, object, or indirect object) is semantically interpreted as the possessor of an NP-argument of the predicate, most generally the theme.[1] This paper considers the status of the external possessor in various languages and whether or not this can be predicted based on other properties of the language. I show on the basis of a sample of twenty-two languages that the surface relation of the external possessor depends upon the language's morphosyntactic argument structure. Also, this paper gives an account of EPCs in Mapping Theory (MT), a revised version of Relational Grammar (RG) that incorporates a level of morphosyntactic argument structure, which is subject to language specific variation. Mapping Theory, in allowing for cross-linguistic variation at this level of structure, makes a straightforward prediction concerning the external possessor.

EPCs have received much attention in the RG literature. Examples from dozens of languages have been discussed. The cross-linguistic data show one fact very clearly: the possessor in EPCs based on transitive clauses takes on direct object properties in some languages, as in (1), but indirect object properties in others, as in (2).[2]

(1) a. Chamorro (Gibson 1992)
Ha fa'gasi-yi yu' si Flory ni magagu-hu.
3SG wash-ASC 1SG PN F OBL clothes-my
'Flory washed my clothes (for me).'

b. Halkomelem (Gerdts 1989: 267, 31)
niʔ tši-ˀqʷ-t-əs ɬə sɬeniʔ kʷθə sqʷəméẏ.
AUX comb-hair-TRANS-3ERG DET woman DET dog
'The woman combed the dog's hair.'

(2) a. Georgian (Harris 1976: 191, iic)
iam gaurecxa perangi gelas.
Ia:ERG she:washed:him:it:II:VC1 shirt:NOM Gela:DAT
'Ia washed Gela's shirt.'

b. Southern Tiwa (Allen et al. 1990: 354, 156f)[3]
Bow-kahun-mu-ban.
2SG:1SG\C-box-see-PAST
'You saw my boxes.'

That the possessor is a direct object is shown in (1a) by the first person clitic pronoun and in (1b) by the fact that the possessor is in straight case, the case used for subjects and direct objects, and the fact that it does not determine genitive agreement on the head noun. In contrast, the possessor in (2a) appears in the dative case, the case used for indirect objects, and the possessor in (2b) determines indirect object agreement (the 1SG portion of the agreement prefix) in the verb complex. I refer the reader to the works cited for additional evidence for the status of the possessor.

In RG the EPC data in (1) are analyzed as possessor ascension constructions; the possessor ascends to take on the grammatical relation (GR) of the host, conforming to the Relational Succession Law (RSL):

(3) Relational Succession Law (Perlmutter and Postal 1983a):
An ascendee assumes within the clause into which it ascends the grammatical relation of its host NP.

The RSL predicts that, in EP constructions with an object host, the possessor is an object, as we see in the data in (1).[4] The data in (2), where the possessor appears to be an indirect object, although the host is a direct object, are problematic for the RSL. Two suggestions have been made concerning such data. First, it has been claimed that some possessors ascend to direct object, while other possessors ascend to indirect object, and thus that the RSL should be abandoned as far as possessor ascension is concerned (Bickford 1986). Second, a possessor union analysis has been proposed for cases involving the possessor as an indirect object (Harris 1976; Rosen 1987). Under the union analysis, the possessive phrase functions like an embedded clause. The possessor and the head are both assigned grammatical relations in the main clause. Unions are not subject to the RSL.

Whatever RG analysis is proposed for EPCs, the fact remains that no prediction has been made concerning which type of EPC will occur in a given language.

In Section 1, I report on a study of EPCs based on a cross-linguistic survey of twenty-two languages. I show that the status of the external possessor in a language is directly related to the number of morphologically-licensed argument positions (MAPs) it has. In Section 2, I present a revised version of RG — Mapping Theory — which encodes MAPs into the final level of structure. After a brief introduction to Mapping Theory, I give an applicative analysis of EPCs. In Section 3, I bring up a second analysis of EPCs, a possessor union analysis, which parallels causative clause union. Section 4 discusses the special case of Kinyarwanda EPCs. Two types of EPCs exist in this language. Mapping Theory easily accommodates the Kinyarwanda data. I claim that EPCs involving alienable possession have an applicative structure, while EPCs involving inalienable possession have a union structure. Thus, we see that two distinct analyses for EPCs are allowed across languages and also within a single language.

I conclude with a brief comparison of Mapping Theory and Relational Grammar with respect to EPC data. MT is much simpler and more constrained than RG. Furthermore, Mapping Theory more closely fits the empirical properties of EPCs in the world's languages.

1. EPCs in twenty-two languages

In this section, I report on a survey of languages. Dubinsky and Rosen's (n.d.) bibliography gives information on RG research on one hundred and five languages. By making a data base of these languages according to the constructions that were claimed to exist in them by the authors of the cited studies, I ascertained that twenty-five languages have EPCs targeting object relations. Furthermore, twenty of these languages had sufficient information reported to allow them to be used in this study. In addition, data from ten recent grammars written in RG-compatible style were added to the database. Two of these, Ika (Frank 1990) and Yimas (Foley 1991) had EPCs and sufficient information about other rules to allow them to be included in the present study. Overall, thirty-five languages with ECPs were surveyed and twenty-two of these had sufficient information to allow them to be included in this study. The languages represent many different language families and many different areas of the world.

For each language, I studied its relational profile (Gerdts 1992b), that is, information regarding the GR-changing rules attested in the language and also the morphological trappings used to express term relations. Table 1 summarizes information about each language with respect to agreement, case, and GR-changing rules. Following the authors' analyses of each language, I indicate for each GR-changing rule given across the top of the table whether the nominal's final status is a direct object (2), an indirect object (3), or an oblique object (4), as indicated in the row for each language.[5] GR-changing rules include demotions of the subject (1) to 2 or 3, advancements of a 3 to 2 or of a benefactive to 2, 3, or 4, causative clause union where the causee is revalued as a 2, 3, or 4, and possessor ascension to 2 or 3. For example, we see in Blackfoot that subjects demote to 2 (in an inverse construction), 3s and benefactives advance to 2, causees in clause union causatives appear as 2s, and possessors ascend to 2. In Albanian, we see that subjects demote to 3, initial 3s in ditransitives remain 3s, benefactives advance to 3, causees appear as 3s, and possessors ascend to 3.

On the basis of this information, it is easy to see the correlation between a language's relational profile and the type of EPC that it exhibits. The A languages are direct-object-centered languages. In these twelve languages, the external possessor has surface direct object properties. The B languages are indirect-object-centered languages. In these nine languages, the external possessor has surface indirect object properties. One language, Kinyarwanda, exhibits a mixed set of properties and thus warrants special discussion (see Section 4).

What property differentiates these two types of languages? The answer is simple: the A and B languages differ in how many nominals they allow as direct arguments. As often noted (see especially Gerdts 1990 and Everett 1988), direct arguments get core morphosyntactic marking: that is, they determine agreement (or pronoun incorporation or cliticization), license surface case as opposed to inherent case, or appear in a fixed word order adjacent to the predicate.[6] A summary of agreement and case is given in the two columns in Table 1 immediately following the language name. Two languages, Indonesian and Kinyarwanda, also make use of SVO word order in differentiating subjects from objects. Reviewing Table 1, we find that the A and B languages have respectively two and three morphosyntactically-licensed argument positions (MAPs).[7]

We conclude on the basis of this evidence that the relational profile of a language is systematically related to its morphosyntactic argument structure. Thus, a theory that can make statements concerning the mapping of grammatical relations to morphosyntactic positions can capture a range of generalizations unavailable to theories that do not make this connection.

Table 1: *Relational Profiles of Twenty-Two Languages*

	Agr	Case	1Dem	3Adv	BenAdv	Causee	PosAsc
A. Blackfoot	1, 2	Ø	2	2	2	2	2
Cebuano	1, 2	Ø		2	2	2	2
Chamorro	1, 2	E, Ab		2	2	2	2
Halkomelem	1, 2	Ø		2	2	2	2
Ika	1, 2	E		2	2	2	2
Indonesian	Ø	Ø		2	2		2
Kalkatungu	1, 2	E, Ab		2	2		2
Korean	Ø	N, A		2		2	2
Okanagan	1, 2	Ø		2	2	2	2
Ojibwa	1, 2	Ø	2	2	2	2	2
Sierra Popoluca	1, 2	Ø		2	2		2
Tzotzil	1, 2	Ø		2	2	2	2
B. Albanian	1; 2, 3	N, A, D	3	= 3	3	3	3
Choctaw	1, 2, 3	N	3	= 3	3	2	3
French	1; 2, 3	D	3	= 3	3	3	3
Georgian	1, 2, 3	E, N, D	3	= 3	3	3	3
German	1	N, A, D	3	= 3, 2	3	2	3
Southern Tiwa	1, 2, 3	Ø		= 3		3	3
Spanish	1; 2, 3	D (2a, 3)	3	= 3, 2	3	3	3
Warlpiri	1, 2, 3	E, Ab, D		= 3	3	3	3
Yimas	1, 2, 3	Ø		= 3	3	3	3
C. Kinyarwanda	1: 2, 3, 4	Ø		= 3	= 4	2/3/4	3i, 2a

Agr = agreement. Under the agreement column, agreement affixes are followed by (,), clitics are followed by (;) and incorporated pronouns are followed by (:).
Case: N = nominative. **A** = accusative. **D** = Dative. **E** = ergative. **Ab** = absolutive.
1Dem = 1 demotion (initial subject demotes to 2 (inverse) or 3 (inversion)).
3Adv = 3 Advancement (initial 3 advances to 2). If there is no advancement of 3s in the language, **=3** appears in this column.
Ben Adv = benefactive advancement (initial benefactive advances to 2, 3, or 4).
Causee = causee in a causative clause union (causee is revalued as 2, 3, or 4).
PosAsc = possessor ascension (the possessor ascends to 2 or 3).
i = inanimate, **a** = animate.
1 = subject, **2** = direct object, **3** = indirect object, **4** = oblique object.

2. Mapping EPCs

The remainder of this paper gives an analysis of EPCs from a Mapping Theory (MT) viewpoint. First proposed in Gerdts (1992b) (see also Gerdts 1992a), MT was designed as a bi-stratal alternative to RG. It has two levels of morphosyntactic structure: a GR tier, corresponding to initial grammatical relations in RG; and a MAP tier, roughly corresponding to final grammatical relations in RG. MAPs are morphosyntactic argument positions defined by a language's trappings (case, agreement, word order). The rules for drawing association lines between the two tiers form the core of the grammar. These parallel the GR-changing rules of RG.[8] However, MT differs from RG in an important respect. In RG, the inventory of grammatical relations and GR-changing rules is available to all languages. In MT, languages differ in the number of MAPs they utilize, and consequently in the constructions they allow.

Following Gerdts 1990, I claim that MAPs are transparently licensed by some morphosyntactic device, the most common being agreement, S(tructural)-Case, and adjacency to the predicate (or a combination of these). Furthermore, Gerdts (1992b) shows that languages vary with respect to the number of MAPs they license; for example, Blackfoot, Halkomelem, and Tzotzil license two, while Albanian, Choctaw, Georgian, and Southern Tiwa license three. The number of MAPs existing in the language directly correlates with the type of associations allowed in the language. Two-MAP languages tend to have linking rules that target the second MAP. Three-MAP languages, in contrast, target a third MAP (e.g. a DAT position) for associations of these types. In RG terms, two-MAP languages are "object-centered" and commonly have 3-2, OBL-2, possessor ascension-2, causee-2, and antipassive constructions. In contrast, three-MAP languages are "indirect object-centered" and commonly have OBL-3, inversion of the subject-3, possessor ascension-3, and causee-3 constructions.

Mapping Theory consists of several modules and rules for relating one module to another. Four perspectives on a nominal are encoded: its thematic relation, its grammatical relation (corresponding to its initial grammatical relation in RG), its MAP (corresponding to its final relation in RG), and its morphosyntactic presentation (i.e. its case, agreement, word order, etc.) For example, the Japanese clause in (4) is given the Mapping Theory representation in (5).

(4) *John ga Mary ni kunsyoo o atae-ta.*
J. NOM M. DAT medal ACC give-PAST
'John gave a medal to Mary.'

(5)

thematic relations:	agent	theme	goal
grammatical relations:	1	2	3
	|	|	|
MAPs:	A	B	C
	|	|	|
presentation:	NOM	ACC	DAT

There are three lexically subcategorized nominals in (5). They are assigned grammatical relations 1 (subject), 2 (direct object), and 3 (indirect object), respectively, following the usual assumptions about the mapping of thematic relations to initial grammatical relations.[9] Each GR is linked to a MAP. MAPs are ordered positions (represented here as A, B, C) linked to morphological presentational statements (for example: NOM case licenses A, ACC case licenses B, and DAT case licenses C). Presentational details are usually omitted in this paper but would be relevant in spelling out the grammar of a specific language. In any given clause, the number of MAPs assigned depends on three things: first, the lexical semantic valence of the verb, second, MAP-reducing or -building morphology, and third, the MAP thresholds set for the language (that is, the maximum and minimum number of MAPs allowed). Japanese is a three-MAP language — it allows a maximum of three direct arguments. Hence A, B, and C are available for linking in (5).

The universal principles for linking GRs to MAPs are given in (6).[10]

(6) Principles for Linking GRs and MAPs:
Saturation Principle: Every MAP must be linked to a GR or cancelled.
Biuniqueness Principle: Every MAP is linked to a single GR (except in multiattachment under coreference), and every GR is linked to at most one MAP.
No Delinking Principle: There are no delinkings.
No Crossing Lines: Association lines cannot cross.

2.1 *Mapping applicatives*

Two types of associations are recognized in the theory. Unmarked associations proceed in a vertical, non-crossing, left-to-right fashion. For example, (5) above shows unmarked association in a three-MAP case. Marked associations, on the other hand, may involve non-vertical linkings, the linking of an extra nominal not lexically subcategorized by the verb, the non-linking of a nominal, or linkings in a right-to-left direction. Marked associations take precedence over unmarked left-to-right linkings. Marked associations are generally subject to morphological conditions. A statement of these conditions and their concurrent effect on argument structure is the biggest task of a Mapping Theory grammar. Some aspects of marked associations will be specified in universal grammar, but other aspects will be subject to parameter setting (see Gerdts 1995).

Some examples of marked association rules are given in (7); these rules are discussed in Gerdts (1992a, 1992b):

(7) a. Applicative: Add a MAP (up to threshold) and link the 3/oblique to the lowest possible MAP.
  b. Antipassive/antidative: Cancel the lowest MAP and do not link the GR above it.
  c. Reflexive: Link both the 1 and the GR above the lowest MAP to the same MAP (and, in some languages, cancel the lowest MAP).
  d. Passive: Do not link the first GR; cancel one or more MAPs.

Furthermore, a quick perusal of these rules reveals that the lowest MAP is the pivotal position in marked associations (other than passive); it is frequently linked or cancelled. This tendency is captured in the following universal principle.

(8) The Last MAP Principle: Marked associations (other than passive) target the last MAP.

Relevant to this paper is (7a), the applicative rule. An applicative in any language adds a MAP if possible, then links the 3/oblique to the lowest MAP. Take the Halkomelem examples in (9) and (10); (9) shows a goal applicative and (10) shows a benefactive applicative.

(9) *niʔ ʔa·m-əs-θám̓š-əs ʔə kʷθə pukʷ.*
AUX give-ADV-TRANS+1OBJ-3ERG OBL DET book
'He gave me the book.' (Gerdts 1988: 94, 18)

(10) *niʔ θə̀y-əłc-θám̓š-əs ʔə kʷθə nə-snə́xʷəł.*
AUX fix-ADV-TRANS+1OBJ-3ERG OBL DET 1POSS-canoe
'He fixed my canoe for me.' (95, 20)

Since (9) and (10) are lexically transitive and Halkomelem is a two-MAP language, MAPs A and B are available for linking. The applicative cannot add a MAP, since the threshold is two in Halkomelem. Nonetheless, the 3 or oblique is linked to the lowest MAP, i.e. B, as (11) shows.

(11)

θ-Rs:	agent	theme	goal/ben
GRs:	1	2	3/OBL
	|		/
MAPs:	A	B	

The 1 links by unmarked association. The 2 is unlinked and therefore gets licensed as a non-argument by peripheral means, such as the preposition in (9) and (10) or by case spread.[11]

Applicatives in three-MAP languages support this approach. Georgian (Harris 1981) has pairs like (12a) and (12b).

(12) a. *gelam šeḳera axali šarvali merabisatvis.*
Gela:ERG he:sewed:it:II:VC1 new trousers:NOM Merab:for
'Gela made new trousers for Merab.' (153, 2a)

b. *gelam šeuḳera axali šarvali merabs.*
Gela:ERG he:sewed:him:it:II:VC1 new trousers:NOM Merab:DAT
'Gela made new trousers for Merab.' (153, 2b)

The representation for (12b), a benefactive applicative, is given in (13).

(13)

θ-Rs:	agent	theme	ben
GRs:	1	2	OBL
	|	|	|
MAPs:	A	B	**C**

Georgian is a three-MAP language, so MAP C is added (represented in boldface) and the benefactive links to it. The 1 and 2 link by unmarked association.

2.2 *Possessor applicatives*

Possessor ascension effects can also be given an MT analysis. For example, in the Korean sentence in (14), the theme nominal is modified by a possessor, as represented by the [POSS] following the 2 in (15).[12]

(14) *Yangswu-ka Swuni-lul elkwul-ul kuli-ess-ta.*
Y.-NOM S.-ACC face-ACC draw-PAST-IND
'Yangsu drew Sooni's face.' (Gerdts 1993: 305, 15)

```
(15)   agent   theme
         1       2[POSS]
         |       /
         A      B
        NOM    ACC
```

We can account for the fact that the possessor takes on the properties associated with the B MAP by adding possessors to the applicative rule in (7a):

(16) Applicative: Add a MAP (up to threshold) and link the 3, oblique, or possessor to the lowest available MAP.

In two-MAP languages such as Korean, the possessor in a possessor applicative based on a transitive clause will link to the B MAP. In contrast, in three-MAP languages, a C MAP is added by the applicative rule and the possessor links to it; for example, see the Choctaw data in (17), as represented in (18).

(17) *Ofi-yat katos ã-kopoli-tok.*
dog-NOM cat 1DAT-bite-PAST
'The dog bit my cat.' (Davies 1986: 10, 18b)

```
(18)   agent   theme
         1       2[POSS]
         |       |    \
         A       B     C
        NOM     ACC   DAT
```

Thus we see that, under an applicative analysis of EPCs, the external possessor will either link to the B MAP or the C MAP, depending upon the MAP threshold of the language.

3. EPCs as possessor union

The previous section gave an applicative analysis of EPCs. Through an applicative rule, the possessor is added as an argument on the GR tier and linked to a MAP. This parallels possessor ascension in RG. A second analysis of EPCs has been proposed within RG — the possessor union analysis (Harris 1976; Rosen 1987; see also Davies 1997; Gerdts 1992c).[13] Under this analysis, EPCs are a type of union, paralleling causative clause union. The possessor and head are seen as occupying an embedded or "downstairs" clause. The possessor revalues as a 3, while the theme inherits the 2 relation in the union stratum, that is, the level of structure where the two clauses combine. This analysis will accommodate EPCs in three-MAP languages. Also, this rule, together with the rule of 3-to-2 advancement, will accommodate EPCs in two-MAP languages.

In this section, I show that it is equally possible to posit a union analysis of EPCs in Mapping Theory. First, I present the MT analysis of causatives. Then I show how this can easily be adapted to EPCs. I conclude that the union analysis of EPCs may be appropriate for some languages, especially those languages in which the EPC has an affectee reading. Thus, both types of analyses for EPCs, applicatives and unions, may be necessary cross-linguistically. Moreover, this opens the possibility for both types of EPCs existing within a single language. I make use of this possibility in the analysis for Kinyarwanda in the following section.

The Mapping Theory analysis of causatives has the following basic features.[14] First, the nominal arguments of the base (in RG terms, the "downstairs" clause) appear in brackets in the position of the theme/2 of the causative. Second, the causee is an outer (in RG terms, an "upstairs") 3 that is co-indexed with the 1 of the base.[15] Third, the MAPs in a causative union will be the number of MAPs of the base plus one per causative, up to the language's theshold. Finally, linking of GRs to MAPs in causatives proceeds in many languages in a right-to-left fashion, though elements of the base that are co-indexed with outer NPs will be skipped over.[16] We can briefly illustrate the effect of the causative rule in two-MAP versus three-MAP languages with the following data. In Swahili, a two-MAP language, a causative based on a transitive such as (19) will not involve the addition of any MAPs.

(19) *Baba a-li-m-fung-ish-a mtoto mlango.*
father he-TEMP-him-close-CAUS-IND child door
'The father made the child close the door.' (Driever 1976: 43)

Thus, as seen in the analysis given in (20), the causee but not the theme will be mapped, given the stipulation that linking in causatives proceeds in a right-to-left fashion.[17]

(20)

θ-Rs:	causer	agent	theme	causee
GRs:	1	$[1_i$	2]	3_i
	|		⟋	
MAPs:	A		B	

However, in the causative of a transitive in a three-MAP language such as Turkish, a MAP will be added, and thus both the theme and the causee can be mapped.

(21) *Dişçi mektub-u müdür-e imzala-t-tɨ.* (Comrie 1985: 323, 80)
dentist letter-ACC director-DAT sign-CAUS-PAST
'The dentist made the director sign the letter.'

(22)

θ-Rs:	causer	agent	theme	causee
GRs:	1	[1_i	2]	3_i
MAPs:	A	B	C	

A similar analysis can be given for EPCs. Paralleling the causee in causatives, there is an "affectee", that is, a non-subcategorized nominal that is affected by the action. The affectee, which is an outer 3, is co-indexed with the possessor.[18] In a two-MAP language such as Tzotzil (Aissen 1987: 126), the affectee links to the B MAP, as indicated by the first person absolutive agreement (B1) on the verb; note that in Tzotzil the possessor also determines NP-internal agreement, the first person ergative agreement (A1) on the theme *jol* 'head'.

(23) *Ch-i-s-toyilan-be j-jol.* (Aissen 1987: 126, 1)
INCMPL-B1-A3-keep.lifting-IO A1-head
'He kept lifting my head.'

(24)

θ-Rs:	agent	theme	affectee
GRs:	1	2[$POSS_i$]	3_i
MAPs:	A	B	

In a three-MAP language, such as Georgian, this analysis would entail the addition of a C MAP to which the affectee would link. Thus, data as in (25) would be represented as in (26).

(25) *vuban xels bavšvs.* (Harris 1976: 170, 25b)
I:wash:him:it:I:VC1 hand:DAT child:DAT
'I am washing the child's hands.'

(26)

θ-Rs:	agent	theme	affectee
GRs:	1	2[$POSS_i$]	3_i
MAPs:	A	B	C

Adopting the affectee analysis accounts for some interesting features of the EPCs found in many languages. First, EPCs in some languages are limited to inalienable possession or verbs of deprivation. There is clearly an element of affectedness in these cases. Also, examples with an external possessor, even when they involve alienable possession, often have a slightly different meaning than the equivalent sentence with only a genitive-marked possessor. For example, Gibson (1992) indicates this extra element of meaning by adding the benefactive to the English gloss for the example in (1a). Second, as Farrell (1994) points out, initializing the affectee as a 3 presumably pre-empts other NPs that would be 3s, given that the Stratal Uniqueness Law (Perlmutter and Postal 1983b) prohibits more than one occurrence of the same GR per level of structure. This explains the fact pointed out by Gibson (1992) that it is not possible to have an EPC in Chamorro if there is a goal NP in the clause. Aissen (1987) points out the same restriction in Tzotzil. In (27), there is a goal but no external possessor, hence the lack of first person absolutive agreement (B1) in the verb complex.

(27) *7a li Petul-e 7i-y-ak'-be j-chij li Xun-e.* (140, 43)
TOP the Petul-CL CMPL-A3-give-IO A1-sheep the Xun-CL
'Petul gave my sheep to Xun.'

The ungrammatical (28) contains both a goal *Xun*, which like other third person absolutives would determine Ø-agreement, and a first person affectee, which determines first person absolutive agreeement (B1) in the verb complex.[19]

(28) **7a li Petul-e, l-i-y-ak'-be j-chij li Xun-e.*
TOP the Petul-CL CMPL-B1-A3-give-IO A1-sheep the Xun-CL
'Petul gave my sheep to Xun.' (140, 44)

If we assume that a principle like the Stratal Uniqueness Law operates on the GR-tier in MT, then the ungrammaticality of data like (28) follows from the the co-occurence of the two 3s on the GR-tier.[20]

The possibility of an affectee analysis for both two-MAP and three-MAP languages suggests that all EPCs might be given this analysis. However, it seems precipitous to abandon the possessive applicative analysis for all languages. For example, Choctaw EPCs contrast with the data given above in that it is possible for a goal to co-occur with an external possessor in that language. Davies (1986: 54, 32) gives examples like the following:

(29) *Hattak-at ohoyo iskali am-im-a:-tok.*
man-NOM woman money 1DAT-3DAT-give-PAST
'The man gave my money to the woman.'

Davies' analysis of this example would be translated into MT as follows, since he argues that the possessor, but not the goal, is a final term:

(30) θ-Rs: agent theme goal
GRs: 1 2[POSS] 3
MAPs: A B C

Furthermore, Davies (1986: 55f) gives an explicit argument, based on reciprocals, that the possessor in Choctaw does not bear a core grammatical relation in the GR-tier.

Thus, we conclude that more than one type of analysis will probably be necessary in order to accommodate EPCs cross-linguistically. Further research is necessary to establish what the essential differences are between these two structures. From the MT viewpoint, either structure is available in both two-MAP and three-MAP languages. So the presence of an external possessor with dative trappings is insufficient justification for positing the affectee analysis in a language. This issue is discussed further in the next section.

4. The Kinyarwanda challenge

Kinyarwanda, according to the data and analyses of Kimenyi (1980), poses an interesting challenge for the view of EPCs given above. Unlike other languages in the sample, Kinyarwanda has two different EPCs. First, Kimenyi shows two ways of expressing inalienable (or part-whole) possession. Example (31a) shows inalienable possession internal to the NP, and (31b) is the corresponding EPC.

(31) a. *Umugóre y-a-shokoj-e umusatsi w'ûmugabo.* (103, 26a)
woman she-PAST-comb-ASP hair of.man
'The woman combed the hair of the man.'

b. *Umugóre y-a-shokoj-e umugabo umusatsi.* (103, 26b)
woman she-PAST-comb-ASP man hair
'The woman combed the man's hair.'

In (31b) both the possessor and the head have object properties. This sentence can be given the following analysis:

(32) θ-Rs: agent theme affectee
GRs: 1 2[POSS$_i$] 3$_i$
MAPs: A B C

In contrast, EPCs with alienable possessors, as in (33b), show different properties.

(33) a. *Umuhuûngu a-ra-som-a igitabo cy'ûmukoôbwa.*
boy he-PRES-read-ASP book of.girl
'The boy is reading the book of the girl.' (98, 5a)

b. *Umuhuûngu a-ra-som-er-a umukoôbwa igitabo.*
boy he-PRES-read-APPL-ASP girl book
'The boy is reading the girl's book.' (98, 5b)

Only the possessor and not the head exhibits object properties, a fact that suggests that EPCs with alienable possessors behave like possessive applicatives in two-MAP languages, represented as follows:[21]

(34) agent theme
1 2[POSS_i]
| /
A B
NOM ACC

Evidence for these two analyses comes from data involving a goal. As predicted, EPCs with inalienable possessors are not grammatical if a goal appears, since the 3 GR is pre-empted by the affectee:[22]

(35) **Umugóre á-r-éerek-a umuhuûngu umukoôbwa amagaru.*
woman she-PRES-show-ASP boy girl legs
'The woman is showing the girl's legs to the boy.' (100, 13b)

In contrast, a goal is possible in an EPC with an alienable possessor:

(36) *Umugóre á-r-éerek-er-a umukoôbwa ibitabo ábáana.*
woman she-PRES-show-APPL-ASP girl books children
'The woman is showing the girl's books to the children.'
(101, 15b)

(37) θ-Rs: agent theme goal
GRs: 1 2[POSS_i] 3
| / |
MAPs: A B C

Since the 3 is not otherwise required to initialize an affectee, a goal bearing the 3 GR is possible.

The problem for the Mapping Theory analysis lies in the fact that Kinyarwanda acts like a three-MAP language with respect to inalienable EPCs, but like a two-MAP language with respect to alienable EPCs. In fact, some constructions in Kinyarwanda can have as many as three NPs having object properties, for instance in clauses with initial 2, 3, and benefactive; or with 2, 3, and applied instrument. These constructions show that Kinyarwanda has a four-MAP threshold.[23] So the alienable EPC, which targets the B MAP rather than introducing a C MAP, is unexpectedly limited.

In this respect, alienable EPCs are like locative applicatives in Kinyarwanda, which also target the B MAP. For example, an applicative like (38) would be given the following representation, since only the locative — not the 2 or 3 — tests to have object properties.[24]

(38) *Umugóre a-rá-hé-er-á-mo ishuûri umuhuûngu ibitabo.*
woman she-PRES-give-APPL-ASP-in school boy books
'The woman is giving the books to the boy in the school.'
(96, 28a)

(39)

GRs:	1	2	3	LOC
MAPs:	A		B	

Locative applicatives contrast with instrumental applicatives such as (40), in which the instrument, the 2, and the 3 all test to have object properties.

(40) *Umugabo y-eerek-eesh-eje ábáana amashusho ímashiîni.*
man he-show-INSTR-ASP children pictures machine
'The man showed pictures to the children with the machine.'
(80, 5b)

Gerdts and Whaley (1991a,b, 1993a) argue for a union analysis for instrumental applicatives. They treat the instrument as an inanimate causee in the outer clause. This analysis is translated into MT as follows:[25]

(41)

θ-Rs:	causer	instr	theme	goal	causee
GRs:	1	$[1_i$	2	3]	3_i
MAPs:	A	B	C	D	

In sum, the generalization is that constructions involving union, that is, inalienable EPCs and instrumental applicatives, allow for the addition of MAPs up to the threshold. In contrast, true applicative structures, that is, alienable EPCs and locative applicatives, do not add MAPs to the structure, but target the B MAP. Clearly, some further exploration of applicative rule statements and the Last

MAP Principle are necessary in order to give a full treatment of Kinyarwanda.

In the interim, the following rule for alienable EPCs in Kinyarwanda fits the facts of the data:

(42) Kinyarwanda alienable EP construction:
  (i) Add an alienable possessor to the GR tier and suffix the applicative morpheme *-ir* to the predicate.
  (ii) Link the alienable possessor to the B MAP and cancel the C MAP, if necessary.

It will be necessary to cancel the C MAP if there is no suitable nominal to the right of the alienable possessor to link to the C MAP. This is a requirement of the Saturation Principle. This will be the case, for instance, in a double EPC. Kimenyi points out that it is possible to have both an alienable and an inalienable EP in the same clause, as in (43).

(43) *Umugabo y-a-vun-i-ye umugóre úmwáana ukuguru.*
man he-PAST-break-APPL-ASP woman child leg
'The man broke the woman's child's leg.' (99, 9c)

In this case, only the alienable possessor has object properties. Both the head and the inalienable possessor lack object properties. This suggests the following analysis.

(44)

θ-Rs:	agent	theme	affectee
GRs:	1	2[POSS$_i$]	3[POSS$_i$]
MAPs:	A	B	ℂ

The C MAP here, introduced by the inalienable possessor applicative, is not linked to a GR and thus is cancelled (indicated by outlining).[26]

MT can also easily accommodate examples that are claimed to have union followed by possessor ascension. For example, Kimenyi (1980) notes that a Kinyarwanda instrument in an instrumental applicative (signalled by the suffix *-iish*) can host a possessor ascension (signalled by the suffix *-ir*).

(45) *Umuhuûngu y-a-andi-iish-ir-ije umukoôbwa*
boy he-PAST-write-INSTR-APPL-ASP girl
íbárúwa íkárámu. (110, 12d)
letter pen
'The boy wrote the letter with the girl's pen.'

In MT terms, the instrumental applicative is treated as a union (see (41) above), as represented in the GR-tier in (46).

(46)	θ-Rs:	causer	instr	theme	causee
	GRs:	1	[1$_i$	2]	3[POSS$_j$]$_i$
	MAPs:	A		B	ℂ

We see in (46) that the alienable possessor (*umukoôbwa* 'girl') links to the B MAP and the C MAP is cancelled, per the rule in (42). This analysis is supported by data presented by Kimenyi showing that only the possessor, and not the theme or the instrument, has object properties.

The stipulative nature of (42) is not totally satisfying, especially given the goal of Mapping Theory to have as much as possible follow from universal principles rather than language-specific statements.[27] Nevertheless, the Kinyarwanda data provide proof that all instances of EPCs cannot be reduced to a single rule. There must be at least two different analyses for EPCs within Kinyarwanda, and presumably these will be available across languages.

5. Conclusion

In this paper, I have investigated External Possession Constructions in Mapping Theory as compared with Relational Grammar.[28] I considered the status of the external possessor in various languages and whether or not this can be predicted based on other aspects of the language. The Mapping Theory analysis of EPCs posits two types of structures: an applicative structure that links the possessor to a MAP, and a union structure that links an affectee coreferent to the possessor to the MAP. For each of these analyses, the rule proceeds differently in different languages, depending on the language's MAP threshold. In two-MAP languages the external possessor will link to the B MAP, while in three-MAP languages the external possessor will link to the C MAP. Under this view of EPCs, there are four possible alternative analyses, but only two are available in any given language.

The RG analysis is very similar to the MT analysis. In RG, two rules are posited, ascension and union. Ascension, claimed to follow the Relational Succession Law (3), results in 2-hood for the possessor. Under a possessor union analysis, the possessor revalues as a 3. However, additional mechanisms are needed to account for the attested data. For many two-MAP languages it is claimed that revaluation to 3 in a union is obligatorily followed by 3-to-2 advancement (Aissen 1987; Gibson 1992; Marlett 1986).[29] So, in fact, RG posits at least three structures for EPCs.[30] Furthermore, no attempt has been made in RG to predict what type of structure will exist in a particular language. Overall, we see that MT does a much better job of limiting the number of analyses necessary to accommodate EPCs cross-linguistically. Also, the MT analyses, since they are always bi-stratal, are simpler. From the point of view of an individual language, the only detail that needs to be stipulated is whether or not the EPC involves an affectee coreferent to the possessor.

Unfortunately, one language in the survey, Kinyarwanda, shows that the MT predictions are too constrained. Kinyarwanda is claimed to be a four-MAP language on the basis of data involving the co-occurrence of three object-like NPs. For example, the initial 2, 3, and benefactive simultaneously display object properties. Thus, we would expect in an EPC based on a transitive verb that the possessor would link to the C MAP. This is what occurs in the case of inalienable EPCs, which test to be affectee union structures in Kinyarwanda. However, in alienable EPCs, the possessor links to the B MAP, even if a C MAP is present in the structure. Thus, we must stipulate that Kinyarwanda EPCs require linking to to the B MAP, superceding the putatively universal Last Map Principle (8). In this respect, alienable EPCs are like locative applicatives, which also target the B MAP. We see that the generalization in Kinyarwanda is that unions obey the Last Map Principle, but applicatives systematically violate them. Further research within Mapping Theory may provide further insight into this quandary. In the interim, consolation can be found in the fact that all other adequate treatments of Kinyarwanda are similarly stipulative.

I conclude on the basis of the EPC data that Mapping Theory is much simpler and more constrained than Relational Grammar. Furthermore Mapping Theory more closely fits the empirical properties of EPCs in the world's languages. Finally, the crucial element of the MT analysis is the language's MAP threshold, which directly correlates to the morphosyntactic trappings of a language. Since these facts are readily accessible to the language learner, ascertaining a language's threshold is often a simple matter. Once the MAP parameter is set, many aspects of the language's syntax, including the status of an external possessor, will follow automatically. Thus, Mapping Theory is plausible from the point of view of learnability.

Acknowledgments

Thanks go to the many people who have given me comments on Mapping Theory, especially Judith Aissen, Cliff Burgess, Bill Davies, Katarzyna Dziwirek, Don Frantz, Pamela Munro, David Perlmutter, Carol Rosen, Lori Samkoe, Nathalie Schapansky, Lindsay Whaley, and many of the participants at the Oregon Conference on External Possession. I greatly appreciate the comments and corrections on this paper from Doris Payne and Charles Ulrich. Thanks also to Carla Hudson for helping compile the data used for Table 1. My research is supported by grants from the Social Science Humanities Research Council of Canada and the SFU President's Research Fund.

Abbreviations

Abbreviations used in this paper: 1 first person (in glosses), 1 subject (in diagrams and text), 2 direct object (in diagrams and text), 3 third person (in glosses), 3 indirect object (in diagrams and text), 4 oblique object, A set A agreement affix (ergative), ACC accusative, ADV advancement, Agr agreement, APPL applicative, ASC possessor ascension marker, ASP aspect, AUX auxiliary, B set B agreement affix (absolutive), BEN benefactive, C agreement prefix (class C NP), CL clitic, CMPL completive aspect, CAUS causative, DAT dative, DET determiner, ERG ergative, GR grammatical relation, I verb series I, II verb series II, INCMPL incompletive aspect, IND indicative, INSTR instrument, IO indirect object, LOC locative, NOM nominative, OBJ object, OBL oblique case marker, PN proper noun unmarked case marker, POSS possessor, PRES present, PAST past, S singular, SUB subject, TEMP temporal marker, TRANS transitive, VC1 verb class 1.

Notes

1 I am limiting the discussion here to EPCs in which the host is a theme in a transitive clause. EPCs based on themes in unaccusative clauses are also possible in many languages. The analyses discussed here straightforwardly handle these constructions. For Relational Grammar and Mapping Theory treatments of this type of EPC in Korean, see Gerdts (1992c, 1993) and the references therein. Also, it has been claimed for some languages that certain oblique nominals can host Possessor Ascension. For alternative treatments of this type of EPC see Davies (1997) and Kimenyi (1980) for Kinyarwanda, and Gerdts (1993) and Maling and Kim (1992) for Korean. Finally, some languages have external possessors in topic or focus positions. In case-marking languages, this usually appears as a double nominative construction. For an RG analysis of this construction in Korean, see Youn (1989). Treatments of topic, focus, relative clause, and cleft constructions have yet to be posited for Mapping Theory.

2 Due to space limitations, I do not repeat the evidence given by the authors for the analyses I refer to. The reader should consult the orginal sources for detailed arguments.

3 Throughout this paper, I am adopting Rosen's (1990) analysis of Southern Tiwa.

4 See Davies (1997) for a discussion of the current status of the RSL.

5 Analyses summarized in the table were taken from the following sources: Albanian (Hubbard 1985), Blackfoot (Frantz 1978, 1981, personal communication), Cebuano (Bell 1983), Chamorro (Crain 1979; Gibson 1992), Choctaw (Davies 1986), French (Legendre 1986; Postal 1990), Georgian (Harris 1976, 1981), German (Wilkinson 1983), Halkomelem (Gerdts 1988, 1989, 1992a), Ika (Frank 1990), Indonesian (Chung 1983; Kana 1986), Kalkatungu (Blake 1982), Kinyarwanda (Gerdts and Whaley 1991a, 1991b, 1993a, 1993b; Kimenyi 1980), Korean (Gerdts 1992c, 1993, and references therein), Ojibwa (Rhodes 1976, 1990; Perlmutter and Rhodes 1989), Okanagan (Hébert 1982), Sierra Popoluca (Marlett 1986), Southern Tiwa (Allen and Frantz 1983; Allen et al. 1990; Rosen 1990), Spanish (González 1988; Tuggy 1980), Tzotzil

(Aissen 1979, 1983, 1987), Warlpiri (Nash 1986), Yimas (Foley 1991). The authors' original analyses were modified in three cases. Cebuano was reanalyzed as an ergative language following Gerdts (1987), Kinyarwanda as a language with three distinct object positions (direct object, indirect object, and oblique object) following Gerdts and Whaley (1991a, 1991b, 1993a, 1993b), and Southern Tiwa as a non-advancement language following Rosen (1990).

6 See Gerdts (1991) for an RG treatment of the two types of case.

7 Furthermore, as Gerdts (1994) argues, nominals that are linked to MAPs are generally more "accessible" than other nominals. For example, they can often be antecedents or targets of reflexives, be relativized, float quantifiers, be passivized, or, sometimes, be raised. In the two-MAP language Nubian (Abdel-Hafiz 1988), 1s and 2s antecede reflexives and raise; in the three-MAP language Albanian (Hubbard 1985), 1s, 2s, and 3s float quantifiers; in the four-MAP language Kinyarwanda (Kimenyi 1980) 1s, 2s, 3s, and BENs relativize and passivize.

8 This paper can only give a brief look at MT and, furthermore, does not compare it with other similar theories. Woolford (1986), which makes use of a tree notation, is perhaps the closest theory in its intention, while Yip et al. (1987), which makes use of linear order, is the closest in notation. Linking Theory (Kiparsky 1988) has greatly influenced the MT rules of marked associations.

9 In developing Mapping Theory, I have relied heavily on the RG treatment of lexical semantics. In RG, it is usually assumed that there is no cross-linguistically valid one-to-one mapping between thematic relations and initial grammatical relations, and therefore these levels are kept distinct. If it proves to be possible to state universally valid rules of argument structure based on thematic relations, perhaps along the lines of Farrell (1994), then the level of grammatical relations will be unnecessary in Mapping Theory.

10 These principles for linking GRs to MAPs are fairly typical in linking theories. See, for example, Ostler (1980), Woolford (1986), and Yip et al. (1987).

11 Thus, the Mapping Theory equivalent to the RG concept of chômeur is simply a non-linked argument. See Farrell (1994) for a discussion of revising RG along these lines.

12 Note that including the possessor in brackets in the GR tier is used only for EPCs. Normally, information within NPs is irrelevant to clause-level GRs and is thus not spelled out in MT.

13 See Blake (1990: 123f) for a summary of Rosen's analysis.

14 The MT analysis of causatives was developed in conjunction with Cliff Burgess. See Burgess (1995) for a discussion of causatives and double causatives in a variety of languages.

15 Analyses of causatives as control structures have been posited elsewhere, including recently Guasti (1996).

16 Linking in causatives in some languages is left-to-right, as discussed in Burgess (1995). For example, in Ilokano the theme rather than the causee links to the B MAP in a causative. Thus, a parameter for the direction of linking in causatives is necessary.

17 Of course, the causer is always linked to the A MAP in an active causative. Thus, the linking parameter will only affect other nominals in the causative.

18 Tuggy (1980) and Farrell (1994: 194f) make a similar claim within RG. Tuggy posits that the affectee is an initial oblique in Spanish. Farrell posits that the affectee is an initial 3 in Chamorro.

19 Alternatively, it could be claimed that Tzotzil lacks a means for licensing non-linked 3s, so that any structure where a 3 could not link would be prohibited. Goals in simple ditransitives are always linked to a MAP. Under this analysis, 3s would differ from 2s, which regularly appear

as non-linked nominals in applicative and antipassive constructions.

20 Farrell (1994) says that the affectee analysis is inappropriate for Tzotzil because Aissen (1987) makes it clear that not all external possessors, especially inanimate ones, can be interpreted to have an affectee meaning. Underlying this comment is the assumption that a language will have a single analysis for all EPCs. I claim here that it is possible for a language to have both a possessor applicative and a possessor union analysis for EPCs, depending in part on semantic factors such as affectedness. Note, however, that in a two-MAP language such as Tzotzil, the two types of EPCs would be associated with identical surface structures. Thus, additional evidence would be necessary to distinguish the two analyses. Furthermore, Farrell's interpretation of affectedness, which seems to require a cognitively aware entity, may be too strong a concept to characterize the outer 3 in languages such as Tzotzil. Something more like "involvement" might be more appropriate. Much more research is necessary both cross-linguistically and within individual languages to determine the range of semantic effects of both types of EPC constructions (see various papers in this volume).

21 RG analyses of these phenomena have been given in Kimenyi (1980), Bickford (1986), and Davies (1997). The idea that alienable external possessors are final 2s but inalienable external possessors are final 3s derives from Bickford. The idea that inalienable EPCs should be analyzed as union constructions derives from Davies.

22 Note, that it is not possible simply to say that the reason this example is ungrammatical is that Kinyarwanda has no means to express a 3 that is not linked. Non-linked 3s appear in locative applicatives (38), as seen in the representation in (39).

23 This is discussed further in Gerdts (1992b). In Gerdts and Whaley (1991b, 1993a, 1993b), the case is made for adding a fourth term relation, a 4, on the basis of the Kinyarwanda evidence.

24 The RG analysis given in Gerdts and Whaley (1991b, 1993a, 1993b) for locative applicatives is that they involve locative-to-3-to-2 advancement. The stipulation that this is a two-step advancement has the same effect as the MT stipulation that the locative links to the B MAP. That is, neither the theme nor the goal will exhibit object properties.

25 Gerdts and Whaley (1993a) argue that there are three object positions having term status in Kinyarwanda: direct object (2), indirect object (3), and oblique object (4). They propose the following version of the instrumental revaluation rule:

(i) Instrumentals are revalued to the term relation immediately below the relation of the lowest ranked nominal in the clause on the hierarchy $1 \rangle 2 \rangle 3 \rangle 4$.

This means that the instrumental will take the first available position on the hierarchy. So, for example, the instrument will be a 3 if the corresponding non-applicative is transitive and a 4 if the corresponding non-applicative is ditransitive. This outcome would be effected automatically in MT under a union analysis given the claim that Kinyarwanda is a four-MAP language, since unions, like applicatives, add MAPs up to threshold.

26 Note that neither the 2 (*ukuguru* 'leg') nor the inalienable possessor (*úmwáana* 'child') can link to the C MAP, due to the No Crossing Lines Principle.

27 The MT analysis of EPCs actually fares no worse in this respect than analyses in other frameworks. For example, Baker's (1988) Government/Binding treatment of Kinyarwanda EPCs limits the discussion of the inalienable possessor construction and the interaction of the two types of EPCs to a footnote.

28 Another potential difference between MT and RG concerns restrictions on the host in EPCs. In MT, hosts are limited to NPs represented in the GR-tier, that is, to arguments of the predicate. RG's Host Limitation Law (Perlmutter and Postal 1983a) limited hosts to terms. However,

Davies (1997) proposes that either the notion "term" be parameterized across languages or that hosts be limited to arguments of the predicate. Assuming this concept can be given a formal definition in RG, there is no real difference between MT and RG in this regard.

29 Intermediate structures are often posited in the analysis of an EPC in order to satisfy the laws of RG, but without empirical support from the language in question.

30 Actually the count is higher if one considers other possible analyses proposed in RG, such as control-style union (Farrell 1994), union with revaluation to 2 (Gibson 1992), affectee-to-3 advancement (Tuggy 1980), and possessor ascension-to-3 (Bickford 1986).

References

Abdel-Hafiz, Ahmed S. 1988. *A Reference Grammar of Kunuz Nubian.* Ph.D. dissertation, State University of New York — Buffalo.

Aissen, Judith L. 1979. "Possessor Ascension in Tzotzil." In L. Martin (ed.), *Papers in Mayan Linguistics.* Columbia, Missouri: Lucas Bros, 89–108.

Aissen, Judith L. 1983. "Indirect Object Advancement in Tzotzil." In D. M. Perlmutter (ed.), *Studies in Relational Grammar 1.* Chicago: the University of Chicago Press, 272–302.

Aissen, Judith L. 1987. *Tzotzil Clause Structure.* Dordrecht: D. Reidel Publishing Company.

Allen, Barbara J., and Donald G. Frantz. 1983. "Advancements and Verb Agreement in Southern Tiwa." In D. M. Perlmutter (ed.), *Studies in Relational Grammar 1.* Chicago: the University of Chicago Press, 303–314.

Allen, Barbara J., Donald G. Frantz, Donna B. Gardiner, David M. Perlmutter. 1990. "Verb Agreement, Possessor Ascension, and Multistratal Representation in Southern Tiwa." In P. M. Postal and B. D. Joseph (eds.), *Studies in Relational Grammar 3.* Chicago: the University of Chicago Press, 321–383.

Baker, Mark C. 1988. *Incorporation: A Theory of Grammatical Function Changing.* Chicago: The University of Chicago Press.

Bell, Sarah J. 1983. "Advancements and Ascensions in Cebuano." In D. M. Perlmutter (ed.), *Studies in Relational Grammar 1.* Chicago: the University of Chicago Press, 143–218.

Bickford, J. Albert. 1986. "Possessor Ascension in Kinyarwanda." *Papers from the Twenty-Second Regional Meeting of the Chicago Linguistic Society.* Chicago: University of Chicago, 129–143.

Blake, Barry J. 1982. "The Absolutive: Its Scope in English and Kalkatungu." In Paul J. Hopper and Sandra A. Thompson (eds.), *Studies in Transitivity* [*Syntax and Semantics* 15]. New York: Academic Press, 71–94.

Blake, Barry J. 1990. *Relational Grammar.* London: Routledge.

Burgess, Cifford S. 1995. "Mapping Multiple Causatives." M.A. thesis, Simon Fraser University.

Chung, Sandra. 1983. "An Object-Creating Rule in Bahasa Indonesia." In D. M. Perlmutter (ed.), *Studies in Relational Grammar 1.* Chicago: the University of Chicago Press, 219–271.

Comrie, Bernard 1985. "Causative Verb Formation and Other Verb-Deriving Morphology." In T. Shopen (ed.), *Language Typology and Syntactic Description,* Vol. III. Cambridge: Cambridge University Press, 309–348.

Crain, Catherine. 1979. "Advancement and Ascension to Direct Object in Chamorro." *Linguistic Notes From La Jolla* 6, 3–32.

Davies, William D. 1986. *Choctaw Verb Agreement and Universal Grammar.* Dordrecht: D. Reidel Publishing Company.

Davies, William D. 1997. "Relational Succession in Kinyarwanda Possessor Ascension." *Lingua* 101: 89–114.

Davies, William D., and Carol Rosen. 1988. "Unions as Multi-predicate Clauses." *Language* 64: 52–88.

Driever, Dorothea. 1976. *Aspects of a Case Grammar of Mombasa Swahili.* [*Hamburger Philologische Studien* 43]. Hamburg: Helmut Buske Verlag.

Dubinsky, Stanley, and Carol Rosen. n.d. *A Bibliography on Relational Grammar through May 1987 with Selected Titles on Lexical Functional Grammar.* Bloomington: Indiana University Linguistics Club.

Everett, Daniel L. 1988. "Clitics, Case, and Word Order in Yagua." *Summer Institute of Linguistics/University of North Dakota Work Papers* 32, 93–142.

Farrell, Patrick Michael. 1994. *Thematic Relations, Relational Networks, and Multistratal Representations.* New York: Garland.

Foley, William A. 1991. *The Yimas Language of New Guinea.* Stanford: Stanford University Press.

Frank, Paul. 1990. *Ika Syntax. Studies in the Languages of Columbia.* Dallas: Summer Institute of Linguistics and the University of Texas at Arlington.

Frantz, Donald. 1978. "Antipassive in Blackfoot." *Papers of the Ninth Algonquian Conference,* 195–203.

Frantz, Donald. 1981. *Grammatical Relations in Universal Grammar.* Bloomington: Indiana University Linguistics Club.

Gerdts, Donna B. 1987. "Antipassives and Causatives in Ilokano: Evidence for an Ergative Analysis of Philippine Languages." In R. McGinn (ed), *Studies in Austronesian Linguistics,* 295–321. Athens: Ohio University Press.

Gerdts, Donna B. 1988. *Object and Absolutive in Halkomelem Salish.* New York: Garland.

Gerdts, Donna B. 1989. "Relational Parameters of Reflexives: The Halkomelem Evidence." In D. B. Gerdts and K. Michelson (eds.), *Theoretical Perspectives on Native American Languages.* New York: State University of New York Press, 259–280.

Gerdts, Donna B. 1990. "Relational Visibility." In K. Dziwirek, P. Farrell, and E. Mejías-Bikandi (eds.), *Grammatical Relations: a Cross-Theoretical Perspective.* Stanford: Center for the Study of Language and Information, 199–214.

Gerdts, Donna B. 1991. "An Outline of a Relational Theory of Case." *Working Papers in Linguistics,* Vol. 1, 25–53, Simon Fraser University.

Gerdts, Donna B. 1992a. "Mapping Halkomelem Grammatical Relations." *Linguistics* 31: 591–622.

Gerdts, Donna B. 1992b. "Morphologically-mediated Relational Profiles." In L. Buszard-Welcher et al. (eds.), *Proceedings of the Eighteenth Annual Meeting of the Berkeley Linguistics Society,* Berkeley: University of California, 322–337.

Gerdts, Donna B. 1992c. "The Syntax of Case-Marked Possessors in Korean." In C. Lee (ed), *Proceedings of the Korean Syntax & Semantics Workshop (Linguistic Society of America Summer Institute, University of California, Santa Cruz, July 1991),* 11–26.

Gerdts, Donna B. 1993. "Mapping Korean Grammatical Relations." *The Fifth (1993) Harvard Symposium on Korean Linguistics,* 299–318.

Gerdts, Donna B. 1994. "Morphosyntactic Argument Structure and NP Accessibility." Paper presented at the Canadian Linguistic Association, Calgary, Alberta.

Gerdts, Donna B. 1995. "The A/B Parameter: A Typology of Unergatives, Passives, and Antipassives." In *Proceedings of the 1995 Annual Conference of the Canadian Linguistic Association, Toronto Working Papers in Linguistics*, 191–201.

Gerdts, Donna B., and Lindsay Whaley. 1991a. "Locatives vs. Instrumentals in Kinyarwanda." In K. Hubbard (ed.), *Proceedings of the Seventeenth Annual Meeting of the Berkeley Linguistics Society: Special Session on African Language Structures.* Berkeley: University of California, 87–97.

Gerdts, Donna B., and Lindsay Whaley. 1991b. "Two Types of Oblique Applicatives in Kinyarwanda." In K. Hunt et al. (eds.), *Proceedings of the Western Conference on Linguistics,* Vol. 4, California State University, Fresno, 138–151.

Gerdts, Donna B., and Lindsay Whaley. 1993a. "Kinyarwanda Applicatives and Some Universal Laws." In T. Heift and P. McFetridge (eds.), *Working Papers in Linguistics,* Vol. 2, Simon Fraser University, 59–88.

Gerdts, Donna B., and Lindsay Whaley 1993b. "Kinyarwanda Applicatives and the 2–AEX." In C. Costas et al. (eds.), *Papers from the Twenty-Eighth Regional Meeting of the Chicago Linguistic Society.* Chicago: University of Chicago, 322–337.

Gibson, Jeanne. 1992. *Clause Union in Chamorro and in Universal Grammar.* New York: Garland.

González, Nora. 1988. *Object and Raising in Spanish.* New York: Garland.

Guasti, M. 1996. "Semantic Restrictions in Romance Causatives and the Incorporation Approach." *Linguistic Inquiry* 27.2: 294–313.

Harris, Alice C. 1976. *Grammatical Relations in Modern Georgian.* Ph.D. dissertation, Harvard University.

Harris, Alice C. 1981. *Georgian Syntax.* Cambridge: Cambridge University Press.

Hébert, Yvonne M. 1982. *Transitivity in (Nicola Lake) Okanagan.* Ph.D. dissertation, University of British Columbia.

Hubbard, Philip L. 1985. *The Syntax of the Albanian Verb Complex.* New York: Garland Publishing, Inc.

Kana, Marit Ann. 1986. *Grammatical Relations in Bahasa Indonesia.* Ph.D. dissertation, Cornell University.

Kimenyi, Alexandre. 1980. *A Relational Grammar of Kinyarwanda.* Berkeley: University of California Press.

Kiparsky, Paul. 1988. "Agreement and Linking Theory." Paper presented at Chicago Linguistic Society 24.

Legendre, Géraldine. 1986. *Topics in French Syntax.* Ph.D. Dissertation, University of California, San Diego.

Maling, Joan, and Soowon Kim. 1992. "Case Assignment in the Inalienable Possession Construction in Korean." *Journal of East Asian Linguistics* 1: 37–68.

Marlett, Stephen A. 1986. "Syntactic Levels and Multiattachment in Sierra Popoluca." *International Journal of American Linguistics* 52: 359–387.

Nash, David. 1986. *Topics in Warlpiri Grammar.* New York: Garland Publishing, Inc.

Ostler, Nicholas. 1980. *A Theory of Case Linking and Agreement.* Bloomington: Indiana University Linguistics Club.

Özkaragöz, İnci Z. 1986. *The Relational Structure of Turkish Syntax.* Ph.D. dissertation, University of California, San Diego.

Perlmutter, David M., and Paul M. Postal. 1983a. "The Relational Succession Law." In D. M. Perlmutter (ed.), *Studies in Relational Grammar 1.* Chicago: the University of Chicago Press, 30–80.

Perlmutter, David M., and Paul M. Postal. 1983b. "Some Proposed Laws of Basic Clause Structure." In D. M. Perlmutter (ed.), *Studies in Relational Grammar 1.* Chicago: the University of Chicago Press, 81–128.

Perlmutter, David M., and Rhodes, Richard. 1989. "Thematic-syntactic Alignments in Ojibwa: Evidence for Subject-Object Reversal." Paper presented at the Linguistic Society of America Summer Institute, Tucson, Arizona.

Postal, Paul M. 1990. "French Indirect Object Demotion." In P. M. Postal and B. D. Joseph (eds.), *Studies in Relational Grammar 3.* Chicago: the University of Chicago Press, 104–200.

Rhodes, Richard A. 1976. *The Morphosyntax of the Central Ojibwa Verb.* Ph.D. dissertation, University of Michigan.

Rhodes, Richard A. 1990. "Ojibwa Secondary Objects." In K. Dziwirek, P. Farrell, and E. Mejías-Bikandi (eds.), *Grammatical Relations: a Cross-Theoretical Perspective.* Stanford: Center for the Study of Language and Information, 401–414.

Rosen, Carol. 1987. "Possessives and the Internal Structure of Nominals." Presented at the 3rd Biennial Conference on Relational Grammar and Grammatical Relations, University of Iowa.

Rosen, Carol G. 1990. "Rethinking Southern Tiwa: the Geometry of a Triple-Agreement Language." *Language* 66: 669–713.

Tuggy, David. 1980. "Ethical Dative and Possessor Omission Si, Possessor Ascension No!" *Workpapers of the Summer Instititute of Linguistics* 24, University of North Dakota, 97–141.

Wilkinson, Edwin. 1983. "Indirect Object Advancement in German." *Proceedings of the Eleventh Annual Meeting of the Berkeley Linguistics Society,* University of California, Berkeley.

Woolford, Ellen. 1986. "The Distribution of Empty Nodes in Navajo: A Mapping Approach." *Linguistic Inquiry* 17.2: 301–330.

Yip, Moira, Joan Maling, and Ray Jackendoff. 1987. "Case in Tiers." *Language* 63.2: 217–250.

Youn, Cheong. 1989. *Korean Multiple Case Constructions: A Relational Account.* Ph.D. dissertation, State University of New York at Buffalo.

PART IV

External Possession, Topics, and Subjects

External Possessor and Logical Subject in Tz'utujil

Judith Aissen
University of California, Santa Cruz

1. Introduction

This paper argues that one important function of external possessor (EP) constructions is to present the possessor as *logical subject* (also sometimes termed *theme* or *topic*). The discussion to follow is based on Tz'utujil,[1] a language in which logical subjects are easy to identify. Analyzing Tz'utujil external possessors (EPRs) as logical subjects makes it possible to correlate two differences between Tz'utujil and English. The first is that while English has only one subject position, Tz'utujil can plausibly be said to have two. Dayley (1985) describes Tz'utujil as being basically VOS, but recognizes SVO as an alternative order. Grimes (1996) classifies Tz'utujil as SVO. The other difference is that Tz'utujil has no lexeme corresponding to the English verb *have*. I suggest that the absence of such a lexeme is related to the word order options Tz'utujil makes available.

In explicating these differences between Tz'utujil and English, it is necessary to tease apart two notions of subject: one is a grammatical function which has to do with phenomena like nominative case and control of agreement. Subject in this sense is the grammatically most prominent nominal in the clause. The other is a cognitive function which has to do with predication. In this sense, which is closer to the Aristotelian sense, the subject "serves to identify or designate what is being discussed".[2] I refer to these as the *grammatical* and the *logical* subject, respectively. The distinction is immediately useful in thinking about the two subject positions in Tz'utujil: one of these, the sentence-final position, is the position for the *grammatical* subject; the other, the sentence-initial position, is the position for the *logical* subject. An important characteristic of Tz'utujil then is the fact that it structurally disassociates these two notions of *subject* in a very visible way. In this respect, Tz'utujil is like Hungarian (Szabolcsi

1994; Kiss 1994) and unlike English. In English, the two notions are largely conflated, with the grammatical subject serving to identify the logical subject.

This difference has significant consequences for the grammar and lexica of the two languages. In English, presentation of some argument as logical subject requires that it be grammatical subject. Accordingly, English has relatively rich syntactic and lexical resources for realizing a range of arguments as grammatical subject (e.g., passive, raising, alternate syntactic frames for many verbs). In Tz'utujil, the realization of logical subject by-passes the grammatical subject. Tz'utujil can thus do without some of the syntactic and lexical resources which in English increase access to grammatical subject position. From this perspective, English *have* can be seen as the lexical means for realizing the semantic possessor as grammatical subject so that it can function as logical subject (Schafer 1997). Given the articulation in English of the logical subject as grammatical subject, English needs such a verb. But Tz'utujil does not, since the possessor can be realized as logical subject without being grammatical subject.

The remainder of the paper grounds these claims more firmly. Section 2 explains how grammatical subject and logical subject are structurally realized in Tz'utujil. Section 3 turns to possessors, and their structural realization as genitives and as logical subjects. It is the realization of possessors as logical subjects which instantiates the EP construction in Tz'utujil. Sections 4 and 5 survey the core instances of this construction in Tz'utujil. Section 6 shows that EPRs are generally limited to unaccusative clauses, but concludes that what is involved has more to do with conceptual semantics or pragmatics than with syntax. Section 7 concludes with a brief discussion of the cross-linguistic implications of the analysis presented here.

2. Structural realization of grammatical and logical subject

Following Dayley (1985: 302), I assume that basic word order in Tz'utujil is V(O)S X. This is exemplified for an intransitive clause in (1a), and for a transitive in (1b). These examples also illustrate that Tz'utujil is a head-marking language: the verb agrees with both subject and object, and possessed nouns agree with their genitives.[3]

(1) a. *X-kam-i ja nuu-tz'ii' rmal b'enéena.*
CMPL-die-IV the A1SG-dog because:of poison
'My dog died because of poison.' Dayley 302

b. *X-uu-loq' ka'i' lı́ibra chuum nuu-tee' iiwiir.*
CMPL-A3SG-buy two pound lime A1SG-mother yesterday
'My mother bought two pounds of lime yesterday.'
Dayley 305

The agreement system is ergative with one set of prefixes (Set A) cross-referencing transitive subjects (ergatives) and a distinct set (Set B) cross-referencing intransitive subjects and direct objects (absolutives). Third person absolutives are not overtly cross-referenced. The same Set A markers also cross-reference genitives on possessed nouns, as in (1a, b). Personal pronouns are generally not pronounced in Tz'utujil. Thus *xkami* 'she/he/it died' and *xuuloq'* 's/he bought it' are perfectly normal. Likewise, the genitives in (1a, b) are not pronounced because they are personal pronouns.

I assume further that the grammatical functions relevant to this paper are phrase-structurally realized, and in terms which can be explicated through Xbar theory. In Xbar theory, all phrases are endocentric, with the head (X) projecting two levels of structure (X′, XP) (Chomsky 1986). As represented in Figure 1, the immediate sisters of the head are its *complements*; the sister of its first projection is its *specifier*. (Linear order is irrelevant here.)

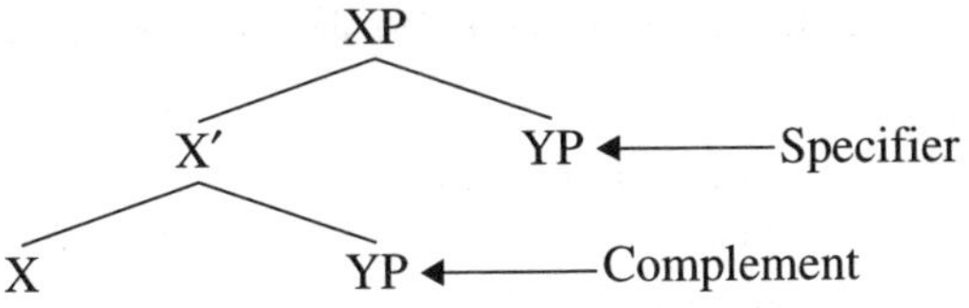

Figure 1: *X-bar Schema*

Basic clause structure in Tz'utujil can be represented by the tree in Figure 2. The basic clause consists of a verb with complement and specifier. The grammatical subject is the specifier of the VP (SpecVP), the grammatical object is the complement of V (CompV). Both complement and specifier of V occur to the right of the head, yielding the VOS order seen in (1).

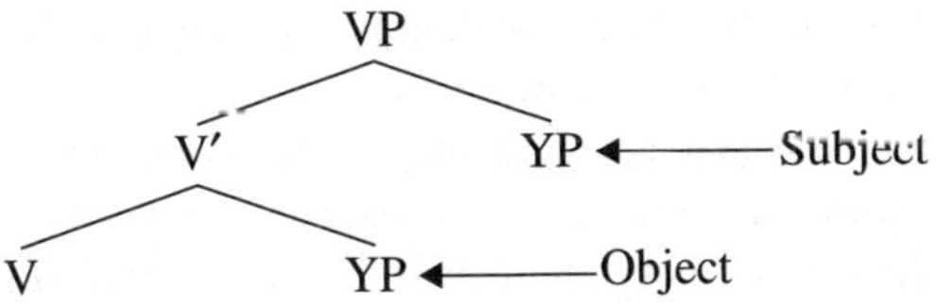

Figure 2: *Tz'utujil Clause Structure*

Visible correlates of grammatical subjecthood in Tz'utujil are thus word order and agreement: control of Set A (ergative) agreement in the case of transitive subjects, and of Set B (absolutive) agreement in the case of intransitive subjects.

As noted earlier, many clauses in Tz'utujil are not verb-initial, but begin with a nominal constituent (bold-faced), one which is most frequently the grammatical subject.

(2) a. ***Je'ee' wa' ch'uu'*** *qas ee utz.*
these fish very B3PL good
'These fish are very good.' Dayley 303

b. ***Ja r-me'al*** *x-ok-i Malincha.*
the A3SG-daughter CMPL-enter-IV Malincha
'His daughter played the role of Malincha.'

c. ***Jar ijqa'n*** *x-uu-ya' rexkeej ch-we.*
the burden CMPL-A3SG-give cramp to-A1SG
'The burden gave me cramps.' Dayley 282

It is the frequent association of grammatical subject with this sentence-initial position which apparently led Grimes (1996) to classify Tz'utujil as an SVO language. But in fact, the sentence-initial position can be occupied by a variety of non-subjects: (3a) shows the direct object in this position, and (3b) shows an oblique:

(3) a. ***Ja w-xaayiil*** *x-in-k'am el San Jwaan.*
the A1SG-wife CMPL-A1SG-take DIR San Juan
'I took my wife to San Juan.' Dict. 198

b. ***Inin*** *x-yaa'-i ja paq ch-we.*
I CMPL-give:PASS-IV the money to-A1SG
'The money was given to me.' Dayley 328

These sentence-initial elements are instances of what I term *logical subject.* I understand logical subject in the sense of Kuroda (1992), who takes logical subject-predicate structure to express the *categorical* judgment of Franz Brentano, as further elaborated by Anton Marty (for references and discussion, see Kuroda; also Horn (1989: 510ff) and Ladusaw (1994)).[4] A categorical judgment involves two acts: first the turning of the mind to an identifiable entity, and second, the ascription of a property to that entity.[5] In a sense which will become clearer when we turn to EPRs, presenting some nominal as logical subject imposes a certain perspective on the situation described, one in which it is construed as a property of the logical subject. In contrast to the categorical judgment is a second judgment type, termed *thetic*. A thetic judgment involves a single act, the simple apprehension of a situation, rather than the dual act involved in a categorical judgment.

The existential sentence is a clear example of a sentence type which expresses a thetic judgment, e.g., *There are mice in the basement.* While the sentence which expresses a thetic judgment may contain a grammatical subject, it will contain no logical subject.

The nature of categorical and thetic judgments leads to certain expectations regarding definiteness. One is that in a sentence expressing a categorical judgment, the logical subject will be definite. This is because the logical subject names the *identifiable* entity involved in such a judgment. The other is that in a sentence expressing a thetic judgment, there should be no corresponding definiteness restriction on the *grammatical* subject. We will show shortly that these expectations are realized in Tz'utujil.

There is another preverbal position which must be distinguished from that occupied by the logical subject. This second position is occupied by a focused element, an interrogative, or an indefinite (Dayley 1985). (I refer to all three as *focus.*) There are syntactic differences between logical subject and focus (Aissen 1992). First, when both occur, the logical subject precedes the focus (underlined), as in (4):

(4) ***Jar iinin*** *xa itzeeneem n-samaajiij.*
the I only sorcery INCMPL:A1SG-work
'I work only sorcery.' Dayley 308

Second, the negation *ma* follows the logical subject, as in (5a), but precedes the focus (5b):

(5) a. ***Ja Taa'*** *ma t-uu-ya' r-paq r-xaayiil.*
the Señor NEG ASP-A3SG-give A3–money A3SG-wife
'The Señor doesn't give money to his wife.' Dayley 314

b. *Ma ch'ooy ta x-tij-ow-i ja kéeso.*
NEG rat IRR CMPL-eat-FOC-IV the cheese
'It wasn't a rat that ate the cheese.' Dayley 322

And third, when the subject of a transitive clause is preverbal, the form of the verb distinguishes logical subject from focus. Focus of the transitive subject requires the special 'focus' verb form found in (5b). The focus verb carries the suffix *-o(w)* and bears no Set A marker. No special verb is required (or allowed) when the logical subject corresponds to transitive subject (cf. (5a)).

Following Aissen (1992), I assume that both the logical subject and the focus are realized structurally within specifier positions of functional projections above VP. There are two such projections, one headed by Inflection ('I') and one by Complementizer ('C'), arranged as shown in Figure 3. The specifiers of both CP and IP occur to the left of their heads. Specifier of CP is occupied by the logical subject,[6] while specifier of IP is occupied by the focus. Negation intervenes between the two specifier positions:

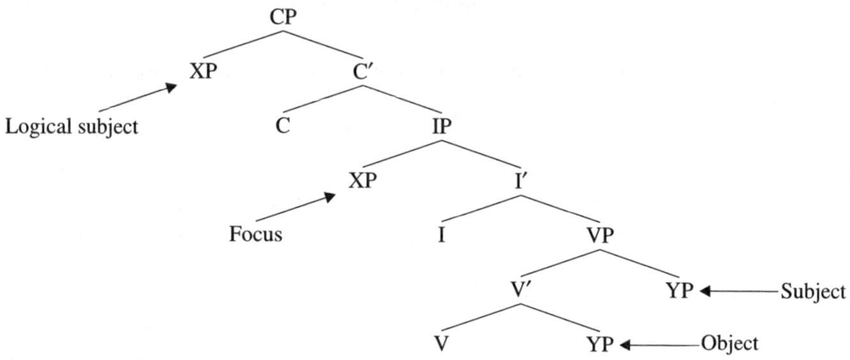

Figure 3: *Tz'utujil Clause with Functional Projections*

Now we can show that (preverbal) logical subject in Tz'utujil is in fact subject to a definiteness restriction, while the (postverbal) grammatical subject is not. The examples in (6) show first that there is no definiteness restriction on the grammatical subject (bold-faced):

(6) a. *X-in-ruu-ti'* ***jun kaab'***.
CMPL-B1SG-A3SG-eat a wasp
'A wasp bit me.'
b. *N-oq-ee-ki-to'-a'* ***oxi' achi'ii'*** *pa jach'*.
INCMPL-B1PL-DIR-A3PL-help-TV three men at harvest
'Three men are coming to help us at harvest.'

However, indefinites cannot occur as logical subjects:[7]

(7) a. ****Jun kaab'*** *x-in-ruu-ti'*.
a wasp CMPL-B1SG-A3SG-bite
('A wasp bit me.')
b. ?***Oxi' achi'ii'*** *n-oq-ee-ki-to'-a'* *pa jach'*.
three men INCMPL-B1PL-DIR-A3PL-help-TV at harvest
('Three men are going to help us with the harvest.')
c. ****Ni majuun*** *x-uu-tij* *ja way.*
no one CMPL-A3SG-eat the tortilla
('No one ate the tortillas.')

(The use of plain transitive verbs in these examples, rather than focus forms, assures that the bold-faced nominals are interpreted as logical subjects. Replacing these verbs with focus forms makes (7a–c) grammatical.) This restriction follows from the conception of logical subject sketched earlier. A categorical judgment ascribes a property to an identifiable entity, and the logical subject names this entity. But indefinites at best introduce discourse referents into the discourse; they do not denote identifiable entities. Thus they are inappropriate logical subjects, and this is why examples (7a–c) are ungrammatical. Examples without a logical subject (e.g., (1), (6)) express thetic judgments (simple descriptions), not categorical judgments. In these cases, there is no existential presupposition associated with the grammatical subject, which may therefore be indefinite, as in (6a, b).[8]

The definiteness effect would also be accounted for if SpecCP were interpreted as the position for the discourse topic. One argument against this is that in complex sentences, embedded SpecCP may be filled by an element distinct from any that fills matrix SpecCP:

(8) a. *W-ojtaq* [*chi* ***jar Aa Xwaan*** *n-ru-k'aj ch'ijch'*].
A1SG-know that the youth Juan INCMPL-A3SG-take car
'I know that Juan drives a car.' Dayley 398

b. ***Ja Ta Mari'y*** *n-uu-ch'ob'* [*chi* ***jar Aa Xwaan***
the Miss María INCMPL-A3SG-think that the youth Juan
x-uu-ch'ey Aa Teeko].
CMPL-A3SG-hit youth Diego
'María thinks that Juan hit Diego.' Dayley 199

This is entirely expected if the clause-initial element is interpreted as logical subject, for the clause is the domain of predication. On the other hand, examples like (8a, b) are puzzling if this element is taken to be discourse topic. The domain of the discourse topic is larger than the clause, and the association of each clause with a distinct discourse topic does not make much sense.

One final point concerns the relation between the logical subject and the associated clause. Dayley (1985: 324ff.) refers to examples like (2)–(5) as involving 'fronting', perhaps suggesting movement of the logical subject to its surface position. Movement would account for the ungrammaticality of examples like (9a, b), with 'hanging topics'. Since the logical subject plays no grammatical role in the associated clause, it would have no source under a movement analysis.

(9) a. ****Ja frúuta*** *qas ki' ja máango.*
the fruit very sweet the mango
'As for fruit, mango is very sweet.'

b. ***Jar Aa Xwaan** kam w-aal.*
the Mr. Juan died A1SG-child
'My daughter died on Juan.'

Nonetheless, I do not assume movement, but rather that the logical subject must be coreferential with a pronoun in the associated clause; i.e., it must *bind* a pronoun.[9] The absence of such a pronoun is what excludes (9a, b). I represent this empty pronoun by *pro* below.

Under the conception sketched above, Tz'utujil phrase structure defines two layers of structure: one internal to VP, which realizes verb-argument structure, and one at the CP level, which realizes logical subject-predicate structure. The structural disassociation of these two sets of relations is one of the most striking properties of Tz'utujil. It is a property which permits nominals other than the grammatical subject to be presented as logical subject using minimal syntactic or lexical resources. The situation in English is quite different. First of all, the standard assumption is that while the subject originates within the VP, it must be raised out of the VP to be licensed as grammatical subject. At surface structure, it occupies the specifier position of a functional projection, usually identified with IP. Second, there is no structural position in English dedicated to the logical subject. Instead, the two 'subject' functions are largely conflated in English. Indeed, one of the important functions of the grammatical subject in English is to identify the logical subject (see Chafe (1976) among others).

3. Possessors

I assume there is a semantic role *possessor*, which is canonically realized as syntactic genitive. In Tz'utujil, genitives (bold-faced in (10)) follow their heads and are cross-referenced on them via Set A prefixes (in (10b), the genitive itself contains a genitive):

(10) a. [*ti r-ujq* [***ja ti xten***]]
DIM A3SG-skirt the DIM girl
'the little girl's skirt'

b. [*ruu-keej* [***n-ata'*** [***pro***]]]
A3SG-horse A1SG-father
'my father's horse'

I assume that the genitive occupies the specifier position of NP which, like the specifier of V, is located to the right of its head.

Suppose the speaker wishes to present the possessor as logical subject, that is, to construe the situation as a property of the possessor. This is easy in Tz'utujil: the possessor surfaces sentence-initially, in the position of the logical subject, and binds a genitive pronoun within the clause.

(11) ***Ja ti xten***$_i$ [*chitoom* [*ti r-ujq* pro$_i$]].
the DIM girl pleated DIM A3SG-skirt
'The little girl has her skirt pleated'. Dict. 75

In (11), *ja ti xten* 'the little girl' is logical subject. By hypothesis, (11) presents the situation of the little girl's skirt being pleated as a property of the little girl. This coincides with the way (11) is translated in the original source: *la patojita tiene plegado su corte,* lit. 'the little-girl has her skirt pleated'. The logical subject in (11) is syntactically integrated into the sentence by virtue of the fact that it binds the genitive of *rujq* 'her skirt'. The head noun agrees with its genitive which, being pronominal, is null. I refer to a logical subject like *ja ti xten* which binds a genitive pronoun as *external possessor* (EPR). This seems appropriate since its only argument role is possessor, and it is located outside the nominal constituent in which that role is assigned (i.e., its construal as possessor is indirect).

The identification of Tz'utujil EPRs with the logical subject predicts that there should be a definiteness restriction on EPRs. This is correct, although demonstrating it is not completely straightforward. First of all, genitives which occur postnominally within the nominal constituent may be indefinite, as in (12a, b):

(12) a. *K'axa-x-i* [*ruu-qul* ***jun ak'aal***] *ch aaq'a'.*
hear-PASS-IV A3SG-voice a child in night
'A child's voice was heard in the dark.'

b. *K'utmaj to* [*r-palaj* ***jun aachi***] *pa wentana.*
appear DIR A3SG-face a man at window
'A man's face was seen at the window.'

The examples in (13), which are synonymous with those of (12), contain sentence-initial genitives which are indefinite. If these are logical subjects, this is contrary to expectation:

(13) a. ***Jun ak'aal*** *k'axa-x-i* [*ruu-qul*] *ch aaq'a'.*
a child hear-PASS-IV A3SG-voice in night
'A child's voice was heard in the night.'

b. ***Jun aachi*** *k'utmaj to* [*r-palaj*] *pa wentana.*
a man appear DIR A3SG-face at window
'A man's face was seen at the window.'

I suggest, however, that these indefinites are in the focus position, not the logical subject position. First, Tz'utujil routinely allows indefinites to occur in the focus position, without focus semantics. This is clear in examples like (14) where the preverbal indefinite cooccurs with the logical subject:

(14) ***Ja n-ata'*** *jun keej x-uu-loq'.*
the A1SG-father a horse CMPL-A3SG-buy
'My father bought a horse.'

Indefinite genitives should then also be possible in focus position. Furthermore, in (13a, b), the indefinite (bold-faced) can be preceded by negation (15a, b), but it cannot precede negation (16a, b). This is a property of the focus, not the logical subject.

(15) a. *Ma* ***jun ak'aal*** *k'axa-x ta [ruu-qul] ch aaq'a'.*
NEG a child hear-PASS IRR A3SG-voice in night
'No child's voice was heard in the night.'
b. *Ma* ***jun aachi*** *k'utmaj to ta [r-palaj] pa wentana.*
NEG a man appear DIR IRR A3SG-face in window
'No man's face appeared at the window.'

(16) a. ??***Jun ak'aal*** *ma k'axax ta [ruuqul] ch aaq'a'.*
b. ??***Jun aachi*** *ma k'utmaj to ta [rpalaj] pa wentana.*

I conclude then that EPRs cannot be indefinite; if they could, examples like (16a, b) would be grammatical. The fact that they cannot follows from the analysis of EPRs as logical subjects.

4. Have

English *have* has a range of interpretations, depending on the syntactic context in which it occurs:

(17) *Jake has a sportscar.* [*Possession*]
Jake has a sportscar in his driveway. [*Location*]
Jake has long hair. [*Permanent property attribution*]
Jake has his beard trimmed. [*Temporary property attribution*]
Jake had his car die on him. [*Experiencer*]

Ritter and Rosen (1993) have suggested that English *have* has no lexical meaning, but is purely functional. Pursuing this further, Schafer (1997) suggests that the function of *have* is to present its postverbal complement as a property of the subject (interpreted as semantic possessor). She interprets sentences with *have* as expressing a categorical judgment, where the postverbal material is interpreted as the logical predicate, and the grammatical subject as logical subject. Diagrammatically:

Grammatical subject	[have XP]
|	|
Logical subject	Logical predicate

Figure 4: *Interpretation of clauses with* ***have***

If this is correct, it is clear why English requires a lexical verb like *have* to realize the possessor as logical subject: in a language where the logical subject is identified by the grammatical subject, presenting the possessor as logical subject requires that the possessor function as grammatical subject. In the absence of a productive rule of possessor ascension which raises the genitive to subject, a verb which lexicalizes the possessor as grammatical subject is required. In English, that verb is *have*.

Schafer's analysis of *have*, coupled with the analysis of Tz'utujil EPRs as logical subject, leads to the expectation that Tz'utujil should have no such verb, for Tz'utujil can realize the possessor as logical subject without involving the grammatical subject. In what follows, we show that all the senses illustrated in (17) are expressed in Tz'utujil through the EP construction, without the use of any verb corresponding to *have*.

4.1 *Possession and location*

The most common EPR in Tz'utujil occurs with the existential predicate *k'ooli*, glossed *be* here. This construction is the standard way to translate the English verb *have* in its possessive sense (cf. Freeze 1992). Dayley (1985: 316) describes this construction as follows:

> In sentences predicating possession, the possessed entity is the subject of *k'ooli*, and it is inflected for possessor with an ergative prefix. If an overt possessor noun phrase occurs in the sentence, it is usually fronted to initial position preceding *k'ooli*, and the subject (i.e. possessed entity) follows *k'ooli*...

The plain existential use of *k'ooli* is illustrated in (18) (nb. *k'ooli* shortens to *k'o* except before pause and before a definite nominal):

(18) *Ee k'o winaq waawe'.*
B3PL be people here
'There are (some) people here.' Dayley 302

The examples in (19a–c) show the EPR construction:

(19) a. ***Ja winaq**$_i$* [*k'o* [*ki-paq* pro$_i$]].
the people be A3PL-money
'The people have money.'

b. *(**Atet**$_i$)* [*k'o jun* [*aa-tz'ii'* pro$_i$]].
you be a A2SG-dog
'You have a dog.' Dayley 316

c. ***Inin**$_i$* [*ee k'o* [*w-ach'aalaal* pro$_i$] *pa taq'aaj*].
I 3PL be A1SG-relatives on coast
'I have relatives on the coast'. Dict. 3

The basic clause in (19c) means 'there are my relatives on the coast', but because of sentence-initial *inin*, the entire sentence is interpreted as a categorical judgment, with the existence of relatives of mine at the coast construed as a property of me. Hence the English translation.

The structure of (19c) is shown in Figure 5 where I assume (contra Dayley) that the nominal headed by *wach'aalaal* occupies (unaccusative) object position. As logical subject, *inin* 'I' surfaces in SpecCP and binds the pronominal genitive (circled) within the unaccusative object (see Szabolcsi (1994) for a very similar analysis of analogous facts in Hungarian).

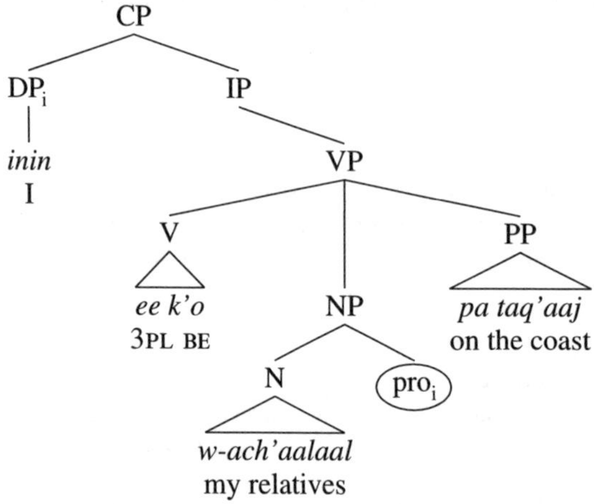

Figure 5: *Structure of (19c)*

Note that the existential predicate has only *wach'aalaal* 'my relatives' as syntactic argument, not *inin* 'I'. Evidence for this is the agreement on the predicate, which is 3rd person plural. The interpretation of *inin* as possessor is the result of its binding the (1st person singular) genitive within the nominal headed by *wach'aalaal*. The existence of this genitive is clear, since *wach'aalaal* agrees with it.[10]

Phrase-structural evidence that *inin* does indeed occupy the same position as other non-possessor logical subjects comes from the fact that it occurs to the left of negation:

(20) ***(Inin**$_i$**)** ma k'o ta [n-paq* pro$_i$].
I NEG be IRR A1SG-money
'I don't have any money.' Dayley 316

Further evidence comes from the fact that it can cooccur with a preposed focus: in (21), the unaccusative object is attracted to focus position by the focus particle *xa* 'only', and the logical subject binds the genitive within the focus.

(21) ***Ja n-ata'**$_i$ [xa r-ek'* pro$_i$] *ee k'ooli.*
the A1SG-father only A3SG-chicken 3PL be
'My father has only chickens.'

Again, the only argument of the predicate is the focused possessum *rek'*. The predicate agrees in number with that nominal (3rd person plural), and not with the logical subject (3rd person singular).[11]

An EPR can bind a genitive within constituents other than the object, yielding clauses which correspond to other variants of English *have*. In (22a, b), the EPR binds into a locative, and in (22c) into a comitative phrase:

(22) a. ***Ja jun ak'aal**$_i$ k'o jun atzabaal [pa r-borsa* pro$_i$].
the a boy be a toy in A3SG-pocket
'The boy has a toy in his pocket.'
b. ***Jar aachi**$_i$ k'o jun ch'a'k [tza' r-chaq* pro$_i$].
the man be a sore on A3SG-buttock
'The man has a sore on his buttocks.' Dict. 2
c. ***Inin**$_i$ k'o paq [w-k'iin* pro$_i$].
I be money A1SG-with
'I have money with me.'

In (22a, b), the situation of the existence of an object in a place is construed as a property of the whole of which the place is part; in (22c), the existence of an object in a place is construed as a property of the place itself.

4.2 *Permanent property attribution*

Both *be* and *have* are used in English to attribute personal characteristics:

(23) a. *The horse's tail is long.*
     b. *The horse has a long tail.*

Example (23a) construes the situation of the horse's tail being long as a property of the tail; (23b) construes it as a property of the horse. The same distinction is drawn in Tz'utujil without the use of any copula verbs. Both construals are based on a clause headed by an adjective predicate 'long' and a single grammatical argument 'the horse's tail'. The difference in construal is determined by whether the possessum is chosen as logical subject, as in the left-hand structure in Figure 6, or the possessor, as in the right-hand structure:

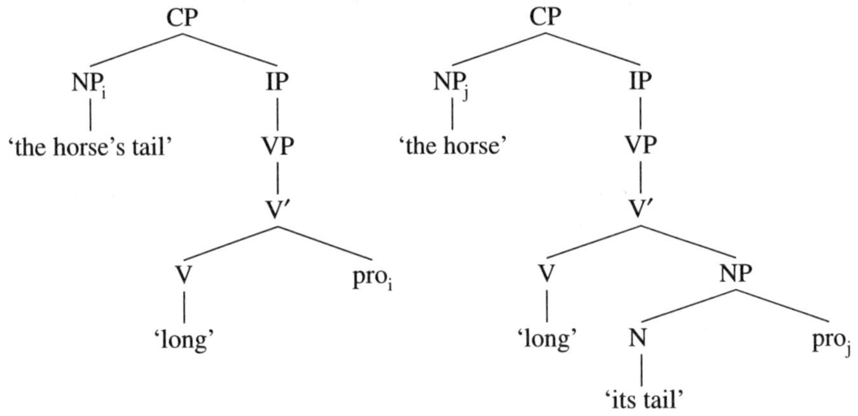

Figure 6: *Structures of (24a, b)*

The examples in (24) show these two construals:

(24) a. [***Ja ruu-jeey ja keej***]$_i$ [*qas nim* pro$_i$].
     the A3SG-tail the horse very big
     'The horse's tail is very long.'
   b. ***Ja keej***$_i$ [*qas nim* [*ruu-jeey* pro$_i$]].
     the horse very big A3SG-tail
     'The horse has a long tail.'

The pair in (25) are similar, but show again that an EPR logical subject is not grammatical subject. The plural agreement in both (25a, b) is determined by the number of the possessum 'testicles', and not by the number of the logical subject, which is plural in (25a), and singular in (25b).

(25) a. [***Ja r-aab'aaj ja wajkax le'***$_j$]$_i$ [*qas ee nimaq* pro$_i$].
the A3SG-testicles the bull DEM very 3PL big:PL
'The testicles of that bull are very big.'

b. ***Ja jun wajkax le'***$_j$ [*qas ee nimaq* [*r-aab'aaj* pro$_j$]$_i$].
the a bull DEM very 3PL big:PL A3SG-testicles
'The bull has very big testicles.' Dict. 1

Native speakers report that pairs like these differ in what is being talked about, an intuition which coincides with our interpretation of the sentence-initial nominal as logical subject.

It is common in Tz'utujil to form a property from an adjective + body part, and apply it to the possessor; but the same construction is used with non-body parts. Entities can be characterized in terms of situations involving their relatives, their possessions, and their mental faculties:

(26) a. ***Jar ajk'ay tana'x***$_i$ [*qas ti utz* [*jun r-mee'aal* pro$_i$]].
the vendor pot very DIM pretty a A3SG-daughter
'The pot vendor has a pretty daughter.' Dict. 9

b. ***Ja n-ata'***$_i$ [*k'aak'a* [*jun ruu-ch'iich'* pro$_i$]].
the A1SG-father new a A3SG-car
'My father has a new car.'

c. ***Ja w-achalii'***$_i$ [*qas utz* [*r-naa'ooj* pro$_i$]].
the A1SG-consuegra very good A3SG-character
'My "consuegra" has very good character.' Dict. 2

4.3 *Temporary property attribution*

Finally, clauses like English *Jake has his beard trimmed* (non-causative sense), which construes the temporary state of Jake's beard as a property of Jake, are translated into Tz'utujil with the EP construction:

(27) a. ***Ja ti xten***$_i$ *chitoom* [*ti r-ujq* pro$_i$].
the DIM girl pleated DIM her-skirt
'The little girl has her skirt pleated.' Dict. 75

b. ***Ja ti miix***$_i$ *jitz'il* [*ruu-q'a'* pro$_i$].
the DIM cat well-tied A3SG-hand
'The cat has its paws well-tied.' Dict. 145

c. ***Ja tz'i'***$_i$ *qas jakajik* [*ruu-chii'* pro$_i$].
the dog very open A3SG-mouth
'The dog has its mouth open.' Dict. 132

The EP construction thus allows the attribution of both individual-level and stage-level properties (roughly, permanent and temporary properties) to the logical subject in Tz'utujil.

4.4 *Conclusion*

The systematic relation between English clauses headed by *have*, and the EP construction in Tz'utujil, follows from their shared semantic-conceptual structure: both construe the denoted situation as a property of an entity interpreted as possessor or location. Because in English logical subject and grammatical subject tend to be conflated, English needs a verb like *have* which lexicalizes the possessor as grammatical subject in order to present it as logical subject. In Tz'utujil, logical subject and grammatical subject are structurally disassociated, so that the possessor can be presented as logical subject without being lexicalized as grammatical subject. This eliminates the need for a verb like *have*.

5. EPR and affectedness

Consider the English pairs in (28)–(31):

(28) a. My grandmother's rib broke.
b. My grandmother broke her rib.

(29) a. Juan's mother died last year.
b. Juan lost his mother last year.

(30) a. The price of corn rose in June.
b. Corn rose in price in June.

(31) a. The girl's tooth fell out.
b. The girl lost a tooth.

In each case, the (a) and (b) examples describe the same situation, but they differ in the way it is presented. Both (29a) and (29b), for example, assert the death of Juan's mother. But (29a) presents the situation in terms of Juan's mother, while (29b) presents it in terms of Juan. The perspectival difference between these examples can be described in terms of logical subject: the logical subject of (29a) is Juan's mother, while that of (29b) is Juan. This coincides of course with differences in grammatical subject, for reasons already discussed. In some cases, the possibility of two perspectives exists because the verb occurs in several syntactic frames (e.g., *break, rise* in (28, 30)); in others, it is the lexical resources of the language which permit a second perspective. It is not possible to say **Juan died his mother* (cf. *Juan broke his arm)*, but the existence of *lose* makes it possible to present the death of Juan's mother as a property of Juan.

Why bother to make these two perspectives available? Apparently because certain situations are readily construed as being either about an entity or about the possessor of that entity. In particular, when a body part, relative, or object that 'belongs' to an individual undergoes a change, the individual him/herself is often affected, and thereby easily construed as the affected entity (the 'end point' of Croft (1994) and Ritter and Rosen (1993), the 'affected' entity of Shibatani (1994), the 'patient' of Jackendoff (1990)). In such cases, it is natural to present the situation as a property of the possessor, i.e. to present the possessor as logical subject. In languages where the grammatical subject identifies the logical subject, an affected possessor will have a claim on the subject relation, and there will be pressure on the language to make resources available for lexicalizing the possessor as grammatical subject.

In Tz'utujil where the logical subject is disassociated from grammatical subject, it should be possible to express construals like those of examples (28b-31b) without lexicalizing the possessor as subject. Indeed, this is exactly what we find. The equivalents of (28b-31b) are expressed in Tz'utujil through the EP construction, where the EPR binds a genitive pronoun. Consider (32), which translates (28b):

(32) ***Ja w-ati't***$_i$ *q'aaj* [*ruu-poox* pro$_i$].
the A1SG-grandmother broke A3SG-rib
'My grandmother broke her rib(s)'.

Despite the translation, the basic clause is intransitive (= 'her rib broke'), as shown by the absence of any Set A (ergative) agreement on the verb. The clause has one syntactic argument, *ruupoox* 'her rib', which I assume is an (unaccusative) object. Being 3rd person, it induces no overt agreement on the verb. The sentence-initial nominal *ja wati't* 'my grandmother' occupies SpecCP, where it is interpreted as logical subject; it binds the genitive pronoun within the object, whence its interpretation as possessor. The structure of (32) is shown in Figure 7:

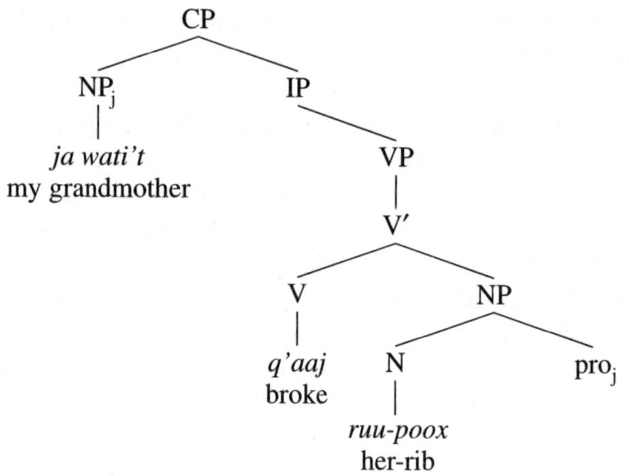

Figure 7: *Structure of (32)*

The syntactic structure of Tz'utujil (32) is significantly different than that of English (28b), despite the intuition that they are equivalent. Their equivalence lies in the fact that they express the same categorical judgment: both construe the situation of my grandmother's rib(s) breaking as a property of my grandmother.

The example in (33) has the same structure, but with a 1st person EPR. Predicate agreement can be only 3rd person, which shows clearly that the logical subject is not grammatical subject.

(33) ***Inin***$_i$ *n-ti'on* /**n-in-ti'on* [*n-wi'* pro$_i$].
I INCMPL-hurt /*INCMPL-B1SG-hurt A1SG-head
'I have a headache.' (= 'me, my head hurts')

Examples (34a – c) are Tz'utujil versions of the English examples (29b, 30b, 31b), all *intransitive* with structures like that shown in Figure 7.

(34) a. ***Jar Aa Xwaan***$_i$ *kam-i* [*ja ruu-tee'* pro$_i$].
the Mr. Juan die-IV the A3SG-mother
'Juan lost his mother last year.'
(='Juan, his mother died last year.')

b. ***Jar iixiim***$_i$ *jote'* [*r-ajil* pro$_i$] *pa taq júnyo.*
the corn rose A3SG-price in when June
'Corn rose in price in June.'
(='Corn, its price rose in June')

c. ***Ja ti xten***$_i$ *x-el jun [r-eey* pro$_i$].
the DIM girl CMPL-exit one A3SG-tooth
'The little girl lost a tooth.'
(='The little girl, her tooth left') Dict. 118

Again, the equivalence of these examples with the corresponding English lies not in the syntax, which is quite different, but in the fact that corresponding examples express the same categorical judgment.

6. Restrictions on the logical subject

All the examples of external possessors that we have discussed so far involve EPRs which bind a genitive within an unaccusative clause, either within the unaccusative object itself, or within an oblique. All the examples of 'fronted' genitives cited in Dayley (1985) and the vast majority of those cited in Dayley et al. (1996) also involve unaccusative clauses. These are core examples in the sense that they occur frequently, and are produced and consistently accepted by speakers in the elicitation situation.

Constructed EP examples where the EPR binds a genitive within a *subject* have a different status. They are harder for speakers to process, speakers disagree with one another about the judgments, and the judgments of individual speakers are themselves inconsistent over time. The reactions that such examples evoke do not seem to justify their classification as ungrammatical; at the same time, as a group, they are degraded compared to EPRs involving unaccusative clauses. The examples in (35) involve unergative clauses: (35a), for example, tries to construe the situation of someone speaking at a meeting as a property of that person's father. The slashes separate judgments of different speakers and/or judgments of the same speaker on different occasions:

(35) a. ✓/?***Jar Aa Lu'***$_i$ *tzijoon-i [ja r-k'ajool* pro$_i$] *chi pa ja*
the Mr. P. speak-IV the A3SG-son at in the
molooj=rii'iil.
meeting
'Pedro's son spoke at the meeting.'

b. ✓/?***Ja nuu-chaaq'***$_i$ *n-samaj [r-mee'aal* pro$_i$] *pa klinika.*
the A1SG-brother INCMPL-work A3SG-daughter at clinic
'My brother's daughter works at the clinic.'

The judgments are similar, perhaps a bit worse, for transitive clauses. Example (36a) tries to construe a woman's visit as a property of her husband:

(36) a. ✓/**Jar Aa Lu'*$_i$ *x-in-uj-r-q'ijl-a'* *kaan [ja*
the Mr. P. CMPL-B1SG-DIR-A3SG-visit-TV DIR the
r-xaayiil pro$_i$] *iiwiir.*
A3SG-wife yest.
'Pedro's wife came to see me yesterday.'

b. ✓/**Ja w-achajiil*$_i$ *n-k'ayij* *keem* *[ja r-aanaa'* pro$_i$]
the A1SG-husband INCMPL-sell weaving the A3SG-sister
pa k'ayib'al.
in market
'My husband's sister sells weaving in the market.'

There are two ways to think about the degraded status of these examples. One is syntactic: the problem might involve the link between the EPR and the null element that it binds. As is well-known, extraction from subjects, and in some cases binding into subjects, is in general more difficult than extraction from (or binding into) objects (Cinque 1990). This would not by itself, however, explain the variation in judgments. Alternatively, the problem might have more to do with the pragmatic or conceptual relation between the logical subject and the property ascribed to it in the EP construction. I sketch this second alternative in a bit more detail, since it seems better able to explain the observed variation in judgments.

There is, first of all, some kind of 'relevance' restriction on the relation between logical subject and predicate: the property applied to the logical subject should be relevant to it. The question of what counts as 'relevance' is a difficult one, but observations of Shibatani (1994) are helpful:

> The participants constituting the event itself, say an agent and a patient of a scene construed as involving a prototypical transitive activity, are optimally relevant to the scene of the event. They show two characteristic features. One is their physical presence and the other, *the affecting and affected roles they play in constituting a transitive event* [emphasis mine, JA]. [470]

There is a preference in Tz'utujil for the logical subject to be interpreted as playing one of the roles mentioned above: 'affecting' (roughly agent) or 'affected' (roughly patient), with the 'affecting' taking priority over the 'affected' in clauses containing both. That is, there is an unmarked association between logical subject and agent in Tz'utujil. This is why Tz'utujil is sometimes described as a SVO language (cf. Grimes 1996). As a consequence, an EPR which binds the genitive within the direct object of a *transitive* clause is not as natural as one which binds into an unaccusative clause.[12] Example (37) is accepted by speakers, but one speaker consistently regards such examples as worse than ones in which the genitive is left *in situ*:

(37) ?***Ja ta Mari'y***$_i$ *x-in-paaxiij* [*ja ruu-t'u'y* pro$_i$].
the Ms. Maria CMPL-A1SG-break the A3SG-pot
'I broke Maria's pot.'

The high naturalness of EPRs in unaccusative clauses in Tz'utujil is thus a consequence of two things: first, the fact that possessors are often patient-like (affected), and second, there is no competing agent. Payne (1997) suggests that EPRs are most often linked to objects of *transitive* clauses, and this is clearly not true in Tz'utujil. The reason, however, is that in Tz'utujil, EPRs are logical subjects, and agents always have priority over non-agents for status as logical subject. The same dynamic is at work in examples like (38a, b), both of which involve an EPR which binds into the oblique phrase *-umaal* 'on account of'. The (a) example, from an unaccusative clause, is perfect; but the (b) example, from an unergative clause, is not as good:

(38) a. ***Ja ya'***$_i$ *x-in-yawaj* [*r-umaal* pro$_i$].
the water CMPL-B1SG-sick A3SG-cause
'I got sick on account of the water,'
i.e. 'The water made me sick.'

b. ?***Ja n-ata'***$_i$ *n-in-samaj* [*r-maal* pro$_i$].
the A1SG-father INCMPL-B1SG-work A3SG-cause
'I'm working on account of my father.'

The speaker's comment on (38b) was that "it's odd because you expect the sentence to be about the father". The problem here seems to be that the verb *samaj* 'work' has an agentive subject, making it difficult to integrate the logical subject into the construal of the situation in an 'affecting' role. This problem does not arise with the unaccusative (38a), which is impeccable. From this perspective, it is not so surprising that EPRs which bind into subjects yield clauses which are less optimal than the core examples. In such cases, the EPR plays neither the role of the 'affecting' party (a role assigned to the grammatical subject), nor the 'affected' (since events denoted by transitive and unergative verbs induce effects on their patients, not on the genitive of the subject).

This leads to the expectation that an EPR could bind into a subject if the denoted property were construed as more relevant to the genitive within the subject than to the subject itself. Two dictionary examples from Dayley et al. (1996) confirm this. Both are syntactically transitive, but semantically unaccusative. Consider (39), which refers to the beating of a heart. This example is semantically one-place, but formally transitive by virtue of being reflexive (roughly, 'heart beats itself'). Note the Set A agreement:

(39) ***Ja w-aanimo*** $_i$ *qas n-uu-k'aq r-ii'* pro $_i$.
the A1SG-heart very INCMPL-A3SG-beat A3SG-self
'My heart is beating.' (=Spanish 'Mi corazón está palpitando')
Dict. 19

Example (39) has a logical subject, which binds the subject of the clause. Like the English (and Spanish) translations, the situation is presented as a property of my heart. However, it is also possible to present it as a property of the person whose heart is beating, as in (40):

(40) ***Ja yaawaa'*** $_i$ *qas n-uu-k'aq r-ii'* [*r-aanimo* pro $_i$].
the patient very INCMPL-A3SG-beat A3SG-self A3SG-heart
'The patient's heart is beating.'
(=Spanish 'Al enfermo le está palpitando el corazón') Dict. 19

The Spanish translation captures better than the English the sense of (40): in the Spanish, the possessor is realized as dative ('of interest') rather than nominal-internally (compare (39)), and occurs in preverbal position.[13] Relevant to us is that in (40), the logical subject is an EP which binds a pronoun within the subject of a transitive clause. Unlike examples (35)–(36), which are degraded, (40) is perfect. The difference is that in (40), the EPR is highly affected, and there is no agent competing for status as logical subject.

Example (41) also suggests the possibility of binding into a subject:

(41) ***Ja josq'il sb'o'*** $_i$ *x-uu-maj ti'oon-eem* [*r-paan* pro $_i$].
the onion cleaner CMPL-A3SG-begin hurt-INF A3SG-stomach
'The onion cleaner's stomach began to hurt.'
(=Spanish 'Al limpiador de cebollas empezó a dolerle el estómago')
Dict. 150

Example (41) quite naturally construes the situation of a stomach beginning to hurt as a property of the person whose stomach is involved. A better English translation might be 'the onion cleaner began to have a stomach ache'. The Spanish translation is closer, since it presents the possessor as dative of interest, external to the nominal and in clause-initial position. Grammatically, *rpaan* 'his stomach' seems to be subject of the aspectual verb *xuumaj*, which is transitive (the object is the clausal complement headed by *ti'ooneem* 'hurt'). If so, then in (41) too, the EPR binds a genitive within the grammatical subject. One might suggest that the logical subject in (41) actually corresponds to the grammatical subject. This would be compatible with the agreement, since the main verb has a 3rd person subject, and the logical subject is 3rd person. But the agreement in (42) shows unambiguously that the logical subject does not correspond to grammatical subject:

(42) ***Jar inin***$_i$*)* *x-uu-maj* /**x-in-maj* *ti'oon-eem*
the I CMPL-A3SG-begin /*CMPL-A1SG-begin hurt-INF
[*n-paan* pro$_i$].
A1SG-stomach
'My stomach began to hurt'.

In (42), agreement on the main verb can only be 3rd person, in agreement with *n-paan* 'my stomach'. I conclude then that the logical subjects in (41, 42) do bind a genitive within the subject. These examples too involve no agent, and the entity denoted by the logical subject is clearly affected.

Examples (35, 36) are questionable for two reasons then: first, it is difficult to see the predicated property as relevant to the logical subject, for it is neither affecting nor affected. Second, these examples contain a distinct agent, which has a prior claim on logical subject.

7. Conclusion

In the larger typology of EP constructions, the Tz'utujil construction is an outlier because the EPR is not realized as a core argument. However, this disassociation from clausal grammatical relations makes the function of the EP construction in Tz'utujil very clear: it is *to present the possessor as logical subject.* I suggest that this is one important function of EP constructions cross-linguistically. If so, the study of EP constructions must engage the question of how the logical subject is articulated in particular languages.

We have identified two ways in which a possessor may be presented as logical subject: it may be realized in a non-argument position which is dedicated to the logical subject, as in Tz'utujil. Alternatively, the possessor may be realized as the grammatical argument of a verb which assigns it a semantic role, as in English. Are there any other possibilities? There is a third strategy, perhaps exemplified by the Sinitic languages (Chappell, this volume) and Chickasaw (Munro, this volume). Contrasts between EP and non-EP constructions in these languages suggest that the function of the EP construction is to present the possessor as logical subject, as in Tz'utujil and English. Syntactically, EP constructions in Sinitic involve a 'multiple subject' construction, and those of Chickasaw involve possessor raising (to subject). Thus, Sinitic and Chickasaw EPRs are grammatical subjects, as in English; but in contrast to English, they are not semantic arguments of the predicate. The third strategy then is one in which the possessor is a core argument of the clause, but is not a semantic argument of the predicate.

Instead, it receives its semantic role from a nominal in the clause. 'Raising' the possessor to subject would be motivated by the need to present it as logical subject, with the 'derived' subject position presumably one which fulfills this function.

The typology described above is sketched in Figure 8.

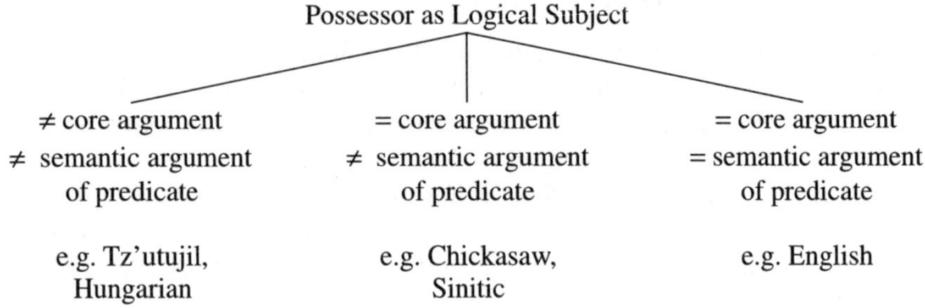

Figure 8: *Realization of Possessor as Logical Subject*

Languages which use the two left-hand strategies should require no verb like *have*, since they have syntactic means to 'raise' a possessor to subject without that possessor being a semantic argument of the verb. Note also that presentation of the logical subject-possessor as a core argument (the middle case) probably need not involve the subject relation. Some of the Spanish examples cited above suggest that possessors can be realized as logical subjects via the indirect object relation, especially in unaccusative clauses.

Finally, Figure 8 suggests that the Tz'utujil-type EP construction might represent the ungrammaticized starting point for the historical development of the EP construction found in Sinitic and Chickasaw. Reanalysis of the Tz'utujil logical subject-possessor as grammatical subject will yield essentially the surface structures of the Sinitic multiple subject construction and Chickasaw possessor raising. From this perspective, the development of the EP constructions in Chickasaw and Sinitic would simply be a special case of the well-known evolution of topics (read, logical subjects) into grammatical subjects (Givón 1976; Li and Thompson 1976).

Acknowledgments

An initial version of this paper was prepared while the author was a fellow at the Center for Advanced Study in the Behavioral Sciences. I am grateful for the financial support provided by NSF Grants #SBR-9022192 and #SBR-9630305, by the UC Office of the President, and the Academic Senate of the University of California, Santa Cruz. This work is primarily based on work with Pablo

Chavajay, from San Pedro La Laguna, Guatemala, and I am grateful to him for his help and insights. I was also able to check most of the material reported here with Marta Navichoc, from the same community. I thank her as well, and also Barbara Rogoff, who facilitated this research in practical ways. Comments from Donka Farkas, Maria Polinsky, and Immanuel Barshi on earlier versions of this paper, and comments and corrections by Pablo Chavajay and Jon Dayley, have been greatly appreciated.

Abbreviations

Abbreviations used in this paper: A1SG Set A, 1st singular, etc; ASP aspect; B1 Set B, 1st person, etc; CMPL completive; DEM demonstrative; DIM diminutive; DIR directional; FOC focus suffix; INCMPL incompletive; INF infinitive; IRR irrealis; IV intransitive verb terminal; NEG negation; SG singular; PL plural; TV transitive verb terminal; ✓ grammatical.

Notes

1 Tz'utujil is a Mayan language of the K'ichean branch, spoken by about 100,000 speakers in the departments of Sololá and Suchitepequéz, Guatemala, south of Lake Atitlán. There are two excellent sources of information on the language: a grammar (Dayley 1985), and a dictionary (Dayley et al. 1996). Examples taken from these two sources are cited as *Dayley* and *Dict*, followed by the page number. All other examples are from my own field notes.

2 *The Encyclopaedia of Philosophy*, ed. Paul Edwards. Vol. 8, p. 33

3 I follow the orthography used in the sources cited in note 1. This orthography is consistent with that proposed by the Academia de las lenguas mayas (1988).

4 Kuroda does not use the term *logical subject*, but *Subject* (with a capital "S"). As Horn (1989: 511) notes, the relevant sense of *subject* is not the logical subject as it might be understood in Montague grammar (as that element which combines with an IV to form a sentence) or in transformational or Relational Grammar (as that element which is the subject at some deep or initial level or representation). The notion is really a psychological or cognitive one.

5 Kiss (1995) proposes a similar interpretation of the corresponding "topic" position in Hungarian, and I have been influenced by her views.

6 In Aissen (1992), I referred to the specifier of CP as the "internal topic". The present paper uses the term "logical subject" instead. In essence, I am proposing here that the internal topic should be interpreted as logical subject, as explicated here.

7 Example (7c) has no version with postverbal subject. Negative indefinites obligatorily front in Tz'utujil to the focus position.

8 The statement that there is no definiteness requirement on the postverbal subject is not quite right: in transitive clauses where both subject and object are 3rd person, the subject cannot be indefinite when the object is definite (cf. Dayley 1985: 319). I believe this is an obviation effect, in the sense of Aissen (1997).

9 A binds B if and only if A c-commands B and A and B are coindexed.

10 In the Ritter and Rosen, and Schafer analyses mentioned earlier, it is not fully clear (to me) how in English, the subject of *have* in *I have money* comes to be interpreted as possessor. Ritter and Rosen (1993) state that the possessive interpretation is a default interpretation. Kayne (1993) accounts for this by deriving the English from a Tz'utujil (or Hungarian) deep structure, i.e., one in which the surface subject of *have* originates as genitive of the postverbal nominal.

11 Note that in (21), the EPR is outside the scope of the focus operator *xa* 'only'. Thus, (21) does not mean 'only my father's chickens exist'.

12 I do not discuss here logical subjects which bind a direct object. These are possible when the subject is 1st or 2nd person, cf. (3a) above. Other configurations are subject to constraints which must be left for another time.

13 The Spanish translations of (39)–(41) are from Dayley et al. (1996).

References

Academia de las lenguas mayas. 1988. *Documento de referencia para la pronunciación de los nuevos alfabetos oficiales.* Guatemala City: Instituto Indigenista Nacional.

Aissen, Judith. 1992. "Topic and Focus in Mayan." *Language* 68: 43–80.

Aissen, Judith. 1997. "On the Syntax of Obviation." *Language* 73: 705–750.

Brentano, Franz. 1924. *Psychologie vom Empirischen Standpunkt*, Vols. I, II. Hamburg: Felix Meiner.

Chafe, Wallace. 1976. "Givenness, Contrastiveness, Definiteness, Subjects, Topics, and Point of View." In Charles Li (ed.), *Subject and Topic.* New York: Academic Press, 25–55.

Chomsky, Noam. 1986. *Barriers.* Cambridge: MIT Press.

Cinque, Guglielmo. 1990. *Types of Abar-Dependencies.* Cambridge: MIT Press.

Croft, William. 1994. "Voice: Beyond Control and Affectedness." In Barbara Fox and Paul Hopper (eds.), *Voice: Form and Function.* Amsterdam and Philadelphia: John Benjamins, 89–117.

Dayley, Jon P. 1985. *Tz'utujil Grammar.* Berkeley: University of California Press.

Dayley, Juan Felipe, Francisco Pérez Mendoza, and Miguel Hernández Mendoza. 1996. *Diccionario tz'utujil.* La Antigua, Guatemala: Proyecto Lingüístico Francisco Marroquín.

Edwards, Paul (ed). 1967. *The Encyclopedia of Philosophy.* New York: Macmillan Publishers.

Freeze, Ray. 1992. "Existential and Other Locatives." *Language* 68: 553–595.

Givón, Talmy. 1976. "Topic, Pronoun, and Grammatical Agreement." In Charles N. Li (ed.), *Subject and Topic.* New York: Academic Press, 149–188.

Grimes, Barbara. 1996. *Ethnologue.* Dallas: Summer Institute of Linguistics.

Horn, Laurence. 1989. *A Natural History of Negation.* Chicago: University of Chicago Press.

Jackendoff, Ray. 1990. *Semantic Structures.* Cambridge: MIT Press.

Kayne, Richard. 1993. "Towards a Modular Theory of Auxiliary Selection." *Studia Linguistica* 47: 3–31.

Kiss, Katalin. 1995. *Discourse Configurational Languages.* Oxford: Oxford University Press.

Kuroda, S.-Y. 1992. *Japanese Syntax and Semantics.* Dordrecht: Kluwer.

Ladusaw, William. 1994. "Thetic and Categorical, State and Individual, Weak and Strong." *Proceedings of the Conference on Semantics and Linguistic Theory 4*. Ithaca, NY: Cornell University, Department of Modern Languages and Linguistics, 220–229.

Li, Charles and Sandra Thompson. 1976. "Subject and Topic: A New Typology of Language." In Charles N. Li (ed.), *Subject and Topic*. New York: Academic Press, 457–489.

Payne, Doris. 1997. "Argument Structure and Locus of Affect in the Maasai External Possession Construction." *Proceedings of the Twenty-third Annual Meeting of the Berkeley Linguistics Society, Special Session on African Languages*. Berkeley: Berkeley Linguistics Society, 98–115.

Ritter, Elizabeth and Sara Thomas Rosen. 1993. "Deriving Causation." *Natural Language and Linguistic Theory* 11: 519–555.

Schafer, Robin. 1997. "Encoding Categorical Judgments in *have* Clauses". Ms.

Shibatani, Masayoshi. 1994. "An Integrational Approach to Possessor Raising, Ethical Datives, and Adversative Passives." *Proceedings of the Twentieth Annual Meeting of the Berkeley Linguistics Society*. Berkeley: Berkeley Linguistics Society, 461–486.

Szabolcsi, Anna. 1994. "The Noun Phrase." In Ferenc Kiefer and Katalin Kiss (eds.), *The Syntactic Structure of Hungarian*, San Diego: Academic Press, 179–274 [*Syntax and Semantics 27*].

The Double Unaccusative Construction in Sinitic Languages

Hilary Chappell
La Trobe University, Melbourne

1. Introduction

The present study examines a syntactically aberrant construction in Sinitic languages which I provisionally label the double unaccusative. This construction represents a clear example of a syntactic construction where the rules of grammar, narrowly understood, are violated: in the double unaccusative, intransitive process verbs take two arguments, one more argument than the verb valency should allow, recalling the "one-too-many-argument" problem described in Shibatani (1994).

The two arguments of the intransitive verb designate possessor (PR) and possessum (PM). Furthermore, the nouns in this possessive relationship occur discontinuously and belong to different constituents. Specifically, the PR appears in the canonical position for grammatical subject (S) clause-initially while the PM appears postverbally in the canonical object position (O). An example of this construction from Cantonese is given below, following the structural formula:

Double unaccusative construction:

$\text{NOUN}_{\text{POSSESSOR}}$ $\text{VERB}_{\text{INTRANSITIVE}}$ $\text{NOUN}_{\text{PART/KIN TERM}}$

Cantonese Yue

(1) 棵 樹 落 咗 好 多 葉
Poh¹ sue⁶ lok⁶ joh² ho² doh¹ yip⁶
$\text{CLASS}_{\text{REF}}$ tree fall PERF very many leaf
'That tree has lost many leaves [more literally: The tree fell very many leaves].'[1]

In this analysis of one type of external possessor construction [EPC] in Sinitic languages, I show that the noun in the canonical preverbal position of syntactic subject acts as the affected PR or experiencer of the event while it is clearly the postverbal noun, in canonical O position, which holds an argument relation with the intransitive verb. Furthermore, I argue that this construction only allows the verb class of unaccusatives, as a specific subtype of intransitive verbs. Unaccusative verbs are intransitive verbs whose single argument is a semantic undergoer but never an agent. This leads to the claim that it is precisely the relationship of inalienable possession (see Chappell and McGregor 1995) which licenses the use of this unusual intransitive construction with two nouns, the 'extra' noun in syntactic S position being semantically a PR.[2] Hence, I conclude that the construction does not represent a double case phenomenon at all.

This kind of construction is significant for language universals and syntactic theory in that Sinitic languages, as can be anticipated from their typological profile, do not use any overt morphological device such as an applicative affix on the verb to adjust the verb valency. Interestingly, this bears similarities to the case for the IlKeekonyokie dialect of Maasai which has various applicative devices but unexpectedly does not use them in the EPC with intransitive verbs taking two arguments (see Payne and Barshi — this volume). Nor is oblique case marking possible on the PR noun in Sinitic languages which could otherwise indicate non-argument status. The conclusion is that this syntactic configuration has to be explained first of all in terms of its semantic and discourse motivation. Hence, this Sinitic construction can provide a limiting case for setting up the common syntactic and semantic parameters for the language universals of EPCs.

2. Previous studies in Sinitic

As is typical for EPCs and topic–comment constructions in Sinitic, this unaccusative construction has been little studied in the literature. It is a topic treated in Mullie (1932), Gao (1969), Wang (1969), Teng (1974a, 1974b) and Modini (1981) for Mandarin and Teng (1995) for Taiwanese Southern Min but, surprisingly, it is only briefly mentioned in Chao's grammar of Mandarin (1968: 323–324, 673–674). Chao classifies his three examples — all with the verb *sǐ* 'die' — as 'inverted subject' sentences. These are sentences where the subject of certain intransitive verbs can occur postverbally, to wit, with verbs of appearance and disappearance. These do not, however, permit an extra argument slot for verbs otherwise subcategorized just for one. Hence, I treat them as a separate construction type with normal valency for intransitive verbs.

Inverted subject construction

$VERB_{INTRANSITIVE}$ NOUN

Mandarin:

(2) 起 霧 了
qǐ wù le
arise fog INC
'There rises a fog.' (Chao 1968: 324)

3. Typological notes on Sinitic languages and the database

Sinitic languages are a sister phylum to Tibeto-Burman languages in the Sino-Tibetan language family located in East and Southeast Asia. Typologically, these tonal languages show analytic or isolating features, though in some Min languages, for example, the development of case markers and complementizers from lexical verbs and the use of a range of nominal suffixes has moved further along the path of grammaticalization than for Mandarin. Complex allomorphy is widespread in Min dialects while tone sandhi can be used as a derivational device in many languages, for example, in the formation of diminutives in Hong Kong Cantonese. In Toishan Cantonese, aspectual distinctions such as for the perfective may also be signalled by tone change.

Mandarin is the official language in the People's Republic of China where it is called *pǔtōnghuà* and also in Taiwan where it is known as *guóyǔ*. Demographically, it has the largest number of speakers of any Sinitic language, spoken by 71.5% of the population in China in one of its dialect forms (Ramsey 1987: 87), and it covers the largest expanse of territory from Manchuria in the northeast of China to Yunnan and Sichuan provinces in the southwest. The other seven main dialect groups fall neatly into almost complementary geographical distribution with Mandarin, covering the east and southeast of China. Sinitic languages can thus be classified into three main groups following Norman (1988):

A. **Northern group**

I. Northern Chinese (Mandarin)
- (i) Northern
- (ii) Northwestern
- (iii) Xiajiang or Lower Yangtze dialects
- (iv) Southwestern

B. **Sinitic languages with a transitional character between the north and south:**

II. Xiang (mainly Hunan province)
III. Gan (Jiangxi province)
IV. Wu dialects such as Shanghainese
(Zhejiang and southern Jiangsu provinces)

C. **Sinitic languages of southeastern China:**

V. Min dialect group (Fujian province)
  (i) Southeastern Min — Taiwanese, Xiamen (Amoy) and Chaozhou (Teochew)
  (ii) Northeastern Min — Fuzhouese[3]
VI. Kejia or Hakka (scattered over Guangdong and Fujian provinces, Taiwan)
VII. Yue dialects such as Cantonese (Guangdong and Guangxi provinces)

Some sinologists also recognize three further dialect groups: these are the Jin dialects in Shanxi province and Inner Mongolia; the Hui dialects found in parts of Anhui, Jiangxi and Zhejiang provinces; and the Pinghua dialects of Guangxi (see Sagart, to appear and Zhang (1996) for further description).

Most of the major dialect groups within Sinitic languages are represented in the database for this analysis. These are the following seven languages.

(a) Mandarin (standard mainland variety of *pǔtōnghuà*; standard Taiwanese Mandarin)
(b) Changsha Xiang
(c) Nanchang Gan
(d) Shanghainese Wu
(e) Southeastern Min — Taiwanese
(f) Hong Kong Cantonese Yue
(g) Hakka[4]

Data from these dialects on unaccusative constructions are used to model the specific syntactic and semantic features of this type of external possessor construction, shared by Sinitic languages, as defined in Payne (1997) and Payne and Barshi (this volume).

3.1 *Basic word order of transitive clauses in Sinitic*

In general, S-V-O (or Agent-Verb-Object) is the basic word order with transitive verbs in Sinitic languages (cf. Norman 1988: 10 and Ramsey 1987: 73). This has been confirmed in recent studies such as Sun (1996) and Tao (1996) for Mandarin and in my own database for seven of the Sinitic languages. Tao's findings in a discourse study of a large corpus of conversational Mandarin show that post-verbal position is the canonical position for transitive objects while transitive agents occur only preverbally (Tao 1996: 122, 201). Matthews and Yip (1994) similarly posit S-V-O as one of the basic word orders for Cantonese. Hence, my analysis takes A-V-O and S-V as the basic word orders for transitive and intransitive predicates respectively.

3.2 *Transitivity in Chinese languages*

The claim is made in the present analysis that the type of EPC under consideration in Sinitic languages is used exclusively with two argument clauses that contain verbs that, in all other syntactic environments, are prototypical one-argument intransitive verbs as far as their case frame goes.

But what are the parameters of transitivity in Sinitic? This needs to be clearly delineated. First, I take transitivity to be a property of the whole clause as in Halliday (1967) and Hopper and Thompson (1980). Verbs which are labile or ambitransitive were excluded from the investigation. These are verbs similar to English *walk, melt* or *march* which can form both transitive and intransitive clauses, the transitive usage being licensed by the causative feature of the construction.

(3) *They walked for many miles.*

(4) *He walked the dog.*

Chao (1968: Chapter 8) defines intransitive verbs in Mandarin as the type which only allows cognate objects such as verbal classifiers, as opposed to transitive verbs which can take any kind of object; Chao proceeds to classify transitive and intransitive verbs into 9 categories. He considers areas of class overlap and finds that, similarly to English, Mandarin has verbs that can form both types of clauses, such as *xià* 'fall, move in a downwards direction', which has a transitive usage in *xià-qī* 'play chess' and *xià-dàn* 'lay eggs'.

I thus excluded pseudo-transitive verbs comparable to English *eat*, which takes either a cognate object from the domain of food or can be used intransitively with the external object understood:

(5) *Can you ring back later? We're eating right now.* [$\text{Verb}_{\text{INTR}}$]

(6) *Jess is eating her favourite Italian dessert, tiramisu.* [$\text{Verb}_{\text{TRANS}}$]

Nor could any of the verbs belong to the type *forget, lose* or *drop* which, though nonvolitional, have a transitive case frame in English and also in many Sinitic languages:

(7) *You dropped your pen on the floor. *You dropped.*

A final diagnostic was that none of the unaccusative clauses could be passivized:

(8) **The tree was fallen many leaves by the wind.*

Wierzbicka (in press) defines prototypical transitivity in terms of an agent, A^{PR}, who "does something to some thing [O^{PR}], because of which, something else happens to O^{PR} at the same time. After this, O^{PR} is not like before. A^{PR} wanted this to happen." She further identifies three core semantic roles of AGENT, PATIENT and UNDERGOER. In her view, S or subject is not a semantic primitive but only a grammatical notion found in certain syntactic contexts that cannot be "linked with any identifiable semantic prototype". I adopt her useful distinction between PATIENT to which an agent does something (found only in prototypical transitive clauses) and UNDERGOER to which something happens (applicable to intransitive clauses of the unaccusative type: *The little boy fell over; I'm scared; You got hurt*). Since the general semantic role of AGENT is defined by Wierzbicka in terms of "X did something," it is thus applicable to agent NPs in both transitive and intransitive clauses (known as 'unergative' clauses: *I cried*; *She snored loudly; The child jumped up and down*). Wierzbicka further defines grammaticalized TOPIC as "I want to say something about Y" wich is relevant to the PR (see section 8).

The predicates in the EPC describe a process involving a change of state that directly affects the UNDERGOER, coded by the noun slotted into postverbal position. This event affects an inalienable PR coded by the noun in preverbal position, the TOPIC. There is no possibility for a prototypical transitive interpretation of a volitional agent acting upon a patient to achieve some desired result state, nor is any degree of transitivity possible such as a causative interpretation. For example, with expressions such as the Mandarin unaccusative EP: *Tā yǎ-le sǎngzi* '3SG go:hoarse PERF throat' 'She went hoarse in the throat', the "surface subject" *tā* '3SG' is not interpreted as responsible for this event in the sense of making her own throat go hoarse (for example, by talking or shouting too much). If a speaker wants to attribute responsibility to the subject, then a causative type of resultative verb compound is more appropriate: *Tā kū-yǎ le sǎngzi* '3SG cry:hoarse PERF throat' 'She cried her throat hoarse' in the sense that she did something which caused the resultant state but without necessarily wanting this to happen.

4. Possession constructions in Mandarin: Double subjects and double objects

The unaccusative construction is not the only EPC which can be found in Sinitic languages. For the purpose of contrast with the main analysis, I briefly digress to describe some other EPCs, using Mandarin data.

4.1 *Double subject construction*

In Chappell (1995), I investigated double subject constructions in Mandarin Chinese discourse, showing that these code an inalienable relationship between a person and body parts, as well as other aspects of the personal domain such as kin and units of social organization.

The double subject or double nominative construction is so labelled due to the feature of the two nouns juxtaposed in sentence-initial position which appear to share a subject-like role vis-à-vis the stative verb in the predicate. Using the semantico-syntactic primes proposed by Dixon (1979, 1994) of A, S and O, and similarly by Comrie (1981), we could label this construction as S_1–S_2–V:

Double subject construction

NP_{WHOLE} NP_{PART} $VP_{STATIVE}$

(9) 我 心 寒
wǒ xīn hán
1SG heart cold
'I felt discouraged.' [Bai 1993: 56]

I showed in Chappell (1995) that for spoken Mandarin from conversational and narrative discourse, lexical NPs as PRs are coded into an intonationally separate unit, preceding the clause with a stative predicate that contains the part noun.

TOPIC-NP_{WHOLE} // SUBJECT-NP_{PART} $VP_{STATIVE}$

(10) 那個 女孩子 個子 顯得 比較 大
Nèige nǚháizi // gèzi xiǎnde bǐjiào dà
that:CLASS girl:child build appear rather big
'That girl, she appeared to be quite big in build.' [Pear 1.0: 200]

In contrast to this, pronominal PRs are typically coded into the same intonation unit or written clause:

(11) 他 朋友 多，人緣 好
Tā péngyou duō, rényuánr hǎo.
3SG friend many popularity good
'He had lots of friends and was very popular [lit. Him — friends were many and popularity good.' [Bai 1993: 51]

The first noun could be categorized as a kind of topic NP when it occurs in its own intonation unit as in (10) above (see also Tao 1996 for a discussion of NP intonation units in Mandarin); it encodes something like affected PR in the pronominal subtype, exemplified in (9) and (11). Apart from the obvious word order distinction, this construction differs from the unaccusative EPC in two main features: (i) the predicate is stative, that is, not the required intransitive process type; and (ii) a person's physical or psychological condition is described, neutral in effect for the PR; that is, neither beneficial nor adversative.

4.2 *A triplet of constructions with discontinuous double objects*

In Mandarin, there are two construction types with transitive verbs that allow what appear to be discontinuous constituents and one with intransitive verbs; these are (i) the passive (of bodily effect), (ii) the *bǎ* construction (with a retained object) and (iii) the unaccusative construction — the subject of this study. Using syntactic primes again in a first *ansatz* on this problem, these three constructions appear to be aligned on an ergative principle of either O_1 PASSIVE MARKER — A — V — O_2 for the passive; A — BA — O_1 — V — O_2 for the *bǎ* construction (that is, with direct objects or semantic patients of transitive verbs); and S_1 — V — S_2 for the unaccusative where S is understood as the semantic undergoer of an intransitive verb. All three constructions are semantically united by virtue of the PR and PM representing the patient or undergoer while, syntactically, they share the feature of discontinuous constituents for the whole and part nouns, described elsewhere in the literature as 'double case'. This appears to confirm Payne and Barshi's hypothesis (this volume) that unaccusative subjects and direct objects (of non EPCs) are highest in accessibility for the formation of EPCs. Examples of each are given below.

(i) Passive of bodily effect: O_1 — PASSIVE MARKER (*ràng/bèi/jiào*) — Agent — V — O_2

The following example illustrates the passive of bodily effect. The passivized subject *zhǔguǎn de Déguórén* 'the German in charge' holds a possessive relationship with the retained object (postverbal noun) *tǔi* 'leg' (see Chappell 1986):

(12) 主管 的 德國人 到 內蒙古 開
Zhǔguǎn de Déguórén dào Nèi Měnggǔ kāi
be:in:charge GEN German to Inner-Mongolia fly
飛機 轟 羊 完 讓 老鄉 用 步槍
fēijī hōng yáng wán, ràng lǎoxiāng yòng bùqiāng
plane scare sheep play PASS villager use rifle
打掉 了 一條 腿
dǎ-diào le yītiáo tǔi
hit-drop PERF one:CLASS leg
'The German who was in charge flew to Inner Mongolia to have fun chasing sheep but had one of his legs shot off by gun-wielding villagers.'
[Beijing 1986: 24]

(ii) *Ba* construction with a retained object:
Agent — TRANSITIVE MARKER (*bǎ*) — O_1 — V — O_2

Similarly, in a subtype of the *bǎ* construction, the noun representing the whole and the PR occurs preverbally (but after the transitive marker *bǎ* as its object), while the noun representing the part is retained postverbally (see also Thompson 1973).

(13) 兩個 人 就 動手 忙 起來 把 魚 括
Liǎngge rén jìu dòng-shǒu máng-qǐlai, bǎ yú guā
two:CLASS person then start:work busy-INC BA fish scrape
了 鱗
le lín.
PERF scale
'Then the two of them got busily to work, scaling the fish' (more literally: took the fish and scraped off their scales).'
[Chen: 1984: 183]

(iii) Unaccusative external possession construction

$\text{NOUN}_{\text{POSSESSOR}}$ $\text{VERB}_{\text{INTRANSITIVE}}$ $\text{NOUN}_{\text{POSSESSUM [PART/KIN TERM]}}$

I analyse the third case of double semantic undergoers below. This third construction type differs from the the passive of bodily effect and the *bǎ* construction with a retained object, in that the main verb is not a transitive but an intransitive unaccusative one: S_1–V– S_2.

The following example from a Mandarin novel codes a relationship between a mass noun and individual items:

(14) 父親 …只 是 白 頭髮 似乎 又 多了
Fùqin zhǐ shi bái tóufa sìhu yòu duō-le
father only be white hair seem again be:many-PERF
幾 根
jǐ gēn
few strand(CLASS)
'As for father, he just had a few more white hairs.'
(more literally: 'As for father — just white hair seems to have increased a few strands.')
[Ding 21:17]

All four types of possession construction in Mandarin are united by the syntactic feature of the whole or PR noun preceding the part; and more significantly, by the general feature of the constructional semantics in coding inalienable possession — something happens to the whole in terms of an event or state affecting a part.

5. The unaccusative EPC in Sinitic languages

In the main analysis which follows, the unaccusative EPC is examined in detail with respect to the seven Sinitic languages of Taiwanese Southern Min, Shanghainese Wu, Changsha Xiang, Cantonese Yue, Gan, Nanchang Hakka and Mandarin.

5.1 *Grammatical relations in the unaccusative EPC*

A defining feature of intransitive and stative verbs is that they take only one argument position. The EPC is striking in that two nouns accompany an intransitive verb and both appear at first blush to have the identical semantic role of undergoer and syntactic role of S. For this reason, I use the term 'double unaccusative'.

Consider the following pair of agnates which shows a semantic relation between the EPC in (15) and its counterpart with a genitive subject in (16):

Unaccusative construction

$[NP_{possessor}]_{patient}$ $VERB_{\substack{intransitive\\ process}}$ $[NP_{possessum}]_{patient}$

Taiwanese Southern Min:

(15) 伊 跛 著 左 腳
I pái tiòh tò-kha
3SG lame RES left-leg
'He has gone lame in the left leg.'

Genitive subject construction:

$[N_{possessor}$ (GEN) $N_{possessum}]_{patient}$ $VERB_{intransitive\ process}$

Taiwanese Southern Min:

(16) 伊 的 左腳 跛 啊
I ê tò-kha pái a
3SG GEN left-leg lame PERF
'His left leg has gone lame.'

In (16) with a genitive subject, only the PM as the head noun of the subject NP holds a core grammatical relation to the verb, namely S; the PR stands in a dependent relation to it. I return to the problem of one or two arguments for the EPC in Section 6 below. In order to decide on the verb valency question, relevant semantic and syntactic features are next presented.

Note that since this study concentrates on the invariant semantic and syntactic features of the unaccusative construction in order to characterize it as a Sinitic construction, only a brief description of variation between Chinese languages is provided. It can, however, be confirmed from the data collected that the range of predicates and metaphors coded by this construction in each language varies widely and quite idiosyncratically with respect to the lexical items used.

5.2 *Range of verb classes*

Two types of intransitive verbs are generally recognized: unaccusative verbs are those whose subject is in the semantic role of undergoer, unergative verbs are those which have agentive subjects, as defined in Levin and Rappaport Hovav (1993). In all seven Sinitic languages investigated, a postverbal subject can co-occur with semantically intransitive predicates such as 'die', 'fall', 'go:rotten', 'go:white', 'go:blind', 'go:bad', 'redden', 'become:more', 'go:hoarse', 'go:numb' and 'get:injured'; that is, with unaccusative verbs. They do not in general co-occur with unergative verbs such as 'run away', 'go' or 'cry'. The exclusion of unergative verbs is shown by the Cantonese example in (17) with *jau*^{2} 'run, leave'. Compare this example with its grammatically well-formed genitive counterpart in (18):

Cantonese Yue
EPC

(17) *佢哋 走 咗 細路
**Kui*^{5}*dei*^{6} *jau*^{2} *joh*^{2} *sai*^{3}*lo*^{6}.
3PL run PERF children

Genitive subject

(18) 佢哋 細路 走 咗
Kui^{5}*dei*^{6} *sai*^{3}*lo*^{6} *jau*^{2} *joh*^{2}.
3PL children run PERF
'Their children have left/run away.'

Table 1 provided in the appendix shows that unergative verbs like 'run' are equally unacceptable in this construction for Taiwanese Southern Min, Changsha Xiang, Nanchang Gan, Shanghainese Wu and Hakka. However, there is one apparent problem for this claim in that Mandarin allows the use of *pǎo* 'run away, flee' in this construction and thus seems at first to constitute a puzzling exception:

Mandarin

(19) 他們 家 跑 了 媳婦
Tāmen jiā pǎo le xífu.
3PL home/family run PERF wife
'Their daughter-in-law (or wife) ran away from home.'

The same Mandarin construction as in (19) could alternatively have many other animate nouns such as *lǎomāzi* '(female) servant'; *yī-qún niú* 'a herd of cattle' or *yītiáo gǒu* ' a dog' in the postverbal slot as the 'escapees', yet these do not necessarily hold an inalienable relation to the preverbal noun (which could also just be *tā* '3SG'). The six other Sinitic languages selected for the database use a different lexeme for 'run away', etymologically distinct from *pǎo*. These are cognates of the verb *jau*^{2} 'leave, run away' in Cantonese (see (17) and (18) above) that has the related meaning of 'leave, walk' in Mandarin [*zǒu*]. Similarly, Mandarin *zǒu* 'leave, walk' cannot be used in this EPC; for example, it cannot be substituted for *pǎo* in (19) above. The explanation for this problem can be better understood if we consider that in examples such as (19), the NP in clause-initial position has a basic locative meaning of 'house' or 'home'. This is often explicitly coded as a locative by means of postpositions such as *-li* 'in' in (20):

(20) 樹林裡 跑出來 兩個 逃兵
Shùlín-li pǎo-chūlai liǎng-ge táobīng.
forest-in run-out two-CLASS deserter
'Out of the forest two deserters came running.'
(more literally: 'Out of the forest came running two deserters.')

Hence, this kind of example in Mandarin can be reclassified as belonging to the type of inverted subject sentence, briefly described in the introduction, whose predicates are restricted to postural verbs and verbs of appearance, disappearance and existence. In this case, *pǎo* 'run:away' is a disappearance verb and the postverbal noun *xífu* 'wife, daughter-in-law' is (arguably) its agentive subject. When optional preverbal NPs are present, they commonly represent a location (see Chao 1968: 671–674; Fan 1996: ch. 8; p.167 for further discussion and examples of the Mandarin inverted subject construction with *pǎo* and preverbal locatives). I thus persist in the claim that unaccusative verbs must be specified for use in the predicate of this Sinitic construction.

In the next section, I argue that there is a semantic rationale behind allowing two undergoer nouns to co-occur with certain intransitive verbs in Sinitic languages: this concerns the fact that the two nouns are related through inalienable possession, either as a part-whole relationship for inanimates, or for body parts and kin with human and animate PRs.

6. Semantic category of the postverbal noun and inalienable possession

The EPC restricts the relationship between the PR and PM to an inalienable one, with part-whole and kin as the main subtypes. The postverbal noun codes either a body part of a human or animate noun, part of an inanimate whole, or kin while the preverbal NP codes the PR. The very first example in the introduction gives an instance of an inanimate part-whole relation coded by the EPC in Cantonese with 'leaf' and 'tree'. Ordinary kinds of material possessions and alienable kinds of ownership cannot be expressed through this construction, however, as comparison of the Cantonese examples (21) and (22) clearly show:[5]

Cantonese Yue

(21) 佢 死 咗 太太
Kui[5] sei[2] joh[2] taai[3]taai[2]
3SG die PERF wife
'He was bereaved of his wife (literally: He died wife).'

Cantonese Yue

(22) *我 嬤嬤 死 咗 啲 花
**Ngoh*^{5} *ma*^{4}*ma*^{4} *sei*^{2} *joh*^{2} *di*^{1} *fa*^{1}
1SG grandmother die PERF CLASS:PL flower
(not: 'My grandmother had her flowers die on her.')

To become grammatical, (22) needs to be reformulated as an S-V-O sentence with a resultative verb compound, as in (23):

Cantonese Yue

(23) 我 嬤嬤 淋 死 咗 啲 花
Ngoh^{5} *ma*^{4} *ma*^{4} *lam*^{4}*–sei*^{2} *joh*^{2} *di*^{1} *fa*^{1}
1SG grandmother soak-die PERF CLASS:PL flower
'My grandmother killed the flowers by overwatering them.'

The category of kin is an interesting, if not idiosyncratic one. The predicate 'to die' cited as the main or only example in some of the references on this construction (Chao 1968; Gao 1969; Wang 1969) turns out to be a singleton in all Sinitic languages surveyed for the category of kin. This generalization includes other synonyms for 'die' such as Mandarin *sàng*, a more formal and polite expression. Semantically similar predicates such as 'get:ill' are not acceptable, despite the fact that they are unaccusative. The following pairs of examples contrast the EPC with agnate genitive subject intransitive sentences in Cantonese and Taiwanese respectively.

Cantonese Yue

(24) *佢 病 咗 太太
**Kui*^{5} *beng*^{6} *joh*^{2} *taai*^{3}*taai*^{2}
3SG be:ill PERF wife

(25) 佢 嘅 太太 病 咗
Kui^{5} *ge*^{3} *taai*^{3}*taai*^{2} *beng*^{6} *joh*^{2}
3SG GEN wife be:ill PERF
'His wife has become ill.'

Taiwanese Southern Min

(26) *我 破病 尪 啊
**Góa phòa-pī*^{n} *ang a*
1SG get:sick husband PERF

(27) 阮 尪 破病 啊
Gún ang phòa-pī^{n} a
1SG:POSS husband get:sick PERF
'My husband got sick.'

Nor are verbs meaning 'get:rich' or 'grow up' permitted.

Why are there such restrictions for kin possession in this construction? In the course of providing an explanation, the category of kin can be used to highlight several further core semantic features of the construction; it has been shown that the unaccusativity requirement generally rules out the co-occurrence of predicates such as 'leave, run away', exemplified above for Cantonese Yue (see 17). This extends to semantically similar unergative verbs such as 'leave (home) the children'.

Shanghainese Wu
Unaccusative EPC:

(28) 伊拉 出道 嘞 伊拉 小人
**I^{53}la^{53} ts'eʔ^{5}dɔ^{13} ləʔ^{2} i^{53}la^{53} ɕiɔ^{34}n̥iŋ^{13}*
3PL leave PERF 3PL children
(not: 'Their children have left on them.')

Genitive construction:

(29) 伊拉 小人 才 出道 嘞
I^{53}la^{53} ɕiɔ^{34}n̥iŋ^{13} zɛ ts'eʔ^{5}dɔ^{13} ləʔ^{2}
3PL children all leave PERF
'All our children have left home (and become independent)'.

This can be usefully compared with European languages such as German where the different types of dative constructions not only allow unaccusative verbs such as 'die', but also unergative verbs such as 'run away':

German

(30) *Mir ist die Frau weggelaufen.*
1SG:DAT is the wife run:away
'My wife ran away on me.'

This leads to the claim that there is an adversity feature, intrinsic to all the Sinitic unaccusative constructions, which rules out unaccusative predicates expressing fortunate events like 'become:rich the son' or even more neutral events like 'grow:up the children'. Only constructions with a genitive subject are acceptable with these predicates:

Taiwanese Southern Min
Unaccusative EPC:

(31) 我 發 囝 阿
**Góa hoat kiá*^{n} *a*
1SG get:rich son PERF

Genitive construction:

(32) 阮 囝 發 阿
Gún kiá^{n} *hoat a*
1SG:POSS son get:rich PERF
'My son got rich.'

Shanghainese Wu
Unaccusative EPC:

(33) *阿拉 大 ▫勒 阿拉 ▫格 小囡
**Aʔ*^{5}*la*^{53} *du*^{13} *leʔ*^{2} *aʔ*^{5}*la*^{53} *kəʔ*^{5} *ɕiɔ*^{34}*nø*^{13}.
1:PL big PERF 1:PL CLASS:POSS children
(not: 'They've had their children grow up on them.')

Genitive construction:

(34) 阿拉 養 大 ▫勒 阿拉 ▫格 小囡
Aʔ^{5}*la*^{53} *ɦiəŋ*^{13}*–du*^{13} *ləʔ*^{2} *aʔ*^{5}*la*^{53} *kəʔ*^{5} *ɕiɔ*^{34}*nø*^{13}.
1:PL raise:big PERF 1:PL CLASS:POSS children
'We've brought up our children.'

None of these situations can be easily interpreted as having any marked effect on the PR, coded as the preverbal subject. This explains why the verb 'get:sick' exemplified in (24) to (27) above for Cantonese and Taiwanese Southern Min does not work, a situation which applies equally to other Sinitic languages. It is an undesirable state of affairs but not one which is sufficiently adversative. For the analogous dative construction in German with a kin PM, these kinds of predicates are similarly proscribed:

(35) German
**Mir sind die Kinder krank/reich/arm geworden.*
1SG:DAT are the children sick/rich/poor become

Hence, even though kin forms a peripheral category in the unaccusative EPC, it can nonetheless be profitably used to display the bundle of features that combine to determine its constructional semantics. In summation, the construction requires an unaccusative predicate which codes an adversative effect on the PR by means of an event that has affected either kin, a part of the body, or part of an inanimate whole, resulting in a marked change of state for the kin or part. More support for these features is provided in the next section on parts of wholes.

6.1 *Part-whole expressions*

The prototype category for the unaccusative EPC involves body parts and their 'owners', the body part being coded into postverbal position and the PR into the preverbal one. A subsidiary category is formed by the inanimate part-whole relation which patterns in the same way as for animates.

Just as for kin, a marked effect on the body part is a primary semantic constraint since the data show that dynamic processes causing changes of state which are short-lived are incompatible; for example, 'get:suntanned (literally: darken the skin)' or 'get:tired in the legs'. In contrast to this, all Chinese languages investigated permit predicates expressing a change to a part of the body which affects one of the main organs of perception or the limbs and results in some kind of dysfunctionality. These include 'go:lame', 'fall:out (hair, teeth)', 'get:injured (hand)' and 'get:broken (hand, arm, leg)'. All languages apart from Taiwanese Southern Min can use the stative verb 'be:many, more' to express the meaning of an increase in some feature such as white hairs or wrinkles. All apart from Changsha Xiang can use a predicate for 'go:bad' with a large number of body parts to generically express some kind of malfunctioning. The majority of languages can also use verbs for 'go:blind' [all except Taiwanese and Xiang] and 'go:deaf' [all except Taiwanese and Shanghainese] in this EPC in combination with the relevant body part. Mandarin and Gan permitted the expression 'go: numb in the legs' while only Mandarin allowed 'go:hoarse in the throat'. I suggest that the restriction on the last two predicates is precisely due to the constraint requiring a marked effect on the body part, and that in this respect Mandarin is somewhat more liberal than other Chinese languages. Furthermore, all these predicates are adversative for the PR. Mullie (1932, 1933) and Fan (1996) give many examples of this pattern for Mandarin, which they treat, like Chao (1968), as a case of subject inversion.

Taiwanese Southern Min

(36) 伊 今年 落 勿會 少 頭毛
I kin-nî^n làu bōe chió thâu-mô·
3SG this:year fall NEG few hair
'He lost quite a lot of hair this year [more literally: He has fallen

not a little hair this year].'

Cantonese Yue

(37) 佢 爛 晒 啲 牙
kui^{5} *laan*^{6} *saai*^{3} *di*^{1} *nga*^{4}
3SG rot COMP CLASS:PL tooth
'All her teeth went bad [more literally: She rotted all teeth].'

Four languages can use the predicate 'go:white (several strands of) hair' [Mandarin, Xiang, Taiwanese, Cantonese]. This is excluded in Shanghainese where the expression is accidentally homophonous with 'pull:out the hair'. The transitive agentive reading apparently overrides the intrepretation for the less frequent unaccusative construction. This predicate is exemplified from Changsha Xiang in (38):

Changsha Xiang

(38) 我 白 噠 幾 根 頭髮 噠
ŋo^{41} *pγ*^{24} *ta*^{21} *tɕi*^{41} *kən*^{33} *təu*^{13}*fa* *ta*^{21}
1SG white PERF several CLASS hair INC
'Several strands of my hair have turned white.'

It is striking to find that the same stative verb for 'white' <u>cannot</u> be used in any of the languages for a beneficial change such as 'go:white in the teeth' or 'go:pale in the skin'.[6] Examples (38) and (39) show this revealing contrast for Xiang.

Changsha Xiang

(39) *□各 隻 細伢子 白 噠 牙齒 噠
**ko*^{24} *tsa*^{24} *ɕi*^{45}*ŋa*^{13}*tsɪ* *pγ*^{24} *ta*^{21} *ŋa*^{13}*ts'ɪ* *ta*^{21}
this CLASS child white PERF teeth INC
(not: 'The child has had her teeth become whiter.')

Other beneficial predicates tested were 'get:smoother skin' to provide a contrast with the (acceptable) 'get:wrinkled skin' or 'become:many wrinkles', not to mention 'go:wavy hair' (as a natural change, not a perm) compared with 'lose' or 'fall:out hair'. All have the consistent result that only adversative changes of state are possible. One apparent counterexample occurs in Fan (1996: 140) for Mandarin (my added glossing and translation):

Mandarin

(40) 他 好 了 瘡疤 忘 了 疼
Tā hǎo le chuāngbā wàng le téng.
3SG good PERF scar forget PERF pain

'He forgot the bitter past after he was relieved of his suffering.'
(more literally: 'He forgot the pain after his wound had healed.')

As a metaphor, (40) does not, however, express a desirable state of affairs. It is used as a criticism when someone shows they haven't learned from a past lesson by making the same mistake again. Hence, in general, the adversative constraint appears to hold.

Inanimate part-whole relations pattern on the person-body part model. Five such examples were tested across Sinitic languages with differing results, which can be viewed in Table 1. These were for 'fall the leaves [tree]' as in (1) above; 'get:punctured (or go:flat) the tire [car]'; 'collapse the roof [house]'; 'go:wrong the leg [chair]' and 'go:rotten to the core [as in fruit and vegetables]'. Only the first predicate with 'fall the leaves [tree]' can be used in all languages surveyed while 'go:flat [tire]' is next highest in acceptability as only the Changsha Xiang speaker cannot use it in this construction. The remaining three predicates had varying patterns of acceptability, as the table shows.

6.2 *Metaphors and other predicates for temperament and disposition*

Metaphors for emotions and personality traits are often formed by body-part terms combined with stative verbs in Chinese languages, as (9) above exemplifies for Mandarin with *heart-cold* for 'discouraged' (see also Chao 1968: 96–100 for a discussion of Mandarin; Matisoff 1978 and Clark 1995 for this widespread phenomenon in Southeast Asian languages). Metaphors and predicates which describe a person's inherent temperament or physical features do not, however, readily lend themselves to use in the EPC since they are semantically stative. These include metaphors meaning 'be easily swayed/credulous [literally: have soft or light ears (depending on the language)]'; 'be jealous [literally: be red in the eyes]' or 'be bad tempered [literally: be bad in the spleen]'.

Such metaphors were used to test the flexibility of the unaccusative EPC in Sinitic languages. The findings confirm the general principle that the small number of acceptable metaphors are those that can be used to code a change in emotion. Furthermore, metaphors coded as unaccusative constructions are generally possible in only a small number of cases across the languages surveyed. Table 1 (Appendix) shows the limited use of metaphors in this EPC. In Changsha Xiang, their use is completely excluded. This restricted occurrence in the unaccusative EPC is the consequence of two factors:

(i) Metaphors with stative verbs of color and quality are often used to describe some inherent personality trait or aspect of a person's disposition. The next two examples with unmarked genitive subjects use a lexicalized metaphor for 'temper' based on the morpheme for 'spleen' with stative verbs that mean 'bad':

Nanchang Gan:

(41) 佢 脾氣 好 壞
tç'ɪe p'itç'i hau fai
3SG temper very bad
'She's very bad-tempered.'

Cantonese Yue:

(42) 佢 脾氣 好 壞
Kui^{5} *pei*^{4}*hei*^{3} *ho*^{2} *waai*^{6}.
3SG temper very bad
'She's very bad-tempered.'

This metaphor cannot form unaccusative EPCs in either language which mean 'Her temper's got worse [more literally: she's got worse in the temper]', despite appropriate aspectual marking.[7] This is shown by (43) and (44):

Nanchang Gan EPC:

(43) *佢 壞 了 脾氣
**tç'ɪe fai lə p'itç'i.*
3SG bad PERF temper

Cantonese Yue EPC:

(44) *佢 壞 咗 脾氣
**Kui*^{5} *waai*^{6} *joh*^{2} *pei*^{4}*hei*^{3}.
3SG bad PERF temper

This particular metaphor could only form an unaccusative EPC in Taiwanese Southern Min with *phái*^{n},[8] yet Cantonese *waai*^{6}, Gan *fai* and Mandarin *huài*, all meaning 'be bad', could be used quite successfully in other predicates with post-verbal body parts to form acceptable EPCs such as 'go bad the teeth' or 'go wrong a (chair) leg' (see Section 6.1 above on part-whole relations coded into the unaccusative EPC). For example, these stative verbs could be used to form expressions such as Mandarin *Tā huài le dùzi* 'He's got diarrhea' [a lexicalization from the literal meaning of 'something has gone wrong in the stomach'] and Taiwanese *I phái*^{n}*-tióh pak-tó· a* [3SG go:wrong-RES stomach PERF 'He's got something wrong with his stomach'] referring to either diarrhea or an unspecific stomach ache. In other words, this particular set of stative verbs has a wide range of application in EPCs due to the generic meaning of something going wrong (whether that be illness, infection, becoming broken, damaged or going rotten).

(ii) In general, the acceptability of stative verbs for color depends on the appropriate aspect marking. Aspect markers which express a change of state are required, if not a durative action process (see also Chao 1968: Chapter 8 for aspect marking possibilities of Mandarin stative verbs). The notable exceptions to this restriction are the transitory emotions of 'go:red the eyes' [Mandarin, Gan, Wu, Yue] as a metaphor for jealousy, and 'go:red the face' [Mandarin, Gan, Wu, Yue] as a metaphor for anger or embarrassment.

For the predicate 'go:red the eyes', Mandarin, Nanchang Gan, Cantonese Yue and Shanghainese Wu allow this collocation in the unaccusative EPC. However, in Shanghainese, it only has the metaphorical meaning of 'get jealous'; in Cantonese it only has the literal meaning of the eyes becoming red due to crying, tiredness or some other cause such as infection,[9] while in Mandarin and Gan, it can be used both metaphorically and literally:

Cantonese Yue unaccusative EPC

(45) 佢 紅 口曬 對 眼 口敢 話: "對 口吾 住 口羅!"
Kui^{5} *hung*^{4} *saai*^{3} *dui*^{3} *ngaan*^{5} *gam*^{2} *wa*^{6}: "*Dui*^{3}–*m*^{4}–*jue*^{6} *loh*^{1}".
3SG red COMP CLASS eye like:this say sorry PART
'She said "Sorry" with reddened eyes.'

Shanghainese Wu unaccusative EPC

(46) 伊 紅 口勒 眼睛
ɦi^{53} *ɦoŋ*^{13} *leʔ*^{2} *ŋɛ*^{13}*tɕiŋ*^{53}
3SG red PERF eye
'He's become jealous.'

The metaphor of 'go:red in the face' for anger or embarrassment can be used in Mandarin, Gan, Wu and Yue, but not in the other three languages (Xiang, Hakka, Min):

Mandarin unaccusative EPC

(47) 我 答不出來 紅 了 臉
Wǒ dá-bu chūlai hóng le liǎn
1SG answer-NEG-out red PERF face
'I couldn't answer and went red in the face.' (Bai 1993: 56)

Nanchang Gan unaccusative EPC

(48) 佢們 爲什麼紅了臉
tɕ'ɪɛmən uei-ɕitli fəŋ ləʔ liɛⁿ?
3PL why red PERF face
'Why have they gone red in the face?'
(e.g. in a context of quarrelling)

In Taiwanese Southern Min, neither of these expressions can be used in the EPC either with literal or metaphorical interpretations. I give one pair of examples with eye-red for 'jealous' to illustrate this contrast in acceptability:

Taiwanese Southern Min unmarked genitive subject construction

(49) 汝目孔赤啊
Lí bȧk-kháng chhiah a
2SG eye-socket red PERF
'You're jealous.'

Taiwanese Southern Min unaccusative EPC

(50) *汝赤目孔啊
**Lí chhiah bȧk-kháng a*
2SG red eye-socket PERF

In several Sinitic languages there is a metaphor based on 'ear' referring to a credulous person, that is, to someone who is easily taken in by others. This metaphor is possible in Mandarin, Yue and Wu with the stative verb 'be:soft' and for Southern Min with the stative verb 'be:light' in genitive or double subject form. However, it is only in Mandarin and Taiwanese Southern Min that an unaccusative form can be found.

Mandarin unaccusative EPC:

(51) 我軟了耳朵就買下好多股票
Wǒ ruǎn le ěrduo, jiu mǎi-xià hǎo duō gǔpiào.
1SG be:soft PERF ear then buy-DIR very many share
'I was so gullible that I bought a lot of shares.'

Taiwanese Southern Min

(52) 伊輕了耳孔啊
I khin liáu hī^{n}khang a
3SG be:light COMP ear PERF
'She's become easier to persuade.'

In Shanghainese, only the double subject construction is available with both literal and metaphorical meanings for 'be:soft in the ears', while the EPC was not acceptable to my informant:

Shanghainese Wu double subject construction:

(53)	迭	口格	小人	耳朵	老	軟	口格
	Diɪʔ^{2}	*kəʔ*^{5}	*ɕiɔ*^{34}*n̠iŋ*^{13}	*n̠i*^{13}*tu*^{34}	*lɔ*^{13}	*n̠yø*^{13}	*kəʔ*^{5}
	this	CLASS	child	ear	very	soft	PART

'This child has very soft ears.' OR: 'This child is quite credulous.'

Shanghainese Wu unaccusative EPC

(54)	迭	口格	小人	軟	口勒	耳朵
	**Diɪʔ*^{2}	*kəʔ*^{5}	*ɕiɔ*^{34}*n̠iŋ*^{13}	*n̠yø*^{13}	*ləʔ*^{2}	*n̠i*^{13}*tu*^{34}
	this	CLASS	child	soft	PERF	ear

(not: 'This child has gone soft in the ears/become credulous.')

The reader is once again referred to Table 1 for the overall patterning of Chinese languages with respect to five different metaphors for emotion or disposition. Note, however, that this only represents a very small sample of the large inventory of metaphors available in each language.

7. Double unaccusative or single argument verb?

Teng (1974b: 81) has argued that the discontinuous possessive construction, as he labels it, can be analyzed as a sentential predicate accompanied by a noun in Experiencer role, that is, the PR. I agree with his analysis of the V–SUBJ$_2$ as a sentential predicate insofar as it is the postverbal noun which consistently holds the relationship of intransitive subject to the main verb. While the PR noun in preverbal position acts as an undergoer semantically ('affected person' or 'affected whole'), it cannot always stand alone with the verb, that is, minus the postverbal 'part' term. Consider the following Mandarin examples (the symbol # indicates syntactically well-formed but semantically odd):

Mandarin

(55)	他	瞎	了;	瘸	了;	聾	了
	Tā	*xiā*	*le;*	*qué*	*le;*	*lóng*	*le*
	3SG	blind	INC	lame	INC	deaf	INC

'S/he's gone blind; lame; deaf.'

(56) *她 多 了; 她 爛 了;
#Tā duō le; #tā làn le
3SG be:many INC 3SG go:rotten INC
'S/he's increased; gone rotten.'

The interpretations for the two clauses in (56) are semantically implausible when used as completed utterances: 'He's increased' and 'She's gone rotten.' In contrast to this, there is no difficulty for the appropriate body part terms to combine with all of these unaccusative predicates, with or without a preceding genitive or PR noun:

(57) 她 的 眼睛 瞎 了; 腿 瘸 了 耳朵 聾 了
(Tā de) yǎnjing xiā le; tuǐ qué le; ěrduo lóng le
3SG GEN eye blind INC leg lame INC ear deaf INC
'(His/her) eyes have gone blind; (His/her) leg has gone lame; (His/her) ear has gone deaf.'

(58) 他 的 皺紋 多 了; 她 的 手 爛 了
Tā de zhòuwen duō le; tā de shǒu làn le
3SG GEN wrinkles be:many INC; 3SG GEN hand rotten INC
'His wrinkles have increased.' 'Her hand got infected.'

If omission of the postverbal PM does not result in an implausible interpretation, then at the minimum a change of meaning is wrought. If we leave out the postverbal kin term 'wife' in Cantonese *Kui*^{5} *sei*^{2} *joh*^{2} *taai*^{3}*taai*^{2} [3SG-die-PERF-wife], then the meaning changes radically from 'He was bereaved of his wife' to 'He died' [*Kui*^{5} *sei*^{2} *joh*^{2}].

A similar situation pertains in the other languages. Here are the same kind of examples from Taiwanese and Cantonese as indicative of the general case:

Taiwanese Southern Min

(59) 伊 加 了 皺痕 *伊 加
I kē liáu jiâu-hûn as opposed to *#I kē-liáu*
3SG be:more COMP wrinkles 3SG be:more-COMP
'He's got more wrinkles.' 'He's increased.'
(more literally: 'He has become more the wrinkles.')

Cantonese Yue

(60) 佢 斷 咗 隻 趾
Kui^{5} *tuen*^{5} *joh*^{2} *jek*^{3} *geuk*^{3}*ji*^{2}
3SG be:broken PERF CLASS toe
'She broke her toe.'

as opposed to

*佢 斷 咗
#Kui⁵ tuen⁵ joh²
3SG be:broken PERF
'She's broken.'

Could it be argued that the postverbal noun is actually an instance of noun incorporation, and thus, that the preverbal PR noun is the real argument, that is, the nominal that holds a relation to the verb?[10] It appears not to be the case given that the stative verb, as has been argued, needs to take aspectual marking, generally in the form of an enclitic or suffix, which thus separates it from the postverbal PM, while the postverbal PM can itself take attributive modification (see examples 1 and 15 above) or be marked by a classifier as in (60), just like any other individuated direct object noun which normally occupies this position.

A stronger case for noun incorporation can be made for certain kinds of double subject constructions, since the body part term precedes the stative verb rather than follows. The sentential predicate of the double subject construction basically has the reverse word ordering to the unaccusative EPC of $[\text{NOUN}_{\text{BODY PART}}\text{–VERB}_{\text{STATIVE}}]_{\text{VP}}$. I noted in Section 6.2 that many of the predicates in these double subject constructions have become fixed expressions, including metaphors, for different kinds of emotions and dispositions. As such, the body part term and the verb act as a unit. Clark (1995) treats similar constructions involving metaphor in several Southeast Asian languages as instances of noun incorporation. In fact, they can be viewed as the lexicalization of the sentential predicate: $[\text{NOUN}_{\text{BODY PART}}\text{–VERB}_{\text{STATIVE}}]$. Chao (1968: 96) gives some examples with *yāo suān* 'waist-sore' where the sentential predicate is treated as a unit for the purpose of the question operation, rather than just the stative verb alone in the VERB-NEG-VERB form:

Mandarin double subject construction:

(61) 你 今兒 還 腰 酸 不 腰 酸 啦?
Nǐ jīnr hái <u>yāo suān</u> bù <u>yāo suān</u> la?
2SG today still waist sore NEG waist sore PART
'Does the small of your back still feel sore today?'
[from Chao (1968: 96)]

Many of these sentential predicates eventually form compounds as the ultimate stage in the lexicalization process. For example, compare the sentential predicate *(tā) xìngzi (tài) jí* [(she) temperament-too-quick] 'She is (too) quick-tempered' with the compound verb it has generated: *xìngzi jí* 'be quick-tempered'. In the compound, the components are bound and brook no insertion of adverbs like *tài* 'too' (see Chao 1968: 99 and Teng 1974a, 1974b, 1995). Teng, in particular, has argued for the necessity of distinguishing fixed NOUN-VERB expressions from true sentential predicates in the double subject construction.

From this we conclude that the postverbal PM holds the core grammatical relation of subject to the unaccusative verb, while the PR noun has a more peripheral status as a kind of topic. Hence, it cannot be upheld that the unaccusative EPC represents the phenomenon of double case, specifically of two semantic undergoers both acting as subject (see, however, McGregor on double case in 'favorite' constructions of Australian languages, this volume). The preverbal slot for the PR as experiencer of an adversative event affecting kin or a body part is not an argument of the verb but fills an extra syntactic slot licensed by the constructional semantics of inalienable possession. Shibatani (1994) discusses similar phenomena in a range of languages, including the Japanese adversative passive and ethical dative constructions.

This does not appear to tally with the definition given in Payne and Barshi (this volume) for EPCs whereby it is the PR that is hypothesized to hold a core grammatical relation and not the PM. This notwithstanding, the syntactic configuration conforms to other aspects of syntax in Chinese languages, such as a general ordering constraint for the whole noun to always precede the part noun (Barry 1975) and the possibility for a small subset of intransitive verbs to form an inverted subject construction with a postverbal subject.

8. Arguments against deriving the unaccusative EPC from a genitive construction

Some theoretical frameworks might treat the unaccusative as having a source construction in an intransitive construction with a genitive NP as subject. Through the process described as PR raising or PR ascension, the dependent PR noun is extracted from a complex genitive subject NP and becomes the new subject with argument status, while the head noun, the PM, is shifted to postverbal position. Apart from the fact that it is difficult to find a motivation for these two syntactic changes to constituency and position, the superficial resemblance between such agnates is quickly dispelled when further syntactic and discourse features are tested.

As Teng (1974a, 1974b) has already observed, the subject as a topical element differs between the two agnate constructions — the genitive and the EP. I reproduce my example (47) as (62) below:

Mandarin

(62) 我 答不出來 紅 了 臉
Wǒ dá-bu-chūlai hóng le liǎn
1SG answer-NEG-out red PERF face
'I couldn't answer and went red in the face.' (Bai 1993: 56)

(63) 我 的 臉 紅 了
Wǒ de liǎn hóng le
1SG GEN face red INC
'My face went red.'

The first example conveys what happened to *wǒ* 1SG 'me,' the schoolboy main character in a first person narrative who is unable to answer the teacher's question; the second in the pair conveys what happened to *wǒ de liǎn* 'my face', and is thus far less affective in meaning. The PR is thus more likely to function as an important discourse topic than the PM, an issue which needs further empirical study.[11]

The affected PR reading of the unaccusative construction is shown neatly by Teng's example (31) (reproduced here as 64 and 65 from Teng (1974b: 465), who uses it, however, to illustrate a pragmatic feature).

(64) 孔子 的 後裔 死 了
Kǒngzi de hòuyì sǐ le
Confucius GEN descendant die INC
'Confucius' descendants died.'

(65) 孔子 死 了 後裔
**Kǒngzi sǐ le hòuyì*
Confucius die INC descendant
?'Confucius lost his descendants.'

Teng explains the unacceptability of (65) in terms of presupposition: Confucius would normally be presupposed as alive in the case of the EPC, whereas this is not relevant for the sentence with the genitive subject in (64). In my view, it is precisely the necessity for the preverbal NP to be an affected PR which enables this interpretation. Hence, it is difficult to uphold a derivational relationship between the two construction types since they serve different discourse functions and display distinct constructional semantics: the genitive construction has a more general meaning of some event affecting a possession — alienable or inalienable, including all kinds of kin relations. It does not code the specific relation of inalienable possession whereby a PR is adversely affected by an event affecting kin or a body part. Nor is the PR in an experiencer role and thus to be presupposed as living (in the case of animate PRs).

Finally, the unaccusative EPC facilitates metaphorical interpretations not always reflected or uppermost in the generally more literal interpretation of the genitive construction. For example, the unaccusative construction in (66) refers to finding the first telltale signs of aging. This interpretation is not implicit in the genitive agnate in (67) which primarily predicates something about 'hair', even though it is, culturally speaking, a valid inference. The same applies to the similar example in the Changsha dialect of Xiang, given in (38).

Taiwanese Southern Min

(66) 我 白 幾若 枝 頭毛 啊
Góa pėh kúi-ná ki thâu-mô· a.
1SG be:white several CLASS hair PERF
'I've got some white hairs now.'

(67) 阮 老爸 的 頭毛 變 白 啊
Gún lāupē ê thâu-mô· (piàn) pėh a
1POSS father GEN hair (change) white PERF
'My father's hair has gone white.'

The final example of this special affinity of the unaccusative EPC for figurative meanings comes from the Shanghai dialect of Wu. It is a kind of hyperbole and is used, for example, when someone carelessly and clumsily bumps into another:

Shanghainese Wu:

(68) 儂 瞎 脱 嘞勒 眼睛 啊
Noŋ^{13} haʔ^{5}təʔ^{5} ləʔ^{5} ŋɛ^{13}tɕiŋ^{53} aʔ^{5}?
2SG be:blind:COMP PERF eye PART
'What's wrong with your eyes? (Can't you see properly?)'
(more literally: 'Have you gone blind in the eyes?')

This analysis of unaccusative EPCs in Sinitic languages shows that they have a different and a more specialized semantic structure when compared with their corresponding genitive constructions. Indeed, only a subset of predicates permissible with a genitive subject has an agnate unaccusative EPC.

9. Conclusion

The core semantic features of the unaccusative EPC are summarized below:

NOUN [EXPERIENCER]	– VERB	– NOUN [UNDERGOER SUBJECT]
POSSESSOR	UNACCUSATIVE INTRANSITIVE	POSSESSUM PART/KIN TERM

(i) A relationship of inalienable possession is coded by this unaccusative type of EPC in Sinitic languages. The whole is coded by the preverbal subject NP and the part by the postverbal NP. The category of kin was shown to be peripheral as its use was restricted to the verb 'die' and its synonyms.

(ii) The predicate is broadly specifiable as an unaccusative intransitive one which requires explicit aspectual modification of an erstwhile stative verb to code a process of change. This change involves an adversative process whereby a part of the body or a part of the whole becomes dysfunctional, if not lost. This component of meaning accounts for the fact that the description of a person's disposition or temperament, typically coded by semantically stative predicates, is similarly proscribed.

(iii) As a corollary of (ii), the change involved must be one that causes a marked effect; hence, transitory processes are not generally coded by this construction, unless metaphor is in use, such as with 'redden the face' for anger or embarassment.

(iv) The genitive counterpart of this construction does not express the same meaning as the unaccusative. This is shown by the fact that the genitive does not always lend itself to metaphorical extension of meaning but has its interpretation restricted to the literal description of a process affecting a part of the given whole. The unaccusative EPC has a different discourse function, focusing on how a process that causes a change in a part affects the whole. The construction with a genitive subject is also unlimited in the kind of predicates it may take, be they unaccusative or unergative, not to mention transitive.

(v) In Sinitic languages, the use of unaccusative verbs in this particular EPC is clearly determined by the constructional semantics. There is no syntactic reason which can explain why 'go:white the hair' is acceptable in several of the Sinitic languages whereas 'go:white the teeth' is not; or why 'go:bad the stomach' is possible in some Chinese languages but not 'go:bad the temper' in the same ones.

(vi) This kind of EPC in Sinitic languages does not make use of any syntactic or morphological mechanism to overtly change the argument structure of the verb. It has been argued that the feature of inalienable possession in its constructional semantics licenses the addition of an extra position for the PR. It represents the affected entity in an adversative process that befalls the associated part.

This EPC corresponds roughly to the type described in Payne and Barshi (this volume) as one where there is no merging of external possession with a noun incorporation process, the PR appears to be a core argument, the PM is not a chômeur and an increase in verb valency has occurred. (This interpretation depends, of course, on the analysis of Dative or Experiencer NPs as either arguments or adjuncts of the clause.) The challenge to Barshi and Payne's conjecture lies in the fact that it is the PM in Sinitic languages — and not the PR — which acts as the core argument — the undergoer subject of an unaccusative verb.

Finally, the unaccusative EPC of Sinitic languages provides another instantiation of the preference of EPCs and noun incorporation constructions for interacting with the syntactic role of the subject of unaccusative verbs and with the direct object in other discontinuous possessive constructions.

Acknowledgments

I thank the following colleagues for their comments, criticisms, ideas and input into this analysis: Mengistu Amberber, Mark Baker, Klaus Ecker, Zygmunt Frajzyngier, Bill McGregor, Marianne Mithun, Doris Payne, an anonymous reviewer and participants at the conference on external possession at the University of Oregon in September 1997.

I would also like to thank the following language consultants: *Mandarin* (*pǔtōnghuà*): Zhang Yanpu; *Taiwanese Mandarin*: Imogen Yu-Chin Chen; *Changsha Xiang*: Yunji Wu; *Nanchang Gan*: Xie Chenglei; *Shanghainese Wu*: Kevin Chen Yao; *Cantonese Yue*: Catherine Ng Chan Kam Chi (Hong Kong); *Taiwanese Southern Min*: Imogen Yu-Chin Chen (Chia-I region); *Huizhou Hakka*: Wu Zhang Zhijing (Kuala Lumpur); *German*: Klaus Ecker; Thekla Wiebusch.

This research forms part of a project entitled "A semantic typology of complex syntactic constructions in Sinitic languages", funded by an Australian Research Council Large Grant (1997–1999) and completed with a Pacific Cultural Foundation subsidy. The final writing up was carried out during a visit to the Research Centre for Linguistic Typology, Australian National University in January and February 1998.

Abbreviations

The abbreviations for grammatical glosses are as follows: BA pretransitive marker, CLASS classifier, COMP completive marker, DAT dative case, GEN genitive marker, INC inceptive or change of state marker, NEG negative marker, PASS passive marker, PERF perfective aspect marker, PL plural, POSS possessive, PART clause-final discourse particle, REF referential use, RES resultative, SG singular.

Notes

1 For the examples, I use *pīnyīn* romanization for Mandarin; Sidney Lau's romanization system for Hong Kong Cantonese Yue; the Church romanization for Taiwanese Southern Min and the International Phonetic Alphabet for Shanghainese Wu, Changsha Xiang and Nanchang Gan.

2 Shibatani (1994) adopts a similar approach in his explanation for the semantic integration into the clause of extra-thematic arguments in ethical datives, indirect adversative passives and possessor raising constructions. It is either the adversative reading or the relationship of inalienable possession which licenses the valency augmentation.

3 Traditionally, the Min group of dialects was classified into Northern and Southern but this has been challenged more recently by Norman (1988) *inter alia*. I adopt Norman's proposed classification here in part, exemplifying only Eastern Min.

4 Only a brief elicitation session was carried out with the Hakka informant to verify that the unaccusative EPC existed in this Sinitic language. For this reason, I do not include Hakka data in the table given in the appendix.

5 Examples used to support the proposed semantic and syntactic features of this construction are intended to be representative for Sinitic, unless otherwise stated. The precise details for each Sinitic language in the survey are given in Table 1.

6 Traditionally, keeping your skin as fair as possible, particularly for women, is desirable; getting tanned is a sign of working outdoors and of a peasant background; it is not culturally desirable.

7 Similarly, in Mandarin, it is not acceptable to use *Tā huài-le píqi* [3SG-bad-PERF-temper] but only *Tā (de) píqi hěn huài* [3SG-(GEN)-temper-very-bad] 'Her temper is bad' or an appositive structure with a nominal predicate N-N: *Tā huài píqi* [3SG-bad-temper] which is also available in Taiwanese: *I chiok pháiⁿ phî-khì* [3SG-enough-bad-temper] 'She's bad-tempered'.

8 The unaccusative form for this expression in Taiwanese can be used in contexts where people's inherited physical qualities and personality traits are being compared: 'She's bad in the skin (she inherited it that way) while he's got it bad in temperament', and so on.

9 The 'red eyes' metaphor for jealousy exists in Cantonese too, but only in the unmarked genitive subject EPC: *kui*^{5} *ngaan*^{5} *hung*^{4} 3SG-eyes-red 'She's jealous [more literally: As for her, the eyes are red]'.

10 I thank Marianne Mithun, the discussant for my paper at the External Possession Conference (U Oregon, September 1997), who suggested this possibility as a further avenue for investigation.

11 I thank an anonymous reviewer for raising this point. The question of discourse topic status of the PR is, nonetheless, beyond the scope of this study. The data is restricted to sentence examples of the unaccusative EPC due to the necessity of eliciting data from seven Sinitic languages.

Appendix

These data were collected over several sessions with each language consultant and have thus been controlled for consistency for individual speakers of each of the representative dialects of the seven Chinese languages.

Due to lack of space, the entire inventory of actual examples is not reproduced here. Hence, it should be noted that there is no intention to imply cognacy of the predicates across Sinitic languages. Not only are the intransitive predicates non-cognate in many cases but so are the aspect markers used to code completed change of state. The examples given in the discussion above provide an adequate indication of this.

Table 1: *Comparison of EPCs in Sinitic languages*

	KIN	Mandarin	Xiang	Gan	Wu	Minnan	Yue
1	die + KIN	✓	✓	✓	✓	✓	✓
2	get ill + KIN	✗	✗	✗	✗	✗	✗
3	run away + KIN	✗	✗	✗	✗	✗	✗
4	grow up + KIN	✗	✗	✗	✗	✗	✗
5	get rich + KIN	✗	✗	✗	✗	✗	✗

	BODY PARTS	Mandarin	Xiang	Gan	Wu	Minnan	Yue
6	go:numb + BP	✓	✗	✓	✗	✗	✗
7	fall:out teeth/hair	✓	✓	✓	✓	✓	✓
8	go:bad + BP	✓	✗	✓	✓	✓	✓
9	go:white teeth/skin	✗	✗	✗	✗	✗	✗
10	go:white hair	✓	✓ [+CLASS]	✓	✗	✓	✓
11	become:more white hairs/wrinkles	✓	✓	✓	✓	✗	✓
12	get:injured + BP	✓	✓	✓	✓	✓	✓
13	get:broken arm/leg	✓	✗	✓	✓	✓	✓
14	go:lame left leg	✓	✓	✓	✓	✓	✓
15	go:deaf right ear	✓	✓	✓	✗	✗	✓
16	go:blind eyes	✓	✓	✓	✓	✗	✓
17	get:hoarse throat	✓	✗	✗	✗	✗	✗

	INANIMATES	Mandarin	Xiang	Gan	Wu	Minnan	Yue
18	fall:leaves	✓	✓	✓	✓	✓	✓
19	go:flat tire	✓	✗	✓	✓	✓	✓
20	collapse roof	✓	✗	✓	✗	✗	✓
21	go:wrong leg (chair)	✓	✓	✓	✗	✓	✓
22	go:rotten core (cabbage)	✓	✗	✓	✗	✓	✗

	METAPHOR	Mandarin	Xiang	Gan	Wu	Minnan	Yue
23	go:red eyes	✓ jealousy, literal mng	✗	✓ jealousy, literal mng	✓ jealousy only	✗	✓ literal mng
24	go:red face	✓anger, embarrassment	✗	✓anger	✓	✗	✓ embarrassment
25	go:soft/light ears	✓	✗	✗	✗	✓	✗
26	go:wrong temper	✗	✗	✗	✗	✓	✗
27	go:wrong belly	✓	✗	✗	✗	✓	✗

Key:

✓	grammatically well-formed unaccusative EPC for which a plausible context can be described
✗	grammatically unacceptable combination of elements for an unaccusative EPC where no interpretation is possible
[+CLASS]	the postverbal part term requires modification by a classifier construction, a bare noun is not grammatically acceptable

References

Bai Xianyong. 1993. *Bai Xianyong Zixuanji* [Anthology of Selected Works of Bai Xianyong]. Hong Kong: Hua Han Publishers.

Barshi, Immanuel and Doris Payne. 1996. "The Interpretation of External Possessors in Maasai." In Lionel Bender and Thomas Hinnebusch (eds.), *Afrikanistische Arbeitspapiere*. Köln: Universität zu Köln, 207–226.

Barry, Roberta. 1975. "Topic in Chinese: An Overlap of Meaning, Grammar and Discourse Function." *Papers from the Parasession on Functionalism.* Chicago: Chicago Linguistic Society, 1–9.

Chao, Yuen-Ren. 1968. *A Grammar of Spoken Chinese*. Berkeley & Los Angeles: University of California Press.

Chappell, Hilary. 1986. "The Passive of Bodily Effect in Standard Chinese." *Studies in Language* 10.2: 271–296.

Chappell, Hilary. 1995. "Inalienability and the Personal Domain in Mandarin Chinese Discourse." In Hilary Chappell and William McGregor (eds.), *The Grammar of Inalienability. A Typological Perspective on the Part-Whole Relation and Terms for Body Parts*. Berlin: Mouton de Gruyter, 465–527.

Clark, Marybeth. 1995. "Where Do You Feel? Stative Verbs and Body Part Terms in Mainland Southeast Asia." In Hilary Chappell and William McGregor (eds.), *The Grammar of Inalienability. A Typological Perspective on the Part-Whole Relation and Terms for Body Parts*. Berlin: Mouton de Gruyter, 529–563.

Comrie, Bernard. 1981. *Language Universals and Linguistic Typology: Syntax and Morphology.* Oxford: Blackwell.

Ding Ling. 1928/1956. "Shafei Nüshi de Riji [Diary of Miss Sophie]." In: *Ding Ling Xuanji* [Selected stories of Ding Ling]. Hong Kong: Wenxue Chubanshe.

Dixon, R.M.W. 1979. "Ergativity". *Language* 55: 59–138.

Dixon, R.M.W. 1994. *Ergativity.* Cambridge: Cambridge University Press.

Fan, Xiao. 1996. *San ge Pingmian de Yufa Guan* [A Three-Dimensional View of Grammar]. Beijing: Beijing Yuyan Xueyuan.

Gao Mingkai. 1969. "Cong Yufa yu Luoji de Guanxi Shuo-dao Zhuyu Binyu" [A Discussion of Subject and Object in Terms of the Relation between Grammar and Logic]. *Yufa Huibian.* Beijing: Zhonghua Shuju.

Halliday, M.A.K. 1956. "Grammatical Categories in Modern Chinese." *Transactions of the Philological Society*, 177–224.

Halliday, M.A.K. 1967. "Notes on Transitivity and Theme in English." *Journal of Linguistics* 3, Part 1, 37–81; Part 2, 199–244.

Halliday, M.A.K. 1968. "Notes on Transitivity and Theme in English." *Journal of Linguistics*, Part 3 in 4: 179–215.

Hopper, Paul and Sandra Thompson. 1980. "Transitivity in Grammar and Discourse." *Language* 56: 251–299.

Levin, Beth and Malka Rappaport Hovav. 1995. *Unaccusativity. At the Syntax-Lexical Semantics Interface*. Cambridge, Mass.: The MIT Press.

Matisoff, James. 1978. *Variational Semantics in Tibeto-Burman*. Philadelphia: Institute for the Study of Human Issues.

Matthews, Stephen and Virginia Yip. 1994. *Cantonese Reference Grammar.* London: Routledge and Kegan Paul.

Modini, Paul. 1981. "Inalienable Possession and the 'Double Subject' Constructions in East Asian." *Cahiers de Linguistique Asie Orientale* 9: 5–15.

Mullie, Joseph M. 1932. *The Structural Principles of the Chinese Language*. Peiping: The Bureau of Engraving and Printing.

Mullie, Joseph M. 1933. "Le Double Nominatif en Chinois." *T'oung Pao* 30: 231–236.

Norman, Jerry. 1988. *Chinese*. Cambridge: Cambridge UP.

Payne, Doris. 1997. "The Maasai External Possessor Construction." In Joan Bybee, John Haiman and Sandra A. Thompson (eds.), *Essays on Language Function and Language Type*. Amsterdam: John Benjamins, 395–422.

Ramsey, S. Robert. 1987. *The Languages of China*. Princeton, NJ: Princeton UP.

Sagart, Laurent. To appear. "Vestiges of Old Chinese Derivational Affixes in Modern Chinese Dialects." In: Hilary Chappell (ed.) *Synchronic and Diachronic Perspectives on the Grammar of Sinitic Languages*.

Shibatani, Masayoshi. 1994. "An Integrational Approach to Possessor Raising, Ethical Datives, and Adversative Passives." *Berkeley Linguistics Society 20*, 461–486.

Sun, Chaofen. 1996. *Word-Order Change and Grammaticalization in the History of Chinese*. Stanford: Stanford UP.

Tao, Hongyin. 1996. *Units in Mandarin Conversation. Prosody, Discourse and Grammar.* Amsterdam: John Benjamins [*Studies in Discourse and Grammar 5*].

Teng Shou-Hsin. 1974a. *A Semantic Study of Transitivity Relations in Chinese*. Taipei: Student Book Co.

Teng Shou-Hsin. 1974b. "Double Nominatives in Chinese." *Language*. 50.3: 455–473.

Teng Shou-Hsin. 1995. "Objects and Verb Complexes in Taiwanese." *Papers from the 1994 Conference on Language Teaching and Linguistics in Taiwan. Vol I: Southern Min.* Taipei: Crane Publishers, 1–22.

Thompson, Sandra A. 1973. "Transitivity and Some Problems with the *ba* Construction." *Journal of Chinese Linguistics* 1.2: 208–221.

Wang, Liaoyi. 1969. "Zhuyu de Dingyi ji qi zai Hanyu zhong de Yingyong" [The definition of subject and its application in Chinese]. *Yuwen Huibian*. Beijing: Zhonghua Shuju.

Wierzbicka, Anna. (in press). Anchoring Linguistic Typology in Semantic Primes. *Linguistic Typology.*

Zhang, Guangyu. 1996. *Min-Ke Fangyan Shigao* [A Draft History of Min and Hakka Dialects]. Taipei: Nantian Shuju.

Zhang, Xinxin and Sang Ye (eds.). 1987. *Beijing Ren: Yibai ge Putongren de Zishu* [Beijing People: Narratives of 100 ordinary people]. Shanghai: Shanghai Wenyi Chubanshe.

External Possession in Creek

Jack B. Martin
College of William and Mary

1. Introduction

In its broadest sense, POSSESSION in linguistics can be viewed as a concept that is centered on ownership and that extends to include instances in which a nominal is stated as being 'within the domain' of a full, referential noun phrase. Such a definition is vague enough structurally to include the various constructions associated with possession and broad enough semantically to include part/whole relations (e.g., *my arm, the leg of the table*), various noun phrase-internal argument relations (*my achievement*, *my election*), and even temporal relations (*next week's picnic*).

The unmarked pattern for possessive constructions in many languages appears to be one in which the possessor (PR) and the nominal it possesses (possessum or PM) form a single noun phrase constituent. Examples of this type will henceforth be referred to as INTERNAL POSSESSION (IP), a term reflecting the influence of König and Haspelmath (1997).

In addition to IP, many languages have a more restricted pattern in which a nominal is interpreted as being 'within the domain' of a full, referential noun phrase, but where, for various reasons, the PR and the PM fail to form a single noun phrase constituent. A classic example of this type of EXTERNAL POSSESSION (EP) is the French 'inalienable' construction (Bally 1926; Hatcher 1944; Kayne 1975; Guéron 1985):

(1) *il* ***me*** *prend le bras*
he me takes the arm
'He takes my arm.' (lit., 'He takes me the arm.')

In the French construction, the external possessor (EPR) is a dative pronominal argument and the PM is usually a body part.

Many other EP constructions are possible. Kuno (1973: 62ff), for example, notes instances in Japanese where both 'thematized' (2a) and 'subjectivized' (2b) noun phrases are interpreted as possessors:

(2) a. *John wa otoosan ga sinda*
John TOP father NOM died
'As for John, his father died.'
b. *John ga otoosan ga sinda*
John NOM father NOM died
'It is John whose father died.'

The French construction in (1) is clearly quite different formally and functionally from the the Japanese constructions in (2). Nonetheless, there are a few connections and themes common to many EP constructions. The presence of an EPR leads to omission of an IPR in the French and Japanese sentences in (1–2), for example. The various constructions are further united historically in that some syntacticians have posited rules of 'possessor ascension' or 'possessor raising' for many types of EP.

This paper treats the phenomenon of EP in Creek, a Muskogean language spoken by several thousand individuals in Oklahoma and Florida. Creek has basic SOV order, a nominative/nonnominative ('oblique') system of case-marking, an elaborate system of verbal grades used for marking aspect, and a somewhat irregular agentive/nonagentive system of person marking on verbs. Like the Western Muskogean languages Chickasaw and Choctaw (Nicklas 1974; Davies 1981a,b, 1986; Munro and Gordon 1982; Payne 1982; Munro 1984; Baker 1988; Broadwell 1990; Munro, this volume), Creek has both IP and EP:

(3) a. ***am**-ífa-t* *î·l-is*
1SG:DAT-dog-NOM die:SG:SUBJ:FGR-IND
'My dog died.' IP
b. *ifá-t* ***am**-î·l-is*
dog-NOM 1SG:DAT-die:SG:SUBJ:FGR-IND
'My dog died.' (lit., 'Dog died for/to me.') EP

In (3a), the first person singular dative prefix *am-* attaches directly to the PM. In (3b), the same possessive prefix appears instead on the verb, suggesting certain parallels to the French pattern in (1).

One goal of this study is to provide the first description of EP in Creek, complementing the description of IP in Martin (1993). I begin by describing the basic structure of EP clauses, followed by a discussion of the contexts in which EP or IP is preferred. I conclude by describing the properties of the construction in terms of a theory of event schemas (Heine 1997). Comparison of the Creek pattern with cognate constructions in the Western Muskogean languages Chickasaw and Choctaw provides a particularly clear view of how cognition, function, and diachrony interact to yield differences and similarities between constructions in language, and how the seemingly unrelated patterns in (1) and (2) can come to overlap in particular languages.

2. The grammar of EP in Creek

The Creek EP pattern I will be describing is illustrated in (3b) above and in (4) below:

(4) *méysti(-n)* *a·tamí-n* ***im***-*áhopa·n-ís*
that:person(-OBL) car-OBL DAT-wreck:LGR-IND
'S/he is wrecking that person's car.' EP

I will consider the structure of (4) first, where the PM is an object. Examples in which the PM is a subject (3b) will be described in 2.2.

2.1 *The EPR is an object of the verb*

The Creek EP pattern in (4) is similar grammatically to the French construction in (1). Thus, the EPR is represented in both languages as an object of the verb and coded in the dative (i.e., in the same way that benefactives are). One indication that the EPR is an object of the verb in Creek is the fact that the verb agrees in person and number with an EPR:

(5)
am-*áhopa·n-ís* 'S/he is wrecking mine / wrecking it for me.'
cim-*áhopa·n-ís* 'S/he is wrecking yours / wrecking it for you.'
pom-*áhopa·n-ís* 'S/he is wrecking ours / wrecking it for us.'
im-*áhopa·n-ís* 'S/he is wrecking his/hers / wrecking it for him/her.'

The forms in (5) all include a dative applicative prefix that attaches to a verb and agrees with its object in the first and second person. The last form *im-* is not restricted to third person, however; instead, it is the bare form of the dative applicative prefix and generally interpreted as third person in most contexts.

In this section, I present additional arguments that the EPR is an object within its clause and external to the PM. Specifically, I argue that (4) has the structure in (6):

(6) EPR and PM as objects:

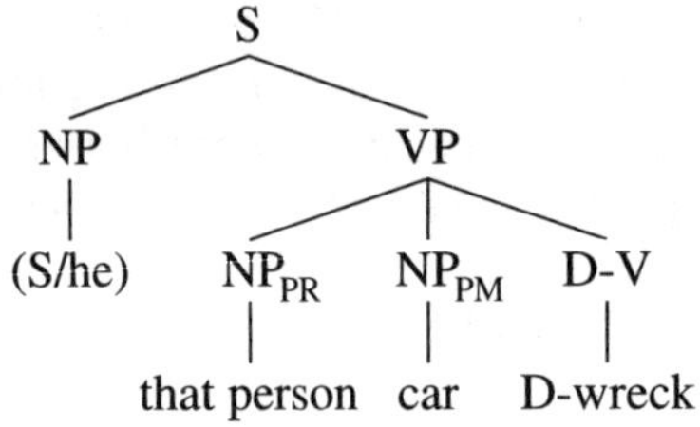

Argument 1: Case marking of the PR

In IP, the PR may not be case marked with nominative *-t* or oblique (nonnominative) *-n*:

(7) *méysti(***-t/*-n**) **im**-a·tamí-n ahópa·n-ís*
that:person-OBL DAT-car-OBL wreck:LGR-IND
'S/he is wrecking that person's car.' IP

In EP clauses where the PM is an object, the PR may be marked in the oblique, as in (4). The EPR thus patterns with other objects of the verb in receiving oblique case.

Argument 2: Adverb placement

In IP, a clause-level element like a locative adverb may not intervene between the PR and PM:

(8) **Bill **fítta-n** sákpa-n nafêyk-ey-s*
Bill outside-OBL arm-OBL hit:HGR-1SG:I-IND
'I hit Bill's arm outside.' IP

In EP, the locative adverb is marginally acceptable in this position:

(9) *?Bill **fítta-n** sákpa-n **in**-nafêyk-ey-s*
Bill outside-OBL arm-OBL DAT-hit:HGR-1SG:I-IND
'I hit Bill's arm outside.' EP

The placement of the adverb between the EPR and PM suggests the PR is itself a clause-level element.

Argument 3: Incorporation of the EPR

Creek allows the indefinite expressions *nâ·ki* 'thing, something,' and *ísti* 'person, someone' to incorporate into the verbs that govern them:

(10) *ifá-t **íst**-a·kk-í·-t ô·-s*
dog-NOM person-bite:LGR-DUR-SAME be:FGR-IND
'The dog bites people.'

In EP, an indefinite EPR may incorporate into the verb:

(11) *sákpa-n* ***íst-im****-a·kk-í·-t* *ô·-s*
arm-OBL person-DAT-bite:LGR-DUR-SAME be:FGR-IND
'S/he bites people's arms.' (said of a dog) EP

In IP, an indefinite PR cannot incorporate into the verb:

(12) **(i)sákpa-n* ***íst****-a·kk-í·-t* *ô·-s*
(3II:)arm-OBL person-bite:LGR-DUR-SAME be:FGR-IND
'S/he bites people's arms.' (said of a dog) IP

In this respect, the EPR patterns with other objects in the language.

Argument 4: Number marking on the verb for the EPR
Creek sometimes has different forms of verbs depending on the number of the theme argument (i.e., the argument stated as being in a position or undergoing a change in state or place):

(13) a. *cá·ni-t* *ifá-n* ***ili·c****-ís*
John-NOM dog-OBL kill:SG:OBJ:LGR-IND
'John is killing the dog.'
b. *cá·ni-t* *ifá-n* ***pasa·t****-ís*
John-NOM dog-OBL kill:PL:OBJ:LGR-IND
'John is killing the dogs.'

As (13) shows, the verb *ili·c-* is used for killing one, while the verb *pasat-* (*pasa·t-* in the lengthened grade) is used for killing two or more.

In addition, Creek has a plural suffix *-ak-* used to indicate that some argument of the verb that is not already specified for number is plural. This suffix may therefore be used to indicate a plural subject:

(14) *ifá-n* *ilí·c-****a·k****-ís*
dog-OBL kill:SG:OBJ-PL:LGR-IND
'They are killing the dog.'

In IP, the plural marker cannot be used to indicate a plural PR:

(15) **cá·ni-t* ***im****-ífa-n* *ilí·c-****a·k****-ís*
John-NOM DAT-dog-OBL kill:SG:OBJ-PL:LGR-IND
'John is killing their dog.' IP

In EP, however, the plural marker may be used to indicate a plural PR:

(16) a. *cá·ni-t* *ifá-n* ***im****-ilí·c-****a·k****-ís*
John-NOM dog-OBL DAT-kill:SG:OBJ-PL:LGR-IND
'John is killing their dog.' EP

b. *cá·ni-t* *ifá-n* ***im****-pasát-****a·k****-ís*
John-NOM dog-OBL DAT-kill:PL:OBJ-PL:LGR-IND
'John is killing their dogs.' EP

In this respect, the EPR in Creek patterns with other arguments of the verb, while the IPR acts as though it is invisible for grammatical categories associated with the verb.

Argument 5: Disjoint reference between the EPR and subject
When the PM is an object, an IPR may be interpreted as referring to the subject of the clause or to another individual:

(17) *í-nki-n* *kawâ·p-is*
3II-hand-OBL raise:FGR-IND
'S/he raised his/her own hand.',
'S/he raised his/her (someone else's) hand.' IP

An EPR, however, is always disjoint in reference with the subject of the clause, just like other pronominal objects:

(18) *í-nki-n* ***in****-kawâ·p-is*
3II-hand-OBL DAT-raise:FGR-IND
'S/he raised his/her (someone else's) hand.'
(not his/her own hand) EP

For independent reasons, dative reflexives are not normally accepted in Creek:

(19) **í-nki-n* ***i·-in****-kawâ·p-is*
3II-hand-OBL REFL-DAT-raise:FGR-IND
'S/he raised his/her own hand.' EP

IP is therefore the only option available in Creek for reflexive activities, even when the context (see Section 3) would normally favor EP:

(20) *i-hókpi-n* *óh-na·fk-ít*
3II-chest-OBL on-hit:LGR-SAME
'[The publican] smote upon his [own] breast…' (Luke 18:13) IP

Pronominal objects in Creek may not be coreferent with other elements in their clause (Martin 1991b: 217). The fact that an EPR must be disjoint from the subject and that IP and EP differ in this respect follows if an EPR is a pronominal object in its clause.

2.2 *The EPR is topicalized when the PM is a subject*

In 2.1 I argued that EP clauses in which the PM is an object have a structure in which the EPR is also an object of the verb. In this section I turn to clauses in which the PM is a subject, as in (21):

(21) *cá·ni ifá-t* ***im***-*î·l-is*
John dog-NOM DAT-die:SG:SUBJ:FGR-IND
'John's dog died.' EP

The EPR in sentences of this type (generally intransitives) continues to behave like an argument of the verb. Thus, the verb agrees for person with the PR:

(22) ***am***-*î·l-is* 'mine died'
cim-*î·l-is* 'yours died'
pom-*î·l-is* 'ours died'
im-*î·l-is* 'his/hers died'

The verb also agrees with an EPR for number:

(23) *im-î·l-is* 'his/hers died'
*im-il-**â·k**-is* 'theirs died'

Yet in some ways the EPR of a PM in subject position behaves as though it has been topicalized. In this section, I present some preliminary evidence suggesting that the sentence in (21) has the structure in (24), in which the EPR has been fronted to clause-initial position:

(24) PM as subject, EPR as topicalized object (cf. (6)):

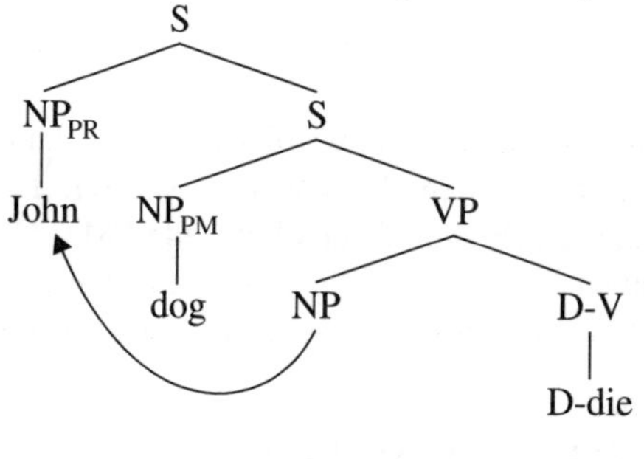

Argument 1: Word order
When the PM is an object, the placement of the EPR is like the placement of other objects, typically occurring after the subject:

(25) *Bill* ***méysti(-n)*** *a·tamí-n* ***im****-áhopá·n-t* *ó·-s*
Bill that:person(-OBL) car-OBL DAT-wreck:LGR-SAME be:LGR-IND
'Bill is wrecking that person's car.' EP

When the PM is a subject, even though it is marked by the dative applicative on the verb, the EPR is frozen in clause-initial position, as in (21). The EPR may therefore not follow the PM when the PM is a subject:

(26) **ifá-t* ***méysti(-n)*** ***im****-î·l-is*
dog that:person(-OBL) DAT-die:SG:SUBJ:FGR-IND
'That person's dog died.' EP

The fact that the EPR continues to pattern with objects in clauses of this type (see (22–23) above) while being restricted to clause-initial position follows if the EPR is obligatorily topicalized in this context.

Argument 2: Case marking
As (4) shows, the EPR may be marked in the oblique when the PM is an object. When the PM is a subject, speakers reject case marking on the EPR:

(27) *méysti****(*-t/*-n)*** *ifá-t* ***im****-î·l-is*
that:person(*-NOM/*-OBL) dog-NOM DAT-die:SG:SUBJ:FGR-IND
'That person's dog died.' EP

The contexts in which case marking is present or absent in Creek are still poorly understood, though new information tends to be case marked and old information tends not to be. The absence of case marking on an EPR of a PM in subject position is consistent with the claim that the EPR in these structures has been topicalized.

2.3 *Status of the PM*

In 2.1 and 2.2, I established the basic structure of Creek EP, claiming that the EPR is an object that is fronted when the PM is a subject. I now turn to grammatical distinctions between IP and EP involving the PM.

In IP, the PM may appear in any of the grammatical roles assigned to definite noun phrases. The PM may thus be a subject (28a, b) or object (28c):

(28) a. *John* ***im****-ífa-t* *î·l-is*
John DAT-dog-NOM die:SG:SUBJ:FGR-IND
'John's dog died.' IP

b. *John* ***im****-ífa-t* *itóci-n* *káhc-is*
John DAT-dog-NOM stick-OBL break:HGR-IND
'John's dog broke the stick.' IP

c. *John hopóywa* ***im****-itocí-n* *káhc-is*
John child DAT-stick-OBL break:HGR-IND
'John broke the child's stick.' IP

In EP, the PM is normally a nonagentive noun phrase. EP is usually rejected in intransitive verbs where the PM acts deliberately:

(29) a. ***am****-ífa* *wo·hk-acók-s*
1SG:DAT-dog bark:SG:SUBJ:LGR-EVID-IND
'My dog is barking.' IP

b. **ifá* ***án****-wo·hk-acók-s*
dog 1SG:DAT-bark:SG:SUBJ:LGR-EVID-IND
'My dog is barking.'
(but acceptable as 'The dog is barking for me.') EP

(30) a. ***am****-ífa* *ta·sk-ís*
1SG:DAT-dog jump:SG:SUBJ:LGR-IND
'My dog jumped (just now).' IP

b. **ifá* ***án****-ta·sk-ís*
dog 1SG:DAT-jump:SG:SUBJ:LGR-IND
'My dog jumped (just now).'
(but acceptable as 'The dog jumped for me.') EP

One exception is verbs of motion, which allow EP even though the subject can be interpreted agentively:

(31) *ifá* ***an****-litk-î·t-t* *o·w-ánk-s*
dog 1SG:DAT-run:SG:SUBJ-CMPL:FGR-SAME be:LGR-PAST-IND
'My dog ran away.' EP

Transitive verbs show similar splits. The PM may not be the subject of an agentive transitive verb (though as (4) shows, the PM may be an object in this context):

(32) **John ifá-t* *itóci-n* ***in****-káhc-is*
ohn dog-NOM stick-OBL DAT-break:HGR-IND
John's dog broke the stick.' EP

With a nonagentive transitive verb, either the subject or the object may be interpreted as the PM:[1]

(33) *łákko-t* *ací-n* ***am****-iyâ·c-is*
horse-NOM corn-OBL 1SG:DAT-want:FGR-IND
'The horse wants my corn.' or 'My horse wants corn.' EP

The PM may be interpreted as a locative and is thus not limited to argument positions:

(34) ***cim**-o·sk-ã̂*
2DAT-rain:LGR-Q
'Is it raining at yours [your place]?' EP

(35) *'ł-**am**-oł-ás*
DIR-1SG:DAT-reach-IMP
'Come over to mine [my place].' EP

The best characterization of the restrictions on the PM in EP seems to be that it must either be nonagentive or a theme. Attempts to restrict the PM to an 'undergoer' may encounter problems with (34); attempts to restrict the PM to absolutive or unaccusative arguments encounter problems with the data in (33–35).

2.4 *Omission of possessive marking on the PM*

Another grammatical point involving EP in Creek concerns the presence or absence of IP when an EPR is present.

Some nouns in Creek (including most body parts and many kinship terms) are obligatorily possessed:

(36) ***ca**-lí* 'my foot', **lí* 'foot'
***an**-híssi* 'my friend', **híssi* 'friend'

In EP clauses in which the PM is not obligatorily possessed, the PM need not have any marker of possession on it:

(37) *ifá-n* ***am**-ilî·c-is*
dog-OBL 1SG:DAT-kill:SG:OBJ:FGR-IND
'S/he killed my dog.' EP

In EP clauses in which the PM is obligatorily possessed, there is double marking of possession internally and externally:

(38) a. ***ca**-sákpa-n* ***an**-káhc-is*
1SG:II-arm-OBL 1SG:DAT-break:HGR-IND
'S/he broke my arm.' EP
b. **sákpa-n **an**-káhc-is*

This is sometimes hard to see in third person forms, but is always apparent in other persons.[2]

The import of this observation is that, as Hyman (1995) observes, omission of possessive marking on the PM is a distinct process from EP: EP can occur without possessor omission (as in (36)), and possessor omission can occur in some languages without EP (as in French *Il a levé le bras*, lit. 'He raised the arm.').

3. Uses of EP

In Creek EP, the PM is usually a part and the PR is usually an experiencer (i.e., an entity interpreted as undergoing sensation or feeling emotion).[3] In some contexts, the PM need not be a part if the PR is an experiencer; in other contexts, the PR need not be an experiencer if the PM is a part:

(39) Prototypical use of Creek EP and extensions:

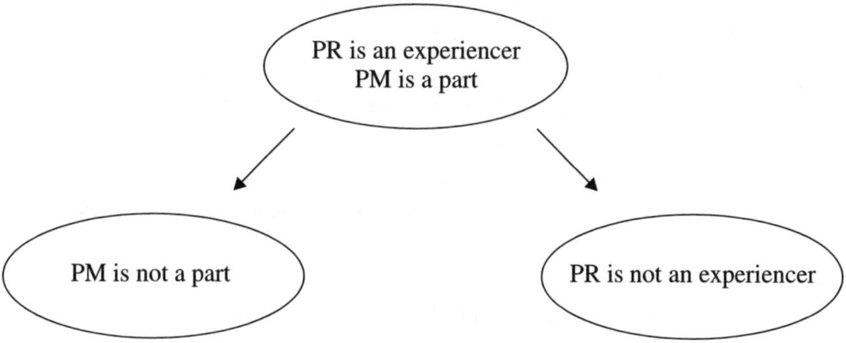

These three basic uses are exemplified in 3.1, 3.2, and 3.3. Section 3.4 discusses instances in which IP is unacceptable; 3.5 turns to the information status of the PR and PM in EP clauses.

3.1 *EP where PR is an experiencer and PM is a part*

EP is routinely used in contexts where one individual affects another individual through action on a part:

(40) *ci-hacko-císka-n itó-n ó*^{n}*hw-ey-t*
2II-ear-edge-OBL wood-OBL have:HGR-1SG:I-SAME
cín-*ɬi·fk-ay-â·n*
2DAT-poke:LGR-1SG:I-when
'When I poke the base of your ear with a stick...' (1992) EP

(41) *i-ká-n* ***in**-náfk-i·* *ha·y-ít* *o·m-êys*
3II-head-OBL DAT-hit-DUR do:LGR-SAME be:LGR-though
'Though [Rabbit] tried to hit [Alligator's] head...' (1991) EP

(42) *i-hácko-n* ***ín**-ta·c-at-í·-s*
3II-ear-obl DAT-cut:LGR-PAST-DUR-IND
'...and smote off his ear...' (Matt. 26:51) EP

(43) *i-ká-n* *s-**in**-náfk-a·k-at-í·-s*
3II-head-OBL INSTR-DAT-hit-PL:LGR-PAST-DUR-IND
'[They took the reed, and] smote him on the head [with it].' (Matt. 27:30) EP

EP is also the automatic choice when a part is in subject position and the PR is either physically affected through direct action on the part or simply inconvenienced by the condition of the part:

(44) *cá-nki-t* ***an**-táck-i·-t* *ô·-s*
1SG:II-hand-NOM 1SG:DAT-cut-DUR-SAME be:FGR-IND
'My hand is cut.' EP

(45) *ca-licíska-t* ***an**-taká·n-i·-t* *ô·-s*
1SG:II-heel-NOM 1SG:DAT-blistered:DUR-SAME be:FGR-IND
'My heel is blistered.' EP

(46) *ca-ná·-t* ***an**-téyy-i·-s*
1SG:II-body-NOM 1SG:DAT-sore-DUR-IND
'My body is sore.' EP

(47) *i-lí-t* ***in**-hasáfk-i·-s*
3II-foot-NOM DAT-swell-DUR-IND
'His/Her foot is swollen.' EP

(48) *cá-nki-t* ***án**-ca·t-ís*
1SG:II-hand-NOM 1SG:DAT-red:LGR-IND
'My hand is bleeding.' EP

(49) *ca-kéyssi-t* ***am**-itiyókc-i·-s*
1SG:II-hair-NOM 1SG:DAT-tangled-DUR-IND
'My hair is tangled up.' EP

3.2 *EP where PR is an experiencer but PM is not a part*

When the PM is not a part, EP is less automatic. With a verb of contact, for example, EP may be used when the PM is a part, but is generally not used when the PM is an item of clothing:

(50) a. *mo·mín í-nki-n* ***ín**-cila·y-at-í·-s*
and 3II-hand-OBL DAT-touch:LGR-PAST-DUR-IND
'...and he touched her hand...' (Matt. 8:15) EP

b. *...in-ká·pa-n cila·y-at-í·-s*
DAT-coat-OBL touch:LGR-PAST-DUR-IND
'...she touched his garment.' (Mark 5:27) IP

When the PR is an experiencer, however, it is clear that EP can be used with nominals other than parts:

(51) ***pom**-ohh-áhkopa·n-ít* ***pon**-líka·f-ít*
1PL:DAT-on-play:LGR-SAME 1PL:DAT-tear.up:LGR-SAME
***pom**-ohh-a-hólwayi·c-í·* *a·ɬ-â·t*
1PL:DAT-on-at-do.bad:LGR-DUR go.about:SG:SUBJ:LGR-when
weyk-ip-áccas
cease-CMPL-must
'...you must cease going around playing on ours [our roof], tearing ours down, and soiling ours.' (1939b) EP

Here Gopher is complaining of Rabbit's activities and their effects on the gophers' subterranean homes. EP is used to show that the gophers are inconvenienced by this activity, even though the PM is not a part of the PR.

Embarrassment is another type of emotion that may lead to use of EP instead of IP with alienables:

(52) *nâ·kitilómha nâ·k* ***an**-hic-iphoy-áɬ-i·-s*
quilt thing 1SG:DAT-see-CMPL:IMPERS-FUT-DUR-IND
kón-cc-in o·w-â·t
think-2SG:I-DIFF be:LGR-when EP
'...if you're thinking, *They'll see my quilts and things...*' (1990)

In this example, a radio announcer is encouraging quilt makers not to be shy about having their work seen at an upcoming competition. EP is used to show that the event results in embarrassment on the part of the quilt makers.

A positive emotion can also lead to the use of EP with alienables:

(53) ***an**-pakpak-í·-s^*
1SG:DAT-bloom-DUR-IND
'Mine [my flowers] have bloomed!' EP

3.3 *EP where PR is not an experiencer but PM is a part*

In many of the examples examined so far, the PR has been interpreted as an experiencer and hence has been animate. Creek allows a second extension of EP to action performed on a part of an inanimate:

(54) *i-li-yopá-n* ***in**-halathéyhc-it*
3II-leg-behind-OBL DAT-take:PL:OBJ:HGR-SAME
'…he took [the dead deer] by the hind legs…' (1936a) EP

(55) *i-ká-n* ***in**-kawáhp-it*
3II-head-OBL DAT-raise:HGR-SAME
'…he lifted [the dead deer's] head…' (1992) EP

(56) *atákła-n li·m-itá-n ko·m-êys íssi tálk-osi-n*
weed-OBL pluck-INF-OBL want:LGR-though leaf only-DIM-OBL
***in**-cáhw-in*
DAT-take:PL:OBJ:HGR-DIFF
'…[he] tried to pull up the weed, but he took off only the leaves…' (1936b) EP

Having a PR that is an experiencer or having a PM that is a part are thus two disjunctive restrictions on the use of EP in Creek.

3.4 *Contexts in which IP is unacceptable*

EP and IP are separate constructions in Creek that are appropriate in different contexts. In some contexts, EP is acceptable where IP is impossible. When the PM is a nominalization, for example, EP is sometimes more natural than IP:

(57) a. *hathá·k-a·t* ***am**-ahopank-â·k-s*
white:RED:LGR-DEF 1SG:DAT-break-PL:FGR-IND
'My white ones broke.' EP

b. *****an**-hathá·k-a·t ahopank-â·k-s*
1SG:DAT-white:RED:LGR-DEF break-PL:FGR-IND
'My white ones broke.' IP

Similarly, some quantifiers can be possessed using EP even when IP is rejected:

(58) a. *omálka-t* ***am**-ahopank-â·k-s*
all-NOM 1SG:DAT-break-PL:FGR-IND
'All of mine broke.' EP

b. **am*-omálka-t* *ahopank-â·k-s*
1SG:DAT-all-NOM break-PL:FGR-IND
'All of mine broke.' IP

These sorts of data make it difficult to claim that EP is derived from IP, since the source structures would themselves be ungrammatical.

3.5 *Information status of the EPR and PM*

In all of the natural examples of EP in my data, the EPR is old information. In fact, the EPR is almost always omitted in examples from texts:

(59) *itokackocí-n î·s-it* *hasní·łka-n*
twig-OBL take:SG:OBJ:FGR-SAME testicle-OBL
*s-**ín**-ho·sk-ín*
INSTR-DAT-scratch:LGR-DIFF EP
'...having taken a twig, [Rabbit] scratches [Wolf's] testicles...' (1939)

There is one example in my textual data of an overt EPR:

(60) ***opá*** *i-tółwa-n* *a·-**im**-ak-tíhh-in*
owl 3II-eye-OBL LOC-DAT-LOC-put.in:PL:OBJ:HGR-DIFF EP
'...he put [crumbled wood bits] in Horned Owl's eyes...' (1939)

In (60), the EPR ('Horned Owl') is one of the main characters and is easily identified, but the storyteller decided to express the EPR anyway.

It is also possible to omit the PM in EP clauses:

(61) ***cin**-típtipi·c-ay-ô·f* *pací·ss-íck-áł-i·-s*
2DAT-slap:LGR-1SG:I-when veer-1SG:I-FUT-DUR-IND
'...when I slap yours [your ear], you veer...' (1992) EP

In IP, however, the PM may never be omitted:

(62) a. *John **in**-káhc-ey-s*
John DAT-break:HGR-1SG:I-IND
'I broke John's.' EP

b. **John káhc-ey-s*
(would mean, 'I broke John.') IP

Speakers accept sentences in which either the PR or the PM in an EP clause is questioned, suggesting that either can be focused:

(63) ***istêy-n*** *sákpa-n* ***in****-nafêyk-íck-a·ˇ*
who-OBL arm-OBL DAT-hit:HGR-2SG:I-Q
'Whose arm did you hit?' EP

(64) *John* ***nâ·ki-n*** ***in****-nafêyk-íck-a·ˇ*
John what-OBL DAT-hit:HGR-2SG:II-Q
'What did you hit of John's?' EP

4. Summary and broader perspectives

The basic properties of Creek EP from the preceding sections are summarized in (65):

(65) Properties of Creek EP:
- The PR is an object (2.1);
- The PR is coded as a benefactive (2.1);
- The PR is fronted when the PM is a subject (2.2);
- IP can be used in a wide range of grammatical contexts, while the uses of EP are more limited. More specifically, the PM may be an object, a subject, or an oblique but is usually not agentive in EP unless it is also a theme (2.3);
- EP is a distinct process from omission of internal marking of possession; internal marking of possession cannot be omitted in Creek EP when the PM is obligatorily possessed (2.4);
- The PR is usually an experiencer and the PM is usually a part, though either one of these conditions alone is sufficient to license EP (3);
- The PR is 'affected' in the sense of: a) being physically harmed by the event or state, as through action on a part; b) benefiting from the event or state; or, c) being harmed or helped psychologically, as by embarrassment or happiness (3);
- EP is not 'derived from' IP: EP and IP are distinct constructions used in different contexts (3.4);
- In texts, the PR is old information and is generally omitted (3.5).

One approach to similar phenomena in the Western Muskogean languages Choctaw and Chickasaw has been to posit a process first labeled 'raising the possessor' by Nicklas (1974: 163) but now more commonly known as 'possessor raising' (Munro and Gordon 1982; Munro 1984; Broadwell 1990; Munro, this volume) or 'possessor ascension' (Davies 1981a,b, 1986). Under these approaches, possessive readings in EP are explained by reducing EP to IP by means of syntactic movement or ascension. No attempt is made to explain how possessive readings arise in IP, however. The fact that EP is more limited than IP in distribution is explained by claiming that the rule responsible for EP has additional conditions associated with it. The absence of EP in a language is described by saying the language lacks the process in question, while the presence of EP in unrelated languages is taken to support the existence of these processes outside of individual languages.

The alternative approach I will pursue here is modeled closely after Heine's (1997) study of possession. Under this approach, languages use various **event schemas** to express abstract notions in concrete terms. Similarities between languages arise in part because similar metaphors are used to express grammatical concepts. 'Possession' as a concept is intrinsic neither to IP nor to EP, but instead emerges pragmatically in at least three distinct contexts:

(a) *The Modifier Schema: NP X modifies Y.* In the Modifier Schema, an NP is portrayed as modifying another nominal attributively, either as a specifier or as a complement.[4] Such a pattern directly encodes the idea that a nominal is 'within the domain' of a noun phrase and thus gives rise to possessive readings. It is the iconic nature of the link between being conceptually 'within the domain' of the PR and syntactically 'internal' to the PM that leads speakers to consider IP to be the unmarked possessive pattern. This is presumably also the reason why so many languages have IP and no other pattern.

(b) *The Goal Schema: Action on or state of Y yields effect to/for X.* The Goal Schema (Heine 1997: 47, 163ff) is used to add a benefactive or malefactive to a clause.[5] When an action or state applies to a part of an entity, any damage or good associated with that entity is transferred to the whole (Bally 1926; Fox 1981; Hyman 1995). Use of benefactive or malefactive coding is thus natural in this context, with possessive readings arising because X and Y must be closely associated for the impact to be transferred. Languages differ in how close this association must be, with Creek coding inanimates as though they were benefactives or malefactives when a part is involved (see 3.3).

(c) *The Topic Schema: (As for) X, (X's) Y (changed/exists, etc.).* In the Topic Schema (Heine 1997: 47, 160ff), a topic is first established and then a statement is made about a subtopic. Examples of this schema are seen in the Japanese examples in (2). One common way to satisfy the 'aboutness' condition holding between a topic and subtopic is for speakers to infer that the topic 'possesses' the subtopic. Such a condition is just as easily satisfied by kinship terms or body parts, so unlike the Goal Schema, the Topic Schema has no special affinity for parts.

These schemas may lead to patterns that are functionally marked, as when less topical elements are positioned too prominently. Such processes as fronting may apply to correct the situation, and reanalysis may subsequently apply to yield a new construction:

(66) The rise of constructions:

Schema
↓
Marked Patterns
↓ ← Discourse Processes, Reanalysis
Unmarked Patterns

Such a chain of events is seen most clearly in the Goal Schema. In this pattern, the EPR is a benefactive or malefactive (i.e., an experiencer). The EPR is thus generally animate and highly topical, tending to be old information in Creek and tending not to be a full noun phrase. As a part, the PM tends to be new information and inanimate.

Many languages prefer old information to precede and to be external to new information. A conflict arises in intransitive uses of the Goal Schema where old information follows new information:

(67) Marked pattern arising in intransitive uses of the Goal Schema:
[SUBJECT [OBJECT [VERB]]]
PM (Part) PR (Exper.)
New info. Old info.

As discussed in 2.2, Creek solves this unstable situation by fronting the EPR in precisely this context, forcing the old information to precede and be external to the new information:

(68) *má honánwa i-lí-t* ***in**-káck-i·-s*
that male 3II-leg-NOM DAT-broken-DUR-IND
[OBJECT$_i$ [SUBJECT [e_i [VERB]]]
Old info. New info.
'That man's leg is broken.' EP (lit., 'That man, the leg is broken to/for him.')

This process is thus similar to the topicalization processes known to apply to experiencer constructions in other languages in which an experiencer begins as an indirect object but is fronted for functional reasons (Cole et al. 1980; Martin 1991a).

These repairs themselves can then lead to further changes. In the Western Muskogean languages Choctaw and Chickasaw, we find that a fronted EPR may be marked in the nominative, much like the Japanese multiple subject construction in (2b):

(69) **Choctaw** (Nicklas 1974: 164)
hattak mat *iyyi't* ***in**-kobafa* *tok*
man that:NOM leg:NOM DAT-break PAST
'That man's leg broke.' EP

The difference between the Creek and Choctaw patterns suggests that the EPR has been fronted in both Creek and Choctaw in this context, but the fronted noun phrase has been reanalyzed as a subject in Choctaw for case marking. The Topic Schema exists independently of the Goal Schema in Choctaw and Chickasaw and also leads to EP; examples like (69), however, show that the two schemas may overlap and harmonize in some contexts.

One remaining question is why internal marking of possession is often absent in EP. The principle at work here also appears to be a functional one: when a possessive relationship is implicit in an EP construction (as when there is a highly topical noun phrase interpreted as a PR), there is a tendency to avoid explicit marking of the IPR. This phenomenon is widespread, found in the French patterns in (1), the Japanese patterns in (2), and the Creek example in (3b). The absence of IP and the presence of EP make it appear that the EPR has been 'raised,' but as shown in 3.4, the two phenomena are distinct.

All of this suggests that the layering of schemas, repairs, and reanalysis yields the appearance of 'constructions,' though these are better understood in terms of cognition, discourse, and history. This should come as no surprise: what is surprising about EP in the Muskogean languages is how easily these factors can be disentangled.

Acknowledgments

I am grateful to Margaret Mauldin, George Bunny, and the late Helen Bunny for help with the Creek data, and to Pam Munro, Aaron Broadwell, Joan Bresnan, Doris Payne, Immanuel Barshi, and Ann Reed for useful suggestions. All mistakes are my own.

Abbreviations

The following conventions are used in this paper: 1SG, 1PL, 2, 3 first person singular, first person plural, second person, third person; I, II agentive and nonagentive series of person markers; CMPL completive; DAT dative applicative; DEF definite; DIFF different subject switch-reference; DIM diminutive; DIR directional; DUR durative; EVID evidential; FGR falling tone grade; FUT future; HGR h-grade; IMP imperative; IMPERS impersonal; IND indicative; INF infinitive; INSTR instrumental; LGR lengthened grade; LOC locative; NOM nominative; OBJ object; OBL oblique; PL plural; PAST past; Q interrogative; RED reduplication; REFL reflexive; SAME same subject switch-reference; SG singular; SUBJ subject; TOP topic. /c/ is an alveopalatal affricate; /V·/ is a long vowel; /V^n/ is a nasalized vowel; /'V/ is an initial short vowel with stress; sentence-final /ˆ/ and /˜/ mark intonation. Creek data cited without a source are elicited.

Notes

1 This sentence is based on the Choctaw equivalent in Davies (1986: 82).

2 In third person forms, a phonological rule sometimes deletes initial /i-/: thus, *i-yanawá* 'his/her cheek' often surfaces as *'yanawá*.

3 Statements made here about frequency are left purposely vague: whether to consider a given sentence as EP or not is often subjective, making quantification difficult.

4 Instead of recognizing a larger Modifier Schema, Heine (1997: 144) establishes subtypes that he calls Location, Source, Goal, Companion, and Topic.

5 I follow Heine (1997) in referring to this pattern as the 'Goal' Schema. It is important to note that the Creek dative applicative adds sources rather than goals to verbs of motion, however, so the term Benefactive Schema would be more appropriate.

References

Baker, Mark. 1988. *Incorporation: A Theory of Grammatical Function Changing*. Chicago: University of Chicago Press.

Bally, Charles. 1926. "L'expression des idées de sphère personnelle et de solidarité dans les langues indo-européennes." In Franz Fankhauser and Jakob Jud (eds.), *Festschrift Louis Gauchat*. Aarau: H. R. Sauerländer, 68–78. [Translated 1995 in Hilary Chappell and William McGregor (eds.), *The Grammar of Inalienability: A Typological Perspective on Body Part Terms and the Part-Whole Relation*. Berlin: Walter de Gruyter, 31–61.]

Broadwell, George Aaron. 1990. *Extending the Binding Theory: A Muskogean Case Study*. University of California, Los Angeles: Ph.D Thesis.

Cole, Peter, Wayne Harbert, Gabriella Hermon, and S. N. Sridhar. 1980. "The Acquisition of Subjecthood. *Language* 56: 719–743.

Davies, William D. 1981a. *Choctaw Clause Structure*. University of California, San Diego: Ph.D Thesis.
Davies, William D. 1981b. "Possessor Ascension in Choctaw." In V. Burke and J. Pustejovsky (eds.), *Proceedings of the NELS 11 Conference*. Amherst: GLSA, University of Massachusetts, 38–57.
Davies, William D. 1986. *Choctaw Verb Agreement and Universal Grammar*. Dordrecht: D. Reidel.
Fox, Barbara. 1981. "Body Part Syntax: Towards a Universal Characterization." *Studies in Language* 5: 323–42.
Guéron, Jacqueline. 1985. "Inalienable Possession, PRO-inclusion, and Lexical Chains." In J. Guéron, H.-G. Obenauer, and J.-Y. Pollock (eds.), *Grammatical Representation*. Dordrecht: Foris, 43–86.
Hatcher, Anna Granville. 1944. "Il me prend le bras *vs.* Il prend mon bras." *The Romanic Review* 35: 156–164.
Heine, Bernd. 1997. *Possession: Cognitive Sources, Forces, and Grammaticalization*. Cambridge: Cambridge University Press [Cambridge Studies in Linguistics 83].
Hyman, Larry. 1995. "The Syntax of Body Parts in Haya." In Hilary Chappell and William McGregor (eds.), *The Grammar of Inalienability: A Typological Perspective on Body Part Terms and the Part-Whole Relation*. Berlin: Walter de Gruyter, 865–90.
Kayne, Richard S. 1975. *French Syntax: The Transformational Cycle*. Cambridge: MIT Press.
König, Ekkehard, and Martin Haspelmath. 1997. "Les constructions à possesseur externe dans les langues de l'Europe." In J. Feuillet (ed.), *Actance et valence dans les langues de l'Europe*. Berlin: Mouton de Gruyter, 525–606.
Kuno, Susumu. 1973. *The Structure of the Japanese Language*. Cambridge, MA: MIT Press.
Martin, Jack B. 1991a. *The Determination of Grammatical Relations in Syntax*. University of California, Los Angeles: Ph.D Thesis.
Martin, Jack B. 1991b. "Lexical and Syntactic Aspects of Creek Causatives." *International Journal of American Linguistics* 57: 194–229.
Martin, Jack B. 1993. "'Inalienable Possession' in Creek (and its possible origin)." *International Journal of American Linguistics* 59: 442–52.
Munro, Pamela. 1984. "The Syntactic Status of Object Possessor Raising in Western Muskogean." In C. Brugman et al. (eds.), *Proceedings of the Tenth Annual Meeting of the Berkeley Linguistics Society*. Berkeley: Berkeley Linguistic Society, UC Berkeley, 634–49.
Munro, Pamela, and Lynn Gordon. 1982. "Syntactic Relations in Western Muskogean: A Typological Perspective." *Language* 58: 81–115.
Nicklas, Thurston D. 1974. *The Elements of Choctaw*. University of Michigan: Ph.D Thesis.
Payne, Doris L. 1982. "Chickasaw Agreement Morphology: A Functional Explanation." In Paul J. Hopper and Sandra A. Thompson (eds.), *Studies in Transitivity*. New York: Academic Press [Syntax and Semantics 15], 351–378.

Texts cited

1936a. Mary R. Haas, Creek Notebook I, University of California, Berkeley.
1936b. Mary R. Haas, Creek Notebook II, University of California, Berkeley.
1939. Mary R. Haas, Creek Notebook XV, University of California, Berkeley.
1990. KWSH broadcast by Spencer Frank of the Seminole Nation News, August 21.
1991. Stories told by Alice Snow, Brighton, Florida.
1992. Stories told by Toney Hill, Norman, Oklahoma.

Chickasaw Subjecthood

Pamela Munro
University of California, Los Angeles

This paper considers the form and behavior of Chickasaw subjects (both underlying and derived) and ways in which the syntax of derived subject constructions becomes more like that of ordinary transitives. Two rules produce derived subjects in Chickasaw: one, the Raised Possessor (RP; Section 2) rule (also known as Possessor Raising), results in an EP construction; the other is an intriguingly similar Oblique Subject rule (OS; Section 4). Derived subjects (Section 5), whose status is confirmed by a number of syntactic traits (Section 3), differ in a number of ways from the "old subjects" of the corresponding pre-RP and pre-OS sentences, which, though still marked nominative, do not otherwise behave like syntactic subjects (Section 6). Chickasaw 'have' sentences seem to derive via RP, but their semantics suggests an independent phrasal status. RP, OS, and 'have' structures are undergoing syntactic reanalysis, with old subjects becoming more like ordinary objects for some speakers (Section 8). However, Chickasaw derived subjects still lack some crucial subject traits, as a comparison of Chickasaw RP with RP in the unrelated but typologically similar language Maricopa reveals (Section 9).

1. Introduction

Chickasaw is an SOV language of the Muskogean family with an accusative case-marking system:[1]

(1) *Ofi'-at kowi'-a̲ lhiyohli.*
dog-NOM cat-ACC chase
'The dog is chasing the cat.'

Nominative case is marked with a suffix *-at*. The syntactic object is marked with the accusative suffix *-a̲*.[2] Zero pronominalization is frequent in Chickasaw: in context, (2) may refer to the same event described in (1):

(2) *Lhiyohli.*
chase
'It is chasing it.'

(There is no gender in Chickasaw: thus, (2) could also mean 'He is chasing it', 'She is chasing him', and so on.)

Chickasaw has an "active" system of verb agreement, with (for the most part) one set of affixes marking active subjects and another set marking patients (mainly subjects of stative verbs and objects of transitive verbs). Following Munro and Gordon (1982), I use the Roman numeral 'I' to gloss affixes from the first set and 'II' for prefixes from the second set,[3] with 'III' indicating prefixes from a third set (formed from the dative prefix *im-*) used for semantic datives of all types.[4] All three classes can reference intransitive subjects, as the first person singular examples in (3) show,[5] and the nominal subject of a verb from any class may be marked as nominative (as in (4)):

(3) a. Class I intransitive verbs: *taloowa-li* 'I sing'; *hilha-li* 'I dance'; *aya-li* 'I go'; *lhabanka-li* 'I snore'; *oppoloka-li* 'I am grouchy'; *chaffa-li* 'I'm one, I'm the one'

b. Class II intransitive verbs: *sa-sipokni* 'I am old'; *sa-malhata* 'I am scared'; *sa-lli* 'I die'; *sa-lhpokonna* 'I dream'; *a-s-okcha* 'I wake up'; *sa-yili'kachi* 'I slither'

c. Class III intransitive verbs: *an-takho'bi* 'I am lazy'; *am-alhchiba* 'I am slow'; *am-ponna* 'I am smart'; *am-ilhlha* 'I am scared'; *a̲-holba* 'I have a vision'; *a̲-hiliya* 'I get bawled out'

(4) *Ihoo-at taloowa.* / *Ihoo-at sipokni.* / *Ihoo-at in-takho'bi.*
woman-NOM sing / woman-NOM be.old / woman-NOM DAT-be.lazy
'The woman sings.' (class I) / 'The woman is old.' (class II) / 'The woman is lazy.' (class III)

Some agreement must be lexically marked (Munro and Gordon 1982): for example, not all the verbs in (3a) are active, volitional, or agentive;[6] many II-subject verbs, like some in (3b), are quite active or volitional; and III-subject verbs are not always clear-cut datives, as the verbs in (3c) show. Cases like *sa-malhata* (a II-subject verb) and *am-ilhlha* (a III-subject verb), both of which mean 'I am scared', show that even fairly fine semantic criteria may not sufficiently differentiate among the three agreement classes.

There is no agreement with third person arguments, as illustrated by the bare verbs in (1–2) and (4). Independent pronouns are used only rarely.

The most basic pronominal agreement pattern for transitive verbs uses a I-marked subject and a II-marked object, as in (5):

(5) *Chi-lhiyohli-li.*
2SG:II-chase-1SG:I
'I am chasing you.'

A common alternative transitive pattern uses a I-marked subject and a dative object. This may be either a derived transitive structure, formed with the addition of the applicative dative prefix *im-* to an independently occurring intransitive verb, as in (6a), or a basic structure, as in (6b): certain dative transitive verbs, such as *i̲-hollo* 'love', do not occur without the dative prefix.

(6) a. *Chin-taloowa-li.*
2SG:III:DAT-sing-1SG:I
'I sing for you.', I sing to you.'

b. *Chi̲-hollo-li.*
2SG:III:DAT-love-1SG:I
'I love you.'

In other less common transitive patterns, the subject triggers II or III pronominal agreement, as with the II-subject verb *banna* 'want' or the III-subject verb *im-alhkaniya* 'forget':

(7) a. *Ofi'-a̲ sa-banna.*
dog-ACC 1SG:II-want
'I want the dog.'

b. *Ofi'-a̲ am-alhkaniya.*
dog-ACC 1SG:III:DAT-forget
'I forget the dog.'

Nominal subjects and objects of all types of transitive verbs may be identically marked with nominative and accusative case respectively. Example (8a) presents a dative transitive sentence (like that in (6b)), with a nominative subject noun and an accusative object noun (cf. the ordinary transitive sentence (1)), while the the II-subject and III-subject sentences in (8b, c) contain identical nominative and accusative subjects and objects:

(8) a. *Hattak-at ofi'-a̲ i̲-hollo.*
man-NOM dog-ACC DAT-love
'The man loves the dog.'

b. *Hattak-at ofi'-a banna.*
man-NOM dog-ACC want
'The man wants the dog.'

c. *Hattak-at ofi'-a im-alhkaniya.*
man-NOM dog-NOM DAT-forget
'The man forgets the dog.'

I know of no syntactic differences among nominal arguments based on the agreement classes of the verbs they are used with. The crucial difference between the transitive patterns in (7) vs. those in (5) and (6) is that verbs like those in (7) may not be used with non-third person objects: there is no way to say 'I want you' or 'I forget you' with a single clause in Chickasaw.

2. Raised possessors in Chickasaw

Chickasaw has several distinct rules that result in the creation of new syntactic subjects. The best described is Possessor Raising (Munro and Gordon 1982; Carden, Gordon, and Munro 1982), which I refer to here as the Raised Possessor rule (RP);[7] this produces what have been called "double subject" constructions:

(9) *Hattak-at im-ofi'-at ishto.* RP
man-NOM DAT-dog-NOM be.big:SG
'The man's dog is big.', 'The man has a big dog.'

(10) *Jan-at foshi'-at in-taloowa.* RP
Jan-NOM bird-NOM DAT-sing
'Jan's bird is singing.'

Although the RP examples (9–10) each contain two nouns, the syntax of these sentences is very different from that of the transitive sentences in (1) or (8). RP sentences have not one, but two, nouns marked with the nominative case suffix *-at*, and they exhibit other syntactic peculiarities. Many such sentences are most naturally translated with the English verb *have* (as in (9)), but they contain no 'have' morpheme — even (10) might be rendered as 'Jan is having her bird sing', though it has none of the sense of forcing that this English translation suggests. Functionally, RP is used when the speaker wants to convey explicitly that the possessor (PR), which is usually human, or at least animate, is more salient in the discourse than the possessum (PM). Crucially, nominative-marked PRs are not semantic subjects of the verbs here — the man in (9) need not be big, and in (10) Jan is probably not singing. Nonetheless, 'man' and 'Jan' are the syntactic subjects of these sentences, as I will demonstrate below.

RP applies to primarily intransitive verbs (some of which, such as 'sing', can occasionally be used with a cognate or other inanimate object). Many different verbs may be used in this construction. As (9) and (10) suggest, for example, the verbs may be agentive ("unergative") or non-agentive ("unaccusative"), volitional or non-volitional, controlled or uncontrolled. However, whether or not a verb may appear in an RP construction is lexically marked: a number of pairs of semantically similar verbs differ according to whether they undergo RP or not.[8] Thus, for example, *hopoba* 'be hungry' undergoes RP, but *tokshila* 'be thirsty' does not; and *toksali* 'work' undergoes RP, but *chokoshkomo* 'play' does not.

As (9–10) illustrate, there are two different forms of the RP rule. In a sentence like

(11) a. *Jan im-ofi'-at illi-tok.*
Jan DAT-dog-NOM die-PERF
'Jan's dog died.'

the subject is the alienably possessed phrase *Jan im-ofi'* 'Jan's dog', with an unmarked PR precedes a PM with a dative prefix. This sentence has two corresponding RP sentences, each with the semantic PR *Jan* as subject:

(11) b. *Jan-at ofi'-at im-illi-tok.* RP, type (a)
Jan-NOM dog-NOM DAT-die-PERF
'Jan's dog died.' > 'Jan had her dog die.'
c. *Jan-at im-ofi'-at illi-tok.* RP, type (b)
Jan-NOM DAT-dog-NOM die-PERF

In the derived sentences (11b, c) the PR no longer appears within the possessed NP, but rather forms a separate, external nominative-marked constituent. Type (a) is the somewhat more common form of the RP rule (also seen in (10)); here, a dative prefix appears on the verb and dative marking is lost from the PM. In Type (b), as in (9), the only surface change is the appearance of the nominative case marker on the PR. I know of no clear syntactic differences between these two varieties of RP in Chickasaw, but verbs vary lexically as to which variety they allow.

I will call the possessed subject phrase in pre-RP intransitive sentences like (11a) the "original subject". In (11b, c) the "raised"[9] semantic PR *Jan* is a "derived subject" and the PM 'dog' is an "old subject". More evidence for the syntactic subjecthood of the derived subject is presented in Section 3.

Evidence that the derived subject is an "external" PR and no longer forms a constituent with the old subject PM in (11b, c) is provided by movement and adverb placement. Thus, for example, the PR in a pre-RP sentence like (11a) can neither be postposed (12a) nor followed immediately by an adverb (12b):

(12) a. **Im-ofi'-at illi-tok Jan.*
*DAT-dog-NOM die-PERF Jan
'Jan's dog died.'

b. **Jan oblaashaash im-ofi'-at illi-tok.*
*Jan yesterday DAT-dog-NOM die-PERF
'Jan's dog died yesterday.'

However, a derived subject (raised semantic PR) like that in (11b) can be postposed or followed by an adverb:

(13) a. *Ofi'-at im-illi-tok Jan-at.* RP
dog-NOM DAT-die-PERF Jan-NOM

b. *Jan-at oblaashaash ofi'-at im-illi-tok.* RP
Jan-NOM yesterday dog-NOM DAT-die-PERF

Because many Chickasaw verbs can take an added dative argument introduced by *im-* (as in (6a)), it might be assumed that the dative prefix on the verb in type (a) RP sentences references a malefactive or benefactive dative argument. Thus, (11b) may look as if it should be related to a sentence like 'The dog died for Jan'. Such doublet constructions exist in some cases, but there is no verb *im-illi* 'to die for'; (11b) cannot be related to a non-RP sentence in which *Jan* is a syntactic argument.

Example (14) illustrates the operation of RP with a non-third person PR:

(14) a. *Am-ofi'-at illi-tok.*
1SG:III:DAT-dog-NOM die-PERF
'My dog died.'

b. *(Anaakoot) ofi'-at am-illi-tok.* RP, type (a)
1SG:NOM dog-NOM 1SG:III:DAT-die-PERF
'My dog died.' > 'I had my dog die.'

c. *(Anaakoot) am-ofi'-at illi-tok.* RP, type (b)
1SG:NOM 1SG:III:DAT-dog-NOM die-PERF

The parenthesized nominative pronouns in the RP sentences (14b, c) are emphatic. As in (11b), the dative prefix is lost from the original subject in (14b), and a III prefix agreeing with the derived PR subject appears on the verb.

RP works differently when the possessed subject is inalienable, as in (15).[10] In the pre-RP sentence (15a), the subject is 'Brenda's eyes'; in (15b) the subject is 'Brenda':

(15) a. *Brenda ishkin-at lakna.*
Brenda eye-NOM be.brown
'Brenda's eyes are brown.'
b. *Brenda-at ishkin-at lakna.* RP
Brenda-NOM eye-NOM be.brown
'Brenda's eyes are brown.' > 'Brenda has brown eyes.'

Non-third person inalienable PRs are marked with a II prefix on the PM: thus *sa-shkin* (1SG:II-eye) is 'my eye'. In the RP sentence (16b), only the (optional) presence of the nominative pronoun corresponding to the PR indicates that RP has occurred; II pronominal agreement remains internal to the PM.[11]

(16) a. *Sa-shkin-at lakna.*
1SG:II-eye-NOM be.brown
'My eyes are brown.'
b. *(Anaakoot) sa-shkin-at lakna.* RP
1SG:NOM 1SG:II-eye-NOM be.brown
'My eyes are brown.' > 'I have brown eyes.'

The description of the different varieties of Chickasaw RP presented in this section illustrates the most conservative form of the rule. Some speakers allow variation in RP sentences, as discussed in Section 8.

3. Chickasaw subject properties

Since the derived subjects of (14c) and (16b) only optionally appear as (emphatic) independent pronouns, these sentences have one version that is identical with the pre-RP sentences (14a) and (16a). However, these identical surface strings have different syntactic structures, one of which has the PM as subject, and one of which has the PR as subject. There are a number of different tests for subjecthood that allow us to clearly identify the subjects of (14c) and (16b) as the first person semantic PR rather than the semantic subject PMs 'dog' and 'eyes'.

As shown in (13a, b), a PR raised to subject by RP can be postposed or followed by an adverb; in contrast, as (12a, b) shows, an old subject whose PR has been raised does not have these properties. While this test effectively differentiates old and derived subjects, it is not a valid test for subjecthood, since all case-marked arguments (including also nominative subjects of non-RP sentences and accusatives) share these features with derived subjects. The subject tests I describe below involve the use of nominative marking, plural *hoo-*, diminutive *-o'si*, and switch-reference and other constructions sensitive to referential identity.[12]

3.1

Chickasaw subjects bear nominative case marking. In an RP sentence, there may be more than one such noun, so nominative marking alone is a necessary but not sufficient test for subject: the syntactic subject in a Chickasaw sentence with neutral word order is its leftmost nominative. A pronominal subject need not appear as an overt independent pronoun (as shown by (14b, c) and (16b)), so the leftmost nominative test is valid only for the fullest form of a Chickasaw sentence, with all arguments specified overtly. By this test, 'I' is the subject of (14b, c), and 'my dog' is the subject of (14a).

3.2

The subject of a Chickasaw sentence, and no other noun, can control the appearance of the third person plural *hoo-* prefix. Although I noted above that third person agreement is always zero, a third person plural argument may optionally trigger the appearance of *hoo-*, regardless of its agreement class:

(17) a. *Hattak-at hoo-aya.*
man-NOM PL-go
'The men go.' (class I subject)
b. *Hattak-at hoo-sipokni.*
man-NOM PL-be.old
'The men are old.' (class II subject)
c. *Hattak-at hoo-im-ilhlha.*
man-NOM PL-DAT-be.scared
'The men are afraid.' (class III subject)

Nouns are not marked for number in Chickasaw, so if *hoo-* were not used, the sentences in (17) would not specify the plurality of their arguments: without *hoo-*, *Hattak-at aya* could mean either 'The man goes' or 'The men go'.[13] When *hoo-* appears, however, as in (17), the plurality of the subject is clear.

Objects may never trigger the appearance of *hoo-*. While (18) could mean 'The men are chasing the dogs', it cannot mean 'The man is chasing the dogs':

(18) *Hattak-at ofi'-a̲ hoo-lhiyohli.*
man-NOM dog-ACC PL-chase
'The men are chasing the dog.', *'The man is chasing the dogs.'

Consider the interaction of RP and *hoo*-marking:

(19) a. *Ihoo i-foshi'-at hoo-taloowa.*
woman DAT-bird-NOM PL-sing
'The woman's birds are singing.', *The woman's bird is singing.'

(19) b. *Ihoo-at foshi'-at hoo-in-taloowa.* RP
woman-NOM bird-NOM PL-DAT-sing
'The women's bird is singing.', *The woman's birds are singing.'

In (19a), the *hoo-* on the verb shows that the original subject 'bird' is plural, while in (19b), the plural noun is the derived subject 'women'. Ex. (19a) could mean 'The women's birds are singing' (since the plurality of the PR 'woman' is not specified), but it cannot mean 'The women's bird is singing'. Ex. (19b) could mean 'The women's birds are singing' (since the plurality of the old subject 'bird' is not specified), but not 'The woman's birds are singing'. Thus, the *hoo-* test differentiates between a sentence in which a PR is a derived subject and one in which it is simply a PR.

3.3

The subject of a Chickasaw sentence, and only the subject, can control the appearance of the diminutive suffix *-o'si* on the verb (Munro 1988). This suffix appears on verbs whose subject is an appropriate diminutive trigger: a small or dear creature, or occasionally a decrepit or pitiable elderly one:

(20) *Chipot-aat pish-o'si.*
child-NOM suck-DIM
'The baby is nursing.'

(21) *Ihoo-at chipot-a pishi-chi. / *...pishi-ch-o'si.* RP
woman-NOM child-ACC suck-CAUS / *...suck-CAUS-DIM
'The woman is nursing the baby.'

Since *chipota* 'child' is an appropriate diminutive trigger, the suffix *-o'si* may follow the verb in (20). The baby is still doing the nursing in the causative sentence (21); however, 'child' is not the subject of that sentence, so the verb cannot be used with *-o'si*.

Now consider the interaction of the diminutive with a possessed subject, before and and after RP:

(22) a. *Ihoo in-chipot-aat pish-o'si.*
woman DAT-child-NOM suck-DIM
'The woman's baby is nursing.'

b. **Ihoo-at chipot-aat im-pish-o'si.* RP
*woman-NOM child-NOM DAT-suck-DIM

Ex. (22a) is fine, since its subject is the PM 'child'. But when the PR 'woman' becomes the subject of (22b) through RP, the suffix *-o'si* cannot appear on the verb, because the sentence no longer has a diminutive subject. Conversely, (23a), without RP, is no good with a diminutive suffix.[14] In (23b), however, the diminutive is used appropriately if the derived PR subject is a baby, even if the dog in question is a Great Dane:

(23) a. *Chipota im-ofi'-at abika. / *...abik-a'si.*
child DAT-dog-NOM be.sick / *...be.sick-DIM
'The baby's dog is sick.'
b. *Chipot-aat ofi'-at im-ambiik-a'si.* RP
child-NOM dog-NOM DAT-be.sick-DIM

Thus, a PR or an old subject cannot serve as a diminutive trigger, but a derived subject may do so.

3.4

The last subject tests in Chickasaw that I will describe here involve marking identity of reference, most importantly through switch-reference morphology. As (24) illustrates, Chickasaw uses switch-reference for monitoring pronominal reference between clauses:

(24) a. *Ofi'-at kowi'-a̱ lhiyohli-hmat sa-kisili-tok.*
dog-NOM cat-ACC chase-REAL=SS 1SG:II-bite-PERF
'After the dog$_i$ chased the cat it$_i$ bit me.'
b. *Ofi'-at kowi'-a̱ lhiyohli-hma̱ sa-kisili-tok.*
dog-NOM cat-ACC chase-REAL:DS 1SG:II-bite-PERF
'After the dog$_i$ chased the cat it$_j$ bit me.'

The system is strictly sensitive to the sameness or difference of the subjects of the subordinate verb to which the switch-reference marker is attached and the higher reference verb. 'Dog', the subject of the 'chase' clause in both sentences, is also the subject of the 'bite' clause in sentence (24a), so the first verb in (24a) is followed by the same-subject (SS) realis subordinator *-hmat*. In (24b), however, the subjects of the two verbs are different, so in this sentence 'chase' is followed by the different-subject (DS) realis subordinator *-hma̱*.[15] Crucially, Chickasaw switch-reference is determined on the basis of identity of reference, not formal identity of agreement markers. Thus, the two clauses in (25) are marked for same-subject, since each has a first person singular subject, even though the first clause has an intransitive II-subject verb (its subject marked with the prefix *sa-*), and the second a transitive I-subject verb (its subject marked with the suffix *-li*):

(25) *Sa-tikahbi-kat ithá̱na-li.*
1SG:II-be.tired-CMPL:SS know-1SG:I
'I know I'm tired.'

Consider the sentences in (26). In these examples, the switch-reference-marked subordinate clauses (bracketed here) have been extraposed; they are marked with forms of the switch-reference markers *-tokat / -toka̱*:

(26) a. *Ihoo-at nokhanglo [im-ofi'-at illi-toka̱].*
woman-NOM be.sad DAT-dog-NOM die-PERF:DS
'The woman is sad that her dog died.'

b. *Ihoo-at nokhanglo [ofi'-at im-illi-tokat].*
woman-NOM be.sad dog-NOM DAT-die-PERF:SS
lower clause RP, type (a)

c. *Ihoo-at nokhanglo [im-ofi'-at illi-tokat].*
woman-NOM be.sad DAT-dog-NOM die-PERF:SS
lower clause RP, type (b)

The embedded clause in (26a) is a non-RP sentence with 'the woman's dog' as its subject; since the subject of the main clause is 'the woman', the embedded clause is marked as having a different subject from the main clause. In (26b, c), the PR 'woman' of the underlying subject in that clause has been subjectivalized. The embedded clauses in (26b, c) have same-subject markers because their derived subjects are the same as the main clause subject, even though the old subject and the main clause subject are different. (*Ihoo* 'woman' is zero-pronominalized in each of the lower clauses, so we cannot see its nominative marking; the fact that the subject-creating rules have applied is inferred primarily from the switch-reference marking.)

3.5

Several other Chickasaw constructions are sensitive to the sameness or difference of subjects. One example is sentences using the verbs *ilahobbi / ahobbichi* 'pretend', as in

(27) a. *Taloowa ilahobbi-li-tok.*
sing pretend:SS-1SG:I-PERF
'I pretended to sing.'

b. *Charles-at taloowa ahobbichi-li-tok.*
Charles-NOM sing pretend:DS-1SG:I-PERF
'I pretended that Charles sang.'

The two verbs here are not synchronically segmentable, since their base verb, *ahobbi*, does not occur alone. The first, *ilahobbi*, is used only when the subject of the lower clause is the same as the pretender (it means something like 'pretend of oneself') and the second, *ahobbichi*, only when the subject of the lower verb is different from the pretender (it means something like 'cause to be pretended'). Although the construction is thus sensitive to the reference of the pretender and the lower subject,[16] there is no switch-reference (or other) marking on the verb of that clause.

Ex. (28) shows how 'pretend' interacts with RP:

(28) a. *Lynn-at im-ofi'-at ishto ahobbichi-tok.*
Lynn-NOM DAT-dog-NOM be.big pretend:DS-PERF
'Lynn pretended her dog was big.'

b. *Lynn-at ofi'-at im-ishto ilahobbi-tok.*
Lynn-NOM dog-NOM DAT-be.big pretend:SS-PERF
lower clause RP, type (a)

c. *Lynn-at im-ofi'-at ishto ilahobbi-tok.*
Lynn-NOM DAT-dog-NOM be.big pretend:SS-PERF
lower clause RP, type (b)

In (28a) there are two clauses, one with 'Lynn' as subject, one with 'Lynn's dog' as subject, so the different-subject 'pretend' verb, *ahobbichi*, is used. In (28b, c), 'Lynn' has been raised to be subject of the lower clause, so the same-subject 'pretend' verb, *ilahobbi*, is used. Even though the first three words of (28a) and (28c) are identical, the choice of 'pretend' verb reveals whether RP has occurred. As with switch-reference, the construction is sensitive to the sameness of the main clause subject and the derived subject of the embedded clause, not that of the old subject.

4. The Chickasaw oblique subject rule

Chickasaw has an Oblique Subject (OS) rule that also produces sentences containing two nominatives. There are two varieties of OS, one with a dative prefix on the verb (as in (29b)), the other without (as in (30b)):[17]

(29) a. *Chihoow-aat ihoo-a̲ im-oktani-tok.*
God-NOM woman-ACC DAT-appear-PERF
'God appeared to the woman.'

b. *Ihoo-at Chihoow-aat im-oktani-tok.* OS
woman-NOM God-NOM DAT-appear-PERF

(30) a. *Hashi'-at Jan-a̲ on-toomi-tok.*
sun-NOM Jan-ACC on-shine-PERF
'The sun shone on Jan.'

b. *Jan-at hashi'-at on-toomi-tok.* OS
Jan-NOM sun-NOM on-shine-PERF

The OS processes take as input transitive sentences containing intransitive verbs such as *oktani* 'to appear' or *toomi* 'to shine' with an added applicative prefix: dative *im-*, *on-* 'on', or *a-* 'against'. Exs. (29a) and (30a) illustrate such applicative transitive sentences — as far as the nominals they contain, these are syntactically identical with simple transitive sentences like (1) above, with a nominative subject and an accusative object. OS sentences like (29b) and (30b) are superficially similar to RP sentences like those in Section 2: they are "double subject" constructions with two nominative-marked nouns, only the first of which is a syntactic subject, and with a verb that may include a dative prefix. As with RP, the derived subject is salient in the discourse, and the sentences can often be paraphrased with 'have': (29b) could be translated 'The woman had God appear to her', and (30b) as 'Jan had the sun shine on her'.

OS also produces non-third person derived subjects, as in (31b) and (32b):

(31) a. *Chihoow-aat (ishnaako̲) chim-oktani-taam?*
God-NOM 2SG:ACC 2SG:III-appear-Q:PERF
'Did God appear to you?'

b. *(Ishnaakoot) Chihoow-aat chim-oktani-taam?* OS
2SG:NOM God-NOM 2SG:III-appear-Q:PERF

(32) a. *Nampanaa'-at (anaako̲) a.sa.shiiyalhchi-taha.*
string-NOM 1SG:ACC 1SG:II:be.tied.on-be.done
'The string is tied onto me.'

b. *(Anaakoot) nampanaa'-at a.sa.shiiyalhchi-taha.* OS
1SG:NOM string-NOM 1SG:II:be.tied.on-be.done

Unlike verbs allowing RP, verbs allowing OS are semantically restricted to "unaccusative" or non-volitional verbs (though as intransitives some of these are I subject (active), others are II subject (non-active)). Ex. (33a) presents a selection of some verbs allowing the first variety of OS (as in (29b, 31b)), and

(33b) presents some verbs allowing the second variety of OS (as in (30b, 32b)). In their pre-OS meaning, none of the verbs in (33) are ordinary active transitives. For example, the last verb in (33b), *o̲-molhchi* 'cover' takes as subject an item or mass that covers something (such as dirt).

(33) a. *im-albina* 'be a camp for' > 'make camp in', *im-alla* 'come to, be born to' > 'give birth to', *im-alhpooba* 'be born to' > 'give birth to', *im-alhtoba* 'be paid to' > 'get paid', *im-ambaanabli* 'run over for' > 'let (something) run over', *im-annoya* 'be told to' > 'have been told, know', *im-á̲lhlhi* 'be faithful to' > 'have be faithful', *im-iksaa* 'be made for' > 'have be made for one', *im-ittola* 'fall away from' > 'drop', *im-i̲hollo* 'be forbidden to' (of a food or drink) > 'have (a food or drink) be forbidden to one', *in-kaniya* 'go away from, get lost from' > 'lose'

b. *a-kallo* 'be tight on' > 'have (something) be tight on one', *a-sítti'ya* 'be pinned on' > 'have pinned on one', *a-shiikoono'wa* 'be knotted onto' > 'have knotted on one', *a-shiila* 'stick onto' > 'have sticking onto', *a-shiiyalhchi* 'be tied on' > 'have tied on', *om-pachili* 'splash on' > 'have (something) splashed on one', *on-toomi* 'shine on' > 'have (something) shine on one', *o̲-molhchi* 'cover' > 'be covered with'

Semantically active or "unergative" verbs with added *im-*, *on-*, or *a-* applicatives may not have those applicatives subjectivalized by OS. Thus, a sentence like (34a) or (35a) with an active verb may not have an added dative or 'on' applicative object subjectivalized by OS: (34b) cannot mean 'The woman has the man sing to her',[18] and (35b) cannot mean 'The woman has the man lie about her':

(34) a. *Hattak-at ihoo-a̲ in-taloowa.*
man-NOM woman-ACC DAT-sing
'The man sings to the woman.'

b. **Ihoo-at hattak-at in-taloowa.* *OS
*woman-NOM man-NOM DAT-sing

(35) a. *Hattak-at ihoo-a̲ o̲-loshka.*
man-NOM woman-ACC on-lie
'The man lies about the woman.'

b. **Ihoo-at hattak-at o̲-loshka.* *OS
*woman-NOM man-NOM on-lie

The derived subject in OS sentences satisfies the same syntactic subject tests as the derived subject in RP sentences. It is the leftmost nominative in the sentence (Section 3.1), and it, not the original subject, controls the interpretation of third person plural prefix *hoo-* (Section 3.2), as shown in (36):

(36) a. *Ofi'-at ihoo-a̲ hoo-in-tamowa-tok.*
dog-NOM woman-ACC PL-DAT-get.lost:PL-PERF
'The dogs got lost from the woman.'

b. *Ihoo-at ofi'-at hoo-in-tamowa-tok.* OS
woman-NOM dog-NOM PL-DAT-get.lost:PL-PERF
'The women had the dogs get lost.', 'The women lost the dogs.'

In the pre-OS sentence (36a), the *hoo-* on the verb is interpreted with the original subject 'dogs' rather than the PR 'woman'. In the OS sentence (36b), however, *hoo-* forces the interpretation that the derived subject 'woman' is plural.

The diminutive suffix *-a'si* (Section 3.3) works similarly in (37):

(37) a. *Chipot-aat ishk-a̲ in-kaniy-a's-tok.*
child-NOM mother-ACC DAT-get.lost-DIM-PERF
'The child got lost from the mother.'

b. *Ishk-aat chipot-aat in-kaniy-(*a's-)tok.* OS
mother-NOM child-NOM DAT-get.lost-(*DIM-)PERF
'The mother had the child get lost from her.', 'The mother lost the child.'

In the pre-OS sentence (37a), 'child' is the subject, so the diminutive suffix may appropriately appear on the verb. In the OS sentence (37b), however, 'mother' has been subjectivalized. Since 'mother' is not an appropriate diminutive trigger, the diminutive suffix may not appear.

The examples in (36) and (37) illustrate how verbs may be lexicalized with new meanings in the OS construction, as suggested by the translations in (33). Although (36b) and (37b) could still be translated with the original subjects 'dog' and 'child', the usual translation would be with 'lose' and the derived subject. Similarly, the verb *im-ittola*, literally 'fall from', is used to mean 'drop' in the OS construction. I return to this question of relexification below.

Switch-reference (Section 3.4) works similarly with OS constructions. In (38a) the lower pre-OS clause has a different subject, 'dog', from the higher subject, 'woman', so a different-subject subordinator is used. In (38b), the dative 'woman' has been subjectivalized in the lower clause, so the two subjects now have the same subject; thus, a same-subject suffix can be used.

(38) a. *Ihoo-at nokhanglo ofi'-at in-kaniya-toka.*
woman-NOM be.sad dog-NOM DAT-get.lost-PERF:DS
'The woman is sad that the dog got lost from her.'
b. *Ihoo-at nokhanglo ofi'-at in-kaniya-tokat.* OS
woman-NOM sad dog-NOM DAT-get.lost-PERF:SS
'The woman is sad that that she lost the dog.'

The 'pretend' constructions (Section 3.5) again are similar. In (39a) the lower center-embedded clause has 'sun' as its subject, so the different-subject 'pretend' *ahobbichi* is used. In (39b) the oblique object 'Lynn' has been subjectivalized, so the same-subject *ilahobbi* is used:

(39) a. *Lynn-at hashi'-at on-toomi ahobbichi-tok.*
Lynn-NOM sun-NOM on-shine pretend:DS-PERF
'Lynn pretended that the sun was shining on her.'
b. *Lynn-at hashi'-at on-toomi ilahobbi-tok.* OS
Lynn-NOM sun-NOM on-shine pretend:SS-PERF

As with the description of RP in Section 2 above, the description of OS presented here illustrates the most conservative forms of the rule. There is even more variation in the treatment of OS, both among speakers and in the speech of single speakers, than there is for RP (Section 8).

5. Derived subjects in Chickasaw

There are a number of similarities between the RP and OS processes that are related to their discourse function of increasing the prominence of the derived subjects.

The new subjects created by both rules are "salient", in that the speaker is more interested in talking about them than about the old subjects. Speakers often consciously choose RP and OS structures in order to highlight the derived subjects. For example, Lizzie Frazier delicately balances the roles of the two characters in the traditional story of "Rabbit and Buzzard" (Munro to appear); in (40), though the original subject is 'Rabbit's bones', inalienable RP is used to make Rabbit a derived subject, since, even when dead, he, rather than his bones, is the focus of interest:

(40) *Rabbit mat foni' ill-aat áyya'sha-ttook miya....* RP
rabbit that:NOM bone only-NOM be.there:PL-rem report
'Only Rabbit's bones were there (they say)...'

However, derived subjects are not simply important in the discourse; they also have a particular syntactic status at the level of the simple clause. Chickasaw has a clause-level topicalization rule (leftward movement), as well as a postposing rule with a somewhat similar pragmatic effect, and morphological means of marking strong topics, focused nominals, and contrastive nominals (Munro and Willmond 1994). None of these movements or markings are correlated with either underlying or derived subjecthood, as revealed by the subject tests in Section 3. And although a derived subject's pragmatic function often seems analogous to that of a topic, derived RP and OS subjects can be either indefinites or questioned, roles that seem incompatible with syntactic topicality:

(41) a. *Kana-hmat ofi'-at im-illi-tok.* RP, type (a)
someone-IND:NOM dog-NOM DAT-die-PERF
'Someone's dog died.'

b. *Kana-hmat im-ofi'-at illi-tok.* RP, type (b)

(42) *Kana-hmat holiss-aat im-ittola.* OS
someone-IND:NOM book-NOM DAT-fall
'Someone dropped their book.'

(43) a. *Kata-haat ofi'-at im-illi-tok?* RP, type (a)
who-INT:NOM dog-NOM DAT-die-PERF
'Whose dog died?'

b. *Kata-haat im-ofi'-at illi-tok?* RP, type (b)

(44) *Kata-haat holiss-aat im-ittola?* OS
who-INT:NOM book-NOM DAT-fall
'Who dropped their book?'

(Chickasaw has several sets of case markers with different discourse and syntactic functions: *-hmat* in (41–42) is an indefinite nominative case marker, and *-haat* in (43–44) is an interrogative nominative marker.)

Non-third persons cannot, in general, be possessed, so it is unremarkable that the old subject of the RP construction must be third person. A pre-OS old subject must also be third person. Both rules have the effect of increasing the grammatical salience of nominals that are more prominent in the discourse than the old subjects, and it would not make sense to do this if the old subjects were speech-act participants

Both RP and OS involve lexical governance. Whether a structually appropriate verb participates in either construction is lexically determined, as is which mode of RP a verb governs.

However, there are some important differences between subjects derived by RP and subjects derived by OS. The most important one concerns thematic role. The derived subject in an RP sentence bears a possessive relationship to the old subject, but is not otherwise a subcategorized argument of the verb of the sentence. In (9), for example, the man may be very small; it is his dog that is big, yet 'man' is a derived subject. In (10) and (11) Jan neither sings nor dies (her bird and her dog do), yet she is the subject in (10) and (11b, c).[19] The derived subjects are syntactic arguments (as shown by the subject tests described in sections 3 and 4) of the RP clauses, but not of the corresponding non-RP sentences. Subjects derived by OS are different, because they always bear a thematic role relative to the derived applicative transitive clauses in which they appear. For example, in (29), both God and the woman are arguments of the derived applicative verb *im-oktani* 'appear to', and in (30), both Jan and the sun are arguments of the derived applicative verb *on-toomi* 'shine on'.

A second difference beween RP and OS is that RP involves no change in surface word order: the PR appears before the PM both in the original sentence and the derived structure. In OS sentences, though, the original applicative object is visibly fronted through the operation of the rule.

A particularly striking difference between RP and OS involves recursion. RP is iterative, as shown by a sentence like (45a), with a complex possessed subject containing several stacked PRs. *Ibiitop* 'ends' is the original subject of 'be burnt' in (45a). The stacked PRs of 'ends' are iteratively raised to subject (from right to left) until finally the most salient nominal, *Jan*, is subjectivalized (45f). Each derived sentence can be shown to have a different subject by the tests discussed in Section 3. There seem to be only processing limitations on this rule.[20]

(45) a. *Jan in-ka̱na' im-ofi' iyyi hishi' ibiitop-at lowa-tok.*
Jan DAT-friend DAT-dog leg hair end-NOM burn-PERF
'The ends of the hair on Jan's friend's dog's legs are burnt.'

b. *Jan in-ka̱na' im-ofi' iyyi' hishi'-at ibiitop-at lowa-tok.* RP

c. *Jan in-ka̱na' im-ofi' iyy-aat hishi'-at ibiitop-at lowa-tok.* RP

d. *Jan in-ka̱na' im-ofi'-at iyy-aat hishi'-at ibiitop-at lowa-tok.* RP

e. *Jan in-ka̱n-aat im-ofi'-at iyy-aat hishi'-at ibiitop-at lowa-tok.* RP

f. *Jan-at in-ka̱n-aat im-ofi'-at iyy-aat hishi'-at*
Jan-NOM DAT-friend-NOM DAT-dog-NOM leg-NOM hair-NOM
ibiitop-at lowa-tok.
end-NOM burn-PERF RP

In contrast, the PR of a semantic dative promoted to subject by OS cannot be raised:

(46) *Jan(*-at) in-kan-aat Chihoow-aat im-oktani-tok.*
Jan(*-NOM) DAT-friend-NOM God-NOM DAT-appear-PERF
'God appeared to Jan's friend.'

The last important difference between RP and OS involves a delicate question of relexification, based on the fact that OS sentences, as noted above, sometimes involve more of a change in meaning than RP sentences (probably because OS, rather like passive, involves an interchange of two separate subject and non-subject constitutents, while RP involves the extraction of one part of a single subject constituent). When *in-kaniya* 'get lost from' is used in OS sentences like (36b), (37b), or (38b) to mean 'lose' or when *im-ittola* 'fall from' is used to mean 'drop' (from the point of view of the derived subject), there is a significant change in meaning that does not seem to occur with RP. Undoubtedly there have been historical cases (as I will suggest in Section 8) where the derived OS meaning eventually completely obscures the original pre-OS sense.

6. Old subjects in Chickasaw

Unlike the derived subjects in RP constructions (as noted in Section 5), Chickasaw old subjects all are semantic subjects (whether agent or theme) acording to the underlying meaning of the verb of their clause. Thus, for example, the old subject 'dog' in (9) is the one that is big, the old subject 'bird' in (10) is the one that sings, and the old subject 'dog' in (11) is the one that dies. In many cases there are lexical selectional restrictions of various sorts that hold between old subjects and RP verbs. Compare (47a) with (47b):

(47) a. *Hattak-at im-ofi'-at ishto.*
'The man's dog is big.'[21] (= (9))
b. *Hattak-at im-ofi'-at hichito.*
man-NOM DAT-dog-NOM be.big:PL
'The man's dogs are big.'

As discussed in Section 3.2, Chickasaw has no number marking on nouns. In most cases, the number of third persons must be inferred from context, but certain verbs have separate forms for singular vs. plural or singular vs. dual vs. plural arguments. One such pair is *ishto* 'be big [singular]' vs. *hichito* 'be big [plural]': speakers insist that only the first can be used with a singular big item, and only the second if more than two big things are involved. In a simple sentence, this involves a distinction between singular vs. plural subject — but in

RP sentences like those in (47), what conditions the speaker's choice of verb is the old subject. In contrast, there are no verbs whose lexical selection is determined by the number or other features of the derived subject.

Chickasaw can thus grammatically indicate the plurality of certain third persons in two ways — lexically, as with the choice of *ishto* vs. *hichito,* as a characteristic of original subjects, and syntactically, with the third person plural *hoo-* prefix (Section 3.2), as a characteristic of surface subjects, including derived subjects.[22]

In this and other syntactic behavior, old subjects in sentences derived by RP and OS seem much like chômeurs in classical Relational Grammar. Not only do they fail to exhibit syntactic subject properties (sections 3 and 4), not only are they restricted to third person, but there are additional ways in which they do not have the pragmatic status of ordinary arguments. For example, all other case-marked nominals can be freely moved to the beginning or the end of a sentence (to show topicality or other discourse roles), but old subjects cannot move away from the position immediately before the verb. Ex. (48) shows that a simple sentence with case-marked subject and object may surface with any word order:[23]

(48) a. *Ofi'-at kowi'-a̲ lhiyohli.*
dog-NOM cat-ACC chase
'The dog is chasing the cat.' (= (1))
b. *Kowi'-a̲ lhiyohli ofi'-at.*
c. *Kowi'-a̲ ofi'-at lhiyohli.*
d. *Ofi'-at lhiyohli kowi'-a̲.* (etc.)

Exs. (49) and (50) show that in an RP or OS sentence, the derived subject may be moved to the end of the sentence, but the old subject may not be preposed before the derived subject or moved after the verb:

(49) a. *Jan-at ofi'-at im-illi-tok.* RP
Jan-NOM dog-NOM DAT-die-PERF
'Jan's dog died.' (= (11b))
b. *Ofi'-at im-illi-tok Jan-at.*
c. * *Ofi'at Jan-at im-illi-tok.*
d. * *Jan-at im-illi-tok ofi'-at.*

(50) a. *Ihoo-at Chihoow-aat im-oktani-tok.* OS
woman-NOM God-NOM DAT-appear-PERF
'God appeared to the woman.' (= (29b))
b. *Chihoow-aat im-oktani-tok ihoo-at.*

c. **Chihoow-aat ihoo-at im-oktani-tok.*[24]

d. **Ihoo-at im-oktani-tok Chihoow-aat.*

In this respect, the status of old subjects is somewhat similar to that of non-case-marked objects. Chickasaw semantic objects can either be marked accusative, as in the examples presented up to now, or left unmarked. Objects without accusative case marking, like 'cat' in (51a), are semantically almost identical to case-marked objects,[25] but they cannot be moved away from their position in front of the verb:

(51) a. *Ofi'-at kowi' lhiyohli.*
dog-NOM cat chase
'The dog is chasing the cat.'

b. *Kowi' lhiyohli ofi'-at.*

c. **Kowi' ofi'-at lhiyohli.*

d. **Ofi'-at lhiyohli kowi.'*[26]

Because of this restricted behavior, the syntactic status of non-case-marked objects seems more like that of incorporated objects in other languages (though these objects' definiteness and specificity do not seem to be restricted), than like that of case-marked arguments. In fact, in rapid speech certain sequences of unmarked object plus verb[27] may be phonologically lenited, as in (52b), the fast speech variant of (52a):

(52) a. *Ofi'-at chokfi abi-tok.*
dog-NOM rabbit kill-PERF
'The dog killed a rabbit.'

b. *Ofi'-at chokf-abi-tok.*
dog-NOM rabbit-kill-PERF

Because of these similarities, it is tempting to consider that the old subject might also be syntactically incorporated in some sense, along with its nominative marking.[28]

Unlike ordinary arguments, old subjects may not be zero-pronominalized. Either or both arguments in an ordinary transitive sentence like (1) may be zero-pronominalized, as shown in (53) (and also (2) above):[29]

(53) a. *Ofi'-at lhiyohli.*
dog-NOM chase
'The dog is chasing it.'

b. *Kowi'-a̲ lhiyohli.*
cat-ACC chase
'It is chasing the cat.'

Zero-pronominalization indicates that an argument is so well understood — or topical — that it need not be identified to the hearer. But although an old subject might be "understood", old subjects cannot be zeroed. If the old subject is zero-pronominalized in the RP sentence (49a), as in (54), the string is meaningless; this sentence cannot be used to say that something of Jan's died.[30] If the old subject is zero in the OS sentence (50a), as in (55), the sentence can only mean 'The woman appeared to him' (an ordinary applicative transitive with a zero-pronominalized object); it cannot mean 'He appeared to the woman' or 'The woman had him appear to her'.

(54) *Jan-at *im-illi-tok.*
*Jan-NOM DAT-die-PERF

(55) **Ihoo-at* *im-oktani-tok.* *as elliptical OS
*woman-NOM DAT-appear-PERF

As noted earlier, certain differences in the pragmatic status of Chickasaw arguments are indicated through choice of case marker: thus, for example, the focused subjects in (56a–c) are marked with the focus nominative *-hoot*; similarly, focused objects can be marked with the focus accusative *-h<u>o</u>,* as in (57):

(56) a. *Ofi'-oot kowi' lhiyohli.*
dog-FOC:NOM cat chase
'A DOG is chasing the cat.'
b. *Ihoo-hoot ofi'-at im-illi.* RP
woman-FOC:NOM dog-NOM DAT-die
'A WOMAN's dog died.'
c. *Ihoo-hoot Chihoow-aat im-oktani-tok.* OS
woman-FOC:NOM God-NOM DAT-appear-PERF
'God appeared to a WOMAN.'

(57) *Ofi'-at kowi'-<u>o</u> lhiyohli.*
dog-NOM cat-FOC:ACC chase
'The dog is chasing a CAT.'

As (56b, c) show, derived subjects may be focused. But old subjects cannot be:[31]

(58) a. **Jan-at ofi'-oot im-illi.* RP
*Jan-NOM dog-FOC:NOM DAT-die
b. **Ihoo-at Chihoow-oot im-oktani-tok.* OS
*woman-NOM God-FOC:NOM DAT-appear-PERF

The failure of old subjects to occur with focus marking seems to indicate less syntactic and pragmatic viability than other arguments have.

Despite this restriction, an old subject may be either questioned or indefinite. Overt indefinite pronominal old subjects are given in (59a, b):

(59) a. *Jan-at nanna-hmat im-illi-tok.* RP
Jan-NOM something-IND:NOM DAT-die-PERF
'Something of Jan's died.'
b. *Jan-at nanna-hmat im-ittola-tok.* OS
Jan-NOM something-IND:NOM DAT-fall-PERF
'Jan dropped something.'

The occurrence of indefinite old subjects in the RP construction is rather surprising, since indefinites otherwise may not be possessed; (59a) looks as if it derives from a source sentence containing the otherwise unacceptable string **Jan i̱-nanna* (Jan DAT-something) 'Jan's something'.

Wh-questions provide additional evidence that old subjects are syntactically different from other nominatives. Chickasaw has a rule of *wh*-movement that optionally fronts a questioned constituent.[32] Questions with fronted *wh*-words, like (60), are judged synonymous with those with *wh*-words in situ:

(60) *Kata-hta̱ ofi'-at lhiyohli?*
who-INT:ACC dog-NOM chase
'Who is the dog chasing?'

A questioned constituent in an embedded clause (like accusative *kata-hta̱* 'who' in (61)) usually surfaces in situ or is fronted only to the beginning of its clause, as in (61a, b),[33] but it may be fronted to the beginning of the whole sentence, before elements of the main clause, as in (61c):[34]

(61) a. *Charles-at ofi'-at kata-hta̱ lhiyohli-ka̱ pí̱s-tok?*
Charles-NOM dog-NOM who-INT:ACC chase-DS see-PERF
'Who did Charles see the dog chase?'
b. *Charles-at kata-hta̱ ofi'-at lhiyohli-ka̱ pí̱s-tok?*
c. *Kata-hta̱ Charles-at ofi'-at lhiyohli-ka̱ pí̱s-tok?*

While the fronting of *wh*-words within their own clauses could result from the simple scrambling/topicalization rules illustrated in (48),[35] scrambling of a nominal out of its clause, as in (61c), is allowed in Chickasaw only with questioned *wh*-words. The non-*wh* object *Jan* cannot be moved out of its clause in (62):[36]

(62) a. *Charles-at ofi'-at Jan-a̱ lhiyohli-ka̱ pí̱s-tok.*
Charles-NOM dog-NOM Jan-ACC chase-DS see-PERF
'Charles saw the dog chase Jan.'

b. *Charles-at Jan-a̲ ofi'-at lhiyohli-ka̲ pí̲s-tok.*
c. **Jan-a̲ Charles-at ofi'-at lhiyohli-ka̲ pí̲s-tok.*

Questioned old subjects behave in a way intermediate between other questioned constituents (like *kata-hta̲* 'who' in (61)) and non-questioned arguments (like *Jan* in (62)).[37] Like any other questioned argument (but unlike a non-questioned old subject), an old subject containing a *wh*-interrogative may be fronted within its clause (63b):

(63) a. *Jan-at nanta-haat im-illi-tok?* RP
Jan-NOM what-INT:NOM DAT-die-PERF
'What of Jan's died?'
b. *Nanta-haat Jan-at im-illi-tok?*
what-INT:NOM Jan-NOM DAT-die-PERF

However, a questioned old subject in an embedded clause may not be fronted out of that clause (64b),[38] unlike other questioned constituents, but like non-questioned arguments:

(64) a. *Charles-at Jan-at nanta-haat im-illi-ka̲ pí̲s-tok?* RP
Charles-NOM Jan-NOM what-INT:NOM DAT-die-DS see-PERF
'What of Jan's did Charles see die?'
(64) b. **Nanta-haat Charles-at Jan-at im-illi-ka̲ pí̲s-tok?*

Thus, *wh*-questions provide further evidence that Chickasaw old subjects cannot serve as the focus of pragmatic attention in the same way that other nominatives do.

7. The Chickasaw 'have' construction

Ex. (65) presents one Chickasaw 'have' sentence.

(65) *Chipot-aat ofi'-at i̲-wáyya'a.*
child-NOM dog-NOM DAT-be.located:SG
'The child has a dog.'

Chickasaw 'have' sentences originate as RP constructions, related to sentences like

(66) *Chipota im-ofi'-at wáyya'a.*
child DAT-dog-NOM be.located:SG
'The child's dog is (there).'

Example (66) is an existential sentence; it could be used, for instance, on looking into a room and seeing the child's dog. There is no single 'have' verb in

Chickasaw: 'have' sentences can be formed with numerous orientational or locational verbs, almost all of which exist in separate forms for singular, dual, or plural subjects.[39]

'Have' sentences like (65) could be derived by the regular application of RP to sentences like (66): the original PR becomes a nominative-marked subject (by the tests in Section 3), the original subject loses its dative prefix but retains its nominative marking, and the verb acquires a dative prefix. However, there is a difference from the RP sentences surveyed in Section 2: the meaning and presupposition of the 'have' sentences is very different from that of their source, since the original sentences presuppose the existence of the possessed objects, while the 'have' sentences are used to assert that existence.

Traditionally, linguistic "rules" are seen as possibly changing emphasis or other pragmatic features, but not basic meaning. We have seen a number of ways in which Chickasaw double-subject constructions are gradually developing independent phrasal status rather than being simply rule-derived variants (with identical truth values) of a group of underlying structures. The interpretation of the 'have' sentences just discussed is strikingly analogous to the relexicalization of many OS sentences ('get lost from' to 'lose', 'fall from' to 'drop', and so on): in each case, the meaning of the double-subject sentence is not predictable from that of the source sentence. Similarly, RP sentences with indefinite old subjects like (59a) have apparent syntactic sources that could not be well-formed surface sentences.

8. Variation and change in Chickasaw derived subject constructions

The 'have' syntax described in Section 7 represents the most conservative variety of Chickasaw. Most speakers use these patterns, and all accept them, but some speakers also produce a different kind of 'have' sentence:

(67) *Chipot-aat ofi' i̱-wáyya'a.*
child-NOM dog DAT-be.located:SG
'The child has a dog.'

The difference between an innovative sentence like (67) and a conservative sentence like (65) is that the old subject 'dog', naming the semantic possession in (67), is no longer marked nominative; rather, it is an unmarked object like that in (51a) above (and could potentially be phonologically incorporated into the verb, as in (52b) above). Conservative speakers do not accept the 'have' construction in (67).

Individual speakers produce similar variants of RP and OS constructions, though the same speakers often describe the conservative variety of these constructions (sections 2 and 4) as "correct". In all these variants, the old subject loses its nominative marking and may even be marked accusative, with the result that the new construction looks like an ordinary transitive sentence rather than a double-subject construction.

Ex. (68) is an example of an RP construction with a non-nominative old subject. The examples in (69) include the OS verbs *in-kaniya* 'get lost from > lose' and *im-ittola* 'fall from > drop'.[40] In both of these, there is no nominative marking on the old subject; in (69b) this noun is phonologically incorporated into the verb.

(68) *Zak-at ofi' im-illi-tok.*
Zak-NOM dog DAT-die-PERF
'Zak's dog died.'

(69) a. *Zak-at holisso in-kaniya-tok.*
Zak-NOM book DAT-get.lost-PERF
'Zak lost the book.'

b. *Tara-at holiss-im-ittola-tok.*
Tara-NOM book-DAT-fall-PERF
'Tara dropped the book.'

RP and OS constructions are often restructured in questions. Even speakers who follow the conservative pattern in using nominative marking on *wh*-old subjects in situ, as in (63a) above and (70a), for example, may switch to accusative marking when the *wh*-phrase is fronted, as in (70b):

(70) a. *Keeli-at ofi' nanta-haat i̲-wáyya'a?*
Keeli-NOM dog what-INT:NOM DAT-be.located:SG
'What kind of dog does Keeli have?'

b. *Ofi' nanta-ho̲ Keeli-at i̲-wáyya'a?*[41]
dog what-FOC:ACC Keeli-NOM DAT-be.located:SG

On occasion, speakers even mark a non-*Wh* old subject with an accusative case marker, as in (71), which also contains an added locative applicative argument:

(71) *Keeli-at i̲-holisso-a̲ holissaapisa' aa-in-kaniya-tok.*
Keeli-NOM DAT-book-ACC school LOC-DAT-get.lost-PERF
'Keeli lost her book at school.'

Probably all speakers have some OS verbs for which they use variable syntactic patterns: an OS pattern with both derived and old subjects marked nominative, and an innovative pattern with the old subject treated as an object. For example, my most conservative consultant volunteers two equivalent forms of a sentence with the verb *im-alhpi'sa* 'be enough for' > 'have enough':

(72) a. *Nipi'-at am-alhpi'sa.* pre-OS / OS
meat-NOM 1SG:III:DAT-be.enough
'The meat is enough for me.' > 'I've had enough meat.'

b. *Nipi'-a̲ am-alhpi'sa.*
meat-ACC 1SG:III:DAT-be.enough
'I've had enough meat.'

Since (72a) does not contain an overt independent pronoun, it could be analyzed (out of context) as either a transitive sentence with 'meat' as subject and a first person dative object, or an OS sentence with the dative subjectivalized and 'meat' a nominative old subject. Subject tests such as switch-reference confirm that either analysis is possible: the sentence is structurally ambiguous. In (72b), however, the old subject has been reanalyzed as an object, acquiring accusative marking, and the sentence is unambiguously transitive.

This example suggests that one possible motivation for the reanalysis of old subjects as objects is that syntactic patterns like that in (72b) are easier for speakers to manipulate and, probably, conceptualize. The typologically unusual multiple nominative structure seen in the conservative RP, OS, and 'have' constructions has puzzled linguists for years, but it must also be harder for speakers to rationalize with more familiar patterns.

Reanalysis may proceed more quickly when structural ambiguity is not possible. The *im-alhpi'sa* sentences in (73) are exactly analogous to those in (72), except that a third person subject is fully specified. In this case, (73a), with a nominative old subject, is judged somewhat questionable; (73b), in which the original semantic subject has been reanalyzed as an ordinary argument, is preferred:

(73) a. ?*Lynn-at nipi'-at im-alhpi'sa.* OS
Lynn-NOM meat-NOM DAT-be.enough
'Lynn has enough meat.'

b. *Lynn-at nipi'-a̲ im-alhpi'sa.*
Lynn-NOM meat-ACC DAT-be.enough

Since Chickasaw thus allows reanalysis of multiple nominative constructions as ordinary transitive constructions, we may wonder if the dative subject transitive pattern, repeated here as (74), had a similar origin:

(74) a. *Ofi'-a̲ am-alhkaniya.*
'I forget the dog.' (= (7b))

b. *Hattak-at ofi'-a im-alhkaniya.*
'The man forgets the dog.' (= (8b))

Im-alhkaniya 'forget' is a dative subject verb that all speakers treat as an ordinary transitive, with a single nominative subject and an accusative object argument. But the pattern in (74a) is exactly the same as that in (72b).

The history of the verb 'forget' is not clear: without the dative prefix, *alhkaniya* means 'be forgotten, be left behind'. Perhaps at some point there was a dative applicative derivative *im-alhkaniya* meaning something like 'be forgotten for', which could have been the source for an OS construction, but this meaning seems a bit unlikely and is not attested synchronically. The semantics of this verb seems more consistent with an RP origin, with earlier stages like those sketched in (75) (I put unattested hypothesized forms within l's):

(75) a. l *Hattak im-ofi'-at alhkaniya.* l
man DAT-dog-NOM be.forgotten
'The man's dog is forgotten.'

b. l *Hattak-at ofi'-at im-alhkaniya.* l RP
man-NOM dog-NOM DAT-be.forgotten

If this scenario is correct, the development from (75b) to the modern (74b) involved more than simple reanalysis of the old subject as an accusative object. There must have been an additional semantic change as well, with the necessary semantic possessive relationship between the derived and original subjects in (75b) lost, since a forgotten object used with the synchronic verb *im-alhkaniya* 'forget' need not be possessed by the subject.

Support for the idea that there may have been interchanges between earlier RP and OS constructions comes from speaker comments on certain OS verbs. Although most speakers volunteer sentences like (76), one speaker rejected this sentence, explaining that *in-kaniya* should be used only with lost items that belong to the subject:

(76) *Preston-at Kayla i-holisso-at in-kaniya-tok.* OS
Preston-NOM Kayla DAT-book-NOM DAT-go.off-PERF
'Preston lost Kayla's book.'

For most speakers, the 'lose' sense of *in-kaniya* seems clearly to derive via OS, since the dative applicative verb exists in the meaning 'go off from', and these speakers do not feel that there is a necessary possessor-of relationship between the derived and old subjects. But since the verb *kaniya* 'go off' exists independently, an RP derivation is also possible, and might be the best account of the grammar of speakers who reject sentences like (76).

If transitive dative subject verbs like *im-alhkaniya* 'forget' may have originated through the reanalysis and lexicalization of earlier OS (or RP) constructions, it is tempting to hypothesize further that transitive II-subject verbs like *banna* 'want' may have had a similar history: the repeated sentences in (77) might derive from earlier subjectivalizations of an earlier verb with a II-marked object, perhaps meaning something like 'attract', as in (78):

(77) a. *Ofi'-a sa-banna.*
'I want the dog.' (= (7a))
b. *Hattak-at ofi'-a banna.*
'The man wants the dog.' (= (8a))

(78) | *Ofi'-at hattak-a banna.* |
dog-NOM man-ACC "attract"
'The dog attracts the man.'

However, there is no evidence for such a development in the meaning of *banna*; we do not otherwise see subjectivalization (passivization) of ordinary transitive objects: OS derived subjects are former applicative objects with an oblique role marked by dative *im-*, *on-* 'on', or *a-* 'against'.

One suggestive similarity between non-I subject transitives like *im-alhkaniya* 'forget' and *banna* 'want' and the derived subject sentences produced by RP and OS is that verbs like *im-alhkaniya* and *banna* may not take non-third person objects, and that RP and OS sentences may not have non-third person old subjects. As noted earlier, in the case of RP sentences this restriction derives naturally from the fact that non-third persons may not be possessed. In the case of OS sentences, the restriction is pragmatic: subjectivalization of an oblique argument is motivated only when the old subject is not a discourse participant. In any case, though, the restriction that objects of non-I subject transitives must be third person would be a logical consequence of an OS or RP origin for these constructions.

9. Typological considerations

In an important paper, Cole et al. argue persuasively on the basis of extensive cross-linguistic data that "transformational (i.e. behavioral) properties, e.g. control of reflexivation and deletability by rules normally affecting only subjects" are consistenty acquired by derived subjects prior to "morphosyntactic (i.e. coding) properties, e.g nominative case and control of verb agreement" (Cole et al. 1980: 719); "such a sequence is the unmarked (and perhaps universal) order of acquisition of subject properties" (p. 720). Thus, for example, the history of the English verb *like* shows that accusative experiencers of this verb exhibited subject behavioral properties such as deletion by Equi, conjunction reduction under identity with a nominative subject, and indefinite subject deletion, long before such experiencers came to be marked nominative (pp. 729–30). The experiencer subjectivalization cases examined by Cole et al. are directly comparable to the types of development seen with Chickasaw OS. RP and the 'have' construction also provide clear cases of changing syntactic subjecthood. Let us consider how the Chickasaw subject properties discussed in sections 3 and 4 above correlate with Cole et al.'s claims.

Clearly, use of nominative case marking (Section 3.1) is a coding property, while control of switch-reference and other such constructions (sections 3.4–5) are behavioral properties. Control of third person plural *hoo-* and diminutive *-o'si* marking seems to be intermediate between the two types of properties, and might be seen as either "coding" or "behavioral". In any case, though, it is clear that Chickasaw presents a range of subject traits.

At first it appears that since Chickasaw derived subjects have all these subject properties, they have fully acquired subjecthood, in Cole et al.'s terms, and nothing more need be said. Indeed, they are approaching this point. But there are two ways in which the derived RP and OS subjects cannot be said to have achieved full subjecthood.

First, even though the derived subjects in a typical RP or OS sentence have the coding property of nominative case marking, this achievement is diluted by the fact that there is always another nominative nominal in these sentences — the old subject, which exhibits none of the other relevant subject properties, but still retains nominative marking (potentially resulting, out of context, in structural ambiguity, as discussed earlier). Only when the old subject loses this anomalous nominative marking, as in the synchronic OS, RP, and 'have' variants described in Section 8, sporadic lexical cases like *im-alhpi'sa* 'be enough', and the hypothesized development of dative transitives like *im-alhkaniya* 'forget', may subject coding be said to have been fully acquired by the derived subject. (This situation seems like a logical but rather unexpected instantiation of Cole et al.'s claims.)

Second (perhaps with the exception of third person *hoo-* marking), derived Chickasaw subjects never acquire the coding property of regular subject-verb agreement. As described in Section 1, Chickasaw has three series of non-third person pronominal agreement markers, known as I, II, and III. Only the I markers unambiguously mark subjects, since the II and III markers may be used to show agreement with both subjects and non-subjects. But derived subjects in RP and OS constructions never indicate agreement with I markers. When such derived subjects are non-third persons, they may trigger three types of verbal agreement: III (dative) agreement (in type (a) RP and dative OS), II agreement (in OS with verbs containing the applicatives *on-* and *a-*), or no agreement at all (in type (b) or inalienable RP) — but they never show I agreement.

It is not the case, incidentally, that Chickasaw never shows a switch from another type of agreement to I marking, so in theory there would be no reason for such a change not to occur. There are two situations (unrelated to changes in subjecthood) when a verb that normally marks a non-third person subject with either II or III agreement instead indicates such a subject with I agreement. The first is when a verb like *hashaa* 'be angry' is used with an added applicative argument. When intransitive, as in (79a), *hashaa* takes a II-marked subject, but when a dative applicative argument is added to the sentence, as in (79b), the subject is marked with a I marker:

(79) a. *Sa-hashaa.*
1SG:II-be.angry
'I am angry.'
b. *Hattak-a̲ i̲-hashaa-li.*
man-ACC DAT-be.angry-1SG:I
'I am angry at the man.'

The second case is when a II- or III-subject transitive verb is used reflexively (reciprocals work similarly). Chickasaw reflexive verbs include a prefix *ili-* and always have I-marked subjects. Thus, when *im-alhkaniya* is used reflexively, as in (80b), its subject agrees with a I marker:

(80) a. *Ofi'-a̲ am-alhkaniya.*
'I forget the dog.' (= (7b), (74a))
b. *Il-im-alhaniya-li.*
REFL-DAT-forget-1SG:I
'I forget myself.'

Thus, there seems to be no direct prohibition against changing non-I subject agreement to I agreement in Chickasaw. It must simply be the case that Chickasaw derived RP and OS subjects do not fully exhibit subject coding properties, in the sense of Cole et al. (1980).

I will close this paper by briefly mentioning a case of PR Raising in another language family in which subjecthood has been acquired more fully than in the Chickasaw case.

The languages of the Yuman family of Southern California, Arizona, and northern Mexico are typologically very similar to Muskogean languages like

Chickasaw: for example, they have SOV and genitive-noun word order, nominative-accusative case marking, switch-reference, and a Subject PR Raising (RP) rule. Consider the following examples from the Yuman language Maricopa (Gordon 1986: 68):[42]

(81) a. *Many m-e'e-ny-sh nyiily-k.*
you 2–hair-DEM-NOM be.black-REAL
'Your hair is black.', 'You have black hair'

b. *Man-sh m-e'e m-nyiily-k.* RP
you-NOM 2–hair 2–be.black-REAL
'You have black hair.'

In (81a), the syntactic subject is the phrase *many m-e'e* 'your hair', which, like all Maricopa subjects, is marked with nominative case. This sentence may be used, as Gordon's translations suggest, either to assert the color of the hair or as a statement of possession, but in (81b), RP applies,[43] and the PR becomes a syntactic subject, acquiring nominative case marking. Gordon notes that in (81b) the semantic PR "has more prominence — it is the focus of attention in the clause" (1986: 68); further the old subject 'hair' "is behaving as though it has become incorporated into the verb. Its position is fixed immediately before the verb; it cannot be marked with any suffixes" (like the "anaphoric" demonstrative suffix *-ny*, which may appear when 'hair' is a syntactic subject (in (81a)) but not when it is an old subject), and it cannot be omitted from the sentence (1986: 68). These facts are strikingly parallel to the Chickasaw ones: the derived subject acquires nominative marking, and the old subject acts incorporated,[44] losing the traits that are pragmatically controlled, such as the ability to move and to take certain markers. As in Chickasaw, derived subjects, not old subjects, serve as switch-reference controllers (Gordon 1983: 85–86). In (82a), the subordinate (first) clause is the pre-RP (81a) (without the independent pronominal PR), so the different-subject marker *-m* is used on the subordinate verb 'be black' (since 'your hair' and 'you' are different). In (82b), the subordinate clause is (81b); here, both subjects are 'you', so the same-subject marker *-k* appears:

(82) a. *M-e'e-ny-sh nyiily-m m-shhot m-lyvii-k.*
2–hair-DEM-NOM be.black-DS 2–be.pretty 2–be.like-REAL
'You are pretty because your hair is black.'

b. *Man-sh m-e'e m-nyiily-k m-shhot m-lyvii-k.*
you-NOM 2–hair 2–be.black-SS 2–be.pretty 2–be.like-REAL
(RP in lower clause)
'You are pretty because your hair is black.', 'You are pretty because you have black hair.'

A derived subject in Maricopa has more fully acquired subject status in Cole et. al's terms than a comparable derived subject in Chickasaw, in two ways: it is the only nominative-marked element in its clause (since Maricopa old subjects like 'hair' in (81b) and (82b) are not marked nominative) and it unambiguously controls subject–verb agreement. In Maricopa, as in Chickasaw, third person arguments like the subjects in (81a) and (82a) are unmarked, but non-third person arguments are marked on the verb. The second person pronominal subject prefix *m-* (which also marks possessive agreement on *m-e'e* 'your hair' and subject agreement on the two parts of 'be pretty' in (82a, b)) appears on the verb 'be black' in the RP sentences (81b) and (82b): even though the second person participant is certainly not black, the grammatical subject of the verb is second person.

Maricopa derived subjects also control plural agreement. Yuman verbs mark plurality by affixation or by ablaut of their stressed vowel (cf. e.g. Gordon 1986: 22–23). Such changes are triggered by collective or distributive features of the subject or the object of the verb, but never, to my knowledge, by features of non-arguments such as a PR. But in RP sentences a plural derived PR-subject may induce plural ablaut of the verb, as in (81b):

(83) a. *M-s'aw m-shent-k?* (RP)
2–child 2–be.one-REAL
'Do you have one child?'

b. *M-s'aw m-shiint-k?* (RP)
2–child 2–be.one:PL-REAL
'Do you (all, each) have one child?' (addressed to many)

Ex. (81a) is an RP sentence in which the second person PR is a derived subject (if an independent pronoun had been used, it would have been marked nominative); semantically, the subject of the verb 'be one' (logically singular) is the PM child (and the PR must also be singular, since *s'aw* means only 'woman's child'). In (81b), the derived subject is plural, so the verb ablauts (with a change from *e* to *ii*) to show that its grammatical subject is plural.

Maricopa RP subjects seem to have achieved grammatical subjecthood more fully than Chickasaw RP and OS derived subjects, perhaps because RP seems to be a much older (and generally less pervasive and productive) rule in Maricopa.

10. Conclusion

In this paper, I have examined two sets of processes in Chickasaw — the RP and OS rules — by which original non-subjects (PRs and datives) become surface syntactic subjects, as demonstrated by a variety of syntactic tests that clearly differentiate these derived subjects from their sentences' original "old subjects". Chickasaw 'have' constructions are an additional special case of the RP construction. In all these sentence types, both derived and old subjects are always marked nominative by conservative speakers, with the result that these surface constructions do not match other transitive or intransitive sentence patterns in the language.

These Chickasaw constructions are changing. Even the most conservative speakers have eliminated the second (old subject) nominative marking in a few lexical cases, and less conservative speakers regularly adapt productive RP, OS, and 'have' structures so that they look more like ordinary transitive sentences.

Nonetheless, the subjects of many types of Chickasaw sentences still fail to exhibit a full range of expected traits, since many clauses contain more than one nominative subject candidate and Chickasaw verb agreement identifies subjects simply and unambiguously only in a minority of cases. The unrelated language Maricopa shows that it is possible for a language with similar rules to treat derived subjects more consistently in terms of case marking and agreement. The Maricopa developments may thus foreshadow a future direction of syntactic change in Chickasaw.

Acknowledgments

This paper is dedicated to the memory of Pollyanna Heath (1913–1997). Except as noted, the Chickasaw data in this paper reflect the speech of Catherine Willmond, to whom I am (as always) extremely grateful. Some aspects of the processes that are the focus of this paper vary for other speakers, as shown in Section 8. I thank the other speakers who have confirmed Mrs. Willmond's judgments and provided the additional data in Section 8, including Frankie Alberson, Adeline Brown, Willie Byars, Lizzie Frazier, Mary James, William Pettigrew, and Thomas Underwood. My recent work on Chickasaw was supported by the Academic Senate of UCLA. Many linguists have stimulated my thinking about the Chickasaw data discussed here over the years; I am especially grateful to Doris Payne for prompting the preparation of this paper and to Carson Schütze for helpful comments on an earlier presentation of it.

Abbreviations

Abbreviations used in this paper: ACC accusative, CMP complement, CAUS causative, DAT dative, DIM diminutive, DS different subject, FOC focus, IND indefinite, INT interrogative, LOC locative, NOM nominative, P plural, PL plural subject, PT perfect/perfective, OS Oblique Subject, Q question, QP past question, REM remote past, RF reflexive, RL realis, RP Raised Possessor, S singular, SS same subject, 1 first person, 2 second person. I, II, and III are explained in the text (see also Munro and Gordon 1982). The orthography is that of Munro and Willmond (1994); underlined vowels are nasalized. A number of phonological rules affect the surface realization of Chickasaw words in the text (see Munro and Willmond 1994). In particular, note that the *im-* of the dative prefix assimilates to the sound that follows it.

Notes

1 My consultants represent all areas of the Chickasaw Nation of Oklahoma in south-central Oklahoma.

2 I give the most common (neutral) forms of these case markers; other forms exist for nouns in different pragmatic roles; cf. Section 6. As described in Section 6, preverbal objects may also be unmarked.

3 As (3a) shows, the first person singular I affix is a suffix, *-li*. All other pronominal affixes are prefixes.

4 I gloss the combination of a non-third person III prefix plus dative *im-* as "III:DAT" (in a deviation from earlier sources, such as Munro and Gordon 1982). Thus, for example, the first person singular dative combination *am-* is glossed "1SG:III:DAT".

5 Chickasaw also has fluid verbs, generally alternating between I (more or less volitional) vs. II (more or less non-volitional) agreement, as with *howita-li* 'I vomited [on purpose]' vs. *sa-howita* 'I vomited [by accident]'. The verbs in (3) can be inflected only for intransitive subjects of the class indicated.

6 Most exceptions to the generalizations presented are idiosyncratic. Quantifier verbs, like *chaffa* 'be one, be the one', constitute an exceptional class: though semantically stative and nonvolitional, they are all I-subject verbs.

7 There is also an Object Possessor Raising rule in Chickasaw (Munro 1984), which I will not consider here. Much of the analysis presented below has profited from discussions with Lynn Gordon and Guy Carden.

8 Mrs. Willmond's judgments regarding whether or not many Chickasaw intransitive verbs may undergo the two varieties of RP (see below) are recorded as syntactic features in Munro and Willmond (1994). The major syntactic class of intransitive verbs that may not undergo RP are those whose subjects are marked with the III set. There are a few minor semantic generalizations: for example, stative verbs referring to color participate only in the form of RP illustrated in (9) and (11c).

9 The use of the term "raised" to refer to these extracted PRs is appropriate within any theory in which a PR of a subject will occupy a lower position in syntactic structure than that subject itself. In addition, the term invites the speculation that possessed phrases in Chickasaw have clausal properties. There is some support for this idea (cf. also work by Jack Martin), but I will not pursue it here.

10 Normally inalienable RP only occurs with inanimate possessed subjects, such as body parts. This restriction does not hold for alienable RP, in which PRs may raise from animate and even human possessed subjects.

11 Thus, with inalienable RP the verb never acquires agreement marking corresponding to the original II possessive marking on the PM, in contrast with type (a) alienable RP (where dative marking might be seen as moving from the PM to the verb). Inalienable RP verbs never have II marking, but certain inalienable RP verbs may have dative marking, as in (i):

(i) *Aaimp-aat iyy-aat (im-)oshta.*
table-NOM leg-NOM (DAT-)be.four
'The table has four legs.'

12 Many other potential subject tests do not provide appropriate evidence of Chickasaw subjecthood in the sentences we are considering here. I do not regard agreement as a valid subject test, since nominals corresponding to pronominals marked with any of the three agreement classes may be underlying subjects (though class I agreement might be seen as a subject test; cf. Section 9). Certain other tests, such as reflexivization and passivization, are appropriate to consider only in the context of transitive sentences. Imperatives are not generally semantically compatible with RP sentences. And so on.

13 Except in this discussion (and regarding (47a)), I use singular translations for convenience only. As we will see, certain verbs lexically require arguments of a particular number.

14 The diminutive suffix would be appropriate here if the dog were a dear little puppy. Crucially, however, its appearance is conditioned by features of the subject, not of a non-subject PR.

15 It is certainly not coincidental that the same-subject switch-reference markers, like the nominative case markers, end in *t*, and the different-subject switch-reference markers, like the accusative case markers, end in a nasalized vowel; cf. Jacobsen (1983), but so far I have seen no convincing synchronic account of this fact. I am grateful to Lynn Gordon for stimulating discussion of Chickasaw switch-reference. There are a variety of different switch-reference markers in Chickasaw, whose use merits further contextual study, following up on work by Payne (1980), Munro and Willmond (1994), and Walker (in preparation), and related to work on the closely related language Choctaw by, e.g., Broadwell (1986) and Williams (1995), as well as preliminary analytical work by Janet Scott [Batchler]. I will not be concerned here with choice of switch-reference marker (as opposed to choice of same- or different-subject marking).

16 Since there is no overt subordinator on the verb I am calling "lower" here, it might be suggested that this construction looks like parataxis. There are several reasons why this is not so. First, the verb of the lower clause in the same-subject *ilahobbi* construction in (27a) is not marked for pronominal subject agreement, as any main clause must be. Second, the lower clause is not independently true, as it would have to be if it were used alone. Finally, unlike an ordinary switch-reference-marked clause, such as those in discussed in Section 3.4, the lower clause may not be postposed. However, the two clauses clearly can refer to separate events, as in

(ii) *Oblaashaash Charles-at taloowa-tok ahobbichi-l-a'chi onnakma̱.*
yesterday Charles-NOM sing-PT pretend:CAUS-1SG:I-IRR tomorrow
'Tomorrow I'll pretend Charles sang yesterday.'

17 In earlier work I have referred to the two varieties of OS (as in (29b), (30b)) as "III-Subjectivalization" and "II-Subjectivalization" respectively.

18 Some speakers would accept (34b) as an RP sentence meaning 'The woman's husband is singing', since 'husband' is *i̱-hattak* (DAT-man).

19 Carden, Gordon, and Munro (1982) argued that Chickasaw RP thus produces violations of the Projection Principle (Chomsky 1981).

20 Elaborated examples like (45f) are rare. But almost all speakers freely volunteer sentences containing at least one instance of multiple RP (and thus a string of at least three nominatives, two derived subjects and one old subject).

21 The number of 'man' here is of course vague, as discussed in Section 3.2: either (47a) or (47b) could be interpreted with 'man' as plural.

22 Historically, the two devices described here are related: the plural 'big' verb *hichito* contains an old form of a plural derivational morpheme related to the *hoo-* prefix. Of course, there are other ways semantic plurality could be indicated, such as by overtly specifying 'a bunch of dogs'.

23 Word orders with both nominals postposed are usually judged less good, though they are sometimes volunteered spontaneously. Thus any restrictions are probably contextual.

24 Examples (50c, d) are acceptable (though implausible) as 'The woman appeared to God', 'God had the woman appear to Him'.

25 In particular, case-marked objects are not more definite or specific than non-case-marked objects; for example, proper names are fully acceptable in either form.

26 There are some poorly understood discourse conditions under which occasional sentences with a final non-accusative object (as in (51d)) are judged acceptable (perhaps involving surprise?). Normally, however, such sentences are rejected in elicitation contexts and are never produced spontaneously.

27 Lenition can occur when the object ends in a vowel or vowel-plus-glottal stop whose syllable is preceded by a heavy syllable, and the following verb starts with a vowel. I normally do not write such fusions, and I have never observed any difference in meaning correlated with this low-level phonological process.

28 This suggestion was made by Bruce Hayes as a comment on part of the analysis in Carden, Gordon, and Munro (1982).

29 I have always assumed that both case-marked and non-case-marked objects could be zero-pronominalized, but in fact there is no easy way to demonstrate this.

30 The judgment that (54) is meaningless is lexically specific. Certain verbs that may be used in an ordinary derived dative applicative form would be interpreted with the nominative noun as (underlying) subject and a zero-pronominalized object.

31 I would assume that non-case-marked objects cannot be focused either; but there are no arguments for this.

32 I am grateful to Aaron Broadwell, Brian Potter, and Andrew Simpson for helpful ideas about Wh movement in SOV languages.

33 The *wh*-word in (61b) could also achieve sentence-initial position through the postposing of the main-clause subject to the very end of the question, as in *Kata-hta̱ ofi'-at lhiyohli-ka̱ pí̱s-tok Charles-at?*

34 It is difficult to find contexts in which a nominative *wh*-word may be felicitously fronted out of a subordinate clause before an element of the main clause. If a lower-clause *wh*-subject is fronted before a main-clause subject, potential ambiguity results, and speakers prefer to interpret the *wh*-nominative as having originated in the higher clause. In (iii), the whole subordinate clause has been fronted between the initial main-clause adverb 'yesterday' and the main-clause subject *Charles*, and *kata-haat* 'who' fronted before the adverb:

(iii) *Kata-haat oblaashaash akanka' ab-a'chi-toko̱ Charles-at ithana-m?*
who-INT.NOM yesterday chicken kill-IRR-DS Charles-NOM find.out-QP
'Who did Charles find out yesterday is going to kill the chicken?'

35 This is what I used to think. In fact, it may not be the most plausible explanation even in these cases. Normally, a switch-reference-marked embedded clause may be freely postposed, as in the examples in 3.4. But an embedded clause containing a *wh*-word may never be postposed, even if the *wh*-word has been fronted: it must occur either in situ, between the higher subject and the main verb, as in (61a), or must be fronted before the higher subject, as in (iii).

36 There is no process that moves a non-*wh* interrogative element out of a lower clause in Chickasaw, regardless of case marking or topicality.

37 I illustrate these facts only for RP old subjects. OS old subjects behave in an entirely comparable manner.

38 Example (64) does not include an example in which the old subject is fronted only within its own clause, as in (63b). This order is fully acceptable when the higher subject is postposed (as described in note 35), but is judged somewhat questionable when the higher subject remains at the beginning of the sentence. It is possible that the problem with (64b) is related to the general difficulty of fronting nominative interrogatives out of embedded clauses (note 36).

39 Such verbs are notionally close to intransitives, but many of them are subcategorized for use with locative objects.

40 Because these sentences have been restructured, an alternative would be to present them with the verbs glossed 'lose' and 'drop'. For consistency, I have retained pre-OS glosses for each instance of these verbs throughout the paper.

41 The speaker who provided (70) alternates between interrogative (a) and focus (b) case marking on *wh*-words.

42 The examples in (81) are cited from Gordon (1986) with spelling adapted following Gordon, Munro, and Heath (in preparation); those in (82) are from Gordon (1983). I have adapted Gordon's glosses to conform with those I use here for Chickasaw. I thank the late Pollyanna Heath for teaching me about Maricopa. This work was supported by the Academic Senate of UCLA.

43 There is considerable support in Yuman for the notion that possessed noun phrases have clausal status (and thus that traditional "raising" is involved here). Cf. Langdon (1978), Gordon (1986: 35–36, 69–70).

44 On occasion, PR agreement (like the *m-* in *m-e'e*) may even be dropped from the Maricopa old subject PM, which then acts like a clitic at the beginning of the verb.

References

Broadwell, George A. 1986. *Choctaw Syntax and the Binding Theory of Switch-Reference*. M.A. thesis, University of California, Los Angeles.

Carden, Guy, Lynn Gordon, and Pamela Munro. 1982. *Raising Rules and the Projection Principle*. LSA Annual Meeting colloquium paper.

Chomsky, Noam. 1981. *Lectures on Government and Binding*. Dordrecht: Foris.

Cole, Peter, Wayne Harbert, Gabriella Hermon, and S. N. Sridhar. 1980. "The Acquisition of Subjecthood." *Language* 56: 719–43.

Gordon, Lynn. 1983. "Switch-Reference, Clause Order, and Interclausal Relationships in Maricopa." In J. Haiman and P. Munro (eds.), *Switch-Reference and Universal Grammar*. Amsterdam and Philadelphia: John Benjamins Publishing Company, 83–104.

Gordon, Lynn. 1986. *Maricopa Morphology and Syntax*. University of California Publications in Linguistics 108. Berkeley: University of California Press.

Gordon, Lynn, Pamela Munro, and Pollyanna Heath. In preparation. Maricopa Dictionary.

Jacobsen, William H., Jr. 1983. "Typological and Genetic Notes on Switch-Reference Systems in North American Indian Languages." In J. Haiman and P. Munro (eds.), *Switch-Reference and Universal Grammar.* Amsterdam and Philadelphia: John Benjamins Publishing Company, 151–84..

Langdon, Margaret. 1978. "The Origin of Possession Markers in Yuman." J. E. Redden (ed.), *Occasional Papers on Linguistics* 2. Carbondale: Southern Illinois University, 33–42.

Munro, Pamela. 1984. "The Syntactic Status of Object Possessor Raising in Western Muskogean." *Berkeley Linguistic Society* 10: 634–49.

Munro, Pamela. 1988. "Diminutive Syntax." In W. Shipley (ed.), *In Honor of Mary Haas.* The Hague: Mouton, 539–56.

Munro, Pamela. To appear. "Chickasaw." In J. Scancarelli and H. K. Hardy (eds.), *The Native Languages of the Southeastern United States.* Lincoln: University of Nebraska Press.

Munro, Pamela, and Lynn Gordon. 1982. "Syntactic Relations in Western Muskogean: A Typological Perspective." *Language* 58: 81–115.

Munro, Pamela, and Catherine Willmond. 1994. *Chickasaw: An Analytical Dictionary.* Norman: University of Oklahoma Press.

Payne, Doris L. 1980. "Switch-Reference in Chickasaw." In P. Munro (ed.), *Studies of Switch-Reference.* [UCLA Papers in Syntax 8], 89–119.

Walker, Cynthia A. In preparation. *An Analysis of Chickasaw Conversation.* Ph.D. dissertation, University of California, Los Angeles.

Williams, Robert S. 1995. *Language Obsolesence and Structural Change: The Case of Oklahoma Choctaw.* Ph.D. dissertation, University of California, Los Angeles.

Part V

The Breadth of External Possession

External Possession in Mohawk

Body Parts, Incorporation, and Argument Structure

Mark Baker
Rutgers University

1. Introduction: the external possession constructions in Mohawk

Suppose that one defines external possession constructions (EPCs) rather broadly as any construction in which an element coded as a verbal pronominal agreement morpheme is interpreted as the possessor of the referent of a noun that appears somewhere in the clause.[1] By this definition, Mohawk has no less than five distinct EPCs, each with its own characteristic properties. All five are mentioned (though not necessarily distinguished) in Michelson's (1991) discussion of closely related Oneida.

Three of the constructions are relatively unremarkable from a typological perspective. First, Mohawk has an alternation that is nearly identical to the well-known English alternation between *I punched John's shoulder* and *I punched John in the shoulder* (see Michelson 1991: sec. 2). Second, there is a construction with verbs of possession or transfer of possession, such as *hninu* 'buy' or *nʌsko* 'steal', in which the indirect object of the verb is understood as the possessor of the direct object (see Michelson 1991: sec. 1). Third, the benefactive/malefactive applicative construction in Mohawk has a reading in which the affected object added by the benefactive morphology is understood as the possessor of the theme of the verb (Michelson 1991: sec. 4). Thus, (1) is often translated as "I washed his car".

(1) *Wa-hi-'sere-ht-óhare-'s-e'.* (Mithun 1984: 868)
FACT-1SG:SUBJ/MASC:SG:OBJ-car-NOM-wash-BEN-PUNC
'I washed his car.' (Better: 'I washed the car for him.')

Each of these kinds of constructions is relatively familiar, and is found in a wide range of languages, including Indo-European ones. Moreover, the Mohawk versions of these constructions have no special properties from a morphological or syntactic point of view. Presumably they arise because of some kind of process of inference (possibly conventionalized) that is grounded by the lexical semantics of the items involved.

However, Mohawk also has two further EPCs that are of more interest with respect to morphosyntax. Thus, the possessor of almost any noun can be coded with verbal object agreement if that noun is incorporated into an intransitive stative verb — i.e., a verb that corresponds roughly to an adjective in English (Michelson 1991: fn. 5; see also Deering and Delisle 1976):

(2) *Ro-[a]nitskwara-tsher-a-hnír-u.*
(NEUT:SG:SUBJ)/MASC:SG:OBJ-chair-NOM-Ø-be.hard-STAT
'His chair is hard.'

In addition, the possessor of a body part noun can be coded with verbal agreement when it is incorporated into virtually any verb, as shown in (3) (Michelson 1991: sec. 4; also Williams (1976) for Tuscarora, Mithun (1984), Mithun (1995), etc.).

(3) *Wa'-khe-hsin-óhare-'.*
FACT-1SG:SUBJ/FEM:SG:OBJ-leg-wash-PUNC
'I washed her leg.'

In this case, benefactive applicative morphology is not needed (and would be unnatural), in minimal contrast to the example in (1).

The constructions in (2) and (3) are interesting for several reasons. First, they are lexically restricted in ways that evoke other aspects of the grammar of Mohawk. For example, the intransitive stative verbs that allow the EPC in (2) are also special in that they only appear in stative aspect (see (24) below). Similarly, the body part nouns that are found in the construction in (3) are also special in that they show "subject" agreement with their possessor when they appear in a locative formation; ordinary alienable nouns retain object agreement with their possessor under these circumstances (see (33)). Second, these two constructions crucially involve noun incorporation. When the noun in question is not incorporated, the verb cannot agree with the possessor:

(4) a. **Ro-hnír-u* *ne anitskwára.*
(NEUT:SG:SUBJ)/MASC:SG:OBJ-be.hard-STAT NE chair.
'His chair is hard.'

b. **Wa-hi-nóhare-'* *ne*
FACT-1SG:SUBJ/MASC:SG:OBJ-wash-PUNC NE
o-kúhs-a'.
NEUT:SG:OBJ-face-NOM.SUFF
'I washed his face.'

However, it is crucially not the case that noun incorporation is an automatic license for external possession in Mohawk (contrary to Postal 1979 and Baker 1985, but in agreement with Mithun 1984, Michelson 1991, and Baker 1996). If the verb is not a stative intransitive and the noun is not a body part noun, then incorporation of a noun into a verb is not sufficient to allow an EPC, as shown in (5).

(5) **Wa-hi-'sere-ht-óhare-'.* (Mithun 1995: 644; Michelson 1991: 760)
FACT-1SG:SUBJ/MASC:SG:OBJ-car-NOM-wash-PUNC
'I washed his car.'

Thus, an interesting combination of lexical factors and morphosyntactic conditions must be met for an EPC to be possible. The contrast between (5) and (3) is a fairly well-known one; it is found in many polysynthetic, noun-incorporating languages (for example, Nahuatl (Launey 1981: 198–199), Mayali (Evans 1991: 275–285); see also Velázquez-Castillo (this volume) on Guaraní and Levy (this volume) on Totonac) and has received some discussion in the literature. The contrast between (5) and (2) is much less familiar, and may be less characteristic of polysynthetic languages as a class; nevertheless, it is probably restricted to this type of language.

Overall, it is not obvious how to give a unified theoretical account of why EPCs are possible under just this combination of conditions. For example, Michelson (1991) has no immediate account of the construction in (2), whereas she tentatively relates the construction in (3) to the English-style alternation between *punch John's shoulder* and *punch John in the shoulder*, which is dubious on empirical grounds (see below). Nevertheless, I will argue that one can explain the basic properties of these two constructions in terms of independently-known properties of their parts, together with a knowledge of the principles and modes of combination that are characteristic of Mohawk, using a style of explanation that is characteristic of formal (generative) grammar. I have already given this kind of an account of (2) (in Baker 1996: ch. 8); a nontechnical review of the analysis is given in Section 3. Section 4 then concentrates on the question of how the theory can be extended to the construction in (3) — something that I failed to do in Baker (1996). A crucial part of this task will be to account for why EP is not always possible in Mohawk: i.e., why sentences like (5) are impossible where the verb is not a stative intransitive and the incorporated noun is not a body part.

2. Some basic properties of Mohawk

First, we must review some basic properties of Mohawk. One obvious property of the language is that it is an almost-pure head marking language, in the sense of Nichols (1986, 1992). Thus, transitive verbs in Mohawk not only may but must agree with their direct objects. Object pronominal agreements are not optional the way they are in (say) Bantu languages or Athapaskan languages:

(6) a. *Sak shako-núhwe'-s ne Uwári.*
Sak MASC:SG:SUBJ/FEM:SG:OBJ-like-HAB NE Mary
'Sak likes Mary.'
b. **Sak ra-núhwe'-s ne Uwári.*
Sak MASC:SG:SUBJ-like-HAB NE Mary

Subject pronominal agreements are also obligatory in Mohawk in a stronger sense than in Indo-European languages. Indo-European languages have subject agreement in finite verb forms, but usually do not in nonfinite clauses where the verb is an infinitive or a participle. No agreement-less infinitival form is possible in Mohawk, even in the complement of try-class verbs.

(7) *K-atenyʌ́t-ha' *(au-sa-ke)-'sere-ht-aserúni-'.*
1SG:SUBJ-try-HAB OPT-ITER-1SG:SUBJ-car-NOM-fix-PUNC
'I am trying to fix the car.'

The actual morphology of agreement in Mohawk is quite complex in several ways that are not directly relevant to the problems at hand; however, a few general remarks may help the reader to better understand the examples. First, subject and object agreements on transitive verbs are usually fused into a single chunk, either morphologically or by idiosyncratic phonological rules. In the glosses I treat these chunks as a single morpheme that expresses both features of the subject and the object; the two sets of features are separated by a slash (see (6)). Second, Mohawk has a so-called active system of agreement, in which some intransitive verbs take one kind of agreement with their sole argument, and other verbs take a different kind of agreement (Mithun 1991, among others). I assume that which kind of agreement a given verb root takes is not synchronically predictable, but is "quirky" agreement, which is determined by a diacritic feature in the lexical entry of the verb. Finally, there are systematic homophonies that hold between the agreement prefixes that show up on intransitive verbs and those that show up on transitive verbs. In particular, the agreement that shows up on a transitive verb that has X as its subject and a neuter object is the same as the agreement that shows up on a "class one" intransitive verb that has X as its sole argument. Similarly, the agreement that shows up on a transitive verb that has a neuter subject and Y as its object is the same as the agreement that shows up on a "class two" intransitive verb, the sole argument of which is Y. Thus, it is natural to call the first type of agreement "subject agreement" and the second type "object agreement", and I use these mnemonic labels in the glosses and some informal discussions. However, the reader should be warned that these morphemes do not always directly reflect the true grammatical relations. These homophonies also suggest that neuter gender arguments are generally expressed by phonologically null agreement morphemes in Mohawk. It is common across languages for the least marked category in an inflectional system to be realized by such a zero morpheme, and I do not take this to be a counter-example to the generalization that verbs always agree with their subjects and objects in Mohawk. However, this does lead to a practical problem, because one cannot always tell whether or not a neuter gender argument is present and is being agreed with by a null morpheme simply by inspecting the surface verb, and in some cases there may be disagreements about this. For this reason, in the glosses I put in parentheses those neuter participants that are inferred from the argument structures of items but that are not directly observable in the morphology.

Given this assumption about neuter arguments, there is only one primary context in which core arguments of the verb are not agreed with in Mohawk: when a noun root functioning as the theme/direct object is incorporated into the verb, the pronominal agreement corresponding to that object is typically omitted (see Baker 1996: sec. 7.4.2).

(8) a. *?*Shako-wir-a-núhwe'-s* *(thíkʌ owirá'a).*
MASC:SG:SUBJ/3OBJ-baby-Ø-like-HAB that baby
'He likes (those) babies.'

b. *Ra-wir-a-núhwe'-s* *(thíkʌ owirá'a).*
MASC:SG:SUBJ-baby-Ø-like-HAB that baby
'He likes (those) babies.'

However, this is the kind of exception that proves a rule, because the incorporated noun can be taken as an alternative form of "head marking". It too has the function of expressing the direct object argument inside the verbal word.

The necessity for some kind of head-marking is arguably the fundamental property of Mohawk and typologically similar languages. In Baker (1996), I call this the "Polysynthesis Parameter", phrasing it as follows.[2]

(9) *The Polysynthesis Parameter* (Baker 1996)
Every argument associated with a head Y must be coindexed with a morpheme in the word containing Y (i.e., with a pronominal agreement factor or an incorporated element).

Of course, to make this condition have content, one needs to add to it a theory of when an agreement factor or an incorporated element is possible. Consider first the condition on agreement, which will play a central role in what follows. For current purposes, I will assume the (slightly simplified) formulation in (10).

(10) Condition on Agreement Relations (CAR) (simplified)
A pronominal agreement factor on a stem X can only be coindexed with a position in the argument structure associated with X.

In essence, this says that a verb can only agree with its own semantic arguments, not with those of (say) the verb of an embedded clause. I take this to be a relatively uncontroversial, minimal theory of agreement.[3]

Significantly, the Polysynthesis Parameter and the CAR apply to nouns as well as to verbs in Mohawk. Ordinary alienable nouns in Mohawk bear a prefix that is cognate to the pronominal agreement prefixes found on verbs; it expresses the gender and (if animate) the number of the referent of the noun. For nouns with neuter referents, this shows up as an invariant *ka-* or *o-* (or their allomorphs), depending on lexical properties of the noun. Nouns with animate referents can show variation for the gender and number of the referent.

(11)	*ká-tshe'*	'bottle'	(*ka-* = NEUT:SG:SUBJ)
	ka-ná'ts-u	'pot, pail'	(*ka-* = NEUT:SG:SUBJ)
	ó-wis-e'	'ice, drinking glass'	(*o-* = *yo-* = NEUT:SG:OBJ)
	o-'neróhkw-a'	'box'	(*o-* = *yo-* = NEUT:SG:OBJ)
	e-ksá'-a	'girl'	(*e-* = *ye-* =FEM:SG:SUBJ)
	ra-ksá'-a	'boy'	(*ra* = MASC:SG:SUBJ)
	rati-ksa'-okú'a	'boys, children'	(*rati* = MASC:PL:SUBJ)
	kuti-ksa'-okú'a	'girls'	(*kuti* = FEM:PL:SUBJ)

When a grammatically neuter noun is possessed,[4] a version of the object agreement prefix shows up, which expresses the person, number, and gender of the possessor. In this case, there is no longer an obvious expression of the neuter referent of the noun, given that neuter "subjects" always trigger zero morphology in the presence of a non-neuter "object", as mentioned above. However, the presence of this element can be inferred from the fact that the possessor can trigger only "object" pronominal agreements, regardless of the lexical properties of the noun root. This is exactly parallel to the way transitive verbs with neuter subjects are inflected in Mohawk (see Baker 1996: ch. 5, 6 for details).

(12) a. *ako-ná'ts-u*
(NEUT:SG:SUBJ)/FEM:SG:OBJ-pot-NOM.SUFF
'her pot'

b. *raó-wis-e'*
(NEUT:SG:SUBJ)/MASC:SG:OBJ-glass-NOM.SUFF
'his glass'

These properties follow from the CAR and the Polysynthesis Parameter if one says that alienable nouns in Mohawk have an argument structure that contains an obligatory subject-like argument that is used in referring or predicating and an optional possessor argument; this is shown in (13).

(13) *na'ts* 'pot' ⟨R, (Possessor)⟩

(Formal syntacticians often call the argument used in referring and predicating the "R" argument, following Williams (1981).) Both of these arguments then must be agreed with — a simple generalization of Mohawk's fundamental head marking nature to the nominal domain.

Finally, consider what noun incorporation (NI) amounts to in these terms. The basic descriptive condition on incorporation is rather well-known: only nouns that function as theme arguments of a verb can be incorporated into that verb. Exactly why this should be so is not important for purposes of this paper (for relevant data and my own view on this, see Baker 1988, 1996; see also Mithun 1984 and many others). However, it will be convenient to state this generalization in the form given in (14), which makes reference to the R argument of nouns that was just introduced.

(14) *Condition on Noun Incorporation*
$[_V$ N+V$]$ is possible only if the R-argument of the noun is coreferential with (coindexed with) the theme argument of the verb.

These then are some of the major "modes of combination" that characterize the morphosyntax of Mohawk as a polysynthetic head-marking language.

3. Stative verbs vs. transitive verbs in EPCs

Next, let us review the essentials of Baker's (1996) account of why stative intransitive verbs allow EP when NI takes place, whereas transitive verbs do not. Additional examples illustrating this generalization are:[5]

(15) a. ***Ro**-nuhs-a-rák-ʌ* *ne Shawátis.*
(NEUT:SG:SUBJ)/MASC:SG:OBJ-house-Ø-be.white-STAT NE John
'John's house is white.'

b. *Te-wak-tsiser-a-'ts-u.*
DUP-(NEUT:SG:SUBJ)/1SG:OBJ-window-Ø-be.dirty-STAT
'My windows are dirty.'

(16) a. **ʌ-hake-natar-a-kwétar-e'.*
FUT-MASC:SG:SUBJ/1SG:OBJ-bread-Ø-cut-PUNC
'He will cut my bread.'

b. **Wa-shako-[a]tya'tawi-tsher-a-rátsu-'.*
FACT-MASC:SG:SUBJ/FEM:SG:OBJ-dress-NOM-Ø-tear-PUNC
'He tore her dress.'

The basic intuition behind the analysis of Baker (1996) was that the impossibility of the examples in (16) and (5) could be related directly to the Polysynthesis Parameter itself. NI constructions are special in that they contain not one but two morphemes with nontrivial argument structures, and the arguments of both must be expressed morphologically. If any argument of either morpheme fails to be agreed with or incorporated, then the Polysynthesis Parameter is violated. This then could be the source of the restrictions we observe.

Thinking in these terms, the table in (17) presents the various types of NI together with the argument structures of the two roots involved.

(17) (i) table + be.hard ⟨R_i⟩ + ⟨$Theme_i$⟩
Simple N + Stative verb
(ii) car + wash ⟨R_i⟩ + ⟨Agent, $Theme_i$⟩
Simple N + Transitive verb
(iii) table + be.hard ⟨R_i, Possessor⟩ + ⟨$Theme_i$⟩
Possessed N + Stative verb
(iv) car + wash ⟨R_i, Possessor⟩ + ⟨Agent, $Theme_i$⟩
*Possessed N + Transitive verb

Here the argument structures of the nouns are as motivated in section 2; the transitive verbs have an ordinary agent-theme argument structure, and the intransitive verbs have only a theme argument. In addition, the R argument of the noun is always coindexed with the theme argument of the verb, in accordance with the Condition on Noun Incorporation in (14). This means that when one says *wa'ke'serehtohare'* 'I washed the car' the thing that is the referent of 'car' is also the thing that is the theme of my washing action. Now of the four possibilities in (17), the only one that is systematically impossible is (iv). This case also has a unique formal property: it is the only one in which the argument structures of the two roots do not stand in a set-subset relationship. In (ii), the only argument of the noun is identified with an argument of the verb, and in (iii) the only argument of the verb is identified with an argument of the noun. In (i) there is complete identity of the two argument lists. However, in (iv) the verb has an argument that is not identified with any argument of the noun (the agent), and the noun has an argument that is not identified with any argument of the verb (the possessor). This seems to be the fatal property of this class of examples. Jumping a bit to conclusions, I offer the following descriptive generalization:

(18) A complex word is possible only if the argument structures of the two components are in a set-subset relationship.

This intuition can be developed into a more formal explanation with one more simple assumption. Before one can check the Polysynthesis Parameter with respect to an example with noun incorporation, one needs to apply agreement, in accordance with the CAR. In order to do this, one needs to know what the argument structure of the stem that one is attaching the agreement to is. Now it is not obvious what the argument structure of these complex examples should be; NI in Mohawk is quite productive, and there is not necessarily a listed lexical entry that can tell us what the argument structure is. What is needed is some kind of function that will derive the argument structure of the compound from that of its parts. Perhaps the simplest imaginable candidate is the "just pick one" rule, given in (19) (compare Chomsky's (1995: ch. 4) discussion of how phrases are labeled in his Minimalist theory).

(19) A complex stem may inherit the argument structure of either one of its component parts, but not both.

What is crucial here is that (19) does not allow the argument structures of the two parts to be added together or composed into a single argument structure; one has to choose one argument structure or the other "as is" and live with the consequences.

Given this, derivations for the crucial examples work as follows. Take first the combination of a possessed noun and an intransitive stative verb, which is possible:

(20)	(i)	*nuhs* 'house'	$\langle R_i, Poss'r_n \rangle$	lexical entry
	(ii)	*rak* 'be.white'	$\langle Theme_i \rangle$	lexical entry
	(iii)	*nuhs-a-rak* 'house-be.white'	$\langle R_i, Poss'r_n \rangle$	by (19)
	(iv)	*ro-nuhs-a-rak-ʌ* (NEUT:SG:SUBJ$_i$)/MASC:SG:OBJ$_n$	$\langle R_i, Poss'r_n \rangle$	by CAR OK by Polysynthesis Parameter

Here the first two lines display the basic lexical properties of the roots. Line (iii) shows the composition of N and V to make a complex stem. At this point, we have to pick what the argument structure associated with this new stem will be. Being foresighted, we pick the argument structure of the noun, because that is the larger of the two. Line (iv) then shows the effect of adding pronominal agreement morphology to the complex stem. By the CAR, we can express via agreement things that are in the argument structure of the stem. In this case, the possessor happens to be there, since we took the argument structure from the original noun; therefore, the complex verb agrees with the understood possessor of the noun root, resulting in an EPC. The verb can also agree with the R argument of the noun, and by doing so it automatically agrees with the theme argument of the verb, since the two are identified (see (14)). In this way, we have succeeded in agreeing with all the arguments of both roots, so the Polysynthesis Parameter is satisfied.

This account explains the fact that this type of EPC is dependent on NI, but in quite a different way from what I suggested in Baker (1988). Recall that if the noun is not incorporated, then the intransitive stative verb cannot bear a pronominal agreement that expresses the possessor of its nominal theme, as shown in (4a), repeated here as (21). (This is true regardless of whether the noun bears possessor agreement or not.)

(21) **Ro-hnír-u* *ne (rao-)anitskwára.*
(NEUT:SG:SUBJ)/MASC:SG:OBJ-be.hard-STAT NE (MASC:SG:POSS)-chair.
'His chair is hard.'

In this case, putting agreement with the possessor on the verb is a straightforward violation of the CAR: the agreement factor on the verb is coindexed with something that is not in the argument structure of that verb. The only argument of the simple verb is its theme, and this is what the verb must agree with. Only when NI forms a complex stem does the possibility of agreeing with arguments of the noun come into the picture.

Next, consider the case of NI into a transitive verb. There are two possible derivations to consider; one of which is (22):

(22)	(i)	*'sere* 'car'	⟨R_i, Poss'r_n⟩	lexical entry
	(ii)	*ohare* 'wash'	⟨$Agent_k$, $Theme_i$⟩	lexical entry
	(iii)	*'sere-ht-ohare* 'car-wash'	⟨R_i, Poss'r_n⟩	by (19)
	(iv)	*wa'-**hi**-'sere-ht-ohare-'* 1SG:SUBJ$_k$/MASC:SG:OBJ$_n$	⟨R_i, Poss'r_n⟩	* by CAR

The early stages of the derivation are the same as before. However, this time when we get to the crucial step at line (iii), there is no best choice for what to pick as the argument structure of the derived stem. Suppose that we pick the argument structure of the noun, which led to a licit EPC in (20). Then at step (iv) the CAR allows agreement with the possessor, but it does not allow agreement with the understood agent of the washing, because that argument is not part of the argument structure associated with the complex stem as a whole. If we make the opposite choice on line (iii), then the CAR allows agreement with the agent of the verb, but it forbids agreement with the possessor of the noun. In short, it is impossible for a Mohawk verb to simultaneously agree with both the agent and the possessor, because these two arguments never exist in the same simple argument structure (and because there is no mechanism for making composite argument structures). If a transitive verb fails to agree with both the agent and the possessor, then there will be a violation of the Polysynthesis Parameter, because the un-agreed-with argument is not expressed by any morpheme in the complex verb. (Note that agents and possessors can never be incorporated in Mohawk (see (14)); hence that way of satisfying the Polysynthesis Parameter is not available either.) In this way, one can account for the basic distribution of the EPC in terms of fundamental observable properties of Mohawk.

One significant feature of this account to note in passing is that none of the theoretical statements it is based on is specific to EPCs. Thus, they should apply in a substantive way to other kinds of examples as well. In Baker (1996: ch. 8), I argue that this is true. In particular, I apply these ideas to the causative and the purposive suffixes of Mohawk, in order to explain why the causative can only attach to verb roots that are intransitive and nonagentive, whereas the purposive can be added to verbs with any number of arguments. If that reasoning is correct, then the EPC is not an isolated phenomenon in Mohawk, but emerges as a special case of a larger pattern of complex verb formation.

Finally, before turning to the body part incorporation construction, it is worth considering eventive intransitive verbs that take a theme as their sole argument: verbs like 'fall' and 'shatter'. At first glance, these verbs seem problematic. They are like stative intransitive verbs in allowing their sole argument to be incorporated, but they differ from them in not allowing an EPC under these circumstances:

(23) a. *Wa'-t-ka-wis-á-hri'-ne'.*
FACT-DUP-NEUT:SG:SUBJ-glass-Ø-shatter-PUNC
'The glass broke.'
b. **Sak wa'-t-**ho**-wis-á-hri'-ne'.*
Sak FACT-DUP-(NEUT:SG:SUBJ)/MASC:SG:OBJ-glass-Ø-break-PUNC
'Sak's glass broke.'

This is rather surprising, since the argument structure of these verbs seems to be identical to that of stative intransitives.

Baker (1996) explains the contrast by adopting Davidson's (1967) influential proposal that eventive verbs have an additional "event" role in their argument structures, which stative verbs lack. One simple piece of motivation for this view is that verbs like *rak* 'be white' differ from eventive verbs like *hri'* 'break' in that *rak* can appear only in the stative aspect, whereas verbs like *hri'* can appear in any of the three basic aspects of Mohawk — punctual, habitual or stative.

(24) *Stative*
a. *Te-yo-hrí'-u.*
DUP-NEUT:SG:OBJ-break-STAT
'It has broken.'
b. *Ka-rák-ʌ.*
NEUT:SG:SUBJ-be.white-STAT
'It is white.'

Punctual
c. *Wa'-t-ká-hri'-ne'.*
FACT-DUP-NEUT:SG:SUBJ-break-PUNC
'It broke.'
d. **Wa'-ká-rak-e'.*
FACT-NEUT:SG:SUBJ-be.white-PUNC
'It was white, became white.'

Habitual

e. *Te-ká-hri'-s.*
DUP-NEUT:SG:SUBJ-break-HAB
'It breaks.'

f. **Ká-rak-s*
NEUT:SG:SUBJ-be.white-HAB
'It whitens.'

This inflectional difference makes sense if one of the functions of the punctual (perfective) and habitual (imperfective) morphemes is to satisfy the event argument of the verb (compare Higginbotham 1985). It follows from this that verbs that have an event argument can take one of these aspects, whereas verbs with no event argument (like *rak*) cannot.[6]

Now, if the argument structure of *hri'* 'break' is actually ⟨Theme, Event⟩, then this is not in a set-superset relationship with the ⟨R, Possessor⟩ argument structure of a possessed noun like *wis* 'glass'. The verbal theme argument is the same as the nominal R argument, but the possessor of the noun bears no relationship to any argument of the verb and the event argument of the verb bears no relationship to any argument of the noun. From this perspective, then, the impossibility of examples like (23b) is what one would expect, given the descriptive generalization in (18). Indeed, it is not hard to generalize the theoretical analysis to explain this case. All that is required is that one generalize the CAR so that it restricts the association of aspect morphemes to event arguments in the same way as it restricts the association of pronominal agreement morphemes to conventional arguments. We then generalize the Polysynthesis Parameter in a similar way, so that it rules out cases where a verb with an event argument does not have a proper aspect suffix. These changes are entirely natural within a Davidsonian approach. Indeed, the ungrammaticality of a form like **ka-hri'* 'it break', with no aspect suffix at all, could be attributed to this generalized Polysynthesis Parameter, whereas the ungrammaticality of (24d) and (24f) could be attributed to the generalized CAR. However, I do not give the revised formulations here, but instead refer interested readers to the discussion in Baker (1996: sec. 8.4).

To summarize so far, we have our answer to why intransitive stative verbs alone allow EP agreement under NI. The crucial fact is that they have the smallest argument structures of any Mohawk verb — so small that they are nondistinct from the argument structure of the incorporated nouns.

4. EPCs involving body part incorporation

Up to this point, I have been reviewing the analysis of Mohawk EPCs given in Baker (1996), showing how it accounts for why EPCs are usually restricted to one particular lexical-semantic class of verbs in terms of independently needed conditions on the inheritance and expression of arguments. The remainder of the article explores how this general analysis can be extended to account for the fact that these lexical restrictions on the verb no longer hold when the incorporated element is a body part noun (BPN). Example (3) showed that EP agreement is possible when a BPN incorporates into a transitive verb; (25) gives other examples of this type, to illustrate something of the range of this phenomenon (the EP agreement is in boldface, for clarity).

(25) a. *Wa-**hi**-'nyuhs-a-ya'k-e'.*
FACT-1SG:SUBJ/MASC:SG:OBJ-nose-Ø-hit-PUNC
'I slapped his nose, I slapped him on the nose.'

b. *Sak wa'-t-**hi**-hsnuhs-áwest-e'.*
Sak FACT-DUP-1SG:SUBJ/MASC:SG:OBJ-finger-Ø-pinch-PUNC
'I pinched Sak's fingers.'

c. ?*T-a-**shako**-ahsit-a-yéna-'.*
CIS-FACT-MASC:SG:SUBJ/FEM:SG:OBJ-leg-Ø-grab-PUNC
'He grabbed her foot.' (sounds good but rarely heard, nonidiomatic)

d. (?)***Ri**-'nyuhs-a-núhwe'-s.*
1SG:SUBJ/MASC:SG:OBJ-nose-Ø-like-HAB
'I like his nose.' (OK, but not every day Mohawk)

In Baker (1996), I failed to give a satisfactory account for why examples like these are possible. All things being equal, they should be ruled out by the same kind of derivation as the one shown in (22). To avoid this consequence, I tentatively assumed that BPNs are not incorporated theme arguments in the same way that other incorporated nouns (INs) are. Rather, I assumed that the putative EPs in examples like (25) are the true themes, and the BP INs function as a kind of adverbial modifier . On this view, the most accurate gloss for (3) would not be 'I washed his face', but rather something like 'I washed him facewise', where the adverbial expression expresses a manner but does not refer (directly) to a face. This is a fairly common analysis; it is adopted very explicitly by Evans (1991: 275–279, 1995) for similar facts in Mayali, for example. It also seems to be more or less what Michelson (1991) has in mind in her very brief discussion of this type of example. However, a more unified analysis would clearly be preferable — especially since this EPC is like the one involving stative verbs in that it requires NI as a conditioning factor (see (4)).

4.1 *Against an adverbial analysis of the body part*

Even putting considerations of conceptual unity aside, there are at least four empirical arguments that point away from analyzing incorporated BPNs as adverbial elements and toward analyzing them as expressions of the theme argument of the verb.

Suppose first of all that the adverbial analysis were true. Then one might expect that the BPN could also appear as an unincorporated adverbial expression, given that NI is generally optional in Mohawk. In a few cases, this expectation seems to be fulfilled. Thus, (26) is a good paraphrase of (25b), with no incorporation and the body part nominal expressed as an obliquely-marked locative adverbial.

(26) *Ra-hsnuhs-á-'ke*
MASC:SG:SUBJ-finger-Ø-LOC
wa'-t-hiy-áwest-e'.
FACT-DUP-1SG:SUBJ/MASC:SG:OBJ-pinch-PUNC
'I pinched him on his fingers.'

However, the striking fact is that this kind of alternative expression is *not* generally available. The unincorporated version in (26) is possible only with a limited number of verbs of physical contact, in which affecting a part of someone counts as affecting the person as a whole.[7] There are many verbs that allow the EP-with-body part-NI construction for which there is no equivalent with the body part expressed as a syntactically separate adverbial.

(27) a. **Ri-núhwe'-s* *ne Sak* (compare (25d))
1SG:SUBJ/MASC:SG:OBJ-like-HAB NE Sak
ra-'nyuhs-á-'ke.
MASC:SG:SUBJ-nose-Ø-LOC
'I like Sak in the nose.'

b. **Ye-hsin-á-'ke* *wa'-khe-nóhare-'.*
FEM:SG:SUBJ-leg-Ø-LOC FACT-1SG:SUBJ/FEM:SG:OBJ-wash-PUNC
'I washed her on her leg.' (compare (3))

For the sentences in (27), the verb's effect on part of a person evidently does *not* equal affecting the person as a whole. But if that is so, then a basic assumption of the adverbial analysis of BP NI sentences is not supported.

A second reason for doubting the adverbial approach comes from discourse anaphora. Suppose that the right gloss of an example like (3) is really 'I washed her legwise', rather than 'I washed her leg'. Then strictly speaking there is no nominal that refers to the body part in the clause. If that is so, then one might expect that pronouns in the subsequent discourse could not refer to the body part — or at least that such pronouns would sound somewhat odd and would require some conscious effort for their interpretation, as is true for an English discourse sequence like *John is a truck-driver. ?It is parked behind the store.* This prediction is not borne out, however: pronouns referring back to the incorporated BPN are entirely natural:[8]

(28) a. *Wa'-uk-**kuhs**-óhare-'* *tánu kwa shéku*
FACT-FEM:SG:SUBJ/1SG:OBJ-face-wash-PUNC and even still
***yo**-nánaw-ʌ*
NEUT:SG:SUBJ-be.wet-STAT
'She washed my face and it (the face) is even still wet.'

b. *Yáhtʌ te-hi-**'nyuhs**-a-núhwe'-s* *ne tsi sótsi*
not NEG-1SG:SUBJ/MASC:SG:OBJ-nose-Ø-like-HAB because too
kowán-ʌ.
NEUT:SG:SUBJ:big-STAT
'I don't like his nose, because it's too big.'

How strong an argument this is depends on one's theory of discourse anaphora, and how easy it is for pronouns to refer to things that are not explicitly mentioned in the previous discourse.[9] But at the very least, the adverbial theory fails to make a substantive prediction that could have distinguished it from the alternative.

A third, more compelling argument is that BP NI in Mohawk has exactly the same distribution as conventional NI. As mentioned in section 2, it is well-known that simple NI is usually possible only if the noun functions as the theme argument of a transitive or intransitive verb. Body part incorporation in Mohawk obeys exactly the same condition. Examples (3) and (25) show amply that the body part can express the theme of a transitive verb; the examples in (29) show that incorporated body parts can also express the themes of eventive unaccusative verbs and stative verbs (see also (42b)):

(29) a. *Wa'-t-ha-[a]t-hsín-ya'k-e'.*
FACT-DUP-MASC:SG:SUBJ-SEMI.REFL-leg-break-PUNC
'His leg broke.' (i.e. 'He broke his leg.')

b. *Sak ra-'nyuhs-owán-ʌ.*
Sak MASC:SG:SUBJ-nose-be.big-STAT
'Sak's nose is big; Sak has a big nose.'

c. *Ra-'nyuhs-a-hútsi-Ø* *ne Sak.*
MASC:SG:SUBJ-nose-Ø-be.black-STAT NE Sak
'Sak's nose is black.'

However, incorporated BPNs cannot be related in a manner or instrument-like fashion to the agent of a transitive or intransitive verb: expressions like 'Sak foot-kicked the tree', 'Mary hand-slapped the table', 'Mary mouth-yelled', or 'Tyer eye-cried' are impossible (see also Evans (1991, 1997) for Mayali). If one treats BP NI in a very different way from simple NI, one risks losing this generalization. In particular, if body parts are analyzed as a kind of adverbial, it is not clear why such an element could not have a subject-oriented reading as well as an object-oriented one. Incorporated adverbs can be interpreted with respect to the agentive subject in Nahuatl; Andrews (1975: 166–169) gives examples like *ni-mācēhual-la-htoa* 'I speak like a peasant' (lit. 'I-peasant-speak'), *ni-tla-mā-huatza* 'I stir something by means of the hands' (lit. 'I-it-hand-stir'), *n-ix-huetzca* 'I smile' (lit. I-face-laugh). This shows that there is no intrinsic reason why an incorporated adverbial cannot have an agent-oriented interpretation. The fact that such interpretations are not possible in Mohawk (and Mayali) thus suggests that these body parts are really incorporated theme arguments, not adverbials.

A final argument comes from incorporation itself. The fundamental advantage of analyzing incorporated BPNs as some kind of adverbial modifier is that it allows the understood possessor to count as the theme; this explains immediately why the understood possessor triggers object-style pronominal agreement on the verb. But if the understood possessor were grammatically an ordinary theme/direct object, then it should be possible in principle for it to incorporate into the verb, given that incorporation of themes is common in Mohawk. But this kind of double incorporation is completely impossible:

(30) a. **T-a-yu-[a]thasterʌ-tsher-a-hsín-ya'k-hu-'*.
CIS-FACT-FEM:SG:SUBJ-pants-NOM-Ø-leg-cut-DISTR-PUNC
'She cut the legs of the pants.'
(Compare: *T-a-ye-hsin-yá'k-hu-' athásterʌ* 'She leg-cut the pants')

b. **Wa'-ke-wir-a-kuhs-óhare-'*.
FACT-1SG:SUBJ-baby-Ø-face-wash-PUNC
'I washed the baby's face.'

Normally, double NI configurations are not allowed in Mohawk. I believe this is precisely because only themes/objects incorporate and there can be at most one such element per clause. However, this explanation does not extend to (30) under the BPN-as-adverb analysis. One might claim that Mohawk has some kind of morphological filter that rules out N-N-V sequences in a single word. But this stipulation is probably not otherwise necessary, and it is rendered dubious by the fact that N-N-V sequences do sometimes occur when the first N-V combination is lexicalized (as in examples with glosses like 'I-milk-water-drink' and 'it-box-door-opened'). On the other hand, if the incorporated BPN is really the theme and the animate element is its grammatical possessor, then the ungrammaticality of (30) follows from the general fact that grammatical possessors never incorporate in Mohawk.

In summary, the analysis of incorporated BPNs as adverbial modifiers fails to make any correct and interesting predictions beyond the facts about agreement that originally motivated it. On the other hand, incorporated BPNs have exactly the same distribution and referential force that clear cases of incorporated theme arguments have in Mohawk. Therefore, we need to develop an analysis of them as such. However, in order to do this, we must face afresh the question of why the verb can have a pronominal agreement that expresses the possessor of the IN if and only if the IN is a BPN.

4.2 *Inherent properties of body part nouns*

To get insight into how this might be done, let us closely compare BPNs with alienably-possessable nouns in contexts other than when the noun incorporates into a verb. In fact, the two classes of nouns have many similarities. Body part expressions can occur as the roots of simple nouns, with no possessor indicated. When this happens, they take a neuter prefix that expresses the referent, just like other nouns in Mohawk. Thus, (31) is comparable to (11) (but note that the prefix is systematically the *o-* form "object" prefix, not the *ka-* form "subject" prefix.)

(31) a. *o-kúhs-a'* 'face'
b. *o-nyúhs-a'* 'nose'
c. *o-káhr-a'* 'eyes'
d. *o-hsnúhs-a'* 'finger(s)'
e. *o-hsín-a'* 'leg'

Such forms are rather rare in natural discourse, but they are the normal citation forms for nouns in vocabulary lists and the like.

BPNs can also take normal possessive agreement, following the same pattern as other nouns: the pronominal agreement prefix registers the person, number, and gender features of the possessor, as well as (implicitly) the neuter referent.

(32) a. *Sak rao-'nyúhs-a' thíkʌ.*
Sak (NEUT:SG:SUBJ)/MASC:SG:POSS-nose-NOM.SUFF that
'That is Sak's nose.'

b. *Ake-nútsi*
(NEUT:SG:SUBJ)/1SG:POSS-head
ra-rást-ha'.
MASC:SG:SUBJ/(NEUT:SG:OBJ)-draw-HAB
'He is drawing my head.' (Deering and Delisle 1976: 230)

c. *Wa'-ke-nóhare-'*
FACT-1SG:SUBJ/(NEUT:SG:OBJ)-wash-PUNC
ako-hsín-a'.
(NEUT:SG:SUBJ)/FEM:SG:POSS-leg-NOM.SUFF
'I washed her leg.'

d. *Ke-núhwe'-s* *ne*
1SG:SUBJ/(NEUT:SG:OBJ)-like-HAB NE
ako-kúhs-a'.
(NEUT:SG:SUBJ)/FEM:SG:POSS-face-NOM.SUFF
'I like her face.'

Thus, it seems that BPNs have (or at least may have) the very same argument structure as other nouns, including an R-argument and an optional possessor argument. In this respect, there is no grammatical difference.

The examples in (32) have some special features of interpretation, however. (32c) and (32d) are elicited examples, and they strike speakers as rather peculiar. In particular, they do not have the normal, inalienably possessed interpretation that one would expect. My consultant remarked that in (32c) it sounds like the leg is not attached to the woman's body, but has been separated from it somehow. Similarly, (32d) really means 'I like her mask' — i.e. her false, separable face. Examples (32a, b) are naturally occurring, but they also come from a special context. Example (32a) was the answer to the question "what is that?", pointing to a hard-to-identify blob in a picture. Here it does not refer to Sak's literal nose, the thing physically attached to his face, but rather to a representation of that thing. Similarly, example (32b) (which is an example from a teaching grammar of when it is permissible to use this form in Mohawk) involves a representation of my head, not the head that is physically attached to my body.

A true inalienably possessed interpretation for unincorporated BPNs is possible, but only if there is a locative suffix on the BPN. Moreover, the pronominal agreement prefix on such BPNs must be a form that is cognate with intransitive subject–class agreement, rather than the usual transitive neuter-plus-object form (Deering and Delisle 1976; Mithun 1995). The examples in (33) are minimal contrasts to those in (32):[10]

(33) a. *Ye-hsin-á-'ke*
FEM:SG:SUBJ-leg-Ø-LOC
wa'-ke-nóhare-'.
FACT-1SG:SUBJ/(NEUT:SG:OBJ)-wash-PUNC
'I washed her (attached) leg.'

b. ?*Ke-núhwe'-s* *ye-kuhs-á-'ke.*
1SG:SUBJ/(NEUT:SG:OBJ)-like-HAB FEM:SG:SUBJ-face-Ø-LOC
'I like her (attached) face.'

c. *Tanu' s-ka'ʌ́nyu* *ne*
and 2SG:SUBJ/(NEUT:SG:OBJ)-examine NE
se-hsnuhs-a-'ké-shu.
2SG:SUBJ-finger-Ø-LOC-PL
'And look at your (attached) hands!' (D&D: 209)

Other nouns can take this same locative suffix, but they cannot undergo the same shift in agreement: the locative form of *ako-núhs-a'* 'her house' is *ako-nuhs-á-'ke* 'at her house', never **ye-nuhs-á-'ke*. Thus, the special "attached" meaning that is characteristic of body parts goes along with a special agreement option. Moreover, these examples have a distant resemblance to the EPC/NI examples in (25), because in (25) like in (33) the BPNs have both a distinctive "attached" interpretation and a special agreement option (the EPC agreement).

There is one other situation in Mohawk in which a predicate bears a single subject-type pronominal agreement, in spite of the fact that it otherwise takes either object-type or transitive pronominal agreement: this is with reflexive verbs. Reflexive verbs in Mohawk are formed by prefixing *atat* to a transitive verb stem. The resulting verb stem is morphologically intransitive, and it means that the agent of the action and the patient of the action are nondistinct. A simple example is:

(34) *S-atát-kʌ.* (D&D: 373)
2SG:SUBJ-REFL-see
'Look at yourself (in the mirror).'

The prefix with these reflexive verb forms is always an intransitive, subject-type agreement form (putting aside a predictable agreement shift that happens in stative aspect forms, mentioned in note 6). Indeed, this generalization overrides other generalizations about agreement in the language. For example, the verb *ati* 'throw' can take a transitive pronominal agreement prefix that represents features of both the subject and object:

(35) *Y-a-huwa-ya't-úti-'* *ne*
TR-FACT-FEM:SG:SUBJ/MASC:SG:OBJ-body-throw-PUNC NE
ra-ksá'a.
MASC:SG:SUBJ-boy
'She threw the boy away.'

Somewhat exceptionally, when this verb has a neuter or incorporated object, it shows object-type agreement with its subject. This is an instance of the "quirky" active agreement in Mohawk mentioned in section 2 (see also Mithun 1991 for discussion).

(36) *Y-a'-akó-[a]ti-'.*
TR-FACT-FEM:SG:OBJ/(NEUT:SG:OBJ)-throw-PUNC
'She threw it away.'

Nevertheless, even this verb takes a subject agreement prefix when it appears in the reflexive form:

(37) *Y-a-**ha**-[a]tat-ya't-úti-'.*
TR-FACT-MASC:SG:SUBJ-REFL-body-throw-PUNC
'He threw himself in.'

Uko 'bump into' is another transitive verb that shows the same behavior. These facts motivate the following generalization about agreement in Mohawk:[11]

(38) If two arguments of a root are coindexed (and hence interpreted as nondistinct in reference), then they are expressed morphologically by an intransitive, subject-class agreement morpheme.

Significantly, the agreement found with unincorporated BPNs in locative expressions is exactly like the one that is found with reflexive verbs; it too falls under the generalization in (38). From a semantic perspective, what is special about BPNs when they have their inalienable interpretation is that the referent of the BPN and its possessor are not two distinct entities. This is comparable to the reflexive clause in (34), where the perceiver and the perceived thing are not two distinct entities. Suppose that we represent this nondistinctness in the way that is usual in formal grammar: by coindexing the arguments in question. Then the argument structure of a BPN used inalienably will be $\langle R_i, Possessor_i\rangle$; (38) says that the pronominal agreement on such a noun will be a single, subject class agreement. This is exactly what we observe in (33). When the referent of the body part noun and the possessor are distinct — represented as $\langle R_i, Possessor_k\rangle$ — then (38) does not apply, and the normal principles of inflecting nouns take over. This gives examples like those in (32).[12] In short, while BPNs have the same gross argument structure as other nouns, they are special in that they can count as reflexive predicates both semantically and inflectionally.

More generally, it is well-known that there is a close relationship between BPNs and reflexive clauses crosslinguistically. Some evidence for this is the fact that body part nouns are used to create anaphoric expressions in many languages. Thus, the equivalent of 'himself' in English is often rendered by a phrase like 'his body' or 'his head' (Pica 1987; Reinhart and Reuland 1991), as in (39) from the Nigerian language Edo.

(39) ***Ò*** *gbé ègbé ẹ́rè.* (O.T. Stewart, personal communication)
he beat body his
'He beat himself.' (lit. 'He beat his body.')

Thus, it should not be a surprise that there is a similarity in the argument structures of reflexive verbs and body part nouns.

4.3 *Explaining the body part EP construction*

Now that we know what the argument structure of a BPN is, we can combine it with the theory of agreement in composite verb stems sketched in section 3. When we do this, the correct results follow immediately, with almost no new assumptions. Example (40) is a prototypical example of an EPC made possible by the incorporation of a BPN:

(40) *Wa-hi-kuhs-óhare-'.*
FACT-1SG:SUBJ/MASC:SG:SUBJ-face-wash-PUNC
'I washed his face.'

The body part has its normal, attached meaning in (40), so the two arguments of the noun are coindexed. The derivation for this example thus proceeds as follows:

(41) (i) *kuhs* 'face' ⟨R_i, Poss'r_i⟩ lexical entry
(ii) *ohare* 'wash' ⟨$Agent_k$, $Theme_i$⟩ lexical entry
(iii) *kuhs-ohare* 'face-wash' ⟨$Agent_k$, $Theme_i$⟩ by (19)
(iv) *wa'-hi-kuhs-ohare-'* ⟨$Agent_k$, $Theme_i$⟩ by CAR
1SG:SUBJ$_k$/MASC:SG:OBJ$_i$ ...satisfies the Polysynthesis Parameter

The derivation in (41) can be contrasted with the minimally different one in (22), where the noun root is the alienably possessed '*sere(ht)* 'car'. The crucial difference is that in the case of *kuhs* 'face', the R and the Possessor are coindexed. Therefore, one can pick the verb's argument structure as the argument structure of the complex stem. Then a prefix is added that agrees with the theme of the verb root, and this automatically results in agreement with both the R argument and the possessor of the BPN. Therefore, the Polysynthesis Parameter is satisfied in this example, accounting for its grammaticality.

Support for this analysis comes from the form of pronominal agreement in body part EPCs when the verb root is intransitive. Example (29) showed that BPNs can be incorporated into intransitive verbs that take theme arguments, and that when this happens the verb agrees with the possessor of the noun. More specifically, the verbs in (29) show subject-class agreement with the possessor; (29a) is repeated as (42a). However, for certain other verbs, an object-class agreement is used in exactly the same circumstances: (42b) is an example.

(42) a. *Wa'-t-**ha**-[a]t-hsín-ya'k-e'.*
FACT-DUP-MASC:SG:SUBJ-SEMI.REFL-leg-break-PUNC
'His leg broke.' (i.e., 'He broke his leg.')

b. *Y-a'-t-**ho**-hsin-a-kétot-e'.*
TR-FACT-DUP-MASC:SG:OBJ-leg-Ø-appear-PUNC
'His leg stuck out.'

This variation is not random. Rather, it is a manifestation of a more elementary difference between verbs like *at-ya'k* 'break' and verbs like *ke'tot* 'appear, 'stick out': *atya'k* always takes subject-class agreement to express its theme argument, whereas *ke'tot* is one of the verbs that takes a "quirky" object-class agreement (cf. Mithun 1991). Thus, 'it broke' is *wa'-te-w-át-ya'k-e'*, with subject class prefix *w-* (an allomorph of *ka-*), whereas 'it appeared' is *y-a'-t-yo-ké'tot-e'*, with object class prefix *yo-*. The general rule is that whatever type of agreement a verb would normally use to express its theme argument is used to express the possessor of the theme argument in the body part EP construction. This is exactly what the theory developed here predicts. When deciding how to inflect a complex stem like *hsin-a-ketot* 'leg-appear', one must choose the argument structure of the verb, rather than the noun, so that the event argument of the verb can be expressed by an aspect suffix. Thus, the pronominal agreement agrees directly with the theme argument of the verb. This agreement encodes the possessor of the BPN, but this is an indirect relationship that exists because the possessor is identified with the theme argument of the verb by a chain of nondistinctness relationships. Therefore, the reflexive agreement rule in (38) (which would call for a subject agreement form) is not applicable to (42b), whereas the lexical specification that *ketot* shows quirky object-type agreement with its theme is relevant.[13]

The next task is to explain why the BPN must be incorporated in order to have an EPC. Unfortunately, this time the desired result does not follow immediately from the CAR, the way the ungrammaticality of (21) did. In a derivation like (41), the pronominal agreement is related most directly to the argument structure of the verb root, and that argument structure is available even without NI.

In practice, the goal is to explain why examples like (43) are bad with any of the three forms that an unincorporated body part can take:

(43) **Ri-núhwe'-s* *(ne) o-'nyúhsa'* /
1SG:SUBJ/MASC:SG:OBJ-like-HAB NE NEUT:SG:OBJ-nose /
rao-'nyúhsa' / *ra-'nyúhs-a-'ke.*
(NEUT:SG:SUBJ/)MASC:SG:POSS-nose / MASC:SG:SUBJ-nose-Ø-LOC
'I like his nose.'

The verb in (43) is perfectly well-formed by itself, with the meaning 'I like him'. Therefore, the real problem is why this verb cannot be properly matched up with the external BPN to get the intended interpretation. For the first two forms of the BPN, there is a straightforward reason: these NPs are grammatically neuter, so they cannot corefer with the masculine singular object of the verb. Thus, these NPs have no syntactic link to any argument position in the clause, and hence have no business appearing there.

This reasoning does not extend to the third form however, both because the BPN may not be grammatically neuter in this case (the only prefix it bears is masculine singular) and because it has locative morphology that allows it to attach to the clause freely as an adjunct. Indeed, sentences of exactly this form are possible when the verb is a verb of physical contact, as shown in (26). What seems to be going on here is this: In NI sentences like (40) the theme argument of the verb is understood as being the same as the referent of the BPN by the normal generalization about NI (see (14)). The referent of the BPN is in turn nondistinct from *but not strictly identical to* the possessor of the BPN. This relationship of nondistinctness is enough to permit the verb to agree with the possessor, but it does not take away the fact that the true theme of the event is really only the body part. In contrast, the grammatical theme of the verb is clearly the person as a whole in (43). Thus the two kinds of sentences are only equivalent for that class of verbs for which affecting the whole really is equivalent to affecting the part. In other cases, the two will differ in their semantic force, such that examples like (43) are semantically anomalous.[14] What remains to be clarified, then, is exactly what the "nondistinctness" relation between the body part and the whole amounts to semantically, such that it justifies treating the two arguments as a single element morphosyntactically, but still stops short of strict semantic identity. Significantly, these same issues arise even with ordinary reflexive constructions. For example, the command in (34) is obeyed even if the addressee does not see his or her whole body in the mirror; seeing only the exterior surface of the front side of the upper half of that body is enough. Here too the perceiver and the perceived are not literally identical, but merely nondistinct, and this is enough to permit a grammatically intransitive form.

It is worth emphasizing that this article is built around a particular intuition about what is special about BPNs. This intuition — familiar from previous literature — is that what makes BPNs special is their quasi-reflexive nature, which comes from the nondistinctness of the body part noun's referent and its possessor.

A common alternative view is that BPNs are special because they are inherently relational: a leg must be a leg of something, for example. This alternative intuition can be expressed by saying that BPNs take possessors as arguments, whereas most other nouns do not (see, for example, Vergnaud and Zubizarreta 1992).

However, example (31) shows that it is simply not true that BPNs require a possessor in Mohawk. Moreover, even if this example were put aside, it would be very difficult to give a unified explanation of the EP facts starting from the alternative hypothesis; for example, it would be hard to distinguish the incorporation of BPNs from the incorporation of alienable nouns that happen to be possessed. Finally, there would be no explanation of the fact that other "inherently relational" nouns such as kinship terms never give rise to EPCs in Mohawk: forms like *I/him-son-washed (meaning 'I washed his son') are completely impossible, for example.

In this paper, I have shown that the first hypothesis leads to a better, more principled account of why external possession is found only when BPNs incorporate. Since the referent of a kinship term like 'son' is a distinct entity from its possessor, this account explains immediately why no EPC is possible with this kind of inalienable possession.

5. Closing remarks: Mohawk EPCs and formal grammar

By way of conclusion, let me step back from the details of the analysis somewhat, in order to reflect on it as an instance of the formal approach to linguistics, and to assess the contribution that this kind of approach can potentially make to a complete understanding of EP phenomena.

First, what makes the account a formal one? Readers who are alert to such things will have noticed that I have not made much use of the distinctive theoretical devices of formal grammar: phrase structure trees, movement transformations, empty categories, and the like. In part, this has been for ease of exposition, since I believe that some of these devices are relevant to a fuller analysis (see Baker 1996). However, the fact that the story can be told without this support shows that the basic ideas are not deeply dependent on those particular devices. Therefore, the analysis can probably be grafted into a different framework easily enough.

More important than the particular mechanisms and terminology, what really makes this work an instance of formal, generative linguistics — Chomskian linguistics in a broad sense — are certain of its very basic, quasi-methodological features. First and foremost, the analysis takes a compositional, "bottom up" approach, in which the properties of a sentence-level phenomenon like EP are explained primarily in terms of the lexical properties of the parts, together with general principles about the available modes of composition. In this view, building sentences out of morphemes is taken to be a bit like building sculptures out of lego blocks: there is a wide diversity of things you can make if you have enough of them, but at low levels what you can make is constrained by the inherent shapes of the pieces. In the case at hand, BPNs have a slightly different "shape" (argument structure) from other nouns; this accounts for why only they can be used to build EPCs. This mode of explanation is characteristic of formal, generative approaches — although it can of course be pursued within functionalist approaches as well.

Second, the present analysis is formal in the sense that its principles are stated in relatively precise, categorical terms so that the consequences of the theory can be examined and evaluated clearly. This makes it possible to test the hypotheses, and progressively deepen and refine the analysis.

Finally, the analysis in this article is Chomskian in that it tries to avoid construction-specific theoretical statements, using instead assumptions that have validity for the language as a whole (and, ideally, for all languages). For example, I have stated no principles the effects of which can be seen only in EPCs. Rather, the claim is that EPCs emerge as a possibility in Mohawk because of an uncontroversial property of the language (it requires head-marking), a simple general principle about how the argument structures of wholes come from their parts (relevant also to verbal derivational suffixes), and a certain meaning-form correlation (seen also in reflexive verbs). In this respect, the approach is in sharp contrast to Construction Grammar, which is built on the basic premise that constructions can have unpredictable properties of their own. Now Chomsky's very strong hypothesis that constructions never have stipulated idiosyncrasies may or may not ultimately be correct. However, I think that the Chomskian discipline of looking for independent motivation for each ingredient of an explanation outside the construction under study is (at least) methodologically useful, because it drives one to find interconnections in the grammar of a language that might otherwise be missed.

In spite of these advantages, it is potentially embarrassing to the formal approach that speakers' actual judgments about things like External Possession are often not cut-and-dried or categorical in the way that formal accounts seem to predict. For example, it is well-known that in many languages there is some fuzziness in what counts as an inalienable possession, and hence some variability in what elements can feed into an EPC. This also seems to be true in Mohawk, as shown by examples like those in (44), where 'sock' and 'car' seem to be treated as BPNs.

(44) a. *Wa-ha-ris-er-akéra-'-ne'.*
FACT-MASC:SG:SUBJ-sock-NOM-stink-INCH-PUNC
'His socks started to smell; He started to smell because of his socks.'

b. *Sak ʌ-ha-[a]te-'sere-ht-ahtʌ́ti-'.*
Sak FUT-MASC:SG:SUBJ-SEMI.REFL-car-NOM-move-PUNC
'Sak pulled out' (lit. 'Sak's car moved; Sak moved in his car')

These are precisely the kind of data that lead some researchers to posit continua and hierarchies of possession. Do they undermine the viability of a formal analysis? I think the answer is no. Crucially, (44a) is only used if the referent of 'he' is wearing the socks at the time, and (44b) assumes that Sak is in the car when it moves. In exactly these circumstances, it makes sense to say that the possessor counts as nondistinct from the possessum with respect to the verbal predicate in question. This nondistinctness then justifies coindexing the R and possessor roles in the argument structure of *ris* 'sock' or *'sere* 'car'. The rest of the account then runs as before. The important thing here is that the "squishiness" can be attributed to how a particular lexical item is used in context. Once these atomic properties are fixed, the grammatical consequences are predictable.[15] If you put squishy bricks into a house-building machine, you get a squishy house; but one should not necessarily infer from this that the machine itself is squishy in its inner workings. It is the same with grammar: no doubt there is plenty of gradation in the domain of the lexicon, but it is not clear that the compositional system is an additional source of gradation.

Acknowledgments

The research for this article was supported by The Social Sciences and Humanities Research Council of Canada, grant 410–95–0979 and FCAR of Quebec, grant 94ER0578. Mohawk is a Northern Iroquoian language spoken in Quebec, Ontario, and New York. General information about the language can be found in Deering and Delisle (1976) and Baker (1996), among other sources. In addition to published sources, new data for this article come from fieldwork done at Kahnawake, Quebec by the author between 1990 and 1995. The two primary consultants in this work were Ms. Grace Curotte and Ms. Carolee Jacobs, who I thank particularly. I also thank Doris Payne, Marianne Mithun, the other participants at the Oregon Conference on External Possession, and three anonymous readers for their detailed comments on this paper, which have led to improvements in the analysis and presentation. Remaining inadequacies are my responsibility.

Abbreviations

The glosses of the Mohawk examples include the following abbreviations: BEN benefactive applicative, CAUS causative, CIS cislocative, DISTR distributive, DUP duplicative, FACT factual mood, FUT future mood, HAB habitual aspect, IMPERF imperfective aspect, INCH inchoative, ITER iterative, LOC locative, NEG negative, NOM nominalizer, NOM.SUFF nominal suffix, OPT optative mood, PL plural, PUNC punctual aspect, REFL reflexive, SEMI.REFL semi-reflexive, STAT stative aspect, TR translocative. Ø is given as the gloss for the epenthetic 'joiner' vowel [a]. Glosses of pronominal agreement morphemes include indication of person/gender (1, 2, MASC, FEM, NEUT)), number (SG, PL), and series (SUBJ (roughly subject), OBJ (roughly object), or POSS (possessor — cognate to object class)). *Ne* is a particle of uncertain significance and so remains unglossed.

Notes

1 There is disagreement whether these morphemes are agreements that reflect properties of the (possibly null) arguments of the verb, or incorporated pronouns that actually are the arguments of the verb. The second view is more widely held, but I happen to hold the first (Baker 1996). As a somewhat incoherent compromise, I often refer to these elements as "pronominal agreements" in this paper.

2 There is one other apparent counter-example to this claim to note: nothing seems to express the theme argument of a ditransitive verb in Mohawk when the theme is not incorporated. In such examples, the transitive pronominal agreement prefix codes the agent and goal arguments, but not the theme. See Baker 1996: sec. 5.3 for discussion of this case.

3 Note however that the CAR does not seem to hold in EPCs in Maasai, according to the data given by Payne (1997). It may be that the CAR is not universal, but is only relevant to polysynthetic languages of the kind defined by (9). This is an interesting issue for future research.

4 Non-neuter nouns cannot be possessed in Mohawk; for example, one cannot say "my boy", but must use a special kinship term like "my son".

5 Mohawk speakers sometimes reject examples like (15b), saying that they have the nonsensical meaning 'I, the window, am dirty'. Crucially this happens only with verbs that lexically select for an object-type agreement prefix. For such verbs, the form of the prefix does not tell whether the incorporated noun is in an alienable relationship to the EP (i.e., interpreted in a parallel fashion to (15b)) or an inalienable one (i.e., interpreted in a parallel fashion to examples like *te-ho-'nyuhs-a-'ts-u* 'His nose is dirty' mentioned in note 13). This can lead to confusion and rejection of the example, just as "garden path" sentences are often rejected in English.

6 I assume that the stative aspect, though traditionally treated as part of the same set as punctual and habitual, actually performs a rather different function, and is more derivational in nature. Evidence for this is the fact that the stative affix can appear inside of derivational suffixes like the causative (e.g. *te-hati-'ts-**u**-st-ha'* (DUP-MASC:PL:SUBJ-be.dirty-STAT-CAUS-HAB) 'They used to make it (be) dirty.') and internally to certain lexicalized compounds. This is never possible with the punctual or habitual affix. It may also be relevant that the stative affix often changes the kind of pronominal agreement prefix that attaches to the verb, as in (24a) compared to (24b) and (24c). The punctual and habitual affixes never have this effect.

In Baker (1996) and an earlier draft of this article I assumed that the [ʌ] at the end of a verb like *rak* 'be white' was synchronically part of the root, and that there was in general no aspect suffix on stative verbs. I thank Marianne Mithun for pointing out several difficulties with this assumption. Nevertheless, there is no doubt that the stative verbs inflect differently from eventive verbs. This is enough to motivate the difference in argument structure that my analysis depends on.

7 The class of verbs that allows (26) is roughly the same as the class of English verbs that allows the alternation between *I punched John's nose* and *I punched John in the nose*.

8 In this respect, Mohawk apparently contrasts with Guaraní (Velázquez-Castillo, this volume), where the incorporated body part cannot be a discourse antecedent.

9 Mithun (1984: 870–71), for example, claims that Mohawk rather freely allows pronouns with no syntactically expressed antecedent. However, it is not clear to me that there is a real difference between English and Mohawk in this respect.

10 An anonymous reviewer suggests that the examples in (33) might be a kind of antipassive. This proposal would explain directly the presence of oblique (locative) morphology on the understood theme; it is also consistent the pronominal agreement prefixes in (33), which can be interpreted as intransitive agreement forms . This proposal could also make a contribution to explaining the ungrammaticality of example (43), which is not fully explained in my account (see note 14). Therefore, it deserves further study.

However, there are some basic objections to this proposal. First, there is no valency-reducing morpheme on the verb, as in prototypical cases of antipassive. Second, the antipassivization would only be possible when the theme is a body part, which is a rather unusual lexical restriction for an antipassivization process. Third, and most importantly, the possibility of expressing a BPN with a spurious locative suffix and a shifted agreement morpheme is not limited to transitive objects. This kind of expression can also be used as the sole argument of an intransitive verb, for example (e.g. *Ra-nʌtsh-á-'ke yo-nawátstar-e'* (MASC:SG:SUBJ-arm-Ø-LOC NEUT:SG:OBJ-be.muddy-STAT) 'His arm is muddy.'). In contrast, antipassive cannot generally apply to the subjects of intransitive verbs. For these reasons, I do not adopt the antipassive analysis here.

11 See Baker (1996: ch. 5) for an attempt to derive this very specific statement from more general properties of agreement in Mohawk.

12 One missing piece of the analysis is an explanation of why reflexive-style agreement is possible if and only if the BPN bears a locative suffix. Thus, examples like (i) are impossible, in contrast to the grammatical (32c) and (33a).

(i) ***Wa'-ke-nóhare-'* *ye-hsín-a'*.
FACT-1SG:SUBJ/(NEUT:SG:OBJ)-wash-PUNC FEM:SG:SUBJ-leg-NOM.SUFF
'I washed her leg.'

I cannot give a full explanation of this within the terms of the present article. However, I suspect that it is related to the independently known fact that bare NPs in Mohawk must be fully referential so that they can corefer with a pronominal element in the clause, whereas locative NPs are not subject to this condition (see Baker 1996: 422).

13 Stative intransitive verbs act just like eventive ones in these respects. For example, *'ts* 'be dirty' takes object-class agreement in both simple clauses (*te-yó-'ts-u* 'It is dirty', with NEUT:SG:OBJ prefix *yo-*) and those involving a body part (*te-ho-'nyuhs-á-'ts-u* DUP-MASC:SG:OBJ-nose-Ø-dirty-STAT 'His nose is dirty', with MASC:SG:OBJ prefix *ho-*). In this, it contrasts with verbs like *hutsi* 'be black', which take subject-class agreement in both situations (see (29b, c)). This pattern is consistent with my theory, although not fully predicted by it.

14 An alternative explanation might be to take the suggestion, mentioned in note 10, that these locative body part phrases are the result of applying antipassive to the clause. Then (43) would be bad simply because the verb has an explicitly transitive pronominal agreement even though antipassivization has applied to detransitivize the clause. However, in addition to the general problems mentioned in note 10, it is not clear how this antipassive proposal would distinguish (43) from the grammatical (26).

15 However, as far as I know, nouns like 'sock' and 'car' never show the special inalienable possession agreement pattern that is characteristic of BPNs when they appear with a locative ending (see section 4.2); i.e., one doesn't find forms like **ra-ris-er-a-'ke* '(at) his sock', even when the person is wearing the sock. Similarly, Mithun (1995) points out that Mohawk has a few noncanonical BPNs like 'hair' and 'blood' that do not take the subject-class pronominal agreement in locative forms, but can be in an EPC when incorporated. As it stands, my theory predicts that these borderline nouns should be equally able to show inalienable agreement in either syntactic environment, as long as the pragmatic context is favorable to a nondistinctness interpretation. If this is not true, something will need to be added to explain why a nondistinctness construction is easier when a noun is incorporated than when it is a locative expression.

References

Andrews, J. Richard. 1975. *Introduction to Classical Nahuatl.* Austin: University of Texas Press.

Baker, Mark. 1985. *Incorporation: A Theory of Grammatical Function Changing.* Ph.D. dissertation, Massachusetts Institute of Technology.

Baker, Mark. 1988. *Incorporation: A Theory Of Grammatical Function Changing.* Chicago: University of Chicago Press.

Baker, Mark. 1996. *The Polysynthesis Parameter.* New York: Oxford University Press.

Chomsky, Noam. 1995. *The Minimalist Program.* Cambridge, MA: MIT Press.

Davidson, Donald. 1967. "The Logical Form of Action Sentences." In N. Rescher (ed.), *The Logic of Decision and Action.* Pittsburgh: University of Pittsburgh Press, 81–120.

Deering, Nora and Helga Delisle. 1976. *Mohawk: A Teaching Grammar.* Kahnawake, Quebec: Thunderbird Press.

Evans, Nicholas. 1991. *A Draft Grammar of Mayali.* ms., University of Melbourne.

Evans, Nicholas. 1995. "The Syntax and Semantics of Body Part Incorporation in Mayali." In Hilary Chappell and William McGregor (eds.), *The Grammar of Inalienability.* Berlin: Mouton de Gruyter, 65–110.

Evans, Nicholas. 1997. "Role or Cast? Noun Incorporation and Complex Predicates in Mayali." In Alex Alsina, Joan Bresnan, and Peter Sells (eds.), *Complex Predicates.* Stanford: CSLI, 397–430.

Higginbotham, James. 1985. "On Semantics." *Linguistic Inquiry* 16: 547–594.

Launey, Michel. 1981. *Introduction à la langue et à la littérature aztèques.* Paris: L'Harmattan.

Levy, Paulette. This volume.

Michelson, Karin. 1991. "Possessor Stranding in Oneida." *Linguistic Inquiry* 22: 756–762.

Mithun, Marianne. 1976. *A Grammar of Tuscarora.* New York: Garland.

Mithun, Marianne. 1984. "The Evolution of Noun Incorporation." *Language* 60: 847–893.

Mithun, Marianne. 1991. "Active/agentive Case Marking and Its Motivations." *Language* 67: 510–546.

Mithun, Marianne. 1995. "Multiple Reflections of Inalienability in Mohawk." In Hilary Chappell and William McGregor (eds.), *The Grammar of Inalienability.* Berlin: Mouton de Gruyter, 633–649.

Nichols, Johanna. 1986. "Head-marking and Dependent-marking Grammar." *Language* 62: 56–119.

Nichols, Johanna. 1992. *Linguistic Diversity in Space and Time.* Chicago: University of Chicago Press.

Payne, Doris. 1997. "The Maasai External Possessor Construction." In Joan Bybee, John Haiman, and Sandra Thompson (eds.), *Esssays on Language Function and Language Type.* Amsterdam: John Benjamins, 395–422.

Pica, Pierre. 1987. "On the Nature of the Reflexivization Cycle." In *Proceedings of NELS 17.* Amherst, MA: Graduate Linguistics Student Association, University of Massachusetts, 483–500.

Postal, Paul. 1979. *Some Syntactic Rules of Mohawk.* New York: Garland.

Reinhart, Tanya and Eric Reuland. 1991. "Anaphors and Logophors: An Argument Structure Perspective." In Jan Koster and Eric Reuland (eds.), *Long-distance Anaphora.* Cambridge: Cambridge University Press, 283–321.

Velázquez-Castillo, Maura. This volume

Vergnaud, Jean-Roger and Maria Luisa Zubizarreta. 1992. "The Definite Determiner and the Inalienable Constructions in French and in English." *Linguistic Inquiry* 23: 595–652.

Williams, Edwin. 1981. "Argument Structure and Morphology." *The Linguistic Review* 1: 81–114.

"Where" rather than "What":

Incorporation of 'Parts' in Totonac

Paulette Levy
Universidad Nacional Autónoma de México

There are two sources, or types, of Noun Incorporation (NI) in Totonac.[1] Both types involve a special part of speech termed Parts. In the first type, a possessed Part term may be incorporated from a direct object NP (1) ((1a–b) with a third person possessor, (1c–d) with a pronominal second person possessor). In the second, a possessed Part may be incorporated from a locative phrase (2). With regard to the rest of Totonac's processes of verb formation, both constructions (1) and (2) are marked in the sense that the conditions under which they are possible can be stated explicitly.

(1) a. *k-pa'qlh-ní:t ix-aqá-n xa:lu.*
1–break-PERF 3:POSS-ear-NMLZR pot
'I have broken the pot's handle.'

b. *k-Ø–aqa-pa'qlh-ní:t xa:lu.*
1–3:OBJ-ear-break-PERF pot
'I have broken the pot on its handle. '
(Lit: 'I have ear-broken the pot.')

c. [From text: The doctors told him]
k-a-ma:-náw
1:INCL-go-PRG-PL:PRG
ka:-chuka:kti:-ni-ya:-n min-cha':xpá:-n.
1:PL-amputate-BEN-ICPL-2:OBJ 2:POSS-leg-NMLZR
'We arc going to amputate your leg.'

d. *k-a-ma:-náw*
1:INCL-go-PRG-PL:PRG
ka:-cha':xpa:-chuka:kti:-ya:-n.
1:PL-leg-amputate-ICPL-2:OBJ
'We are going to leg-amputate you.'

(2) a. *ka-wili-' tlamank nak kim-pa:xtú:-n*!
IMP-sit:CAUS-2 pot LOC 1:POSS-side-NMLZR
'Put the pot besides me!'
(Lit: 'Put the pot by my side!')

b. *ka-kim-pa:xtu:-wili-' tlamank!*
IMP-1:OBJ-side-sit:CAUS-2 pot
'Put the pot besides me!'

c. *ka-wili-' tlamank nak ix-pa:xtú:-n Juan/chiki'!*
IMP-sit:CAUS-2 pot LOC 3:POSS-side-NMLZR Juan/house
'Put the pot besides Juan/the house!'

d. *ka-Ø–pa:xtu:-wili-' tlamank Juan/chiki'!*
IMP-3:OBJ-side-sit:CAUS-2 pot Juan/house
'Put the pot besides Juan/the house!'

Both (1b, d) and (2b, d) are instances of external possession constructions (EPCs) as they are defined in this book. The erstwhile possessor is marked as one of the core arguments of the verb, signalled by the object paradigm; the possessor is expressed nowhere else in the clause. Semantically, the Totonac EPCs have clear locative components, a fact which has not been particularly noted for EPCs in other languages. The Totonac incorporated Parts also give diachronic insight into the typological appearance of applicatives in EPCs.

We restrict our definition of NI in Totonac only to those cases in which both an analytic and a synthetic paraphrase are possible. When no analytic form is possible, Part+V forms are considered instances of lexical composition. This is not just because no analytical paraphrase is possible, but because its absence also entails a whole cluster of properties which mark them as clear cases of tighter lexical composition: the meaning of the compound is non-compositional, the compounded Part cannot be omitted in many cases, the process is not fully productive (i.e., not all 'parts' can go into the preverbal slot), the compounded nominal can have a variety of notional relationships to the verb including that of being semantically related to the subject of a transitive verb (cf. Levy 1994b).

Example (1) represents a very common type of NI. Since Sapir's early analysis (1911), it is commonly observed that if a language incorporates at all, it will allow incorporation of the semantic noun-class denoting 'body-parts'. Furthermore, the incorporated noun is clearly cognate with its non-incorported counterpart. Mithun (1984: 856) calls this Type II NI in which the valence of the verb is not altered, and which serves to foreground or background certain participants in the clause.

Example (2) shows a rarer type of incorporation. Usually, when locatives are incorporated, they are either sanctioned by a locative applicative (Kimenyi for Kinyarwanda as quoted in Baker, 1988: 238), or else body-parts-cum-locatives appear in a type of EPC in which the locative body part term is still maintained in a phrase case-marked as locative and the possessor is marked in the verb as a core participant, as in Oneida (Michelson 1991). The peculiarity of the Totonac construction in (2) is that the incorporated Part acts as an adposition-cum-applicative, and the NPs in the clause are, therefore, not case-marked. This type of NI is not directly discussed by Mithun (1984), but is implied in her hierarchy which describes what semantic roles incorporated nouns can bear relative to the verb: Patient of a transitive verb > Patient of an intransitive verb > Instrumental/Locative (Mithun 1984: 875).

1. Background information

Before discussing the parameters for the two types of Totonac NI, we present some background information about Totonac Parts. A principal point in this analysis is that the specific possessor-possessum relations found in Totonac EPCs are both locative, albeit of a different type in each case.

The Parts class in Papantla Totonac is language- and culture-specific. It is a large formal class of bound morphemes (ca. 90 elements), biuniquely defined by its co-occurrence with verb roots to form complex verb bases, but very extensively used in other constructions.[2] It is by no means confined to human or animal 'body-parts'. A good approximation to the semantic characterization of the class is 'visible segmentations of a pre-existing whole,' where the whole may be any kind of entity. Given the extent of the constructions in which Parts appear, and given their frequency in text and in the lexicon, one can say without doubt that the class is very productive, i.e., the language has elaborated this domain.

Although the label chosen for the class appeals to a notional characterization (i.e., the semantic feature that all members of the class share), it is important to point out that membership in the class, and the formal, semantic, and pragmatic characteristics of its elements are language specific. This means that not every thing that a non-Totonac speaker could construe as a 'part' belongs to the Totonac Part class.

A few examples of monomorphemic Part terms are listed here. When appropriate, the first gloss is a translation where the denotatum is human; the second is a more schematic gloss that tries to convey the trait shared by all the uses of the morpheme. Alternatives are sound-symbolically related: *ak(a)-*, *aq-* 'head', 'extreme of longest axis' (inference of verticality in many combinations)';

laka-, laqa- 'face', '2D, flat' (inference of visibility)'; *pa:-* 'belly', '3D, having volume (not flat), container-like'; *mak-, maq-* 'skin, body', 'circular, spherical'; *kilh-, qalh-*'mouth, lip', '1D, edge, opening'.

Even within monomorphemic Parts, there are some whose denotation is non-corporeal and which start to have a more locative sense even in translation: *pi:-* 'area inside an angle'; *paj-* 'interval between two straight lines'. When we abandon the domain of the human body and look at the plurimorphemic nomenclature for the house, we are struck by the fact that there are no morphemes for referents such as 'door' or 'window' (concepts which are named with Spanish loanwords and which can be better thought of as 'functional parts'). In contrast, there seems to be an enormous nomenclature for specific locations in a house. For example, *tanqi:-* can mean either 'interior angle of wall and floor' or else 'the strip of ground under the eave at the back of the house'. *Qi:kilhti:-* indicates 'space under the eave, all around'. That is, once we abandon the realm of terms for which individuated nouns are used in many non-Totonac languages, it is far easier to think in terms of places, to think of Parts as non-reified subregions.

In support of the idea that Parts do not name inherently reified subregions, note that in examples (1a, c, 2a, c) Parts have to be nominalized by adding *-N* in order to be used as independent nouns. The case for a nominalization analysis of the Totonac Part terms in (1a, c, 2a, c) is plausible because there are no basic (i.e., non-derived) nouns ending in *-N*.[3] Generally, nouns ending in *-N* are deverbatives of various semantic types. Members of the class of Parts are clearly non-verbal, since they do not accept verbal affixes; but nonetheless, the forms in (1a, c, 2a, c) exemplify the only other type of noun that ends in *-N*.

2. Incorporation from a possessed direct object

As we have said, incorporation from a possessed direct object is very common typologically. Its main syntactic characteristic is that it does not alter the valence of the verb. Example (1b), repeated here for ease of reference, shows a NI/EP construction in which the possessor is third person.

(1) a. *k-pa'qlh-ní:t ix-aqá-n xa:lu.*
1–break-PERF 3:POSS-ear-NMLZR pot
'I have broken the pot's handle.'

b. *k-Ø-aqa-pa'qlh-ní:t xa:lu.*
1–3:OBJ-ear-break-PERF pot
'I have broken the pot on its handle.'

For first and second persons, the strongly preferred construction is the synthetic one, i.e., the EPC (3).

(3) *ki-maka-qa'xi-'.*
1:OBJ-hand-hit-2:SUBJ:CMPL
'You hit me on the hand.'
k-maka-qa'xí-n.
1:SUBJ-hand-hit-2:OBJ:CMPL
'I hit you on the hand.'

Only when the body-part is very topicalized do we find the analytic internal possession construction with a first or second person possessor in the direct object. Example (1c) illustrates. It is from a two-page narrative which recounts what happened to one of the narrator's relative's legs as a result of diabetes.

(1) c. [The doctors told him]
k-a-ma:-náw *ka:-chuka:kti:-ni-ya:-n*
1:INCL-go-PRG-PL:PRG 1:PL-amputate-BEN-ICPL-2:OBJ
min-cha':xpá:-n.
2:POSS-leg-NMLZR
'We are going to amputate your leg.'

In this short narrative, the noun *cha:'xpá:n* 'leg' appears twelve times. The narrative could in fact be named "The story of a leg". Observe that in (1c), the object pronoun in the verb is sanctioned by the Benefactive suffix *-ni*.

Both (1a) and (1b) are transitive. Totonac has only two series of pronominal affixes, one for subject, and the second references non-subject. Transitive verbs (either inherently so, or via derivation) are defined by the fact that they take the non-subject series directly, i.e., without further affixation. In addition, there are several applicative morphemes (Benefactive, Commitative, Instrumental) that change the valence of the verb; in such cases the non-subject series signals the added relation (as in 1c). Totonac does not have a promoting passive, but rather has a backgrounding detransitivizing construction that involves the suffix *-nan* 'unspecified object' (UNSP:OBJ). This suffix blocks the occurrence of a direct object NP and yields an intransitive verb, very often with the reading of habitual action. As we can see in (4), both the simple verb *p'aqlh-* 'break' and the complex verb base *aqapa'qlh-* 'ear:break' are transitive. These are elicited examples. Although they are possible in the system, they are not habitually employed because they do not express habitual actions. The context given was one in which a daughter systematically breaks everything in the kitchen. In this same context, a derivation with *-nan* occurs in the deverbative agentive noun (5).

(4) *Para pa'qlh-nam-para-ya-'*
If break-UNSP:OBJ-REIT-ICPL-2
*(*xa:lu), k-a-ma ma:kxtajni:-ya:-n.*
(*cup) 1–go-PRG punish-ICPL-2:OBJ
'If you keep on breaking (being a habitual breaker of things), I am going to punish you.'

Para aqa-pa'qlh-nam-para-ya-'
If ear-break-UNSP:OBJ-REIT-ICPL-2
*(*xa:lu), k-a-ma ma:kxtajni:-ya:-n.*
(*cup) 1–go-PRG punish-ICPL-2:OBJ
'If you keep ear-breaking [all sorts of things], I am going to punish you.'

(5) *pa'qlh-ná-' jaí' cu'ma:t.*
break-UNSP:OBJ-NMLZR this girl
'This girl is [a systematic] breaker.'

aqa-pa'qlh-ná-' jaí cu'ma:t.
ear-break-UNSP:OBJ this girl
'This girl is a handle-breaker.'
(The equivalent of our saying with irony: "She is a specialist in breaking cup's handles.")

I have argued extensively elsewhere for the fact that when both analytic and synthetic paraphrases of type (1) are possible, the analytic construction is semantically and pragmatically marked with respect to other types of Part+V compounds and with respect to the synthetic counterpart (Levy 1999). This is particularly so for first and second person possessors (see ex. 3). A Part can be unpacked ("excorporated") only under certain conditions. The verb must express high affect on the undergoer, entailing physical contact with the undergoer, and in a majority of cases a change of state in the undergoer. The genitival phrase must express a part/whole relationship in which the Part is a visible, segmentable part of a pre-existing whole, and in this sense the Part is possessed by the whole. This is one very specific type of possessor-possessum relationship.

The synthetic form, in turn, does not express this type of part/whole relationship, but rather exploits the fact that a visible, segmentable part of a whole is a location on the whole, so that incorporated parts of type (1) restrict the meaning of the head verb with respect to locus of affect. With first or second person possessors, the only possible interpretation in the synthetic construction is that of a body-part, and the operating principle seems to be that the affectee is the person. The Part only denotes locus of affect.

3. Incorporation from a locative phrase

The second type of Totonac NI is incorporation into a verb from a subcategorized locative phrase containing a possessive construction (2); (2b) illustrates NI with a first pronominal object, and (2d) illustrates it with two third person NPs.

(2) a. *ka-wili-' tlamank nak kim-pa:xtú:-n!*
IMP-sit:CAUS-2 pot LOC 1:POSS-side-NMLZR
'Put the pot besides me!'

b. *ka-kim-pa:xtu:-wili-' tlamank!*
IMP-1:OBJ-side-sit:CAUS-2 pot
'Put the pot besides me!'

c. *ka-wili-' tlamank nak ix-pa:xtú:-n Juan/chiki'!*
IMP-sit:CAUS-2 pot LOC 3:POSS-side-NMLZR Juan/house
'Put the pot besides Juan/the house!'

d. *ka-Ø–pa:xtu:-wili-' tlamank (*nak) Juan/chiki'!*
IMP-3:OBJ-side-sit:CAUS-2 pot (*LOC) Juan/house!
'Put the pot besides Juan/the house!'

As seen in (2d), when incorporation takes place the locative complement cannot be case-marked.

Incorporation from a locative phrase is practically restricted to the four Locative Existentials in their stative, inchoative and causative forms, respectively *wi:*, *tawi:la*, *wi:lí* 'sit'; *ya:*, *ta:yá*, *ya:wá* 'stand'; *ma:*, *tamá:*, *tra'mí:/ma:pí'* 'lie'; *waka'*, *tawaká'*, *ma:waká'* 'hang'. These verbs are subcategorized for a locative complement, marked on the complement NP by the locative marker *nak* (2a, c, 6). Both the stative and inchoative forms are bivalent (6a, b), while the causative is trivalent (6c).

(6) a. *Wi: kin-ti:kú' nak chi'ki.*
sit:3:STAT 1:POSS-father LOC house
'My father is is the house'.

b. *Tawi:la-ma kin-ti:kú' nak silla.*
sit:3:INC-PRG 1:POSS-father LOC chair
'My father is sitting on the chair'.

c. *Ka-wili-' puqi' nak mesa!*
IMP-sit:CAUS-2 gourd LOC table
'Put the gourd on the table!'

Since third person singular subject and object are zero, the trivalent nature of the causative may not be immediately transparent. However, it can be demonstrated by the plural marker on the verb, *ka:-*, which only signals that one or more of the core arguments is plural. In (7), *ka:-* shows that the following are core arguments: the argument bearing the Locative relation (7a), the argument bearing the Theme relation (7b, 8), and the argument bearing the Effector role as syntactic subject in (2d) above.

(7) a. *ka-ka:-pa:xtu:-wili-' tlamank Pedro y Juan*!
IMP-PL:OBJ-side-sit:CAUS-2 pot Pedro and Juan
'Put the pot besides Pedro and Juan!'

b. *ka-ka:-pa:xtu:-wili-' wa'q kin-tlamank-ká'n mesa!*
IMP-PL:OBJ-side-sit:CAUS-2 all 1:POSS-pot-PL:POSS table
'Put all our pots besides the table!'

(8) *ka-ka:-ak-ya:wa-' wa'q ki-libruh-ká'n Juan!*[4]
IMP-PL:OBJ-head-hang.CAUS-2 all 1:POSS-bokk-PL:POSS Juan
'Put all our books on Juan's head!'

When a Locative Existential functions as an existential, the locative complement is optional (9).

(9) *Ni: ti wi:.*
NEG someone sit:3:STAT
'There isn't anyone'.

For incorporation of type (2) to occur, it has to be from a possessed NP of the form "its-Part N" governed by the locative marker. In the incorporated forms, the Part term functions as an incorporated adposition-cum-applicative, at least in the sense of sanctioning a non case-marked additional core participant. The object series denotes the possessor. The possessor must appear as a core argument in the clause, since the incorporated verb form must fill up all its valences.

Not all instances of Part+Locative Existential Verb are cases of type (2) incorporation. The main diagnostic of those which are not is that they do not allow non-incorporated, i.e., analytic, counterparts. The remainder of this section explores the semantic conditions which predict when an analytic counterpart can occur.

Thus far we have seen that the head of an incorporating verb must be a Locative Existential, and we might be tempted to think this is all that is necessary. However, while having a Locative Existential head verb is necessary, it is not a sufficient condition for predicting which Part + $V_{\text{Locative existential}}$ complex verbs can indeed have an analytic counterpart. For example, (10) shows three arguments and in this respect is parallel to (2). But an analytic paraphrase of the (2b) type is impossible.

(10) a. *k-ka:-ak-ya:wa-lh li:takaxtay ki-lakcu:maján.*
1–PL:OBJ-head-stand:CAUS-CMPL ornament 1:POSS-little:girls
'I put the ornaments on the heads of my little girls.'

b. **k-ka:-ya:wa-lh li:takaxtay (nak) ix-aqxa'qa*
1–PL:OBJ-stand:CAUS-CMPL ornament LOC 3:POSS-head
ki-lakcu:maján.
1:POSS-little:girls
'I put the ornaments on the heads of my little girls.'

The possibility of having an analytic counterpart construction also does not depend on the semantic nature of the argument that fills the locative valence. Both in those cases that allow an analytic construction and in those that disallow it, the Locative argument can be either [+Human] or [–Human].

The verb bases that cannot excorporate their Part morpheme differ from the ones that can unpack them in several respects. First, compound verbs that lack analytic counterparts can take the unspecified object morpheme, which surfaces in deverbative derivations (11).

(11) *pa:-tawaka'-ná-'*
belly-hang:INC-UNSP:OBJ-NMLZR
'apron'

Second, in a compound verb without an analytic counterpart, the Part term can notionally refer to any core argument as the locus of affect, such as the subject in (12a) or the object in (12b).

(12) a. *María ak-ta:ya-lh xanat.*
Mary head-stand:INC-CMPL flower
'Mary put a flower on her head.'

b. *Tiku ak-ya:wa-pá jaí' stapu?*
who head-stand:CAUS-REIT:CMPL this bean
'Who sowed over these beans?' (Lit. 'Who sowed [another bean] again on the head of these beans?')

This points to just a semantic or pragmatic relation between the arguments and the compound verb on the principle that a segmentation of a pre-existing Whole entails the Whole. For these complex verbs, the Part does not signal which of the arguments will express the Whole. The Part only signals locus of affect; the information needed to identify which is the affected argument is retrieved pragmatically. Thus in (13), which is about an imaginary circus act, it is impossible to know whether it is John or Peter standing on the other's head.

(13) *ak-taya:-lh* *Pedro Juan.*
head-stand:INC-CMPL Peter John
'John$_i$ stood Peter on his$_i$ head.' or
'Peter$_i$ stood John on his$_i$ head.' or
'John stood on Peter's head.' or
'Peter stood on John's head.'

Verbs that have both analytic and synthetic forms do not display these properties. Rather, for verbs which have both analytic and synthetic possibilities, the synthetic incorporated Part is only in coreference with the analytical Whole noun that appears always as an obligatory non-subject complement, i.e., a Locative Object-cum-possessor. The semantic relation expressed by this particular incorporating clause is one of a locative event which locates a Figure with regards to a Ground; the Part simply restricts the search domain.

Whether a verb has both a synthetic and an analytic construction, or not, depends then on the semantic characteristics of the Locative Phrase that is governed by the locative marker *-nak* and contains the possessed NP. That is, the condition that enables one to predict whether a complex verb base of the form Part + Locative$_{\text{Existential Verb}}$ may have an analytic counterpart is whether *the complex base* (and not just the head) has a lexical semantic component indicating that the Part is used as a point of reference, that it, in effect, should mean 'put-besides', 'put-behind', etc. Analytic paraphrases, then, cannot be predicted from the class of verbs heading the construction (in this case, locative existentials), nor from a representation of the underlying syntactic-like relations of the Locative Phrase, since Parts have not grammaticalized as independent adpositions.

As a general rule for practically all Part terms,[5] it has to be noted that in genitival constructions a reading as a 'place on X' or as a 'point of reference (location) with respect to X' seems to be largely pragmatically derived. Observe (14), where the difference between the readings of a 'place on the tree' versus a 'point of reference with respect to the tree' seems to be inferred only from knowledge about *tawila:na* 'they are sitting' and *taqusma:na* 'they are flying'.

(14) *Spitu, nak ix-aqspú':n-n* *ki'wi tawila:na.*
bird LOC 3POSS-top-NMLZR tree 3PL:are:sitting
'The birds, they are on the top of the tree.'

Spitu, nak ix-aqspú':n-n ki'wi taqusma:na.
bird LOC 3POSS-top-NMLZR tree 3:are:flying
'The birds are flying over the tree.'

Saying that 'place on X' vs. 'point of reference with respect to X' readings depend on pragmatics does not entail that the pragmatic inference is attributable just to knowledge of the world. On the contrary, in Totonac the inference seems to derive regularly from the larger linguistic co-text. For example, 'place on X' vs. 'point of reference with respect to X' situations determine the selection of different locative existentials and in those cases, the combination with the specific locative existential employed forces either a 'place on X' or a 'point of reference with respect to X' reading of the genitive NP governed by *nak* LOC (15).

(15) a. *Nak ix-qí:-n chiki' tawaka:'na tlamank.*
LOC 3POSS-back-NMLZR house 3:hanging pot
'The pots are hanging on the back [wall] of the house.'
b. *Nak ix-qí:-n chiki' tawila:na tlamank.*
LOC 3POSS-back-NMLZR house 3:sitting pot
'The pots are [sitting] at the back of the house.'

In (15), the choice of locative existential is correlated to a 'place' vs. 'reference point' situation: if the pots are on the wall, one must use *tawaka':na* 'hanging' (15a); if they are on the floor, it must be *tawila:na* 'sitting' (15b). Accordingly, the reading of *ixqí:n* is 'on the back (wall)' in (15a), while it is 'at the back of (the house)' in (15b). One could conceive of most Parts as underspecified with regard to this parameter, receiving their specification from larger context. Complex verb bases furnish just that: a larger co-text that fixes the unspecified feature.

In sum, it is the semantic difference between a 'place on X' versus a 'point of reference with regard to X' which allows us to predict whether a synthetic Part + Locative Existential complex will allow or disallow an analytic paraphrase. Only in cases where the lexical meaning of the synthetic form implies a 'point of reference with regard to X' do we have the analytical paraphrases. The incorporating complex verbs should, in effect, mean something like 'put-besides', 'put-behind', etc. The other necessary components are not enough in themselves, as analytic paraphrases do not depend on the nature of the verb heading the construction, nor do they depend on a representation of the underlying syntactic relations of the Locative Phrase. The latter is because Parts have not grammaticalized to independent adpositions in this construction. Rather, the possibility of an analytical counterpart depends on compositionality having fixed one or the other of the possible readings of Parts.

4. Two different types of locative relations

We have seen that both types of NI/EP constructions in Totonac have to do with the expression of locative relations. In Incorporation from an object NP, the Part delimits the locus of affect of the predicate, the 'place' where the action of the predicate takes place (cf. 1). In Incorporation from a locative phrase (cf. 2), the Part morpheme expresses a reference point with respect to another participant in the event from which one can compute the location of the event.

When both co-occur, locus of affect is coded by the Part incorporated into the verb complex; location of the event is coded by a locative phrase, as in (16) from text.

(16) *ta-laqxti:-waka'-lh nak maqachu'nqni.*
INGR-temple-hit-CMPL LOC fence
'(The grandmother) got hit on the temples, on the fence.' (2h88)

That there are two distinct, contrasting meanings is clear from the opposition between (17a) and (17b), which involve the same basic root predicate:

(17) a. *jaí' ni:ma k-chi'pa-ní:t nak ki-makán.*
this REL 1–grab-PERF LOC 1POSS-hand
'this one that I have grabbed in my hand' (r86)
b. *ki-maka-chi'pa-ni:t-a'.*
1OBJ-hand-grab-PERF-2
'You have grabbed me on my hand.'

An exact parallel is found in many languages. In English and Spanish, to take two familiar examples, both types of locative relations can be coded by the same formal means; but it is clear that they are two distinct types even in those languages from the zeugma effect of sentences like *He hit himself on the head and on the fence*. In English the first type can alternatively be coded in an Internal Possession Construction as a direct object: *I hit my head.* In Spanish, it can be coded also as a direct object but it requires an EP Construction with the dative marking the possessor (18).

(18) *Le golpeé la cabeza.*
3DAT hit:1:PAST the head
'I hit him on the head.'

In Totonac, both types of locations are expressed through the use of Part morphemes, but each exploits a different semantic property of Totonac Parts: they can be construed as subregions of a whole (places on the whole), or they can be construed as reference points on-or-relative-to an entity (points that are useful for projecting a region with regard to that entity). 'Place on entity' readings are associated with Incorporation from an object NP; 'location of the event with regard to a reference object' readings are associated with Incorporation from a Locative Phrase.

I hope to have shown that Totonac Parts — a prominent part of speech in the language — do not serve to deploy arguments but have as one of their functions the expression of different locative relations in a polysynthetic language that has no adpositions. These different locative relations derive naturally from different interpretations of the specific part/whole relation expressed by the language-specific class of Parts.

Genitival phrases that express locative relations are wide spread, being, for instance, one of the defining Mesoamerican areal features (Campbell, Kaufman, and Smith-Stark 1986: 545). Parts-cum-locatives are also a very common phenomenon, widely distributed for instance in Africa (Heine 1989), and in Oceania (Bowden 1991). The most common development is that 'parts' tend to grammaticalize as adpositions (Svoru 1993). In Totonac they are incorporated into the verb, and the locative relation is expressed by means of an external possessor construction.

Acknowledgments

I am indebted to Doris Payne for editorial work well beyond the call of duty. All remaining flaws are, alas, mine. Gracias a Natalio García, Martha, Mingo, Lito, Sixta Gómez por permitirme atisbar las bellezas de su lengua. Kilhaqamantitá'.

Abbreviations

Abbreviations used in this paper: 1, 2, 3 first, second, third person (usually subject unless otherwise specified); 1D, 2D, 3D one, two, or three dimensional; CAUS causative, CMPL completive aspect, DAT dative, IMP imperative, INC inchoative, INCL inclusive, INGR ingressive, INST instrumental, LOC locative, NEG negative, NMLZR nominalizer, OBJ object, PERF perfective aspect, PL plural, POSS possessive, PRG progressive, REIT reiterative, REL relative, STAT stative, V verb.

Notes

1 Totonacan consists of seven varieties of Totonac, plus three of Tepehua (Egland and Bartholomew 1983). The Totonacan family has almost 250,000 speakers. This paper deals with

Papantla Totonac, which is one of the main varieties in terms of number of speakers (ca. 80,000) and which is spoken is the northern part of the state of Veracruz, on the Gulf Coast of Mexico. Transcription follows a version of the practical orthography in which *x* = /š/, *ch* = /č/, *c* =/¢/, *lh* = /ƚ/, *j* = /h/, *V'* = laryngealized vowel, *V:* = long vowel; when the accent falls on a syllable other than the penult, it is indicated by an acute accent over the accented vowel.

2 Basically, Parts are used as (a) the main compound formation device for all four major lexical classes, (b) in the genitive construction with a locative meaning that we will discuss below, (c) and they are the lexical material which, probably through a process of heterosemy, consitutes the class of numeral classifiers; cf. Levy (1994a).

3 *-N* = /-n/ after vowel, /-ni/ after consonant.

4 Singular Theme, plural Locative is not possible.

5 Of the basic five dimensions ('front', 'back, 'over', 'under', 'besides') only 'front' has two forms. One form implies mostly 'place' *laka-,* 'at the front'; the other, *lakati:-* 'in front of' has a reading of 'location with respect to a reference point'.

References

Baker, Mark C. 1988. *Incorporation. A Theory of Grammatical Function Changing.* Chicago: The University of Chicago Press.

Bowden, John. 1991. *Behind the Preposition. Grammaticalization of Locatives in Oceanic Languages.* MA thesis, University of Auckland.

Campbell, Lyle, T. Kaufman, and T. Smith-Stark. 1986. "Meso-America as a Linguistic Area." *Language* 62: 530–70.

Egland, Steven and Doris Bartholomew. 1983. *La Inteligibilidad Interdialectal en México: Resultado de algunos Sondeos.* México: Instituto Lingüístico de Verano.

Heine, Bernd. 1989. "Adpositions in African Languages." *Linguistique Africaine* 2: 77–127.

Levy, Paulette. 1994a. "How Shape Becomes Grammar: On the Semantics of Part Morphemes in Totonac." Working Paper 29, Cognitive Anthropology Research Group at the Max Planck Institute for Psycholinguistics. Nijmegen, The Netherlands.

Levy, Paulette. 1994b. "Base Verbal en Totonaco". In Carolyn MacKay and Verónica Vázquez (eds.), *Investigaciones Lingüísticas en Lenguas Mesoamericanas.* México: UNAM, 227–262.

Levy, Paulette. 1999. "From 'Part' to 'Shape': Incorporation in Totonac and the Issue of Classification by Verbs." *International Journal of American Linguistics.*

Michelson, Karin. 1991. "Possessor Stranding in Oneida." *Linguistic Inquiry* 22: 756–762.

Mithun, Marianne. 1984. "The Evolution of Noun Incorporation." *Language* 60: 847–894.

Sapir, Edward. 1911. "The Problem of Noun Incorporation in American Languages". *American Anthropologist* 13: 250–282. [Reprinted in William Bright, (ed.). 1990. *The Collected Works of Edward Sapir.* Vol V: *American Indian Languages.* Berlin: Mouton, 27–60.]

Svoru, Soteria. 1993. *The Grammar of Space.* Amsterdam and Philadelphia: John Benjamins Publishing Company.

External Possessor in Oluta Popoluca (Mixean)

Applicatives and Incorporation of Relational Terms

Roberto Zavala Maldonado
University of Oregon, Universidad de Guadalajara, and Max Planck Institute for Psycholinguistics

Introduction

Oluta Popoluca (Mixe-Zoquean) presents two major constructions comparable to what have been characterized in the literature as external possessor constructions (EPC). The first EPC occurs with monovalent and bivalent verb roots affixed by their corresponding applicative which alters the argument structure of the clause. The applicative increases the valence of the verb allowing the semantic possessor of a nominal phrase to be treated as an extra core argument directly dependent on the derived verb. The second EPC is a noun incorporation construction which occurs when the semantic possessor of a nominal phrase is coded as a direct dependent of the verb and the semantic possessed noun combines with the verb root to make a complex verb (Mithun 1984).

EPCs in which the semantic possessor is expressed as a direct dependent of the verb have internal possessor (IP) counterparts, that is, constructions in which the possessor occurs as a dependent of the nominal phrase only.

Two different applicative constructions code the possessor as a direct dependent of the verb. The two applicative affixes are the prefix *küj-* which occurs with monovalent verb roots, and the suffix *-ja:yʔ* which occurs with monovalent, bivalent and trivalent verb roots.[1]

Küj-, glossed as APPL2, changes patient-oriented monovalent verbs into non-agentive bivalent verbs. The derived verbs select for two core arguments: a theme/patient and a malefactive/benefactive. In a non-applicative clause the possessor is a dependent of the only core argument of the clause, as in (1a), where the first-person possessor *tan=* is a direct dependent of the nominal and is an internal possessor (IP). In the applicative counterpart (1b), the semantic possessor is expressed in two slots within the clause. The first-person absolutive proclitic *ta=* is a direct dependent of the verb and is an external possessor (EP). Simultaneously, the first person possessor *tan=* is a direct dependent of the nominal.

(1) a. IP Construction with Monovalent Verb
Ø=ʔo:k-u=k *tan=majaw*
B3(ABS)=die-CMPL=ANIM A1(POSS)=wife
'My wife died.'

b. EP Construction with *küj-* Derived Bivalent Verb
*ta=**küj-**ʔo:k-ü-w=ak* *tan=majaw*
B1(ABS)=APPL2–die-INV-CMPL=ANIM A1(POSS)=wife
'My wife died on me (or I got affected by the fact that my wife died).'

Oluta Popoluca (OP) presents a second applicative, *-ja:yʔ*, APPL1 (with its allomorphs *-ay*, *-aʔ*, *-jay*, *-aʔx*), which changes agentive bivalent verbs into trivalent verbs and monovalent verbs into bivalent verbs. The applicative *-ja:yʔ* occurs in double-object constructions and allows semantic benefactives, datives, recipients and some locatives to be construed as primary objects of ditransitive clauses (Dryer 1986, Comrie 1982). Transitive clauses with a possessed patient or theme can be paraphrased with ditransitive (applicative) clauses in which the verb root is suffixed with *-ja:yʔ*. In this type of clause the semantic possessor (PR) is expressed in two slots: a) as IP of the secondary object, and b) as the primary object of the clause. Sentence (2b) is the EP counterpart of (2a).

(2) a. IP Construction with Transitive Verb
tu:max=ak *ʔi=pa:t-u=k* *tan=majaw*
Thom=ANIM A3(ERG)=find-CMPL=ANIM A1(POSS)=woman
'Thom found my wife.'

b. EP Construction with V-*ja:yʔ* Ditransitive Verb
tu:max=ak ***ta****=pa:t-**aʔx**-ü-w=ak*
Thom=ANIM B1(ABS)=find-APPL1–INV-CMPL=ANIM
tan*=majaw*
A1(POSS)=woman
'Thom found my wife for me (Thom found my wife and I benefited from that).'

The suffix *-ja:yʔ* also occurs with monovalent roots. Intransitive clauses with a theme and a possessed location can be paraphrased with transitive clauses in which the monovalent root is suffixed with *-ja:yʔ*. In this type of clause the PR is expressed in two slots: a) as IP of the locative phrase, and b) as the second direct core argument of the clause. Sentence (3b) is the EP counterpart of (3a).

(3) a. *Ø=ʔit-u=k* *xi:mu* *tan=tük-mü*
B3(ABS)=exist-CMPL=ANIM Simon A1(POSS)=house-LOC
'Simon was in my house.'

b. ***ta****=ʔit-****aʔx****-ü-w=ak* *xi:mu*
B1(ABS)=exist-APPL1–INV-CMPL=ANIM Simon
tan*=tük-mü*
A1(POSS)=house-LOC
'Simon was in my house.'

The constructions illustrated in (1b) and (3b) have not been discussed in the literature of Mesoamerican languages as cases of EP. In contrast, the construction in (2b) has been the focus of intensive research within the Relational Grammar framework and has been characterized as a prototypic case of possessor ascension in at least three Mesoamerican languages: Tzotzil (Mayan) (Aissen 1979, 1987), Sierra Popoluca (Mixe-Zoquean) (Marlett 1986), and Huastec (Mayan) (Constable 1989).[2] Aissen, Marlett and Constable have argued that in the applicative construction the possessor of the patient has ascended out of the noun phrase into the clause where it bears a noninitial grammatical relation, i.e., the direct object grammatical relation, whereas the possessum (PM) has acquired the chômeur relation.

In contrast to non-applicative constructions (1a, 2a, 3a), applicative constructions (1b, 2b, 3b) indicate that the PR of the theme/patient or location has been beneficially or adversely affected by the action.

Noun incorporation (NI) is a very prolific process in OP. From a typological point of view OP is of special interest because it allows incorporation not only of themes, instruments and locatives, but also of agents of transitive verbs. OP presents the four types of noun incorporation proposed by Mithun (1984). Within the typology suggested by Mithun, Type II NI (manipulation of case) advances a dependent of an argument position or an oblique argument into the case position vacated by the incorporated noun. Type II NI is the second major strategy in OP for coding the PR as a direct dependent of the clause. In this construction the PM is not a core argument of the clause since it occurs incorporated in the verb, whereas the PR is expressed as a direct core argument of the clause. This is illustrated in (4b).

(4) a. Possessor as dependent of the possessed noun
Ø=ye:k-u *tan=puʔpu*
B3(ABS)=grow-CMPL A1(POSS)=belly
'My belly grew.'

b. EP by NI
*ta=**pu?pu-**ye:k-u*
B1(ABS)=belly-grow-CMPL
'My belly grew.' (Lit. I belly-grew)

This type of NI does not change the syntactic valence of the verb complex. The verb complex (verb root plus incorporated noun) in (4b) stays intransitive. The transitive verbs *tun* 'to make' and *?e:p* 'to see' in (5) keep all the properties of transitive verbs when the PM is incorporated.

(5) a. *tan=**kü:k-**tun-pe* *na?ka*
A1(ERG)=hole-make-INCMPL.T board
'I am making a hole in the board.'
b. *tan=**?unak-**?e:p-u=k* *chuwa*
A1(ERG)=son-see-CMPL=ANIM John
'I took care of John's son.'

The most frequently incorporated nouns within Type II NI are body-part terms (4b) and names of excretions (Fox 1981); but kinship terms (5b) and items referring to parts of wholes (5a) are also attested with some verb roots. The incorporated noun can refer to the possessum of: the theme of agentive bivalent verbs (5), the only argument of monovalent verbs (4), the location of non-agentive bivalent verbs (6), or the goal/recipient/location (primary object) of trivalent verbs (7b).

(6) *ta=**yo?k-**tük?i:y?-ü-w* *tzu?chi*
B1(ABS)=throat-go.into-INV-CMPL meat
'I choked on the meat.' (Lit. the meat went into my throat or the meat throat-went.into me)

(7) a. Possessor as dependent of the possessed noun
tan=tu:t?-ay-u=k *?inyeksyon xi:mu=k*
A1(ERG)=put-APPL1–CMPL=ANIM injection Simon=ANIM
?i=tewa-jem
A3(POSS)=buttocks-LOC
'I put an injection in Simon's buttocks.'
b. EP by NI
*tan=**tewa-**tu:t?-ay-u=k* *?inyeksion*
A1(ERG)=buttocks-put-APPL1–CMPL=ANIM injection
xi:mu=k
Simon=ANIM
'I put an injection in Simon's buttocks.'

In what follows I will discuss in detail the two major strategies used in OP to code the PR of a nominal as a direct core argument of the clause (Table 1).

Table 1: *Structures of the Two External Possessor Constructions in OP*

EPC1: applicative
beneficiary$_i$ + [*küj*-V] (possessor$_i$ + possessum)
beneficiary$_i$ + [V-*ja:yˀ*] (possessor$_i$ + possessum)

EPC2: noun incorporation
possessor + [possessum-V]

I will examine the properties of the two applicative constructions and compare them with other double-object constructions present in OP. The properties of clauses with the applicative *-ja:yˀ* will be compared with analogous clauses in Tzotzil and Sierra Popoluca. I will argue that this type of clause in OP should be characterized as a double-object construction, rather than indirect object to direct object advancement as proposed for Tzotzil (Aissen 1987), or direct object advancement as proposed for Sierra Popoluca (Marlett 1986). I will also argue that a possessor ascension analysis for this type of applicative construction cannot be sustained in OP.

The OP NI strategy which allows coding the PR as a core argument of the clause will be compared with another type of NI present in the language. This comparison will establish the distinctive semantic and morphosyntactic properties of Type II NI. The contrast of Type II NI in OP with analogous constructions in other languages is of special interest because Type II NI in OP allows incorporation of semantic possessed locatives and possessed recipients, which is crosslinguistically rare or unreported.

This paper is organized as follows: Section 1 introduces the basic morphosyntactic facts of OP that are necessary for understanding the type of constructions discussed in the following sections. Section 2 discusses the two types of applicative clauses. Section 3 surveys the Type II NI strategy. Finally, Section 4 summarizes the findings.

1. Generalities of Oluta Popoluca

1.1 *Person marking and aspectual marking in main independent clauses*

OP is a head-marking, ergative and inverse language. The multimorphemic verb carries information regarding the core arguments of the clause, aspect, mode, directionals, valence increasers (five applicatives, two causatives) and decreasers (passive), reflexive, negation, incorporated nominals and adverbs. OP distinguishes independent and dependent clauses (Clark 1981). Dependent clauses are structures following matrix verbs, auxiliaries and adverbs. Independent and dependent clauses follow different patterns for marking aspect, person and inversion. The language has two different paradigms of aspect markers. One aspectual paradigm only occurs in independent clauses, and the other only in dependent clauses. Each paradigm distinguishes incompletive, completive and irrealis aspects (Table 2).

Table 2: *Aspect Markers for Independent and Dependent Clauses*

	Independent	Dependent
Incompletive	*-pa* (intransitive) *-pe* (transitive)	*-i/-e*
Completive	*-u*	*-i*
Irrealis	*-am* (direct) *-an...pa* (inverse)	*-aʔn* (direct) *-aʔne* (inverse)

OP is a head-marking language. The core arguments of the clause do not need to be expressed by nominals or pronouns external to the verb complex. The core arguments are inferred from the morphology which marks person, plurality and inversion on the verb. OP has three different sets of person markers that I will refer to as Set A, Set B and Set C (Table 3).[3] Three persons in the singular and four persons in the plural are distinguished. The paradigm for the four plural persons is formed from the same proclitics that appear in the singular with addition of the plural suffixes. The vowel of the suffix *-Vt,* which signals first and second-person plural, copies the vowel occurring immediately before. The suffix *-ütz* distinguishes first-person plural exclusive from first-person plural inclusive. The suffix *-küx* appears in parenthesis in Table 3 to indicate that this morpheme, in agreement with third-person plural core participants, is optional.

In main independent clauses either a Set A or a Set B proclitic precedes the verb. Set A has an ergative distribution: actor of transitive verb (8). Set B has an absolutive distribution: the only participant of monovalent predicates (9a), second participant of agentive-bivalent verbs (the non-actor of transitive verbs) (9b), second participant of bivalent non-agentive verbs (9c), and third participant of trivalent verbs (primary object of ditransitives) (9d).

(8) A = Ergative for Independent Clauses
__tan__=ʔixkap-u=na=k *jeʔ ma:wro*
A1(ERG)=know-CMPL=still=ANIM DEF Mauro
'I still knew Mauro.' {re/255}

Table 3: *Paradigms of the Three Sets of Person Markers*

	Set A	Set B	Set C	Plural Markers	EXCL
P 1	*tan*	*ta*	*tax*	*-Vt*	*-ütz*
E					
R 2	*min*	*mi*	*mix*	*-Vt*	
S					
O 3	*ˀi*	*Ø*	*ta*	*(-küx)*	
N					

(9) B = Absolutive for Independent Clauses

a. Only argument of monovalent
ta=*nükx-pa* *tan*=*na:x-mü*
B1(ABS)=go-INCMPL.I A1(POSS)=earth-LOC
'I am going to my town.' {Tr/177}

b. Non-actor of agentive bivalent (transitive)
ta=*ko:chikx-ü-pa*=*k* *tzanay*
B1(ABS)=take.care-INV-INCMPL.I=ANIM snake
'(The snake) takes care of me.' {Llo/132}

c. Second participant of non-agentive bivalent
ta=*ˀit-küx-ü-w*=*ak* *yoxetunpaˀ-tük*
B1(ABS)=exist-3PL-INV-CMPL=ANIM worker-PL
'I had workers.' (Lit. 'Workers existed on me.') {reb275}

d. Third participant of trivalent (ditransitives)
ta=*tun-aˀx-ü-w*=*ak* *tan*=*kama-nak*
B1(ABS)=do-APPL1–INV-CMPL=ANIM A1(POSS)=corn.field-DIM
'He prepared my little cornfield for me.' {CTr/35}

Set A may also mark the possessor of nouns as in (9a) and (10).

(10) A = Possessor
tan=*majaw*
A1(POSS)=woman
'my wife'

A second marking pattern for both aspect and person is displayed by dependent clauses (embedded clauses following adverbs, auxiliaries and matrix predicates). In dependent clauses the aspect markers are selected from the right column of Table 2. In this type of clause Set C has an ergative distribution (11), whereas Set A has an absolutive distribution (12a–d).

(11) Set C = Ergative for Dependent Clauses
mü:t=ak *jem* ***tax**=yaktij-i* *tzanay*
and=ANIM there C1(ERG)=abandon-CMPLD snake
ʔi=yak-ʔo:k-w-aʔ
A3(ERG)=CAUS-die-CMPL=RLVZR
'...and there I abandoned the snake that I killed.' {Co/108}

(12) Set A = Absolutive for Dependent Clauses
a. Only argument of monovalent
jaʔmej=mpok ***tan**=nükx-i* *ʔü:tz*
in.that.way=also A1(ABS)=go-INCMPLD I
'In that way I also go.' {Ve/226}

b. Non-actor of agentive bivalent (transitive)
ʔoyamej=k ***tan**=yakkay-e-j*
properly=ANIM A1(ABS)=feed-INCMPLD-INVD.I
'She feeds me properly.' {Tr/384}

c. Second participant of non-agentive bivalent
jupaʔ=k *xuʔni* ***min**=ʔit-i-j*
how.many=ANIM dog A2(ABS)=exist-INCMPLD-INVD.I
'How many dogs do you have?'

d. Third participant of trivalent (ditransitives)
de-jem ***tan**=nüm-aʔx-e-j=ak*
from-there A1(ABS)=say-APPL1–INCMPLD-INVD.I=ANIM
min=yaktzükx-am *yaʔaj kane:la*
A2(ERG)=roast-IRR this cinnamon
'After that they say to me: "You are going to roast cinnamon."' {C22/16}

From the distribution of the person markers in independent and dependent clauses, it is clear that OP follows an ergative-absolutive alignment. Table 4 summarizes the type of clauses in which the three sets of person markers occur and the functions assigned to each set in independent and dependent clauses.

1.2 *Direct and inverse marking*

In addition to the ergative–absolutive alignment, OP distinguishes two types of clauses: direct vs. inverse. Clauses with more than one core participant, that is, clauses with bivalent and trivalent verbs, have to follow either the direct (8, 11, 13) or the inverse (9b–d, 12b–d, 14) marking pattern.

Table 4: *The Three Sets of Person Markers (Ergative Alignment)*

Type of Clause Function	*Independent*	*Dependent*
Ergative	A	C
Absolutive	B	A

(13) Direct

a. ***tan=****tze:k-pe=k* *chuwa*
A1(ERG)=scold-INCMPL.T=ANIM John
'I am scolding John.'

b. ***ˀi****=machiˀt-u=k* *xuˀni*
A3(ERG)=release-CMPL=ANIM dog
'(When he arrived at that place) he released the dogs.'
{Ve/72}

(14) Inverse

a. ***ta=****tze:k-****ü****-pa=k* *chuwa*
B1(ABS)=scold-INV-INCMPL.I=ANIM John
'John is scolding me.'

b. *jaˀ=xü=k* ***Ø****=ni:tza:yˀˀi:yˀ-****ü****-pa* *maktaxko tüˀkxan*
he=EVID=ANIM B3(ABS)=illuminate-INV-INCMPL.I four candle
'Four candles are illuminating him, it is said.'

A clause is coded as direct when the first participant of the clause (the actor in transitives) outranks the second (theme/patient in transitives) or third (goal/benefactive/ malefactive/locative in ditransitives) participant of the same clause in saliency (person, animacy or topicality). A clause is coded as inverse when the opposite is true, that is, when the second or third participant outranks the first participant of the clause in saliency (Dryer 1991, 1994; Gildea 1994; Givón 1994a, 1994b). The two distinct alignments are schematized in (15). In the direct alignment, (15a), the highest participant on the argument hierarchy (AH) coincides with the highest participant on the saliency hierarchy (SH). In the inverse, (15b), the highest participant on the argument hierarchy does not coincide with the highest participant on the saliency hierarchy.

(15) a. **Direct Alignment**
AH: *Agent* > Theme/Patient > Location/Experiencer/Benefactive/Goal
SH: *High-salience participant* > Low-salience participant

b. **Inverse Alignment**
AH: *Agent* > Theme/Patient > Location/Experiencer/Benefactive/Goal
SH: Low-salience participant < *High-salience participant*

In the direct pattern the person proclitic on the verb is ergative and refers to the actor. In the inverse, the person proclitic is absolutive and refers to the nonactor (patient/goal/benefactive). Direct clauses differ from inverse clauses not only in person marking but also in aspect and directive marking.[4] There are two incompletive markers: *-pe* for transitive clauses (13a) and *-pa* for intransitive clauses (9a). The suffix *-pe* occurs in direct clauses (13a), whereas the suffix *-pa* occurs in inverse clauses (14). The verb in direct clauses does not take any directive marker; in contrast, the verb in inverse clauses occurs with one of the following inverse suffixes: *-ü* in independent clauses, and *-y* (inverse completive) or *-j* (inverse incompletive) in dependent clauses.

Table 5 schematizes the distribution of the direct and inverse patterns for a transitive verb.

Table 5: *Direct and Inverse Patterns in Transitive Clauses*

Non-actor / *Actor*	1	2	3
1	INV (REFL)	LOCAL.DIR	DIR
2	LOCAL.INV	INV (REFL)	DIR
3	INV	INV	INV (REFL)/ DIR (3:3′)/INV (3′:3)

As in many other languages with inverse morphology (Klaiman 1992, 1993; DeLancey 1981b; Zavala 1994), OP codes certain combinations of the transitive paradigm obligatorily as direct; whereas other combinations of the same paradigm are coded obligatorily as inverse. The combinations 1:3 and 2:3 are direct. The combinations 3:1 and 3:2 are inverse. Transitive clauses with a Speech Act Participant (SAP) actor and a SAP nonactor display a third pattern which differs morphologically from the direct and the inverse pattern described above. This third pattern is known in Algonquian studies as *local* (Hockett 1966; Delancey

1981a) but will not be discussed here.[5] Suffice it to say that the 1:2 combination follows a direct subpattern whereas the 2:1 combination follows an inverse subpattern. The reflexive and reciprocal combinations are coded as inverse. Finally the 3:3 combination can be coded as direct or inverse depending on whether the most salient participant (in animacy or topicality) is the actor (13b) (direct 3:3') or the nonactor (14b) (inverse 3':3) of the clause.

1.3 *Verb root classes*

On the basis of formal and semantic criteria (e.g., valency and semantic role frame), seven classes of underived verb roots can be recognized in OP. There are three classes of bivalent roots, three classes of monovalent roots, and one class of trivalent root:

Bivalent:	**TV1** (Transitive with IV1 counterpart)
	TV2 (Transitive with IV2 counterpart)
	NON-AGT-BV (Non-agentive bivalent)
Monovalent:	**IV1** (Agent-oriented intransitive with TV1 counterpart)
	IV2 (Patient-oriented intransitive with TV2 counterpart)
	Plain-IV2 (Patient-oriented intransitive)
Trivalent:	**DV3** (Ditransitive)

The TV1 and TV2 bivalent roots select for an agentive first participant (actor) and for a non-agentive second participant (non-actor) (Hopper & Thompson 1980). These are the canonical transitive verb roots. All transitive verb roots have intransitive non-derived counterparts. The two classes of transitive verbs can be established on the basis of the thematic structure of their intransitive counterparts. TV1 verbs have an agent-oriented ("active" or "unergative") intransitive counterpart such as *tun* 'do, make', *tzo:kˀ* 'pay' and many others. TV2 verbs have patient-oriented ("non-active" or "unaccusative") intransitive counterparts, such as *ˀawtzoˀ* 'close', *mutz* 'break' and many others.

Non-agentive bivalent verbs (NON-AGT-BV) also select for two semantic arguments. But these verbs select a theme/patient (absolutive) as first argument and a location or experiencer (absolutive) as second argument. In (16) the first-person absolutive marker preceding the NON-AGT-BV *ˀit* 'have, exist in a location' is the second selected argument of the verb (the location). The nominal phrase *yoxetunpaˀtük* 'workers', which triggers third-person plural agreement on the verb, is the first selected argument (the theme). These two characteristics corroborate the fact that the verb in (16) is bivalent and that both the theme and the location are core arguments.

(16) ***ta***=*ʔit-küx*-***ü***-*w*=*ak* *yoxetunpaʔ-tük*
B1(ABS)=have-3PL-INV-CMPL=ANIM worker-PL
'I had workers.' (Lit. 'Workers existed to me.') {reb275}

The second difference between canonical transitive verb roots and NON-AGT-BV roots is that TV1 and TV2 can take either the direct or the inverse pattern. In contrast, NON-AGT-BV verbs can appear only in clauses that follow the inverse pattern. However, some members of the NON-AGT-BV class have Plain-IV2 verbs as their monovalent lexical counterparts. For instance bivalent *ʔit* 'have, exist in a location' has the Plain-IV2 counterpart *ʔit* 'exist'. The "notional direct" pattern, that is, the pattern where the theme outranks the location in saliency, cannot be expressed with the bivalent NON-AGT-BV verb. A verb following the "notional direct" pattern necessarily belongs to the Plain-IV2 class. In this construction, the theme (signaled by the absolutive first-person marker) is the only core argument of the clause (17). The locative participant is expressed by an oblique phrase.

(17) "Notional Direct" Counterpart of NON-AGT-BV
ta=*ʔit-pa* *tü:yan*-***pi***
B1(ABS)=exist-INCMPL.I hammock-LOC
'I am on the hammock.'

In addition to *ʔit*, other members of the NON-AGT-BV class are: *ʔut* 'like', *ʔom* 'crave', *may* 'endure at a LOC', *ʔoy* 'have', *tzi:yʔ* 'stick on LOC', *jo:y* 'lack, miss something', *toy* 'burn on LOC', *tzuʔkx* 'get pricked on LOC', and many others.

NON-AGT-BV verbs allow incorporation of the first argument (theme) (18), and incorporation of the possessed nominal of the second argument (location) (19).

(18) a. Non-incorporated Theme
ta=*ʔom*-***ü***-*w* ***kayan***
B1(ABS)=crave-INV-CMPL food
'I have a craving for food.'

b. Incorporated Theme
ta=***kayan***-*ʔom*-***ü***-*w*
B1(ABS)=food-crave-INV-CMPL
'I have a food-craving.' (Lit. 'I have food-craving.')

(19) Incorporated Location
a. *ta*=***yoʔk***-*tükʔi:yʔ-ü-w* *tzuʔchi*
B1(ABS)=throat-go.into-INV-CMPL meat
'I choked on the meat.' (Lit. 'The meat went into my throat.')

b. *ta=**küx-ˀit-ü-pa*** *chipin*
B1(ABS)=body-have-INV-INCMPL.I smallpox
'I have smallpox on my body.' (Lit. 'I body-have smallpox .')

A subset of NON-AGT-BV verbs has the semantic theme conflated on the verb stem (Zavala 1997, 1998).[6] That is, verbs of this subset cannot express their selected theme with a nominal external to the verb complex. Verbs with conflated theme are: *mu:kˀ* 'be drunk', *jip* 'catch a cold, have the flu', *jotan* 'be angry, be mad', *jayyüˀk* 'be happy', *ka:na-ˀax* 'be salty', *ke:ye-ˀax* 'be a sinner', *ˀo:pik-ˀax* 'be foamy' and many others.

Monovalent verbs (IV1, IV2 and Plain-IV2) are prefixed by the absolutive person marker (Set B in independent clauses and Set A in dependent clauses). IV2 and Plain-IV2 verbs are patient-oriented. Plain-IV2 verbs do not have an underived bivalent counterpart. The causative prefix *yak-* derives transitive verbs from Plain-IV2 verbs. Some examples of plain-IV2 with their causative counterparts are: *ˀo:k* 'die'/*yak-ˀo:k* 'kill', *tij* 'stay'/*yak-tij* 'abandon', *toy* 'be hot'/*yak-toy* 'burn', *mi:nˀ* 'come'/*yak-mi:nˀ* 'bring' and many others. IV2 and Plain-IV2 ("unaccusatives") verbs accept nominal incorporation, whereas IV1 ("unergatives") verbs do not.

Two dissimilar semantic interpretations obtained in the applicative *küj-* (APPL2) construction provide another test which distinguishes IV1 (agent-oriented) verbs from IV2 and Plain-IV2 (patient-oriented) verbs. An abilitative or indirect causative interpretation is obtained with IV1 (unergative) verbs. A benefactive or malefactive interpretation is obtained with IV2 and Plain-IV2 (unaccusative) verbs.

The DV3 class has a single member. *Mo:yˀ* 'give' is the only OP underived verb which selects for three semantic participants: actor, theme, and recipient. Some syntactic rules concerning *mo:yˀ* and other derived trivalent verbs operate on the basis of a primary vs. secondary object asymmetry, whereas some other rules operate on the basis of the theme vs. recipient asymmetry.

2. External possessor and applicatives

OP has multiple applicatives, which alter the argument structure of verbs. *Toj-* (instrumental), *mü:-* (comitative), *-ja:yˀ* (*-ay*, *-aˀx*, *-aˀ*, *-jaˀ*) and *kuj-* allow thematically peripheral arguments to be treated as direct core arguments. These include: instrumentals, locatives, associatives, benefactives, malefactives, recipients, and addressees. *Toj-*, *mü:-* and *-ja:yˀ* occur with monovalent or bivalent roots to derive bivalent and trivalent stems. *Küj-* changes monovalent verb roots into bivalent stems. In what follows I discuss the applicatives *küj-* and *-ja:yʔ*. These both allow an EP interpretation when the possessor of a nominal subcategorized by the verb is construed as a direct dependent of the verb stem.

2.1 *The küj- construction and external possession*

Sentences (20a–b) illustrate the *küj-* construction.

(20) a. *ta=**küj-**ʔo:k-küx-ü-w=ak* *piyu-tük*
B1(ABS)=APPL2–die-3PL-INV-CMPL=ANIM chicken-PL
'The chickens died on me.'

b. *Ø=**küj-**kaʔ-küx-ü-w=ak* *tük*
B3(ABS)=APPL2–descend-3PL-INV-CMPL=ANIM house
yoxetunpaʔ-tük
worker-PL
'The house fell down on the workers.' (The workers were adversely affected by the fact that the house fell down)

The *küj-* construction with a patient-oriented verb root expresses a benefactive or a malefactive reading. For instance, *ʔo:k* 'die' and *kaʔ* 'descend' belong to the Plain-IV2 class, selecting for a single theme participant. In contrast, the applicative verb stems in (20) are bivalent and select for a theme (first argument) and a benefactive/malefactive (second argument). Both are core arguments of the clause, and both can trigger third-person plural agreement on the verb (20a theme, 20b benefactive/malefactive). Only the second argument (benefactive/malefactive) is overtly indicated by the absolutive person marker. This is evident in (20a) where the absolutive marker *ta=* refers to the malefactive participant. The verb stem always carries the inverse suffix since the benefactive/malefactive outranks the theme in saliency, whereas the theme outranks the benefactive/malefactive in the argument hierarchy (see 15).

The argument structure of verb stems derived with *küj-* is very similar to the argument structure of NON-AGT-Bivalent underived verbs. Both verb types are bivalent, are not agentive, and carry an inverse suffix. However, only NON-AGT-Bivalent roots include a second non-agentive participant in their argument structure; verbs such as *ʔit* 'exist in a location, have' do not need *küj-* in order to include a second core argument.

(21) *mo:k ta=ka:=ʔit-ü-pa-:t*
corn B1(ABS)=NEG=have-INV-INCMPL.I-SAP.PL
'We do not have corn.' {C6/38/12}

In contrast, verbs such as *ʔo:k* 'die' and *kaʔ* 'descend' cannot be construed as non-agentive bivalent verbs without *küj-* (22).

(22) a. * *ta=ʔo:k-küx-ü-w=ak* *piyu-tük*
B1(ABS)=die-3PL-INV-CMPL=ANIM chicken-PL
(Intended reading: 'The chickens die on me.')
b. **Ø=kaʔ-küx-ü-w=ak* *tük* *yoxetunpaʔ-tük*
B3(ABS)=descend-3PL-INV-CMPL=ANIM house worker-PL
(Intended reading: 'The house fell down on the workers.')

However, with *küj-* they can include the extra-thematic benefactive/malefactive within their argument structure.

Applicative clauses with a possessed first argument (theme) can be interpreted as EPCs when the PR of the theme is coreferential with the benefactive/malefactive introduced by the applicative. In (23) the PR is expressed in two slots within the clause. The possessor *min=* is coreferential with the absolutive person marker *mi=*, which signals the malefactive/benefactive extra-thematic participant.

(23) *mi=küj-ma:jʔ-ü-w=ak* *min=majaw*
B2(ABS)=APPL2–sleep-INV-CMPL=ANIM A2(POSS)=woman
'Your wife fell asleep on you.'

The *küj-* construction with an EP interpretation is used when the PR of the theme is construed as affected. An intransitive counterpart of the *küj-* construction is used when the PR of the theme is not highlighted as affected (24).

(24) *Ø=ma:jʔ-u=k* *min=majaw*
B3(ABS)=sleep-CMPL=ANIM A2(POSS)=woman
'Your wife fell asleep.'

There are *küj-* constructions where the PR of the theme is not coreferential with the argument introduced by the applicative. In (25) *min=* refers to the second-person PR of the theme; whereas the absolutive *ta=*, before the verb root, refers to the first-person malefactive introduced by the applicative *küj-*.

(25) ***ta=****küj-ʔo:k-ü-w=ak* ***min=****majaw*
B1(ABS)=APPL2–die-INV-CMPL=ANIM A2(POSS)=woman
tan=küʔ-pi
A1(POSS)=hand-LOC
'Your woman died on me, on my hands.'

Sentences such as (25) clearly show that a "possessor ascension" analysis of clauses such as (23) is unfortunate. That is, it is not the case that the applicative "promotes" the dependent of the theme (the possessor) to an argument position and that the theme nominal is "demoted" to the chômeur relation. In both (23) and (25), the applicatives introduce an extra semantically-relevant participant into the clause. The derived verb now has two core arguments. The EP reading in (23) is obtained only when the extra participant (the malefactive/benefactive) introduced by the applicative is coreferential with the PR of the theme. However, constructions such as (25), where the malefactive is not coreferential with the PR of the theme, clearly show that the extra core argument of *küj-* constructions cannot be analyzed as a hypothetical "copy" of the PR of the theme.

2.2 *The applicative -ja:yʔ and external possession*

Two EPC subtypes share the applicative *-ja:yʔ* (*-ay*, *-aʔx*, *-aʔ*, *-jaʔ*). One construction is ditransitive and the other is transitive. I will discuss first the general characteristics of double object (ditransitive) constructions and then I will present the two EPC subtypes.

2.2.1 *Double object constructions*

As mentioned above, *mo:yʔ* 'give' is the only underived trivalent verb root in OP. But sentences with a theme/patient as second participant and a benefactive/malefactive/recipient/addressee/locative as third participant are expressed as double object constructions when the applicative *-ja:yʔ* is added to canonical transitive verb roots (TV1, TV2). In (26b) *ʔi=yoʔwe* 'her husband' functions as the primary object of the clause in the applicative construction. In contrast, the third participant of non-applicative clauses is marked as an oblique argument (26a).

(26) a. *kayan ta=tu:tʔ-i* ***wew-pi*** ***tra:ste-jot-pi***
food C3(ERG)-put-CMPLD there-LOC container-inside-LOC
'She put the food there, inside the container.' {C18/8/28}

b. *ʔi=nükx-i=xü=k*
A3(ABS)=go-CMPLD=EVID=ANIM
*ta=tu:tʔ-**aʔ**-i=k* *nü:n* ***ʔi=yoʔwe***
C3(ERG)=put-APPL1–CMPLD=ANIM tortilla A3(POSS)=husband
'She went to leave the tortillas with her husband.' {C18/8/28}

Both secondary and primary objects of ditransitive constructions can be expressed with unflagged nominals and both can trigger third-person plural agreement on the verb (27). Thus, secondary and primary objects are core arguments of ditransitive clauses.

(27) a. Plural Agreement with the Theme (secondary object)
*tan=mü:mi:nˀ-**küx**-ay-u=k* *metzko kawa:yu le:ncho*
A1(ERG)=bring-3PL-APPL1–CMPL=ANIM two horse Lencho
'I brought two horses to Lencho.'

b. Plural Agreement with the Recipient (primary object)
*tan=mü:mi:nˀ-**küx**-ay-u=k* *tan=kawa:yu*
A1(ERG)=bring-3PL-APPL1–CMPL=ANIM A1(POSS)=horse
yoxetunpaˀ-tük
worker-PL
'I brought my horse to the workers.'

A quantifier binding rule indicates syntactic asymmetries among the two objects of ditransitives by targeting the theme. Only the theme can bind with preverbal quantifiers. This is illustrated in (28) where the reading in which the quantifier binds the recipient is ruled out.

(28) *taˀna=k* *tax=mü:mi:nˀ-küx-aˀ-i=k* *kawa:yu-tük*
many=ANIM C1(ERG)=bring-3PL-APPL1–CMPL=ANIM horse-PL
yoˀojwa-tük
man-PL
'I brought many horses to the men.' (*not* 'I brought horses to many men.')

In contrast, the primary vs. secondary object distinction, where the only object of transitives is treated the same as the recipient of ditransitives, controls the three following rules. First, the primary object is overtly marked by the person marker on the verb in the inverse (cf. *mi=* in 29).

(29) *pün **mi=**juy-**aˀx**-anüpa* *tü:nˀi*
who B2(ABS)=buy-APPL1-IRR.INV shit
'Who is going to buy shit from you?' {vend/160}

Second, the primary object functions as the subject in passives of ditransitives. This is illustrated in (30) where the absolutive marker *mi=* refers to the recipient. This type of passive follows the inverse pattern as sketched in (15b) since the outranking participant in the argument hierarchy (the theme) does not match with the highest ranking participant of the clause in terms of saliency (the recipient).

(30) *jeˀ kafet **mi=**yak-tzo:kˀ-aˀx-anüpa*
that coffee B2(ABS)=PASS-pay-APPL1–IRR.INV
'You are going to be paid for that coffee.' {Trab/665}

Third, the actor binds with the primary object in reflexives (31a) and reciprocals (31b) of ditransitive constructions.

(31) a. *ni-tu:t?-a?x-a-j* *tan=kü?kumu*
REFL-put-APPL1–IMP-INV.I A1(POSS)=ring
'Wear my ring!' (Lit. 'Put my ring on you!') {PR/AA}

b. *je?tük=ak* *Ø=ni-pa:t-küx-a?x-ü-w=ak*
they=ANIM B3(ABS)=RECIP-find-3PL-APPL1–INV-CMPL=ANIM
me:nyu *mü:t=ak* *?i=jayko-tük*
money and=ANIM A3(POSS)=sister-PL
'They$_i$ and their$_i$ sisters found money for each other.' {A/RE}

In sum, clauses with TV1 and TV2 verb roots can register an extra-thematic third participant as primary object once the verb root takes the applicative *-ja:y?*. Both the theme and the applicative participant are core arguments in ditransitive clauses; however, what would be an extra-thematic participant for the simple root is treated by most rules as the preferred syntactic object argument in the applicative construction. In what follows I will argue that what has been treated as possessor ascension in other Mesoamerican languages is a type of double object construction in OP.

2.2.2 *External possession and the double object construction*

Similar to *küj-* constructions, a subset of double object constructions has an EP interpretation. The EP reading is obtained when the extra-thematic applied argument is coreferential with the PR of the theme/patient. Sentences (32)–(34) illustrate double object constructions with EP interpretation.

(32) *tan=tükaw=ak* *ta=yakke:k?-**a?x**-ü-pa*
A1(POSS)=father=ANIM B1(ABS)=remove-APPL1–INV-INCMPL.I
tan=tu:min
A1(POSS)=money
'My father takes my money away from me.' {C8/57/50}

(33) *min=tuku* *pün* *mi=ko:puj-**a?x**-anüpa=a?*
A2(POSS)=cloth who B2(ABS)=wash-APPL1–IRR.INV=RLTVZR
'Who is washing your clothes?' {C22/93/253}

(34) *?ü:tz=koj=k=e?* *pro:we-nak* *tan=ja:=yakjüntzi:y?-**ay**-pe*
I=only=ANIM=CLEFT poor-DIM A1(ERG)=MIR=burn-APPL1–INCMPL.T
?i=tü?kxan *tan=jayxe?paj*
A3(POSS)=candle A1(POSS)=daughter.in.law
'I am the only little poor one who burns candles for my daughter-in-law (who has died).' (Lit. 'I am the only poor one who burns my daughter-in-law's candles.') {c11a/75/879}

Sentences such as (32)–(34) have the same formal properties as any other double object construction. First, both the possessed theme (secondary object) and the applied extra-thematic argument (primary object) can trigger third-person plural agreement on the verb. Second, both secondary and primary objects can occur as unflagged nominals and both are core arguments of the clause. Third, the primary object is overtly signaled with the person marker in the inverse pattern (32)–(33). Fourth, the primary object of an active ditransitive with EP interpretation is the subject of the passive counterpart (35)–(36).

(35) ***ta****=yak-tu:tˀ-aˀx-ü-w* *tan=japoyˀu:ki*
B1(ABS)=PASS-put-APPL1–INV-CMPL A1(POSS)=breakfast
'I got my breakfast.' (Lit. 'My breakfast was put to me.'){C22/83}

(36) *jeˀ pa:jjaykak=tük ˀi=kawa:yo-nak*
DEM forest's.spirit=PL A3(POSS)=horse-DIM
Ø*=yak-kay-aˀx-ü-w=aˀ*
B3(ABS)=PASS-eat-APPL1–INV-CMPL=ANIM
'The horses of the spirits of the forest were eaten.' {C8/82/43}

And fifth, the actor of ditransitives with EP interpretation binds with the primary object in reflexives (37) and reciprocals.

(37) ***ta****=ni-yu:k-aˀx-ü-w* *tan=koˀpak* *mü:t tuku*
B1(ABS)=REFL-hide-APPL1–INV-CMPL A1(POSS)=head with rag
'I hid my head with the rag.' {P/AA/13}

The ditransitive construction with an EP interpretation is used when the PR of the secondary object is construed as an affected participant (benefactive or malefactive). A transitive counterpart is used when the PR of the theme is not highlighted as affected (38)–(40).

(38) *nükx-pa ta=mü:-kapx-e* ***tan****=tzüˀ*
go-INCHI.I C3(ERG)=ASSOC-talk-INCMPLD A1(POSS)=mother
'He is going to talk to my mother.' {AA/ND:208}

(39) *ˀi=wüj-pe=k* ***tan****=me:nyu*
A3(ERG)=untie-INCMPL.T=ANIM A1(POSS)=money
'She unties my money.' {AA/ND:268}

(40) *jeˀ=k ˀi=juy-am* ***min****=ka:xa*
that=ANIM A3(ERG)=buy-IRR A2(POSS)=coffin
'He is going to buy your coffin (when you die).' {AA/ND:289}

Tzotzil (Aissen 1979, 1987), Sierra Popoluca (Marlett 1986) and Huastec (Constable 1989) have equivalent constructions to those in (32)–(34). This type of structure has been treated as possessor ascension (PA). Aissen, Marlett, and Constable have argued that the PR of the theme is raised to "clausal 3" or indirect object which advances to "clausal 2" or direct object, putting the "initial 2" (the possessed theme) in "chômage". The analysis offered for these languages cannot be extended to the equivalent construction in Oluta Popoluca for two reasons. First, the "initial 2" or possessed theme in OP maintains syntactic properties which are distinctive for core clausal arguments. The fact that the possessum of the theme can trigger third-person plural agreement on the verb and the fact that it occurs as an unflagged nominal corroborates its core argument status. There is not convincing evidence demonstrating that the secondary object in OP is an inert argument or "final chômeur". Second, for OP, it cannot be sustained that the primary object of the clause in sentences such as (32)–(34) makes no semantic contribution beyond that made in its function as PR of the theme, as argued by Aissen (1987: 128) for Tzotzil. The primary object coreferential with the PR of the secondary object of ditransitives always refers to an affected participant. OP has ditransitive sentences in which the PR of the secondary object is not coreferential with the primary object of the clause. Cases such as (41)–(43) clearly demonstrate that the primary object bears an extra-thematic relation which is independent of the PR of the theme. In (41) the primary object is first person, whereas the PR of the secondary object is second person.

(41) *je? tye:mpo* ***tan****=jo?n-küx-a?x-i-y*
DEM time A1(ABS)=steal-3PL-APPL1–CMPLD-INVD.C
min*=piyu*
A2(POSS)=chicken
'In those times they robbed your chickens from me.'

In (42) the primary object is third person, whereas the PR of the secondary object is first person.

(42) ***tan****=welado:ra-wok tan=yakjüntzi:y?-küx-ay-pe*
A1(POSS)=candle-DIM A1(ERG)=light-3PL-APPL1–INCMPL.T
tan=?esta:mpa-wok
A1(POSS)=Saints'.images-DIM
'I light my little candles to the little images of my Saint.'
{c11a/84/945}

In (43) the primary object is third person, whereas the PR of the secondary object is second person.

(43) *tan=mü:nükx-ay-u=k* ***min=tü*ˀ*kxan*** *ˀa:nima*
A1(ERG)=take.along-APPL1–CMPL=ANIM A2(POSS)=candle dead
'I took your candles to the dead.' {PA2C/9}

Thus, these two facts clearly indicate that the secondary object is not an inert argument, that the third participant bears a thematic relation other than just PR of the theme, and that the EP interpretation of double object constructions is only obtained in those subcases when the PR of the theme is coreferential with the primary object of the clause.

Marlett (1986: 375) has pointed out that Sierra Popoluca's trivalent verbs (i.e., verbs such as 'give' and 'sell' which do not use the applicative in ditransitive sentences with a dative participant) carry the applicative when the theme is possessed. This is taken by Marlett as evidence that the applicative registers the PR of the theme and not an extra third participant since recipients of underived trivalent verbs act as core arguments by default. Similar to Sierra Popoluca, *mo:y*ˀ 'give' in OP does not take the applicative when the recipient acts as the primary object. This is illustrated in (44) where the first person absolutive *ta=* refers to the recipient (primary object) and the verb occurs without *-ja:y*ˀ.

(44) *ta=mo:y*ˀ*-küx-ü-w=ak* *metzko kawa:yu le:ncho*
A1(ABS)=give-3PL-INV-CMPL=ANIM two horse Lencho
'Lencho gave me two horses.'

The OP verb *mo:y*ˀ can take the applicative only when a fourth participant is included in the argument structure of the clause. This is illustrated in (45) where the PR of the theme is coreferential with the extra participant which is not licensed by the argument structure of the underived verb. OP cases such as (45) cannot be analyzed as PA either, since the participant added via the applicative is not a copy of the PR of the theme. The added argument refers to an affected benefactive or malefactive participant similar to what has been traditionaly called "dative of interest" in languages such as Spanish.

(45) *Lencho=k* *ta=mo:y*ˀ***-a*ˀ*x***-*ü-nü-w=ak*
Lencho=ANIM A1(ABS)=give-APPL1-INV-already-CMPL=ANIM
tan=kawa:yu=k xi:mu
A1(POSS)=horse Simon
'Lencho already gave my horse to Simon instead of me.'

In sum, a PA analysis proposed for the EP construction in other Mesoamerican languages is inadequate to account for the morphosyntactic facts that the equivalent construction with the applicative *-ja:y*ˀ shows in OP. Contrary to the PA analysis, I have argued that the participant introduced by the applicative is always a semantically relevant extra-thematic argument of the clause, which refers to the affected participant. It has an EP interpretation only when the primary object is coreferential with the PR of the theme.

2.2.3 *Constraints on the applicative construction in OP and other Mesoamerican languages*

The applicative construction discussed as PA in other Mesoamerican languages presents two constraints. First, the applicative is prohibited when the subject of the clause is coreferential with the PR of the "initial direct object." This constraint is not attested in OP. Sentences in which the subject is coreferential with the PR of the direct object must be expressed as transitive clauses in Sierra Popoluca, Tzotzil and Huastec. In contrast, the OP version of 'Wash your faces!' or 'I found my food' can be expressed with a transitive clause (46a, 47a) or a ditransitive reflexive clause (46b, 47b) where the subject is coreferential with both the PR of the secondary object and the primary object of the clause.

(46) a. *puj-ü-:t* *min=wintojkü:k-tek*
wash-IMP-SAP.PL A2(POSS)=face-SAP.PL
'Wash your faces!'

b. *ni-puj-aʔx-üj-ü-:t* *min=wintojkü:k-tek*
REFL-wash-APPL1-INV-IMP-SAP.PL A2(POSS)=face-SAP.PL
'Wash your faces!' (Lit.: 'Wash yourselves your faces (for your benefit)!'

(47) a. *tan=pa:t-nü-w* *tan=kayan*
A1(ERG)=find-already-CMPL A1(POSS)=food
'I found my food already.'

b. *ta=ni-pa:t-aʔx-ü-nü-w* *tan=kayan*
B1(ABS)=REFL-find-APPL1-INV-already-CMPL A1(POSS)=food
'I found my food already.' (Lit.: 'I found myself my food (for my benefit).'

The second constraint proposed for Sierra Popoluca, Huastec and Tzotzil is that an EP interpretation of ditransitive clauses is only obtained when the possessed nominal is an "initial direct object" (e.g., 'He ate my beans'). That is, the EP interpretation is not obtained in applicative constructions when the possessed nominal is the "initial subject" or "oblique" of an intransitive or transitive clause. In Tzotzil, Huastec and Sierra Popoluca, 'My mother slept' and 'My mother ate beans' cannot be rendered with applicative constructions. In OP 'My mother slept' is expressed with an intransitive clause and 'My mother eats beans' with a transitive clause. However, the OP versions of 'My mother slept on me (I am affected by the fact that my mother slept)' and 'My mother ate tortillas instead of me' are rendered with applicative constructions.

(48) *ta=küj-ma:jʔ-ü-w=ak* *tan=tzüʔ*
B1(ABS)=APPL2–sleep-INV-CMPL-ANIM A1(POSS)=mother
'My mother slept on me.' ('I am affected by the fact that my mother slept.)'

(49) *tan=tzüʔ=k* *ta=kay-aʔx-ü-w=ak* *nü:n*
A1(POSS)=mother=ANIM B1(ABS)=eat-APPL1–INV-CMPL=ANIM tortilla
'My mother ate tortillas instead of me.'

The construction in (48) and (49) is not treated as PA by Aissen (1987: 135–138) and Marlett (1986: 379) since they claim that the extra argument introduced by the applicative refers to "an initial benefactive, malefactive or recipient," whereas in the "true" ditransitive possessor ascension construction the argument introduced by the applicative is thematically irrelevant to the clause. Above (2.1. and 2.2.2) I argued that the argument introduced by the applicative is not just a "copy" of the PR of the nominal involved, as has been claimed by Marlett (1986) for Sierra Popoluca. That is, in OP neither (48)–(49) or (32)–(34) can be analyzed as PA since the extra argument is always thematically relevant to the clause.

2.2.4 *The applicative* ***-ja:yʔ*** *with patient-oriented verbs*

The applicative *-ja:yʔ* occurs not only with TV1 and TV2 verb roots, but also derives bivalent predicates (50b, 51b) from patient-oriented monovalent predicates (IV2). Such derived stems appear in constructions in which the PR of an oblique locative nominal is coreferential with the argument introduced by the applicative. The possessed locative nominal is then an obligatory constituent of the clause. Thus, applicative constructions illustrated in (50b)–(51b) are transitive and have an EP interpretation since an affected participant which is coreferential with the PR of an oblique argument is simultaneously coded as a direct dependent of the derived verb. The intransitive counterparts (50a)–(51a) do not have an EP interpretation.

(50) a. *Ø=ʔit-u=k* *xi:mu* *tan=tük-mü*
B3(ABS)-exist-CMPL=ANIM Simon A1(POSS)=house-LOC
'Simon was in my house.'

b. *ta=ʔit-aʔx-ü-w=ak* *xi:mu*
B1(ABS)=exist-APPL1–INV-CMPL=ANIM Simon
tan=tük-mü
A1(POSS)=house-LOC
'Simon was in my house (and this affected me).'

(51) a. *Ø=ʔo:k-u=k* *xi:mu* *sa:ra=k* *ʔi=tük-mü*
B3(ABS)=die-CMPL=ANIM Simon Sara=ANIM A3(POSS)=house-LOC
'Simon died at Sara's home.'
b. *ʔi=ʔo:k-ay-u=k* *xi:mu* *sa:ra=k*
A3(ERG)=die-APPL1–CMPL=ANIM Simon Sara=ANIM
ʔi=tük-mü
A3(POSS)=house-LOC
'Simon died at Sara's home (and this affected Sara).'

The main features of this type of applicative constructions are: the bivalent verb stem is formed with a monovalent verb root suffixed with *-ja:yʔ*; the first core argument is signaled by the ergative person marker when the verb follows the direct pattern (51b); the second core argument is signaled by the absolutive person marker when the verb follows the inverse pattern (50b); and the possessed locative nominal remains oblique.

The EP interpretation in this type of applicative construction is only obtained with patient-oriented verb roots. Sentences with agent-oriented verb roots suffixed with *-ja:yʔ* are ditransitive and do not require a locative nominal as a constituent of the clause.

Applicative clauses equivalent to (50b)–(51b) have not been reported in other Mesoamerican languages. A PA analysis is very unlikely here since the "host" of the PR which hypothetically ascends to direct object is a locative oblique. Obliques are ruled out as "hosts" by the Host Limitation Law of Relational Grammar (Marlett 1986).

3. External possessor and noun incorporation

OP has complex verbs formed with a noun stem immediately preceding a verb stem. These will be referred to as noun incorporation (NI) constructions (Evans 1996). Several morphological and phonological properties distinguish an incorporated noun from a non-incorporated noun. Incorporated nouns precede the verb stem and follow the person marker, negative marker, valence reducers and increasers (applicatives, passives, causatives), some modals, and incorporated adverbs. Non-incorporated nouns precede or follow the verb complexes which consist of the verb stem and several affixes. Bisyllabic nouns receive stress in the first syllable when they are incorporated, whereas the same type of nouns receive their stress in the last syllable when they are not incorporated. Finally, some nouns exhibit a reduced form when they are incorporated.

OP exhibits the four types of noun incorporation suggested by Mithun (1984). I will discuss only Type II. This type allows the possessor of a noun to occur as a foregrounded participant of the clause by coding it as a direct dependent of the verb. At the same time, the semantic possessum is backgrounded and is incorporated into the verb complex.

3.1 *Type II noun incorporation and external possessor*

Type II NI has been identified in the literature as a subtype of "possessor ascension" or "possessor raising" (Mithun 1996; Velázquez-Castillo 1995). Type II NI is used when the speaker focuses on the effects of the event or state on the PR instead of on the possessed. In OP there are different subtypes of Type II NI. Each subtype can be identified based on the class of verb and the semantic role of the incorporated noun.

Type II NI is possible with agentive bivalent verbs (TV1, TV2) (52), patient oriented intransitives (IV2) (53), non-agentive bivalent verbs (54), and underived and derived trivalent verbs (55), (56). IV1 (agentive monovalent) verbs do not allow NI.

(52) a. IP Construction. TV1 Verb
tan=ʔe:p-pe=k *chuwa* *ʔi=ʔunak*
A1(ERG)=see-INCMPL.T=ANIM John A3(POSS)=son
'I am taking care of John's son.'

b. Type II NI.
*tan=**ʔunak-**ʔe:p-pe=k* *chuwa*
A1(ERG)=son-see-INCMPL.T=ANIM John
'I am taking care of John's son.'

(53) a. IP Construction. IV2 Verb
Ø=ye:k-u *tan=puʔpu*
B3(ABS)=grow-CMPL A1(POSS)=belly
'My belly grew.'

b. Type II NI.
*ta=**puʔpu-**ye:k-u*
B1(ABS)=belly-grow-CMPL
'My belly grew.' (Lit. 'I belly-grew.')

(54) a. IP Construction. NON-AGT-Bivalent Verb
ta=ʔit-ü-pa *chipin* *tan=**küx-**jem*
B1(ABS)=body-have-INV-INCMPL.I smallpox A1(POSS)=body-LOC
'I have smallpox on my body.'

b. Type II NI.
*ta=**küx-**ʔit-ü-pa* *chipin*
B1(ABS)=body-exist-INV-INCMPL.I smallpox
'I have smallpox on my body.'

(55) a. IP Construction. Non-derived Trivalent Verb
tan=mo:yʔ-am=ak *wope le:ncho ʔi=tewa-jem*
A1(ERG)=give-IRR=ANIM blow Lencho A3(POSS)=buttock-LOC
'I will hit Lencho in his buttocks.'

b. Type II NI.
*tan=**tewa-**mo:yʔ-am=ak* *wope le:ncho*
A1(ERG)=buttocks-give-IRR=ANIM blow Lencho
'I will buttocks-hit Lencho.'

(56) a. IP Construction. Derived Trivalent Verb
tan=tu:tʔ-ay-u=k *ʔinyeksyon xi:mu=k*
A1(ERG)=put-APPL1–CMPL=ANIM injection Simon=ANIM
ʔi=tewa-jem
A3(POSS)=buttocks-LOC
'I put an injection in Simon's buttocks.'

b. Type II NI.
*tan=**tewa-**tu:tʔ-ay-u=k* *ʔinyeksion*
A1(ERG)=buttocks-put-APPL1–CMPL=ANIM injection
xi:mu=k
Simon=ANIM
'I put an injection in Simon's buttocks.'

The semantic role of the incorporated possessum varies with respect to each verb class. TV1, TV2 and IV2 verbs can incorporate the theme/patient possessum. Non-Agentive-Bivalent verbs can incorporate the locative/benefactive possessum. Trivalent verbs can incorporate the possessed subregion (a location) referring to the recipient/benefactive/locative noun.

In contrast to Type I NI (Mithun 1984), Type II NI does not reduce the syntactic valence of the verb. In (52b) above, the verb remains transitive (the actor is indexed by the ergative person marker and the verb takes *-pe,* incompletive for transitive verbs, in the direct). The semantic PR, but not the semantic possessum, functions as the second core argument in transitive clauses with Type II NI. This is supported by two facts. First, the PR appears indexed by the person marker on the verb in both inverse (57) and passives (58).

(57) *ta=**ʔunak-**ʔe:p-ü-pa=k* *chuwa*
A1(ABS)=son-see-INV-INCMPL.I=ANIM John
'John is taking care of my son.'

(58) *ta=yak-**ʔunak-**ʔe:p-pa*
A1(ABS)=PASS-son-see-INCMPL.I
'My son is being watched.'

Second, the PR, and not the possessum, binds with the actor in reflexive clauses.

(59) *tan=wa:nʔpe tan=yakniʔo:kanej **ta=**ni-**yoʔk-**xotz-anüpa*
I.want to.kill.myself B1(ABS)=REFL-neck-tie-IRR.INV
'I want to kill myself, I am going to tie myself on the neck.'
{c11a/37/618}

The PR is also treated as a core argument when the verbs involved in Type II NI are monovalent, non-agentive-bivalent, and trivalent.

Tu:tʔ 'put' and *jik* 'spread', among others, allow double incorporation. The noun referring to the semantic theme occupies the position closer to the verb root, whereas the noun referring to the possessed location precedes the incorporated theme (60c). In (60b) the incorporation of the theme makes it possible for the locative phrase, which includes a PR and a possessed nominal, to occupy the direct object position. In (60c) both the theme and the possessed nominal of the locative phrase are incorporated. The PR of the locative nominal functions as the second core argument of the clause.

(60) a. *tan=tu:tʔ-u* *tzoy* *le:ncho ʔi=puʔpu-pi*
A1(ERG)=put-CMPL remedy Lencho A3(POSS)=stomach-LOC
'I put remedy on Lencho's stomach.'

b. *tan=**tzoy-**tu:tʔ-u=k* *le:ncho*
A1(ERG)=remedy-put-CMPL=ANIM Lencho
ʔi=puʔpu-pi
A3(POSS)=stomach-LOC
'I remedy-put on Lencho's stomach.'

c. *tan=**puʔpu-tzoy-**tu:tʔ-u=k* *le:ncho*
A1(ERG)=stomach-remedy-put-CMPL=ANIM Lencho
'I stomach-remedy-put on Lencho.'

3.1.1 *Incorporated nouns and external possessors*

Incorporated nouns in Type II NI refer to items which are inalienable or in close association with their possessors, such as body parts (54)–(56), kinship terms (58), excretions (61), relational nouns (62), and parts of wholes (63).

(61) *ta=**nüʔpin**-pitzüm-pa*
B1(ABS)=blood-go.out-INCMPL.I
'I am bleeding.'

(62) *ta=nükx-am tax=**natz**-witti:yʔ-i*
B1(ABS)=go-IRR C1(LOCAL)=behind-walk-INCMPLD
'I am going to walk behind you.' {C7/45/53}

(63) *tan=**pak**-mo:t-pe chiʔwa*
A1(ERG)=seed-grind-INCMPL.T squash
'I am grinding squash seeds.'

Alienable nouns do not undergo incorporation under Type II NI. Thus, compare (61)–(63) with the ill-formed expressions (64)–(66) involving alienable incorporated nouns.

(64) **ta=**xuʔni**-pitzüm-pa*
B1(ABS)=dog-go.out-INCMPL.I
(Intended meaning: 'My dog is leaving.')

(65) **tan=**kama**-witti:yʔ-pe*
A1(ERG)=corn.field-walk-INCMPL.T
(Intended meaning: 'I am walking in his corn-field.')

(66) **tan=**ʔükxi**-mo:t-pe=k xi:mu*
A1(ERG)=corn-grind-INCMPL.T=ANIM Simon
(Intended meaning: 'I am grinding Simon's corn.')

The PR expressed as a dependent of the verb can be animate or inanimate (63), (67).

(67) *tan=**wintoj**-top-am me:xa*
A1(ERG)=face-clean-IRR table
'I will clean the table (<'table's face').'

Thus, animacy does not play a key role in determining whether a PR can enter into the Type II NI construction. The only restriction is that the PR has to be in close association with the incorporated possessed item by physical contiguity or by a close kinship relation.

3.1.2 *Productivity and lexical compounding*

The NI examples (53)–(56) have unincorporated paraphrases in which the PRs are dependents of nominals functioning as core arguments of the verb. There are, however, many N-V compounds which do not exhibit non-incorporated paraphrases. For instance, the compound verb *yoʔk-tükʔi:yʔ* 'choke on' does not have an analytic counterpart in which the possessed noun *tan=yoʔk-tu* 'my throat' appears as an independent phrase.

(68) a. *ta=**yoʔk-**tükʔi:yʔ-ü-w* *tuʔchi*
B1(ABS)=throat-enter-INV-CMPL meat
'I choked on the meat.' (Lit. 'The meat went into my throat.')
b. **Ø=tükʔi:yʔ-u* *tzuʔchi tan=yoʔk-tu-pi*
B3(ABS)=enter-CMPL meat A1(POSS)=throat-SUFF-LOC
(Intended meaning: 'I choked on the meat.')

Many N-V compounds are verbs which diachronically arose out of Type II NI constructions. The nouns of these compounds were originally body-part terms or relational nouns, but synchronically are never found as independent nouns. For instance, the incorporated morphemes *koʔ-* 'head, top', *ʔüx-* 'back', *natz-* 'behind', and *ni:-* 'body, surface' are part of many verb compounds, none of which have unincorporated counterparts in which the bound morpheme appears in an independent possessed nominal phrase.[7]

(69) a. ***koʔ-* Compounds:** *koʔ-wop* 'cut on top', *koʔ-niʔt* 'bend a protuberant part', *koʔ-kaʔtz* 'prune on top', *koʔ-jeʔpx* 'be hooked'
b. ***ʔüx-* Compounds:** *ʔüx-ton* 'push someone', *ʔüx-kep* 'hound someone', *ʔüx-kaʔtz-jo:y* 'pull a vegetable from the back',*ʔüx-poj* 'kick'
c. ***natz-* Compounds:** *natz-wit* 'follow', *natz-kep* 'look for someone', *natz-ʔe:p* 'to spy on someone', *natz-wop* 'to hit in the back', *natz-piyüʔkʔi:yʔ* 'to run after someone'
d. ***ni:-* Compounds:** *ni:-ta:tzʔ* 'urinate on someone', *ni:-jeʔtz* 'pull leaves off', *ni:-ju:m* 'scrub a surface', *ni:-pen* 'massage'

Other cases of Type II NI have resulted in compounds with a specific meaning which is compositionally opaque; that is, the meaning of the whole cannot be predicted from the meaning of its parts. As an illustration, consider the cases in (70).

(70) a. *ʔaw-pa:t* mouth-reach 'kiss someone'
b. *koxo-tünni:yʔ* knee-stand.up 'kneel down'
c. *koʔ-ju:x* head-cover 'be a godmother of someone'
d. *win-kaʔtz* eye-cut 'clear up the field'

Thus, both the fact that there are frozen compounds without analytic paraphrases and compounds with non-compositional meaning make it clear that Type II NI is a lexical process which cannot be derived syntactically (Baker 1993). This view has been defended by Mithun (1984), Rosen (1989), and Velázquez-Castillo (1995), among others.

4. Summary and conclusions

In this paper I have discussed the two mechanisms used in OP to encode the semantic possessor of an argument as a direct dependent of the verb.

The double object construction and other applicative constructions code the PR of a nominal as a clausal argument, and cannot be analyzed as PA constructions. In the analyses offered for other Mesoamerican languages it has been claimed that the ditransitive applicative clause is a PA construction. The PA analysis is based on the assumption that the argument introduced by the applicative does not have semantic relevance to the clause. The PA analysis presupposes that the applicative argument is a copy of the PR of the "initial direct object." I have offered semantic and syntactic evidence which confirm that the applicative argument is not a copy of the PR but an extra participant with semantic relevance to the clause. My claim is that the EP interpretation of the various applicative constructions is obtained when the PR of the nominal in argument position is coreferential with the extra argument introduced by the applicative. A second assumption of previous PA analyses has been that the possessed nominal phrase becomes a chômeur once the PR has ascended to a clausal argument position. This second assumption was also found to be unsubstantiated for the three OP applicative constructions discussed.

Type II noun incorporation is the second construction used to code the PR of an argument as a direct dependent of the verb. All verbs except agentive-monovalent ones exhibit Type II NI. The semantic roles of the incorporated nouns in Type II NI are: themes/patients, locatives and benefactives. The inalienable nouns which occur incorporated on the verb are all relational nouns referring to body parts, excretions, kinship terms and parts of wholes. The incorporated nouns do not maintain any properties of core arguments. Several tests which identify core arguments showed that the PR instead functions as a clausal argument. Finally, formal and semantic behavior of several N-V compounds, which originated out of Type II NI constructions, was presented to support the claim that this type of incorporation is not syntactically but lexically governed.

Applicative constructions with EP interpretation share some features with Type II NI construction. Both constructions are possible when the PR is conceptualized as affected by the state or action described by the predicate. The theme/patient of bivalent or monovalent verbs is the preferred target for the EP construction. The next preferred role is the locative of non-agentive monovalent or bivalent verbs. The EP interpretation is also available for the third argument of trivalents via Type II NI but it is not available via the applicative construction. Type II NI shows the common restrictions found in other languages of the world with respect to which type of possessed items are accessible for the EP constructions, i.e., only parts of wholes and inalienable nouns can be incorporated. In contrast, the applicative constructions discussed allow the EP interpretation with all kinds of possessed items. This can be explained when one considers that the double object and benefactive (*küj-*) constructions allow the special EP interpretation whenever several structural conditions are satisfied but do not have particular restrictions with respect to the semantics of the nouns functioning as themes.

Acknowledgments

The Oluta Popoluca data come from fieldnotes and texts collected, transcribed and analyzed by the author, gathered during several field seasons which began in the summer of 1994. Field research was made possible through Universidad de Guadalajara, Universidad Nacional Autónoma de México, and CONACYT (1994–1995). Three fieldwork seasons were funded by the following grants received by Kaufman and Justeson: National Geographic Society (#5319–94), and National Science Foundation (SBR-9411247 and SBR-9511713). The Max Planck Institute for Psycholinguistics has financed the investigation from the beginning of 1996 until the present. I am grateful to Antonio Asistente, Lorenzo Molina, Rafaela Santander, Jesús de los Santos, Inez Díaz, Nicolasa de los Santos, Josefa de los Santos, Otilio de Dios, Victor González, Alfredina Asistente, Ruperta Pérez, Mario Melchor, Tomás de los Santos, Bonifacio Canuto and the late Bartolo Flor, Agripino Molina, Claudio Pavón, and Criserio Molina for their continuous cooperation, patience, and generosity. Special thanks also to Felix Ameka, Connie Dickinson, Doris Payne and Søren Wichmann for their comments and suggestions. Any errors are my own responsibility.

Abbreviations

Abbreviations used in this paper: A set A person markers (ergative for independent, absolutive for dependent, possessor marker); ABS absolutive; ANIM animate clitic; ASSOC associative applicative; APPL1 applicative which brings recipients, benefactives, malefactives and locatives into the verb argument structure; APPL2 benefactive, malefactive applicative; B set B person markers (absolutive for independent); C set C person markers (ergative for dependent); CAUS causative; CMPL completive for independent; CMPLD completive for dependent; DEF definite article; DEM demonstrative; DIM diminutive; EP external possessor; ERG ergative; EXCL exclusive; EVID evidential; IMP imperative; INCL inclusive; INCMPLD incompletive for dependent; INCMPL.I incompletive for independent intransitive; INCMPL.T incompletive for independent transitives; INV inverse for independent; INVD.C inverse for dependent completive; INVD.I inverse for dependent incompletive; INV.LOCAL inverse for local constructions; IP internal possessor; IRR irrealis for independent; IRRD irrealis for dependent; IRR.INV irrealis plus inverse; LOC locative postposition; LOCAL local marker (1:2) or (2:1); MIR mirative; NEG negative; NMZR nominalizer; OP Oluta Popoluca; PASS passive; PL plural; POSS possessor; RECIP reciprocal; REFL reflexive; RLTVZR relativizer; SAP speech act participant (first and second person); SAP.PL plural for speech act participants; SUFF unknown suffix; 1 first person; 2 second person; 3 third person; 3PL third person plural agreement.

Notes

1 Monovalent roots are the equivalent of intransitive verbs in other languages. Bivalent roots are the equivalent of both intransitive and transitive verbs in other languages. See discussion below.

2 Sierra Popoluca is also known in the literature as Soteapan Zoque.

3 The person markers are proclitics which occur as independent morphemes or as reduced bound forms. In examples I represent them in their unreduced shape.

4 DeLancey (1981b) uses directive to refer to morphemes that explicitly signal inverse or direct.

5 The local pattern in OP also presents a direct vs. inverse alternation.

6 The term *conflation* is borrowed from Talmy (1985). I use it for the lexicalization pattern in which the inherent semantics of a predicate convey an action or state in addition to a selected participant of that predicate. The conflated participant cannot be expressed by a nominal external to the verb. An English example is the verb *water* in examples like: *I watered the plants. I watered water on the plants* is bad since the explicit theme is already conflated in the verb.

7 Wichmann (1995: 533–536) has reconstructed the forms **hü(x)-* 'back', **ʔaw-* 'pertaining to the mouth', **ni:-* 'surface, corporeal' and **nah-* 'circumvention' as derivational verbal morphemes already present in Proto-Mixe-Zoque.

References

Aissen, Judith. 1979. "Possessor Ascension in Tzotzil." In Laura Martin (ed.), *Papers in Mayan Linguistics.* Columbia, Missouri: Lucas Brothers, 89–108.

Aissen, Judith. 1987. *Tzotzil Clause Structure*. Dordrecht: Reidel.

Baker, Mark C. 1993. "Noun Incorporation and the Nature of Linguistic Representation." In W. A. Foley (ed.), *The Role of Theory in Language Description.* Berlin-New York: Mouton de Gruyter, 13–44.

Clark, Lawrence E. 1981. *Diccionario Popoluca de Oluta.* México, D.F.: Summer Institute of Linguistics.

Comrie, Bernard. 1982. "Grammatical Relations in Huichol." In Paul J. Hopper and Sandra A. Thompson (eds.), *Studies in Transitivity*, *Syntax and Semantics, Vol. 15*. New York Academic Press, 95–115.

Constable, Peter G. 1989. *Basic Clause Structure in Veracruz Huastec*. Unpublished MA Thesis, University of North Dakota.

DeLancey, Scott. 1981a. "An Interpretation of Split Ergativity and Related Patterns." *Language* 51:626–57.

DeLancey, Scott. 1981b. "The Category of Direction in Tibeto-Burman." *Linguistics of the Tibeto-Burman Area* 6.1:83–101.

Dryer, Matthew. 1986. "Primary Objects, Secondary Objects, and Antidative." *Language* 62: 808–845.

Dryer, Matthew. 1991. "Subject and Inverse in Kutenai." In J. Redden (ed.), *Papers from the American Indian Languages Conference, University of California at Santa Cruz, Occasional Papers in Linguistics* 16. Carbondale, Ill.: University of So. Illinois, 183–192.

Dryer, Matthew. 1994. "The Discourse Function of the Kutenai Inverse." In T. Givón (ed.), *Voice and Inversion*. Amsterdam: John Benjamins, 65–69.

Evans, Nicholas. 1996. "The Syntax and Semantics of Body Part Incorporation in Mayali." In Hilary Chappell and William McGregor (eds.), *The Grammar of Inalienability*. Berlin: Mouton de Gruyter, 65–110.

Fox, Barbara. 1981. "Body Part Syntax: Towards a Universal Characterization." *Studies in Language* 5:323–342.

Gildea, Spike. 1994. "Semantic and Pragmatic Inverse: 'Inverse Alignment' vs. 'Inverse Voice' in Carib of Surinam." In T. Givón (ed.), *Voice and Inversion*. Amsterdam: John Benjamins, 187–230.

Givón, T. ed. 1994a. *Voice and Inversion*. Amsterdam: John Benjamins.

Givón, T. 1994b. "The Pragmatics of De-transitive Voice: Functional and Typological Aspects of Inversion." In T. Givón (ed.), *Voice and Inversion*. Amsterdam: John Benjamins, 3–43.

Hockett, Charles. 1966. "What Algonquian is Really Like." *International Journal of American Linguistics* 32: 59–73.

Hopper, Paul and Sandra A. Thompson. 1980. "Transitivity in Grammar and Discourse." *Language* 56:251–299.

Kaufman, Terrence S. 1993. *Mije-Sokean Comparative Grammar*. Pittsburgh: University of Pittsburgh. MS.

Klaiman, M. H. 1992. "Inverse Languages." *Lingua* 88:227–261.

Klaiman, M. H. 1993. "The Relationship of Inverse Voice and Head-marking in Arizona Tewa and other Tanoan Languages." *Studies in Language* 17:343–70.

Marlett, Stephen A. 1986. "Syntactic Levels and Multiattachment in Sierra Popoluca." *International Journal of American Linguistics* 52:359–87.

Mithun, Marianne. 1984. "The Evolution of Noun Incorporation." *Language* 60:847–94.

Mithun, Marianne. 1996. "Multiple Reflections of Inalienability in Mohawk." In Hilary Chappell and William McGregor (eds.), *The Grammar of Inalienability*. Berlin: Mouton de Gruyter, 633–650.

Rosen, Sara. 1989. "Two Types of Noun Incorporation." *Language* 65:294–317.

Talmy, Leonard. 1985. "Lexicalization Patterns: Semantic Structure in Lexical Forms." In Timothy Shopen (ed.), *Language Typology and Syntactic Description*. Vol 3, *Grammatical Categories and the Lexicon*. London: Cambridge University Press, 57–149.

Velázquez-Castillo, Maura. 1995. "Noun Incorporation in Guaraní." *Linguistics* 33:673–709.

Wichmann, Søren. 1995. *The Relationship Among the Mixe-Zoquean Languages of Mexico*. Salt Lake City: University of Utah Press.

Zavala, Roberto. 1994. "Inverse Alignment in Wastek." *Función* 15/16:27–81.

Zavala, Roberto. 1997. "Inverse Clauses with Non-Agentive Bivalent Verbs in Oluta Popoluca (Mixe-Zoquean)." Nijmegen: Max Planck Institute. MS.

Zavala, Roberto. 1998. *Oluta Popoluca Trilingual Dictionary.* Nijmegen: Max Planck Institute. MS.

Syntactic Roles vs. Semantic Roles

External Possession in Tukang Besi

Mark Donohue
University of Sydney

1. Introduction

This paper examines external possession (EP) constructions, and attempts to determine which is more salient in determining the grammaticality of a particular EP construction: the syntactic roles hierarchy (elsewhere referred to as the *grammatical functions hierarchy*, or the *obliqueness hierarchy*), or the thematic hierarchy, a ranked list of semantic (or thematic) roles. Evidence for the relative salience of one hierarchy over the other is drawn from an examination of the role that they both play in determining the grammaticality of EP in Tukang Besi, an Austronesian language from central-eastern Indonesia, and a brief look at EP in other languages.

Based on the data observed and the generalizations drawn from them, we conclude that a theory of grammar which is exclusively based on grammatical functions (or privileged structural positions which are underlying governed by the verb) cannot account for the restrictions observed. Neither is a theory purely based on semantic principles adequate for a model of the constraints on EP, and an attempt to formulate a model which combines features of both these approaches, within the framework of Lexical-Functional Grammar (LFG; Bresnan 1982; Andrews 1996; among others), is presented. The relevance of pragmatic information is highlighted, and a space in the model is made available for it, though this is not the focus of the discussion.

2. Semantic roles and grammatical functions

Various authors have made reference to the explanatory power of a thematic hierarchy, i.e., a ranked listing of the semantic roles that may be borne by arguments and adjuncts of a verb. One of the more recent of these proposals is that put forward by Bresnan and Kanerva (1989), with the following hierarchy:

agent > beneficiary > goal/experiencer > instrument > theme/patient > locative

The idea of this hierarchy as an explanatory tool in grammar is by no means uncontroversial; explicit arguments have been made against it by Schachter (1992) and Rugemalira (1994). Enough evidence exists, however, to assume that individual semantic roles do play a part in the grammars of languages (Simango 1995; M. Donohue 1996b). The working definitions of the different semantic roles I leave to Andrews (1985), but for the purposes of this article assume a definition of *theme* as 'the argument which is affected or undergoes a change of position as a result of the verbal activity' and *patient* as 'the argument which is a theme that further undergoes a change of state as a result of the verbal activity'. Other versions of a thematic hierarchy also exist, such as the version proposed by Foley and Van Valin (1984: 59):

agent > effector > locative > theme > patient

Foley and Van Valin's *effector* corresponds to *instrument* as I use the term; their *locative* corresponds to Bresnan and Kanerva's *beneficiary*, *goal*, and *locative*. See Bresnan and Kanerva (1992) for comments on the differences between these two hierarchies (and others), and justifications for some of the differences. I assume the version of the thematic hierarchy proposed in Bresnan and Kanerva (1989) for purely empirical reasons — see Donohue 1995b for details of the argumentation. I would like to modify it in one regard, in order to emphasize the difference between CORE (terms, nuclear, direct, sister to V or Spec position) and OBLIQUE (peripheral, case assigned by a P) arguments. To this end, noting that all occurrences of locative arguments are oblique, I would propose a subset of the hierarchy that applies to only core arguments, as below:

agent > beneficiary > goal/experiencer > instrument > theme > patient

Both core and oblique lists of arguments refer to positions on this hierarchy, but are in turn ranked with respect to each other — this is a point I shall return to in Section 6.

3. Tukang Besi

Tukang Besi is an aberrant Philippine-type language,[1] with a very mixed syntactic typology, based in Southeast Sulawesi. Orthographic {b} and {d} represent imploded stops; {ʔ} represents a glottal stop. The NOMINATIVE (in the sense employed by Bell 1976, 1983, and Kroeger 1993, to refer to the morphological means used to encode a grammatical subject) case *na* and non-nominative CORE case *te* are used to mark the core nominal arguments of the verb.[2] Prefixes indexing the person and number of the subject are obligatorily present on the verb, which also takes agreement markers for object (arguably (pronominal) clitics, but written here as affixes for simplicity; the analysis does not affect the issues discussed here) if the object argument is nominative. In addition to these two basic transitive sentence types,[3] there is also a passive voice.[4] The paradigm of voice alternations may be illustrated with sentences (1)–(4):

Basic transitive clause, object is nominative:

(1) *No-ʔita-ʔe na ʔobu te kalambe.*
3R-see-3OBJ NOM dog CORE girl
'The /A girl saw the dog.'

Basic intransitive clause:

(2) *No-wila-mo na ʔobu.*
3R-go-PF NOM dog
'The dog is going.'

Basic transitive clause, subject is nominative:

(3) *No-ʔita te ʔobu na kalambe.*
3R-see CORE dog NOM girl
'The girl saw a/(the) dog.'

Passive clause:

(4) *No-to-ʔita-mo na ʔobu.*
3R-PASS-see-PF NOM dog
'The dog was seen.'

In these sentences, the difference between (1), (3) and (4) is explainable through the assignment of degrees of prominence in the discourse; both (1) and (3) represent ongoing discourse strategies, and show focus on the dog and the girl, respectively. In (4), on the other hand, the emphasis is on the event, with no regard for the seer, and very little discourse prominence paid to the dog. Unlike *te kalambe* in (1), the *by*-phrase in a passive clause may not be mentioned, either as a core or an oblique argument, though it is assumed that there is an actor that causes the action to take place.

Only one set of object agreement markers may be present on a verb:

(5) *No-huʔu-ko (*-ʔe)*
3R-give-2SG.OBJ-3OBJ
'She gave (* it) to you.'

Note that in (5) the recipient/goal is marked on the verb as the object of the verb. With the verbs *huʔu* 'give' and *kahu* 'send' (and these verbs alone), a nominal recipient is likewise morphologically marked identically to a direct object, with the nominative or non-nominative core case, though differentiated syntactically. This is in marked contrast to the treatment of beneficiaries, which are morphologically marked with a prepositional/serial verb construction *ako te*, and which may never (outside of applicative constructions) appear in the same morphological guise (in terms of case marking or object agreement) as the object of a main verb.

Possession is indicated phrasally by the use of either a possessive affix, for pronominal possession; or a genitive phrase, for possession by a full nominal or emphatic possession by a pronominal (the alternatives are mutually exclusive). An example of each is given below, and the full set of pronominal possessive suffixes is shown in (8):

(6) *No-ʔelo-ʔe na ana-su.*
3R-call-3OBJ NOM child-1SG.POSS
'She called my child.'

(7) *Ku-ʔelo-ʔe na ana nu wulumbaʔa-su.*
1SG-call-3OBJ NOM child GEN neighbor-1SG.POSS
'I called my neighbor's child.'

(8)

1SG *-su*	1PA *-mami*	1PL *-nto*
2SG *-ʔu*		2PL *-miu*
	3(SG/PL) *-no*	

The same suffixes are used for all forms of phrasal possession, and so there is no alienable/inalienable distinction at a phrasal level. The question of the semantics of possession of different possessums is thus irrelevant, since we are dealing with a category that has the same grammatical realization regardless of the semantics involved, and so may be considered to be represented in the same way. Thus, for example, we find the same suffix *-su* on all of *te atesu* 'my heart/liver/emotions', *te limasu* 'my hand', *te amasu* 'my father', *te wunuasu* 'my house', *te* *pidisu* 'my rubbish', *te karajaasu* 'my work', *te karajaaʔasu* 'the place where I work, my working place', and for some more verbal expressions, such as *te iʔitasu* 'the thing that I saw', *te ibaluakosu* 'the thing that was bought for me', etc.

4. External possession in Tukang Besi: Basics

The following sections present details of the EP construction in Tukang Besi, concentrating on the presentation of data. Attempts at a full generalization or explanation will be delayed until later.

4.1 *Transitive objects*

The ability of transitive objects to appear in EP constructions is illustrated by the following sentences. Sentences (9) and (10) show the basic forms of a clause without EP, and (11) is the equivalent sentence with an EP construction. The pragmatic difference between (10) and (11) is that in (11) there is more emphasis (pragmatic salience, prominence, focus) on the identity of the possessor and the possessor's relationship to the directly affected object (the testability of this pragmatic salience is discussed in more detail in Section 4.4). The sentence in (11) is more likely to enrage the addressee, since it is structuring the information in such a way as to show that the speaker construes the event of striking to have a great(er) degree of effect on the possessor (the addressee in this case), and so maximizes the personal affront, whereas (10) emphasizes the assault on the cousin alone, and not the consequences for the addressee.

(9) *No-peku te tolida-ʔu.*
3R-backfist CORE cousin-2SG.POSS
'He backfisted your cousin.'

(10) *No-peku-ʔe na tolida-ʔu.*
3R-backfist-3OBJ NOM cousin-2SG.POSS
'He backfisted your cousin.'

(11) *No-peku-ko na tolida-ʔu.*
3R-backfist-2SG.OBJ NOM cousin-2SG.POSS
'He backfisted your cousin.'

It is worth noting that there is no EP equivalent of (9), a point to which I shall return in Section 4.4. That is, a sentence of the form shown in (12) is ungrammatical:

(12) **No-peku te tolida-ˀu te ikoˀo.*
3R-backfist CORE cousin-2SG.POSS CORE 2SG

In (12) grammaticality fails primarily because the verb selects for one non-nominative object, yet the clause contains two non-oblique, non-nominative arguments. This is not a universal restriction, since an underived verb like *huˀu* 'give', or many derived verb forms involving applicative or causative morphology, allow two (or more) non-nominative core arguments, as in (13):[5]

(13) *No-huˀu te raja te tuduˀa.*
3R-give CORE king CORE slave
'They gave a slave to the king.'

An important restriction applies to the status of the object in an EP construction: it must be directly affected, adversely, by the action specified by the verb. Compare (11) with the ungrammatical (14):

(14) **No-ˀita-ko na tolida-ˀu.*
3R-see-2SG.OBJ NOM cousin-2SG.POSS
'He saw your cousin.'
(Good with the reading: 'Your cousin saw you.' for different reasons)

Even a pragmatic context to make the fact of being seen obviously adverse does not make an EP construction grammatical if the verb itself does not adversely affect the object. This is illustrated in the more extended piece of discourse given in (15). The '[A/B]' in this example, and examples following, is used when two minimally different alternatives are considered, and the grammaticality of each is judged.

(15) *I molengo molengo atu, no-mai min(a) i ito.*
OBL long.ago that 3R-come from OBL there:higher
'(When it happened) back then, they came from the north.'

Te amai sanggila no-rato-lolaha, no-rato ako
CORE 3PL pirate 3R-arrive-search 3R-arrive PURP
na-l[um]olaha-ˀe…
3I-search.SI-3OBJ
'Those pirates came searching, they came to hunt for …'

na mi(a) u kampo. Kaˀasi, te iai-su
NOM person GEN village alas CORE ySi-1SG.POSS
'… the villagers. Alas, …'

[**no-ˀita-aku* / *no-ˀita-ˀe*] *te* *amai jaˀo. No-tangkapu-aku*
3R-see-1SG.OBJ 3R-see-3OBJ CORE 3PL evil 3R-catch-1SG.OBJ
'… that evil lot saw my little sister. They caught her / *me …'

na *iai-su* *maka* *no-ala-ˀe* *kua melai.*
NOM ySi-1SG.POSS and.then 3R-fetch-3OBJ ALL far
'… and carried her off far away.'

In (15) it is clear that the fact that the narrator's sister was spotted by the pirates had very adverse consequences on the sister, and also by extension on the narrator as evidenced by the use of an EP construction at the end of the fourth line in *Notangkapuaku.* In spite of this, and in spite of the fact that the sighting of the sister by the pirates must be construed as adversely affecting the sister, and by extension the speaker, an attempt to substitute *noˀitaaku* for *noˀitaˀe* in the narrative is viewed as totally unacceptable. Clearly there is more than simple adverse-affectedness at work in determining eligibility for EP constructions. In addition to the pragmatic requirement that the possessor be construed as being affected by the verb clause, the possessum must also be directly affected; that is, it must bear a theme or patient semantic role.[6]

In (11) the possessive marking is still present on the original NP, as well as appearing on the verb; a clause with EP in which the possessum appears without possessive marking in the original NP (if the object is represented as a full NP, and not simply referred to by pronominal affixation alone, as in (15)) is ungrammatical, as seen in (16):

(16) **No-peku-ko* *na* *tolida.*
3R-backfist-2SG.OBJ NOM cousin

Faced with sentences such as these, Tukang Besi speakers *can* interpret the sentence to mean 'Your cousin backfisted you', but the sentence is clearly marked as a substandard production by a language learner, and not the sort of utterance to be produced by a native speaker (the grammatical version of the speakers' interpretation would be *Nopekuko te tolida*). Similarly, it is not possible to express the possessor in an independent noun phrase (*na ikoˀo* or *te ikoˀo* in (17)); it must be marked by a possessive suffix in the NP with the possessum, as in (11).

(17) **No-peku-ko* *na* *tolida-ˀu* [*na* / *te* *ikoˀo*].
3R-backfist-2SG.OBJ NOM cousin-2SG.POSS NOM CORE 2SG

This restriction means that, in effect, the only possessors that may appear in EP constructions are bound pronominals;[7] there is no means by which a nominal possessor can appear in a clause and be interpreted as the possessor of an argument, other than in an attributive genitive phrase, as seen in (18) and (19), which do not display EP. Sentences (20) and (21) show attempts at EP with full nominal possessors, with nominative or non-nominative possessums, respectively.[8] Sentence (20) is ungrammatical because it contains two nominative NPs, with no grammatically expressed possessive link between them and no means of determining which is the subject. Sentence (21) similarly shows two NPs with no expressed possessive relationship between the two, but (because of the different case marking employed) is interpretable as a simple transitive clause.

(18) *No-peku te tolida nu ama-su.*
3R-backfist CORE cousin GEN father-1SG.POSS
'He backfisted my father's cousin.'

(19) *No-peku-ˀe na tolida nu ama-su.*
3R-backfist-3OBJ NOM cousin GEN father-1SG.POSS
'He backfisted my father's cousin.'

(20) **No-peku-ˀe na tolida na ama-su.*
3R-backfist-3OBJ NOM cousin NOM father-1SG.POSS
'He backfisted your cousin.'
(equally bad for any other translation)

(21) *No-peku-ˀe na tolida te ama-su.*
3R-backfist-3OBJ NOM cousin NOM father-1SG.POSS
*'He backfisted my father's cousin.'
(Good with the non-EP reading 'My father backfisted the cousin,' not necessarily 'his cousin', compare with (14))

Finally, the possessum must refer to a body part or cosanguineal kin term in order to appear in an EP construction.[9] Compare the grammatical EP constructions in (11) and (22) with the ungrammatical (23), and the more subtly ungrammatical (24). The latter of these two ungrammatical sentences has a kin term that is not cosanguineal, that is, is related only by marriage, and so is not eligible to appear in an EP construction.

(22) *No-ban-siku-aku na talapihi-su.*
3R-BREAK-elbow-1SG.OBJ NOM temple-1SG.POSS
'He elbowed me in the temple.' (i.e., the part of my head to the side of my forehead)

(23) **No-peku-ko na katumpu-ˀu.*
3R-backfist-2SG.OBJ NOM house.post-2SG.POSS
'He backfisted your house post.'

(24) **No-peku-ko* *na* *sanggalapa-ʔu.*
3R-backfist-2SG.OBJ NOM wife's.sister's.husband-2SG.POSS
'He backfisted your brother-in-law-in-law.'

Interestingly, this same class of objects is also picked out by a restriction surrounding the incorporating verb *hoto-* 'have'. In this case, a construction with a body part or cosanguineal kin term is ungrammatical, but one with (for example) *katumpu* or *sanggalapa* is grammatical.

We may conclude, then, that transitive verbs which allow EP are quite restricted in the form of the clause in which EP can be found. These restrictions can be summarized as follows:

- the possessor must be more salient than the possessum ('pragmatic focus')
- the object must be nominative (and so the verb must appear with object agreement)
- the object must be adversely affected *directly* by the action specified in the verb (that is, the possessum must be a theme or patient, the affectedness of which malefactively impinges on the possessor)
- the possessor must be pronominal, and expressed as a bound suffix
- the possessor must not appear in a separate NP
- the possessum must be a cosanguineal kin term or body part (the class of 'inalienable' possession) of the external possessor

Notice that there is no restriction as to the person/number categories that may be used in EP, as is found in some languages (e.g., Kanum, which restricts non-body part EP to first person singular only, while allowing body part EP for all persons); in Tukang Besi any person or number category may be represented.

4.2 *Intransitive subjects*

In this section we shall see that, in addition to the Os discussed above which are eligible for EP, certain intransitive subjects are also found with EP constructions.

Sentence (25) shows an intransitive subject with an affected theme argument, and (26) is the same sentence with EP; again, the same pragmatic factors apply as were discussed in 4.1; compare these sentences with (9)–(11).

(25) *No-mobela na* *tolida-ʔu.*
3R-wound NOM cousin-2SG.POSS
'Your cousin is wounded.'

(26) *ʔU-mobela* *na* *tolida-ʔu.*
2SG.R-wound NOM cousin-2SG.POSS
'Your cousin is wounded.'

Most of the restrictions listed at the end of Section 4.1 apply to intransitive EP as well, namely the requirement that the possessor may not appear in a separate NP (and may only be pronominal), that the possessive suffixes on the possessum be retained, and that the possessum be inalienable. These are illustrated in (27)–(29); compare (28) with (26).

(27) *ˀU-mobela na ikoˀo [na / te] tolida-ˀu.
2SG.R-wound NOM 2SG NOM CORE cousin-2SG.POSS
'Your cousin is wounded.'

(28) *ˀU-mobela na tolida.
2SG.R-wound NOM cousin
'Your cousin is wounded.'

(29) *ˀU-mobela na sanggalapa-ˀu.
2SG.R-wound NOM wife's.sister's.husband-2SG.POSS
'Your wife's sister's husband is wounded.'

Regarding affectedness, we can state that not only must the possessum be affected, but it must bear a theme/patient semantic role; an affected experiencer is not eligible to appear in an EP construction, thus restricting intransitive EP to a subclass of the unaccusative verbs. Compare (26) above with (30), illustrating the ungrammaticality of agentive subjects in EP constructions; and (31) with (32), showing that experiencer subjects also may not appear in this construction (see M. Donohue 1996a for further morphological exemplification of this split):

(30) *ˀU-koni na tolida-ˀu.
2SG.R-laugh/smile NOM cousin-2SG.POSS
'Your cousin is smiling.'

(31) *ˀU-moˀaro na tolida-ˀu.
2SG.R-hungry NOM cousin-2SG.POSS
'Your cousin is hungry.'

(32) *ˀU-maˀeka na tolida-ˀu.
2SG.R-afraid NOM cousin-2SG.POSS
'Your cousin is scared.'

We can conclude that in addition to the requirement that an intransitive argument must be adversely affected in order to display EP, it must furthermore be a theme or patient.

4.3 *Restrictions: Semantic roles or syntactic roles?*

We have seen that, in Tukang Besi, the principal determining factor for eligibility to trigger EP is the semantic role of the affected item; only arguments bearing a theme or patient semantic role may exhibit EP, and all such arguments appear eligible for EP construction, regardless of whether they are transitive objects or intransitive subjects. The only direct morphological effect that the syntactic role of the possessum has is in determining the position of the EP marking on the verb — as the examples show, when the possessum is the subject of the verb, the EP is marked with subject agreement on the verb; and when the possessum is object of the verb, the EP is marked with object agreement on the verb. In terms of the thematic hierarchy mentioned earlier, these are the lowest positions available for core arguments. The span of the thematic hierarchy that defines the set of arguments eligible for EP constructions is shown in (33):

(33) The thematic hierarchy and EP in Tukang Besi
agent > beneficiary > goal/experiencer > instrument > theme > patient
Available for EP

The ineligibility of non-affected themes to show EP has already been demonstrated for transitive verbs; the ungrammaticality of other semantic roles is shown in (34)–(37) (since no transitive verbs have agent or beneficiary objects in Tukang Besi, applicative verbs have been used in (34) and (35)):

Agent:

(34) *ʔ*U-wila-ngkene-aku na tolida-su*
2SG.R-go-COM-1SG.OBJ NOM cousin-1SG.POSS
'You went with my cousin.'

Beneficiary:

(35) *ʔ*U-ala-ako-aku na tolida-su te kau rumpu*
2SG.R-fetch-APPL-1SG.OBJ NOM cousin-1SG.POSS CORE firewood
'You fetched some firewood for my cousin.'

Goal:

(36) *ʔ*U-hoti-aku na tolida-su*
2SG.R-donate-1SG.OBJ NOM cousin-1SG.POSS
'You donated (food) to my cousin.'

Instrument:[10]

(37) *ʔ*U-pake-aku* *na* *poda-su*
2SG.R-use-1SG.OBJ NOM knife-1SG.POSS
'You used my knife.'

Intransitive sentences have been shown in (26) and (30)–(32); there are no intransitive verbs which take a beneficiary, goal or instrument subject. The absence of transitive subjects is also explained by reference to the semantic role information: there are no transitive subjects that are themes or patients, and so none satisfy the filter seen in (33).[11] There is no need to refer to the syntactic roles hierarchy in order to determine the eligibility of an argument for EP in Tukang Besi.

4.4 *Restrictions: Grammatical functions and voice*

From the evidence so far we might conclude that semantic role identity is the only factor playing a part in determining the grammatical status of EP in Tukang Besi. Nevertheless, it does appear that grammatical relations do play a role as well: as mentioned earlier, the language is a Philippine-type language, and displays the kind of voice system (a la Kroeger 1993) that can not be characterized in terms of syntactic roles (A, S and O). Rather, a pragmatically determined grammatical 'subject' is selected, and marked with NOMINATIVE case (the discourse basis of the two basic transitive clause types presented in Section 3). Importantly, the nominative argument is unique in terms of pragmatic salience and preferred grammatical function status.

We have seen that there is a restriction in Tukang Besi that the argument which exhibits EP must be in nominative case, whether it is an O or (trivially) an S. This point has already been exemplified in (9), and shall not be repeated here. What is worth noting, however, is that, since this voice system operates on the basis of pragmatic salience, we have clear morphosyntactic evidence that EP in Tukang Besi depends on pragmatics as much as it does on semantic roles,[12] and that syntactic roles such as the usually defined '(grammatical) subject' (S and A) and 'object' (O), or structural positions corresponding to these notions, do not play a role in this construction.[13]

5. The grammatical status of the possessor and the possessum

Having established the semantic, pragmatic and syntactic restrictions placed on the possessum in an EP construction, we need to examine the grammatical status of both the possessum and the possessor. Although the possessum is marked with nominative case (see (11) and elsewhere for examples), the position of the possessor might be expected to be the (syntactically) nominative argument. Compare (11) with (38):

(38) *No-peku-ko* (*na iko*ʔ*o*).
3R-backfist-2SG.OBJ NOM 2SG
'He backfisted you.'

We are then faced with, superficially, two morphologically nominative arguments, when only one syntactically nominative argument (= grammatical subject) is allowed per clause. A test for grammatical subjecthood that is fairly robust in Philippine-type languages is the ability to launch floating quantifiers; this test is also valid in Tukang Besi. Examples (39) and (40) illustrate the ability of the nominatively marked argument in a simple clause to launch a quantifier, and the inability of that floated quantifier to refer to a non-nominative argument:

(39) *Saba*ʔ*ane no-lemba-*ʔ*e na kaluku te amai.*
all 3R-carry.on.shoulder-3OBJ NOM coconut CORE 3PL
'They carried all the coconuts.'
*'All of them carried the coconuts.'

(40) *Saba*ʔ*ane no-lemba te kaluku* (*na amai*).
all 3R-carry.on.shoulder CORE coconut NOM 3PL
'All of them carried the coconuts.'
*'They carried all the coconuts.'

In a clause with EP, it is clearly the possessor that launches the floating quantifier, not the possessum.

(41) **Saba*ʔ*ane no-peku-ko na tolida-*ʔ*u.*
all 3R-backfist-2SG.OBJ NOM cousin-2SG.POSS
'He backfisted all of your cousins.'

(42) *Saba*ʔ*ane no-peku-komiu na tolida-miu sa-mia.*
all 3R-backfist-2PL.OBJ NOM cousin-2PL.POSS 1–CLASS
'He backfisted the cousin of you all.'

We must therefore conclude that the morphological nominative case on the possessum NP is not a reflection of grammatical subject status, which is assigned to the possessor. The appearance of a morphological nominative case on arguments without grammatical subject status has precedents in other parts of the grammar; in a passive clause, for instance, the 'subject' is marked with nominative case, but does not display any nominative syntactic properties:

(43) (**Saba?ane*) *no-to-lemba* *na* *kaluku.*
all 3R-PASS-carry.on.shoulder NOM coconuts
'(All of) the coconuts were carried.'[14]

Another argument against the possessum bearing the grammatical subject relation is that in combination with reciprocal prefixes, the possessum appears without nominative case marking, though this cannot be fully explored here.

The core/oblique status of these morphologically nominative but syntactically non-subject possessed arguments is difficult to determine; all that can be said with certainty is that they are outside the VP.

6. Models of EP eligibility

Looking beyond the Tukang Besi data, it appears that EP only rarely applies to arguments other than the core arguments of the verb; I shall take as a working hypothesis the assumption that sentences such as (44) are of at best marginal grammaticality in other languages, just as they are ungrammatical in Tukang Besi:[15]

(44) I-put-you [the rice] [in [your pot]]

(45) **Ku-tau-ko* *te* *bae* *i* *pansi-?u.*
1SG-put-2SG.OBJ CORE rice OBL pot-2SG.OBJ
'I put the rice in your pot.'

This non-occurrence of EP from an oblique possessum is predicted from semantic factors that are inappropriate for EP in this sort of example (low affectedness of the possessor, wrong alienability relationship). This non-occurrence may therefore not necessarily represent a core / oblique distinction, but nevertheless gives an empirical basis for us to restrict our search to non-oblique arguments.

I shall briefly compare the EP construction in Tukang Besi with that in a sample of other languages which display substantially different restrictions on EP. These languages have been selected on the basis of an examination of EP constructions in a much wider range of languages, and are each representative of a 'class' of EP constructions found cross-linguistically.

6.1 *Tzotzil*

In Tzotzil (Mayan, data from Aissen 1987),[16] it appears that EP applies only to the object of the verb, but that there is not such a range of restrictions as to the semantic nature of the verbal activity. The following sentences show similarities between the Tukang Besi and Tzotzil EP constructions (examples (46)' and (47)' have the same translations as (46) and (47)):

Object with and without EP:

Tzotzil:

(46) *A-mil* *k-ol.*
2SG.ERG-kill 1SG.POSS-child
'You killed my child.' (1987: 141)

(47) *A-mil-b-on* *jutuk k-ol.*
2SG.ERG-kill-APPL-1SG.ABS one 1SG.POSS-child
'You killed my child.' (1987: 126)

Tukang Besi translations:

(46′) *ˀU-hoko-mate-ˀe* *na* *ana-su.*
2SG.R-FACT-die-3OBJ NOM child-1SG.POSS

(47′) *ˀU-hoko-mate-aku* *na* *ana-su.*
2SG.R-FACT-die-1SG.OBJ NOM child-1SG.POSS

The differences between the two languages are shown in the contrast in grammaticality between (48) and (48)', illustrating EP with an unaccusative verb,[17] and (49) and (49)', illustrating the ability for non adversely-affected objects to appear in EP structures in Tzotzil, but not in Tukang Besi (the translations are the same in both languages). In both languages EP with an unergative verb is ungrammatical. These data are summarized in Table 1:

Tzotzil:

(48) **L-i-cham-be* *j-tot.*
COMP-1SG.ABS-die-APPL 1SG.POSS-father
'My father died.' (1987: 138)

(49) *L-a-j-nup-be* *ta be* *l-a-tot-e.*
COMP-2SG.ABS-1SG.ERG-meet-APPL on road the-2SG.POSS-father-CL
'I met your father on the road.' (1987: 126)

Tukang Besi:

(48′) *Ku-mate na ama-su.*
1SG-die NOM father-1SG.POSS

(49′) **Ku-po-ʔawa-ngkene-ko te ama-ʔu i tonga*
1SG-REC-get-COM-2SG.OBJ CORE father-2SG.POSS OBL middle
nu sala.
GEN road

Table 1: *Extension of EP constructions in Tzotzil and Tukang Besi:*

	O		S		A
	unaffected	affected	affected	unaffected	unaffected
Tzotzil	✓	✓			
Tukang Besi		✓	✓		

Syntactic role-based and Semantic role-based systems

These data show us that different languages have different tolerances for syntactic or semantic role identity in EP constructions. In the next sections I shall present representative examples of different restrictions on EP eligibility in different languages.

6.2 *Northern Pomo*

The ability of affected theme/patient intransitive subjects (but not agentive ones) to appear in EP constructions is not limited to Tukang Besi; similar facts have also been reported for Northern Pomo. O'Connor (1992: 262–284) discusses the use of the term 'Absolutive' as a description of the range of arguments that may display EP (p. 276–277), and notes that the semantic relation between the possessed body part and the possessor is such that 'any affect (sic) on a body part beyond basic physiological sensations will still, due to the normal undetachability of a body part, have consequences, pragmatic, social or otherwise, for the possessor' (p. 267).

O'Connor does mention the possibility of an agentive argument as a possessor (p. 267), but later (p. 276) notes that 'Agentive subjects may also be ruled out …' A careful check of the whole book reveals that none of the EP examples that she quotes include any agentive possessors. We thus find languages like Tukang Besi and Northern Pomo, in which the semantic role of the possessum is the most important factor in determining eligibility to appear in an EP construction, and ones like Tzotzil (and many others; see papers in this volume), in which the determining factor is objecthood: the lowest ranked (core) syntactic role, as opposed to the lowest ranked (core) semantic role(s).

6.3 *Choctaw*

Looking in the other direction, we also find languages in which EP extends to include the entire range of intransitive verbs; grammatically equivalent sentences comparable to (47)–(49) are given in (50)–(53) from Choctaw (Muskogean, Davies 1986) (similar facts are explicitly reported for Southern Tiwa by Allen et al. 1990).[18]

Choctaw: Object with EP; affected possessor:

(50) *Mĩko am-ofi-t takkon i-apa-tok.*
chief 1POSS-dog-NOM apple 3DAT-eat-PAST
'My dog ate the chief's apple.' (1986: 51)

Non-affected:

(51) *Alla towa ĩ-chim-pila-li-tok.*
child ball 2DAT-3DAT-throw-1NOM-PAST
'I threw your ball to the child.' (1986: 59)

Subject with EP; unaccusative/affected possessor:

(52) *Iyyi-t ã-hottopa-h.*
leg-NOM 1DAT-hurt-PRED
'My leg hurts.' (1986: 46)

Unergative / non-affected:

(53) *Sa-shki hoshi-t ĩ-hika-tok.*
1POSS-mother bird-NOM 3DAT-fly.SG-PAST
'My mother's bird flew.' (1986: 59)

Tukang Besi allows EP constructions in situations analogous to (50) and (52), but does not permit EP with a non-affected object possessum like that in (51), or with a non affected possessum subject such as that in (53). Although Choctaw allows a wider range of intransitive subjects in EP constructions than Tukang Besi, neither permits EP with transitive subjects.

6.4 *Kanum*

Many languages, exemplified here with Kanum ('Pama-Nyungan', southern New Guinea; M. Donohue 1997) shows a highly restricted (proto-typical?) form of EP, in which the possessum must be both object of the verb, and an affected theme/patient, as seen in the following set of examples. In (54) and (55) the object prefix and subject suffix, respectively, are appropriate for the possessum object and the subject. In (56) we see an object prefix that indexes the person and number values of the possessor; this is not possible for the non-affected object in (58). In (57) the person/number values of the possessor may not be reflected in the subject suffixes, or the form of the verb (which in this case shows different forms for singular and plural subjects), showing that EP is not possible for unaccusative subjects, even when affected.

Kanum: No EP:

(54) *Nsâne klawo s-nkw-nt.*
1SG.DAT child OBJ-hit.linearly-T.PAST.SG.SUBJ
'S/he hit my child.'

(55) *T-ayngkângk-ns mllä-ny nsâne yempoka klawo.*
UNACC-fall.PL-T.PAST.PL.SUBJ stone-LOC 1SG.DAT two child
'My two children fell on the stone.'

Object with EP:

(56) *Nsâne klawo b-nkw-nt.*
1SG.DAT child 1SG.OBJ-hit.linearly-T.PAST.SG.SUBJ
'S/he hit my child.'

No EP possible:

(57) **T-ayngkânt-y mllä-ny nsâne yempoka klawo.*
UNACC-fall.SG-T.past.SG.SUBJ stone-LOC 1SG.dat two child
'My two children fell on the stone.'

(58) **Nsâne klawo byew-y.*
1SG.DAT child 1SG.OBJ:see-T.PAST.SG.SUBJ
'S/he saw my child.'

Kanum is clearly the most restrictive language examined so far in terms of the range of situations that allow EP; both semantic role information (affected theme/patient) and syntactic role information (object of a transitive verb) are required in order to judge the grammaticality of an utterance. Transaltions of all of the grammatical Kanum EP constructions are also grammatical in Tukang Besi, which additionally allows EP with a sentence such as (57) (which is comparable to (48′)). In the next section we shall examine a language with extremely unrestricted EP, IlKeekonyokie Maasai.

6.5 *IlKeekonyokie Maasai*

In IlKeekonyokie Maasai (Payne 1997) it appears that EP may occur with any argument of a verb, including possessums which are transitive subjects. Interestingly, the possessor in an EP construction is always expressed as the object of the verb (with a verbal prefix for first (*áa-*) or second (*(ɛ)kí-*) person object; this analysis of the prefixes differs from that in Payne), even when the possessum is the subject (third person, or plural, arguments have no corresponding object prefix; although these possessors may appear in EP constructions with object possessums (p. 403–404), Payne does not give examples of a third person nominal possessor in an EP construction with a subject possessor).

This construction can be seen in (59), showing the two interpretations possible for an EP construction in a transitive clause in IlKeekonyokie Maasai. The 1SG marked on the verb can be interpreted as the possessor of either the subject or the object of the clause.

(59) *Áa-ból* *ɔl-páyyàn* *ɔ-sandúkù.*
1SG.OBJ-open MASC.SG-man.NOM MASC.SG-box.ACC
(i) 'My husband will open the box.'
(ii) 'The man will open my box.' (414–415)

Given that IlKeekonyokie Maasai allows even transitive subjects to be the possessum in an EP construction, it is worthwhile noting that there do not seem to be any restrictions on the semantic roles or affectedness of the possessum; given that transitive subjects are the least affected arguments in any clause, and that they typically bear semantic roles associated with the highest parts of the semantic hierarchy, this is to be expected. Other examples show that EP is not restricted in terms of the intransitive subjects it can take, nor the degree of affectedness of the object of a transitive verb:

(60) *Áa-búúk* *en-kínè.*
1SG.OBJ-shout FEM.SG-goat.NOM
'My goat will bleat.'
(grammatical for IlKeeonyokie Maasai; 411, 413)

(61) *Áa-dɔ́l ɛ́n-káyná.*
1SG.OBJ-see FEM.SG-arm.ACC
'He/she/they see my arm.' (403)

Clearly, IlKeekonyokie Maasai has very few restrictions on the semantic or syntactic role that the possessum must bear, requiring only that it not be an oblique. (Payne 1997: 406 explicitly notes that "in no dialect, however, can EPs be interpreted as owning obliques.")

6.6 *Summary and models*

The five different types of EP that I have described are summarized in Table 2, indicating that a wide range of restrictions on external possession constructions is found, extending from the most highly restricted cases in which only highly affected objects are available for EP constructions, to the more liberal Choctaw pattern in which any argument apart from a transitive subject may appear in an EP construction, regardless of the semantic roles involved, and the highly liberal IlKeekonyokie Maasai form of EP.

Table 2: *The range of arguments eligible for EP*

	O		S		A
	unaffected	affected	affected	unaffected	unaffected
Tukang Besi		✓	✓		
Kanum		✓			
Tzotzil	✓	✓			
Choctaw	✓	✓	✓	✓	
IlK. Maasai	✓	✓	✓	✓	✓

To model this within a formal theory of grammar, we will need to have both semantic role information and information concerning the grammatical function present at the same level of grammar; in M. Donohue (1996b) I argue for this need with regard to relativization strategies, following Andrews (1996). A proposed entry for a verb such as 'see' is that given in (62), in which both a semantic specification of the content of the verb and the semantic roles of the verb participants are given. These participants can be mapped onto argument position in the verb's subcategorization frame following the conventions of Lexical Mapping Theory (Bresnan and Moshi 1990):

(62) PRED: [LCS 'see' (Semantics of 'see') ⟨experiencer, theme⟩ / TERM LIST ⟨__, __⟩]

Given the four different language types (with respect to semantic role or syntactic role restrictions on EP) shown in Table 2, we can model the different restrictions on EP in terms of these two lists: the subcategorization list and the thematic hierarchy list. This is shown in (63)–(67). Tukang Besi only refers to the semantic role of an argument regardless of its syntactic position, whereas Tzotzil and Choctaw only refer to the position in the subcategorization list. Tzotzil specifies the position that is outranked by at least one other argument, thus delimiting the argument which has the grammatical function OBJECT; Choctaw specifies the lowest ranked argument position (which may or may not be outranked by another argument), thus specifying the absolutive position. Kanum requires reference to both the thematic hierarchy (specifying the lowest set of semantic roles), and the subcategorization list (functioning as Tzotzil and Choctaw, respectively, in specifying object and absolutive positions). Finally, IlKeekonyokie Maasai simply refers to transitive arguments that are subcategorized for by the verb; beyond this stipulation, there is no need to refer to either semantic role (on the thematic heirarchy list) or syntactic role (on the subcategorization list) for two participant verbs.

(63) EP in Tukang Besi
TERMS ⟨ …, thm/pt, … ⟩
Available for EP

(64) EP in Kanum
TERMS ⟨ __, thm/pt ⟩
Available for EP

(65) EP in Tzotzil
TERMS ⟨ __ , __ ⟩
Available for EP

(66) EP in Choctaw
TERMS ⟨ (__), __ ⟩
Available for EP

(67) EP in IlKeekonyokie Maasai

TERMS ⟨ ..., ___, ... ⟩
|
Available for EP

Notice that the final specification for availability to EP does not have to refer to notions such as subject or object, but merely specifies the relative position on an ordered subcategorization list of (core) verbal arguments, and in some cases also requires reference to the specific semantic roles borne by that argument.

With the conventions for availability to EP relegated to a language-specific level, all we need ensure is that all the information required is present at the same level of the grammar. In addition to the information schematized in (63)–(67), the model also needs to refer to a degree of pragmatic salience. While I believe that a separate level of pragmatic information representation (a pragmatic-structure, suggested by Bresnan and Mchombo 1987) is the correct solution to the problem of pragmatic input to syntax, given a conventional LFG framework we can represent a pragmatic component in the functional structure. In this way we arrive at an EP structure as seen in (68) (based on C. Donohue 1996). The presence or absence of pragmatic focus determines the choice of which set of features (those of the possessor, or those of the possessum) appears expressed as the direct grammatical function. Reference to the semantic role information of the arguments, specified in the lexical conceptual structure of the verb, determines availability from a semantic role standpoint; and also rules out the transitive subject from consideration in most languages, since transitive subjects are the most highly ranked arguments in any subcategorization frame. For some languages the possessor, if expressed, must be assigned more pragmatic focus than the object; this is the case reported for Maung, mentioned earlier. In other languages, such as Tukang Besi, the focus may be on either the possessor or the possessum. In Tukang Besi the choice of pragmatic focus is made morphologically explicit through the assignment of the grammatical subject properties, assumed to be modeled by a structure like that in (69), representing the voice system typical of most Philippine-type languages (in this case, an Object Voice).

(68)

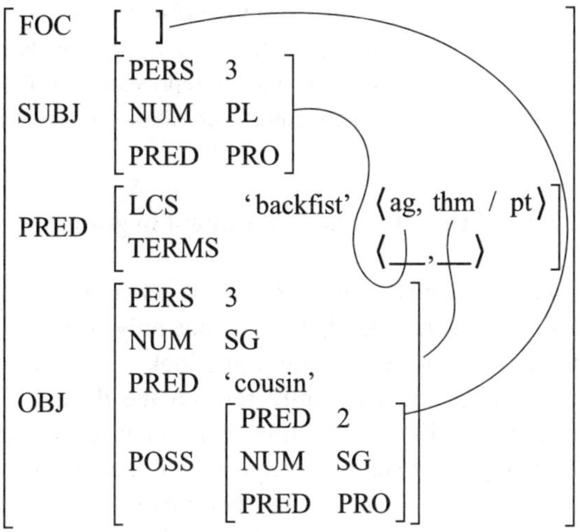

(69)

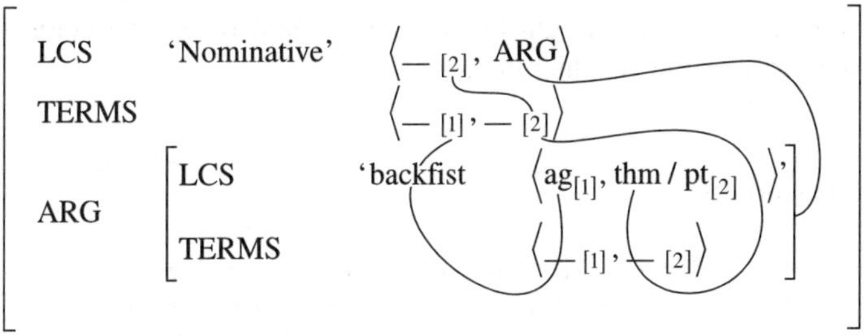

The functional structure in (68), which follows the conventions in Andrews 1996, shows the value of representing the semantic role information as equally accessible as the syntactic role information (which is deducible from knowledge of positioning in the subcategorization frame). The linking conventions, shown here as lines linking positions in the functional structure, indicate that the identity of the subcategorized-for object of the verb has not changed; but that pragmatic factors, namely focus, have overridden the normal assignment of this argument to be the alternative to the agent in the voice system. In (68) the linking is from the possessor to the focus position, rather than from the possessum, and so the possessor is taken as the nominative argument.

The fact that pragmatic factors such as focus have a strong correlate with voice selection is well known (see, among others, Givón ed. 1994); thus, information on focus feeds into the voice system, presented in (69). Tukang Besi has a Philippine-style focus system, but with two core arguments regardless of the choice of actor voice or object voice; this is represented in the term list of the 'nominative predicate', which is an obligatory derivation on any verbal predicate.

7. Conclusion: EP and the informational content in grammar

From the preceding discussion we can see that an account of EP in Tukang Besi does not refer to the syntactic roles hierarchy, but only needs to refer to the thematic role of the possessum. A cross-linguistic look at variation in EP shows that different languages do not necessarily rely on the thematic hierarchy to determine eligibility for an EP construction, but can take the syntactic roles hierarchy as their starting point (in most languages conflated with the notion of grammatical subjecthood, or 'pivot' versus 'non-pivot'), or a combination of syntactic roles and semantic roles. Importantly, based on the evidence presented in the previous section, we cannot assign either one of these hierarchies as the dominant factor cross-linguistically, nor account for the variation with just one or the other of the two hierarchies.

Abbreviations

Abbreviations used in this paper (some portmanteau morphemes are glossed with a combination of these, such as Tukang Besi *-ko* '2SG.OBJ', second person singular object): 1 first person, 2 second person, 3 third person, ABS absolutive, ACC accusative, APPL applicative, ARG argument of predicate, ART article, BREAK forceful verbaliser, CAUS causative, CL class, CLASS classifier, COM comitative (agentive applicative), COMP completive, CORE (non-nominative) core, DAT dative, EP external possession, ERG ergative, FEM feminine, FOC focus, GEN genitive, I irrealis, LCS lexical-conceptual structure, LOC locative, MASC masculine, NI noun incorporation, NOM nominative, NUM number, OBJ object, OBL oblique, PA paucal, PASS passive, PAST past, PERS person, PF perfective, PL plural, POSS possessive, PRED predicate, PRO pronominal, PURP purposive, R realis, SG singular, SI subject infix, T.PAST today's past, TERMS core verbal arguments, TOP topic, UNACC unaccusative.

Notes

1 By this I refer to the morphosyntactic patterns found in the majority of the indigenous languages of Taiwan, the Philippines, Madagascar and western Indonesia (particlularly Borneo).

2 For the rest of this article I shall refer to the core arguments of the verb as subject and object with something approaching the traditional use of these labels, referring to S and A vs. O, respectively (I shall use Dixon's (1979, etc.) terms A, S and O for convenience, to refer to what

are also known as transitive subject, intransitive subject, and transitive object, respectively. For a more rigorous, empirical, definition, see Andrews 1985: 68).

3 The antipassive analysis of the Philippine voice system does not work, certainly not for Tukang Besi. It could be argued that there is really only one basic transitive clause type, the form shown in (1), and that (3) is an 'antipassive' derivation from it; indeed, similar analyses have been proposed for other Philippine-type languages. Problems with this analysis for Tukang Besi are that we have to assume that there is no explicit antipassive morphology on the verb, whereas there is explicit passive morphology in the passive voice, with the prefix *to-*; that the 'antipassive', not the active, clause is used as input to the passive derivation, which cannot appear with object suffixes; that the *by*-phrase in the 'antipassive' is still a core argument of the verb, not an oblique (demonstrable by time-adverb placement restrictions, and case-marking choices); and that the derived 'subject' of an antipassive clause (the seer, in (3)) behaves differently with respect to relativization than does either the derived subject of a passive clause, or the subject of an intransitive verb. For these reasons I have adopted the analysis of Tukang Besi as showing a voice system which I describe as being 'Philippine-type', not adequately characterizable as either nominative-accusative with passives or ergative-absolutive with antipassives.

4 Although the derived subject of the passive verb is marked by the nominative *na*, it bears none of the syntactic properties normally associated with such an argument.

5 It is worth noting that applicative morphology is *not* permitted with EP constructions; compare (11) with (11′):

(11′) **No-peku-ako-ko* *na* *tolida-ʔu.*
3R-backfist-APPL-2SG.OBJ NOM cousin-2SG.POSS
'They backfisted your cousin.'

This sentence is not valid as a benefactive applicative clause either (*'They backfisted your cousin for you.'), since the base object of the verb, cousin, is marked nominatively, when, given the existence of an applied object, that object will appear in nominative case. A grammatical applicative construction would be that shown below, with non-nominative case marking on *tolidaʔu*.

No-peku-ako-ko *te* *tolida-ʔu*
3R-backfist-APPL-2SG.OBJ CORE cousin-2SG.POSS
'They backfisted your cousin for you(r benefit).'

Equally important is the fact that (11) without the NP (that is, *Nopekuko* only) is the normal way to say 'He backfisted you.' and that the NP is required for the EP reading, an unusual finding for a language like Tukang Besi with extensive zero anaphora and many verb-only clauses.

6 Of course, a claim about the kinds of semantic roles that an argument may bear is equivalent to a claim about the event structure of the verb; and so the restriction may be explained in terms of verbal types. There is no difference between these two approaches other than the terminology used.

7 Equally, any bound pronominal (first, second or third person, singular or plural) may show EP. The examples in this paper concentrate on first and second person singular possessors, since they are the possessors most frequently found in EP constructions, but examples like

(11″) *No-peku-kita* *na* *tolida-nto*
3R-backfist-1PL.OBJ NOM cousin-1PL.POSS
'They backfisted our cousin.'

are perfectly acceptable. EP with a third person possessor is harder to demonstrate, since the object clitic representing the possessor will necessarily be *-ʔe*, the same as that used for the possessum; but variation in the interpretation of reciprocal constructions shows that this, too, is a grammatical option (Donohue 1995a: 289–291).

8 It is worth noting at this point that EP is not recursive in Tukang Besi, and that it is not possible, for instance, for the possessor of *ama* in (19) to exhibit external possession and be marked on the verb:

(19′) **No-peku-aku na tolida nu ama-su.*
3R-backfist-1SG.OBJ NOM cousin GEN father-1SG.POSS

9 Note that in the case of a body part there is no question of 'construal of affectedness' on the part of the speaker, since a possessor is necessarily affected by an action affecting any of her or his body parts.

10 Evidence that *na podasu* in (37) bears an instrumental role, and not a theme role, is found in the restrictions on different relative clause strategies, as reported in M. Donohue (1996b).

11 There is not a requirement that the transitive subject bear a particular semantic role in order for EP to be grammatical. The object of a verb like *raho* 'affect' may exhibit EP, even though the subject is clearly not an agent, as long as the object is highly affected.

No-raho-ko na tolida-ʔu te kinda.
3R-affect-2SG.OBJ NOM cousin-2SG.POSS CORE lightning
'The lightning struck your cousin.'

12 This cannot be taken as a universal principle, however. In Maung, Capell and Hinch (1970: 62) note that EP is obligatory in all cases where possessive prefixes may be used on nouns (body parts and certain kinship relations). For example, we may cite

ŋan-ɛjan da ŋa-wija
1SG.OBJ-see ART.CL.IV 1SG.POSS-hair
'You see my hair.'

which apparently does not have a paraphrase with internal possession.

13 Other languages, such as Tagalog (Kroeger 1993: 32–33), seem to refer to the grammatical status (grammatical subject) of the possessed argument as well as its syntactic/semantic roles, allowing only nominative affected Os to show EP.

14 The 'agreement' on the verb in this example is somewhat misleading, since a verb in a passive clause does not need to agree with its erstwhile subject, and may always display a third person 'dummy' agreement marker:

Notosepamo na iaku is as acceptable as *Kutosepamo* (*na iaku*)
3R-PASS-kick-PF NOM 1SG 1SG-PASS-kick-PF NOM 1SG

for 'I was kicked.'

15 For instance, Davies (1986: 60) mentions that 'possessors cannot ascend from hosts bearing oblique relations", and cites the fact that in Choctaw sentences such as

Chokka chim-ia-li-tok
house 2DAT-go-1NOM-PAST

can only mean 'I went to the house for you', and not *'I went to your house'. Choctaw, interestingly, has constraints AGAINST the appearance of 'most kinship terms marked with the inalienable prefix' (1986: 58):

**Ishki-t ã-himmita-h*
mother-NOM 1DAT-young-PRED
'My mother is young.'

For Northern Pomo, O'Connor (1992: 283) mentions a possible counter to the claim that EP must be related to a core argument, but does note that 'not all such sentences are acceptable', suggesting that this is not a productive EP construction.

16 From my limited sample, it appears that Tzotzil is (at least treated as) representative of the majority of languages with EP constructions.

17 See Merlan (1985) and Mithun (1991) for discussion of the range of parameters that can reflect the unergative / unaccusative distinction in a given language.

18 It is probably significant that the EP constructions in Choctaw and Southern Tiwa use the dative agreement set to index the possessor on the verb and not the accusative set of affixes, which (in the main) mark more highly affected arguments. More cross-linguistic work on the differences between EP constructions with accusatively marked possessors and datively marked possessors is needed to verify this as a correlate of the data, or accident of the sample.

References

Aissen, Judith L. 1987. *Tzotzil Clause Structure*. Dordrecht: Riedel Publishing Company.

Allen, Barbara J., Donald G. Frantz, Donna B. Gardiner and David M. Perlmutter. 1990. "Verb Agreement, Possessor Ascension, and Multistratal Representation in Southern Tiwa." In David M. Perlmutter (ed.), *Studies in Relational Grammar 3*. Chicago: University of Chicago Press, 321–383.

Andrews, Avery. 1985. "The Major Functions of the Noun Phrase." In Timothy Shopen (ed.), *Language Typology and Syntactic Description: Volume I, Clause Structure*. Cambridge: Cambridge University Press, 62–154.

———. 1996. *Lexical Functional Grammar*. Course notes, Australian Linguistics Institute, Canberra.

Baker, Mark. 1988. *Incorporation: A Theory of Grammatical Function Changing*. Chicago: University of Chicago Press.

Bell, Sarah. 1976. *Cebuano Subjects in Two Frameworks*. PhD thesis, Massachusetts Institute of Technology.

———. 1983. "Advancements and Ascensions in Cebuano." In David M. Perlmutter (ed.), *Studies in Relational Grammar 1*. Chicago: University of Chicago Press, 143–218.

Bresnan, Joan (ed.). 1982. *The Mental Representation of Grammatical Relations*. Cambridge: MIT Press.

Bresnan, Joan and Jonni Kanerva. 1989. "Locative Inversion in Chichewâ: a Case Study of Factorization in Grammar." *Linguistic Inquiry* 20: 1–50.

———. 1992. "The Thematic Hierarchy and Locative Inversion in UG: A Reply to Schachter's Comments." In Tim Stowell and Eric Wehrli, (eds.), *Syntax and Semantics 26: Syntax and the Lexicon*. New York: Academic Press, 111–125.

Bresnan, Joan and Sam A. Mchombo. 1987. "Topic, Pronoun, and Agreement in Chichewâ." *Language* 63: 741–782.

Bresnan, Joan and Lioba Moshi. 1990. "Object Asymmetries in Comparative Bantu Syntax." *Linguistic Inquiry* 20: 147–185.

Capell, A. and H. E. Hinch. 1970. *Maung Grammar, Texts and Vocabulary*. The Hague: Mouton.

Davies, William D. 1986. *Choctaw Verb Agreement and Universal Grammar*. Dordrecht: Riedel.

Dixon, R.M.W. 1979. "Ergativity." *Language* 55 (1): 59–138.

Donohue, Cathryn. 1996. "A Note on External Possession." MS, UCLA Department of Linguistics.

Donohue, Mark. 1995a. *The Tukang Besi Language, of Southeast Sulawesi, Indonesia*. Doctoral dissertation, Australian National University. To appear in Mouton de Gruyter's Grammar Library series.

———. 1995b. "The Thematic Hierarchy: Evidence from Causatives and Applicatives in Tukang Besi." Paper presented at the Second conference of the Austronesian Formal Linguistics Association. Montréal, Canada: March 25th 1995.

———. 1996a. "Split-intransitivity in Tukang Besi." *Oceanic Linguistics* 35 (2): 294–305.

———. 1996b. "Relative Clauses in Tukang Besi: Grammatical Functions and Thematic Roles." *Linguistic Analysis* 26 (3–4): 159–173.

———. 1997. "External Possession and Kanum". Talk at Concordia University, Montreál, Québec, 10 October 1997. To appear in *Concordia Working Papers*.

Dowty, David. 1991. "Thematic Proto-roles and Argument Selection." *Language* 67: 547–619.

Fillmore, Charles J. 1968. "The Case for Case." In Emmon Bach and Robert Harms, (eds.), *Universals in Linguistic Theory*. New York: Holt, Rinehart and Winston, 1–81.

Foley, William A. and Robert D. Van Valin. 1984. *Functional Syntax and Universal Grammar*. [Cambridge Studies in Linguistics series 38]. Cambridge: Cambridge University Press.

Givón, T. (ed.). 1994. *Voice and Inversion*. Amsterdam: John Benjamins.

Hopper, Paul J. and Sandra A. Thompson. 1980. "Transitivity in Grammar and Discourse." *Language* 56:251–299.

Kroeger, Paul. 1993. *Phrase Structure and Grammatical Relations in Tagalog*. Stanford University: CSLI publications.

Merlan, Francesca. 1985. "Split Intransitivity." In Johanna Nichols and Anthony Woodbury (eds.), *Grammar Inside and Outside the Clause: Some Perspectives From the Field*. Cambridge: Cambridge University Press, 324–362.

Mithun, Marianne. 1984. "The Evolution of Noun Incorporation." *Language* 60 (4): 847–895.

———. 1991. "Active/Agentive Case Marking and its Motivation." *Language* 67 (3): 510–546.

O'Connor, Mary Catherine. 1992. *Topics in Northern Pomo Grammar*. New York: Garland.

Payne, Doris. 1997. "The Maasai External Possessor Construction." In Joan Bybee, John Haiman and Sandra A. Thompson (eds.), *Essays on Language Function and Language Type*. Amsterdam: John Benjamins, 395–422.

Rugemalira, Joseph M. 1994. "The Case Against the Thematic Hierarchy". *Linguistic Analysis* 24: 62–81.

Schachter, Paul. 1992. "Comments on Bresnan and Kanerva's 'Locative Inversion in Chichewâ: A Case Study in Factorisation in Grammar.'" In Tim Stowell and Eric

Wehrli (eds.), *Syntax and Semantics 26: Syntax and the Lexicon*. New York: Academic Press, 103–110.
Simango, Ron. 1995. *The Syntax of Bantu Double Object Constructions*. PhD dissertation, University of Columbia, South Carolina.

External Possession in Sahaptian

Noel Rude
Confederated Tribes of the Umatilla Indian Reservation

Sahaptian (written with final *-ian*) is the name of a language family from the Columbia Basin of the Pacific Northwest of the United States. It contains two closely related but mutually unintelligible languages, Sahaptin (with final *-in*) and Nez Perce. There is considerable dialect variation within Sahaptin, which Rigsby (1965) organizes into three clusters, Northwest, Northeast, and Columbia River Sahaptin. Examples cited in this paper are labeled either Sahaptin or Nez Perce, and the Sahaptin examples are Columbia River unless otherwise noted.

This paper treats external possession (EP) mostly in Sahaptin, with occasional reference to Nez Perce (the rudiments of the Nez Perce system have already been described elsewhere, e.g. Rude 1986a). There are three sections to the paper. The first discusses grammatical relations, the second describes the structures of external possession, the third adds detail in regard to complex genitive constructions. The third section is added to illustrate the extreme complexity of the syntax of EP in Sahaptian. It is not a trivial part of the language.[1]

1. Grammatical relations

Word order is extremely "free" in both Sahaptian languages. It serves only a discourse-pragmatic function (see Rude 1992a); it never distinguishes subject from object. The Sahaptian languages nevertheless have well defined grammatical relations. These are marked through a system of noun case inflections, verbal pronominals, and pronominal enclitics. The Sahaptian languages, in other words, are about equally head marking and dependency marking. I will only hit the highlights of the system here. Those interested in a fuller description should consult Rigsby and Rude (1996), Aoki (1966, 1970), and Rude (1986b, 1994).

1.1 *Nominal case marking*

True syntactic transitivity is coded in Sahaptian by both accusative and ergative cases. Nouns and independent pronouns are case marked, and there is concord between a noun and its modifier.[2]

1.1.1 *The accusative case*

The direct object is case marked by *-na* in Sahaptin (*-nan* in NW Sahaptin) and by /-nen/ in Nez Perce.[3] Accusative case marking is obligatory for humans (1, 2).

(1) *á-q̓inu-ša=aš ɨwínš-na*
3ABS-see-IMPERF=1SG man-ACC
'I see the man.' (Sahaptin)

(2) *ʔe-héx-c-e háama-na*
3ABS-see-IMPERF-SG.NOM man-ACC
'I see the man.' (Nez Perce)

1.1.2 *The ergative case*

Transitive subjects are case marked three different ways in Sahaptin. When the direct object is 3rd person, the subject is unmarked for case (3):

(3) *i-q̓ínu-ša ɨwínš inɨ́it-na*
3NOM-see-IMPERF man house-ACC
'The man sees the house.' (Sahaptin)

When the direct object is a Speech Act Participant (SAP), the subject is case marked ergative via *-nɨm* (4):

(4) *i-q̓ínu-ša=aš ɨwínš-nɨm*
3NOM-see-IMPERF man-ERG
'The man sees me.' (Sahaptin)

In 3rd person on 3rd person transitive constructions, the agentive subject is case marked associative in the inverse (5). Compare the associative in (6).

(5) *pá-q̓inu-ša ɨwínš-in*
INV-see-IMPERF man-ASSOC
'The man sees him.' (Sahaptin)

(6) *wiyánawi-ya=ataš ɨwínš-in*
arrive-PAST=1PL.EXC man-ASSOC
'I arrived *with* the man.' (Sahaptin)

In Nez Perce, the subject of a transitive verb may be unmarked for case but only if the object is (or would be if present) also unmarked for case (7). I call this construction the antipassive.

(7) *hi-héxn-e háama ˀiníit*
3NOM-see-PAST man house
'The man saw a house.' (Nez Perce)

All other transitive subjects are case marked ergative with /-nim/, whether the object is a SAP (8) or 3rd person (9).

(8) *hi-héxn-e háama-nm*
3NOM-see-PAST man-ERG
'The man saw me.' (Nez Perce)

(9) *pée-xn-e háama-nm*
3/3–see-PAST man-ERG
'The man saw him.' (Nez Perce)

1.2 *The genitive case*

The genitive is marked by *-nim* (with allomorphs *-nm* and *-m*) in Nez Perce (10) and by *-(n)mí* in Sahaptin (11).

(10) *háama-nm sík̓em*
man-GEN horse
'the man's horse' (Nez Perce)

(11) *ɨwinš-mí k̓usi*
man-GEN horse
'the man's horse' (Sahaptin)

Though the possessor noun probably most often precedes the possessum, there is no clearly defined noun phrase in Sahaptian. Possessor and possessum are frequently discontinuous within the clause, as in the following.

(12) *ɨwinš-mí i-wiyánawi k̓usi*
man-GEN 3NOM-arrive.PF horse
'The man's horse has arrived.' (Sahaptin)

(13) *sík̓em hi-páayn háama-nm*
horse 3NOM-arrive.PF man-GEN
'The man's horse has arrived.' (Nez Perce)

When a pronoun is inflected with an oblique case, the genitive regularly co-occurs (14). In Nez Perce this is generally true only for pronouns, but in Sahaptin human nouns are also so treated (15).[4]

(14) *ku=taš ana maaní anáw á-sapk̓ukɨn-x̣ naa-mí-yay*
and=1PL.EXC REL however like 3ABS-gather-HAB 1PL-GEN-BEN
'and whichever way we gather them *for* ourselves' (NE Sahaptin)

(15) *i-kʷí-ya tanan-maa-mí-yay*
3NOM-do-PAST person-PL-GEN-BEN
'he or she did it *for* the people' (Sahaptin)

1.3 *Pronominal prefixes*

1.3.1 *Nominative and absolutive pronominals*

Third person arguments are marked by verbal prefix. The subject of an intransitive verb is coded by *hi-* in Nez Perce and by its cognate *i-* in Sahaptin. The pronominal is referential (16a and 17a) or expresses subject-verb agreement (16b and 17b). Note that if the subject in these examples were not 3rd person, this pronominal would not occur.

(16) a. *hi-páayn*
3NOM-arrive.PF
'*He* has arrived.'
(Nez Perce)

b. *hi-páayn háama*
3NOM-arrive.PF man
'The man has arrived.'
(Nez Perce)

(17) a. *i-wiyánawi*
3NOM-arrive.PF
'*He* has arrived.'
(Sahaptin)

b. *i-wiyánawi ɨwínš*
3NOM-arrive.PF man
'The man has arrived.'
(Sahaptin)

Another 3rd person pronominal, Nez Perce *ʔe-* (18) and Sahaptin *á-* (19),[5] similarly codes a direct object when the subject is a SAP:

(18) a. *ʔe-twíikin*
3ABS-follow.PF
'I have followed *him.*'
(Nez Perce)

b. *ʔe-twíikin ʔáayato-na*
3ABS-follow.PF woman-ACC
'I have followed the woman.'
(Nez Perce)

(19) a. *á-twana-š=naš*
3ABS-follow-PF=1SG
'I have followed *him/them.*'
(Sahaptin)

b. *á-twana-š=naš ɨwínš-na*
3ABS-follow-PF=1SG man-ACC
'I have followed the man.'
(Sahaptin)

The distribution of *á-* is a bit more complex in NW Sahaptin. It also codes the subjects of intransitive verbs. For example, (19a) and (19b) above are grammatical in NW Sahaptin, but so are (20a) and (20b).[6] The exact functional distinction between *i-* and *á-* in NW Sahaptin is not very well understood at this time. Because *á-* marks the objects of transitive verbs and the subjects of intransitive verbs (in NW Sahaptin), I have labeled it absolutive (ABS). As we shall see later, this pronominal also marks external possession for 3rd person. These examples can also have a possessive reading, depending on context. The point to note is that in either situation, *á-* marks a core grammatical relation.[7]

(20) a. *á -wiyanawi*
3ABS-arrive.PF
'*He* has arrived.'
'*His* has arrived.'
(NW Sahaptin)

b. *á-wiyanawi iwínš*
3ABS-arrive.PF man
'The man has arrived.'
'*Her* man has arrived.'
(NW Sahaptin)

The pronominal *á-* is ungrammatical with an oblique object (as in 21 with the oblique *tilaakinmíyaw* 'to the woman'). If 'to the woman' is advanced to direct object in a directive construction (as in 22 with the accusative *tílaakina*), then there is agreement with *á-*. The pronominal *á-* thus codes only core grammatical relations, never obliques.

(21) *wína-š=naš tilaaki-nmí-yaw* (**á-wina-š=naš tilaaki-nmí-yaw*)
go-PF=1SG woman-GEN-ALL
'I have gone to the woman.' (Sahaptin)

(22) *á-winan-awa-š=naš tílaaki-na*
3ABS-go-DIR-PF=1SG woman-ACC
'I have gone to the woman.' (Sahaptin)

1.3.2 *The inverse*

The Sahaptin pronominal *pá-* marks *inverse* voice. The significance this has for EP is that the inverse *pá-* is a transitivity marker. With SAP participants this means transitive action from 2nd to 1st person (23a), as contrasted with *direct* action from 1st to 2nd person (23b).

(23) a. *pá-q̓inu-ša=nam*
INV-see-IMPERF=2PL
'You see me.' (Sahaptin)

b. *q̓ínu-ša=maš*
see-IMPERF=1SG/2SG
'I see you.' (Sahaptin)

With 3rd person participants *pá-* implies that the direct object is more topical than the subject, e.g., (24a) contrasted with (24b). The inverse differs from a passive in that the agent is not demoted but rather remains a core syntactic argument and accusative case marking is preserved on the patient noun (see Rude 1994).

(24) a. *ɨwínš-na <u>pá</u>-q̓inu-ša*
man-ACC INV-see-IMPERF
'He sees *the man.*' (Sahaptin)

b. *ɨwínš-na <u>i</u>-q̓ínu-ša*
man-ACC 3NOM-see-IMPERF
'*He* sees the man.' (Sahaptin)

In Nez Perce the equivalent pronominal /pé-/ marks only transitive action from 3rd to 3rd person. Unlike the Sahaptin inverse (where the direct object is primary topic), the subject remains the primary topic and the direct object is secondary topic in the Nez Perce construction.

(25) *ˀáayato-na* pée-xn-e háama-nm
woman-ACC 3/3–see-PAST man-ERG
'The man saw the woman.' (Nez Perce)

1.3.3 *Plural markers in Nez Perce*

Nez Perce (in part optionally) marks nominative subjects for plural by verbal affix. Certain aspectual suffixes have special plural forms, e.g. the imperfective *-s*:

(26) a. *hi-kúu-s-e*
3NOM-go-ASP-SG.NOM
'He is going.' (Nez Perce)

b. *hi-kúu-s-e háama*
3NOM-go-ASP-SG.NOM man
'The man is going.' (Nez Perce)

(27) a. *hi-ku-s-íix*
3NOM-go-ASP-PL.NOM
'They are going.' (Nez Perce)

b. *hi-ku-s-íix háham*
3NOM-go-ASP-PL.NOM men
'The men are going.' (Nez Perce)

Otherwise the prefix *pe-* (or *pa-* by vowel harmony) marks the subject plural:

(28) a. *hi-kú-ye*
3NOM-go-PAST
'He went.' (Nez Perce)

b. *hi-kú-ye háama*
3NOM-go-PAST man
'The man went.' (Nez Perce)

(29) a. *hi-pe-kú-ye*
3NOM-PL.NOM-go-PAST
'They went.' (Nez Perce)

b. *hi-pe-kú-ye háham*
3NOM-PL.NOM-go-PAST men
'The men went.' (Nez Perce)

Number marking in the Nez Perce verb is indifferent to person. Note that the same aspectual forms distinguish number in 1st person subjects (30a and 30b) and that *pe-* also marks plural for 1st person subjects (31b).

(30) a. *kúu-s-e*
go-ASP-SG.NOM
'I am going.' (Nez Perce)

b. *ku-s-íix*
go-ASP-SG.NOM
'We are going.' (Nez Perce)

(31) a. *kú-ye*
go-PAST
'I went.' (Nez Perce)

b. *pe-kú-ye*
PL.NOM-go-PAST
'We went.' (Nez Perce)

Nez Perce number marking operates on a strictly nominative-accusative basis. Another prefix, /nés-/, marks plural objects:

(32) *hi-nées-hex-c-e* *ha?áyato-na*
3NOM-PL.ACC-see-ASP-SG.NOM women-ACC
'He sees the women.' (Nez Perce)

Sahaptin *pa-* is the plural counterpart of *i-* (compare 33a and 33b with 17a and 17b above).

(33) a. *pa-wiyánawi*
3PL.NOM-arrive.PF
'*They* have arrived.'
(Sahaptin)

b. *pa-wiyánawi* *awínš-ma*
3PL.NOM-arrive.PF men-PL
'The men have arrived.'
(Sahaptin)

1.4 *Second position pronominals*

In Sahaptin, second position pronominals obligatorily code SAP (1st and 2nd person) arguments when they are either subject or object. These pronominals, given in Table 1, are indifferent to case. They mark only *core* (Perlmutter 1983) or *actant* (Tesnière 1959) grammatical relations. In transitive clauses case is distinguished by the 3rd person pronominal which is prefixed to the verb. The second position pronominals mark the subjects of intransitive verbs (34).

Table 1. *Sahaptin second position pronominals*

	Singular	Plural
1st person exclusive	*=naš* (*=aš*, *=š*)	*=nataš* (*=ataš*, *=taš*)
1st person inclusive		*=na* (NW *=nan*)
2nd person	*=nam*	*=pam*
1st to 2nd person	*=maš*	*=mataš*

(34) *ɨwínš=naš wá ín*
and=1SG be I
'*I* am a man.' (Sahaptin)

The second position pronominals also code the subjects (35) and objects (36) of transitive verbs.

(35) *šín-a=naš á-laak-ša*
who-ACC=1SG 3ABS-forget-IMPERF
'Who am *I* forgetting?' (Sahaptin)

(36) *čáw=naš mún i-wáwyan-a*
NEG=1SG when 3NOM-whip-PAST
'He never whipped *me*.' (Sahaptin)

"Direct" transitive action (i.e., 1st to 2nd person) is marked by the complex pronominals: =*maš* when both participants are singular and =*mataš* when one or more is plural:

(37) *ku=maš ní-ta x̣ax̣áyk*^{w}
and=1SG/2SG give-FUT money
'and *I* will give *you* money' (Sahaptin)

(38) *áw=mataš nána-ta Nixyáwi-kan*
now=1PL2 take-FUT Pendleton-toward
'*I* will take *you folks* toward Pendleton now.' (Sahaptin)

Just as with the pronominal prefix *á-*, neither are oblique (benefactive, allative, versative, ablative, locative, instrumental) arguments coded by the second position pronominals. Such arguments always occur as independent pronouns.

(39) *pa-wína-m-a inmí-kan* (**pa-wína-m-a=aš inmí-kan*)
3PL.NOM-go-CSL-PAST mine-VERS
'They came *toward me*.' (Sahaptin)

1.5 *Summary*

Grammatical relations are integral features of both Sahaptian languages. They have clear behavioral properties (see, for example, Rude 1997b), and they can be defined morphologically. The morphology, as discussed above, includes nominal case markers, verbal affixes, and pronominal enclitics (2nd position in Sahaptin). These properties are summarized in Table 2.

Table 2. *Morphology of grammatical relations*

SUBJECT	Nez Perce	Sahaptin
Nominal case marking		
Ergative	*-nim*	*-nɨm*
Absolute	-Ø	-Ø
Verb affixation		
Nominative (3rd pers.)	*hi-*	*i-*; PL *pa-*
Absolutive (3rd pers.)	*ʔe-*	*á-*
Inverse		*pá-*
3rd/3rd	*pée-*	
Number	SG *-en* PL *pe-/-in*	
SAP enclitics	*=x*, *=m*, etc.	*=naš*, *=nam*, etc.
OBJECT		
Nominal marking		
Accusative	*-ne/-p*	*-na(n)/-áp/-p*
Verb affixation		
Absolutive (3rd pers.)	*ʔe-*	*á-*
Inverse		*pá-*; PL *patá-*
3rd/3rd	*pée-*	
Number	PL *nées-*	
SAP enclitics	*=x*, *=m*, etc.	*=naš*, *=nam*, etc.

2. External possession

In this section, I argue that Sahaptian has EP constructions, in which the possessor holds a core grammatical relation to the verb.

2.1 *Intransitive clauses*

2.1.1 *'Have' constructions*

The notion corresponding to English 'have' is expressed with an intransitive clause with copula in Sahaptian. The possessor holds a core grammatical relation and the possessum is expressed by a predicate noun. An SAP subject is coded by a 2nd position pronominal, the one irregularity being that a complex pronominal (*=maš* 'you' singular, *=mataš* 'you' plural) — which otherwise marks 2nd on 1st person transitive action — encodes 'you' (41). A 3rd person subject is coded by the pronominal prefix *á-*. If an independent pronoun occurs, it is in the genitive case.

(40)	a.	*wá-š=naš ǩúsi* be-TNS=1SG horse '*I* have a horse.' (Sahaptin)	b.	*wá-š=naš inmí ǩúsi* be-TNS=1SG my horse '*I* have a horse.' (Sahaptin)
(41)	a.	*wá-š=maš ǩúsi* be-TNS=1SG/2SG horse '*You* have a horse.' (Sahaptin)	b.	*wá-š=maš imíin ǩúsi* be-TNS=1SG/2SG your horse '*You* have a horse.' (Sahaptin)
(42)	a.	*á-wa ǩúsi* 3ABS-be horse '*He/they* has/have a horse.' (Sahaptin)	b.	*á-wa pɨnmíin ǩúsi* 3ABS-be his/her horse '*He* has a horse.' (Sahaptin)

To force the 'be' reading, *=naš* must be accompanied by a stressed nominative pronoun, e.g., as in (43b) (compare 43a). Since (44b) and (45b) are otherwise morphologically distinct from (44a) and (45a), the pronouns *ím* 'you' and *pɨ́n* 'he' are contrastive and thus optional.

(43)	a.	*wá-š=naš (inmí) ǩúsi* be-TNS=1SG my horse '*I* have a horse.' (Sahaptin)	b.	*wá-š=naš ín ǩúsi* be-TNS=1SG I horse '*I* am a horse.' (Sahaptin)
(44)	a.	*wá-š=maš (imíin) ǩúsi* be-TNS=1SG/2SG your horse '*You* have a horse.' (Sahaptin)	b.	*wá-š=nam (ím) ǩúsi* be-TNS=2SG you horse '*You* are a horse.' (Sahaptin)
(45)	a.	*á-wa (pɨnmíin) ǩúsi* 3ABS-be his/her horse '*He* has a horse.' (Sahaptin)	b.	*i-wá (pɨ́n) ǩúsi* 3NOM-be he/she/it horse '*It* is a horse.' (Sahaptin)

It is suggested that (43a), (44a), and (45a) are EP constructions because of the presence of the SAP pronominals *=naš* and *=maš* and the 3rd person pronominal *á-*. These only encode core arguments in clauses without a possessor. Just as English 'have' allows for the possessor to be subject, so these Sahaptin constructions allow for the possessor to be subject. This is accomplished by another lexeme in English. In Sahaptin it is another grammatical construction. Compare (46), (47), and (48) without EP. The pronominal *i-* expresses concord with the possessum and the pronominal *á-* with the possessor.

(46) *i-wá inmí ƙúsi*
3NOM-be my horse
'The horse is mine.' (Sahaptin)

(47) *i-wá imíin ƙúsi*
3NOM-be your horse
'The horse is yours.' (Sahaptin)

(48) *i-wá pɨnmíin ƙúsi*
3NOM-be his/her horse
'The horse is his.' (Sahaptin)

2.1.2 *Other EP constructions*

The reason for presenting the 'have' constructions in §2.1.1 is not so much to argue that they should independently qualify for EP status, but that exactly the same *construction* is optionally extendable to all other intransitive clauses. There the possessor is subject and the possessum is — for lack of a better term — chômeur.[8]

(49) a. *wiyánawi-š=naš ƙúsi*
arrive-PF=1SG horse
'*My* horse has arrived.'
(Sahaptin)

b. *wiyánawi-š=naš inmí ƙúsi*
arrive-PF=1SG my horse
'*My* horse has arrived.'
(Sahaptin)

(50) a. *wiyánawi-š=maš ƙúsi*
arrive-PF=1SG/2SG horse
'*Your* horse has arrived.'
(Sahaptin)

b. *wiyánawi-š=maš imíin ƙúsi*
arrive-PF=1SG/2SG your horse
'*Your* horse has arrived.'
(Sahaptin)

(51) a. *á-wiyanawi ƙúsi*
3ABS-arrive.PF horse
'*His/their* horse has arrived.'[9]
(Sahaptin)

b. *á-wiyanawi pɨnmíin ƙúsi*
3ABS-arrive.PF his/her horse
'*His* horse has arrived.'
(Sahaptin)

Now, is the construction in (49–51) really external possession? As we shall see, the possessor has all the appearance of an intransitive subject, that is, with the exception of one feature: The nominal (a stressed pronoun in 49b, 50b, and 51b) remains an oblique genitive. This is also true when the possessor is a full noun, as in (52). So can we really speak of EP here?

(52) *á-wiyanawi ɨwinš-mí k̓úsi*
3ABS-arrive.PF man-GEN horse
'The man's horse has arrived.' (Sahaptin)

That this is a clear example of EP (aside from the genitive *-mí*) is suggested by the verbal morphology, because the construction is optional, and because when it does occur the possessor (not the possessum) is the discourse topic or pivot (for which see Rude 1986a). These factors are discussed in the sections that follow immediately below.

2.1.2.1 *Second position enclitics*. That the 'have' constructions in 2.1.1. and the "other EP constructions" in 2.1.2. are examples of external possession is demonstrated by the presence of the 2nd position pronominal enclitics when the possessor is an SAP. These pronominals otherwise code only core/actant arguments, they do not code oblique arguments (Section 1.4).

2.1.2.2 *The absolutive pronominal*. Note that *á-*, which codes the 3rd person possessor, is the same pronominal that codes 3rd person objects (core-actant arguments) and also, optionally in NW Sahaptin, 3rd person nominative subjects of intransitive verbs. In fact Sahaptin *á-* (and Nez Perce *ˀe-*) provides a good test for transitivity. Verbs in Sahaptian are inherently either intransitive or transitive. The grammatical relation coded by this pronominal prefix (whether direct object or possessor subject), varies accordingly, e.g. if Nez Perce *ˀe-* (or Sahaptin *á-*) translates as 'his', I classify the verb as inherently intransitive, as in (53). If it translates as 'him', I classify the verb as inherently transitive, as in (54).

(53) *ˀa-páayn-a*
3ABS-go-PAST
'*His* arrived.' (Nez Perce)

(54) *ˀa-táamyan-a*
3ABS-hit-PAST
'I hit *him*.' (Nez Perce)

Nez Perce *ˀe-* and Sahaptin *á-* always mark a core grammatical relation, either a direct object (on a transitive verb) or an EP possessor subject (on an intransitive verb).

2.1.2.3 *Number agreement in Nez Perce.* There is another test for core grammatical relationhood in Nez Perce, and this is number agreement (Section 1.3.3). In EP constructions the number markers mark the possessor as singular (55a and 56a) or plural (55b and 56b).[10]

(55) a. *ʔa-páay-c-a*
3ABS-go-ASP-SG.NOM
'*His* is arriving.' (Nez Perce)

b. *ʔa-páay-c-ix*
3ABS-go-ASP-PL.NOM
'*Theirs* is arriving.' (Nez Perce)

(56) a. *ʔa-páayn-a*
3ABS-go-PAST
'*His* arrived.' (Nez Perce)

b. *ʔa-pa-páayn-a*
3ABS-PL.NOM-go-PAST
'*Theirs* arrived.' (Nez Perce)

2.1.2.4 *Optional status of the construction.* The last evidence I shall cite to show that we are dealing with a genuine EP situation has to do with the the fact that the construction is optional. For example, there is no EP in (57) (as indicated by subject-verb agreement via *i-*), whereas in (58) there is EP (i.e., *á-* expresses subject-verb agreement with the possessor).

(57) *i-wiyánawi ɨwinš-mí x̣áy*
3NOM-arrive.PF man-GEN friend
'The man's *friend* has arrived.' (Sahaptin)

(58) *á-wiyanawi ɨwinš-mí x̣áy*
3ABS-arrive.PF man-GEN friend
'*The man*'s friend has arrived.' (Sahaptin)

Here again we can use the nominative number agreement test in Nez Perce. If, for example, we pluralize the possessum, then there can be plural subject-verb agreement only in the *hi-* construction (i.e., with *pa-* in 59), not in the *ʔa-*marked EP construction (60).

(59) *hi-pa-páayn haama-nm láwtiwaa-ma*
3NOM-PL.NOM-arrive.PF man-GEN friend-PL
'The man's friends have arrived.' (Nez Perce)

(60) *ʔa-páayn haama-nm láwtiwaa-ma*
3ABS-arrive.PF man-GEN friend-PL
'The man's friends have arrived.' (Nez Perce)

If, however, we pluralize the possessor, then we get plural subject-verb agreement only in the EP construction (marked by *ʔa-* in 62), not in the non-EP construction (marked by *hi-* in 61).

(61) *hi-páayn hahám-nim láwtiwaa*
3NOM-arrive.PF men-GEN friend
'The men's friend has arrived.' (Nez Perce)

(62) *ʔa-<u>pa</u>-páayn hahám-nim láwtiwaa*
3ABS-PL.NOM-arrive.PF men-GEN friend
'The men's friend has arrived.' (Nez Perce)

The point of this section has been to illustrate the optionality of the process, and therefore to show that EP plays a semantic or functional role.[11] In the introduction to the abstracts for these papers, Doris Payne notes that "EP constructions are most widely employed when the speaker construes a situation as having a clear effect (often psychological or emotional, rather than physical) on the possessor." This is most likely true in Sahaptian, but such information is difficult to obtain (without coaxing from the linguist). Speakers sometimes invoke respect, e.g., 'my father' is supposedly less respectful with EP than without. One thing that is clear, though, is that EP plays a discourse-pragmatic function: The EP argument maintains topic continuity, i.e., it serves the same basic discourse function as subject (see Rude 1986a). In (63) topic continuity is maintained between possessor subject ('his') and the regular nominative subject ('he') via the pronominals *á-* and *i-*.

(63) *ášam <u>á</u>-wiyanawi-ya wáƛ̓i ku ánay <u>i</u>-wiyánawi-ya*
wife 3ABS-arrive-PAST first and after 3NOM-arrive-PAST
'*His* wife arrived first and *he* arrived after.' (Sahaptin)

The 3rd person EP prefix *á-* also maintains topic continuity with a plural subject (coded by *pa-* in 64).

(64) *ana tún <u>á</u>-wa mɨšk^w yáamkt, k̓^w apɨ́n <u>pa</u>-sápsik̓^w a-ta čná*
REL what 3ABS-be belief that 3PL.NOM-teach-FUT here
'The things which are *their* beliefs, those *they* will teach here.'
(Sahaptin)

2.1.3 *Summary*

Either the possessor or the possessum can be subject in an intransitive clause. In Sahaptin a 1st person external possessor is marked by the enclitic *=naš*, a 2nd person external possessor by *=maš*, and a 3rd person external possessor by *á-*. Otherwise the possessum (always 3rd person) controls verbal agreement via *i-*.

In Nez Perce a possessum (like ordinary 3rd person subjects) controls verbal agreement with *hi-*. An external SAP possessor controls zero verbal agreement and an external 3rd person possessor controls agreement via *ʔe-*. In a non-EP construction the possessum controls number agreement, and in an EP construction the possessor controls number agreement.

2.2 *Transitive clauses*

There are four principle strategies for coding possessed objects: 1) detransitivization, 2) accusative concord between possessum and possessor, 3) accusative case marking on the possessum when the possessor is not coded as a noun or independent pronoun, and 4) external possession. The strategies available and their distribution depend, among other things, on whether or not the possessor is coreferential with the grammatical subject.

2.2.1 *Possessor coreferential with subject*

In Sahaptin the first three strategies (not EP) obtain when the possessor is coreferential with the subject. When the possessum is not a kinship term,[12] and when transitivity is maintained (as, e.g., with absolutive agreement *áw-* in 65), an independent possessive pronoun must have accusative concord.

(65) *kúuš=naš áw-ɨn-x̣a inmí-maaman miyánaš-maaman*
thus=1SG 3ABS-tell-HAB my-ACC.PL child-ACC.PL
'thus I tell my children' (Sahaptin)

The same strategy obtains in Nez Perce (66).

(66) *ˀe-héxn-e ˀíinim-ne miyaˀás-na*
3ABS-see-PAST my-ACC child-ACC
'I saw my (own) child.' (Nez Perce)

Otherwise there is an obligatory detransitivization whereby the erstwhile object is neither case marked nor referenced with a pronominal prefix (67, 68, 69).

(67) *lɨmq̓í-ša=aš áčaš*
close.eyes-IMPERF=1SG eye
'I am closing my eyes.' (Sahaptin)

(68) *i-lúluk-ša (pɨnmín) miyálas*
3NOM-nurse-IMPERF his/her baby
'She is nursing her (own) baby.' (Sahaptin)

(69) *héexn-e (ˀíinim) miyáˀc*
see-PAST my child
'I saw my (own) child' (Nez Perce)

If the possessum is a kinship term, 1st person forms (such as *naˀíłas* 'my mother') are case marked with the regular accusative (i.e., *-na* in 70); 2nd person forms (such as *íł* 'your mother') are case marked with the special accusative *-áp* (71); and 3rd person forms (such as *pčá* '(his/her) mother') are case marked with the special accusative *-pa* (72). Full transitivity is maintained in each instance.

(70) *á-túuk-šan-a=aš* *naˀíłas-na*
3ABS-see-IMPERF-PAST=1SG my.mother-ACC
'I saw my (own) mother.' (NE Sahaptin)

(71) *á-túuk-šan-a=nam* *ił-áp*
3ABS-see-IMPERF-PAST=2SG your.mother-ACC
'You saw your (own) mother.' (NE Sahaptin)

(72) *i-túuk-šan-a* *pčá-pa*
3NOM-see-IMPERF-PAST mother-ACC
'He saw his (own) mother.' (NE Sahaptin)

A similar strategy can be seen in Nez Perce where *naˀtóot* 'my father' (73) and *ˀiṁtóot* 'your father' (74) are case marked with *-ap*. Detransitivization, however, is obligatory with *píst* '(his/her) father' (75).

(73) *ˀe-héxn-e* *naˀtóot-ap*
3ABS-see-PAST my.father-ACC
'I saw my (own) father.' (Nez Perce)

(74) *ˀe-héxn-e* *ˀiṁtóot-ap*
3ABS-see-PAST your.father-ACC
'You saw your (own) father.' (Nez Perce)

(75) *he-héxn-e* *píst*
3NOM-see-PAST father
'He saw his (own) father.' (Nez Perce)

Such forms as Sahaptin *pčá* '(his/her) mother' and Nez Perce *píst* '(his/her) father' can occur with independent pronouns. If so, there is accusative concord with the possessum and transitivity is maintained (76, 77).

(76) *á-tuuk-šan-a=ataš* *naamí-na pčá-na*
3ABS-see-IMPERF-PAST=1PL.EXC our-ACC mother-ACC
'We saw our (own) mother.' (NE Sahaptin)

(77) *pe-héxn-e* *núunim-ne pisí-ne*
3PL.NOM-see-PAST our-ACC father-ACC
'We saw our (own) father.' (Nez Perce)

2.2.2 *Possessor not coreferential with subject*

Three grammatical constructions (detransitivization, accusative concord, and external possession) occur when the possessor is not coreferential with the subject. Detransitivization occurs only when the possessum is nonhuman and relatively nontopical (78, 79). The possessor retains its genitive case marking.

(78) *pa-nák̓x̣tu-ša niimí tamánwit*
3PL.NOM-revive-IMPERF our law
'They are reviving our law.' (NW Sahaptin)

(79) *hi-ttóola-ya ʔáayato-m tiwíyext*
3NOM-forget-PAST woman-GEN advice
'He forgot the woman's advice.' (Nez Perce, Phinney 1934: 30:7)

There are two possibilities when the possessum is human (or topical). First, there may be accusative concord; i.e., both the possesor and possessum are case marked accusative (80, 81).

(80) *á-ykɨn-x̣an-a=aš inmí-nan pšɨ́t-nan*
3ABS-hear-HAB-PAST=1SG my-ACC father-ACC
'I used to hear my father.' (NW Sahaptin)

(81) *pe-kiyuu-t̓ipéecwi-s-e ʔimim-né peqéex̣-ne*
3/3–marry-DES-IMPERF-SG.NOM your-ACC sister's.son-ACC
'She wants to marry your sister's son.' (Nez Perce, Aoki 1979: 10:36)

Possessor nouns, at least in Sahaptin, may also show accusative concord (82). (Note again that the noun phrase is not a well developed constituent in Sahaptian. Possessor and possessum are often separated from each other, as in 82.)

(82) *pšɨ́t-na=aš á-q̓inu-ša ɨwinš-mí-na*
father-ACC=1SG 3ABS-see-IMPERF man-GEN-ACC
I see the man's father (Sahaptin)

Second, the possessor may be external, in which case it is the direct object and the possessum has no case marking and controls no verbal or enclitic agreement. The verb carries the applicative suffix (83, 84).[13]

(83) *patá-naksklik-ay-ša paanáy wáwnak^{w}šaš*
3PL.NOM/3ACC-twirl-APPL-IMPERF 3SG.ACC body
'They are twirling his body.' (Sahaptin)

(84) *ʔiceyéeye-ne páhap páa-ʔnaxpayk-aʔy-s-ix*
Coyote-ACC daughter 3/3–bring-APPL-IMPERF-PL.NOM
'They are bringing Coyote's daughter.' (Nez Perce, Phinney 1934: 273:11)

The Sahaptian applicative construction codes both external possessors and objectified benefactives — (85), for example, is ambiguous in this regard. It corresponds to (86) where 'horse' is in the genitive case and to (87) where 'horse' is in the benefactive case.

(85) *áw-ani-yay-a=aš k̓úsi-na tawtnúk*
3ABS-make-APPL-PAST=1SG horse-ACC medicine
'I made medicine *for* the horse.' or
'I made the horse*'s* medicine.' (Sahaptin)

(86) *aní-ya=aš k̓úsi-nmí tawtnúk*
make-PAST=1SG horse-GEN medicine
'I made the horse*'s* medicine.' (Sahaptin)

(87) *áw-ani-ya=aš k̓úsi-yay tawtnúk-na*
3ABS-make-PAST=1SG horse-BEN medicine-ACC
'I made the medicine *for* the horse.' (Sahaptin)

2.3 *Summary*

External possession is possible only when the possessor is not coreferential with the subject. It contrasts with detransitivized constructions (when the possessum is nonhuman and nontopical and the possessor is also not highly topical) and with constructions in which there is accusative concord between possessor and possessum. The direct object in Sahaptian, which contrasts with demoted objects, is clearly a secondary topic (see Rude 1986b, 1988, 1994, 1997b). Where there is accusative concord, the possessum is secondary topic; and where there is EP, the possessor is secondary topic (see Rude 1986a).

3. Complex constructions

3.1 *Multiple possessors*

The Sahaptian system of kinship terms allows for the unambiguous contrasts illustrated below.[14] The first three examples are with an intransitive verb. In (88) the possessum or head noun is subject, in (89) the lower possessor is an EP subject, and in (90) the higher possessor is EP subject.

(88) *natutasa-nmí i-winanín k̓úsi*
my.father-GEN 3NOM-run.away.PF horse
'My father's *horse* has run away.' (Sahaptin)

(89) *natutasa-nmí á-winanin k̓úsi*
my.father-GEN 3NOM-run.away.PF horse
'My *father's* horse has run away.' (Sahaptin)

(90) *inmí=š pšɨt-nmí winanín k̓úsi*
my=1SG father-GEN run.away.PF horse
'*My* father's horse has run away.' (Sahaptin)

The next three examples illustrate the same phenomenon with a transitive verb. In (91) there is no grammatical object and neither possessor is external, in (92) the lower possessor is external (i.e., direct object), and in (93) the higher possessor is external (i.e., direct object).

(91) *i-q̓ínu-šan-a natutasa-nmí k̓úsi*
3NOM-see-IMPERF-PAST my.father-GEN horse
'He saw my father's horse.' (Sahaptin)

(92) *i-q̓ínw-ay-šan-a natútasa-na k̓úsi*
3NOM-see-APPL-IMPERF-PAST my.father-ACC horse
'He saw my *father's* horse.' (Sahaptin)

(93) *i-q̓ínw-ay-šan-a=aš pšɨt-nmí k̓úsi*
3NOM-see-APPL-IMPERF-PAST=1SG father-GEN horse
'He saw *my* father's horse.' (Sahaptin)

3.2 *Feeding from the directive*

Both Sahaptian languages have constructions which "promote" an oblique semantic case role to direct object (see Rude 1991a). Most typically (but not necessarily always) this oblique argument is human. For example, in (94) an oblique allative noun is case marked *-yaw*. In the directive construction in (95), however, the oblique case role is coded by the verbal suffix *-awa* and the noun is case marked accusative.

(94) *i-wínan-a ɨníit-yaw*
3NOM-go-PAST house-ALL
'He went *to* the house.' (Sahaptin)

(95) *i-wínan-awan-a miyúux̣-na*
3NOM-go-DIR-PAST chief-ACC
'He went *to* the chief.' (Sahaptin)

This human noun is coreferentially possessed in (96) and hence the case marker *-pa* occurs. When the possessor is not coreferential, EP is required (97). In other words, the directive (and other such constructions, see Rude 1986b, 1991a) feeds the EP applicative.

(96) *i-wínan-awan-a pčá-pa*
3NOM-go-DIR-PAST mother-ACC
'He went *to* his (own) mother.' (Sahaptin)

(97) *i-wínan-awa-y-a pčá*
3NOM-go-DIR-APPL-PAST mother
'He went *to his* (someone else's) mother.' (Sahaptin)

3.3 *Genitive subject of complement*

3.3.1 *Subject complement*

The subject in a nominalized construction is regularly put in the genitive case. This genitive is subject to external possession, i.e., as a core argument of a main clause. The process is optional. In the following sentences with subject complements, there is EP in (98) and no EP in (99).

(98) *ku* k^{w}*ná i-wɨ́šayčɨn-x̣an-a*
and there 3NOM-stay-HAB-PAST
tanan-maa-mí káˀwi-t wíwnu-na
person-PL-GEN feast.first-NMLZR huckleberries-ACC
'*And the people feasting first on the huckleberries* would stay there.' (Sahaptin)

(99) *ku* k^{w}*ná á-wšayčɨn-x̣an-a*
and there 3ABS-stay-HAB-PAST
tanan-maa-mí káˀwi-t wíwnu-na
person-PL-GEN feast.first-NMLZR huckleberries-ACC
'And *the people* feasting first on the huckleberries *would stay there*.' (Sahaptin)

3.3.2 *Object complement*

A main verb and complement with nominalized verb undergo clause merger in Sahaptian (the words can occur in any order).[15] The subject in an object complement can be construed either as a genitive subject of the complement (100) or as a dative object of the main verb (101), with the latter considered a species of raising.

(100) *pa-tq̓íx̣-šan-a tilaaki-nmí wína-t-ay*
3PL.NOM-want-IMPERF-PAST woman-GEN go-NMLZR-BEN
'They wanted the woman to go along.' (Sahaptin)

(101) *pa-tq̓íx̣-šan-a tilaaki-nmí-yaw wína-t-ay*
3PL.NOM-want-IMPERF-PAST woman-GEN-DAT go-NMLZR-BEN
'They wanted the woman to go along.' (Sahaptin)

Constructions with dative object (marked by *-yaw* in Sahaptin, as in 101) are subject to "dative shift" where the dative NP can also become the direct object. Example (101) is no exception, as the alternative coding strategy in (102) shows (see Rude 1997b).

(102) *pa-tq̓íx̣-šan-a tílaaki-na wína-t-ay*
3PL.NOM-want-IMPERF-PAST woman-ACC go-NMLZR-BEN
'They wanted the woman to go along.' (Sahaptin)

If the subject of the complement is construed as a possessor (as in 110 above), it is then subject to external possession, as (103) shows.

(103) *pa-tq̓íx̣n-ay-šan-a tílaaki-na wína-t-ay*
3PL.NOM-want-APPL-IMPERF-PAST woman-ACC go-NMLZR-BEN
'They wanted the woman to go along.' (Sahaptin)

This dual origin (whether historical or synchronically motivated) explains the optionality of the applicative (compare 102 and 103) when the subject in an object complement becomes the direct object of the matrix verb. When there is no applicative marker, the derivation is as in (104).

(104) [possessor]-ACC < [possessor]-GEN-DAT (by "dative shift")
[possessor]-GEN-DAT < [possessor]-GEN (by "raising")

The applicative occurs when the derivation (or construal) is as in (105).

(105) [possessor]-ACC < [possessor]-GEN (by "EP raising")

3.4 *Summary*

The data suggest the syntactic hierarchy in (106) for accessibility to EP, where the criterion is the grammatical relation of the genitive construction. In Sahaptian more obligatory EP situations arise with O, and EP is excluded entirely from A.

(106) A > S > O

Aside from the syntactic distribution suggested in (106), topicality is perhaps the most salient feature of EP in Sahaptian (see Rude 1986a). The more topical the possessor (in contrast to the possessum), the more likely it will be externally possessed (and the possessum downgraded). However, the humanness of the possessum is a complicating factor. If the possessum is human, the likelihood for EP in the direct object increases.

Given that "EP constructions are most widely employed when the speaker construes a situation as having a clear effect (often psychological or emotional, rather than physical) on the possessor" (Payne and Barshi, this volume), one can see here a direct relation to topicality. The core participants in a discourse (coded as subjects and objects) are also the most topical, and these certainly ought to be those arguments most affected (emotionally and otherwise) by the events and states described.

Although we can explain this tight interplay between syntax, semantics and discourse, we must not forget the validity of all three linguistic domains (see Givón 1995). Grammatical relations, topicality, semantic case roles, and affectedness (emotional and otherwise) are all dissociable to one degree or another, and it is unlikely that we can reduce the function of EP, at least universally, to any one of these domains.

Acknowledgments

Support for this research was provided by the Confederated Tribes of the Umatilla Indian Reservation, by Cátedras Patrimonial Nivel II (Consejo Nacional de Ciencia y Tecnología, México, 1994–1996), and by the National Science Foundation (BNS 8919577). I also wish to thank the many Sahaptin and Nez Perce consultants with whom I have worked over the years. Though too numerous to mention them all individually, I would like to single out in particular Inez Spino Reves and Lucy Yettona John (Columbia River Sahaptin), Elizabeth Jones (Northeast Sahaptin), and Lottie Moody (Nez Perce).

Abbreviations

Abbreviations used in this paper: 1 First person; 2 Second person; 3 Third person; - Affix boundary; = Clitic boundary; A transitive subject; ABS Absolutive; ACC Accusative; ALL Allative; APPL Applicative; ASP Aspect; ASSOC Associative; CSL Cislocative; CR Columbia River; DAT Dative; EP External Possession; EXC Exclusive; FUT Future; GEN Genitive; HAB Habitual; IMPV Imperfective; INC Inclusive; INSTR Instrument; LOC Locative; MOD Modal; NMLZR Nominalizer; NE Northeast; NEG Negative; NW Northwest; NOM Nominative; O grammatical object; PF Present perfect; PL Plural; PP Past participle; PST Past; REL Relative; REFL Reflexive; S intransitive subject; SAP Speech Act Participant; SG Singular; TNS Tense; VRS Versative; Y/NQ Yes-No question.

Notes

1 Though there is no grammatical gender in Sahaptian, I use 'he/him' unless the original context dictates otherwise.

2 Ergative case marking is not equal to marking the semantic agent (Dixon 1994). The ergative case is a *transitive* subject (whether agent or dative) and thus is as much a marker of transitivity as is the accusative case. See Rude (1991b, 1997a) for speculation on the diachronic development of both noun cases in Sahaptian.

3 I generally cite Nez Perce morphemes in angled brackets, e.g. /-nen/, rather than *-ne*. Nez Perce phonology is complex (much more so than Sahaptin), and this will eliminate the need to cite all the various allomorphs.

4 The Sahaptian oblique noun cases include a benefactive, allative/dative ('to'), versative ('toward'), ablative, locative, and instrumental. Note that underlined morphemes in the examples are italicized in the translation.

5 This has a morphophonemic variant *ˀew-* in Nez Perce and *áw-* in Sahaptin.

6 Also unlike NE and CR Sahaptin (and Nez Perce), NW Sahaptin also allows zero in this environment, e.g. *wiyánawi* 'he/she/it has arrived' and *wiyánawi ɨwínš* 'the man has arrived'.

7 This intransitive subject function in NW Sahaptin may be old, *i-* and *á-* having once marked a proximate-obviative contrast. If so, this might help explain the pathway for the present EP function of *á-*.

8 *Chômeur* is a handy term borrowed from Relational Grammar (Perlmutter 1983).

9 As explained earlier, this clause — apart from a broader context — would be ambiguous in NW Sahaptin (not in CR or NE Sahaptin, nor is the equivalent construction in Nez Perce ambiguous). In NW Sahaptin this could mean either 'His/their horse has arrived' or 'He/they has/have arrived'. This point is not pertinent to the discussion at hand, except for what it might have to say in regard to the historical development of *á-* as an EP marker. It is mentioned only for the sake of those who may have some knowledge of NW Sahaptin, such as through the texts preserved in Jacobs (1929).

10 For a detailed discussion of the Sahaptian inflectional suffix complex, see Rude (1996).

11 Languages abhore absolute synonymy, and thus where a construction is "optional" one looks

for less obvious semantic distinctions and/or discourse-pragmatic function. See Givón (1984, 1990).

12 For a fuller treatment of the grammar of kinship terms, see Rude (1989).

13 The applicative morphemes are historically *-ʔey and *-ʔini, both of which can be identified as originally verbs for 'give' (see Rude 1991). Both morphemes are found in Nez Perce and in NE Sahaptin where their occurrence is morphophonemically conditioned. Only *-ʔey occurs in CR Sahaptin and only *-ʔini NW Sahaptin.

14 Examples (98–103) are from Warm Springs Sahaptin (a CR dialect) and are taken from Rude (1997b).

15 For more extensive description of the Sahaptin dative shift, see Rude (1992b).

References

Aoki, Haruo. 1966. "Nez Perce and Proto-Sahaptian Kinship Terms." *International Journal of American Linguistics* 32: 357–368.

Aoki, Haruo. 1970. *Nez Perce Grammar.* Berkeley and Los Angeles: University of California Press. [University of California Publications in Linguistics, Vol. 62].

Aoki, Haruo. 1979. *Nez Perce Texts.* Berkeley and Los Angeles: University of California Press. [University of California Publications in Linguistics, Vol. 90].

Dixon, R. M. W. 1994. *Ergativity.* Cambridge: Cambridge University Press. [Cambridge Studies in Linguistics, Vol. 69].

Givón, T. 1984, 1990. *Syntax: A Functional-Typological Introduction.* Vols. 1&2. Amsterdam and Philadelphia: John Benjamins.

Givón, T. 1995. *Functionalism and Grammar.* Amsterdam and Philadelphia: John Benjamins.

Jacobs, Melville. 1929. *Northwest Sahaptin Texts, 1.* Seattle: University of Washington Press, 175–244. [University of Washington Publications in Anthropology, Vol. 2, No. 6].

Perlmutter, David (ed.) 1983. *Studies in Relational Grammar 1.* Chicago: University of Chicago Press.

Phinney, Archie. 1934. *Nez Percé Texts.* New York: Columbia University Press. [Columbia University Contributions to Anthropology, Vol. 25].

Rigsby, Bruce. 1965. *Linguistic Relations in the Southern Plateau.* Unpublished PhD dissertation, University of Oregon.

Rigsby, Bruce, and Noel Rude. 1996. "Sketch of Sahaptin, a Sahaptian Language." In Ives Goddard (ed.), *Languages.* Washington: Smithsonian Institution, 340–366. [Handbook of North American Indians, Vol. 17. National Museum of Natural History. Washington: Smithsonian Institution.]

Rude, Noel. 1986a. "Discourse-Pragmatic Context for Genitive Promotion in Nez Perce." *Studies in Language* 10: 109–186.

Rude, Noel. 1986b. "Topicality, Transitivity, and the Direct Object in Nez Perce." *International Journal of American Linguistics* 52: 124–153.

Rude, Noel. 1988. "Ergative, Passive, and Antipassive in Nez Perce: A Discourse Perspective." In Masayoshi Shibatani (ed.), *Passive and Voice*. Amsterdam and Philadelphia: John Benjamins, 547–560.

Rude, Noel. 1989. "The Grammar of Kinship Terms in Sahaptin." In Scott DeLancey (ed.), *Papers from the 1989 Hokan-Penutian Languages Workshop*. Eugene, Oregon: University of Oregon, 87–95. [University of Oregon Papers in Linguistics 2].

Rude, Noel. 1991a. "Verbs to Promotional Suffixes in Sahaptian and Klamath." In Elizabeth C. Traugott and Bernd Heine (eds.), *Approaches to Grammaticalization Vol. II*. Amsterdam and Philadelphia: John Benjamins, 185–199. [Typological Studies in Language 19]

Rude, Noel. 1991b. "On the Origins of the Nez Perce Ergative NP Suffix." *International Journal of American Linguistics* 57: 24–50.

Rude, Noel. 1992a. "Word Order and Topicality in Nez Perce." In Doris L. Payne (ed.), *Pragmatics of Word Order Flexibility*. Amsterdam and Philadelphia: John Benjamins, 193–208. [Typological Studies in Language 22].

Rude, Noel. 1992b. "Dative Shifting in Sahaptin." *International Journal of American Linguistics* 58: 316–321.

Rude, Noel. 1994. "Direct, Inverse and Passive in Northwest Sahaptin." In T. Givón (ed.), *Voice and Inversion*. Amsterdam and Philadelphia: John Benjamins, 101–119. [Typological Studies in Language 28].

Rude, Noel. 1996. "The Sahaptian Inflectional Suffix Complex." In Victor Golla (ed.), *Proceedings of the Hokan-Penutian Workshop*. Berkeley: Department of Linguistics, 51–89. [Survey of California and Other Indian Languages, Report 9, series editor Leanne Hinton].

Rude, Noel. 1997a. "On the History of Nominal Case in Sahaptian." *International Journal of American Linguistics* 63: 113–143.

Rude, Noel. 1997b. "Dative Shifting and Double Objects in Sahaptin." In T. Givón (ed.), *Grammatical Relations*. Amsterdam and Philadelphia: John Benjamins, 323–349. [Typological Studies in Language 35].

Tesnière, Lucien. 1959. *Éléments de syntaxe structurale*. Paris: Klincksieck.

External Possession Constructions in Nyulnyulan Languages

William McGregor
Katholieke Universiteit Leuven

1. Introduction

Many Australian Aboriginal languages exhibit a set of constructions, used in the expression of certain types of possession, that satisfy three conditions: (i) the possessor (PR) and the possessum (PM) are designated by distinct NPs, which (ii) show the same case-marking morphology; and (iii) the PR, rather than the PM, is cross-referenced by a bound pronominal. Such languages include, among others, Gooniyandi (McGregor 1985), Warlpiri (Hale 1981), Jaru (Tsunoda 1981: 196ff), many Western Desert varieties (e.g., Ngaanyatjarra (Glass and Hackett 1970: 67), Luritja (Heffernan 1984: 65), and Wangkajunga (my field notes), and Nyulnyulan languages. Example (1) illustrates the construction in a Nyulnyulan language.

(1) *ngaji juyu marru nyily* ***mi****-nyjun* — Yawuru
INTER you head headache 2MIN:NOM-say
'Do you have a headache?' (More literally, 'Do you ache head?')
(Hosokawa 1991: 428)

Observe that the underlined words do not form an NP (see below and section 2; also McGregor 1985); neither shows a case-marking postposition, indicating that both are in the absolutive; and it is the PR *juyu* 'you', rather than the PM *marru* 'head' that is cross-referenced by the second person pronominal prefix *mi-* to the inflecting verb -JI 'say, do'.

Payne (1997: 395) defines an external possession construction (EPC) as any construction expressing a possessive relation by means of coding the PR in a core grammatical relation (argument, participant role), in an NP external to the NP designating the PM. Possessive constructions in Nyulnyulan languages meet these criteria iff they satisfy conditions (i) and (iii).[1] Condition (i) is an obvious requirement; (iii) is necessary since argument roles in these languages are by definition those that are cross-referenced by a bound pronominal to the inflecting verb (see McGregor 1997: 113). Conversely, any possessive construction satisfying these two conditions will clearly also satisfy Payne's criteria. Many, though not all, EPCs satisfy condition (ii) as well. Those that do will be referred to as Identically Marked Constructions (IMCs); those satisfying just (i) and (iii), as Differently Marked Constructions (DMCs).

This paper has three main aims. The first is to provide an overview of the range of EPC types in Nyulnyulan languages. As expected, EPCs exist in which the PR serves as unaccusative intransitive subject and direct object. But there also exist EPCs in which the PR is unergative intransitive subject, transitive subject, and some types of oblique object, thus refuting the commonly held view that transitive subjects cannot serve as the PRs in EPCs — "are not accessible to possessor raising" in relational grammar parlance.[2]

A second aim is to characterize the semantics of EPCs. It will be argued that they express a particularly close relation between the PR and PM, such that the PM falls within the personal domain of the PR (Bally 1995; Chappell and McGregor 1995), in regard to the referent situation. Furthermore, in IMCs the involvement of the PM in the situation is more intimate than in DMCs.

The third aim is to identify differences among the languages in terms of their usage of EPCs. Specifically, it is shown that Western Nyulnyulan languages (Bardi, Jawi, Nyulnyul, Jabirrjabirr, Nimanburru, and Ngumbarl) employ EPCs less commonly than do Eastern Nyulnyulan languages (Warrwa, Nyikina, Yawuru, and Jukun). Moreover, they use non-EPCs in circumstances in which Eastern languages strongly prefer EPCs. It is proposed that this difference in construction preference correlates with a morphological difference: Western languages show a system of pronominal prefixes to a small set of the most inalienable Ns (McGregor 1995); this system is absent from the Eastern languages, thereby necessitating the use of EPCs to express inalienable relationships.

The present paper represents the first cross-linguistic investigation of EPCs in Nyulnyulan languages. In fact, to date, they have been described in detail in just one language, namely Yawuru; Hosokawa (1995) represents a comprehensive investigation of the semantics of the constructions, extending the account furnished in Hosokawa (1991). Luckily, however, resources available to me include a considerable number of examples of EPCs in many of the languages.[3]

Before we go any further, an important issue needs to be confronted. It is widely believed that the status of NP units is questionable in the average, non-configurational, Australian language (see e.g., Hale 1981 [cf., however, Hale 1983], and Blake 1983). In such languages no contrast could exist between internal possession (IP) — i.e., possession expressed within NPs, also called attributive possession — and external possession. For Nyulnyulan languages, however, the status of NPs is undeniable. Not only is discontinuity of putative NPs rare in all of the languages, but also postposition placement is determined by NP structure: case-marking postpositions almost always occur one per phrase, attached to the first word of the unit. Thus there is scope for a contrast between EPCs and IPCs in Nyulnyulan languages.

2. IPCs in Nyulnyulan languages

All Western Nyulnyulan languages, as well as an idiolect of Warrwa (an Eastern language), show pronominal prefixes to fifty or so nominals, the majority of which refer to body parts. According to McGregor (1995: 263–265), whether or not an N in Nyulnyul is prefixing is semantically conditioned. Prefix-taking Ns are those that represent aspects of the personal domain of all normal human beings, and include the most inalienable body parts (the least detachable, most central to the person, including eyes, mouth, foot, hand, etc.), as well as personal representations such as shadows, names, reflections, souls, etc. The same appears to hold for other languages that show the system.

In NPs, no Nyulnyulan language distinguishes between alienable and inalienable possession.[4] IP is marked in one of two ways, either: (a) by an oblique or emphatic possessive pronominal designating the PR and an N(P) designating the PM, as in (2); or (b) by two NPs, one designating the PR, the other designating the PM, linked by a third person oblique pronominal (usually the minimal form, but occasionally the augmented form, if the number of the PR is non-minimal), as in (3) and (4). The order of units in both types is free, although the phrases almost always remain contiguous.

(2) { *jan* 1MIN:OBL / *janijirr* 1MIN:EMPH } *yil* dog — Nyulnyul
'my dog'

(3) *walangk jin* *ibal jan* — Jabirrjabirr, Nyulnyul
spear 3MIN:OBL father my
'my father's spear' (Nekes and Worms 1953: 532)

(4) *bin wamb ni-mal jin* Nyulnyul
this man 3SG-hand 3MIN:OBL
'this man's hand'

In Nyikina and Yawuru there is another means of marking IP: by dative marking of the PR, optionally accompanied by a possessive pronominal encliticised to the PM, as shown by (5) and (6). (According to Stokes 1982: 386, in Nyikina omission of the pronominal enclitic is possible only for certain inalienably possessed items such as kin and dogs.)

(5) *wamba-ni muk yi-ndiny-Ø marnin-ji yila* Nyikina
man-ERG hit 3MIN:NOM-did-3MIN:ACC woman-DAT dog
'The man hit the woman's dog.' (Stokes 1982: 69)

(6) *linyju-yi durrkarrang-jina* Yawuru
policeman-DAT car-3MIN:OBL
'the policeman's car' (Hosokawa 1991: 246)

How the various means of expressing IP in Eastern Nyulnyulan languages contrast semantically remains unclear. Stokes (1982: 385) suggests that the third person oblique pronoun as possessive marker tends to occur with inanimate PRs in Nyikina; Hosokawa (1991: 247) suggests that in Yawuru it is associated with generic PRs, and is frequently used in classification, whereas the dative construction tends to be used when the PR is definite. (Both may be correct; however, neither provides convincing justification.)

3. Identically marked external possession constructions

Two main types of Identically Marked EPCs are found in Nyulnyulan languages: a transitive construction, in which the PR serves as an "object" (a "double object construction"), and an intransitive construction in which the PR serves as subject (a "double subject construction"). In both constructions the PR and PM NPs are unmarked by a postposition. It seems likely that they exist(ed) in every Nyulnyulan language. In addition, it is possible to find IMCs involving the PR in all core roles — though no single language shows all possibilities. Sections 3.1 and 3.2 deal with the two primary types, in order; section 3.3 discusses the less common ones.

3.1 *PR as transitive object*

In IMCs in transitive clauses the PR and PM NPs are almost always unmarked, and only the PR is cross-referenced by the accusative pronominal enclitic, indicating that it serves as an object argument. This is illustrated by examples (7) and (8):[5]

(7) *kinya-na kirwa Ø-namana-**ngayu**, kanyjingana-na,*
this-ERG bad 3MIN:NOM-put-1MIN:ACC lightning-ERG
nimidi ngajanu. Warrwa
leg my
'I got a shock from the lightning, in my leg.' (More literally, 'The lightning made me bad my leg.')

(8) *baawa dab nga-nandiny-**Ø** nimala* Warrwa
child touch 1MIN:NOM-caught-3MIN:ACC hand
'I touched the child on the hand.' (More literally, 'I touched the child hand.')

In (7) it is clear that the first person pronominal enclitic *-ngayu* cannot cross-reference the PM, which is a third person NP. Moreover, the ellipsed NP *ngayu* 'I' (see note 4) would not form an NP with *nimidi ngajanu* 'my leg', for reasons outlined in section 2 above. For the same reasons *baawa ... nimala* (child ... hand) does not constitute an NP in (8). It might be objected that in examples such as (8) it is impossible to tell whether the accusative pronominal enclitic cross-references the PR or the PM, since both are third person singular. While it is true that this cannot be settled by inspection alone, evidence can be adduced that demonstrates that it must be the PR that is cross-referenced. To propose that the Ø pronominal enclitic in (8) cross-references the body part NP *nimala* 'hand' would require the identification of another construction type satisfying conditions (i) and (ii) of section 1, but not (iii). Instead, (iii′), which states that the PM rather than the PR is cross-referenced by a bound pronominal to the inflecting verb, would be satisfied. The problem is that all of the available evidence indicates that — ignoring reference — examples such as (8) are semantically identical with examples such as (9), which are transitive IMCs, with the pronominal enclitic unquestionably cross-referencing the PR. There is no justification whatever for proposing an additional class of constructions satisfying (i), (ii) and (iii′).

(9) *dab nandiny-**ngayu** nimala* Warrwa
touch 3MIN:NOM-caught-1SG:ACC hand
'He touched me on the hand.' (More literally, 'He touched me hand.')

In transitive IMCs it is typically the case that a person suffers as a result of action taking effect at or on a body part. It is the person him/herself who is actually engaged in the action, while the body part represents the specific place at which it is localised (see further McGregor 1985 and section 5 below).

3.2 *PR as intransitive subject*

In the intransitive IMC there is a pair of unmarked NPs, one designating the PR, the other the PM. Only the PR is cross-referenced by a pronominal prefix to the verb, as shown by (10), in which the prefix *nga-* to the inflecting verb -JI 'say' cross-references the PR *ngayu* 'I', not the PM *nga-lma* 'my head'. Note furthermore that (as per section 2) *ngayu nga-lma* (I my-head) does not constitute an NP. Comparable examples exist in the other languages; see e.g., Hosokawa (1995) for Yawuru examples.

(10) *ngayu nga-lma bingbal* ***nga****-nyjan* Warrwa
I 1SG-head sore 1MIN:NOM-say
'I've got a sore head.' (More literally, 'I am sore head'.)

Most intransitive IMCs designate painful, undesirable states a person suffers, which are typically localised in the part of the body specified by the PM NP. However, the state need not necessarily be either painful or undesirable: in (11), for instance, it is highly desirable, as it prognosticates success in the card game *kunts*; and in (12), one of the few examples in which this construction is used to refer to movement of a body part, it is neutral.[6]

(11) *kinyingk min kura jawal kinyingki ni-mbala-b* ***in****-ngurlun*
that TEMP game story this 3SG-leg-REL 3SG:NOM-feels
amburiny Bardi
man
'This is the story of what happens in that game when a person has a feeling in his leg.' (Ejai 1986b: 275)

(12) *jalmarra dubdub* ***Ø****-jan jalmarra jina* Warrwa
bird flap 3MIN:NOM-says feather 3MIN:OBL
'Bird is flapping its wings.'

Intransitive IMCs are not restricted to unaccusatives in Nyulnyulan languages (as they are in some languages — e.g., Payne 1997). Unergative subjects are also permissible, for instance, in intransitive reflexive/reciprocal clauses:[7]

(13) *kinya waarru* ***Ø****-banjiny nalma* Warrwa
this scratch 3MIN:NOM-exchanged head
'He scratched his head.' (More literally, 'He scratched himself head.')

Finally, most Nyulnyulan languages show a marked intransitive construction, the medio-active (or quasi-passive — Hosokawa 1991, 1995; McGregor forthcoming a). This construction shows the ergative-absolutive "case frame" of a transitive clause, but the pronominal prefix to the inflecting verb cross-references the unmarked NP, rather than the ergatively marked NP as in transitive clauses. Medio-actives designate happenings that befall people (usually), as in (14), and thus presumably involve unaccusative subjects. IMC variants are common in Yawuru (Hosokawa 1995: 166).

(14) (*ngayu*) ***nga****-lurranda kungkulu-manyjan nyamba-ni jungku*
I 1MIN:NOM-burnt hair-only this-ERG fire
'The fire only burnt my hair.' (Hosokawa 1991: 436) Yawuru

In examples (7) and (10)–(12) the NP designating the PM contains information about the PR — indicated by a pronominal prefix in (10) and (11), and by a free oblique pronoun in (7) and (12). On the other hand, in examples (8) and (9), no such indication is provided within the PM NP. Whilst PR marking by pronominal affixes is obligatory (in languages which exhibit the system), the marking of the PR by a free possessive pronominal or a separate NP is not obligatory, and is less common than non-marking. Yawuru seems to be unique in precluding indication of the PR in the PM NP (Hosokawa 1995: 167, 169, 172).

3.3 *PR in other roles*

Nyikina and Nyulnyul show an IMC in which the PR serves as transitive subject, as in (15) and (16). The ergatively marked PM NP designates a body part used instrumentally to effect the action, and is not available for alienable possessions, which must be marked by the instrumental postposition *-ngany*. This construction is, however, quite rare in both languages: instrumental body parts are almost always represented by instrumental NPs in non-EPCs.

(15) *ngayi-ni malbulu* ***nga****-nkulalmany-Ø nimarrangka-ni*
I-ERG coolamon 1MIN:NOM-made-3MIN:ACC hand-ERG
'I made the coolamon with my hands.' (Stokes 1982: 126) Nyikina

(16) *bardi* ***nga****-naw-Ø nga-marl-in kinyingk walangk*
grip 1SG:NOM-gave-3MIN:ACC 1SG-arm-ERG this spear
'I gripped the spear by/with my hands.' Nyulnyul

Strangely, the corresponding construction in Yawuru shows the PM ergatively marked, but the PR unmarked (Hosokawa 1995: 255) — see example (21) below.

Finally, there are just a few examples (all in Warrwa) of IMCs with the PR in a type of oblique argument role that I have elsewhere dubbed Affected (McGregor 1990: 330–332, 1997: 97, 113), since it represents someone who is indirectly affected by the situation. In these examples the PR and PM are designated by NPs marked by the same local postposition, and the PR is cross-referenced by an oblique pronominal enclitic on the inflecting verb. Consider (17), in which the NPs are marked by the locative postposition. Clearly the person is affected in some way by the situation — by the snake's presence — however, the snake is not represented as acting on him. The PM, the man's back, indicates more precisely the part of the body at which the situation took effect; this construction is available only for such inalienable possessions — *ninja* 'back' could not be replaced by e.g., *burrkurru* 'car', or *mayarra* 'house' — indicating that it is indeed an EPC.

(17) *yaalu Ø-jarra-**jina*** *nyinka-n, ninja-n jina.*
stand 3MIN:NOM-stood-3MIN:OBL this-LOC back-LOC his
'(The snake) stood up behind his back.' Warrwa

Summing up, all Nyulnyulan languages show IMCs in which the PR serves as an intransitive subject or transitive object. Intransitive subjects are not necessarily unaccusative, although these are perhaps the most frequent. Other IMC are much rarer, and may be restricted to certain languages. The most glaring absence is of a double subject transitive IMC: it is attested in just two languages, and then rarely; such IMCs are common in many nearby languages (e.g., Gooniyandi (McGregor 1985) and Warlpiri (Hale 1981)).

4. Differently marked external possession constructions

Various external possession constructions with different morphological marking of the PR and PM are found in Nyulnyulan languages; most of these seem to be language specific. The PR may serve as transitive object or intransitive subject, but rarely as transitive subject. The PM may be marked by an ergative, locative, or ablative postposition, or (rarely) by none. Obviously conditions (i) and (iii) (section 1) are satisfied. Space permits no more than an outline of the most common possibilities.

DMCs with the PR as direct object are — in contrast with the corresponding IMCs — quite restricted. Most languages have a construction in which the

PM is marked by the ablative postposition, indicating a part of an animate being's body at which an action of grasping or holding takes effect, as in (18). In Nyulnyul the PM may be marked by the locative postposition, specifying the place where the action took effect — the point on the object at which the (violent) physical connection with the subject occurred, as in (19). These constructions are not available for anything bar parts of the object's body, and since they satisfy (i) and (iii), are EPCs.

(18) *makarra-ngkawu nga-nandiny-**Ø*** *bani* Warrwa
tail-ABL 1MIN:NOM-caught-3MIN:ACC goanna
'I grabbed the goanna by the tail.'

(19) *buy-in i-nar-**ngay*** *nga-mird-uk* Nyulnyul
ant-ERG 3SG:NOM-speared-1MIN:ACC 1SG-leg-LOC
'Ant(s) bit me on the leg.'

Where the PR is an intransitive subject, the PM may take the locative postposition, at least in Bardi and Nyulnyul, as in (20).

(20) *joororrjooroorr* ***nga**-laban nga-mird-on* Bardi
rheumatism 1SG:NOM-have 1SG-knee-LOC
'I have rheumatism in my knee.' (Aklif 1991)

Yawuru seems to be the only language which shows DMCs with the PR as transitive subject. In fact, there are two types: one has the PR unmarked, the PM ergatively marked (21); the other has the PR ergatively marked, and the PM locatively marked (22).

(21) *buu **wal**-ju-Ø* *(jungku) nilirr-ni* *juyu*Yawuru
blow 2minNOM:will-say-3MIN:ACC fire mouth-ERG you
'You blow the fire with your mouth.' (Hosokawa 1991: 255)

(22) *(ngayu-ni) kamba yila **nga**-nyjanbarn-Ø* *niwal-kun janu*
I-ERG that dog 1MIN:NOM-kicked-3MIN:ACC foot-LOC my
'I kicked the dog with my foot.' (Hosokawa 1991: 433) Yawuru

In other Nyulnyulan languages body part instruments are normally marked by the instrumental postposition *-ngany*. Although these constructions satisfy conditions (i) and (iii), they are not EPCs since they do not actually encode a relationship of possession between the two NPs: the body part term can always be replaced by an NP designating an artifact, indicating that that item had been used instrumentally. The possessive relation is no more than a contextually engendered interpretation. The same condition — that it must specify the possessive relation — also precludes certain other constructions, involving ergative-, ablative- or locative-marked PMs.

5. The semantics of EPCs

In this section it is argued that EPCs express the meaning that the PR and the PM referents are very closely associated with one another, such that the PM falls within the personal domain or sphere of the PR (Bally 1995; McGregor 1985; Chappell and McGregor 1995), in the context of the situation designated by the clause. In this restricted domain, the PR and PM may be considered to be inalienably related, inseparable from one another. Moreover, it is the PR that is most centrally involved in the situation, in its 'directionality' (or transitivity); the PM is involved only as a consequence.

It is also proposed that the two primary types of EPC, IMCs and DMCs, contrast semantically in terms of the manner in which the PM is involved in the situation vis-à-vis the PR. IMCs indicate that the two are involved in the same way in regard to what might be considered to be the more "semantic" case roles (marked by the postpositions); DMCs indicate that they are involved in rather different ways. According to certain parameters, IMCs liken the involvement of the PM in the situation to the involvement of the PR; DMCs, by contrast, liken the involvement of the PM to the circumstantial involvement of an external entity. Seen in these terms, IMCs indicate the closest association between the PR and PM, while DMCs represent conceptually more distant associations. In both cases the PR and PM are considered to be conceptually distinct; contra Hale (1981), there is no sense in which they are identified (see also McGregor 1985: 212), even though the PM shows little individuation.

5.1 *The meaning of EPCs*

The claim that EPCs indicate a particularly close association between the PR and the PM in relation to the referent situation is supported by two types of evidence: restrictions on the PM, and contrasts with non-EPC constructions.

As the examples cited above show, PMs are typically parts of the PR's body. Usually they are parts that would be considered to be the most inalienable, those which are most central to the characterisation of a human being as a person; these include the head, hands, feet, arms, legs, mouth, eyes and ears. Fingernails and toenails, hair, and bodily exuviae are not particularly inalienable, and rarely occur as PMs in EPCs. Significantly, the most inalienable items are those parts which are designated by prefixing Ns in the Western Nyulnyulan languages (McGregor 1995).

PMs in EPCs are not, however, restricted to inalienably possessed body parts. Also included are various entities that may be considered to fall within the domain of a person's essential 'self', particularly personal representations such as names,[8] images (23), shadows, reflections, footprints, one's native country, and a person's *rayi* 'conception totem, dreaming'. So also may be some items of apparel, particularly hats, headbands, and belts, as well as at least one once incurable disease, namely leprosy (24).[9] (Hosokawa 1991: 446–447 provides a number of Yawuru examples; see also McGregor 1985 for comparable Gooniyandi examples.)

(23) *ngirrandiny-jarri-**yawu*** *bilirr wamba-na* Warrwa
they:got-SEQ-1&2MIN:ACC spirit man-ERG
'The men took our photograph.' (More literally, 'The men got us spirit.')

(24) ***nga**-mamalkinjin* *yik jan* Jabirrjabirr, Nimanburru, Nyulnyul
***nga**-malkinjin* *iik an* Bardi
1SG:NOM-conceal:self sick 1MIN:OBL
'I conceal my sickness (leprosy).' (More literally, 'I conceal myself my sickness.') (Nekes and Worms 1953: 359, 601)

The above represent the main types of entity occurring as PMs in EPCs across the Nyulnyulan languages. No language exhibits the full range in the available corpora, and a number show only a small subset; most likely this reflects inadequacies in the corpora rather than genuine differences between the languages. (This hypothesis, however, remains to be tested.) Other PMs, such as bodily exuviae, kin, pets, tools, vehicles, houses, and so on, which are difficult to conceive of as falling into a human being's personal domain, are not attested in EPCs.

For most EPCs it is possible to find agnate non-EPCs involving the same PM. The meaning contrasts between the two constructions further support my proposals concerning the semantics of EPCs. We now briefly examine a few illustrative agnate pairs in which the PR in the EPC and the PM in the non-EPC serve in core grammatical roles.

Let us first consider the role of transitive subject. As we have seen, in Nyulnyul and Nyikina there is an IMC in which the PR can bear this role (section 3.3). This may be contrasted in both languages with an equally rare non-EPC in which the PM serves as the transitive subject, and is cross-referenced by a nominative pronominal prefix to the verb, as in (25) and (26), where the pronominal prefixes (*i-* and *yi-*) cross-reference the body part NPs rather than the first person PRs.

(25) *nga-mbal-in* *i-ninjudar-ngay* Nyulnyul
1SG-foot-ERG 3SG:NOM-tripped-1MIN:ACC
'My foot tripped me.'

(26) *kujarra-ni niyambalu ngajanu-ni yi-nkany-ngayu* Nyikina
two-ERG foot my-ERG 3MIN:NOM-carried-1MIN:ACC
'My two feet took me.' (Stokes 1982: 285)

In (25) the person's foot is not under the control of the PR but acts as if it were an independent entity such as a stick, that might inadvertently trip the person; and in (26) the feet are being treated as though they are external to the PR, and might have the capability of carrying the person, like a vehicle, perhaps irrespective of the person's volition. By representing the PM as transitive subject it is implied that it is engaged independently in the action.[10] Examples (25) and (26) contrast sharply with (15) and (16), where the body parts are being very deliberately used by the person to achieve the actions.

A different set of agnates in Nyikina and Nyulnyul lends additional support to the claim. These involve the PR as transitive subject, and the PM either ergatively marked (an IMC) or instrumentally marked (a non-EPC). In the IMC (examples are (15) and (16)), the PM seems to show a greater degree of agentivity, being more actively involved than in the non-EPC, where the role of the PM is more instrument-like; that is, the PM behaves more like the PR in the IMC, but more like an independent though controlled entity in the non-EPC. This suggestion is consistent with Stokes' observation (1982: 83) that the ergative marking "seems to occur most often with body parts towards the periphery of the body (hands and feet)" — these appendages being the prototypical instruments.

Similarly, when a potentially inalienable PM, rather than its PR, serves as intransitive subject there is a suggestion that the person is not in control, that the PM is engaged in the action inadvertently, not as a consequence of the engagement of the PR. Moreover, the situation is typically confined to PM, and does not also apply to the PR. These observations are illustrated by (27) and (28). In (27) it is the arm that is involved in the situation of breaking; moreover, this not as a consequence of the involvement of the person in this situation: the speaker is not engaged in the process of breaking, which is restricted to the body part. And (28) describes the involuntary movement of parts of a dead body.

(27) *nga-nyjaluny-jarri warany-mirri nimarla Ø-ngunyjuluny-janu*
1MIN:NOM-fell-SEQ other-EMPH hand 3MIN:NOM-broke-1MIN:OBL
'When I fell over I broke one arm.' Warrwa

(28) *i-ngkalkalamanan ni-marla akal ni-yarda* Bardi
3SG:NOM-was:moving:around 3SG-arm and 3SG-body
'His hand and body were moving around.' (Metcalfe 1975: 190)

Again, the situation is similar when a potentially inalienable PM serves as a direct object. In contrast to the corresponding EPC, the non-EPC suggests that the PM is involved in the action to the exclusion of the PR, or that the PM is completely affected. Thus, in (29), it is just the head that is seen, not the entire person; and in (30) the head is completely shaved of hair.

(29) *kinya-na Ø-jalan-janu* *ngajanu nalma* Warrwa
this-ERG 3MIN:NOM-sees-1MIN:OBL my head
'He can only see my head.'

(30) *a-njarrka-Ø* *nga-lma boonyja!* Bardi
2SG:NOM-will:shave-3MIN:ACC 1SG-head completely
'Shave my head completely!' (Aklif 1991)

5.2 *Semantic contrasts between IMCs and DMCs*

I have suggested that IMCs and DMCs contrast semantically, with IMCs indicating a higher degree of inalienability than DMCs. This is because the involvement of the PM in the referent situation is more like that of the PR in IMCs than it is in DMCs. In DMCs it is more like a spatial-circumstance, with the PM in most cases being marked by a postposition marking a locational relation of some sort. Diagrammatic iconicity is manifest.

Four sets of evidence support this proposal. First, the range of PMs in IMCs is least restricted, and covers all of the types identified at the beginning of the previous subsection: body parts, personal representations, clothing, and diseases. On the other hand, possessa appear to be restricted to parts of the body in DMCs. These are the only items which can readily serve both as spatial locations, sources, and so on, and at the same time as inalienables. Personal representations and diseases are in the main too abstract to be treated as spatial locations; and while items of clothing may be considered as locations, treating them as such effectively distances them from the person to the extent that it is difficult to conceive of action involving them as impinging on the personal domain of the wearer.

Second, in certain cases, agnate IMCs and DMCs exist. These contrast semantically, the PM being more intimately and thoroughly involved in the situation in an IMC than in the corresponding DMC. For instance, in Nyulnyul, agnate IMCs and DMCs exist in which the PR serves as transitive object, and the PM is either unmarked or locatively marked. IMCs are used typically when the PM is more affected by the situation; DMCs when the PM is less affected, which may be because the action is restricted to a part of the PM, or because the PM shows no obvious physical manifestation of the effects of the situation.

Thus, whereas the situation referred to by (31) involves a number of ants (note the plural third person prefix in the verb), that referred to by (19) might involve a single ant. In (31), the speaker's body part is apparently being bitten all over, rather than in one place, as may be the case in (19) — and thus it is more affected by the situation.

(31) *nga-marl buy-in kad ingirr-aw-**ngay*** Nyulnyul
1SG-arm ant-ERG bite 3PL:NOM-gave-1SG:ACC
'Ants bit me on the arm.'

Similar agnates can be found (in Bardi and Nyulnyul) when the PR is an intransitive subject — for example, (11) and (20) above. In the IMC in (11) the PM seems to be completely involved in the experienced feeling, which is apparently a single telic event involving the whole leg; by contrast, in the DMC in (20) the knee is less strongly affected — the rheumatism is probably experienced only part of the time, and as a background uncomfortable, but not consuming, pain.

5.3 *Differences between Eastern and Western Nyulnyulan languages*

The discussion of section 5.1 presumes a uniformity across the Nyulnyulan languages in the meanings of EPCs. Although I believe this is by and large correct, there are undeniable differences between the two major genetic subgroups in regard to their usage of IMCs. Eastern languages employ EPCs much more frequently than do Western languages; Western languages use non-EPCs (with the PM in core roles) about as frequently as EPCs, and in contexts in which Eastern languages strongly prefer EPCs. For instance, in describing physical states of body parts, Eastern Nyulnyulan languages almost always employ EPCs, as in (10) above and:

(32) *ngurr **nga**-ndin nimarla* Nyikina
swollen 1MIN:NOM-say hand
'My hand is swollen.' (More literally, 'I am swollen hand.') (Nekes and Worms 1953: 484)

(33) *mangar **nga**-ngaran niwal janu* Yawuru
stiff 1MIN:NOM-become foot 1MIN:OBL
'My foot has gone to sleep.' (More literally, 'I am becoming stiff my foot.') (Nekes and Worms 1953: 370)

In Western languages, by contrast, the PM is normally treated as intransitive subject in a non-EPC except when the person-PR is seriously or permanently affected. Thus compare the following two examples, the first (representing a temporary state) being a non-EPC, the second (designating a permanent condition) an IMC:

(34) *walm i-nyji nga-marl* Nyulnyul
shrivel 3SG:NOM-say 1SG-arm
'My hand is cramped.'

(35) *walm* ***nga****-nyji nga-kad* Nyulnyul
shrivel 1SG:NOM-say 1SG-body
'I became paralysed.' (More literally, 'I am shriveled my body.')

Similarly, in many environments in which the "double object" IMC would be employed in Eastern Nyulnyulan languages, a plain transitive clause with the PM as object is frequently employed in Western languages. Again, it appears that the IMC is used in Western languages when the PR is more seriously affected, in particular when the PR experiences the situation as a strong sensation.[11]

This difference between the two branches of the family does not reflect any major difference in the emic-semantics of their EPCs. In both branches a particularly close association between the PR and the PM is encoded by an EPC. The difference lies in the circumstances in which this is marked, and along with this, the circumstances in which the PR is assigned a role in the 'directionality' of the situation. In Western Nyulnyulan languages the person must be more involved in the situation — must experience it more strongly, suffer more from it — than in Eastern languages, in order to be encoded in a core grammatical role in an EPC.

This difference, it is suggested, is a consequence of retention of the system of pronominal prefixes to Ns in the Western Nyulnyulan languages, which, as mentioned in section 2, define a class of inalienable Ns. The availability of this system permits indication of a close relation between the PR and PM by means other than the EPC. This system is not available in the Eastern languages (except in rudimentary form in one Warrwa idiolect), which means that inalienability can only be expressed by EPCs.

The following diachronic scenario is suggested. With the grammaticisation of the system of pronominal prefixes to Ns from the "double object" construction in proto-Nyulnyulan (as per McGregor 1995), and consequent loss of this and other IMCs, an expressive gap emerged. It would no longer have been possible to indicate that any parts of the body (or personal representation) other than those designated by prefixing Ns were intimately associated with a person in a certain event; nor, conversely, would it have been possible to indicate that a part designated by a prefixing N was not intimately associated with the person in the event. This motivated the re-emergence of EPCs, though they were restricted to cases in which the effect on the PR was most significant. Later, with the loss of the system of pronominal prefixes to Ns in the Eastern languages came an expansion of the EPCs to cover cases in which the effect on the PR was less significant.

6. Conclusion

This paper has described various EPCs in the Nyulnyulan family, and discussed the meanings associated with them. It has proposed that they express a type of inalienability: that is, they indicate that a close relationship obtains between the referents of two NPs, such that one falls within the personal domain of the other (Bally 1995; Chappell and McGregor 1995), in the context of a particular situation. The PM's involvement in the situation is dependent on the PR's.

There are important differences among the various types of inalienability expressed grammatically in Nyulnyulan languages (see also Mithun 1995). The most restricted type is associated with nominal prefixation (mainly in Western subgroup); included are just the most personal parts of the body, and representations of the self — what is essential to the definition of any person as a person, irrespective of individual traits (McGregor 1995). The least restricted is encoded by IMCs, which admit probably all parts of the body (though not exuviae), as well as a large set of personal representations, some items of clothing, and certain diseases. DMCs lie in between, being apparently restricted to parts of the body.

The PR in an EPC serves (by definition) in a core grammatical role, including (in some languages) transitive subject, and oblique objects. The PM does not serve in a core grammatical role. What grammatical relations does it enter into? According to Relational Grammar, it becomes a chômeur, and thus serves in no (surface) grammatical relation. By contrast, I take the view that it does enter into a grammatical relation. In particular, it is grammatically related to the PR by a type of dependency relation (McGregor 1997). It is beyond the scope of this article to present evidence for this suggestion.

Finally, this paper has of necessity painted the picture in broad brush strokes, ignoring many matters of detail. Much more work needs to be done on EPCs in the surviving Nyulnyulan languages, particularly on the similarities and differences among them.

Acknowledgments

This is a revised version of a paper presented to the Conference on External Possession and Noun Incorporation, University of Oregon, 7–10 September 1997. I am grateful to Doris Payne and Immanuel Barshi for inviting me to participate, thus stimulating me to do the long-planned research, and to the audience for useful comments. I am also grateful to Doris Payne for extensive and thorough critiques of previous versions; needless to say, she is not responsible for remaining inadequacies. My fieldwork on Nyulnyul and Warrwa was supported by grants from the Australian Research Council (Grant A58930745 and A59332055), the Australian Institute of Aboriginal and Torres Strait Islander Studies, and the National Aboriginal Languages Program; an ARC Research Fellowship (A9324000) provided opportunity to carry out the research away from the field. My greatest debts are, of course, to my language instructors, Carmel Charles (Nyulnyul), and Maudie Lennard and Freddy Marker (Warrwa).

Abbreviations

Abbreviations used in this paper: ABL ablative; ACC accusative; AUG augmented number; DAT dative; DMC differently marked construction; EMPH emphatic; EPC external possession construction; ERG ergative; IMC identically marked construction; INTER interrogative; IP internal possession; IPC internal possession construction; LOC locative; MIN minimal number; NOM nominative; OBL oblique; SG singular; PL plural; PM possessum; PR possessor; REL relativiser; SEQ sequential; and TEMP temporal. The first three integers indicate the three person categories. For clarity, the PR is indicated by a single underline, the PM by a double underline; bound pronominals to inflecting verbs that cross-reference PRs in EPCs are shown in bold. Orthography used is consistent across the languages, with the exception of Bardi, which employs an additional vowel symbol, *o*. Sources for all numbered examples are indicated, except those from my own field notebooks.

Notes

1 Obviously crucial to this definition is the recognition that a construction encodes a possessive relation. Possession being a difficult concept to pin down precisely, however, it is not usually possible to uncontentiously classify constructions as possessive. For present purposes I assume as an operational requirement that the construction must be restricted to circumstances in which one of the NPs can only be replaced by a small range of NPs of certain types. A construction that is available to an unrestricted range of NPs, it cannot encode possession, and thus cannot be an EPC.

2 This is not new information. Hale (1981) and McGregor (1985) mention and provide examples of EPCs with transitive subject PRs, in Warlpiri and Gooniyandi respectively. One wonders whether these works have been ignored because they present inconvenient facts, at variance with cherished theory-driven presumptions.

3 The main sources of data are: my own field notes for Nyulnyul and Warrwa; Stokes (1982) for Nyikina; Hosokawa (1991, 1995) for Yawuru; Metcalfe (1975), Ejai (1986a, 1986b), and Aklif (1991) for Bardi; and Nekes and Worms (1953) for Bardi, Nyulnyul, Jabirrjabirr, Nimanburru, Yawuru, and Nyikina.

4 Stokes (1982: 384–385) suggests that the distinction is made in Nyikina, inalienable possession being sometimes marked by simple apposition of the two N(P)s. However, her examples are clearly EPCs. And in Nyulnyul, some examples in which apposition might appear to mark inalienable possession actually involve classification of the PM by the PR, as in *burruk ni-wal* (kangaroo 3SG-tail) 'kangaroo tail' (see also McGregor 1990: 261).

5 Example (7), like a number of other examples cited below, does not show an external NP *ngayu* designating the PR. This is a consequence of the fact that NPs are generally ellipsed if they convey given (predictable) information; this is particularly likely to happen for first and second person arguments, since they are (by definition) cross-referenced in the inflecting verb, and thus their referents are generally retrievable. As far as I can tell, in all examples in which the PR NP has been ellipsed it could be included, though no doubt to do so would sound prolix and pedantic. The bolded cross-referencing pronominals indicate at least the person and number of the ellipsed PR, and its clausal role (given the transitivity of the clause).

6 Examples (11) and (12) can be identified as EPCs for precisely the reasons adduced in Section 3.1 for example (8): the two underlined nominals in both examples must constitute separate NPs, and the cross-referencing pronominal prefix to the inflecting verb must cross-reference the PR.

7 Although, as Doris Payne has pointed out (pers.comm.), subjects of reflexive/reciprocal intransitive clauses in some languages are unaccusatives, there is no evidence that this is so in Nyulnyulan languages. The fact that the subject of a reflexive/reciprocal such as (13) can be marked by the ergative postposition surely indicates that it is unergative. (This fact does not, by the way, indicate that reflexive/reciprocal constructions are transitive — see McGregor forthcoming b.) For similar reasons, intransitive subjects of bodily movement clauses such as (12) are also unergative.

8 As Hosokawa (1995: 183) observes, this applies particularly to a person's Aboriginal name, and less so to his or her European name, which is considered more alienable.

9 Articles of clothing and diseases are not, of course, prototypical inalienables. Nevertheless, in certain circumstances they may be considered to be inalienable: clothing, by virtue of close physical proximity when worn, and the fact that a person's appearance is thereby changed; incurable diseases because of the permanent association with the person.

10 In keeping with this, bodily exuviae, which cannot be entirely controlled, frequently serve as transitive subjects, as in e.g. the Nyulnyul *ngurnd-in i-nmin-ngay* (piss-ERG 3SG:NOM-puts-1MIN:ACC) 'I want to do a piss' (more literally, 'Piss puts me').

11 An exception is where body parts are severed. Usually these actions are represented by non-EPCs, even though they must surely involve high effect on the person. The explanation for this at first rather puzzling state of affairs is that severing of body parts is (fortunately!) not the norm for real-world situations involving persons, and requires that the action be directed particularly to the part; actions directed to the person which merely manifest themselves in a part of the person's body (i.e. in which the part serves as an intermediary) do not normally result in the severance of the part. This underlines the fact that general principles are involved, which may contextualise in different, seemingly contradictory ways.

References

Aklif, Gedda. 1991. [Bardi fieldnotes.] Electronic files held in the Australian Institute of Aboriginal and Torres Strait Islander Studies Library.

Bally, Charles. 1995. "The Expression of Concepts of the Personal Domain and Indivisibililty in Indo-European Languages." In Hilary Chappell and William McGregor (eds.), *The Grammar of Inalienability: a Typological Perspective on Body Part Terms and the Part-Whole Relation.* Berlin and New York: Mouton de Gruyter, 31–61.

Blake, Barry. 1983. "Structure and Word Order in Kalkatungu: the Anatomy of a Flat Language." *Australian Journal of Linguistics* 3: 143–175.

Chappell, Hilary and McGregor, William. 1995. "Prolegomena to a Theory of Inalienability." In Hilary Chappell and William McGregor (eds.), *The Grammar of Inalienability: a Typological Perspective on Body Part Terms and the Part-Whole Relation.* Berlin and New York: Mouton de Gruyter, 3–30.

Ejai, Tudor. 1986a. "Punitive Expedition Against the Bardi." In Luise Hercus and Peter Sutton (eds.), *This is What Happened: Historical Narratives by Aborigines.* Canberra: Australian Institute of Aboriginal Studies, 151–164.

Ejai, Tudor. 1986b. "The Killing of the 'Bilikin' Brothers." In Luise Hercus and Peter Sutton (eds.), *This is What Happened: Historical Narratives by Aborigines.* Canberra: Australian Institute of Aboriginal Studies, 140–149.

Glass, Amee and Dorothy Hackett. 1970. *Pitjantjatjara Grammar: A Tagmemic View of the Ngaanyatjara (Warburton Ranges) Dialect.* Canberra: Australian Institute of Aboriginal Studies.

Hale, Ken. 1981. "Preliminary Remarks on the Grammar of Part-Whole Relations in Warlpiri." In John Hollyman and Andrew Pauley (eds), *Studies in Pacific Linguistics in Honor of Bruce Biggs.* Auckland: Linguistic Society of New Zealand, 333–344.

Hale, Ken. 1983. "Warlpiri and the Grammar of Non-configurational Languages." *Natural Language and Linguistic Theory* 1: 5–47.

Heffernan, John. 1984. *Papunya Luritja Language Notes.* Papunya: Papunya Literature Production Centre.

Hosokawa, Komei. 1991. *The Yawuru Language of West Kimberley: a Meaning-based Description.* PhD thesis, Australian National University.

Hosokawa, Komei. 1995. "'My Face *Am* Burning!': Quasi-passive, Body Parts, and Related Issues in Yawuru Grammar and Cultural Concepts." In Hilary Chappell and William McGregor (eds.), *The Grammar of Inalienability: a Typological Perspective on Body Part Terms and the Part-Whole Relation.* Berlin and New York: Mouton de Gruyter, 155–192.

McGregor, William. 1985. "Body Parts in Kuniyanti Clause Grammar." *Australian Journal of Linguistics* 5: 209–232.

McGregor, William. 1990. *A Functional Grammar of Gooniyandi.* Amsterdam: John Benjamins.

McGregor, William. 1995. "Nominal Prefixing in Nyulnyul." In Hilary Chappell and William McGregor (eds.), *The Grammar of Inalienability: a Typological Perspective on Body Part Terms and the Part-Whole Relation*. Berlin and New York: Mouton de Gruyter, 251–292.

McGregor, William. 1997. *Semiotic Grammar.* Oxford: Oxford University Press.

McGregor, William. forthcoming a. "The Medio-Active Construction in Nyulnyulan Languages." *Studies in Language*.

McGregor, William. forthcoming b. "Reflexive and Reciprocal Constructions in Nyulnyulan Languages." In Zygmunt Frajzyngier and Traci Curl (eds.), *Reciprocals: Forms and Functions*. Amsterdam: John Benjamins.

Metcalfe, Christopher. 1975. *Bardi Verb Morphology.* Canberra: Pacific Linguistics.

Mithun, Marianne. 1995. "Multiple Reflections of Inalienability in Mohawk." In Hilary Chappell and William McGregor (eds.), *The Grammar of Inalienability: a Typological Perspective on Body Part Terms and the Part-Whole Relation*. Berlin and New York: Mouton de Gruyter, 633–649.

Nekes, Herman and Ernest A. Worms. 1953. *Australian Languages.* Fribourg: Anthropos Institut.

Payne, Doris. 1997. "The Maasai External Possessor Construction." In Joan Bybee, John Haiman and Sandra A. Thompson (eds.), *Essays on Language Function and Language Type*. Amsterdam: John Benjamins: 395–422.

Stokes, Bronwyn. 1982. *A Description of Nyigina: A Language of the West Kimberley, Western Australia*. PhD thesis, Australian National University.

Tsunoda, Tasaku. 1981. *The Djaru Language of Kimberley, Western Australia.* Canberra: Pacific Linguistics.

On the Properties of Emai Possessors

Ronald P. Schaefer
Southern Illinois University, Edwardsville

1. Introduction

This paper examines constraints governing possessor constructions in Emai, a Benue-Congo language of Nigeria's Edoid group (Bendor-Samuel 1989). These constructions show variable order of the possessor (PR) and possessum (PM). An external possessor (EPR) precedes its PM; an internal possessor (IPR) follows its PM. To initiate analysis of these constructions, I rely on schema theory, particularly as articulated in Heine's (1997) discussion of the grammaticalization of event schemas. I hypothesize that event schemas frame the PR as a location in Internal Possession (IP) constructions and as a topic in External Possession (EP) constructions. The linguistic properties characterizing these constructions are then investigated through a more detailed examination of PR animacy, PM inalienability and verb type. Each of these dimensions constrains order relations between PR and PM. I conclude that externalized possessors reflect predication-affected topics resulting from a situation type incorporating event change.

2. Schema theory

Schema theory holds to the assumption that linguistic expression for some grammatical domains extends to other domains. Often this is due to the latter's relatively more abstract conceptual nature. Schemas unite significant structural features culled from a number of related situations, and they reflect situations frequently encountered in human experience. As event schemas, they assume a propositional form, bringing together in structural templates stereotypes of significant participants and their relations. Event schemas from one domain thus serve as the source for grammatical morphemes used to encode another domain.

According to Heine (1997), five event schemas or structural templates characterize attributive possession constructions in the world's languages. These schemas are location, companion, goal, source and topic. Through a process of grammaticalization, each can serve as the source for a grammatical expression of relations between PR and PM. Two event schemas relevant to the grammatical structure of Emai's possession constructions are the location schema and the topic schema. Each exhibits a distinct structural configuration. The location schema construes the PR as a location where the PM is located. In the possession construction (1) from Maninka, the locative postposition *la* construes the PR *Mamadu* as a place relative to the PM *báara*.

(1) *Mamadu lá báara*
Mamadu at work
'Mamadu's work'

In contrast, the topic schema views the PR as a participant whom the speaker wishes to re-establish as relevant to the universe of discourse. In most, but not all realizations of the topic schema, the PR precedes the PM and is cross-referenced as a pronominal on the PM. Afrikaans illustrates this schema neatly with the PR *die boer* positioned initially in the phrase and cross-referenced by the pronoun *se* modifying the PM *huis*.

(2) *die boer se huis*
the farmer his house
'the farmer's house'

3. Emai possession constructions

Emai exhibits relatively strict SVO word order incorporating verb serialization. In its possession domain, Emai reflects two event schemas. They account for a word order contrast and lay the foundation for delineating constraints affecting External Possession constructions.

The location schema serves as the structural template for IP constructions in Emai. The latter take the form in (3), where the PM *úkpun* precedes the nominal PR *o̱lí ó̱mo̱he* and the pronominal PRs *o̱í*, *iyáín*, *e̱é̱*, *avbá*, *amáí*, and *me̱*. For the current generation of Emai speakers, each pronoun allows the associative morpheme *ísi* except first person singular *me̱*, which, for the previous generation, took the form *e̱mé̱* and accepted the associative morpheme. The *ísi* particle exhibits an obligatory high low tone and induces the obligatory lowering of the first of a sequence of high tones in its complement (cf. the citation form *ólí ómohe* 'the man' in (3a)).[1]

(3) a. *úkpún ísi olí ómohe*
cloth ASSOC the man
'the man's cloth'

b. *úkpún ísi oí / iyáín*
cloth ASSOC his their
'his / their cloth'

c. *úkpún ísi eé / avbá*
cloth ASSOC your:SG your:PL
'your (SG) / your (PL) cloth'

d. *úkpún ísi amáí*
cloth ASSOC our
'our cloth'

e. *úkpún me*
cloth my
'my cloth'

Realization of the location schema in Emai is derived through grammaticalization of a locative construction framed by the verb *si* (4). This verb exhibits contrasting senses in conjunction with the proximity particle *kee*. In one sense it conveys the spatial proximity of two locative entities, its subject (e.g., *ólí íme* 'the farm') and *kee*'s complement (e.g., *ekin* 'market'). Non-locative entities like animate *ólí ófe* 'the rat' must be framed as locations by a relative clause of place (4b). Failure to do so results in ungrammaticality (4c).

(4) a. *ólí íme sí kéé ekin*
the farm be near market
'The farm is near the market.'

b. *ébé ólí ófé ri sí kéé íwé me*
where the rat be be near house my
'Where the rat is is near my house.'

c. **ólí ófe sí kéé íwé me*
the rat be near house my
'The rat is near my house.'

Si's other senses convey motion of a subject (5a) or direct object (5b) participant relative to a location, or express a relation of social or psychological proximity between two human participants (5c).

(5) a. *óli ómohe sí kéé udéken*
the man move near wall
'The man moved near the wall.' *'The man is near the wall.'

b. *óli ómohe sí óli agá kéé udéken*
the man move the chair near wall
'The man moved the chair near the wall.'

c. *óli ómóhé sí kéé óli okposo*
the man move near the woman
'The man developed a closer relationship with the woman.'

Si never expresses spatial proximity without *kee* (6a), although it is found without *kee* in the sense 'to drag' (6b).

(6) *a. *óli ímé sí ekin*
the farm be market
'The farm is near the market.'

b. *óli ómohe o ó si olí úi*
the man SC CONT drag the rope
'The man is dragging the rope.'

The hypothesis assumed for this paper is that *si* in its locative sense (4) served as a structural template for a grammaticalization process leading to the associative morpheme *ísi*. Grammaticalized as part of this process was the erstwhile subject concord particle *í-*, whose tonal properties reflect the Emai subjunctive (Schaefer 1998). That is, it imposes low tone on *si* which in turn lowers the first of a high tone sequence in associative phrase complements (e.g., *éwé ísi olí ómohe* 'the man's goat'). The *i-* particle's potential for grammaticalization and tonal imposition is also evident in the marker for right dislocation (RD), which incorporates the verb *khi* 'to exist.' The RD marker *íkhi* manifests an obligatory low tone on the erstwhile verb *khi*, an obligatory high tone on the ertswhile subject marker *í-*, and induces lowering of the first of a high tone sequence in its complement *olí ómohe*.

(7) *óli okposo gbé ói, íkhi olí ómohe*
the woman kill him RD the man
'The woman killed him, that is the man.'

As for EP constructions, I hypothesize their structural template to be the topic schema. In (8a), the PR *oí* 'her' is framed as topic by its phrase initial position relative to the PM *úhunmi*. Although some languages express the PR not only as a topic but also as a pronominal modifier of the PM, this is not the case in Emai.

The lack of cross-referencing on the PM is consistent with the fact that modifying PRs fail to occur when the PR referent is previously expressed in a clause (8b). Modifying PRs are interpreted with disjoint reference relative to a preceding noun (8a).

(8) a. *ó̱li okposo déé ó̱í úhunmi ré*
the woman lower her head DISP
'The woman lowered her (someone else's) head.'
b. *ó̱li okposo déé úhunmi ré*
the woman lower head DISP
'The woman lowered her (own) head.'

To illustrate the linear order contrast between IP and EP constructions, consider (9a) and (9b), both of which are grammatical but only one of which shows an externalized PR.

In an IP construction, the PM *úkpun* 'cloth' precedes the associative particle *ísi* and the PR *oje* 'Oje' (9a), whereas in an EP construction the PR *ójé* precedes the PM *úkpun* (9b).

(9) a. *o̱ nwú úkpún ísi oje mó̱é̱*
he take cloth ASSOC Oje have
'The youth took hold of the cloth of Oje.'
'The youth held the cloth of Oje.'
b. *ó̱lí ó̱vbekhan nwú ójé úkpun mó̱é̱*
the youth take Oje cloth have
'The youth took hold of Oje's cloth.'
'The youth held Oje by the cloth.'

If we assume that EP constructions instantiate a topic schema and that externalized PRs are topics, we cannot escape addressing the nature of "topic". As the discourse literature emphasizes (Brown and Yule 1983; Levinson 1983; and Clark 1996), the notion of topic has evolved with different senses. One of these defines topic as a relation between a discourse participant and the overall structure of discourse. A topic, then, is what a discourse is about. A second definition specifies topic as a relation between a discourse participant and an utterance. A topic under this definition is what an utterance is about.

Common to these definitions is an "aboutness" relation. I propose extending this relation to predication-affected topics, i.e., externalized possessors. (See Givón 1984 for a distinct but related proposal under the rubric of secondary topic.) As a topic, I take the shift in position between the IP and EP constructions to reflect a shift in information value. Through the shifted position, the speaker intends to activate the discourse status of the PR and thereby make the hearer aware that the event change expressed by the predicate affects the PR. Change in this case applies to location (movement of an entity from one place to another), possession (transfer of an entity from one person to another), or state (alteration in the material integrity of an entity). The predication-affected topic thus consists of a discourse participant affected in some measure by event change. Transitive change-of-state verbs are directly related to lexical arguments serving as direct objects. If affectedness were the only criterion for a predication-affected topic, these lexical arguments would be expressed by the topic schema. Since the lexical arguments of Emai's transitive change-of-state verbs are not expressed by the topic schema, a predication-affected topic must be indirectly related to the predication. PRs bear exactly this relation, since they are linked by a possession relation to a PM serving as lexical argument.

If we view externalized PRs as predication-affected topics, we would not expect their uniform occurrence across all grammatical positions. In fact, EP constructions in Emai never occur in subject position, where one finds only the IP construction.

(10) a. *órán ísi oje gúó̱ghó̱ á*
tree ASSOC Oje break CS
'The tree of Oje broke.'
b. **ójé óran gúó̱ghó̱ á*
Oje tree break CS
'Oje's tree broke.'

Likewise, EPRs fail to appear in indirect object position following the indirect object particle *li* (11b).

(11) a. *o̱lí ó̱mo̱he nwú o̱lí úkpun lí o̱vié̱n ísi oje*
the man give the cloth APPL slave ASSOC Oje
'The man gave the cloth to the slave of Oje.'
b. **o̱lí ó̱mo̱he nwú o̱lí úkpun lí ójé o̱vié̱n*
the man give the cloth APPL Oje slave
'The man gave the cloth to Oje's slave.'

EPRs are never found as either first (12a–b) or second object (12c–d) in double object constructions.

(12) a. *o̱ fí é̱wé ísi oje úkpóran*
he hit goat ASSOC Oje stick
'He hit the goat of Oje with a stick.'

b. **o fí ójé éwe úkpóran*
he hit Oje goat stick
'He hit Oje's goat with a stick.'

c. *e míéé óvbékhán ísi oje úkpún ísi óli okposo*
they receive youth ASSOC Oje cloth ASSOC the woman
'They received from the child of Oje the cloth of the woman.'

d. *e míéé ójé óvbekhan ólí ókpósó úkpun*
they receive Oje youth the woman cloth
'They received from Oje's child the woman's cloth.'

Lastly, EP is never realized in focus position (13b), left-dislocated (topicalized) position (13d), or right-dislocated position (13f).

(13) a. *úkpún ísi oje lí ólí ókpósó nwú móé*
cloth ASSOC Oje PF the woman carry have
'It was the cloth of Oje that the woman held.'

b. *ójé úkpun lí ólí ókpósó nwú móé*
Oje cloth PF the woman carry have
'It was Oje's cloth that the woman held.'

c. *úkpún ísi oje, óli okposo nwú ói móé*
cloth ASSOC Oje the woman carry it have
'As for the cloth of Oje, the woman held it.'

d. **ójé úkpun, óli okposo nwú ói móé*
Oje cloth the woman carry it have
'As for Oje's cloth, the woman held it.'

e. *óli okposo nwú ói móé, íkhi ukpún ísi oje*
the woman carry it have RD cloth ASSOC Oje
'The woman held it, that is the cloth of Oje.'

f. **óli okposo nwú ói móé, íkhi ojé úkpun*
the woman carry it have RD Oje cloth
'The woman held it, that is Oje's cloth.'

EP constructions, however, are realized in direct object and locative complements. Each will be examined for restrictions imposed by features of PM, PR and verb.

4. Possessum constraints

Constraints on possessa in EP constructions reflect an inalienability hierarchy. Salient indices on this hierarchy include body parts (BP), associated possessions like clothing items (AP), and non-associated possessions (NAP). A PM higher on the inalienability hierarchy is more likely to induce EP, all other conditions being met.

BP < AP < NAP

PM constraints apply equally within direct object and locative complement noun phrases. For direct objects, EPRs are acceptable when the PM is a body part. Corresponding IP constructions often require an interpretation at odds with the "usual" circumstances of the world, "!" designating such pragmatic oddity. It is easier to assume that the PM *óbo̲* 'hand' is attached to the PR *oje* 'Oje' (14b), than to assume that the PM is detached from the PR (14a). In detachment circumstances IPRs are obligatory.

(14) a. !*ó̲lí ó̲vbekhan nwú óbó̲ ísi oje mó̲é̲*
the youth take hand ASSOC Oje have
'The youth took hold of / held the hand of Oje.'
b. *ó̲lí ó̲vbekhan nwú ójé óbo̲ mó̲é̲*
the youth take Oje hand have
'The youth took hold of / held Oje's hand.'

When the PM is not a body part but an item closely associated with the PR, e.g., a piece of clothing, EPRs and IPRs in direct object complements appear under differing conditions. EPRs require physical contact between PM and PR, i.e., the cloth must be worn by Oje (15a). IP constructions require a non-contact relation, i.e., the cloth is not worn by Oje (15b).

(15) a. *ó̲lí ó̲vbekhan nwú ójé úkpun mó̲é̲*
the youth take Oje cloth have
'The youth took hold of / held Oje by the cloth.'
b. *ó̲lí ó̲vbekhan nwú úkpún ísi oje mó̲é̲*
the youth take cloth ASSOC Oje have
'The youth took hold of / held the cloth of Oje.'

A PM which is neither a body part nor a closely associated item strictly disallows application of EPRs. EP constructions are never acceptable with a non-associated PM, as in the case of *agógó* 'gong' (16).

(16) a. **ó̲lí ó̲vbekhan nwú ójé agógó mó̲é̲*
the youth take Oje gong have
'The youth took hold of / held Oje's gong.'
b. *ó̲lí ó̲vbekhan nwú agógó ísi oje mó̲é̲*
the youth take gong ASSOC Oje have
'The youth took hold of / held the gong of Oje.'

PM constraints specified by the inalienability hierarchy apply as well to the locative complements of verbs and postverbal particles. An EPR in locative complements does not immediately precede the PM. It precedes the locative preposition *vbi* and immediately follows a verb or postverbal particle.

EPRs in locative complements are acceptable with a body-part PM, assuming normal pragmatic conditions. It is more natural to assume that the PR *oje* 'Oje' is alive and that he is inalienably linked to the PM *égbe* 'body' (17a), than to assume the opposite (17b). With an inalienable PM, EPRs are acceptable, while IPRs are generally not. However, if Oje were dead, an IP construction would be acceptable (17b) and an EP construction would not (17a).

(17) a. *o nwú úkpun ó ójé vbí égbe*
he put cloth CL Oje LOC body
'He put a cloth onto Oje's body.'
b. !*o nwú úkpun ó vbí égbé ísi oje*
he put cloth CL LOC body ASSOC Oje
'He put a cloth onto the body of Oje.'

For a closely associated PM in locative complements, both EP and IP constructions are acceptable, although again under differing conditions. An EPR requires physical contact, i.e., the PM *úvbierun* 'hat' must be worn by the PR *oje* 'Oje' (18a). IP constructions demand an alienable condition where the hat is not worn by Oje (18b).

(18) a. *o nwú ikhumi ó ójé vbí úvbierun*
she put charm CL Oje LOC hat
'She put a charm onto Oje's hat.'
b. *o nwú ikhumi ó vbí úvbíérún ísi oje*
she put charm CL LOC hat ASSOC Oje
'She put a charm onto the hat of Oje.'

A non-associated PM, the lowest position on the inalienability hierarchy, absolutely disallows EPRs in locative complements. It requires IP constructions, such as (19b) with *agá* 'chair' as PM.

(19) a. **o nwú ébe ó ójé vbi agá*
he put book CL Oje LOC chair
'He put a book onto Oje's chair.'
b. *o nwú ébe ó vbi agá ísi oje*
he put book CL LOC chair ASSOC Oje
'He put a book onto the chair of Oje.'

5. Possessor constraints

PRs in Emai EP constructions are constrained in part by their animacy value. Acceptability of EPRs correlates in large measure with PR position on the animacy hierarchy (Dixon 1979; Comrie 1981; Croft 1990), where 1PL stands for first person, 2PL for second, 3PL for third, PN for proper name, HN for human noun, AN for non-human animate noun and IN for inanimate noun. Nouns higher (more leftward) on the hierarchy tend to participate in EP constructions when lower nouns do not.

1PL < 2PL < 3PL < PN < HN < AN < IN

The animacy hierarchy, as it interacts with the inalienability hierarchy, appears to affect EPRs equally in direct object and locative complement positions. Beginning at the lower end of the hierarchy, we find that EPRs in either direct objects or locative complements are never realized by inanimate nouns. The inanimate noun *imáto* 'car' cannot occur as an externalized PR in a direct object (20b) or a locative complement (20d).

(20) a. *o̱ kpé úghégbé ísi imáto á*
he wash mirror ASSOC car CS
'He washed off the mirror of the car.'
b. **o̱ kpé imátó ughegbe á*
he wash car mirror CS
'He washed off the car's mirror.'
c. *o̱ kú ame̱ kú ó̱ vbí úghégbé ísi imáto*
he throw water throw CL LOC mirror ASSOC car
'He splashed water onto the mirror of the car.'
d. **o̱ kú ame̱ kú ó̱ imátó vbi ughegbe*
he throw water throw CL car LOC mirror
'He splashed water onto the car's mirror.'

EPRs in both grammatical relations, however, include non-human animate nouns. The animate noun *ó̱ó̱kho̱* 'chicken' participates in EP constructions in direct objects under conditions of inalienability (21a), i.e., the leg is attached to the chicken, whereas it fails to do so under alienability (21b), i.e., the leg is detached from the chicken.

(21) a. *o̱ nwú ó̱lí ó̱ó̱khó̱ awe̱ ó̱ vbi erain*
he put the chicken leg CL LOC fire
'He put the chicken with its leg into the fire.'

b. *o̱ nwú áwé̱ ísi oókho̱ ó̱ vbi erain*
he put leg ASSOC chicken CL LOC fire
'He put the leg of the chicken into the fire.'

Animate nouns in locative complements occur as EPRs under conditions of inalienability. Consider *e̱nye̱* 'leopard' in (22a) (i.e., its tail is attached). Under conditions of alienability, *e̱nye̱* occurs as an IPR (22b) (i.e., its tail is detached).

(22) a. *o̱ ré̱ íza ó̱ ó̱lí é̱nyé̱ vbí úkpiriai*
he put footstep CL the leopard LOC tail
'He stepped onto the leopard's tail.'

b. *o̱ ré̱ íza ó̱ vbí úkpíríáí ísi e̱nye̱*
he put footstep CL LOC tail ASSOC leopard
'He stepped onto the tail of the leopard.'

Inanimate and non-human animate nouns aside, human possessors in EP constructions reflect the animacy hierarchy as it interacts with the inalienability hierarchy, with tense, and with definiteness of their modifier. Under normal pragmatic conditions and with a highly inalienable PM (e.g., a body part), full noun PRs like *okposo* 'woman' in direct object and locative complements show up as EPR when marked as definite, for instance by the definite determiner *ó̱li*.

(23) a. *ohí tóó ó̱lí ókpósó éto á*
Ohi burn the woman hair CS
'Ohi burned up the woman's hair.'

b. *!ohí tóó étó ísi ó̱li okposo á*
Ohi burn hair ASSOC the woman CS
'Ohi burned up the hair of the woman.'

c. *o̱ kú ame̱ kú ó̱ ó̱lí ókpósó vbí égbe*
he throw water throw CL the woman LOC body
'He splashed water onto the woman's body.'

d. *!o̱ kú ame̱ kú ó̱ vbí égbé ísi ó̱li okposo*
he throw water throw CL LOC body ASSOC the woman
'He splashed water onto the body of the woman.'

Full nouns in both direct object and locative complements are not externalized when indefinite. *Okposo* fails as EPR when unmodified or when modified by the quantifier *ó̱so* 'certain, some' (24b, d).

(24) a. *ohí tóó étó ísi okposo / okpósó ó̱so á*
Ohi burn hair ASSOC woman woman some CS
'Ohi burned up the hair of a woman / some woman.'

b. **ohí tóó ókpósó / ókpósó óső éto á*
Ohi burn woman woman some hair CS
'Ohi burned up a woman's / some woman's hair.'

c. *o kú ame kú ó vbí égbé ísi okposo /okpósó óso*
he throw water throw CL LOC body ASSOC woman woman some
'He splashed water onto the body of a woman / some woman.'

d. **o kú ame kú ó ókpósó / ókpósó óső vbí égbe*
he throw water throw CL woman woman some LOC body
'He splashed water onto a woman's / some woman's body.'

Full nouns positively marked for definiteness (*óli okposo*) combine with an associated PM to optionally allow EPRs in direct objects (25a–b) and locative complements (25c–d).

(25) a. *ohí tóó ébé ísi óli okposo á*
Ohi burn book ASSOC the woman CS
'Ohi burned up the book of the woman.'

b. *ohí tóó ólí ókpósó ébe á*
Ohi burn the woman book CS
'Ohi burned up the woman's book.'

c. *o kú ame kú ó vbí úkpún ísi óli okposo*
he throw water throw CL LOC cloth ASSOC the woman
'He splashed water onto the cloth of the woman.'

d. *o kú ame kú ó ólí ókpósó vbí úkpun*
he throw water throw CL the woman LOC cloth
'He splashed water onto the woman's cloth.'

Proper name and third person pronoun PRs with strongly inalienable PMs are externalized from direct object (26b) and locative complement (26d).

(26) a. *ohí tóó étó ísi oí / ísi oje*
Ohi burn hair ASSOC her ASSOC Oje
'Ohi burned up the hair of hers / Oje.'

b. *ohí tóó óí / ójé éto á*
Ohi burn her Oje hair CS
'Ohi burned up her / Oje's hair.'

c. !*o kú ame kú ó vbí égbé ísi oí / ísi oje*
he throw water throw CL LOC body ASSOC hers ASSOC Oje
'He splashed water onto the body of hers / Oje.'

d. *o̲ kú ame̲ kú ó̲ o̲í / ójé vbí égbe*
he throw water throw CL her Oje LOC body
'He splashed water onto her / Oje's body.'

Proper names and third person pronouns with an associated PM are also acceptable, although third person pronouns pose some difficulties for judgments of grammaticality in decontextualized sentences. This problem appears tied to a speaker's ability to fashion a suitable referent for the pronoun outside a specific discourse context. EPRs pose no acceptability problem in discourse contexts, since they frequently occur in Emai oral tradition narratives (Schaefer 1995). Accordingly, third person pronouns as well as proper names linked to associated PMs serve as EPRs in direct objects (27a–b) and locative complements (27c–d).

(27) a. *ohí tóó ébé ísi o̲í / oje á*
Ohi burn book ASSOC her Oje CS
'Ohi burned up the book of hers / Oje.'

b. *ohí tóó o̲í / oje ébe á*
Ohi burn her Oje book CS
'Ohi burned up her / Oje's book.'

c. *o̲ kú ame̲ kú ó̲ vbí úkpún ísi o̲í / oje*
he throw water throw CL LOC cloth ASSOC her Oje
'He splashed water onto the cloth of hers / Oje.'

d. *o̲ kú ame̲ kú ó̲ o̲í / ójé vbí úkpun*
he throw water throw CL her Oje LOC cloth
'He splashed water onto her / Oje's cloth.'

Second person possessors aligned with a body part PM in direct object or locative complements reveal a distinct constraint on EP constructions. They fail to appear as EPRs in perfective tense/aspect (e.g., Emai's completive present (28b) and completive past (28c) are distinguished by contrasting tonal melodies on their subjects, *aleke* and *áléké*, respectively). Perfective tense/aspect with EP constructions establishes a conflict between the speaker's presumption that the hearer is unaware that an event change affected the PR and the status of the second person referent as PR. How can second person hearers under normal pragmatic conditions not be aware that they were affected by an event?

This conflict between the speaker's presumption of PR knowledge and the hearer as a PR dissolves at future points on the time axis. The time frame in which hearers are asserted to be unaware of the event change effect on themselves is subsequent to the moment of utterance. Externalized second person pronouns, therefore, are acceptable in clauses marked for future occurrence by auxiliaries such as anticipative *ló̱* 'be about to' (28d) and predictive *ló̱* 'will' (28f). As in Emai's perfective, the anticipative and predictive functions of *ló̱* differ by a tonal melody on the subject (e.g., *aleke* vs. *áléké*, respectively). Unlike the perfective, the tense contrast in (28d) and (28f) is confined to time axis points subsequent to the moment of utterance.

(28) a. *aleke tóó étó ísi eé̱ á*
Aleke burn hair ASSOC your CS
'Aleke burned up the hair of yours.'
b. **aleke tóó wé̱ éto á*
Aleke burn your hair CS
'Aleke burned up your hair.'
c. **áléké tóó wé̱ éto á*
Aleke burn your hair CS
'Aleke burned up your hair.'
d. *aleke ló̱ too wé̱ éto á*
Aleke ANTI burn your hair CS
'Aleke is about to burn up your hair.'
e. **aleke kú ame̱ kú ó̱ vbí égbé ísi eé̱*
Aleke throw water throw CL LOC body ASSOC yours
'Aleke splashed water onto the body of yours.'
f. *áléké ló̱ ku ame̱ kú ó̱ wé̱ vbí égbe*
Aleke PRED throw water throw CL your LOC body
'Aleke will splash water onto your body.'
g. **aleke kú ame̱ kú ó̱ wé̱ vbí égbe*
Aleke throw water throw CL your LOC body
'Aleke splashed water onto your body.'

Under normal pragmatic conditions and with a highly inalienable PM (e.g., a body part), the first person PR *me̱* in completive present tense/aspect is externalized from direct objects (29b) and from locative complements (29d).

(29) a. !*ohí tóó étó me̱ á*
Ohi burn hair my CS
'Ohi burned up the hair of mine.'
b. *ohí tóó mé̱ éto á*
Ohi burn my hair CS
'Ohi burned up my hair.'

c. *!o̱ kú ame̱ kú ó̱ vbí égbé me̱*
he throw water throw CL LOC body my
'He splashed water onto the body of mine.'

d. *o̱ kú ame̱ kú ó̱ mé̱ vbí égbe*
he throw water throw CL my LOC body
'He splashed water onto my body.'

Compared to an inalienable PM, an associated PM with a first or second person PR under normal pragmatic conditions does not require an EP construction. Under conditions of associated inalienability but contrastive tense, first and second person PRs optionally serve as EPRs in direct objects (30a–d), and locative complements (30e–h).

(30) a. *aleke tóó ébé me̱ á*
Aleke burn book my CS
'Aleke burned up the book of mine.'

b. *aleke tóó mé̱ ébe á*
Aleke burn my book CS
'Aleke burned up my book.'

c. *aleke tóó ébé ísi e̱é̱ á*
Aleke burn book ASSOC your CS
'Aleke burned up the book of yours.'

d. *áléké ló̱ too wé̱ ébe á*
Aleke PRED burn your book CS
'Aleke will burn up your book.'

e. *aleke kú ame̱ kú ó̱ vbí úkpún me̱*
Aleke throw water throw CL LOC cloth my
'Aleke splashed water onto the cloth of mine.'

f. *aleke kú ame̱ kú ó̱ mé̱ vbí úkpun*
Aleke throw water throw CL my LOC cloth
'Aleke splashed water onto my cloth.'

g. *aleke kú ame̱ kú ó̱ vbí úkpún ísi e̱é̱*
Aleke throw water throw CL LOC cloth ASSOC yours
'Aleke splashed water onto the cloth of yours.'

h. *aleke ló̱ ku ame̱ kú ó̱ wé̱ vbí úkpun*
Aleke ANTI throw water throw CL your LOC cloth
'Aleke is about to splash water onto your cloth.'

6. Event constraints

Thus far, EPR acceptability has reflected constraints captured by hierarchies for the animacy of the PR and inalienability of the PM. One might assume that a convergence of these hierarchies, specifically their leftmost indices, would consistently lead to acceptable EP constructions. This conclusion, however, is not warranted. EP constructions also appear constrained by verb type, specifically one articulating change, as opposed to stativity or activity.

Throughout the immediately preceding section, verbs linked to EP constructions expressed change of state (30b), i.e., the book underwent a change of state with respect to its material integrity; and change of location (30f), i.e., the water changed its location from where it was to the cloth. To show how change of possession interacts with inalienability and animacy to control EP constructions, consider the verb complex *doo nwu* 'to steal.' Provided animacy and tense conditions are met, EP constructions containing an associated PM (e.g., *é̱we* 'goat') are acceptable with human noun PRs (31b, d). By virtue of the verb complex *doo nwu* 'to steal,' the goat becomes a possession of the woman, and no longer is in the PR's possession.

(31) a. *ó̱li okposo dóó é̱wé me̱ / ísi o̱í / ísi oje nwú*
the woman steal goat my ASSOC his ASSOC Oje carry
'The woman stole the goat of mine / his / Oje.'

b. *ó̱li okposo dóó mé̱ / ó̱i / ójé é̱we nwú*
the woman steal my his Oje goat carry
'The woman stole my / his / Oje's goat.'

c. *ó̱li okposo dóó é̱wé ísi e̱é̱ nwú*
the woman steal goat ASSOC your carry
'The woman stole the goat of yours.'

d. *ó̱li okposo ló̱ doo wé̱ é̱we nwú*
the woman ANTI steal your goat carry
'The woman is about to steal your goat.'

As the following will show, non-change verbs (those encoding perceptions, activities with no inherent change and statives) tend not to admit EPRs. Moreover, verbs which inherently fail to encode event change do not accept EPRs. However, when event change is introduced by a postverbal particle or conventional metaphor, these same verbs admit EPRs. It is thus situation type (verb + postverbal particle or conventional metaphor) rather than verb type itself which constrains EP constructions.

Turning to event constraints, consider the convergence of inalienability and animacy in the direct object of a cognition verb, such as the visual perception verb *zawo* 'see.' Under conditions of high inalienability of the PM (i.e., a body-part) and high animacy of the PR (i.e., 1PL pronoun), EPRs fail to occur with *zawo*. Regardless of PR animacy, in fact, EPRs never occur with any perception verb.

(32) a. **aleke záwó mé / óí / ójé akon*
Aleke see my his Oje tooth
'Aleke saw my / his / Oje's tooth.'
b. **áléké ló zawo wé akon*
Aleke PRED see your tooth
'Aleke will see your tooth.'

Zawo only accepts IP constructions (33).

(33) *aleke záwó ákón me / ísi eé / ísi oí / ísi oje*
Aleke see tooth my ASSOC your ASSOC his ASSOC Oje
'Aleke saw the tooth of mine / yours / his / Oje.'

EP constructions are restricted not only by perception verbs. Intransitive verbs of motion such as *o* 'to enter,' when referring to location change of a human entity in subject position, accept IP constructions.

(34) *ólí ómohe ó vbí íwé me / ísi eé / ísi oí / ísi oje*
the man enter LOC house my ASSOC your ASSOC his ASSOC Oje
'The man entered the house of mine / yours / his / Oje.'

In contrast, regardless of PR position on the animacy hierarchy, modifier definiteness or tense, the verb *o* does not admit EPRs in its locative complement when referring to location change of a human entity.

(35) a. **ólí ómohe ó mé / óí / ójé vbi iwe*
the man enter my his Oje LOC house
'The man entered my / his / Oje's house.'
b. **ólí ómohe ló o wé vbi iwe*
the man ANTI enter your LOC house
'The man is about to enter your house.'

Nonetheless, if definiteness of PR and tense conditions are met, this same verb with the same locative complement allows EPRs when specifying an event schema encoding a conventional metaphor with the sense 'to engulf.' Event change which construes *erain* 'fire' as engulfing *iwe* 'house' affects the associated PM *iwe* directly and the PR *ójé*, *óí* or *mé* indirectly. The change of state metaphorically expressed by the verb *o* and its participants allows, indeed requires, EPRs with pronouns as well as names and nouns positively marked for definiteness (36b, d).

(36) a. *erain ó ójé / ó̱í / mé̱ vbi iwe*
fire enter Oje his my LOC house
'Fire engulfed Oje's / his / my house.'

b. **erain ó vbí íwé ísi oje / ísi o̱í / me̱*
fire enter LOC house ASSOC Oje ASSOC his my
'Fire engulfed the house of Oje / his / mine.'

c. *erain ló̱ o wé̱ vbi iwe*
fire ANTI enter your LOC house
'Fire is about to engulf your house.'

d. **erain ó vbí íwé ísi eé̱*
fire enter LOC house ASSOC your
'Fire engulfed the house of yours.'

A conventional metaphor for the sense 'stuck' also leads to EP constructions. It is framed by an event schema incorporating the verb *o*, the subject *isie̱in* 'pepper' and the locative *e̱o* 'eye.' The stuck sense shows *isie̱in* undergoing a change of location relative to the highly inalienable PM *e̱o*, thus affecting the PR *mé̱*, *ójé* or *ó̱í*. EPRs are grammatical (37a, c), while IPRs are not.

(37) a. *isie̱in ó mé̱ / ójé / ó̱í vbi e̱o*
pepper enter my Oje his LOC eye
'Pepper stuck in my / Oje's / his eyes.'

b. **isie̱in ó vbí é̱ó me̱ / ísi oje / ísi ó̱i*
pepper enter LOC eye my ASSOC Oje ASSOC his
'Pepper stuck in the eyes of mine / Oje / his.'

c. *ísíé̱ín ló̱ o wé̱ vbi e̱o*
pepper PRED enter your LOC eye
'Pepper will stick in your eyes.'

d. **isie̱in ó vbí é̱ó ísi eé̱*
pepper enter LOC eye ASSOC your
'Pepper stuck in the eyes of yours.'

A conclusion warranted by the preceding facts is that event or situation type, rather than verb type per se, governs Emai EP constructions. At the core of the event type admitting EPRs is change: location change of a moving entity, possession change of a transferred entity, or state change of an entity.

Under this change hypothesis, verbs encoding simple activities should not allow EP constructions. Accordingly, verbs like *e* 'to eat' in the completive present (38) fail to admit EP constructions.

(38) **ohí é mé̱ / ójé émae*
Ohi eat my Oje food
'Ohi ate my / Oje's food.'

E allows only IP constructions in simple clauses.

(39) *ohí é émáé me̱ / ísi oje*
Ohi eat food my ASSOC Oje
'Ohi ate the food of mine / Oje.'

However, when *e*'s complement includes the terminal particle *léé* 'to finish Ving, already,' EPRs across the animacy hierarchy are acceptable, provided tense and definiteness conditions are met (40b, d). The terminal particle carries an implication of absolute change in the quantity of its direct object, i.e., *émae* 'food' is entirely consumed rather than simply eaten from.

(40) a. *ohí é émáé me̱ / ísi oje léé*
Ohi eat food my ASSOC Oje TERM
'Ohi finished eating all the food of mine / Oje.'
b. *ohí é mé̱ / ójé émae léé*
Ohi eat my Oje food TERM
'Ohi finished eating all my / Oje's food.'
c. *ohí é émáé ísi e̱é̱ léé*
Ohi eat food ASSOC your TERM
'Ohi finished eating all the food of yours.'
d. *ohí ló̱ e wé̱ émae léé*
Ohi ANTI eat your food TERM
'Ohi is about to finish eating all your food.'

Other activity verbs behave in a similar fashion. The verb *vun* 'to uproot' absent the terminal particle does not allow EP constructions.

(41) a. *ohí vún émá me̱ / ísi oje*
Ohi uproot yam my ASSOC Oje
'Ohi uprooted the yam of mine / Oje.'
b. **ohí vún mé̱ / ójé éma*
Ohi uproot my Oje yam
'Ohi uprooted my / Oje's yam.'

In conjunction with the terminal particle *léé*, *vun* with an inalienably associated PM admits an EPR (42).

(42) a. *ohí vún mé̱ / ójé éma léé*
Ohi uproot my Oje yam TERM
'Ohi finished uprooting all my / Oje's yam.'
b. *ohí ló̱ vun wé̱ éma léé*
Ohi ANTI uproot your yam TERM
'Ohi is about to finish uprooting all your yam.'

Postverbal particles and conventional metaphor thus impact EPR acceptability. They give rise to situations articulating a change of location, possession or state. Along with PR animacy and PM inalienability, it is situation or event change which controls EPR acceptability.

7. Residual problems

I have tried to suggest that Emai EP constructions are governed by interaction of the inalienability hierarchy, the animacy hierarchy, and the situation type incorporating change. Nonetheless, some verbs not yet considered show asymmetry in their acceptability of EPRs which is somewhat puzzling.

One of these problem areas centers on the transitive verb *gbe* in its 'kill' sense. Direct objects of *gbe* allow EP constructions only with first person PRs (43), remaining pronouns as well as full nouns and names being ungrammatical. A puzzling aspect of these facts is that despite an associated PM and a change of state verb, only first person is acceptable.

(43) a. *e gbé é̱wé me̱*
they kill goat my
'They killed the goat of mine.'
b. *e gbé mé̱ é̱we*
they kill my goat
'They killed my goat.'
c. *e gbé é̱wé ísi oje*
they kill goat ASSOC oje
'They killed a goat of Oje.'
d. *e *gbé ójé é̱we*
they kill Oje goat
'They killed Oje's goat.'

e. *e gbé é̱wé ísi e̱é̱*
they kill goat ASSOC your
'They killed a goat of yours.'

f. **é ló̱ gbe wé̱ é̱we*
they PRED kill your goat
'They will kill your goat.'

Although unacceptability beyond first person could arise from some combination of factors constraining EP constructions, it may be the speaker's inability to posit a lack of awareness of PR affectedness beyond the first person that is operating. Third person, proper name, and full noun PRs with associated PMs might be particularly vulnerable to the speaker's confidence level in asserting a lack of awareness of PR affectedness. As a reflection of a grammaticalization process evolving through time, it might also be that first person pronouns constitute PRs most likely to be externalized. They represent the speaker's highest level of confidence about the change affecting the PR, i.e., the speaker. If so, this contrasts with Heine's (1997) claim that lexical nouns precede pronouns in the evolution of constructions which appear syntactically similar to Emai EP constructions.

Another puzzling verb is *ríi* 'to be located.' With the inalienable PM *awe̱* 'leg' in its locative phrase, this verb, too, only allows EP constructions in first person (44b). Why would an apparently stative verb admit an EPR and then only in first person? Concerning the former, notice that the situation encoded by *ríi* and its participants in (44) reflects a change of location (e.g., the wound presumably was not on the leg at some prior point), which only first person PRs can confidently be held accountable for.

(44) a. **e̱mai ríi vbí áwé̱ me̱*
wound be LOC leg my
'A wound is on the leg of mine.' / 'A wound got on my leg.'

b. *e̱mai ríi mé̱ vbi awe̱*
wound be my LOC leg
'A wound is on my leg.'

c. *e̱mai ríi vbí áwé̱ ísi e̱é̱/ ísi o̱í/ísi oje*
wound be LOC leg ASSOC your ASSOC his ASSOC Oje
'A wound is on the leg of yours / his / Oje.'

d. **e̱mai ló̱ ri wé̱ vbi awe̱*
wound ANTI be your LOC leg
'A wound is on your leg.'

e. **e̱mai ríi ó̱í / ójé vbi awe̱*
wound be his Oje LOC leg
'A wound is on his / Oje's leg.'

If linked to an associated rather than inalienable PM (45b), the verb *ríi* does not allow EPRs even with first person PRs.

(45) a. *évbii ríi vbí úkpún me̱ / ísi eé̱ / ísi o̱í / ísi oje*
oil be LOC cloth my ASSOC your ASSOC his ASSOC Oje
'Oil is on the cloth of mine / yours / his / Oje.'

b. **évbii ríi mé̱ / wé̱ / ó̱í / ójé vbí úkpun*
oil be my your his Oje LOC cloth
'Oil is on my / your / his / Oje's cloth.'

When *ríi* involves an inalienable PM (unlike the associated PM of (45)), first and third person PRs show EP constructions, as do full nouns and names. Second person pronouns fail since *ríi* never accepts the future tense particle *ló̱* with its predictive or anticipative functions. Nonetheless, the situation type encoded in (46) is possession change, albeit temporary, affecting the grammatical subject, *ó̱pia* 'cutlass.' It remains to be seen whether other instances of EPRs can be accounted for by the change situation type and how residual cases like these can be more fully accounted for.

(46) a. *ó̱píá ísi o̱í ríi mé̱ vbí óbo̱*
cutlass ASSOC his be my LOC hand
'A cutlass of his is in my hand.'

b. **ó̱píá ísi o̱í ríi wé̱ vbí óbo̱*
cutlass ASSOC his be your LOC hand
'A cutlass of his is in your hand.'

c. **ó̱píá ísi o̱í ríi vbí óbó̱ ísi eé̱*
cutlass ASSOC his be LOC hand ASSOC your
'A cutlass of his is in the hand of yours.'

d. *ó̱píá ísi eé̱ ríi ó̱í vbí óbo̱*
cutlass ASSOC your be his LOC hand
'A cutlass of yours is in his hand.'

e. *ó̱píá me̱ ríi ó̱í vbí óbo̱*
cutlass my be his LOC hand
'A cutlass of mine is in his hand.'

8. Conclusion

This paper has examined the syntactic, semantic and pragmatic properties associated with externalization of the PR in the Edoid language Emai. Limited to direct object and locative complements, this process is constrained by inalienability and animacy hierarchies as well as specific restrictions concerning tense, PR definiteness and situation type. Neither inalienability nor high animacy narrowly defined is required for EP constructions, while tense and definiteness constrain participation of second person pronoun and human noun PRs, respectively. One of the principal conclusions of this analysis is that EP constructions, signaling a shift in the pragmatic status of PRs, are realized through activation of a topic schema brought about by a situation type incorporating change.

Acknowledgments

Analysis of data incorporated in this paper was supported by a grant from the National Science Foundation, SBR #9409552. Principal consultant on this project was Professor Francis Egbokhare of the University of Ibadan, Nigeria, without whose assistance this paper could not have been completed. For useful comments on the substance and form of this paper, I am indebted to Doris Payne, Mitzi Barker, and Immanuel Barshi.

Abbreviations

Abbreviations used in this paper: ANTI anticipative, APPL applicative, ASSOC associative, CONT continuous aspect, CL change of location, CS change of state, DISP displacement, LOC locative, PF positive focus, PRED predictive, R relator, RD right dislocation, SC subject concord, TERM terminal.

Notes

1 Orthographic conventions for Emai are consistent with those in Schaefer (1987), where *o̱* represents a lax mid back vowel, *e̱* a lax mid front vowel and *vb* a voiced bilabial approximant.

References

Bendor-Samuel, J. (ed.). 1989. *The Niger-Congo Languages*. New York: University Press of America.

Brown, Gillian and George Yule. 1983. *Discourse Analysis*. New York: Cambridge University Press.

Clark, Herbert. 1996. *Using Language*. New York: Cambridge University Press.

Comrie, Bernard. 1981. *Language Universals and Linguistic Typology*. Chicago: University of Chicago Press.

Croft, William. 1990. *Typology and Universals*. New York: Cambridge University Press.

Dixon, R.M.W. 1979. "Ergativity." *Language* 55: 59–138.

Givón, Talmy. 1984. *Syntax: A Functional-Typological Introduction. Volume 1*. Philadelphia: John Benjamins.

Heine, Bernd. 1997. *Possession: Cognitive Sources, Forces, and Grammaticalization*. New York: Cambridge University Press.

Levinson, Stephen. 1983. *Pragmatics*. New York: Cambridge University Press.

Schaefer, Ronald. 1987. *An Initial Orthography and Lexicon for Emai: An Edoid Language of Nigeria*. Bloomington: Indiana University Linguistics Club.

Schaefer, Ronald. 1995. "On the Discourse Function of Possessor Movement in Emai Prose Narratives." In Pamela Downing and Michael Noonan (eds.), *Word Order in Discourse*. Philadelphia: John Benjamins, 487–515.

Schaefer, Ronald. 1998. "Tone and Mood in Emai." Paper presented at Annual Meeting of the Linguistics Society of America. New York.

From Interest to Ownership

A Constructional View of External Possessors

Mirjam Fried
University of Oregon

1. Introduction

The empirical focus of this paper is a collection of Czech sentence patterns in which one constituent appears to require a possessive construal with another nominal in the sentence.[1] This configuration of a possessor-possessum relationship, in which the possessor is expressed externally to the nominal containing the possessum, is briefly illustrated in (1) below; the possessor is obligatorily marked by the dative case and represents an extra syntactic element, not an argument supplied by the valence of the predicate:

(1) a. *Petr* *zryl* *Honzovi*
Peter:NOM:SG:MASC dig:up:PP:SG:MASC Honza:DAT:SG:MASC
zahradu.
garden:ACC:SG:FEM
'Peter dug up Honza's yard.'

b. *Petrovi* *se* *rozbilo* *auto.*
Peter:DAT:SG:MASC REFL break:PP:SG:NEUT car:NOM:SG:NEUT
'Peter's car broke down.'

This pattern contrasts with internally expressed possessors, which require a special possessive form[2] and have to agree in case, number, and gender with the possessum, as shown in (2):

(2) a. *Petr* *zryl* *Honzovu*
Peter:NOM:SG:MASC dig:up:PP:SG:MASC Honza:POSS:ACC:SG:FEM
zahradu.
garden:ACC:SG:FEM
'Peter dug up Honza's yard.'

b. *Petrovo* *auto* *se*
Peter:POSS:NOM:SG:NEUT car:NOM:SG:NEUT REFL
rozbilo.
break:PP:SG:NEUT
'Peter's car broke down.'

The primary concern of this paper is the external possessor's (EPR) role in the clause structure. This aspect of the EPR phenomenon is far from fully understood, as indicated by the growing body of EPR literature (Berman 1982; Blake 1984; Shibatani 1994; Payne 1997a, 1997b; and papers in this volume), and revolves around several interrelated questions that will be addressed in this study: the semantic relationship between EPRs and thematic arguments with the same case marking, the structural source of EPRs as an extra syntactic element, and the relationship between EPRs and the head predicates. I will also explore the relationship between externally and internally expressed possessors, such as shown in (1) vs. (2), at least to the extent that it is directly relevant to the questions posed above. I will demonstrate that proper characterization of the EPR pattern involves several contributing factors, including the clause structure, the nature of the possessor, the inherent semantics of the possessum, and the semantic valence introduced by a given predicate.

The analysis of the Czech data will also lead to addressing two broader issues that keep reappearing in EPR research. One has to do with identifying semantic categories that play a role in syntax. I will provide evidence that the syntax-semantics interface must operate with semantic features more elementary than traditional semantic roles such as agents, patients, etc. and that it must allow layering of fine-grained semantic specifications; the semantic category in question will be the notion of 'affectedness'. The other area concerns the question of why, cross-linguistically, the construal of external possession is only rarely attested with transitive subjects. This tendency will be attributed to the main function of EPRs, which is to highlight the consequences an event may have for the possessor.

The paper is organized as follows. Section 2 establishes structural constraints on possessive construal in different clause types, leading to some preliminary generalizations about EPRs. Section 3 studies semantic principles that govern the distribution of EPRs as compared to internal possessors, completing the description of Czech EPRs. Section 4 explores the notion of 'affectedness', concentrating on the semantic features associated with Czech datives in general, and proposes a constructional treatment of EPRs. Section 5 returns to the restrictions on EPR construal, focusing on the preference for possessive construal with absolutive arguments and raising questions about representing 'affectedness'.

2. The syntax of Czech EPRs

One of the parameters along which EPRs can be evaluated concerns the structural conditions on the possessor-possessum relationship, namely, what syntactic constituents can serve as the possessum. The introductory pair of examples in (1) shows that Czech allows EPRs in both transitive and intransitive sentences and at first blush, the possessive construal appears to follow the pattern commonly found across languages: the EPRs can possess transitive objects, illustrated in (3), and intransitive subjects (4–5); we may further note that the intransitive clauses include both derived intransitives, such as the passive or agent-demoting reflexive in (4a) and (4b), respectively, and lexical intransitives, particularly the so-called unaccusative[3] variety (5):

(3) a. *Stavbaři nám úplně zničili*
builder:NOM:PL:MASC 1PL:DAT entirely destroy:PP:PL:MASC
zahradu.
garden:ACC:SG:FEM
(i) 'The builders completely destroyed our back yard.'
(ii) *'Our builders completely destroyed a/the yard.'

b. *Maminka chlapci ten*
mom:NOM:SG:FEM boy:DAT:SG:MASC that:ACC:SG:MASC
prst pofoukala.
finger:ACC:SG:MASC blow:on:PP:SG:FEM
(i) 'My/his$_i$ mom [soothed] the boy's$_i$ [injured] finger by blowing on it.'
(ii) *'The boy's mother [soothed] someone else's [injured] finger by blowing air on it.'

(4) a. *Zatím mu byly do němčiny*
for:now 3SG:MASC:DAT be:PP:PL:FEM into German:GEN:SG:FEM
přeloženy jen některé povídky
translate:PASS:PL:FEM only some:NOM:PL:FEM story:NOM:PL:FEM
'So far only some of his short stories have been translated into German.'

b. *Už se ti ta rána*
already REFL 2SG:DAT that:NOM:SG:FEM wound:NOM:SG:FEM
zacelila?
make:whole:PP:SG:FEM
'Has your wound healed yet?'

(5) a. *Dětem konečně trochu zčervenaly*
child:DAT:PL:FEM finally a:bit turn:red:PP:PL:FEM
tváře.
cheek:NOM:PL:FEM
'The cheeks of the children finally turned [healthy] pink.'

b. *Zvoní ti budík.*
ring:PR:3SG 2SG:DAT alarm:clock:NOM:SG:MASC
'Your alarm clock is ringing.'

c. *Už nám kvete i šeřík.*
already 1PL:DAT bloom:PR:3SG also lilac:NOM:SG:MASC
'Even our lilac is in bloom now.

There are, however, additional options, easily found especially with intransitive verbs. The examples in (6–8) below show sentences that contain an extra oblique constituent, thus offering an additional nominal that could be, at least in principle, owned by EPR. Notice that many of these obliques indeed turn out to be construed as belonging to EPR at the expense of the subject:

(6) a. *Spadlo mu do oka*
fall:PP:SG:NEUT 3SG:MASC:DAT in eye:GEN:SG:NEUT
smítko.
dust:NOM:SG:NEUT
'A speck of dust got into his eye.'

b. *Spadl mu do polívky*
fall:PP:SG:MASC 3SG:MASC:DAT into soup:GEN:SG:FEM
vlas.
hair:NOM:SG:MASC
'His hair fell into his/someone else's soup.'

(7) a. *Před domem se nám*
before house:INS:SG:MASC REFL 1PL:DAT
propadla silnice.
collapse:PP:SG:FEM road:NOM:SG:FEM
'In front of our house the road collapsed.'

b. *Na zámku jim straší*
on chateau:LOC:SG:MASC 3PL:DAT haunt:PR:3SG
Bílá Paní.
white:NOM:SG:FEM lady:NOM:SG:FEM
'Their chateau is haunted by the [spirit of] the White Lady.'

(8) a. *Pod stolem se ti válí*
under table:INS:SG:MASC REFL 2SG:DAT lie:around:PR:3SG
několik knížek.
several:NOM:SG book:GEN:PL:FEM
(i) 'There are a few books under your table.'
(ii) 'A few of your books are under the table.'

b. *Několik knížek se ti*
several:NOM:SG book:GEN:PL:FEM REFL 2SG:DAT
válí pod stolem.
lie:around:PR:3SG under table:INS:SG:MASC
(i) 'A few of your books are under the table.'
(ii) 'There are a few books under your table.'

On a closer look, it becomes obvious that we must also consider the semantics of the potential possessum; for that purpose I will assume a possessive hierarchy as follows:[4]

(9) body parts > kinship relations > close alienable entities > distant alienable entities

The data in question suggest a clear division between body parts and other types of possessa. The examples in (6) demonstrate that in intransitive clauses body parts are always interpreted as belonging to EPR, regardless of the grammatical function of the possessum; (6a) shows possessive construal with an oblique phrase, while in (6b) the possessum is obligatorily the nominative and the construal of the oblique is determined by context. In order to avoid this automatic interpretation, the body part would have to be explicitly marked as belonging to someone else:

(10) *Do polívky mu spadl*
into soup:GEN:SG:FEM 3SG:MASC:DAT fall:PP:SG:MASC
něčí vlas.
someone:POSS:NOM:SG hair:NOM:SG:MASC
'Someone's hair fell into his soup.'

Once we start moving down the possessive hierarchy, though, the construal options become more fluid. In order to see what plays a role in determining the possessum, it is instructive to study the examples in (7) and (8). In both variants in (7) the possessive relationship holds unambiguously between the EPR and the oblique because in either case the oblique outranks the nominative on the possessive hierarchy as the potential possessum: the referents of the nominative NPs in these particular examples are hardly, if at all, possessible. We may also note that (7b) is equally felicitous whether the referent of the dative is literally the owner of the chateau or simply a generically interpreted entity with loose association to it, without any real ownership (e.g., a settlement in the chateau's vicinity). In contrast to (7), the same clause structure shown in (8) displays different construal patterns in that both (8a) and (8b) are ambiguous in the same way. The ambiguity, however, need not be a mystery either. Presumably, books and tables fall on about the same point of the possessive hierarchy and consequently, there may not be any clear preference for either one as the possessum.[5] Finally, it may be interesting to note that in order to get both nominals to be the possessum, EPR cannot be used; instead, both nominals must appear with an internally expressed possessor:

(11) *Pod tvým stolem se válí*
under your:INS:SG:MASC table:INS:SG:MASC REFL lie:around:PR:3SG
několik tvých knížek.
several:NOM:SG your:GEN:PL:FEM book:GEN:PL:FEM
'Several of your books are under your table.'

Relevant configurations in transitive sentences are somewhat harder to come by, but when they do occur, they obey the same general principles. Consider the examples in (12) and (13) below, each of which contains a subject, object, and an oblique. There, too, the interference of the possessive hierarchy is evident. In these examples the oblique is higher on the hierarchy than the direct object and therefore is construed as the possessum:

(12) *Z tváře mi doktor*
from cheek:GEN:SG:FEM 1SG:DAT doctor:NOM:SG:MASC
vyoperoval malý nádor.
operate:PP:SG:MASC small:ACC:SG:MASC tumor:ACC:SG:MASC
'From my cheek the doctor removed a small tumor.'

(13) *Před domem už jim díry*
before house:INS:SG:MASC already 3PL:DAT hole:ACC:PL:FEM
vyspravili.
fix:PP:PL:MASC
'In front of their house, all the holes got fixed.' (lit. 'in front of their$_i$ house [they]$_j$ have fixed all holes.')

In light of these facts it does not come as a surprise that subjectless clauses also allow EPRs, which are then construed with whatever oblique nominal is present, as briefly illustrated below:

(14) *Teklo nám do kuchyně.*
flow:PP:SG:NEUT 1PL:DAT into kitchen:GEN:SG:FEM
'There was a leak in our kitchen (i.e. there was a way for rain to get into our kitchen).'

In purely structural terms, then, the attested patterns yield a somewhat cumbersome generalization: possessive construal occurs with non-subject nominals (direct or oblique) in all types of clauses (transitive, intransitive, atransitive) and can also occur with intransitive subjects. However, this generalization requires an additional provision which says that if a sentence contains more than one nominal that would satisfy the structural condition, a specific construal depends on the nominals' relative ranking on the possessive hierarchy.

3. Semantics of the EPR pattern

3.1 *Background*

In order to get a complete picture of the EPR phenomenon, it is also necessary to consider EPRs against the background of other possessive expressions. While Czech does not distinguish formally between different types of possessed entities, it does use a variety of strategies to express possession. With respect to the analysis of EPRs, two alternatives are particularly relevant.

One possibility is to express the possessor internally to the NP that contains the possessum, as in the following example showing a possessive pronoun:

(15) *jeho knihy/nos/matka*
'his books/nose/mother'

NP-internal possessors (IPRs) are, in principle, possible all across the possessive hierarchy, including body parts, but this generalization holds only if we abstract away from any contextual or semantic considerations. For example, the IPR strategy appears to be prohibited in certain environments, such as illustrated in (16); the reflexive possessive pronoun *svůj* 'self's' indicates that a non-subject nominal is possessed by the subject:

(16) a. *zatnout (*svoje) zuby, vypláznout*
clench:INF (*self's) tooth:ACC:PL:MASC, stick:out:INF
*(*svůj) jazyk*
(*self's) tongue:ACC:SG:MASC
'to clench one's teeth, to stick one's tongue out'

b. *Políbil* (*??svou/??mou) matku* *na*
kiss:PP:SG:MASC (??self's/??my) mother:ACC:SG:FEM on
*(*její) tvář.*
(*her) cheek:ACC:SG:FEM
'He$_i$ kissed [his$_i$/my] mother$_j$ on [her$_j$] cheek.'

The examples in (16) represent an alternative strategy for expressing possession, whereby the interpretation of a possessive relationship is left to context, without any overt marking on either the possessor or the possessum. In fact, zero marking is the most neutral strategy used with entities that are in a close whole/part relationship: it is obligatory with body parts and strongly preferred with kinship relations. But the same lack of overt marking commonly occurs with other kinds of possession as well, often leading to ambiguities:

(17) a. *Prodal* *jsem* *auto.*
sell:PP:SG:MASC AUX:1SG car:ACC:SG:NEUT
'I sold my/a car.'

b. *Žena* *se* *na nic*
woman:NOM:SG:FEM REFL on nothing:ACC:SG:NEUT
neptala.
NEG:ask:PP:SG:FEM
(i) '[My] wife didn't ask any questions.'
(ii) 'The woman didn't ask any questions.'

In cases such as these, a possessive reading is necessarily conditioned pragmatically and ambiguities are resolved by context.

3.2 *External vs. internal possessors*

Another source of semantic restrictions on the use of IPRs emerges from their competition with EPRs. The differences in their distribution are governed by several intersecting parameters that lead to various modifications of the possessor-possessum relationship. Let us start with a handful of examples that contrast an EPR in the (a) version with an IPR in the (b) version, noting that the two variants are not synonymous:

(18) a. *Zryl* *už* *jsi* *matce*
dig:up:PP:SG:MASC already AUX:2SG mother:DAT:SG:FEM
zahradu?
garden:ACC:SG:FEM
'Have you dug up mother's yard for her?'

b. *Zryl už jsi matčinu*
dig:up:PP:SG:MASC already AUX:2SG mother:POSS:ACC:SG:FEM
zahradu?
garden:ACC:SG:FEM
'Have you dug up mother's yard?'

(19) a. *Zavraždili mu i bratra.*
murder:PP:PL:MASC 3SG:MASC:DAT also brother:ACC:SG:MASC
'They murdered his_i brother on him_i, too.'

b. *Zavraždili i jeho bratra.*
murder:PP:PL:MASC also his brother:ACC:SG:MASC
'They murdered his brother, too.'

(20) a. *Šlapal* jí po kytkách.
step:PP:SG:MASC 3SG:FEM:DAT over flower:LOC:PL:FEM
'He stepped all over her flowers [and it won't make her very happy].'

b. *Šlapal po jejích kytkách.*
step:PP:SG:MASC over her:LOC:PL flower:LOC:PL:FEM
'He stepped all over her flowers.'

The examples in (18–19) differ from (20) in transitivity, but all three pairs show a similar difference in interpreting the possessive relationship as presented in the (a) and (b) variants. The EPR version in (18a) implies that the possessor has some interest in the event of yard digging; specifically, *matka* 'mother' is cast as someone who will benefit from it, either because she is the current owner of the yard (the most natural reading), or because she is in charge of maintaining it and had someone do it for her (however, this would be much more commonly expressed by a prepositional phrase dedicated to this particular benefactive interpretation: *za matku* 'instead of mother'). In contrast, the IPR form in (18b) only asserts that the yard was, at some point, in mother's possession and she need not even be alive at the time the sentence is uttered. The phrase *matčinu zahradu* in (18b) could easily mean 'the yard that used to be mother's'; such a reading is impossible in (18a). Similarly, the IPR version in (19b) is a clinical description of what happened to someone's brother, whereas the use of EPR in (19a) speaks to the fact that the result of the event somehow concerns the possessor. The difference between (20a) and (20b) is more subtle but follows the same general pattern: the use of EPR in (20a) implies that the stepping on the flowers will have consequences that are of interest to their owner; no such implication can be construed in (20b), which simply describes someone's path.

The crucial difference between EPRs and IPRs thus lies in whether or not the possessor is affected by the circumstances expressed by the predicate: while IPR expresses only possession, EPR has the additional property of 'affectedness'. This observation is further confirmed by the fact that an IPR can sometimes co-occur, however marginally, with an EPR. The example (21a) below uses an IPR phrase, while (21b) contains an EPR alongside the optional possessive pronoun.

(21) a. *Všechny jeho pacienty ošetřila.*
all:ACC:PL:MASC his patient:ACC:PL:MASC take:care:PP:SG:FEM
'She took care of all his patients.'

b. *Všechny (jeho) pacienty mu ošetřila.*
all:ACC:PL:MASC (his) patient:ACC:PL:MASC 3SG:MASC:DAT take:care:PP:SG:FEM
'She took care of all his patients for him.'

The sentence in (21b), where both IPR and EPR are present, is admittedly awkward stylistically, but it is not ungrammatical and it provides important evidence that the use of EPR is possible even when its role as a possessor is clearly played down by the presence of a plain, NP-internal possessor; at the same time, the circumstances described by (21b) are always interpreted as benefiting the possessor, regardless of whether the possessive pronoun *jeho* 'his' is included or not.

There are also cases in which only one and not the other possessive expression can be used, and the gaps are quite telling. Starting with the restrictions on IPRs, consider the examples in (22) and (23). They are structurally comparable to those in (20) above and yet, the IPR versions in both (22b) and (23b) are pragmatically very odd, as indicated by the symbol '#', while the form in (20b) is perfectly coherent:

(22) a. *Šlapal jí na nohy.*
step:PP:SG:MASC 3SG:FEM:DAT on foot:ACC:PL:FEM
'He stepped on her feet.'

b. #*Šlapal na její nohy.*
step:PP:SG:MASC on her:ACC foot:ACC:PL:FEM
'He stepped on some feet of hers.'

(23) a. *Mamince se točila hlava.*
mom:DAT:SG:FEM REFL spin:PP:SG:FEM head:NOM:SG:FEM
'Mom was feeling dizzy.'

b. #*Maminčina* *hlava* *se* *točila.*
mom:POSS:NOM:SG:FEM head:NOM:SG:FEM REFL spin:PP:SG:FEM
'A head my mom owns was spinning.'
*'Mom was feeling dizzy.'

The relevant issue here is the nature of the possessum. In particular, when the possessum is a *bona fide* body part (i.e., attached to the body), the use of IPR is prohibited. The IPR forms in (22b) and (23b) are not necessarily ungrammatical, but they shift the interpretation of the possessum, forcing a reading in which the body part is understood as an alienable entity and not something that is physically part of the possessor. The IPR version in (22b) invokes the image of a heap of foot-like objects being stepped on and (23b) is a description of an autonomous head-like object spinning around; here the contrast with the intended meaning associated with the conventionalized EPR-based expression in (23a) is particularly striking (cf. similar facts in Polish, as discussed by Frajzyngier 1997). This patterning is pragmatically consistent with the affected nature of the EPR: if a body part is affected, its possessor is necessarily affected as well. It is, therefore, conceivable for a language to develop at least a preference for an EP pattern in contexts in which a body part is presented as an affected argument; in Czech this preference has been fully grammaticized as the only option. Notice, however, that the use of EPR with body parts does not extend to contexts in which the body part is not an affected argument. As the following pair of examples illustrates, a possessive relationship cannot be construed with a transitive subject even if its referent is a body part, as in (24b); only IPR is possible in this structural context (24a):

(24) a. *Jeho šediny* *nikoho* *nedojímaly.*
his grey:hair:NOM:PL:FEM nobody:ACC NEG:touch:PP:PL:FEM
'His grey hair didn't win [him] any sympathy.' (lit. 'his grey hair didn't move anybody')

b. **Šediny* *mu* *nikoho*
grey:hair:NOM:PL:FEM 3SG:MASC:DAT nobody:ACC
nedojímaly.
NEG:touch:PP:PL:FEM

The role of the affectedness feature is further confirmed by certain gaps in the use of EPRs, which occur regardless of the type of possessum. Some examples are given below; notice that the sentences in (25–27) are structurally identical to those in (18–19) but the EPR versions in (25b), (26b), and (27b) are ungrammatical:

(25) a. *Už jste viděli jejich zahradu?*
already AUX:2PL see:PP:PL:MASC their garden:ACC:SG:FEM
'Have you seen their yard yet?'

b. **Už jste jim viděli zahradu?*
already AUX:2PL 3PL:DAT see:PP:PL:MASC garden:ACC:SG:FEM
'Have you seen their yard [for/on them]?'

(26) a. *Dvořákovu hudbu miloval.*
Dvořák:POSS:ACC:SG:FEM music:ACC:SG:FEM love:PP:SG:MASC
'He loved Dvořák's music.'

b. **Dvořákovi hudbu miloval.*
Dvořák:DAT:SG:MASC music:ACC:SG:FEM love:PP:SG:MASC
'He loved Dvořák's music [for/on him].'

(27) a. *Neslyšel ani její budík.*
NEG:hear:PP:SG:MASC neither her:ACC alarm:clock:ACC:SG:MASC
'He didn't even hear her alarm clock.'

b. **Neslyšel jí ani*
NEG:hear:PP:SG:MASC 3SG:FEM:DAT neither
budík.
alarm:clock:ACC:SG:MASC
'He didn't even hear her alarm clock [for her].'

In order to explain the difference between the two sets of examples we need to consider the semantics of the head predicates. All the verbs in (18–20) could be classified as 'contact' predicates in that their second argument is either a patient, as with the (strongly) transitive verbs *zrýt* 'dig up' or *zavraždit* 'murder' in (18) and (19), or a spatial endpoint impacted by a motion event, as is the case with *šlapat* 'step on' in (20). The inherent affectedness of the second argument in events of this kind presents a natural environment for the possibility that the second argument's possessor may also be affected in some way. In contrast, verbs of perception/experience, such as *vidět* 'see', *slyšet* 'hear', *milovat* 'love', do not imply any tangible affectedness of their second argument and, therefore, it is not likely that the owner can be naturally cast as being affected either. Put differently, it is not clear in what way the owner of the yard in (25a), for example, would be affected by somebody else's visual perception of it. It should not be too surprising, then, that the use of EPR with weakly transitive predicates, such as verbs of perception, is impossible. This patterning is also consistent with the restrictions on EPR as they have been reported for other languages (O'Connor 1994; Payne 1997b).

It must also be noted that the ungrammaticality of the EPR versions in (25–27) is not just a question of felicitous context, as evidenced by the following examples describing situations in which the second argument could be construed as at least potentially affected:

(28) a. *Zavraždili/*milovali mu bratra.*
murder/*love:PP:PL:MASC 3SG:MASC:DAT brother:ACC:SG:MASC
'They murdered/*loved his brother on him.'

b. *Zavraždili/milovali jeho bratra.*
murder/love:PP:PL:MASC his brother:ACC:SG:MASC
'They murdered/loved his brother.'

(29) a. *Lékař jí nohu ošetřil/ *viděl.*
doctor:NOM:SG:MASC 3SG:FEM:DAT leg:ACC:SG:FEM take:care/ *see:PP:SG:MASC
'The doctor has taken care of/*seen her wounded leg for her.'

b. *Lékař její nohu *ošetřil/ viděl.*
doctor:NOM:SG:MASC her:ACC leg:ACC:SG:FEM *take:care/ see:PP:SG:MASC
'The doctor has *taken care of/seen her wounded leg.'

The examples in (28) juxtapose a strongly transitive verb *zavraždit* 'murder' (repeating the examples from (19)) and the verb *milovat* 'love', showing that the latter cannot co-occur with EPR even though it is pragmatically plausible to expect that loving a human being (as opposed to music, as in (26) above) may have an effect on that person. In (29a), too, the possibility of inferring that the doctor's seeing somebody's wounds may have consequences for the wounded person is not enough to license the verb *vidět* 'see' in an EP pattern. The apparent difference between *zavraždit* 'murder' and *ošetřit* 'take care of' in (28b) and (29b), respectively, follows from the nature of the possessum: recall that EPR is obligatory with body parts, thus ruling out the use of IPR in (29b). However, this requirement does not prevent the co-occurrence of an IPR with the verb *vidět* 'see', since the use of EPR requires that the body part be an affected argument, as already demonstrated. And similarly, (27b) cannot be used even in a context in which 'he' was asked to listen for the alarm clock; the verb *slyšet* 'hear' simply excludes any possibility of volitional involvement on the part of the hearer, who, therefore, cannot be ordered to hear for anyone's benefit.

The examples in (28) and (29) are particularly valuable for establishing the crucial characteristics of EPRs. The fact that only potential or contextually motivated affectedness of the possessum does not automatically extend to its possessor must be taken as evidence that the affectedness feature is an inherent part of the EP pattern, not just something that can be inferred from context or from the possessive relationship alone. The gaps in the use of either EPR or IPR can, then, be explained as incompatibility between this intrinsic property of EPR and the semantics of other sentence elements, particularly the semantics of the head verb and the possessum.[6]

3.3 *Summary*

The facts presented so far lead to the conclusion that EPRs in Czech show several properties that are consistent with crosslinguistically observed patterns. EPRs can occur in both transitive and intransitive clauses but possessive construal is restricted to certain complements only; it is common with transitive objects, unaccusative subjects, and various obliques; it is rare with unergative subjects (this issue will be taken up in Section 5.1); and prohibited with transitive subjects. Within these structural limits, the distribution of EPRs is sensitive to several semantic/pragmatic factors: (i) the possessor's involvement in the event, (ii) the type of the head predicate, and (iii) the type of the possessum. First, the use of EPR is possible only when the possessor is cast as somehow affected, positively or adversely, by the circumstances described by the predicate; otherwise, only non-EPR expressions of possession are permitted. Consistent with this requirement, predicates that do not have any affected argument are less likely to welcome EPRs (e.g., verbs of perception or unergative predicates). And finally, if there are multiple nominals, all of which satisfy both the structural and semantic constraints on EPRs, possessive construal is determined by the potential possessum's relative place on the possessive hierarchy: the higher ranking entity will be construed as possessed by EPR and ambiguity will result in cases when the competitors rank about the same. In addition, body parts represent a special class in that they require the use of EPR, provided that the conditions on structure and predicate semantics are satisfied.

This web of relationships and constraints leaves us with several questions. One issue is the source of the EPR nominal, as it clearly is not supplied by the valence of the head predicates. Another question is whether, and in what way, EPRs are related to other dative-marked nominals, and this goes hand in hand with the most intriguing problem, which is the nature of the 'affectedness' feature. In the remainder of this paper, I will concentrate on these issues.

4. Analysis

4.1 *Theoretical background*

First, a brief theoretical digression is in order. The analysis will be based on the assumption that the basic units of linguistic structure are meaning-form pairs, in keeping with cognitively oriented approaches to grammar (Fillmore 1988; Langacker 1991; Goldberg 1995; van Hoek 1995). I will use the framework of Construction Grammar (Fillmore 1988; Fillmore, Kay & O'Connor 1988; Fillmore & Kay 1995), which offers a particularly convenient way of addressing the problem at hand. Its main features relevant to the subsequent discussion can be summarized as follows. The basic building blocks are meaning-form pairs called grammatical constructions, which represent conventional patterns of linguistic structure. Each construction may contain several layers of information (syntactic, semantic, pragmatic, etc.) and all of this is organized into two main domains: the external characteristics of the construction as a whole and its internal make-up. The internal structure is represented by box diagrams that are nested inside the larger construction and that carry information about the construction's constituents. A skeletal version of a verb-headed construction as an example is shown in Diagram 1.[7]

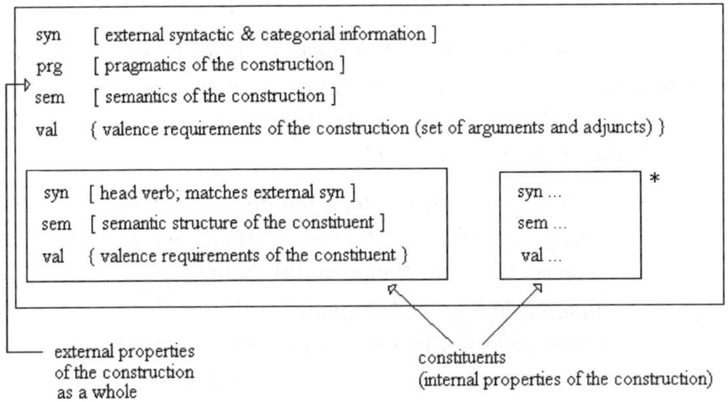

Diagram 1. Constructional template.

Information about co-occurrence restrictions is represented in the form of feature structures, which are lists of attribute-value pairs. Constructions can be combined with one another creating ever more complex patterns, and the combinatorial possibilities are regulated by the principles of unification, which ensure that attributes with contradictory values fail to combine. This property puts Construction Grammar in the family of other unification-based frameworks, such as Lexical Functional Grammar (Bresnan 1982), Head-Driven Phrase Structure Grammar (Pollard & Sag 1987), and others. Moreover, constructions may be clustered through a network of inheritance relations so that constructions that share a particular feature (or a set of features) form (hierarchical) groupings of mutually related construction types and subtypes.

Constructions that are headed by complement-taking entities must address, among other things, the alignment between predicate-specific participants, as projected from the lexicon, and their surface expression. This association is mediated by the predicate's valence, and canonical mapping between valence elements and syntax is handled by an inventory of 'linking' constructions. The head predicate and its arguments contribute certain properties to any larger construction they occur in; but a construction, as a complex grammatical object, is not just a sum of its parts: it may modify some of the features contributed by its subconstituents as well as add properties of its own. This means that the structure of any given clause need not be just a straightforward projection of its head but may be a combination of elements originating from multiple sources.

4.2 *Affectedness and case marking in Czech*

Let us first address the dative form. In Czech, two-place predicates that express an action directed at an endpoint fall into two major subclasses. One class, illustrated in (30), marks the second argument by the accusative, while the other, shown in (31), requires dative marking:

(30) *Políbil/pozdravil/rozzlobil/uhodil* *je/*jim.*
kiss/greet/make:angry/hit:PP:SG:MASC 3PL:ACC/*DAT
'He kissed/greeted/angered/hit them.'

(31) *Vládl/ublížil/překážel/pomohl*
rule/cause:grief/be:in:the:way/help:PP:SG:MASC
*celému/*celé* *městu/*město.*
whole:DAT/*ACC:SG:NEUT city:DAT/*ACC:SG:NEUT
'He ruled over/caused grief for/was in the way of/helped the whole city.'

The verbs in (30) are semantically transitive and their second argument is a patient, i.e., an entity that is directly affected by the action, either through physical manipulation or through some causal effect. In contrast, the verbs in

(31) express an action for someone's benefit or to someone's detriment, with a less immediate, more abstract effect on the second argument; this kind of 'mental' affectedness is more reminiscent of the traditional notion of *dativus (in-)commodi* (notice, incidentally, that most of the English equivalents in (31) code the second argument in oblique phrases, not as direct objects), and is generally consistent with broadly understood goals, which are always coded in the dative in Czech, whether prepositional or plain.[8]

Within the scope of this paper, it is not necessary, or even practically possible, to explore the complex network of connections between the various ways in which goal-like participants can be instantiated. Suffice it to say that the special kind of affectedness associated with Czech EPRs holds at least a family resemblance relationship to several thematic datives (cf. also Berman's 1982 classification of 'affected datives' in Hebrew). In addition to the class of dative-taking verbs exemplified above, the most salient example of the connection is provided by the highly productive experiential datives, shown below, that appear with predicates of uncontrolled experience:

(32) a. *Ulevilo se jí.*
relieve:PP:SG:NEUT REFL 3SG:FEM:DAT
'She started feeling better.'

b. *Tahle barva se mu*
This:NOM:SG:FEM color:NOM:SG:FEM REFL 3SG:MASC:DAT
nikdy nelíbila.
never NEG:appeal:PP:SG:FEM
'He never liked this color.' (lit. 'this color never appealed to him')

The dative complement is a core participant, often the only participant as in (32a), and semantically represents an entity that undergoes certain involuntary states, physical or mental. Another related use is the dative that appears with a handful of verbs of 'belonging', illustrated in (33), where the lexical meaning of the verb casts the affectedness explicitly as ownership:

(33) *Auto patří Petrovi.*
car:NOM:SG:NEUT belong:PR:3SG Peter:DAT:SG:MASC
'The car belongs to Peter.'

This use of the dative case is also related to marking the recipient role associated with verbs of 'giving'; the difference between the two verb classes has to do with the nature of the event types they represent. While the ownership with the verbs of 'belonging' is treated as a constant property in an existential expression, it is necessarily a dynamic relation with the verbs of 'giving'.

What is of particular interest with respect to EPRs are sentences of the following kind:

(34) a. *Budu ti (v Praze) překážet.*
FUT:1SG 2SG:DAT (in Prague:LOC:SG:FEM) be:in:the:way:INF
'(In Prague,) I'll be in your way.'

b. *Budu ti (při práci) překážet.*
FUT:1SG 2SG:DAT (at work:LOC:SG:FEM) be:in:the:way:INF
'I'll be hindering you(r work).'

Both examples are based on a dative-taking verb (*překážet* 'be in the way') and contain one additional, optional constituent (locative, in this case) that further specifies the circumstances of the event. The variant in (34a) is a straightforward instance of the dative-marked argument as exemplified in (31). Example (34b), however, provides evidence that when that same argument can be felicitously construed possessively, an EPR reading arises: 'work' is a possessible entity and can, therefore, form a possessum-possessor relationship with the dative nominal; 'Prague', on the other hand, cannot easily enter into any such relationship and does not trigger a possessive reading.

The observation that a thematic dative can be also construed possessively is taken as the first step toward establishing an explicit connection between the thematic dative(s) and EPR. The second step concerns the question of how this dative may turn up as an extra constituent that cannot be treated as an argument of the head verb.

4.3 *'Free' dative of interest*

The following series of examples illustrates the problem:

(35) a. *Pršelo.*
rain:PP:SG:NEUT
'[It] rained.'

b. *Petrovi pršelo.*
Peter:DAT:SG:MASC rain:PP:SG:NEUT
'Peter had rain.'

(36) a. *Na dovolené Petrovi pršelo.*
on vacation:LOC:SG:FEM Peter:DAT:SG:MASC rain:PP:SG:NEUT
'[It] rained during Peter's vacation.'

b. *Na horách Petrovi pršelo.*
on mountain:LOC:PL:FEM Peter:DAT:SG:MASC rain:PP:SG:NEUT
'Peter had rain [while he was] in the mountains.'

The basic form in (35a) shows that the head predicate *pršet* 'rain' does not have any valence and normally does not occur with any complement. In (35b) a dative nominal is added and the sentence now reports a situation in which the event of raining had definite consequences for whatever activity the referent of the dative NP was engaged in. Thus, (35b) is an instance of an affected argument in a clause whose head predicate clearly does not introduce any such participant. This configuration is further expanded in (36) by adding an optional locative phrase, which may or may not be construed as belonging to the dative NP, depending on the NP's possessibility (note the parallel with the two variants in (34) above). The result is a structure that has all the ingredients associated with the EP pattern: it contains a dative nominal that (i) is an extra syntactic element, (ii) shows the special kind of affectedness, and (iii) can be construed as a possessor of another nominal in the clause.

In order to account for the dative NP in sentences such as (35b), I propose to start with the assumption that there is a regular linking relationship between the Czech dative and the semantic roles clustered around the semantic notion of goal-ness. In constructional terms this means that there is a linking construction that specifies minimally the following association (very roughly):

$$\text{val}\ \left\{ \begin{bmatrix} \text{syn} & [\ \text{case DAT}\ ] \\ \text{role} & [\ \theta\ \ \text{GOAL}\ ] \end{bmatrix} \right\}$$

Diagram 2. Dative Linking Construction.

For the purpose of this paper it is not crucial to go into the representational detail of this particular construction nor to work out how exactly this construction relates to all the other datives, i.e., whether it is directly inherited by other linking constructions or whether we are dealing with synchronically less transparent relationships that may be, perhaps, traceable only as a historical connection. The important point is that the construction in Diagram 2 identifies a very salient relationship (Poldauf 1962; Mluvnice Češtiny 1986, cf. also Haspelmath in this volume), one that apparently extends beyond the predicates whose valence inherently requires it (hence the traditional term 'free dative' used by the Czech grammarians). An extension of this kind can be described as an emancipation process in which a particular linking relationship becomes conventionalized to such a degree that it takes off as an independent grammatical pattern. The new construction continues to carry (some of) the original meaning shaped by the event type associated with specific lexical predicates (Fried 1995; in spirit compatible with Goldberg 1995) but it also contains additional properties of its own.

Under these assumptions we can posit a special meaning-form pair that represents a specific, crystallized version of the general linking relationship(s) associated with Czech datives. The basic features of this linking construction, which I will call Dative of Interest (following Poldauf 1962), are presented in Diagram 3, using a somewhat simplified version of the box notation used in Construction Grammar.

```
prg   [ 'introduce an interested party' ]
sem   [ 'circumstances described by the predicate have significant consequences
        for the interested party, whose referent is not in control of the event' ]
val   { [ syn    [case      DAT]      ] }
      { [ sem    [animate   + ]       ] }
      { [ role   [θ  'interest']      ] }
```

Diagram 3. Dative of Interest Construction.

It is built into the construction that the constituent it licences, the 'interested party' has the following properties: it is affected in a particular way, it is an animate entity associated with a particular semantic role,[9] and it is always coded in the dative. When the Dative of Interest construction (DI) is inherited by another construction, it has the effect of adding a dative nominal to the valence of the head predicate and the result is another, more complex construction (DI is thus what Kay & Fillmore 1997 classify as an adjunct construction).

The specification of DI in Czech is quite straightforward, but additional restrictions and special features may, of course, appear in other languages that use an affected dative of this kind. It seems, for example, that this 'free' dative is restricted to pronominal expressions in French (Authier & Reed 1992); it is also conceivable that a language my further narrow down the kind of 'interest' associated with the DI construction so that it is conventionalized in a benefactive (or malefactive) reading only. Any such conditions would be simply part of the DI construction, representing its idiosyncratic features, which set it further apart from the thematic datives.[10] It remains to be established whether positing DI is sufficient to account for the EPR phenomenon, or whether an additional construction is necessary in Czech.

4.4 *EPR as a special case of the dative of interest*

We have seen that the dative-marked arguments can sometimes be interpreted as possessors if the clause contains a possessible nominal; recall the examples in

(34) and (36). At first glance, it might seem desirable to treat EPRs as a parallel phenomenon, the only difference being that the dative in (36) is of the constructional type, supplied externally by the DI construction, while in (34) it is thematic. Such an approach would effectively treat the possessive aspect of the EPR phenomenon as a pragmatic problem, where the possessive relationship would be inferred from context, depending on whether or not a given sentence contains a possessible item or not. Support for this view could be drawn from the fact that there are frequent cases of what appears to be an indeterminacy between plain interest and EPR, as shown below:

(37) *Uříznu ti nohu.*
cut:FUT:1SG 2SG:DAT leg:ACC:SG:FEM
(i) 'I'll cut your leg off.' (EPR)
(ii) 'For you I'll cut a leg.' (interest)

(38) *Žena mu do rána zemřela.*
woman:NOM:SG:FEM 3SG:MASC:DAT by morning die:PP:SG:FEM
(i) 'By morning his wife was dead.' (EPR)
(ii) 'By morning the woman died on him.' (interest)

(39) *Alena mu obě*
Alena:NOM:SG:FEM 3SG:MASC:DAT both:ACC:PL:FEM
knihy přeložila.
book:ACC:PL:FEM translate:PP:SG:FEM
(i) 'Alena translated both of his books for him.' (EPR)
(ii) 'Alena translated both of the books for him.' (interest)

All of these sentences contain an externally supplied dative and a possessible entity which, in turn, allows the dative to be construed possessively. Such indeterminacy would, after all, be in keeping with the general tendency in Czech to leave possession open to interpretation, without any grammatical marking.

Other facts, however, speak against this analysis. For one thing, even when multiple interpretation is in principle possible, there is an overwhelming tendency to apply the possessive reading, including configurations in which there are no readily possessible items. An example is provided by the following sentence:

(40) *(Stavbařům) natekla do příkopu*
(builder:DAT:PL:MASC) flow:PP:SG:FEM into ditch:GEN:SG:MASC
voda.
water:NOM:SG:FEM
'Water filled the ditch (to the construction workers' dismay).'

This example does not offer any obvious possessor-possessum relationship and yet, there is a sense in which the ditch is felt by speakers to 'belong' to the builders; as one speaker put it, "the builders are working on it and so in that sense it is theirs". A similar observation has been also made about affective datives in Hebrew (Berman 1982). But even more importantly, many instances of the extra dative allow *only* a possessive reading; especially interesting examples are in (7) and (8): all of those sentences have two candidates for being a possessum, none of them particularly high on the possessive hierarchy, and yet, one of them must always be selected; the interpretation of plain interest is not an option there. And finally, the structural restrictions on possessive construal cannot be addressed by DI alone, as it does not follow from its specification which nominal(s) can be interpreted as the possessum under the EPR reading, such that it (i) excludes transitive subjects and (ii) motivates the idiosyncratic use of unergative subjects. No such restrictions are associated with the use of DI, precisely because it lacks the possessive dimension as one of its inherent characteristics.

All of this suggests that there is a special grammatical construction that shares certain properties with DI but adds features of its own. In particular, it must be made explicit that EPRs represent interest overlaid with possession and that the co-occurence of these two semantic features is subject to specific grammatical constraints, rather than being a matter of pragmatic plausibility. The essence of the proposed construction is captured in the informal description in (41) below, which minimally makes clear one fundamental difference between the DI and EPR constructions in that the former is still just a linking construction, i.e., one that targets a particular valence element and expects to simply unify with a valence-bearing lexical item, while the latter is a verb-headed grammatical pattern that is internally structured:

(41) EP Construction (EPC)

Constructional properties:

a. inherit Dative of Interest (this accounts for the 'interest'-based affectedness and case marking of EPR);

b. introduce a possessive frame with its two participants (possessor and possessum) and specify their relationship to the rest of the construction;

Internal properties:

c. restrict the alignment possibilities for the argument that will be supplied by the head predicate and will serve as the possessum.

A more detailed representation of EPC is in Diagram 4, which should be read as follows. This construction introduces a POSSESSION frame (following

Fillmore's 1982 notion of 'interpretive frames') that must be incorporated into the overall interpretation of any EP pattern. This general requirement is indicated by the coindexing (↓↑) between the external semantics of EPC and the semantics of the head predicate; the latter brings along, among other things, its own semantic frame and its list of participants. However, the incorporation process does not amount to simply 'adding up' the two components, but is constrained in a specific way. The semantics of the possessor will incorporate the semantic information provided by the inherited DI, resulting in the semantically complex 'affected possessor'. The possessum, on the other hand, must unify with the inherent semantics of yet another participant; this is indicated by the notation #2[ ] & #3[ ] in the external semantics. The internal structure of EPC tells us that the prospective possessum will be supplied by the valence of the head predicate, but the selection is further restricted: the corresponding nominal must be ultimately interpretable as having a 'non-agentive' role in order to remain compatible with the inherent affectedness of the possessor. Specifically, if the possessum is linked to an agentive argument, the unification between #2 and #3 ought to fail. In reality, there are two possible outcomes with respect to this mapping, depending on the source of the agentive argument: while transitive agents always fail, unergative agents can be sometimes accommodated, with a shift in interpretation. I will return to this issue in Section 5.

```
inherit  DI
syn      [ head [cat V] ]
sem  ↓4 [ frame  POSSESSION
              Possessor   #1[ ]
              Possessum   #2[ ] (subject to possessive hierarchy) & #3[ ] ]
val      { #3 [ role  [ θ  'non-agentive']]}

  syn      [ head [cat V] ]
  sem  ↑4  [ frame  X
                Part.  #3[ ] ]
  val      {...#3[  ]...}
```

Diagram 4. EP Construction.

The effect of inheriting DI as part of EPC is spelled out in Diagram 5, which is a combination of Diagrams 3 and 4; the information contributed by DI is in italics.

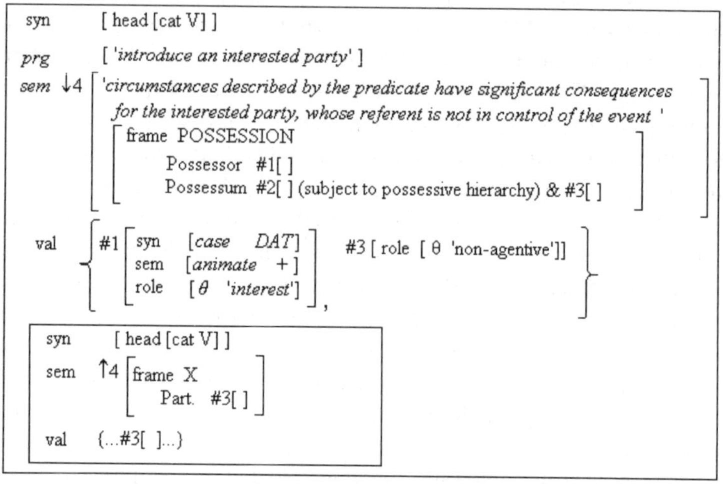

Diagram 5. Fully specified EPC.

With respect to theoretical implications about the status of semantic roles, this representation captures several important points. (i) A layered approach of this kind does not treat the notions ‘possessor’ or ‘possessum’ as semantic roles on a par with agents, patients, etc. but, rather, as a particular semantic property that can be imposed on such roles in specific grammatical contexts. (ii) The semantic role provisionally labeled ‘interest’ must be specified in such a way that the argument bearing this role (#1 in the diagrams) cannot unify with the affected argument (such as patients or other affected datives) in the valence of the head verb. And (iii), the requirement of a ‘non-agentive’ role for the possessum (#3) must be defined in such a way as to permit unification with just the right role-types in the valence of the head verb (patients, themes, locatives, etc.). These issues are the topic of Section 5.

5. Affectedness and event structure

5.1 *Possessive construal revisited*

We have established that Czech displays a clear preference for possessive construal with transitive objects, oblique complements expressing certain spatial endpoints (targets of a dynamic event or static locations in which an event takes place), and unaccusative subjects. Equally clearly, possessive construal is impossible with transitive subjects. I suggest that this patterning follows from the semantics of EPC and particularly from its focus on the affectedness of the possessor.

Poldauf's (1962: 342) formulation that the interest — whether in its basic meaning or overlaid with possession — is located at the end of an event, thus expressing a 'resulting interest', strikes me as particularly helpful in capturing the generally acknowledged relationship between EPRs and complete situations (cf. also Berman 1982; Authier & Reed 1992; O'Connor 1994). According to this view there is a definite connection between the affectedness of EPRs and endpoints, rather than starting points, of events; patient-like participants, goals, or locations are more consistent with highlighting affectedness than participants that bring about the effect (agents, causes, etc.). Such a connection is further supported by the observation that interest can be so easily interpreted as ownership, as is the case, for example, in Czech or Hebrew (Berman 1982); it is a manifestation of a simple, intuitive assumption that if an entity is affected, its possessor is likely to be affected as well. As a result, we can expect patients, themes, locations, and the like, rather than agents, to be compatible with an affected possessor.

Semantic analysis of this kind predicts that unergative subjects should be fairly low on the hierarchy of possible possessive construal. As already mentioned, unergatives occur only infrequently in Czech; nevertheless, they are not impossible, as evidenced by the following sentences:

(42) a. *Ta holka Aleně vůbec nejedla.*
that:NOM:SG:FEM girl:NOM:SG:FEM Alena:DAT:SG:FEM not:at:all NEG:eat:PP:SG:FEM
'That daughter of Alena's was a fussy eater.'

b. *Studenti jim tam hrozně kradli.*
student:NOM:PL:MASC 3PL:DAT there terribly steal:PP:PL:MASC
'Their students were horrible thieves.'

These examples have one conspicuous property in common: they do not express an action, as would be expected, given the lexical meaning of the head predicates (*jíst* 'eat', *krást* 'steal'); instead, they have a distinctly stative flavor. Put differently, in order for these predicates to work at all in EPC they have to be construable as reporting a state rather than an action whose instigator simply might be possessed by the referent of an EPR nominal. Consequently, they tend to have a habitual interpretation: (42a) is best paraphrased as 'Alena's$_i$ daughter was in the habit of not eating properly and it annoyed her$_i$' and (42b) as 'their$_i$ students were thieves and their$_i$ own reputation was, therefore, on the line'. It is also clear that the stative reading must be attributed to EPC because it does not obtain when the dative nominal is absent, as shown below on the verb *jíst* 'eat':

(43) *Ta* *(její)* *holka* *vůbec*
that:NOM:SG:FEM (her:NOM) girl:NOM:SG:FEM not:at:all
nejedla.
NEG:eat:PP:SG:FEM
'That girl (of hers) ate nothing.'

This variant does not imply a habitual reading but describes a one-time act. The example in (43) could be naturally continued by a comment such as 'I saw her plate — she didn't touch the food at all', which would be incoherent as a follow-up to (42a). Notice also that the agentive interpretation in (43) holds whether or not an internally expressed possessor is present.

This outcome can be taken as additional evidence that (i) affectedness of the possessor is a crucial feature of EPRs, (ii) the affectedness must be built into the meaning of EPC, rather than just inferred from context, and (iii) a grammatical construction can impose an interpretation that may modify the intrinsic semantics of its subcomponents. Without a special construction (EPC), the shift in meaning observed with the unergative predicates could not be easily accounted for. Nevertheless, the possibility of causing a shift in meaning is not free or random. In particular, it follows from the properties of EPC that the agent of a transitive verb must fail as a potential possessum since transitive predicates offer a better candidate (namely, the patient) to satisfy automatically the 'non-agentive' requirement on the possessum. Possessive construal with transitive agents/subjects in a language like Czech would thus be possible only at the point when the affectedness feature of the possessor would become bleached and EPR could then be used as an expression of possession only.

5.2 *Affectedness*

The preceding discussion finally brings us to the question of how the affectedness characteristic of EPRs should be handled by the syntax-semantics interface.

In this section, I will briefly outline the main issues and suggest a direction for further work on this problem.

First of all, the Czech material provides good evidence that the notion of affectedness is not an exclusive feature of patients. But in order to accommodate the fact that affectedness may come in various shapes, we must allow the possibility that morphosyntactic processes may be sensitive to semantic features smaller than standard semantic roles.

Another major question concerns the inventory of semantic roles. With respect to EPRs, the issue is what role this constituent is associated with or, put differently, how the notion of 'interest' or 'mental affectedness' fits in. It should be evident that EPRs cannot simply be patients in the traditional sense since they occur alongside indisputable patients in transitive clauses without violating the bi-uniqueness condition (whether or not the two semantic entities may use the same surface expression in some languages is a separate matter). Evidently, Czech EPRs share something both with patients (namely, their affectedness) and with dative-marked roles (the goal-like dimension, which includes the benefactive/malefactive component, for example). In order to get a more accurate picture of these relationships, we must opt for those approaches to semantic roles that do not make the feature 'affected' an exclusive property of patients but work, instead, with a more abstract semantic relation that represents simply an endpoint of an event (various conceptions of such a relation can be found in Foley & Van Valin 1984; Klaiman 1988; Croft 1992; Kemmer 1993; Fried 1995). Based on the data discussed in this paper, I envision the endpoint-based approach discussed below as one way of incorporating the semantics of EPRs into the domain of semantic roles.

I assume a frame-based, layered approach to semantic roles (Fried 1995, 1997; drawing primarily on Fillmore 1977, 1982; Wilkins 1987; and Jackendoff 1987), in which individual roles are defined as relational concepts derived from a small inventory of generalized event patterns. The roles are further assumed to be compositional, defined as specific clusters of certain elementary semantic notions such as motion, intention, affectedness, etc., each of which is assigned a particular value (positive, negative, or unspecified). The event patterns are organized into two major layers, spatial and causal, and the relationship between them is mediated by a more abstract pattern that consists of a Starting Point and Endpoint. In the context of EPRs, our primary concern is the Endpoint relation, which can be instantiated, roughly speaking, either as a patient (in the causal layer) or as a number of other relations in the spatial layer, including goals, locations, beneficiaries, or certain experiencers. The Czech material suggests that the notion of affectedness could be associated with the general Endpoint and from there passed onto its various instantiations, roughly divided into two categories: direct, or full, affectedness (patient-like) vs. indirect affectedness (goal-like), each of which can be further modified by manipulating the values in the feature-value pairs, yielding a cluster of subtly different but still related semantic roles.

With respect to EPRs it means that we could account for their special kind of affectedness as well as for the dative coding by positing a family of roles that would subsume what I have been labeling 'interest' together with dative-marked experiencers, recipients, beneficiaries, and the like. It should be added that while the network of event patterns and roles is assumed to be available universally, it does not follow that all languages must code EPRs in the dative; they obviously do not. Nevertheless, it ought to be more likely that EPRs will take a form linked to one of the roles clustered around the Endpoint (e.g., patient, benefactive, recipient, locative), than one associated with clearly unaffected roles (e.g. agent, source, instrument, etc.). All of the endpoint roles are modifications of the general feature 'affectedness', reflecting what it might mean to be the locus of effect in different event patterns. (The issue of how exactly we should go about setting up the matrices of attribute-value pairs in order to represent each modification is, then, a technical question of implementing this proposal.)

Locating the affectedness feature in the network of semantic roles does not, of course, address the possessive dimension of EPRs. But as was discussed in Section 4, the possessive relation must be introduced by a special grammatical construction, as a feature that occurs only in particular configurations of participants (cf. a similar account for Maasai in Payne, in press).

6. Conclusion

The goal of this paper was two-fold: to give a detailed description of the EPR pattern in Czech and to address several theoretical problems raised by EPRs. Within issues specific to the study of the EPR phenomenon, I concentrated primarily on the restrictions on possessive construal and the competition between EPRs and IPRs. I argued that both issues can be best captured by a semantically based analysis, centered around the valence of the head predicate and its interaction with the possessor-possessum relation. More specifically, EPRs are treated primarily as entities associated with a particular kind of affectedness, here called 'interest', and introduced by a special grammatical construction that regulates their distribution. The affectedness of EPRs is also key to accounting for the crosslinguistically attested patterns of possessive construal, which tend to favor affected (or at least non-agentive) roles as the potential possessum.

On a more general level, the data discussed in this paper highlight the need for (i) a sufficiently articulated semantic component that can capture subtle semantic distinctions below the level of traditional semantic roles, such as the distinction between different types of affectedness (Czech provides useful material in this respect since its case marking shows sensitivity to such fine-grained distinctions), and (ii) a framework that can accommodate instances in which sentential structure is not just a projection of the head predicate but may combine features supplied by a variety of sources (valence, constructional requirements, inherent semantic properties of nominals, and pragmatic conditions), all serving as equal contributors in building up larger grammatical units.

Acknowledgments

I wish to acknowledge those who contributed to this work at various stages, by reading early versions of this paper and offering helpful feedback and discussion: Andreas Kathol, Paul Kay, Alan Timberlake, and the editors of this volume.

Abbreviations

Abbreviations used in this paper: NOM nominative, DAT dative, ACC accusative, GEN genitive, LOC locative, INS instrumental, POSS possessive, MASC/FEM/NEUT masculine/feminine/neuter, REFL reflexive, SG/PL singular/plural, PR present, FUT future, PP past participle, PASS passive, AUX auxiliary, NEG negative, INF infinitive.

Notes

1 The data used in this study come from a variety of sources: utterances collected randomly by the author from the speech of a handful of speakers from Central and Northern Bohemia, made-up examples tested on those speakers, and data from other publications (particularly Poldauf 1962 and Mluvnice češtiny 1986, the academic grammar of Czech, which covers both spoken and written Czech). The grammaticality judgements reflect both the author's speech and the other sources used.

2 I will be glossing this form as POSS; it is morphologically distinct from the genitive case, which is governed by various verbs and prepositions and is glossed as GEN throughout this paper.

3 I am using this term strictly in the semantic sense, as a convenient label for intransitive predicates that do not introduce any agentive argument. Similarly, the term 'unergative' will be used to mean intransitive predicates whose valence does contain an agentive argument. Neither term is intended to imply any theory-specific structural claims.

4 It is possible that additional criteria, such as proximity, as suggested by Shibatani 1994, might play a role in the choice of a possessum. I will not be concerned with this aspect of the construal.

5 The two versions are not perfectly equivalent, as indicated by the switched order of the possible readings: (8a) is more likely to construe the oblique as the possessum, while (8b) is more likely to select the nominative. It appears that this difference correlates with the distribution of the topic function, which in Czech is marked by sentence-initial placement: notice that the topical element is the oblique in (8a) and the nominative in (8b).

6 It is also possible that the distribution of IPRs vs. EPRs interacts to some degree with discourse structure, most likely showing sensitivity to the notion of 'newsworthiness' (cf. a number of papers in Payne 1992). This dimension of the EPR phenomenon will be ignored here because it is not directly relevant to the issues explored in this paper.

7 The following abbreviations and symbols will be used in the diagrams: val 'valence', syn 'syntax', sem 'semantics', prg 'pragmatics', cat 'lexical category', Part. 'participant', θ 'thematic', the symbol # is a unification index, a set of square brackets [] encloses an attribute-value pair, a set of curly brackets {} encloses a list of valence elements (arguments and adjuncts), and the downward arrow ↓ indicates that the external semantics includes the semantics of the constituent marked by the upward arrow ↑.

8 In addition to a difference in case marking, these predicates also exhibit different syntactic behavior. For example, only the verbs in (30) can form promotional passives, as shown in (i), while the dative-taking verbs cannot (ii):

(i) a. *Byl tím velmi rozzloben.*
be:PP:SG:MASC 3SG:NEUT:INS very anger:PASS:3SG:MASC
'He was very angered by it.'

(ii) b. **Byl jimi velmi ublížen.*
be:PP:SG:MASC 3PL:INS very cause:grief:PASS:SG:MASC
'He was really hurt by them.

9 For the moment this is not intended as a claim about whether or not 'interest' should be understood as a semantic role in the traditional sense. For the immediate purposes of this discussion, it is meant merely as a claim that this dative nominal carries with it a particular semantic feature (or a set of features) that plays a role in morphosyntax. I will return to this issue in Section 5.

10 In fact, the classification of 'affected datives' in Hebrew, as presented by Berman 1982, would lend itself very well to the constructional treatment sketched out here. The differences among her four types ('non-participating affectee', experiencer, benefactee and its subtypes, and reflexive) could all be captured through changes in specifications of the basic DI construction, resulting in a family of DI constructions.

References

Authier, J.-Marc and Lisa Reed. 1992. "Case Theory, Theta Theory, and the Distribution of French Affected Datives." *West Coast Conference on Formal Linguistics* 10: 27–39.

Berman, Ruth A. 1982. "Dative Marking of the Affectee Role: Data from Modern Hebrew." *Hebrew Annual Review* 6: 35–59.

Bresnan, Joan (ed.). 1982. *The Mental Representation of Grammatical Relations*. Cambridge MA: MIT Press.

Blake, Barry J. 1984. "Problems for Possessor Ascension: Some Australian Examples." *Linguistics* 22: 437–453.

Croft, William. 1985. "Indirect Object 'Lowering'." *Berkeley Linguistic Society* 11: 39–51.

Croft, William. 1992. "Voice: Beyond Control and Affectedness." In Barbara Fox and Paul Hopper (eds.), *Voice: Form and Function*. Amsterdam: John Benjamins, 89–117.

Fillmore, Charles J. 1977. "Case for Case Reopened." In Peter Cole and Jerrold Sadock (eds.), *Syntax and Semantics 8: Grammatical Relations*. New York: Academic Press, 59–82.

Fillmore, Charles J. 1982. "Frame Semantics." In The Linguistic Society of Korea (ed.), *Linguistics in the Morning Calm*. Seoul: Hanshin Publishing Company, 111–137.

Fillmore, Charles J. 1988. "Mechanisms of Construction Grammar." *Berkeley Linguistic Society* 14: 35–55.

Fillmore, Charles J. and Paul Kay. 1995. *Construction Grammar.* Manuscript. University of California at Berkeley.

Fillmore, Charles J., Paul Kay, and Mary Catherine O'Connor. 1988. "Regularity and Idiomaticity in Grammatical Constructions." *Language* 64: 501–538.

Foley, William and Robert Van Valin. 1984. *Functional Syntax and Universal Grammar.* Cambridge: Cambridge University Press.

Frajzyngier, Zygmunt. 1997. "EP and NI as Coding Means: A System Interactional Approach." Paper presented at the Oregon Conference on External Possession and Related Noun Incorporation.

Fried, Mirjam. 1995. *Grammatical Subject and Its Role in the Grammar of Case Languages*. University of California, Berkeley Ph.D. dissertation.

Fried, Mirjam. 1997. "In the Garden Swarms with Bees: a Linking Challenge." Paper presented at the Annual Meeting of the Linguistic Society of America in Chicago.

Goldberg, Adele E. 1995. *A Construction Grammar Approach to Argument Structure.* Chicago: University of Chicago Press.

Jackendoff, Ray. 1987. "The Status of Thematic Relations in Linguistic Theory." *Linguistic Inquiry* 18: 369–411.

Kay, Paul and Charles J. Fillmore. 1997. "Grammatical Constructions and Linguistic Generalizations: the *What's X doing Y* Construction." Manuscript. University of California at Berkeley.

Kemmer, Suzanne. 1993. *The Middle Voice.* Amsterdam: John Benjamins.

Klaiman, Miriam. 1988. "Affectedness and Control: a Typology of Voice Systems." In Masayoshi Shibatani (ed.), *Passive and Voice*, 25–84.

Langacker, Ronald. 1991. *Foundations of Cognitive Grammar, vol 2: Descriptive Application*. Stanford: Stanford University Press.

Mluvnice Češtiny (The Czech Grammar). 1986. Praha: Academia.

O'Connor, Mary Catherine. 1994. "The Marking of Possession in Northern Pomo: Privative Opposition and Pragmatic Inference." *Berkeley Linguistic Society* 20: 387–401.

Payne, Doris L. (ed.). 1992. *Pragmatics of Word Order Flexibility*. Amsterdam: John Benjamins.

Payne, Doris L. 1997a. "The Maasai External Possessor Construction." In John Haiman et al. (eds.), *Essays on Language Function and Language Type*. Amsterdam: John Benjamins, 395–422.

Payne, Doris L. 1997b. "Argument Structure and Locus of Affect in the Maasai External Possession Construction." *Berkeley Linguistic Society 23. Special Session on African Languages, 98–115.*

Poldauf, Ivan. 1962. "Místo dativu ve výstavbvě věty ('Sentence structure and the role of the dative')." *Acta Universitatis Carolinae, Slavica Pragensia* IV: 335–345.

Pollard, Carl and Ivan Sag. 1987. *Information-Based Syntax and Semantics*, Vol.1. Stanford CA: Center for the Study of Language and Information (CSLI).

Shibatani, Masayoshi. 1994. "An Integrational Approach to Possessor Raising, Ethical Datives, and Adversative Passives." *Berkeley Linguistic Society* 20: 461–486.

van Hoek, Karen. 1995. "Conceptual Reference Points." *Language* 71: 310–340.

Wilkins, Wendy. 1987. "On the Linguistic Function of Event Roles." *Berkeley Linguistic Society* 13: 460–472.

External Possession, Reflexivization and Body Parts in Russian

Vera I. Podlesskaya Ekaterina V. Rakhilina
Institute of Cultural Anthropology,
Russian State University of Humanities

1. Introduction

This paper surveys basic syntactic techniques for expressing the relationship between a body part and its possessor in Russian, focusing on external possession constructions. We examine conditions allowing pronominalization by means of reflexive pronouns in the case of external possession.[1] Our main goal is to provide a coherent semantic and pragmatic account for the particular pattern of syntactic configurations exhibited by the various constructions in this family of construction types. In Russian, the range of allowable body part (BP) possession constructions depends on the semantic and pragmatic character of the relationship between the possessor and his/her/its body part, as represented by the lexical meaning of the head verb as well as conventionalized metaphorical extensions of this meaning.

Russian is one of the many Indo-European languages that allow so-called "possessor raising"[2] constructions, often classified as "dative of interest", "ethical", "benefactive", or "sympathetic dative" (cf., inter alia, Cienki 1993; Wierzbicka 1988 and the bibliography there). This type of construction is exemplified in (1):

(1) *Postiraj mne, požalujsta, rubašku*
wash:IMP I:DAT please shirt:ACC
'Wash me the shirt, please.'

The animate dative nominal in these constructions is "extra-thematic," in that this argument is not licensed by the head verb, or 'is not part of the case frame of the head' verb (Shibatani 1994: 465). The referent of the dative nominal is always affected by the action denoted by the head verb (Rakhilina 1982; Wierzbicka 1988: 169–236). The notion of affectedness will be discussed in detail in the next section, but, for now, we shall focus on the fact that the relationship between the referents of the dative nominal and the accusative nominal is usually, but not exclusively, possessive. In (2), for instance, the actual possessor of the shirt is marked internally to the direct object constituent:

(2) *Postiraj mne, požalujsta, papinu sinjuju rubašku*
wash:IMP I:DAT please father:POSS:ACC blue:ACC shirt:ACC
'Wash father's blue shirt for me, please.'

When a direct object is a BP nominal[3], the possessive interpretation is forced in Russian (as well as in many other languages where similar dative constructions are observed, as pointed out in Shibatani 1994). In this case, the referent of the dative nominal is interpreted as the possessor of the BP and no simultaneous internal possessor marking is allowed:

(3) *Petja slomal Vase (*svoju / *ego /*
Petja:NOM has.broken Vasja:DAT (*REFL:POSS:ACC / *he:POSS:ACC /
**Petinu / *Vasinu) ruku*
*Petja:POSS:ACC / *Vasja:POSS:ACC) arm:ACC
'Petja has broken Vasja's arm.' Lit. 'Petja has broken [for/on] Vasja [the] arm.'

An important point to notice here is the fact that, without the extra-thematic dative, if a Russian verb has an animate subject and a BP noun as another core argument (usually a direct object), it is the animate subject that is interpreted as the possessor and, normally, the possessor is not simultaneously expressed internally to the direct object constituent (either by a possessive pronoun, or by a reflexive possessive pronoun, or by a possessive adjective):

(4) *Petja slomal (*svoju / *ego / *Petinu)*
Petja:NOM broke (*REFL:POSS:ACC / *POSS:ACC / *Petja:POSS:ACC)
ruku
arm:ACC
'Petja$_i$ broke [his$_i$] arm.'

This means that, when the internal possessor marking is blocked, it is the presence or absence of the extra-thematic dative argument that indicates the actual possessor of the body part. Since in the absence of the dative argument the possessor is unambiguously associated with the referent of the subject, one could expect that there should be no need of reflexivization in sentences like (3) and (4) above. However, alongside (3) and (4), the following dative construction with the reflexive *sebe* is also possible:

(5) *Petja slomal sebe ruku*
Petja:NOM broke REFL:DAT arm:ACC
'Petja$_i$ broke his$_i$ arm.' Lit. 'Petja$_i$ broke [for/on] himself$_i$.[the] arm.'

Moreover, the reflexive pronoun *sebe* as an extra-thematic dative argument may occur even with verbs that describe situations where the possessor of the body part can be no one else but the animate figure expressed by the subject. This happens in constructions that we will conventionally label "pseudo possessor raising" (see Section 3 for further discussion):

(6) *Ona stërla Ø / sebe / *ej nogu*
she:NOM rubbed Ø / REFL:DAT / *she:DAT foot:ACC
'She gave herself a blister.' Lit. 'She$_i$ rubbed Ø / [for/on] herself$_i$ [the] foot [sore].'

The Russian verb *steret'* here has the meaning 'to get blisters because your shoes rub' and you simply cannot describe rubbing someone else's foot with this particular verb. Hence, the reflexive pronoun is not necessary for pointing out the actual possessor. In other words, again, the reflexive pronoun appears here not for reference disambiguation, and, thus, must have some other functional motivation.

On the other hand, not all verbs that allow BP nominals as direct objects also allow extra-thematic dative arguments — reflexivized or not. Verbs of perception and sensation, for instance, usually force the internal possessor marking and do not allow dative constructions:

(7) *Ja ljublju (*sebe /*tebe) tvoi svetlye volosy*
I:NOM love (*REFL:DAT /*you:DAT) your:ACC fair:ACC hair:ACC
'I love your fair hair.'

Thus, some verbs with BP direct objects in Russian allow an extra-thematic dative argument (sometimes with its further reflexivization) even in cases where there seems to be no reason for it, while others prohibit it even in cases where there are no obvious contraindications.

In this paper we will argue that, in addition to pure syntactic restrictions, there are also semantic and pragmatic factors controlling the phenomenon and that among them the lexical meaning of the head verb should be considered as one of the most decisive.

The paper consists of two major divisions, Section 2 and Section 3. In Section 2, we will compare possessor raising and possessor splitting constructions — two basic Russian constructions in which a possessive relationship is necessarily entailed between a BP nominal and a animate nominal, and where the possessor is expressed externally to the constituent which contains the (inalienably) possessed item. We try to show that it is mainly the lexical meaning of the head verb that controls the choice between possessor raising and possessor splitting patterns. Then, in Section 3, we discuss the conditions that allow or favor reflexivization in possessor raising constructions. We would like to advance a coherent semantico-pragmatic account that combines the lexical meaning of the verb, the semantic contribution made by the dative construction per se, and the semantic effect of reflexivization.

2. Basic BP external possession constructions in Russian

Russian has two distinct BP external possession constructions with extra-thematic arguments, namely, possessor splitting and possessor raising.[4] In the possessor splitting construction, the possessor is a core argument (usually a direct object marked with the accusative) of the head verb, while a BP nominal is an extra-thematic argument specifying the most "affected" BP. This argument is expressed by a directional preposition plus the BP nominal in the case required by the preposition — normally, dative or accusative.

(8) *Griša* *poceloval* *Mašu* *v* *guby*
Griša:NOM kissed Maša:ACC in lips:ACC
'Griša kissed Maša on the lips.'

(9) *Maša* *udarila* *Grišu* *po* *ščeke*
Maša:NOM hit Griša:ACC on cheek:DAT
'Maša hit Griša on the cheek.'

Possessor raising constructions, in contrast, have a BP nominal as a core argument (usually a direct object) of the head verb while the possessor is an extra-thematic argument marked with the dative. In other words, while in possessor splitting constructions it is the possessor and **not the BP** that fills in the valency slot opened by the head verb, in possessor raising constructions, it is the BP and **not the possessor** that fills in the relevant valency slot:

(10) *Babuška* *pomyla* *vnuku* *ruki*
grandmother:NOM washed grandson:DAT hands:ACC

'Grandmother washed the grandson's hands.' Lit.'...washed [for/on] grandson [the] hands'

(11) *Vrač obrabotal bol'nomu ranu*
doctor:NOM dressed patient:DAT injury:ACC
'The doctor dressed the patient's injury.' Lit. '...dressed [for/on] [the] patient [the] injury.'

In possessor splitting constructions the BP nominal can be omitted while the possessor nominal cannot:

(12) *Griša poceloval Mašu v guby*
Griša:NOM kissed Maša:ACC in lips:ACC
'Griša kissed Maša on the lips.'
⇒ *Griša poceloval Mašu*
Griša:NOM kissed Maša:ACC
'Griša kissed Maša.'

but not

⇒ **Griša poceloval v guby*
Griša:NOM kissed in lips:ACC
'Griša kissed on the lips.'

In possessor raising constructions, by contrast, the possessor nominal can be omitted while the BP nominal cannot:

(13) *Vrač obrabotal bol'nomu ranu*
doctor:NOM dressed patient:DAT injury:ACC
'The doctor dressed the patient's injury.' Lit. '...dressed [for/on] [the] patient [the] injury.'
⇒ *Vrač obrabotal ranu*
doctor:NOM dressed injury:ACC
'The doctor dressed the injury.'

but not

⇒ **Vrač obrabotal bol'nomu*
doctor:NOM dressed patient:DAT
'The doctor dressed [for/on] the patient.'

Thus, in possessor splitting constructions the BP nominal is a peripheral argument, while the possessor nominal is a core argument. In possessor raising constructions, vice versa, the possessor nominal is a peripheral argument, while the BP nominal is a core argument.[5]

The main function of possessor raising constructions is to show personal affectedness of the possessor (see for details Rakhilina 1982; Wierzbicka 1988: 169–236). The semantic element that could be conventionally labeled as 'affectedness' must be a part of the lexical meaning for those verbs that allow possessor raising. Using the framework outlined in Wierzbicka 1988: 169–236, we will demonstrate below that a difference in 'affectedness' may be the only difference between two almost synonymous verbs. This explains the fact that one verb allows integration of the possessor as an extra-thematic dative argument while another does not.

A good example of the lexically motivated possessor raising in the BP domain is given by a group of Russian verbs that denote different ways of 'touching'. Verbs that describe operating with the object itself, without any possible consequences for its possessor, normally disallow possessor raising, except in very limited contexts. For instance, the verb *potrogat'* 'to touch' is normally used with the internal possessor, or with possessor splitting, as in *(14)*, but not with possessor raising, cf. *(15)*:

(14) *Potrogaj eë za kolenku*
touch:IMP she:ACC for knee:ACC
'Touch her on the knee'

but

(15) ??*Potrogaj ej kolenku*
touch:IMP she:DAT knee:ACC
'Touch her knee.' Lit. 'Touch [for/on] her [the] knee'

The verb *potrogat'* allows possessor raising only in contexts like (16):

(16) *Po-moemu u neë temperatura. Potrogaj*
[it seems to] me by she:GEN fever:NOM touch:IMP
ej lob!
she:DAT forehead:ACC
'She seems to have fever. Feel her forehead!' Lit. 'Touch [for/on] her [the] forehead'.

The natural interpretation of (16) is 'touch her forehead to see if she has fever'. Here the verb *potrogat'* is a contextual synonym to the verb *poščupat'* 'to feel (to touch in order to find out something)'. The latter easily allows possessor raising which in BP possession constructions is interpreted as 'touching the BP in order to find out the state of the possessor'. One may use (17) with reference to a child who just came in after playing in the snow:

(17) *Nado poščupat' emu nogi, ne promočil li?*
[it.is].necessary touch.and.check:INF he:DAT feet:ACC NEG got:wet Q
'[We] should feel his feet: maybe he got wet'. Lit. 'touch-and-check [for/on] him [the] feet'

The verb *naščupat'* 'to find by groping', on the other hand, refers only to the fact of touching an object **as a whole**, and its parts cannot be specified. Therefore, the verb does not allow possessor splitting, cf. (18). It implies no affectedness of the possessor, and, therefore, it blocks possessor raising as well, cf. (19), and, thus the only possibility is to use the internal possessor, as shown in (20):

(18) **Ona naščupala ego v temnote za lokot'*
she:NOM groped he:ACC in darkness:LOC on elbow:ACC
'She found [and touched] him on the elbow in the darkness.'

(19) **Ona naščupala v temnote emu lokot'*
she:NOM groped in darkness:LOC he:DAT elbow:ACC
'She found [and touched] [for/on] him the elbow in the darkness.'

(20) *Ona naščupala v temnote*
she:NOM groped in darkness:LOC
ego lokot'
his:ACC elbow:ACC
'She found [and touched] his elbow in the darkness.'

Another example of lexical constraints on possessor raising is given by Russian verbs that denote greeting gestures. The degree of personal affectedness of the possessor may depend on the way the BP is involved in a culturally institutionalized gesture. For example, "kissing on the chin" (in the Russian cultural paradigm) is nothing more than specifying where a person was kissed. "Hand-kissing", on the other hand, is a sort of conventionalized gesture that requires that the recipient is personally affected, being the one who is greeted by this gesture. That is why the former is naturally described with possessor splitting (see 21 as opposed to 22), while the latter with possessor raising (see 23 as opposed to 24):

possessor splitting

(21) *On poceloval eë v podborodok*
he:NOM kissed she:ACC in chin:ACC
'He kissed her on the chin.'

but

(22) ??*On poceloval eë v ruku*
he:NOM kissed she:ACC in hand:ACC
'He kissed her on the hand.'

possessor raising

(23) *On poceloval ej ruku*
he:NOM kissed she:DAT hand:ACC
'He kissed her hand.' Lit. 'He kissed [for/on] her [the] hand.'

but

(24) ??*On poceloval ej podborodok*
he:NOM kissed she:DAT chin:ACC
'He kissed her chin.' Lit. 'He kissed [for/on] her [the] chin.'

Possessor raising is allowed in Russian not only from the direct object, but also from noun phrases introduced by directional prepositions. These noun phrases normally express the goal of movement. Here again, the BP nominal and not the possessor is required to satisfy the valency of the head verb, and the possessor is raised to show its personal affectedness. Compare the two sentences with the verb *nastupit'* 'to tread (over/on)' which keeps the possessor internally marked when the item, e.g. 'carpet' in (25), is alienably possessed, but forces possessor raising from the prepositional phrase in combination with a BP nominal, as in (26):

(25) *Ona nastupila na ego kovër (grjaznymi botinkami)*
she:NOM trod on his:ACC carpet:ACC dirty:INSTR boots:INSTR
'She trod over his carpet (in [her] dirty boots).'

(26) *Ona nastupila emu na nogu*
she:NOM trod he:DAT on foot:ACC
'She trod on his toe'. Lit. '...[for/on] him on [the] foot '

Possessors raised from phrases headed by directional prepositions may be expressed not only with "plain" dative case, but also with the preposition *k* 'to[ward]' plus dative. Thus (27) may have two variants — *k nemu* 'to[ward] he:DAT' and *emu* 'he:DAT':

(27) *Ona sela k nemu / emu na koleni*
she:NOM sat:down to[ward] he:DAT / he:DAT on knees:ACC
'She sat on his knees'. Lit. '...to[ward] him / him on [the] knees '

The possessor cannot be marked with *k* when his/her personal affectedness goes beyond pure spatial changes. Thus, the raised possessor in (28) can only be used with the plain dative, but not with *k* plus dative, because 'she' experiences not just that the shawl is moved from some place to her shoulders, but also that she feels now warmer and more comfortable:

(28) *On* *nabrosil* *šal'* *ej* / **k* *nej*
he:NOM threw:over shawl:ACC she:DAT / *to[ward] she:DAT
na pleči
on shoulders:ACC
'He threw the shawl over her shoulders.'

Similarly, one and the same expression with a BP may allow both plain dative and *k* plus dative in its direct meaning, but forbids *k* plus dative when used metaphorically:

(29) *Rebënok* *sel* *emu* / *k* *nemu* *na šeju*
child:NOM sat:down he:DAT / to[ward] he:DAT on neck:ACC
'The child$_i$ sat on his$_j$ neck'. Lit. 'him / to[ward] him on the neck' (pure spatial interpretation)

but

(30) *Rebënok* *sel* *emu* / **k* *nemu* *na šeju*
child:NOM sat:down he:DAT / *to[ward] he:DAT on neck:ACC
'The child$_i$ sat on his$_j$ neck'. Lit. 'him / *to[ward] him on the neck' i.e. "stopped earning money relying only on his financial help" (metaphoric interpretation).

In this section we have attempted to show that the lexical meaning of a head verb (or sometimes even the lexical meaning of a given combination of a head verb and a BP noun, cf. 'kissing someone's hand' vs. 'kissing someone's chin' in (21)–(24) above) can block, allow or favor the expression of extra-thematic arguments by means of possessor splitting, "plain" dative and prepositional dative possessor raising. In the next section we will demonstrate that the lexical meaning of a head verb controls also reflexivization in possessor raising BP constructions.

3. Reflexivization in possessor raising BP constructions: Some correlations between reflexivization and semantic reflexivity

A verb with an animate subject and a BP nominal as its other core argument may express the three following types of situations.

Type (A). Situations where the animate entity expressed by the subject is obligatorily the possessor of the body part. Thus, for (31) the only possible interpretation is that the tongue I bit was my own :

(31) *Ja prikusil [*ego] jazyk*
I:NOM bit [*his] tongue:ACC
'I bit [my] tongue.'

One simply cannot describe biting someone else's tongue with this particular verb.

Type (B). Situations where the animate entity expressed by the subject may or may not be the possessor of the body part. Thus, for (32) two interpretations are possible: 'my own ear' and 'someone else's ear' (though 'my own ear' reading is more natural):

(32) *Ja dotronulsja do uxa*
I:NOM touched at ear:GEN
'I touched [the] ear.'

For disambiguation it is necessary to specify the possessor, e.g. by means of a possessive pronoun.

Type (C). Situations where the animate entity expressed by the subject cannot be the possessor of the body part. Thus, in (33) *požat' ruku* 'to shake one's hand' means a sympathetic gesture and the body part involved cannot belong to the person expressed by the subject:

(33) *On požal mne ruku*
he:NOM shook I:DAT hand:ACC
'He shook my hand.' Lit. 'he shook [for/on] me [the] hand.'

We may say that types (A), (B) and (C) differ in degrees of **semantic** reflexivity, such that type (A) is the most semantically reflexive and type (C) is the least semantically reflexive.

In the next sections we will point out possible correlations between semantic and syntactic reflexivity. In other words, we will try to show that, depending on its lexical meaning, the head verb may block, allow or favor reflexivization of the extra-thematic argument and, furthermore, the extra-thematic argument substituted for a reflexive pronoun may differently contribute to the general meaning of the construction. The discussion in the next sections is restricted to verbs that don't allow the possessor of the related body part to be expressed, and those that allow the possessor to be expressed either internally or with "plain" dative possessor raising.

3.1 *Strong semantic reflexivity*

3.1.1

"Absolute" semantic reflexives are "verb plus BP noun" combinations that describe those relatively rare actions that are performed exclusively with a part of one's own body, normally, with some emotional or communicative motivation. Among them are, for instance, *stisnut' zuby* 'clench [one's] teeth (in a determined or angry way)', *priščurit' glaza* 'to squint [one's eyes],' *prikusit' jazyk* 'bite [one's] tongue (also in the figurative sense, i.e., to refrain from speaking)'. Possessors in these constructions cannot be expressed, either internally or externally:

(34) *On priščuril*
he:NOM squinted
**svoi* / **sebe* / **ego* / **emu* *glaza*
*REFL:POSS:ACC / *REFL:DAT / *he:POSS:ACC / *he:DAT eyes:ACC
'He squinted.'. Lit. 'He squinted [the] eyes'

3.1.2

Some semantically reflexive "verb plus BP noun" combinations do not allow external possessor, but allow what might be called "the descriptive reflexive" — the reflexive internal possessor that optionally appears together with some other internally expressed attribute of the BP noun. Compare the following two examples:

(35) *Maša namorščila lob*
Maša:NOM wrinkled brow:ACC
'Maša$_i$ wrinkled [her$_i$] brow.'

(36) *Maša namorščila Ø/svoj ušiblennyj lob*
Maša:NOM wrinkled REFL:POSS:ACC hurt:ACC brow:ACC
'Maša$_i$ wrinkled Ø/her$_i$ hurt brow.'

In (35) and (36) the brow unambiguously belongs to Maša, because wrinkling is a semantically reflexive action that can be performed exclusively with one's own brow. So the possessive reflexive adjective *svoj* is not needed for disambiguation in (36). It appears to show that the involved body part deserves special characterization. Sometimes when this characterization is implied by the context, the possessive reflexive adjective may appear even without any other attribute, as in (37) below, where the brow is characterized "internally", by the diminutive suffix *ik*:

(37) *Ne moršči svoj lob-ik!*
NEG wrinkle:IMP REFL:POSS:ACC brow-DIM:ACC
'Don't wrinkle your [nice, cute, pretty etc.] brow.'

Other examples of semantically reflexive "verb plus BP noun" combinations that allow the internal possessor marked with the "descriptive" reflexive include: *obliznut' guby* 'lick [one's] lips', *nadut' guby* 'pout [one's lips]', *vysunut' jazyk* 'to stick [one's] tongue out.' These constructions with the BP noun as a direct object are functionally very close to semantically reflexive constructions with BP nouns as instrumental objects — the latter also allow internal possessors marked with the "descriptive" reflexives:

(38) *Ščenok viljal svoim pušistym xvostom*
puppy:NOM wagged REFL:POSS:INSTR fluffy:INSTR tail:INSTR
'A puppy$_i$ wagged his$_i$ fluffy tail.' Lit. '...with his$_i$ fluffy tail'

3.1.3
Some semantically reflexive "verb plus BP noun" combinations allow what we call "pseudo possessor raising", cf. example (6) in Section 1. In these constructions the optional reflexive pronoun in the dative case (*sebe*) is, again, not needed for reference disambiguation:

(39) *Ona propoloskala Ø / sebe / *emu gorlo*
she:NOM gargled Ø / REFL:DAT / *he:DAT throat:ACC
'She gargled'. Lit. 'She$_i$ gargled Ø / [for/on] herself$_i$ [the] throat.'

Gargling presumes operating only with one's own mouth or throat, so the reflexive is not necessary for pointing out the actual possessor. Some other examples of semantically reflexive "verb plus BP noun" combinations that allow "pseudo possessor raising" include: *steret' sebe nogu* 'to rub [oneself] a foot [with a shoe]' (i.e. 'to get blisters, because the shoes rub'), *rastjanut' sebe myšcu* 'to strain [oneself] a muscle', *otrastit' sebe borodu* 'to grow [oneself] a beard.' The dative reflexive pronoun, when used with the verbs of these group, emphasizes the following two points: (a) the situation is either initiated by the subject / = possessor ('gargling'), or results from the action initiated by the subject / = possessor ('rubbing one's foot', e.g. as a result of putting on new shoes), and (b) the situation has a long-lasting visible effect on the subject / = possessor.

3.2 *Weak semantic reflexivity*

In this section we will describe three main types of the "verb plus BP noun" combinations that code activities involving body parts whose possessors are not obligatorily coreferential with the subject.

3.2.1

Expressions like *otkryt' rot* 'to open [one's] mouth', *zakryt' glaza* 'to close [one's] eyes', *povernut' golovu* 'to turn [one's] head', *sognut' ruku* 'to bend [one's] arm' — prototypically are semantic reflexives but allow non-reflexive use under special conditions.

When used prototypically as semantic reflexives they either have the unmarked possessor, as in (40), or allow "the descriptive" reflexive internal possessor (cf. Section 2.1.2.), as in (41):

(40) *On naklonil golovu*
he:NOM bowed head:ACC
'He$_i$ bowed [his$_i$] head'.

(41) *On naklonil svoju seduju golovu*
he:NOM bowed REFL:POSS:ACC grey:ACC head:ACC
'He$_i$ bowed his$_i$ grey head'.

The unmarked or internal possessor in the above examples presume the natural interpretation "the body part movement caused by psychoenergy" (cf. Rakhilina 1982). An important point to notice here is the fact that in Russian the same set of verbs is used to describe actions performed naturally with a part of one's own body as well as actions performed with a part of other person's body: *naklonit' golovu* means 'to bow [one's] head' and 'to push [someone's] head down'; *podnjat' ruku* means 'to raise [one's] hand' and 'to lift [someone's] hand' etc. Unlike English, which has a lexical opposition available, Russian makes use of dative possessor raising constructions to describe actions that cannot be performed in a natural way and need someone's help:

(42) *On naklonil Maše golovu*
he:NOM bowed Maša:DAT head:ACC
'He pushed Maša's head down. Lit. 'He bowed [for/on] Maša [the] head'.

In other words, the verbs of this group require the dative external possessor to express the unnatural non-reflexive sense. These cases might be called "the disabled dative" (cf. also the opposition "direct vs. indirect bodily actions" in

Wierzbicka 1988: 169–237). The dative external possessor may keep the "disabled" reading even when it is pronominalized by the reflexive pronoun. This is possible when the animate entity referred to by the subject performs an action with his/her own body part in an unnatural way with additional effort, manipulation or an instrument:

(43) *On naklonil sebe golovu*
he:NOM bowed REFL:DAT head:ACC
'He$_i$ pushed his$_i$ head down. Lit. 'He$_i$ bowed [for/on] himself$_i$ [the] head'.

3.2.2

Some "verb plus BP noun" combinations may elicit different semantic interpretations depending on whether the subject is coreferential to the possessor of the body part, or not. Thus, "damaging" verbs including *slomat'* 'break', *porezat'* 'cut', *pocarapat'* 'scratch', etc., denote activities when used non-reflexively (to damage someone's BP), but denote states as a result of some activity when used reflexively (to get one's own BP damaged):

(44) *Kakoj-to bandit slomal Pete ruku*
some thug:NOM broke Pet'a:DAT arm:ACC
'Some thug has broken Petja's arm.' Lit. '…[for/on] Petja [the] arm'

(45) *Petja slomal Ø / sebe ruku*
Pet'a:NOM broke Ø / REFL:DAT arm:ACC
'Petja$_i$ broke Ø / his$_i$ arm.' Lit. 'Petja$_i$ broke Ø / [for/on] himself$_i$ [the] arm.'

The dative reflexive marker in (45) is optional. Its function is the same as in the case of semantically reflexive verbs discussed in Section 3.1.3.: it emphasizes that (a) the situation is either initiated by the subject / = possessor ('Petja deliberately broke his arm,' e.g., to avoid military service), or results from the action initiated by the subject / = possessor ('Petja intentionally did something [e.g. went somewhere, although he was told not to do that] and, as a result, he broke his arm'), and (b) the situation has a long-lasting visible effect on the subject / = possessor. Without the dative reflexive pronoun *sebe*, (45) can refer only to an accidental event.[6]

3.2.3

Some "verb plus BP noun" combinations disallow possessor raising when used as semantic reflexives, but allow the dative possessor raising when used non-reflexively. These are normally combinations like *čistit' zuby* 'brush teeth' or *myt' ruki* 'wash hands' that denote actions that can be performed on both one's own and someone else's BP, but, when performed on one's own BP, are usually ritualized, habitual actions. Compare (10), repeated below as (46), with the raised possessor, and (47) with obligatorily zero-marked possessor:

(46) *Babuška pomyla vnuku ruki*
grandmother:NOM washed grandson:DAT hands:ACC
'Grandmother washed the grandson's hands.' Lit.'...washed [for/on] grandson [the] hands'

(47) *Babuška pomyla ruki*
grandmother:NOM washed hands:ACC
'Grandmother$_i$ washed [her$_i$] hands.'

4. Conclusions

We have examined several basic syntactic configurations in which possessors can be expressed externally to the corresponding possessed noun phrase in Russian: possessor splitting, possessor raising with the possessor expressed in the plain dative case, and possessor raising with the possessor expressed as the dative case object of the preposition *k*. Our central claim is that the lexical meaning of the verb, especially its semantic reflexivity, motivates the particular pattern of syntactic configurations that it allows. We have intentionally restricted our discussion to the domain of body parts as an example of inalienable possession. In other words, we have kept the "natural" relationship between the participants constant in order to figure out what other components of the verbal meaning can be reflected in the surface grammar of "raising" and "splitting".

A question for further study inevitably arises: how are the listed configurations used beyond the BP domain? It is clear, at least, that semantically reflexive verbs exist beyond the BP domain, and, moreover, they allow reflexivization following "the pseudo possessor raising" pattern. To give just two examples, consider the verbs *prisvoit'* 'to appropriate (to take something for one's own use without permission)', and *vzjat' v žëny / mužja* 'to marry (to take somebody as one's wife / husband)'. These verbs are easily used with a reflexive pronoun in the position of a dative ("raised") argument:

(48) *On prisvoil Ø / sebe den'gi kompanii*
he:NOM appropriated Ø / REFL:DAT money:ACC company:GEN
'He$_i$ has appropriated Ø / [to / for] himself$_i$ [some of the] company's money.'

(49) *On vzjal Ø / sebe v žëny Veru*
he:NOM took Ø / REFL:DAT in[to] wives Vera:ACC
'He married Vera." Lit. 'He$_i$ took Vera Ø / [to / for] himself$_i$ as a wife.'

The reflexive pronoun as a dative argument in the above examples it is not necessary for reference disambiguation: being semantically reflexive, these verbs cannot mean that one appropriates something to/for someone else, but only for oneself. Similarly, one cannot take somebody as a wife for someone else, but only for oneself. As in the BP domain, pseudo possessor raising here brings in the idea of intentionality and a long-lasting visible effect on the subject/possessor.

Thus, the following issue awaits further research: to what extent can the external possession patterns be exploited by the surface grammar beyond the BP domain? We believe that the study presented here has at least established the basis for further movement towards the solution of this problem.

Acknowledgments

This research was partially supported by the Russian Foundation for Humanities (grant 96–04–06396). An earlier version of this paper was presented at the External Possessor Conference, Eugene, Oregon, September 1997. We would like to thank Doris Payne and an anonymous reviewer for their helpful comments. We owe a lot to Barbara Partee and Jakov Testelec for discussing the semantic issues related to reflexivization and possessor raising. We are especially indebted to Thomas Payne whose insightful remarks significantly improved both the content and the style of this paper.

Abbreviations

Abbreviations used in this paper are: ACC accusative, DAT dative, DIM diminutive, GEN genitive, IMP imperative, INF infinitive, INSTR instrumental, LOC locative, NEG negative, NOM nominative, Q question, POSS possessive adjective / pronoun, REFL reflexive pronoun.

Notes

1 The term "reflexivization" is restricted in this paper only to the syntactic process, namely, triggering the reflexive pronoun. We do not discuss morphological reflexivization, i.e., the category marked on the verb with suffix *s'/sja* and connected with verbal transitivity.

2 Following M. Shibatani, we shall use the term possessor raising "without subscribing to a derivational account that 'raises the possessor' out of the adnominal position" (Shibatani 1994: 461).

3 The names of the covering of hair on the head and body of humans and animals, as well as the names of damaged areas of the body, like 'wounds', or 'blisters', are also included in the class of BP nominals in this paper.

4 In this paper we will not discuss how the described patterns of external possession in Russian correlate with the so called existential possession constructions (in which the possessor is marked with the preposition *u* 'by' plus the genitive noun). The insightful results in this area can be found in Iordanskaja-Mel'čuk 1995; Cienki 1993; Padučeva 1985, inter alia.

5 Taking into consideration this symmetry, it would be more consistent to use the term "BP lowering" for what we call possessor splitting; we, however, prefer to keep the term "possessor splitting" which is well established in Russian language studies (cf. Apresjan 1974: 153–156).

6 We are grateful to B. Partee for drawing our attention to the fact that externalization of the possessor in English is sometimes also used to mark the intentionality of the referred action. For example, possessor splitting in *I hit John on the arm*, as well as in *I hit myself on the arm*, forces the intentional reading of the sentences, while *I hit my arm [on the door]* typically refers to an accidental event.

References

Apresjan, Jurij. 1974. *Leksičeskaja semantika*. Moskva: Nauka.

Cienki, Alan. 1993. "Experiencers, Possessors, and Overlap Between Russian Dative and *u* + Genitive." *Berkeley Linguistic Society* 19: 76–89.

Iordanskaja, Lidija and Igor Mel'čuk. 1995. "**Glaza Maši golubye vs. Glaza u Maši golubye:* Choosing Between Two Russian Constructions in the Domain of Body Parts." *The Language and Verse of Russia.* [*UCLA Slavic studies, new series*, 2]: 147–171.

Padučeva, Elena. 1985. *Vyskazyvanie i ego sootnesënnost' s dejstvitel'nost'ju.* Moskva: Nauka.

Rakhilina, Ekaterina. 1982. "Otnošenie prinadležnosti i sposoby ego vyraženija v russkom jazyke (datel'nyj possessivnyj)." *Naučno-texničeskaja informacija. Serija 2,* 2: 24–30.

Shibatani, Masayoshi. 1994. "An Integrational Approach to Possessor Raising, Ethical Datives, and Adversative Passives." *Berkeley Linguistic Society* 20: 461–486.

Wierzbicka, Anna. 1988. *The Semantics of Grammar*. Amsterdam: John Benjamins.

Possessor Raising in a Language That Does Not Have Any

Maria Polinsky
University of California at San Diego

Bernard Comrie
Max Planck Institute

Introduction

Most studies of external possession have focused on the cases where a non-argument (possessor) becomes an argument. This change from the status of a subconstituent (i.e. constituent within a clause constituent) to that of an argument is known in the literature as Possessor Raising (or Possessor Ascension).[1]

For an example of Possessor Raising, consider the following minimal pair from Chukchi; in (1a), the possessor is a constituent in the object NP, in (1b) it is an argument of the clause (the possessum nominal is incorporated in the verb):

(1) Chukchi (Polinskaja & Nedjalkov 1987: 254)

a. *əməlʔo kelʔ-in məng-ət čəwi-nenet.*
all devil-POSS arm-ABS:PL cut-AOR:3SG→3PL
'He cut off all the arms on the devil(s).'
*'He cut off the arms of all the devils.'

b. *əməlʔo kelʔe-t məngə-čwi-nenet.*
all devil-ABS:PL arm-cut-AOR:3SG→3PL
'He cut off the arms of all the devils.'
?'He cut off all the arms on the devils.'

The comparison between (1a) and (1b) reveals a number of interesting morpho-syntactic and semantic effects associated with Possessor Raising. In (1a), 'devil(s)' is a constituent of the object and it cannot float the quantifier; in (1b), 'devils' is the direct object which floats the quantifier. From a semantic view-point, the main emphasis in (1a) is on the change of state undergone by the arms; any change in the state of the possessor is inferential, and as an inference, can be canceled (e.g., (1a) can have the continuation "... but the devils did not even notice that"). In (1b), the emphasis is on the change of state undergone by the devils (for details, see Polinskaja and Nedjalkov 1987; see also O'Connor 1996 for similar effects in Northern Pomo). Note also that the examples in (1) feature the inalienable possession relationship, the type most commonly involved in Possessor Raising constructions.

Thus, from the syntactic viewpoint, Possessor Raising creates an independent clausal argument out of a constituent of an NP. The main semantic effects associated with Possessor Raising consist of:[2]

(i) the entailment of a significant change of state in the referent of the possessor (this may or may not mean that a significant change of state in the referent of the possessum is no longer relevant);
(ii) the aboutness condition associated with the referent of the possessor.

The inseparability of the syntactic and semantic effects of Possessor Raising has rarely been questioned. In this paper, we would like to focus on the separability of this particular syntax and this particular semantics. We will examine a language — Tsez — where the semantic and pragmatic features associated with Possessor Raising occur without their relevant syntactic counterpart, that is, without the alternation between a constituent of an NP and an independent clausal argument. To account for such a split in effects, we will propose an analysis in terms of the satisfaction of semantic constraints which allow the interlocutors to override a syntactic violation. At the end of the paper we will discuss the cross-linguistic and theoretical questions raised by such an analysis.

1. The Tsez puzzle

In this section, we will examine the formation of Tsez relative clauses and we will show that Tsez violates the well-known Accessibility Hierarchy and island constraints.

1.1 *Preliminary information on Tsez*

Tsez, also known by its Georgian name Dido, is a member of the Nakh-Daghestanian (Northeast Caucasian) language family spoken in the west of the Daghestan Republic, Russia, by about 14 thousand speakers.

Tsez is a non-rigid verb-final language with a rich case system. Case-marking operates on an ergative-absolutive basis, with the ergative case for the subject of a transitive verb, and the absolutive case (identical to the citation form) both for subjects of intransitive verbs and for direct objects of transitive verbs, cf. (2a, b), (3):

(2) a. *už-ā kidbe-r gagali teƛ-si.*
boy-ERG girl-DAT flower:ABS give-PAST.WIT
'The boy gave a flower to the girl.'
b. *uži Ø-ik'i-s*
boy:I:ABS I-go-PAST.WIT
'The boy went.'

(3) *už-ā ˤono-d ažo y-eč'-si.*
boy-ERG ax-INS tree:II:ABS II-cut-PAST.WIT
'The boy cut the tree with an ax.'

The first and second person singular pronouns, exceptionally, do not distinguish between the absolutive and ergative functions morphologically, i.e., each one has a single form for these functions, cf. (4) and (5):

(4) *di γˤutk-ā Ø-iči-x.*
me:I house-INESS I-live-PRES
'I [man speaking] live in the house.'

(5) *di čorpa r-ac'-xo.*
me soup:IV:ABS IV-eat-PRES
'I am eating the soup.'

Most, though not quite all, vowel-initial verbs agree in noun class with their absolutive argument (see Polinsky 1995 for details). Tsez has four noun classes in the singular, indicated by roman numerals, merging to two (I versus II-IV) in the plural. The class I singular prefix is null. These features are illustrated in sentences (2)–(5). In (3), the verb takes the class II singular prefix *y-*, agreeing with the class II singular noun *ažo* 'tree'.

We would also note that Tsez has the phenomenon of null anaphora, whereby arguments that are recoverable from context can be omitted. Thus, in an appropriate context, the verb *teƛ-si* 'give-PAST.WIT' on its own would be an appropriate utterance.

Our primary interest in this paper is the formation of certain relative clauses in Tsez; we will first present a general overview of Tsez relativization and then discuss what we call relative clauses with Possessor Raising effects.

1.2 *Tsez relative clause formation: General overview*

The major relative clause formation strategy in Tsez is a participial construction. The relative clause, indicated in the following examples by means of enclosure in square brackets, normally precedes the head noun, though other orders are not excluded (for details, see Comrie et al. forthcoming). In the relative clause, what would be a finite verb in the corresponding main clause appears as a participle, e.g. the past participle in *-ru*, the present participle in *-xosi*.[3] Within the relative clause, there is no indication of the role that the referent of the head noun plays in that relative clause. Thus, in examples (6)–(8), corresponding to main clause (2a), repeated here for convenience, there is no indication within the relative clause that the referent of the head functions as subject of 'give' in (6), as direct object in (7), and as indirect object in (8). As these examples illustrate, relativization is possible on each of subject, direct object, and indirect object:

(2) a. *užā kidbe-r gagali teƛ-si.*
boy-ERG girl-DAT flower:ABS give-PAST.WIT
'The boy gave a flower to the girl.'

(6) [*kidbe-r gagali tāƛ-ru*] *uži*
girl-DAT flower:ABS give-PAST.PART boy:ABS
'the boy who gave a flower to the girl'

(7) [*už-ā kidbe-r tāƛ-ru*] *gagali*
boy-ERG girl-DAT give-PAST.PART flower:ABS
'the flower that the boy gave to the girl'

(8) [*už-ā gagali tāƛ-ru*] *kid*
boy-ERG flower:ABS give-PAST.PART girl:ABS
'the girl to whom the boy gave a flower'

It is also possible to relativize on various obliques and on constituents of infinitival constructions and of participial complement constructions (for details, see Comrie 1995; Comrie and Polinsky 1998a).

Despite the wide-ranging possibilities of relativizing on various arguments and adjuncts, Tsez relativization is not without limitations. It is usually impossible to relativize on objects of comparison and on genitives; the latter constraint is illustrated by (9):[4]

(9) a. *uži-s* $\gamma^{w\text{ʕ}}$*ay b-oxi-n b-ik'i-s.*
boy-GEN1 dog:III:ABS III-run-GER III-go-PAST.WIT
'The boy's dog ran away.'

b. *[*γ^wʕ ay* *b-oxi-n* *b-āk'i-ru*] *uži* *ʕiyay-xo.*
dog:III:ABS III-run-GER III-go-PAST.PART boy:ABS cry-PRES
'The boy whose dog has run away is crying.'

(10) a. *už-ā* *r-iču-s* *eni-s* *ʕoƛ.*
boy-ERG IV-break-PAST.WIT mother-GEN1 spindle:IV:ABS
'The boy broke the mother's spindle.'

b. *[*už-ā* *r-āču-ru* *ʕoƛ*]
boy-ERG IV-break-PAST.PART spindle:IV:ABS
eniy *ʕiyay-xo.*
mother:ABS cry-PRES
'The mother whose spindle the boy broke is crying.'

The ill-formedness of (9b) and (10b) is consistent with the accessibility hierarchy (Keenan and Comrie 1977), shown in a slightly modified version in (11). A possible generalization could be that the relativization cut-off point in Tsez is *before* genitives:[5]

(11) Subject > Object > Oblique > Genitive > Object of comparison

However, some genitives in Tsez do permit relative clause formation, in violation of (11) as well as of subjacency and certain island constraints.

1.3 *Tsez relative clause formation: Possessors*

Consider the pairs (12a, b), (13a, b), and (14a, b), where the (b) examples show relativization on a possessor.

(12) a. *kidbe-s* *xot'o* *b-oƛ-xo.*
girl-GEN1 foot:III:ABS III-hurt-PRES
'The girl's foot is hurting.'

b. [*xot'o* *b-oƛ-xosi*] *kid* *ʕiyay-xo.*
foot:III:ABS III-hurt-PRES.PART girl:ABS cry-PRES
'The girl whose foot is hurting is crying.'

(13) a. *uži-s* *obiy* *Ø-exu-s.*
boy-GEN1 father:I:ABS I-die-PAST.WIT
'The boy's father died.'

b. [*obiy* *Ø-āxu-ru*] *uži* *ʕiyay-xo.*
father:I:ABS I-die-PAST.PART boy:ABS cry-PRES
'The boy whose father died is crying.'

(14) a. *učiteli-s cim b-izi-x*
teacher-GEN1 anger:III:ABS III-rise-PRES
'The teacher is angry (lit.: The teacher's anger is rising).'

b. [*cim b-izi-xosi*] *učitel ˁiyay-xo.*
anger:III:ABS III-rise-PRES.PART teacher:ABS cry-PRES
'The teacher who is angry (lit.: whose anger is rising) is crying.'

These examples contrast with (10b), which shows that possessors within an argument of a transitive clause cannot be relativized, and with (9b), which shows that not all intransitive clauses permit relativization of possessors, either. Additionally, the examples just presented also violate island constraints (Ross 1967). For an illustration of the fact that Tsez does, indeed, respect the Complex NP Constraint, consider the following ungrammatical examples in (15b) and (15c) (the English 'translations' violate similar constraints and are given in double quotes to indicate literal translation):

(15) a. *dā-r* [$_{NP}$[$_{IP}$ *už-ā k'et'u žāk'-ru(-λi)*]
me-DAT boy-ERG cat:ABS hit-PAST.PART(-NMLZR)
xabar] *r-iy-xo.*
story IV-know-PRES
'I know the story that the boy beat the cat.'

b. *[*dā-r* [[*k'et'u žāk'-ru(-λi)*] *xabar*]
me-DAT cat:ABS hit-PAST.PART(-NMLZR) story
r-iy-xosi] *uži ˁiyay-xo.*
IV-know-PRES.PART boy:ABS cry-PRES
"The boy that I know the story that (he) beat the cat is crying."

c. *[*debe-r* [[*k'et'u žāk'-ru(-λi)*] *xabar*] *λā*]
thou-DAT cat:ABS hit-PAST.PART(-NMLZR) story who:ERG
r-iy-xo?
IV-know-PRES
"Who do you know the story that (he) beat the cat?"

We are now ready to formulate the problem we need to address: what determines the selective relativization of possessors in intransitive clauses?

2. Possessor raising?

There could be several possible approaches to explaining selective relativization of genitives. In this section we will examine the possibility that the relativization of genitives is preceded by Possessor Raising — the genitive becomes an argument and is then allowed to relativize because Tsez generally relativizes arguments (as shown above). In other words, the solution that we will present (and refute) would be to claim that (12)–(14), unlike (9), (10), involve Possessor Raising constructions. The closest analogy in English are sentences of the type 'the foot is hurting the girl' or 'the father died on the boy'. The semantics of possession in these tentative cases is quite typical, as (12) and (14) involve inalienable possession, and (13) involves a kinship relation (which often shows effects similar to those of inalienable possession).

2.1 *Characteristics of predicates in possessor relatives*

Let us start with the observation that the predicates in possessor relatives are intransitive and their semantics is non-agentive, which suggests that these could be unaccusative predicates. We were unable to find strong unaccusativity diagnostics in Tsez; the diagnostic which we are going to describe below is not without limitations, and we would regard our results with caution.

Tsez transitives and some intransitive verbs can derive iterative forms by means of the suffix *-nod-/-anad-*, compare (16a), (16b) for transitives and (16c–f) for intransitives:

(16)	a.	*ħaƛu-*	—	*ħaƛ^{w}anad-* 'drink'
	b.	*ħaƛ-*	—	*ħaƛanad-* 'butt (with horns)'
	c.	*k'oλi-*	—	*k'oλanad-* 'jump'
	d.	*ˤiya-*	—	*ˤiyanad-* 'cry'
	e.	*uti-*	—	*utnod-* 'turn around'
	f.	*ħapλi-*	—	*ħapλinod-* 'bark'

Intransitive verbs that do take the suffix *-nod-/-anad-* are semantically agentive, as in (16c–f). On the other hand, intransitives that do not co-occur with this suffix are non-agentive, a typical semantic correlate of unaccusativity, e.g.:

(17)	a.	*oƛ-*	—	**oƛnod-* 'hurt'
	b.	*izi-*	—	**izinod-* 'rise'
	c.	*ƛaħu-*	—	**ƛaħ^{w}anad-* 'tear' (intr.)
	d.	*-exu-*	—	**ex^{w}anad-* 'die'
	e.	*-oq-*	—	**-oqanad-* 'stay, be; become'
	f.	*meši-*	—	**mešinod-* 'light up'

The reason this diagnostic is of limited use is that for certain classes of intransitives, for example, verbs expressing permanent states ('stay') or irreversible events ('die'), it is unclear whether it is the morphosyntax or the sheer incompatibility of the verbal meaning with the semantics of habituality that blocks forms such as **iyanad-* 'know (iterative)' or **ex^{w}anad-* 'die (iterative)'.

The limitations of this diagnostic notwithstanding, it is sufficient for our purposes because it reveals that only unaccusative predicates can occur in possessor relative clauses.[6,7]

Cross-linguistically, it is common for absolutives to host Possessor Raising (cf. Aissen 1987: Ch. 8), which makes unaccusatives a natural class of verbs to occur in a Possessor Raising construction. (Why Tsez transitives resist such Possessor Raising is a separate issue.) We can, therefore, hypothesize that possessor relatives (as (12b), (13b), and (14b)) are formed from clauses with Possessor Raising. In other words, the possessor is not relativized directly while in the genitive position but, rather, undergoes Possessor Raising first.

2.2 *Silent Possessor Raising?*

If Possessor Raising does indeed occur, we should, ideally, expect to observe it in finite clauses. However, the absence of such clauses does not constitute evidence against Possessor Raising, because in principle, Possessor Raising can also occur as a "way station" to other processes, such as extraction. We will refer to this "way station" function as Silent Possessor Raising.

Let us first present the evidence that Tsez does not have an independent Possessor Raising construction. In general, when Possessor Raising occurs, it does so through one of two routes: either as an applicative construction, where the possessor becomes an argument and the possessum nominal remains an argument, or as a construction where the possessum nominal is an adjunct and the possessor assumes an argument position. For Tsez, the latter option is ruled out by the agreement facts. The possessum nominal in the relative clause is in the absolutive and therefore triggers agreement (recall that Tsez agreement is determined by the absolutive NP), as in (18a).[8] If the possessor assumed the single argument status in the relative clause, then the predicate of the relative clause would be expected to show its class, as in (18b), where 'hurt' agrees with 'the girl'. As this example shows, such a scenario is ungrammatical:

(18) a. [*xot'o* *b-oƛ̄-xosi*] *kid* *ˁiyay-xo.*
foot:III:ABS III-hurt-PRES.PART girl:II:ABS cry-PRES
'The girl whose foot is hurting is crying.' (=(12b))

b. *[*xot'o* $Ø_i$ *y-oƛ̄-xosi*] *kid*$_i$ *ˁiyay-xo.*
foot:III:ABS Ø:II II-hurt-PRES.PART girl:II:ABS cry-PRES
'The girl who is hurting in the foot is crying.'

Thus, if Possessor Raising is an option, we would expect it to be an applicative construction which adds another argument in the absolutive case. (Below, we consider the possibility of coding the added argument in some other case.) The internal grammar of Tsez does allow for the possibility of more than one argument being expressed by the absolutive because Tsez has the so-called biabsolutive construction, where the core arguments of certain periphrastic verb forms are agent and patient (Polinsky 1995; Comrie forthcoming), cf.:

(19) *uži čorpa r-iš-xo Ø-ičāsi yoƛ.*
boy:I:ABS soup:IV:ABS IV-eat-PRES.GER I-being is
'The boy is eating soup.'

Although this case marking possibility is available in principle, it is not available to encode an added possessor, as shown by the completely uninterpretable (20):

(20) **uži obiy Ø-exu-s.*
boy:I:ABS father:I:ABS I-die-PAST.WIT
'The boy's father died.'

Let us now consider the possibility of expressing the added possessor in an oblique case — after all, as long as the possessum is in the absolutive and determines agreement, the possessor can be expressed as an adjunct because adjuncts relativize freely (see above). A role close to possessor, Goal, can be expressed in Tsez by dative or possessive[9] (depending on whether or not possession transfer is permanent or temporary; cf. the dative in (2) above). However, the oblique encoding of a possessor is also ungrammatical:

(21) **uži-r/uži-q obiy Ø-exu-s.*
boy-DAT/boy-POSS father:I:ABS I-die-PAST.WIT
'The boy's father died.'

Thus, there are no independent finite clauses in Tsez that would illustrate Possessor Raising. This leaves us with the possibility of Silent Possessor Raising.

Under Silent Possessor Raising, the possessor, which presumably becomes an argument, should be able to show argument effects. One such effect is the antecedence of reflexives and reciprocals. In our work (Polinsky and Comrie 1997; forthcoming) we show that reflexives and reciprocals in Tsez are clause-bound and that they can be anteceded by both subject and object (with a preference for subject). Assuming that the possessor is extracted from the relative clause, its trace can still antecede a reflexive; given the possible argument status of the possessum nominal, we can expect the reflexive to be at least ambiguous.[10] Similar logic applies to the reciprocals. However, we see that examples

(22) and (23) below are not ambiguous since the possessor nominal cannot antecede a reflexive or reciprocal, which is a serious blow to the Silent Possessor Raising analysis.

(22) [*nesā nesi-z*$_{i/*j}$ *ʕaƛ-ā* *obiy*$_i$ *Ø-āxuru*] *žek'u*$_j$ *ʕiyay-xo.*
REFL-GEN2 village-INESS father:I:ABS I-died man:ABS cry-PRES
'The man$_j$ whose father$_i$ died in his$_{i/*j}$ village is crying.'
(lit.: The man that the father died on in his village is crying.)

(23) [*eni-obiy*$_i$ *sidā side-z*$_{i/*j}$ *ʕaƛ-λ-āy*
parents:IPL:ABS RECIP-GEN2 village-INESS-ABL
b-ok'āλ-ru] *xexbi*$_j$ *ʕiyay-xo.*
IPL-disappear-PAST.PART children:ABS cry-PRES
'the children$_j$ whose parents$_i$ disappeared from each other's$_{i/*j}$ village'

Next, if there were to be Silent Possessor Raising, we would expect *wh*-questions to be fed by such Silent Possessor Raising. However, (24a, b) are completely ungrammatical, regardless of the position of the *wh*-word:

(24) a. **šebi* [*xot'o* *b-oƛ-xosi*] *ʕiyay-xo?*
WH:ABS foot:III:ABS III-hurt-PRES.PART cry-PRES
b. *[*xot'o* *b-oƛ-xosi*] *šebi* *ʕiyay-xo?*
foot:III:ABS III-hurt-PRES.PART WH:ABS cry-PRES
'Who is crying whose foot hurts?'

Other effects associated with argumenthood are untestable given the limitations of non-agentive predicates — for example, it is impossible to come up with plausible examples of control structures. Altogether, we have no evidence for Silent Possessor Raising and we do have sufficient evidence against it.

Tsez is not the only language where effects associated with Possessor Raising can occur in the absence of Possessor Raising as such. For example, in Maithili, verb-possessor agreement is common but there is also no independent evidence to support Possessor Raising (Stump and Yadav 1988).

Since there is no independent evidence for Possessor Raising, positing it for (12)–(14) would make the analysis circular. Moreover, there are other violations of the Accessibility Hierarchy in Tsez which cannot be explained by Possessor Raising anyway — these include the relativization of complements of postpositions (see Comrie and Polinsky 1998a for details) and the occasional relativization of constituents of adverbial clauses, as in (25):[11]

(25) a. *qaraqy-ā gagali b-oγ-nosi ix*
bush-ERG flower:III:ABS III-bring-TEMP spring:III:ABS
b-āy.
III-come:FUT
'When the bush blooms, spring will come.'

b. [*gagali b-oγ-nosi ix*
flower:III:ABS III-bring-TEMP spring:III:ABS
b-ay-xosi] *qaraq*
III-come:FUT bush
'the bush that, when it blooms, spring will come'

Other syntactic possibilities which could be considered here include proper government (Rizzi 1990) and DP/NP contrasts (Chung 1991; Stowell 1991). It is beyond the scope of this paper to articulate both analyses at length. Let us just mention that the proper government analysis is problematic given that only genitives in subjects of unaccusatives relativize, whereas genitives which are constituents of absolutive objects do not (see (10b) above, where the possessor 'mother' is a constituent of the object NP in a transitive clause). The DP/NP contrast would predict extraction to be impossible out of NPs (cf. Chung 1991), but there is no independent evidence for treating the genitive-containing argument of an unaccusative as a DP and all other genitive-containing arguments as NPs.

To conclude this section, Silent Possessor Raising and some other syntactic solutions fail to account for the selective relativization of genitives. Our preliminary survey of a number of unrelated languages suggests that selective relativization of genitives is a fairly common occurrence, found, for example, in Maori (Polinsky and Comrie 1996), in Kambera (Klamer 1994: 309), in Chamorro (Chung 1991), in Tauya (MacDonald 1990: 16).

3. A semantic account of selective relativization of genitives

3.1 *Overriding syntactic ill-formedness*

As a viable alternative, we would like to suggest an analysis specifying appropriateness conditions on possessor relatives. In this analysis, we assume that there are certain syntactic conditions on relativization and that those conditions are respected. Roughly, the conditions state that relativization is possible on clausal constituents but not permitted on constituents within those constituents, i.e. subconstituents. Relativization of subconstituents is therefore ill-formed. However, it can be tolerated if certain semantic or pragmatic conditions are met, and it is these conditions that we are going to examine below. As we present our proposal, we will refer to the conditions in question as semantic. However, our conception of semantics is broader than usual — it subsumes both the truth-conditions on the well-formedness of utterances and appropriateness conditions as long as they are potentially formalizable, for example, in terms of semantic properties.

From a syntactic standpoint, the extraction of a possessor nominal out of a clause constituent is ill-formed — this is demonstrated by (9b), (10b), and (24). However, the syntactic ill-formedness can be overridden by the appropriate semantics. To override the structural ill-formedness, the hearer has to assign a plausible interpretation to the association between the head NP and an unexpressed constituent in the attributive clause. If a plausible interpretation can be assigned, as has been the case in the examples examined so far, then the resulting relative clause construction is judged acceptable. If no such plausible interpretation can be assigned, then the resulting relative clause is judged unacceptable.

Let us start with the reason why possessor relatives as in (12)–(14) *are* accepted as well-formed. We can approach this question in terms of an overall analysis of relative clauses, whereby the hearer has to extract a plausible interpretation that will link together the head noun and the attributive clause. In many instances, the argument structure of the verb in the relative clause will give a reasonably clear indication of which constituent is missing from the relative clause, as in the interpretation of (6)–(8), though this procedure is complicated slightly by the need to bear in mind the general possibility of null anaphora in Tsez.

However, one can achieve a slightly broader perspective by considering the notion of "frame" (Fillmore 1982; 1985) rather than just the argument structure of the verb. A particular lexical item will evoke a frame consisting of a number of other items that must be present in order to complete its semantics. Thus, the verb 'give' evokes a giver, a recipient, and a gift. Predicates with such general semantics as 'be located' or 'go' will evoke a time and place at which the situation in question holds. The plausibility of a particular relative clause is then determined primarily by the availability of the corresponding head noun in the frame of the lexical verb in question.

3.2 *Semantic conditions on appropriateness*

We would now like to specify two semantic conditions which, if met, allow possessor relatives to be interpretable. Returning to the possessor examples above, 'foot', being a body part, necessarily evokes the concept of the person or animal to whom the foot belongs. Likewise, 'father', being a relational concept, necessarily evokes the concept of the "possessor" of that father, i.e. the child; whereas 'boy', for instance, being nonrelational, does not invoke a frame. In other words, the crucial examples (12)–(14) involve a relational noun or a noun expressing inalienable possession. Such nouns have an argument structure of their own; that is, they are linked to their respective possessors in the linguistic structure. In a *typical* situation in the real world, the referents of such nouns do not exist independently of something else. More specifically, their existence is contingent on:

(i) the existence of another referent or
(ii) a specific situation in which they undergo an apparent change of state.

The contingency condition in (i) represents the reference point relationship in which one referent (R_i) is accessed indirectly, via another (R_j), and the latter referent is cognitively accessible (Chafe 1987; Langacker 1993; Taylor 1996). The possession relationship is a particular case of the reference point relationship, whereby the possessor corresponds to R_j and the possessum to R_i. We would like to propose that it is not just the accessibility of Rj that determines the reference point relationship, but rather the satisfaction of contingency condition (i) by both R_j and R_i.

All the relativizations on genitives in Tsez involve pairs of referents which satisfy contingency condition (i) — the possessor is under the presupposition of existence and the possessum cannot exist independently of it (relational nouns; inalienables; whole-part configurations).

Next, Tsez allows relativization on genitives if the predicate of the relative clause is unaccusative. Semantically, predicates that allow relativization on genitives are intransitives that normally take a patient-like argument. This patient-like argument, therefore, satisfies contingency condition (ii) above in that it does not exist independently outside the described event and/or it undergoes a significant change of state in that event. The change of state condition is actually more restrictive than is usually assumed (for example, as in Dowty 1991). Tsez seems to have the restriction that the change of state has to manifest itself in apparent results. For example, if an entity is broken or disappears, its pieces or its absence from the actual location constitute the apparent outcome of the expressed event. If someone suffers in the course of an event, this certainly can be construed as change of state but this change of state may not be apparent to an observer. Likewise, if a participant goes from full to hungry, everyday logic dictates that the change of state occurs but may not manifest itself in an obvious way. Psych-verbs, which do not participate in possessor relatives despite their structural appropriateness (see note 5), commonly imply a change of the experiencer's state but the change is once again not apparent to an observer.

Assuming this logic is correct, what diagnostics are available to a linguist to distinguish apparent results from the more obscure ones? We are not ready to give a definite answer here; rather, we would like to propose some preliminary diagnostics which can hopefully be tested in a cross-linguistic way. One possible diagnostic, suggested to us by Beth Levin (personal communication), is whether or not the change of state in question regularly constitutes the *intended* result of a prior causal event (mostly accomplishments). For example, the state of being clean is an intended result of the event of cleaning, whereas the state of suffering is possible on its own.

The second possible diagnostic, although it is not cross-linguistically valid, is offered to us by the internal grammar of Tsez, which has a morphologically marked distinction between witnessed (evidential) and unwitnessed (non-evidential) events in the past (for details, see Comrie and Polinsky forthcoming). In the declarative, past events which are witnessed are marked by the suffix *-s(i)*, whereas unwitnessed past events are marked by the suffix *-n(o)*. Verbs which can participate in possessor relatives and which, ostensibly, imply an apparent change of state, occur freely in the witnessed form (cf. (12a), (13a), (14a)). Verbs which do not imply an apparent change of state are more likely to occur in the unwitnessed form (if the participant is not first person). Their occurrence in the witnessed form, therefore, constitutes a semantically more complex case, where additional information is available. For instance, compare the contrast between (26a) which is only an inference concerning the girl's state and (26b) which, according to speakers of Tsez, suggests that the girl directly informed someone that she was hungry:

(26) a. *kid* *mek'u-n.*
girl:ABS be.hungry-PAST.UNWIT
b. *kid* *mek'u-s.*
girl:ABS be.hungry-PAST.WIT
'The girl was hungry.'

Unfortunately, both diagnostics sketched here, the semantic one and the language-internal one, are not categorical. There are two possible reasons for this: either the diagnostics touch upon a semantic feature which is in itself not categorical or they simply need to be worked out in more detail. We leave this question open.

3.3 *Applying the semantic conditions*

We are now ready to turn to the ill-formed genitive relatives as in (9b), repeated here:

(9) b. *[*γ^wˤay* *b-oxi-n* *b-āk'i-ru*] *uži* *ˤiyay-xo.*
dog:III:ABS III-run-GER III-go-PAST.PART boy:ABS cry-PRES
'The boy whose dog has run away is crying.'

Note that contingency conditions (i) and (ii) are both violated in (9). First, the existence of the dog is not uniquely dependent on the existence of the boy, and second, the predicate 'go away' is clearly agentive and entails the independent existence of its single argument prior to the event (Dowty 1991).

In (27), which can be compared with (13), the reference-point relation between the possessum and the possessor holds, and contingency condition (i) is therefore met; however contingency condition (ii) is not satisfied because the verb is agentive/unergative. As a result, (27b) is judged unacceptable, in contrast to (13b):

(27) a. *uži-s* *obiy* *Ø-ik'i-s.*
boy-GEN1 father:I:ABS I-go-PAST.WIT
'The boy's father went away.'
b. *[*obiy* *Ø-āk'i-ru*] *uži* *ˤiyay-xo.*
father:I:ABS I-go-PAST.PART boy:ABS cry-PRES
'The boy whose father went away is crying'

In (28), the predicate meets contingency condition (ii) but there is no unique reference point relationship between the referent of the possessor and the referent of the possessum. The relative clause formed on the genitive is judged marginal:

(28) a. *uži-s* *ca* *b-ok'eλ-si.*
boy-GEN1 star:IIIABS III-disappear-PAST.WIT
'The boy's star disappeared.'
b. ?[*ca* *b-ok'āλ-ru]* *uži* *ˤiyay-xo.*
star:III:ABS III-disappear-PAST.PART boy:ABS cry-PRES
'The boy whose star disappeared is crying.'

At this point, it seems that Tsez requires that both (i) and (ii) be met in order for the relativization on genitives to occur. However, the marginal acceptability of (28b) (as opposed to the ill-formedness of (27b)) suggests that the two contingency conditions could be reduced to one, namely (ii): sentence (28) satisfies condition (ii) because the star undergoes a significant change of state.[12] If this generalization holds cross-linguistically, the possession relationship could be represented as involving a locative predicate ('be at/with') which would be a particular instance of an unaccusative type verb (Benveniste 1960; Chvany 1975; Baker 1996; and many others). This would be a highly desirable result, but since more work is needed to confirm it, we will commit ourselves only to the conjunction of (i) and (ii).

To conclude this section, we have argued that the relativization of possessors (and some other subconstituents, see (25) above) should be distinguished from the canonical relativization of arguments. Relative clauses modifying possessors are syntactically ill-formed and are simply *interpreted* as acceptable; see Haig (1996) and Matsumoto (1996) for accounts of Japanese relativization including pragmatic considerations.[13] The relationship between the possessum and the possessor across clause boundary is subject to appropriateness conditions which need to be satisfied in order for the structure to be felicitous. These conditions are similar to the semantic conditions observed under Possessor Raising across languages.

4. Questions for further study

We have examined a language in which there is no independent evidence for Possessor Raising as a syntactic phenomenon but there are certain semantically driven effects normally associated with Possessor Raising, such as the implicature that the possessor undergoes a significant change of state as the result of the event expressed. The existence of languages such as Tsez raises a number of general questions which we would like to mention here.

The first question we would like to raise is whether or not the opposite of the Tsez situation is possible, namely, the presence of the syntactic effects of Possessor Raising in the absence of the semantics associated with them. Tzotzil data discussed by Aissen (this volume) seem to fit this criterion — as Aissen shows, there is no clear semantics of affectedness or change of state of the possessor referent involved in Tzotzil. There is some comparative evidence on dialects of Ostyak (a Uralic language) and on Western/Eastern Armenian which suggests that this might be the case (Ackerman and Nikolaeva 1997; Sigler 1996).

Our findings suggest several further questions: If the correlation between the syntactic and semantic/pragmatic aspects of Possessor Raising is indeed not watertight, then the commonly known Possessor Raising (external possessor) constructions represent the grammaticalization of a particular case. What can lead to such a grammaticalization? What can prevent it? Where else do natural languages apply the semantic/pragmatic corollaries of Possessor Raising without any syntactic change?

Finally, our results suggest that Tsez relativization of possessors is driven by their semantic/pragmatic interpretation. Despite the common perception of pragmatics as a fairly unconstrained domain, we have made an attempt here to formulate the conditions that determine the appropriateness of possessor relatives. If such attempts as ours prove fruitful, we might move forward in our understanding of the ways in which semantics and pragmatics affect grammatical expression in a direct way.

Conclusions

In this paper, we have examined the possibility of a dissociation between syntax and semantics, which normally correlate in Possessor Raising constructions.

We have argued, for Tsez, that semantic effects associated with Possessor Raising can actually occur in the absence of Possessor Raising syntax. We have shown that the constraint against relativization of genitives in Tsez is overridden for genitives if the possessor and possessum are in a highly predictable relation and/or the predicate of the relative clause is an intransitive unaccusative verb. These conditions generally characterize the standard cases of Possessor Raising; in the Tsez case, the missing component is the syntactic one.

The cross-linguistic separation between Possessor Raising syntax and Possessor Raising semantics suggests that the more familiar cases of Possessor Raising may represent the grammaticalization of what is otherwise an independent phenomenon.

Acknowledgments

This work was supported in part by NSF grant SBR-9220219 and by UCSD Senate Grant #960940S. We are indebted to Ramazan Rajabov and Arsen Abdulaev for sharing with us their judgments on and insights into the Tsez language. We are grateful to Immanuel Barshi, Helma van den Berg, Knud Lambrecht, Ron Langacker, Doris Payne, David Perlmutter, and the participants in the External Possession Conference for their criticisms and comments. The final result, with all its errors and fallacies, is our sole responsibility.

Abbreviations

Abbreviations used in this paper: ABS absolutive; AOR aorist; DAT dative; ERG ergative; ESS essive; GEN1 genitive-1; GEN2 genitive-2; GER gerund; INESS inessive; NMLZ nominalizer; PL plural; PRES present; PRES.PART present participle; PAST.PART past participle; PAST.WIT past witnessed; RECIPR reciprocal; REFL reflexive; SG singular; TEMP temporal converb. The numerals I through IV are used to indicate noun classes, but only where relevant to the point being made; the first person pronoun is glossed 'me'.

Notes

1 Although these terms imply a derivational account of the relevant phenomena, the non-argument-to-argument alternation can be analyzed either derivationally or representationally. We do not commit ourselves to a specific analysis here.

2 Semantic conditions are understood broadly, i.e., including both truth-conditional semantics and those elements of meaning that are often treated as "pragmatic", e.g. 'aboutness' (Reinhart 1982) or pragmatic existential presupposition (Kempson 1975).

3 The past participle in *-ru* changes the vowel preceding the last consonant of the stem into *ā*.

4 The genitive-1 in *-s* is used when the genitive is dependent on an absolutive noun, the genitive-2 in *-z* otherwise.

5 Tsez does not allow the relativization of objects of comparison either.

6 There is, however, a wrinkle to this generalization: there are many unaccusative verbs that seem not to occur in possessor relatives. Consider, for example, the verbs *mekwad-* (**mekwanad-*) 'be hungry', *eč'aħi-* (**eč'aħinod-*) 'be in a hurry', which do not permit possessor relatives:
(i) *[*obiy eč'aħi-xosi*] *uži ˤiyay-xo.*
father be in a hurry-PRES.PART boy:ABS cry-PRES
'The boy whose father is in a hurry is crying.'
We will return to this problem in Section 3.

7 Psych-verbs, which take the experiencer in a locative case and the stimulus in the absolutive, are unable to participate in possessor relatives.

8 See also examples (13), (14) above.

9 The case we are calling possessive belongs to the set of local cases (Comrie and Polinsky 1998b); it is not to be identified with genitive.

10 Since the clauses we consider are intransitive, it is impossible to test for reflexives in an argument position. If we were to adopt the narrow definition of reflexives as occurring in argument positions only (Reinhart and Reuland 1993), this would undermine our results, but does not eliminate the crucial difference between possessors, which cannot antecede reflexives, and olique arguments, which can serve as reflexive antecedents (Polinsky and Comrie 1997).

11 In order to understand (25), the reader should bear in mind that 'bloom' is expressed by an N-V compound verb (lit. 'flower-bring').

12 One could argue that the verb 'go away' used in (27) also entails a significant change of state, but this still fails to save the appropriateness of (27b). Note that verbs of motion can be construed either as implying a change of state or as implying voluntary action. We propose that it is the latter semantic component that is prominent in *ik'i-* 'go'. Note also that with regard to iterative formations, *ik'i-* patterns with the verbs in (16), while *ok'eλ-* does not, patterning with the verbs in (17) above. This also underscores the difference between these two verbs, suggesting that *ik'i-* is unergative and *ok'eλ-* unaccusative.

13 Our account for Tsez and the accounts for Japanese by Haig and by Matsumoto converge in

recognizing the relevance of pragmatic factors in the interpretation of relatives. There is, nevertheless, a significant difference — the cited works suggest that pragmatics or semantics should replace syntax for Japanese, and we propose for Tsez that syntactic rules are still valid but can be overridden by pragmatics.

References

Ackerman, Farrell, and Irina Nikolaeva. 1997. "Identity in Form, Difference in Function: The Person/Number Paradigm in W. Armenian and N. Ostyak." Paper presented to the LFG-97 Conference, University of California at San Diego.

Aissen, Judith. 1987. *Tzotzil Clause Structure.* Dordrecht: Reidel.

Baker, Mark. 1996. "On the Structural Positions of Themes and Goals." In Johan Rooryck and Laurie Zaring (eds.), *Phrase Structure and the Lexicon*. Dordrecht: Kluwer, 7–34.

Benveniste, Emile. 1960. "'Être' et 'avoir' dans leurs fonctions linguistiques." *Bulletin de la Société de linguistique de Paris* 55: 89–106.

Chafe, Wallace. 1987. "Cognitive Constraints on Information Flow." In Russell Tomlin (ed.), *Coherence and Grounding in Discourse.* Amsterdam: John Benjamins, 21–51.

Chung, Sandra. 1991. "Functional Heads and Proper Government in Chamorro." *Lingua* 85: 85–134.

Chvany, Catherine. 1975. *On the Syntax of BE-Sentences in Russian*. Columbus: Slavica.

Comrie, Bernard. 1995. "Relative Clauses and Related Constructions in Tsez." Paper presented to NSL-9, University of Chicago.

Comrie, Bernard. Forthcoming. "Valency Changing Derivations in Tsez." In Robert M.W. Dixon and Alexandra Y. Aikhenvald (eds.), *Changing Valency*. Cambridge: Cambridge University Press.

Comrie, Bernard, and Maria Polinsky. 1998a. "Form and Function in Syntax: Relativization in Tsez." In Michael Darnell, Edith Moravcsik, Michael Noonan, Frederick Newmeyer and Kathleen Wheatley (eds.), *Functionalism and Formalism, vol.2: Case Studies*. Amsterdam: John Benjamins.

Comrie, Bernard, and Maria Polinsky. 1998b. "The Great Daghestanian Case Hoax." In: Anna Siewierska and Jae Jung Song (eds.), *Case, Typology and Grammar: In Honor of Barry J. Blake*. Amsterdam: John Benjamins, 95–114.

Comrie, Bernard, and Maria Polinsky. Forthcoming. "Evidentials in Tsez". In Zlatka Guentchéva (ed.), *L'énonciation médiatisée II*. Louvain: Peeters.

Comrie, Bernard, Maria Polinsky, and Ramazan Rajabov. Forthcoming. "Tsezian Languages." In Alice Harris and Rieks Smeets (eds.), *Caucasian Languages.* New York: Curzon Press.

Dowty, David. 1991. "Thematic Proto-Roles and Argument Selection." *Language* 67: 547–619.

Fillmore, Charles J. 1982. "Frame Semantics." *Linguistics in the Morning Calm.* Seoul: Hanshin, 111–138.

Fillmore, Charles J. 1985. "Frames and the Semantics of Understanding." *Quaderni di Semantica* 6/2: 222–254.

Haig, John H. 1996. "Subjacency and Japanese Grammar: A Functional Account." *Studies in Language* 20: 53–92.

Keenan, Edward L., and Bernard Comrie. 1977. "Noun Phrase Accessibility and Universal Grammar." *Linguistic Inquiry* 8: 63–99.

Kempson, Ruth. 1975. *Presupposition and the Delimitation of Semantics.* Cambridge: Cambridge University Press.

Klamer, Marian. 1994. *Kambera, a Language of Eastern Indonesia.* Ph.D. Dissertation, Vrije Universiteit, Amsterdam.

Langacker, Ronald W. 1993. "Reference-Point Constructions." *Cognitive Linguistics* 4: 1–38.

MacDonald, Lorna, 1990. *A Grammar of Tauya.* Berlin-New York: Mouton de Gruyter.

Matsumoto, Yoshiko. 1996. "Interaction of Factors in Construal: Japanese Relative Clauses." In Masayoshi Shibatani and Sandra Thompson (eds.), *Grammatical Constructions: Their Form and Meaning.* Oxford: Clarendon Press, 103–24.

O'Connor, Mary Catherine. 1996. "The Situated Interpretation of Possessor-Raising." In Masayoshi Shibatani and Sandra Thompson (eds.), *Grammatical Constructions: Their Form and Meaning.* Oxford: Clarendon Press, 125–56.

Polinskaja [=Polinsky], Maria, and Vladimir Nedjalkov. 1987. "Contrasting the Absolutive in Chukchee: Syntax, Semantics, and Pragmatics." *Lingua* 71: 239–70.

Polinsky, Maria. 1995. "Tsez Agreement: The Trivial and the Unusual." Paper presented to NSL-9, University of Chicago.

Polinsky, Maria, and Bernard Comrie, 1996. "Relativizing Genitives in Austronesian." Paper presented to the Third Austronesian Formal Linguistics Association (AFLA-3), UCLA, April, 1996.

Polinsky, Maria, and Bernard Comrie. 1997. "Reflexivization in Tsez." Paper presented to NSL-10, University of Chicago.

Polinsky, Maria, and Bernard Comrie. Forthcoming. "Anaphoric Logophors: Reflexivization in Tsez." To appear in a festschrift.

Reinhart, Tanya. 1982. *Pragmatics and Linguistics: An Analysis of Sentence Topics.* Indiana University Linguistics Club.

Reinhart, Tanya, and Eric Reuland. 1993. "Reflexivity." *Linguistic Inquiry* 24: 657–720.

Rizzi, Luigi. 1990. *Relativized Minimality.* Cambridge, Mass.: MIT Press.

Ross, John R. 1967. *Constraints on Variables in Syntax.* Ph.D. dissertation, Massachusetts Institute of Technology. (Published 1986 as: *Infinite Syntax.* Norwood, NJ: Ablex.)

Sigler, Michele. 1996. *Clause Structure in Western Armenian.* Ph.D. dissertation, Massachusetts Institute of Technology.

Stowell, Tim. 1991. "Determiners in NP and DP." In Katherine Leffel and Denis Bouchard (eds.), *Views on Phrase Structure.* Dordrecht: Kluwer, 37–56.

Stump, Gregory, and Ramawatar Yadav. 1988. "Maithili verb agreement and the Control Agreement Principle." *Chicago Linguistic Society* 24, 2: 304–21.

Taylor, John R. 1996. *Possessives in English. An Exploration in Cognitive Grammar.* Oxford: Clarendon Press.

Author Index

Language Index

Subject Index

N

O

Q

R

W

X

In the series TYPOLOGICAL STUDIES IN LANGUAGE (TSL) the following titles have been published thus far:

1. HOPPER, Paul J. (ed.): *Tense-Aspect: Between semantics & pragmatics.* 1982.
2. HAIMAN, John & Pamela MUNRO (eds): *Switch Reference and Universal Grammar. Proceedings of a symposium on switch reference and universal grammar, Winnipeg, May 1981.* 1983.
3. GIVÓN, T.: *Topic Continuity in Discourse. A quantitative cross-language study.* 1983.
4. CHISHOLM, William, Louis T. MILIC & John A.C. GREPPIN (eds): *Interrogativity: A colloquium on the grammar, typology and pragmatics of questions in seven diverse languages, Cleveland, Ohio, October 5th 1981-May 3rd 1982.* 1984.
5. RUTHERFORD, William E. (ed.): *Language Universals and Second Language Acquisition.* 1984 (2nd ed. 1987).
6. HAIMAN, John (Ed.): *Iconicity in Syntax. Proceedings of a symposium on iconicity in syntax, Stanford, June 24-26, 1983.* 1985.
7. CRAIG, Colette (ed.): *Noun Classes and Categorization. Proceedings of a symposium on categorization and noun classification, Eugene, Oregon, October 1983.* 1986.
8. SLOBIN, Dan I. & Karl ZIMMER (eds): *Studies in Turkish Linguistics.* 1986.
9. BYBEE, Joan L.: *Morphology. A Study of the Relation between Meaning and Form.* 1985.
10. RANSOM, Evelyn: *Complementation: its Meaning and Forms.* 1986.
11. TOMLIN, Russel S.: *Coherence and Grounding in Discourse. Outcome of a Symposium, Eugene, Oregon, June 1984.* 1987.
12. NEDJALKOV, Vladimir (ed.): *Typology of Resultative Constructions. Translated from the original Russian edition (1983). English translation edited by Bernard Comrie.* 1988.
14. HINDS, John, Shoichi IWASAKI & Senko K. MAYNARD (eds): *Perspectives on Topicalization. The case of Japanese WA.* 1987.
15. AUSTIN, Peter (ed.): *Complex Sentence Constructions in Australian Languages.* 1988.
16. SHIBATANI, Masayoshi (ed.): *Passive and Voice.* 1988.
17. HAMMOND, Michael, Edith A. MORAVCSIK and Jessica WIRTH (eds): *Studies in Syntactic Typology.* 1988.
18. HAIMAN, John & Sandra A. THOMPSON (eds): *Clause Combining in Grammar and Discourse.* 1988.
19. TRAUGOTT, Elizabeth C. and Bernd HEINE (eds): *Approaches to Grammaticalization, 2 volumes (set)* 1991
20. CROFT, William, Suzanne KEMMER and Keith DENNING (eds): *Studies in Typology and Diachrony. Papers presented to Joseph H. Greenberg on his 75th birthday.* 1990.
21. DOWNING, Pamela, Susan D. LIMA and Michael NOONAN (eds): *The Linguistics of Literacy.* 1992.
22. PAYNE, Doris (ed.): *Pragmatics of Word Order Flexibility.* 1992.
23. KEMMER, Suzanne: *The Middle Voice.* 1993.
24. PERKINS, Revere D.: *Deixis, Grammar, and Culture.* 1992.
25. SVOROU, Soteria: *The Grammar of Space.* 1994.
26. LORD, Carol: *Historical Change in Serial Verb Constructions.* 1993.
27. FOX, Barbara and Paul J. Hopper (eds): *Voice: Form and Function.* 1994.
28. GIVÓN, T. (ed.) : *Voice and Inversion.* 1994.
29. KAHREL, Peter and René van den BERG (eds): *Typological Studies in Negation.* 1994.

30. DOWNING, Pamela and Michael NOONAN: *Word Order in Discourse.* 1995.
31. GERNSBACHER, M. A. and T. GIVÓN (eds): *Coherence in Spontaneous Text.* 1995.
32. BYBEE, Joan and Suzanne FLEISCHMAN (eds): *Modality in Grammar and Discourse.* 1995.
33. FOX, Barbara (ed.): *Studies in Anaphora.* 1996.
34. GIVÓN, T. (ed.): *Conversation. Cognitive, communicative and social perspectives.* 1997.
35. GIVÓN, T. (ed.): *Grammatical Relations. A functionalist perspective.* 1997.
36. NEWMAN, John (ed.): *The Linguistics of Giving.* 1998.
37. RAMAT, Anna Giacalone and Paul J. HOPPER (eds): *The Limits of Grammaticalization.* 1998.
38. SIEWIERSKA, Anna and Jae Jung SONG (eds): *Case, Typology and Grammar. In honor of Barry J. Blake.* 1998.
39. PAYNE, Doris L. and Immanuel BARSHI (eds.): *External Possession.* 1999.
40. FRAJZYNGIER, Zygmunt and Traci S. CURL (eds.): *Reflexives. Forms and functions.* n.y.p.
41. FRAJZYNGIER, Zygmunt and Traci S. CURL (eds): *Reciprocals. Forms and functions.* n.y.p.
42. DIESSEL, Holger: *Demonstratives. Form, function and grammaticalization.* n.y.p.